standard catalog of® CHEVELLE
1964-1987

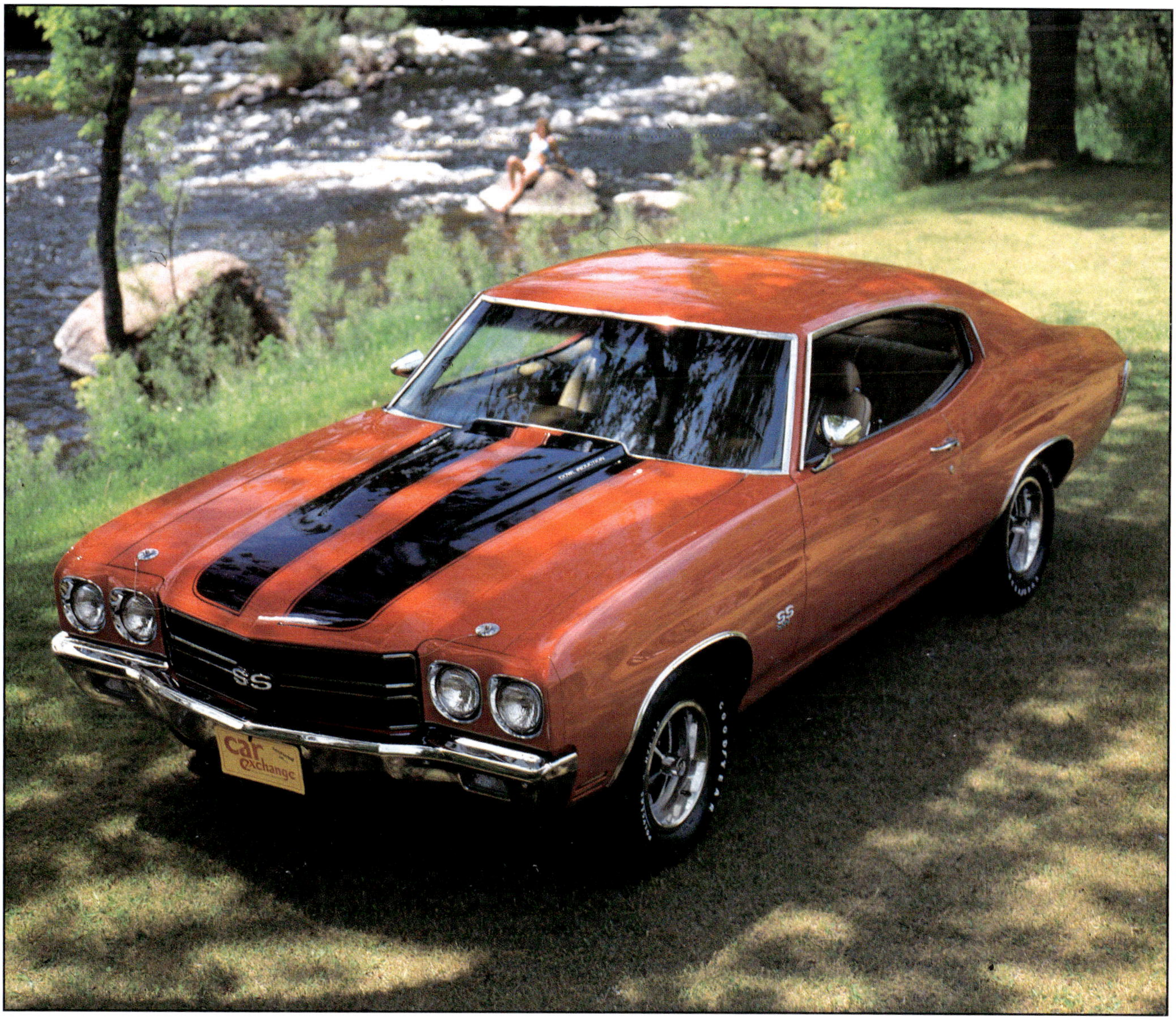

John Gunnell

©2003 by Krause Publications
All rights reserved.

No portion of this publication may be reproduced or transmitted in any form or by any means, electronic or mechanical, including photocopy, recording, or any information storage and retrieval system, without permission in writing from the publisher, except by a reviewer who may quote brief passages in a critical article or review to be printed in a magazine or newspaper, or electronically transmitted on radio or television.

Please call or write for our free catalog of publications. Our toll-free number to place an order or obtain a free catalog is (800) 258-0929.

700 East State Street • Iola, WI 54990-0001
715-445-2214 • 888-457-2873
www.krause.com

Library of Congress Catalog Number: 2002113153
ISBN: 0-87349-575-6

Acknowledgements

Special thanks to: Tony Hossain, Scott Settlemire, Jerry Heasley, Dan Lyons, Mike Mueller, Robert Genat, Donna Williams, Daniel Carr, Ed Hughes, and Larry Kinsel and the staff at GM Media Archives.

Front cover photography:
A 1971 Chevelle SS (Daniel B. Lyons photo); a 1967 Chevelle SS 396 (Daniel B. Lyons photo); a 1966 Chevelle Malibu convertible (Jerry Heasley photo).

Back cover photography:
A 1965 El Camino and Chevelle SS (Mike Mueller photo).

To my friend and first photographer Mike Carbonella. I hope this inspires you to go out and get that '70 Super Sport before it's too late.

— *John Gunnell, December 23, 2002*

Contents

Introduction 6	1970 47
Chevelle	1971 55
1964 9	1972 64
1965 14	1973 70
1966 21	1974 76
1967 26	1975 81
1968 33	1976 86
1969 39	1977 91

Malibu	1981 107
1978 96	1982 111
1979 100	1983 114
1980 104	

El Camino

1964 119
1965 123
1966 127
1967 130
1968 133
1969 136
1970 139
1971 144
1972 147
1973 150
1974 153
1975 157
1976 161
1977 165
1978 168
1979 172
1980 175
1981 178
1982 181
1983 185
1984 188
1985 190
1986 192
1987 195

Sprint

1971 199
1972 203
1973 205
1974 207
1975 209
1976 211
1977 213

Caballero

1978 216
1979 220
1980 220
1981 224
1982 226
1983 230
1984 234
1985 236
1986 238
1987 241

Price Guide 243

Introduction

Chevelle!
The '55 Chevy, Spectacularly Reinvented

"Though its sales are already greater than those of the entire Ford Motor Company, Chevrolet has for 1964 prepared a whole new line of intermediate models in an effort to win more sales. Last week Chevrolet General Manager S.E. "Bunkie" Knudsen showed to the press the auto that is expected to do the job: the new Chevelle. Impressed by its clean and handsome styling, Detroit's normally undemonstrative auto reporters broke into spontaneous applause."

Time Magazine, August 30, 1963

If ever an automobile epitomized GM's design philosophy of the early 1960s, it was the clean, razor-edged 1964 Chevelle. This all-new Chevy entry in the "mid-size" car category seemed so right for so many people with its "1955 Chevy-like" dimensions, classic good looks and sporty appeal of the top-of-the-line Malibu SS series. Initial V-8 choices were limited to 195- and 220-hp versions of the venerable 283, but things heated up considerably in the spring of 1964 with the addition of the 327 V-8 to the option list. The '64 Chevelle was a complete line of cars — with 11 models, including coupes, sedans, hardtops and wagons.

The public loved the Chevelle, and the critics approved, too. *Motor Trend* said in March 1964 that "Somehow, we couldn't help feeling we'd driven the Chevelle before, about eight years ago. It's basically very similar to the popular 1955 Chevrolet — a shade shorter in overall length and height, but with the same basic engine/chassis combination."

It's always fun to stuff a big engine in a light car. And with the mid-1965 announcement of the Chevelle SS 396, the balance of power in the muscle car wars shifted dramatically to Chevrolet. The limited-production (only 201 built) Malibu SS 396 was enthusiastically endorsed by the editors of *Motor Trend*, *Hot Rod* and *Car and Driver*.

After the limited rollout of 1965, volume production of the Chevelle SS 396 began in 1966. This new breed of Super Sport emphasized brute force at an affordable cost. Relegated to the options list were bucket seats, floor console and wheel covers. The emphasis was under the hood, where the 396 V-8 was available in a choice of 325-, 350 or 375-hp versions.

The Chevelle SS 396 continued into 1967 as America's top-selling intermediate performance car.

In 1968, a racy-looking new generation of Chevelle SS 396 was set loose — and Woodward Avenue would never be the same. Sitting on a tight 112-inch wheelbase (sedans and wagons were longer), the Chevelle coupes and convertibles took the long-hood/short deck formula to daring lengths. Power trains remained unchanged, but that hardly mattered

One year later, "No More Mr. Nice Guy" was bold declaration of a Chevrolet ad showcasing the entire lineup of '69 Super Sports and the '69 Corvette. Another defiant advertisement, showing a tough-looking Chevelle SS 396, proclaimed it the "Class Bully."

Fact is, the '69 Chevelle SS 396 was a take-no-prisoners street machine from day one. Styling was simple, and spectacular. The 396 V8 engines ranged from fierce to fearsome.

So what was the ultimate heavyweight champion of the muscle car era? Well, an excellent case can be made for the 1970 Chevelle SS 454. In its LS6 version, the hp rating was a ground-pounding 450. Appropriately, this monster was wrapped in some seriously sexy bodywork. Maybe it should not be surprising that, at a 2002 classic car auction, an LS6 SS 454 Chevelle sold for $172,000. The SS 454 is an icon for a whole era that seemed to disappear in an instant as the economy tanked, insurance rates skyrocketed, and engine emission controls began to sap V-8 power.

After 1970, as muscle car sales collapsed, Chevelle remained America's undisputed midsize sales leader with a handsome array of Malibu coupes, sedans, wagons and convertibles.

Today, 40 years after America first got to know Chevelle, the award-winning Chevy Malibu still represents superb value in an affordable midsize automobile. Acclaim by consumer publications and popularity with owners serves to ensure a bright future for the nameplate that was once the terror of Woodward Avenue.

"Perhaps Bunkie Knudson said it best in his 1963 press conference when asked about the origins of the Chevelle nameplate. 'It's a coined name,' he replied. 'It doesn't mean anything.' There was a ripple of laughter, so Knudson added: 'But we'll make it mean something.' The laughter ceased."

Automotive News, August 26, 1963

—By Tony Hossain

(Tony Hossain works for Campbell-Ewald Advertising of Warren, Michigan, Chevrolet's advertising agency.)

Chevelle

1964-1977

1964

The 1964 Chevelle was an all-new model from Chevrolet.

Anticipating a general improvement in the market for cars priced and sized below regular models, Chevrolet introduced the Chevelle for 1964. It was the U.S. auto industry's only all-new car that year. It fit between the compact Chevy II and full-size Chevrolet models. "You're looking at Chevelle — the only thing that could come between Chevrolet and Chevy II," said one Chevrolet advertisement featuring a blue Malibu Super Sport Coupe. In another ad, the Chevelle was lauded for "the way it fits between parking meters." Industry observers quickly dubbed the Chevelle a "senior compact." Assembly of Chevelles was initially quartered at plants in Baltimore, Kansas City and a brand new factory in Fremont, California. Due to strong sales, additional factories were used for Chevelle production later in the year. The Chevelle was styled with square-looking lines like the 3-year-old Chevy II, but it had curved side-window glass and an emphasis on width that combined to give it a more distinctive look. The grille featured 10 main segments, with the eight nearest the center formed by seven vertical moldings and crisscrossing horizontal molding. The dual, round headlights were housed in the outer segments with the grille texture around them and rounded outer ends. Amber-colored, rectangular front parking lights were housed in the otherwise solid front bumper. Chevrolet advertised "wide-opening doors" and "family-size trunk space" and said it provided "a Fisher Body-ful of head room, legroom and shoulder room inside." Four engines and four transmissions were offered in the Chevelle when it was introduced. They ranged from a 120-hp in-line six-cylinder engine to a 220-hp V-8 and from a three-speed stick shift to a Powerglide automatic. The Chevelle chassis featured a completely new perimeter frame. Chevrolet's exciting newcomer came in 11 models arranged in three series. Both the Chevelle 300 and Chevelle Malibu lines offered two- and four-door sedans and station wagons. A convertible body style was exclusive to the upper series. A Malibu SS (for Super Sport) series was also available. Counting sixes and V-8s, there were 22 distinct offerings to Chevelle buyers.

I.D. NUMBERS

Vehicle identification numbers (VIN) embossed on a plate welded to the left front door hinge pillar post facing the driver. The first symbol designates the model year: 4=1964. The second and third symbols designate the series: (six-cylinder) 53=Chevelle 300, 55=Malibu, 57=Malibu SS; (V-8) 54=Chevelle 300, 56=Malibu, 58=Malibu SS. The fourth and fifth symbols designates body type: 11=two-door sedan, 15=two-door six-passenger station wagon, 35=four-door six-passenger station wagon, 37=two-door Sport Coupe, 45=four-door nine-passenger station wagon, 67=two-door convertible and 69=four-door sedan. The sixth symbol designates the assembly plant location: A=Atlanta, Georgia, B=Baltimore, Maryland, G=Framingham, Massachusetts, H=Fremont, California, K=Kansas City, Missouri, and L=Los Angeles, California. The last six symbols are the sequential unit production number at the specific factory. The Fisher Body tag riveted to the top of the cowl on the left side of the car below the hood provides additional vehicle identification information. The FISHER BODY

CHEVELLE

STYLE NUMBER (ST) consists of a prefix identifying model year and four or more symbols identifying the series and body style (example: 64-13867 for a V-8-powered 1964 Malibu SS convertible). The BODY NUMBER consists of a prefix designating assembly plant and the sequential unit production number at the specific factory (example: B 100001 is the first car built at the Baltimore factory). The TRIM NUMBER (TR) identifies upholstery.

COLORS

(900) Tuxedo Black, (905) Meadow Green Metallic, (908) Bahama Green Metallic, (912) Silver Blue Metallic, (916) Daytona Blue Metallic, (918) Azure Aqua Metallic, (919) Aqua Lagoon Metallic, (920) Almond Fawn Metallic, (922) Ember Red, (932) Saddle Tan, (936) Ermine White, (938) Desert Beige, (940) Satin Silver, (943) Goldwood Yellow on Malibu SS only and (948) Palomar Red Metallic. Interior colors of Fawn, Aqua, Red, Blue, Saddle, White and Black were available on specific models with specific exterior paint colors.

ENGINE CODES

Appear on the right side of six-cylinder blocks behind the distributor and right front of V-8 engine blocks: (194 cid/120 hp six) GH, GJ, KC, KD, G, GB, GF, GG, GK, GL, GM, GN, K, KB, KJ and KH; (230 cid/140 hp six) BL, BM, BN, BP, LL, LK, LM and LN; (283 cid/195 hp V-8) J, JA and JD; (283 cid/220 hp V-8) JG, JH; (327 cid/250 hp V-8) JQ, JT and SR; (327 cid/300 hp V-8) JR, SS.

CHEVELLE 300 — SERIES 53/54 (6-CYL/V-8)

The base level Chevelle 300 came with thin bright metal body side moldings. A small badge shaped like the Chevrolet chevron decorated the trailing edge of the rear fenders and carried the "300" designation on a black background. The Chevrolet name was spelled out in chrome letters on the edge of the hood and rear deck lid and the Chevelle name was spelled out on the front fender tips. Standard equipment included a sturdy all-welded rugged steel frame with welded torque-box design, metal inner front fender liners, a long-life exhaust system, high-level ventilation through dual vents in the front cowl side panels with individual knob controls for each, push-button outside door handles, an inside rearview mirror, an enclosed steering column, a rheostat-controlled lighted instrument cluster (with a dial speedometer, fuel gauge, oil pressure indicator light, engine temperature indicator light and generator indicator light), a five-position ignition switch, direction signal indicators, an ash tray, a radio speaker grille in top of the instrument panel, a locking glove box, a counter-balanced hood and rear deck lid, a diaphragm-spring type single dry disc clutch with two facings, Safety-Master self-adjusting brakes, 14-inch wheels with tubeless tires, a 54-plate 44-amp-hour 12-volt battery, a high-output heater and defroster, foam front seat cushions, dual interior sun visors, an easy-car vinyl headlining, electric windshield wipers, a color-keyed steering wheel with horn ring, an automatic cigarette lighter, a key-locking glove compartment, front seat belts and five black sidewall tires. The seats inside the Chevelle 300 models came in neat, new patterned fabrics trimmed with leather-grain vinyl. The vinyl-coated rubber floor mats were color-keyed and featured an attractive spatter design. Other quality interior details included a half-circle steering wheel horn ring, padded armrests front and rear and dual rear ashtrays. Chevelle 300 interiors were available in four colors — fawn, aqua, red or blue — depending upon the buyer's exterior color selection. The two-door six-passenger station wagon was exclusive to this series and is a desirable collector car today. The Chevelle 300 station wagons combined long-wearing fabrics with vinyl trim and had vinyl-coated rubber floor mats. All Chevelle six-passenger station wagons came with a vinyl-coated rubber mat on their load floor. On the Chevelle 300 wagon's load area sidewalls was a vinyl-coated textured metal. All wagons featured textured-metal seatbacks and tailgate inner surface filler panels protected with a protective coating of vinyl.

Model Number	Body/Style Number	Body Type & Seating	Factory Price	Shipping Weight	Production Total
CHEVELLE 300 SERIES 53 (6-CYL)					
53	11	2d sedan-6P	$2,231	2,825 lbs.	Note 1
53	69	4d sedan-6P	$2,268	2,850 lbs.	Note 1
53	15	2d wagon-6P	$2,528	3,050 lbs.	Note 1
53	35	4d wagon-6P	$2,566	3,130 lbs.	Note 1
CHEVELLE 300 SERIES 54 (V-8)					
54	11	2d sedan-6P	$2,339	2,955 lbs.	Note 1
54	69	4d sedan-6P	$2,376	2,980 lbs.	Note 1
54	15	2d wagon-6P	$2,636	3,170 lbs.	Note 1
54	35	4d wagon-6P	$2,674	3,250 lbs.	Note 1

NOTE 1: Individual body style production is not available; see production notes following Malibu SS listing below.

CHEVELLE MALIBU – SERIES 55/56 (6-CYL/V-8)

The Chevelle Malibu came with bright metal body side moldings that widened on the rear flanks of the car and had a center indent with contrasting white finish on this portion. The trailing edge of the rear fenders carried a bright metal Malibu script. The rocker panels were trimmed with wide bright metal moldings. The rest of the trim was similar to that of the 300. In addition to all of the features that were standard on the Chevelle 300, the Malibu featured a deluxe steering wheel with a horn ring, back-up lights, a lighted glove compartment and an electric clock. The Malibu sport coupe and Malibu sedans were upholstered in deluxe pattern cloth accented with metallic treads and had leather-look vinyl trimmings. The Malibu convertible featured an all-vinyl interior Deep-twist carpeting and bright metal highlights were found inside all Malibus, along with a deluxe steering wheel with a half-circle horn ring and deep-twist carpeting. Interior color choices, keyed to exterior colors were fawn, aqua, red, blue and saddle. Malibu station wagons were upgraded to all-vinyl upholstery and deep-twist carpeting and the three-seat wagon had a vinyl-coated textured metal load floor. Another upscale touch was leather-grain vinyl on the load area sidewalls.

Model Number	Body/Style Number	Body Type & Seating	Factory Price	Shipping Weight	Production Total
CHEVELLE MALIBU SERIES 55 (6-CYL)					
55	69	4d sedan-6P	$2,349	2,870lbs.	Note 1
55	37	2d sport coupe-6P	$2,376	2,850lbs.	Note 1

The Chevelle Malibu Super Sport convertible was an appealing first-year vehicle.

55	67	2d convertible-6P	$2,587	2,995 lbs.	Note 1
55	45	4d wagon-9P	$2,744	3,240 lbs.	Note 1
55	35	4d wagon-6P	$2,647	3,140 lbs.	Note 1
CHEVELLE MALIBU SERIES 56 (V-8)					
56	69	4d sedan-6P	$2,457	2,995 lbs.	Note 1
56	37	2d sport coupe-6P	$2,484	2,975 lbs.	Note 1
56	67	2d convertible-6P	$2,695	3,120 lbs.	Note 1
56	45	4d wagon-9P	$2,852	3,365 lbs.	Note 1
56	35	4d wagon-6P	$2,755	3,265 lbs.	Note 1

NOTE 1: Individual body style production is not available; see production notes following Malibu SS listing

CHEVELLE MALIBU SS SERIES 57/58 (6-CYL/V-8)

"Everyone has a bit of swashbuckler in him," said the first Chevelle catalog, in an obvious example that 1964 was a pre-political-correctness era. "And one sure way to get it out is to get behind the wheel of an all-new Malibu Super Sport coupe or convertible." The Chevelle Malibu was clearly identified by the "SS"-in-a-chrome-circle badges at the trailing edge of each rear fender and on the right-hand side of the rear body panel. The Malibu SS did not have bright metal mid-body side moldings like other Malibus. Instead, the entire profile from the fender tops to the wheel lips and rocker panels was outlined in bright metal. Standard equipment included a heater and defroster, foam front seat cushions, electric windshield wipers, front seat belts, five black sidewall tires, vinyl upholstery, padded arm rests, a deluxe steering wheel with a horn ring, back-up lights, a glove compartment light, an electric clock, carpeting, front bucket seats upholstered in soft vinyl flanked by bright metal moldings, a sporty center console housing the floor-mounted straight-line shift lever for the Powerglide automatic transmission or a stick shift for the four-speed synchro-mesh transmission, special engine gauges and special wheel covers with a radial pattern centered around an exclusive Super Sport emblem and a vented design to allow brake cooling. Used car books of the era listed prices and weights for Malibu SS six-cylinder models and there was nothing in the catalog to suggest you couldn't get one, but industry production records indicate that only V-8s were built. Malibu SS interiors came in a choice of seven color-keyed combinations including Fawn, Aqua, Red, Blue and Saddle, plus the Chevelle-exclusive choices of white or black.

Model Number	Body/Style Number	Body Type & Seating	Factory Price	Shipping Weight	Production Total
CHEVELLE MALIBU SS SERIES 57 (6-CYL)					
57	37	2d sport coupe-6P	$2,538	2,875 lbs.	Note 1
57	67	2d convertible-6P	$2,749	3,020 lbs.	Note 1
CHEVELLE MALIBU SS SERIES 58 (V-8)					
58	37	2d sport coupe-6P	$2,646	3,000 lbs.	Note 1
58	67	2d convertible-6P	$2,857	3,145 lbs.	Note 1

NOTE 1: Individual body style production is not available; see production notes below.

PRODUCTION NOTES

NOTE 1 Production of all 1964 Chevelles by body style was:
sport coupe 134,670   convertible 23,158
4-door sedan 113,816   2-door sedan 22,568
4-door wagon 41,374   2-door wagon 2,710

NOTE 2 Industry statistical breakouts show 142,034 Chevelle sixes and 196,252 Chevelle V-6s were built.

NOTE 3 Additional statistics record series production, in rounded-off figures, as follows:

Chevelle 300 (6-cyl)	53,000
Chevelle 300 (V-8)	15,300
Total	68,300
Malibu (6-cyl)	62,100
Malibu (V-8)	86,900
Total	149,000
Malibu SS (6-cyl)	0
Malibu SS (V-8)	67,100
Total	67,100
Wagons (6-cyl)	17,100
Wagons (V-8)	26,900
Total	44,000

NOTE 4 Production by factory was:

Code	Factory	Production	Code	Factory	Production
B	Baltimore	80,829	H	Fremont	25,033
K	Kansas City	107,862	L	Los Angeles	43,760
*	Bloomfield	11,856	A	Atlanta	68,931
G	Framingham	15			

(*) Bloomfield was not actually a factory but an export shipping point for cars actually built at other plants.

ENGINES

CHEVELLE 300, MALIBU, MALIBU SS BASE 194-CID, 120-HP SIX-CYL: Overhead-valve. Cast-iron block. Bore and stroke: 3.562 x 3.25 in. Displacement: 194.4 cid. Compression ratio: 8.5:1. Brake hp: 120 at 4400 rpm. Taxable hp: 36.00. Torque: 177 lbs.-ft. at 2400 rpm. Seven main bearings. Hydraulic valve lifters. Crankcase capacity: 4 qt. (add 1 qt. for new filter). Cooling system capacity: 10.5 qt. (add 1 qt. for heater). Carburetor: Rochester one-barrel Model 7023105. Three-speed manual transmission standard; three-speed overdrive and Powerglide transmissions optional.

CHEVELLE 300, MALIBU, MALIBU SS OPTIONAL 230-CID, 155-HP SIX-CYL: Overhead-valve. Cast-iron block. Bore and stroke: 3.875 x 3.25 in. Displacement: 230 cid. Compression ratio: 8.5:1. Brake horsepower: 155 at 4400 rpm. Taxable hp: 36.00. Torque: 215 lbs.-ft. at 2000 rpm. Seven main bearings. Hydraulic valve lifters. Crankcase capacity: 4 qt. (add 1 qt. for new filter). Cooling system capacity: 10.5 qt. (add 1 qt. for heater). Carburetor: Rochester one-barrel Model 7023003. Three-speed manual transmission standard; three-speed overdrive and Powerglide transmissions optional.

CHEVELLE 300, MALIBU, MALIBU SS BASE 283-CID, 195-HP V-8: Overhead-valve. Cast-iron block and head. Bore and stroke: 3.875 x 3.00 in. Displacement: 283 cid. Compression ratio: 9.25:1. Brake hp: 195 at 4800 rpm. Taxable hp: 48. Torque: 285 lbs.-ft. at 2400. Five main bearings. Hydraulic valve lifters. Crankcase capacity: 4 qt. (add 1 qt. for new filter). Cooling system capacity: 16 qt. (add 1 qt. for heater). Carburetor: Rochester 7024101 two-barrel. Three-speed manual transmission standard; three-speed overdrive and Powerglide transmissions optional.

CHEVELLE 300, MALIBU, MALIBU SS BASE 283-CID, 220-HP V-8: Overhead valve. Cast-iron block and head. Bore and stroke: 3.875 x 3.00 in. Displacement: 283 cid. Compression ratio: 9.25:1. Brake hp: 220 at 4800 rpm. Taxable hp: 48. Torque: 295 lbs.-ft. at 3200. Five main bearings. Hydraulic valve lifters. Crankcase capacity: 4 qt. (add 1 qt. for new filter). Cooling system capacity: 16 qt. (add 1 qt. for heater). Carburetor: Rochester 7024024 four-barrel. Three-speed manual transmission standard; three-speed overdrive, four-speed manual and Powerglide transmissions optional.

CHEVELLE 300, MALIBU, MALIBU SS OPTIONAL 327-CID, 250-HP 327 V-8: Overhead-valve. Cast-iron block and head. Bore and stroke: 4.00 x 3.25 in. Displacement: 327 cid. Compression ratio: 10.50:1. Brake hp: 250 at 4400 rpm. Taxable hp: 51.20. Torque: 350 lbs.-ft. at 2800. Five main bearings. Hydraulic valve lifters. Crankcase capacity: 4 qt. (add 1 qt. for new filter). Cooling system capacity: 15 qt. (add 1 qt. for heater). Carburetor: (Chevelle) Rochester 7024125 four-barrel.; (Chevrolet full-size) Carter 3846247 four-barrel. Three-speed manual transmission standard; three-speed all-synchromesh, four-speed manual and Powerglide

This Malibu convertible was decked out in Goldwood Yellow.

Ed Hughes photo

1964

The flashy new 1964 Chevelle had wide-ranging appeal, thanks in part to 22 different engine-body style combinations.

transmissions optional.

CHEVELLE 300, MALIBU, MALIBU SS OPTIONAL 327-CID, 300-HP V-8: Overhead-valve. Cast-iron block and head. Bore and stroke: 4.00 x 3.25 in. Displacement: 327 cid. Compression ratio: 10.50:1. Brake hp: 300 at 5000 rpm. Taxable hp: 51.20. Torque: 360 lbs.-ft. at 3200. Five main bearings. Hydraulic valve lifters. Crankcase capacity: 4 qt. (add 1 qt. for new filter). Cooling system capacity: 15 qt. (add 1 qt. for heater). Dual exhaust. Carburetor: Carter 3826004 four-barrel. Three-speed manual transmission standard; three-speed all-synchromesh, four-speed manual and Powerglide transmissions optional.

CHEVELLE MALIBU SS OPTIONAL 327 V-8: Overhead-valve. Cast-iron block and head. Bore and stroke: 4.00 x 3.25 in. Displacement: 327 cid. Compression ratio: 11.00:1. Brake hp: 365 at 6200 rpm. Taxable hp: 51.20. Torque: 350 lbs.-ft. at 4000. Five main bearings. Hydraulic valve lifters. Crankcase capacity: 4 qt. (add 1 qt. for new filter). Cooling system capacity: 15 qt. (add 1 qt. for heater). Dual exhaust. Carburetor: Holley 3858399 four-barrel. Three-speed manual transmission standard; three-speed all-synchromesh and four-speed manual transmissions optional.

Note This engine was advertised in mid-year sales literature and was the first engine installed in an El Camino tested by *Hot Rod* magazine, but the 365-hp option was cancelled at the last minute.

CHASSIS

Wheelbase: 115 in. Overall length: (wagon) 198.8 in.; (car) 193.9 in.. Width: 74.6 in. Overall height: (convertible) 52.9 in.; (sport coupe) 52.8 in.; (sedan) 53.2 in. and (station wagon) 55.1 in. Front tread: 58 in. Rear tread: 58 in. Turning circle: (curb-to-curb) 41.9 ft.; (wall-to-wall) 44.7 ft. Overall steering ratio: (standard) 28.0:1; (power) 20.4:1. Luggage capacit in usable cubic feet: (coupe) 16.7; (sedan) 16.8; (convertible, top up) 16.5; (convertible, top down) 15.5. Tires: (wagons) 7.00 x 14; (car) 6.50 x 14. Four-wheel coil suspension. Four-link rear suspension. Ball-race steering gear.

OPTIONS

RPO L77 220-hp V-8 ($53.80). RPO L30 250-hp V-8 ($94.70). RPO L74 300-hp V-8 $137.75. RPO M10 three-speed overdrive transmission ($107.60). RPO M-35 Powerglide transmission ($188.30). RPO M40 four-speed manual transmission ($188.30). RPO G80 Positraction rear axle ($37.70). Optional 3.36:1 rear axle ratio ($2.20). RPO T60 heavy-duty battery ($7.55). RPO J65 sintered metallic brake linings ($37.70). RPO K79 heavy-duty generator ($10.80). RPO K77 heavy-duty generator ($21.55). RPO K81 heavy-duty generator ($64.60). RPO K02 temperature-controlled fan ($16.15). RPO VO1 heavy-duty radiator ($10.80). RPO G66 Super-lift rear air shocks ($37.70). RPO F40 special suspension for Malibu SS ($3.80), for other Chevelles ($4.85). RPO J50 power brakes ($43.05). RPO N40 power steering ($86.10). RPO A31 power windows ($102.25). RPO CO6 power convertible top ($53.80). RPO A41 power front seat, except not available in Malibu SS ($64.40). RPO C60 Four-Season air conditioning ($363.70). RPO C65 custom air conditioning ($317.45). RPO ZO1 Comfort & Convenience group including inside day/night rearview mirror, two-speed windshield wipers and windshield washers ($30.15). RPO AO1 tinted glass, all windows ($31.25). RPO AO2 tinted windshield ($19.95). RPO V31 front bumper guards ($9.70). RPO V32 rear bumper guards ($9.70). RPO B70 padded instrument panel ($18.30). RPO N33 Comfortilt steering wheel ($43.05). RPO U63 AM push-button radio ($58.65). RPO U60 AM manual radio ($50.05). RPO ZO2 radio group including push-button radio and rear speaker ($72.10).

OPTION INSTALLATION RATES

Automatic transmission (65.1 percent). Four-speed manual transmission (8.2 percent). V-8 engine (59.7 percent). Six-cylinder engine (40.3 percent). Radio (57 percent). Heater (96.3 percent). Power steering (30.1 percent). Power brakes (10.2 percent). Power seat (0.2 percent). Power windows (0.7 percent). Power rear wagon window (4.7 percent). Bucket seats (20.7 percent). Tilt steering (1.0 percent). White sidewall tires (64.6 percent). Windshield washers (54.2 percent). Tinted windshield only (36.3 percent). All tinted glass (13.3 percent). Back-up lights (84.5 percent). Air conditioning

The '64 Chevelle's square appearance was similar to the Chevy II.

(8.9 percent). Positraction (8.0 percent). Full wheel covers (55.7 percent). Overdrive (1.4 percent). Based on model year production of 338,286 units.

HISTORICAL FOOTNOTES

Dealer introductions of new Chevrolet cars occurred on Sept. 28, 1964. Semon E. Knudsen remained as general manager of Chevrolet Division. From the first appearance of prototypes in July 1963 to the end of that calendar year Chevelle output reached 113,780 units, which made it Chevy's second most popular line. Model year production was 338,286 Chevelles which represented 4.3 percent of total U.S. auto production for the year. The 1964 Malibu SS sport coupe with the 283-cid 195-hp V-8 did 0 to 60 mph in 9.7 seconds and the quarter mile took 17.4 seconds.

"On display Thursday, Sept. 24," said the two-page advertisement featuring a blue, 327-powered Chevelle Malibu Super Sport Coupe. "Despite its smashing first year's success, we've made Chevelle for '65 even more exciting to look at, drive and enjoy. It's more graceful, with elegant new front end styling. What an improved ride! It's smoother, softer, easier handling, because it has softer coil springs, an improved rear suspension and extra body insulation."

The 1965 Chevelles were mildly restyled. The nose was veed slightly outward and a new grille was used. It featured a wide horizontal center bar carrying an elongated Chevrolet emblem in the center. There were four narrower horizontal molding above the center bar and four below it. The entire ensemble was surround by a heavier bright metal molding. The Chevrolet name was seen on the lip of the hood, above the grille. At the rear were new taillamps. General 1965 styling features included dual headlights, amber parking and turn lights, a corrosion-resisting anodized aluminum grille, a bright windshield reveal molding, a bonded-in windshield, parallel-action electric wipers, a Fisher body with high-level air inlet, a double-wall cowl, flush-and-dry rocker panels, front fender skirts, fork-type door locks and a welded all-steel perimeter frame.

Two sixes and three V-8s were offered at first, with three additional V-8s added during the year. The sizzling new 375-hp V-8 was aimed directly at the new muscle car market created by the Pontiac GTO and made the SS 396 a direct competitor to the "Goat." All Chevelle engines had an automatic choke, oil filter, positive crankcase ventilation, a Delcotron generator and 6,000-mile or 60-day oil changes. All V-8s had an oil-wetted paper air filter element. All Chevelles came with six months or 6,000 miles chassis lubrication.

This sport coupe is one of only 201 Z16 Chevelle Malibu SS 396s made in 1965.

I.D. NUMBERS

VIN embossed on a plate welded to the left front door hinge pillar post facing the driver. The first symbol 1 designates Chevrolet. The second and third symbols designate the series: (Six-cylinder) 31=Chevelle 300, 33=Chevelle 300 Deluxe, 35=Malibu, 37=Malibu SS; (V-8) 32=Chevelle 300, 34=Chevelle 300 Deluxe, 36=Malibu, 38=Malibu SS. The fourth and fifth symbols designates body type: 11=two-door sedan, 15=two-door six-passenger station wagon, 35=four-door six-passenger station wagon, 37=two-door sport coupe, 67=two-door convertible and 69=four-door sedan. The sixth symbol designates the model year: 5=1965. The seventh symbol designates the assembly plant location: A=Atlanta, Georgia, B=Baltimore, Maryland, G=Framingham, Massachusetts, H=Fremont, California and K=Kansas City, Missouri. The last six symbols are the sequential unit production number at the specific factory. The Fisher Body tag riveted to the top of the cowl on the left side of the car below the hood provides additional vehicle identification information. The Fisher Body STYLE NUMBER (ST) consists of a prefix identifying model year and four or more symbols identifying the series and body style (example: 65-13867 for a V-8-powered 1965 Malibu SS convertible). The BODY NUMBER consists of a prefix designating assembly plant and the sequential unit production number at the specific factory (example: B 100001 is the first car built at the Baltimore factory). The TRIM NUMBER (TR) identifies upholstery.

COLORS

(A) Tuxedo Black, (C) Ermine White, (D) Mist Blue, (E) Danube Blue, (H) Willow Green, (J) Cypress Green, (K) Artesian Turquoise, (L) Tahitian Turquoise, (N) Madeira Maroon), (P) Evening Orchard, (S) Sierra Tan, (W) Glacier Gray and (Y) Crocus Yellow. Interior colors of Fawn, Turquoise or Red were available with specific exterior paint colors.

ENGINE CODES

Codes appear on the right side of six-cylinder blocks behind the distributor and right front of V-8 engine blocks: (194 cid/120 hp six) AA, AC, AG, AH, AK, AL, AN, AR; (230 cid/140 hp six) BK, BN, BY, BZ, CA, CB, CC, CD; (283 cid/195 hp V-8) DA, DB, DE; (283 cid/220 hp V-8) DG, DH; (327 cid/250 hp V-8) EA, EE; (327 cid/300 hp V-8) ED, EF; (327 cid/350 hp V-8) EC, ED; (396 cid/375 hp V-8) IX.

CHEVELLE 300 — SERIES 131/132 (6-CYL/V-8)

Chevelle 300 models had bright lower body sill moldings, Chevelle 300 rear fender nameplates and emblems, bright ventipanes (vent windows), bright windshield moldings, bright rear window reveal moldings, single unit taillamps with bright bezels, rear bumper back-up light opening covers and small hubcaps. The Chevelle 300 interior featured pattern cloth and vinyl trim (with all-vinyl trim on station wagons) in a standard grade

Chevelle

cloth, a foam-cushioned front seat, a cigarette lighter and a vinyl floor covering. Standard equipment included a heater and defroster, electric windshield wipers and front seat belts.

Model Number	Body/Style Number	Body Type & Seating	Factory Price	Shipping Weight	Production Total
CHEVELLE 300 SERIES 131 (6-CYL)					
131	11	2d sedan-6P	$2,109	2,870 lbs.	Note 1
131	69	4d sedan-6P	$2,146	2,900 lbs.	Note 1
131	15	2d wagon-6P	$2,400	3,140 lbs.	Note 1
CHEVELLE 300 SERIES 132 (V-8)					
132	11	2d sedan-6P	$2,215	3,010 lbs.	Note 1
132	69	4d sedan-6P	$2,251	3,035 lbs.	Note 1
132	15	2d wagon-6P	$2,505	3,275 lbs.	Note 1

NOTE 1: Individual body style production is not available; see production notes following Malibu SS listing below.

CHEVELLE 300 DELUXE SERIES 133/134 — (6-CYL/V-8)

Chevelle 300 Deluxe models had bright body side moldings, bright lower body sill moldings, Chevelle 300 rear fender nameplates and emblems, bright ventipanes (vent windows), bright windshield moldings, bright rear window reveal moldings, single unit taillamps with bright bezels, rear bumper back-up light opening covers, small hubcaps, higher body side trim strips, bright roof drip cap moldings and bright rear cove outline moldings (except on station wagons). The Chevelle 300 Deluxe interiors were trimmed in plusher vinyl-and-cloth combinations with all-vinyl door trim. They featured a unique dual-spoke steering wheel with horn ring. Standard equipment included a heater and defroster, foam front seat cushions, electric windshield wipers, automatic front-door dome light switches, front seat belts and padded armrests.

Model Number	Body/Style Number	Body Type & Seating	Factory Price	Shipping Weight	Production Total
CHEVELLE 300 DELUXE SERIES 133 (6-CYL)					
133	11	2d sedan-6P	$2,183	2,870 lbs.	Note 1
133	69	4d sedan-6P	$2,220	2,910 lbs.	Note 1
133	35	4d wagon-6P	$2,511	3,185 lbs.	Note 1
CHEVELLE 300 DELUXE SERIES 134 (V-8)					
134	11	2d sedan-6P	$2,288	3,010 lbs.	Note 1
134	69	4d sedan-6P	$2,326	3,050 lbs.	Note 1
134	35	4d wagon-6P	$2,616	3,320 lbs.	Note 1

NOTE 1: Individual body style production is not available; see production notes following Malibu SS listing below.

CHEVELLE MALIBU — SERIES 135/136 (6-CYL/V-8)

Cars in the Malibu series had the following items added to or replacing Chevelle 300 Deluxe equipment: special grille paint treatment, color-accented body side moldings, bright wheelhouse moldings, Malibu rear fender scripts with Chevelle emblems, bright hood windsplit moldings, ribbed upper and lower cove trim panels (ribbed tailgate lower trim on station wagons), back-up lights in the rear bumper, luxurious pattern cloth-and-vinyl interior trims, color-keyed deep-twist floor carpeting, a foam-cushioned rear seat, a specific dual-spoke steering wheel with horn ring, an electric clock, a bright glove compartment facing molding with series nameplate and a glovebox light.

Model Number	Body/Style Number	Body Type & Seating	Factory Price	Shipping Weight	Production Total
CHEVELLE MALIBU SERIES 135 (6-CYL)					
135	69	4d sedan-6P	$2,299	2,945 lbs.	Note 1
135	37	2d sport coupe-6P	$2,326	2,930 lbs.	Note 1
135	67	2d convertible-6P	$2,532	3,025 lbs.	Note 1
135	35	4d wagon-6P	$2,590	3,225 lbs.	Note 1
CHEVELLE MALIBU SERIES 136 (V-8)					
136	69	4d sedan-6P	$2,405	3,080 lbs.	Note 1
136	37	2d sport coupe-6P	$2,431	3,065 lbs.	Note 1
136	67	2d convertible-6P	$2,637	3,160 lbs.	Note 1
136	35	4d wagon-6P	$2,695	3,355 lbs.	Note 1

The 1965 Malibu SS could be ordered with either of two six-cylinder engines, or one of three different V-8s.

NOTE 1: Individual body style production is not available; see production notes following Malibu SS listing below.

CHEVELLE MALIBU SS SERIES 136/137 — (6-CYL/V-8)

A clean, sporty appearance was created for the Chevelle Malibu SS by the use of wide bright body sill moldings, rear lower fender moldings, back-up lights, Malibu SS rear fender scripts, wheel trim covers, SS emblems on the rear deck lid, a black-accented grille, a black rear cove (or a silver cove on cars with black exterior finish), specific Super Sport wheel covers, front bucket seats with bright trim ends, a center console with four-speed manual or automatic transmissions and an all-vinyl luxury interior. Special instrument panel features included an electric clock, a lighted glove box, temperature, ammeter and oil pressure gauges.

Model Number	Body/Style Number	Body Type & Seating	Factory Price	Shipping Weight	Production Total
CHEVELLE MALIBU SS SERIES 136 (6-CYL)					
137	37	2d sport coupe-6P	$2,484	2,980 lbs.	Note 1
137	67	2d convertible-6P	$2,690	3,075 lbs.	Note 1
CHEVELLE MALIBU SS SERIES 136 (V-8)					
138	37	2d sport coupe-6P	$2,590	3,115 lbs.	Note 1
138	67	2d convertible-6P	$2,796	3,210 lbs.	Note 1

NOTE 1: Individual body style production is not available; see production notes below.

CHEVELLE MALIBU SS 396 — (V-8)

Regular Production Option Z16 was the mid-1965 Chevelle SS 396 package. It included a 396-cid, 375-hp V-8 with dual exhausts, chrome engine accents, impact-extruded pistons, molybdenum-coated piston rings, special alloy connecting rods and four-bolt main bearing caps. The drive train featured an 11-in. diaphragm clutch, the M20 four-speed manual transmission, a 3.25-in. diameter one-piece drive shaft and a heavy-duty 12-bolt rear axle with a special 8.875-in. ring gear. The suspension featured 1.06-in. diameter front and rear stabilizer bars, shot-peened ball joint struts, cast iron wheel hubs, special shock absorbers and a special heavy-duty suspension with stiffer front and rear springs. The drum brakes were special 11 x 2.75-in. units up front and 11.0 x 2.00-in. units at the rear. The 7.65 x 14 Firestone Super Sport nylon cord tires were mounted on 6.00 x 14-inch wheels. Also included were a 160-mph speedometer, power steering with 15.0:1 gearing and 4.0 turns lock-to-lock and an AM/FM Multiplex stereo radio. A large-capacity cooling system was provided to cool the "big-block" V-8. Specific exterior trim included Malibu SS front fender emblems, a special rear cove treatment and "396 Turbo-Jet" front fender emblems. An SS 396 emblem was mounted in the dash. Fifteen-inch diameter simulated mag-style wheel covers were included in the $1,501 option package. Only 201 Chevelle Malibu SS 396s were made in 1965.

Model Number	Body/Style Number	Body Type & Seating	Factory Price	Shipping Weight	Production Total
138	37	2d sport coupe-6P	$4,091	3,115 lbs.	Note 1
138	67	2d convertible-6P	$4,297	3,210 lbs.	Note 1

NOTE 1: Individual body style production not available; see production notes below.

PRODUCTION NOTES

NOTE 1 Model-year production of all 1965 Chevelles was 384,894 units.
NOTE 2 Industry statistical breakouts in rounded-off numbers show 137,200 Chevelle sixes and 206,700 Chevelle V-8s were built in 1965.
NOTE 3 Additional statistics record series production, in rounded-off figures, as follows:

Chevelle 300 (6-cyl)	26,500
Chevelle 300 (V-8)	5,100
Total	**31,600**
Chevelle 300 Del. (6-cyl)	32,000
Chevelle 300 (V-8)	9,600
Total	**41,600**
Malibu (6-cyl)	56,400
Malibu (V-8)	95,800
Total	**152,200**
Malibu SS (6-cyl)	8,600
Malibu SS (V-8)	72,500
Total	**81,100**
Wagons (6-cyl)	13,800
Wagons (V-8)	23,800
Total	**37,600**

(*) Malibu SS V-8 production included 201 Chevelle Malibu SS 396 models.
NOTE 4 Production by factory was:

The stylish Malibu in Madeira Maroon.

CHEVELLE

There is no mistaking that this 1965 Chevelle had the Z16 option, which included a 375-hp, 396-cid V-8 with dual exhaust.

Code	Factory	Production	Code	Factory	Production
B	Baltimore	83,876	H	Fremont	50,215
K	Kansas City	108,697	*	Bloomfield	2,940
A	Atlanta	50,467	G	Framingham	47,699

(*) Bloomfield was not actually a factory but an export shipping point for cars actually built at other plants.

ENGINES

CHEVELLE 300, MALIBU, MALIBU SS BASE 194-CID, 120-HP SIX-CYL: Overhead-valve. Cast-iron block. Bore and stroke: 3.562 x 3.25 in. Displacement: 194.4 cid. Compression ratio: 8.5:1. Brake hp: 120 at 4400 rpm. Taxable hp: 36.00. Torque: 177 lbs.-ft. at 2400 rpm. Seven main bearings. Hydraulic valve lifters. Crankcase capacity: 4 qt. (add 1 qt. for new filter). Cooling system capacity: 11 qt. (add 1 qt. for heater). Carburetor: Rochester one-barrel Model 7023105.

CHEVELLE 300, MALIBU, MALIBU SS OPTIONAL 230-CID, 140-HP SIX-CYL: Overhead-valve. Cast-iron block. Bore and stroke: 3.875 x 3.25 in. Displacement: 230 cid. Compression ratio: 8.5:1. Brake hp: 140 at 4400 rpm. Taxable hp: 36. Torque: lbs.-ft. 220 at 1600 rpm. Seven main bearings. Hydraulic valve lifters. Crankcase capacity: 4 qt. (add 1 qt. for new filter). Cooling system capacity: 11 qt. (add 1 qt. for heater). Carburetor: Rochester one-barrel Model 7023105.

CHEVELLE 300, 300 DELUXE, MALIBU BASE, MALIBU SS OPTIONAL 283-CID, 195-HP V-8: Overhead-valve. Cast-iron block and head. Bore and stroke: 3.875 x 3.00 in. Displacement: 283 cid. Compression ratio: 9.25:1. Brake hp: 195 at 4800 rpm. Taxable hp: 48. Torque: lbs.-ft. 285 at 2400. Five main bearings. Hydraulic valve lifters. Crankcase capacity: 4 qt. (add 1 qt. for new filter). Cooling system capacity: 16 qt. (add 1 qt. for heater). Carburetor: Rochester 7024101 two-barrel.

CHEVELLE 300, 300 DELUXE, MALIBU, MALIBU SS OPTIONAL 283-CID, 220-HP V-8: Overhead-valve. Cast-iron block and head. Bore and stroke: 3.875 x 3.00 in. Displacement: 283 cid. Compression ratio: 9.25:1. Brake hp: 220 at 4800 rpm. Taxable hp: 48.0. Torque: 295 lbs.-ft. at 3200. Five main bearings. Hydraulic valve lifters. Crankcase capacity: 4 qt. (add 1 qt. for new filter). Cooling system capacity: (add 1 qt. for heater). Carburetor: Rochester 7025127 four-barrel.

CHEVELLE 300, 300 DELUXE, MALIBU, MALIBU SS OPTIONAL 327-CID, 255-HP V-8: Overhead-valve. Cast-iron block and head. Bore and stroke: 4.00 x 3.25 in. Displacement: 327 cid. Compression ratio: 10.50:1. Brake hp: 250 at 4800 rpm. Taxable hp: 51.20. Torque: 355 lbs.-ft. at 3200. Five main bearings. Hydraulic valve lifters. Crankcase capacity: 4 qt. (add 1 qt. for new filter). Cooling system capacity: 14 qt. (add 1 qt. for heater). Carburetor: Rochester 7024127.

CHEVELLE, MALIBU, MALIBU SS OPTIONAL 327-CID, 300-HP V-8: Overhead-valve. Cast-iron block and head. Bore and stroke: 4.00 x 3.25 in. Displacement: 396 cid. Compression ratio: 10.50:1. Brake hp: 300 at 5000 rpm. Taxable hp: 51.20. Torque: 360 lbs.-ft. at 3200. Five main bearings. Hydraulic valve lifters. Crankcase capacity: 4 qt. (add 1 qt. for new filter). Cooling system capacity: 15 qt. (add 1 qt. for heater). Carburetor: Carter 3851761. Sales code: L35.

CHEVELLE MALIBU SS OPTIONAL 327-CID, 350-HP V-8: Overhead-valve. Cast-iron block and head. Bore and stroke: 4.00 x 3.25 in. Displacement: 327 cid. Compression ratio: 11.00:1. Brake hp: 350 at 6000 rpm. Taxable hp: 51.20. Torque: 360 lbs.-ft. at 3200. Five main bearings. Hydraulic valve lifters. Crankcase capacity: 4 qt. (Add 1 qt. for new filter). Cooling system capacity: 15 qt. (Add 1 qt. for heater). Carburetor: Holley 3883150 or Rochester 7026201 four-barrel. Engine code: EC or ED.

CHEVELLE SS OPTIONAL 396-CID, 375-HP V-8: Overhead-valve. Cast-iron block and head. Bore and stroke: 4.09 x 3.76 in. Displacement: 396 cid. Compression ratio: 11.0:1. Brake hp: 375 at 5600 rpm. Taxable hp: 53.60. Torque: 415 lbs.-ft. at 3600. Five main bearings. Hydraulic valve lifters. Crankcase capacity: 4 qt. (Add 1 qt. for new filter). Cooling system capacity: 22 qt. (Add 1 qt. for heater). Carburetor: Holley 3893229 four-barrel. Sales code: L37. Engine code: IX.

Note: Midyear option; only 201 Chevelle Z11 coupes with the L37 V-8 were built in late 1965.

CHASSIS

Wheelbase: 115 in. Overall length: (wagon) 201.4 in.; (car) 196.6 in. Width: 74.6 in. Overall height: (convertible) 52.9 in.; (sport coupe) 52.8 in.; (sedan) 53.2 in. and (wagon) 55.1 in. Front tread: 58 in. Rear tread: 58 in. Turning circle: (curb-to-curb) 41.9 ft.; (wall-to-wall) 44.7 ft. Overall steering ratio: (standard) 28.0:1; (power) 20.4:1. Luggage capacity in usable cubic feet: (coupe) 16.7; (sedan) 16.8; (convertible, top up) 16.5; (convertible, top down) 15.5. Tires: (wagons) 7.35 x 14; (car) 6.95 x 14. Four-wheel coil suspension. Four-link rear suspension. Ball-race steering gear.

OPTIONS

Four-season air conditioning ($363.70). Rear antenna, replacing front, except on station wagon (no cost). Positraction rear axle ($37.60). Optional rear axle ($2.20). Heavy-duty battery ($7.55). Heavy-duty body equipment for Chevelle 300 four-door sedan ($18.30). Special metallic brake facings ($37.70). Front bumper guards ($9.70). Rear bumper guards, except station wagons ($9.70). Heavy-duty chassis equipment for Chevelle 300 four-door sedan with air conditioning or 140-hp engine ($19.40). Heavy-duty clutch, six-cylinder ($5.40). Comfort and convenience package A for Chevelle 300 and Chevelle 300 Deluxe ($40.90). Comfort and convenience package A for Malibu and Super Sport ($30.15). Comfort and convenience package B for Chevelle 300 and Chevelle 300 Deluxe ($50.60). Comfort and convenience package B for Malibu and Super Sport ($39.85). Transmission oil cooler, with Powerglide ($16.15). Rear windshield defroster, sedan and sport coupe ($21.55). Dual exhaust, with 250-hp V-8 ($21.55). Temperature controlled fan with V-8b ($16.15). 42-amp Delcotron generator ($10.80). 55-amp Delcotron generator, standard with air conditioning ($21.55). 62-amp Delcotron generator for cars without air conditioning and no power steering ($75.33). Tinted glass in all windows ($31.25). Tinted windshield only ($19.95). Heater and defroster deletion for cars without air conditioning ($72 credit). Tri-volume horn ($14). Instrument panel safety pad ($18.30). Station wagon luggage rack ($43.05). Two-tone paint ($16.15). Power brakes ($43.05). Four-way power seat, not available in Chevelle 300, Malibu SS or

The 1965 Malibu SS convertible came with a starting price of $2,690 for the six-cylinder version and $2,796 with the base V-8.

CHEVELLE

This pristine 1965 Malibu SS convertible came with a 283-cid V-8 and plenty of amenities from the time period, including power steering, air conditioning, power top and a tinted windshield.

with four-speed transmission ($64.60). Power steering ($86.10). Station wagon power tailgate window ($26.90). Convertible power top ($53.80). Power windows on all except Chevelle 300 ($102.25). Heavy-duty radiator, not available with air conditioning or transissionb oil cooler ($10.80). Manual radio and antenna ($50.05). Push-button radio and antenna ($58.65). Push-button radio and rear speaker, except convertible ($72.10). AM/FM push-button radio ($136.70). Rear seat speaker, except convertible ($13.45). Black vinyl roof on coupes and sport coupes ($75.35). Front seat belt deletion ($11 credit). Deluxe seat belts with retractors ($7.55). Station wagon divided second seat ($37.70). Heavy-duty rear shock absorbers ($37.70). Sport-styled steering wheel ($32.30). Comfortilt steering wheel with Powerglide or four-speed manual transmission ($43.05). Heavy-duty front and rear suspension, except station wagons and Malibu SS ($4.85). Heavy-duty front and rear suspension on station wagons and Malibu SS ($3.80). Tachometer for V-8 models ($48.45). Five 6.95 x 14 white sidewall tires ($28.70 additional for models with 6.95 x 14 standard). Five 7.35 x 14 black sidewall tires ($7.80 additional for models with 6.95 x 14 standard). Five 7.35 x 14 white sidewall tires ($39.70 additional for models with 6.95 x 14 standard). Five 7.75 x 14 black sidewall tires ($22.25 additional for models with 6.95 x 14 standard). Five 7.75 x 14 white sidewall tires ($54.10 additional for models with 6.95 x 14 standard). Five 7.75 x 14 black sidewall nylon tires ($39.25 additional for models with 6.95 x 14 standard). Five 7.75 x 14 white sidewall tires ($73.20 additional for models with 6.95 x 14 standard). Five 7.35 x 14 white sidewall tires ($31.90 additional for models with 7.35 x 14 standard). Five 7.75 x 14 black sidewall tires ($14.45 additional for models with 7.35 x 14 standard). Five 7.75 x 14 white sidewall tires ($46.30 additional for models with 7.35 x 14 standard). Five 7.75 x 14 black sidewall nylon tires ($31.45 additional for models with 7.35 x 14 standard). Five 7.75 x 14 white sidewall nylon tires ($65.40 additional for models with 7.35 x 14 standard). Five 7.75 x 14 black sidewall nylon tires ($17.90 additional for models with 7.75 x 14 standard). Four-speed manual transmission ($188.30). Three-speed overdrive transmission ($107.60). Powerglide transmission with six-cylinder models ($188.30). Powerglide transmission for V-8 models ($199.10). Full wheel covers, except Malibu SS ($21.55). Simulated wire wheel covers, except Malibu SS ($75.35). Simulated wire wheel covers on Malibu SS ($57.05).

OPTION INSTALLATION RATES

Automatic transmission (67.3 percent). Four-speed manual transmission (10.3 percent). V-8 engine (62 percent). Six-cylinder engine (38 percent). Radio (64.3 percent). Heater (98 percent). Power steering (33.2 percent). Tilt steering (2.4 percent). Power brakes (7.7 percent). Power seat (0.2 percent). Power windows (0.5 percent). Power rear wagon window (3.1 percent). Bucket seats (21.4 percent). Seat belts (92.1 percent). White sidewall tires (66.1 percent). Windshield washers (58.1 percent). Tinted windshield only (38.9 percent). All tinted glass (14.2 percent). Back-up lights (84.5 percent). Air conditioning (11.1 percent). Dual exhaust (8.2 percent). Positraction (6.1 percent). Full wheel covers (55.2 percent). Overdrive (1.4 percent percent). Based on model-year production of 343,894 units.

HISTORICAL FOOTNOTES

According to *Motor Trend*, the 396-cid 375-hp Chevelle could do 0 to 60 mph in 6.7 seconds and covered the quarter mile in 15.3 seconds at 96 mph. According to *Car Life*, the 375-hp Chevelle could do 0 to 60 mph in 6.5 seconds and covered the quarter mile in 14.9 seconds at 98 mph. Allocations of these cars were supposed to be to Chevrolet officials only and Chevrolet General Manager "Bunkie" Knudsen had a personalized version. However, a limited number of the cars were sold to the public.

This 1966 Chevelle had the L78 optional 396 engine and came in Tuxedo Black.

A new body graced 1966 Chevelles, with forward-thrusting front fenders, new body contour lines, wider-appearing anodized aluminum grille and new rear body cove treatment. The new body was more curvaceous and had a slight "Coke bottle" shape with the rear fenders bulging upwards.

The dual round headlights were moved closer together, like they had been in 1964, rather than the "barbell" look of the 1965 units. The grille had nine vertical members behind four full-wide horizontal moldings. In the center of the grille was the Chevelle name, except on the hot version, which had a big SS badge with the numbers 396 below it. The grille moldings got the black-out treatment on the SS 396 muscle car. Rectangular, amber-colored front parking lamps sat in the bumper, below the headlights. The bumper on either side of the front license plate indentation had rectangular air slots. At the rear were rectangular lights that curved into the body edges with square back-up lenses at the inboard edge. A Chevrolet emblem decorated the center of the rear body panel on Chevelle 300 and Malibu models. The SS 396 had the word Chevelle in place of the Chevy badge and an SS 396 logo on the right-hand side. The back bumper was solid with a center license plate indentation. The rear of the sport coupe roof had a unique "flying buttress" treatment with the backlight hooded by the sail panels.

There was also a two-seat, four-door station wagon, but the relatively rare two-door wagon disappeared. A new four-door hardtop — called a sport sedan in Chevrolet lingo — joined the model mix in some series. Other offerings consisted of two- and four-door sedans, a two-door hardtop (or sports coupe) and a convertible.

I.D. NUMBERS

VIN embossed on a plate welded to the left front door hinge pillar post facing the driver. The first symbol 1 designates Chevrolet. The second and third symbols designate the series: (six-cylinder) 31=Chevelle 300, 33=Chevelle 300 Deluxe, 35=Malibu; (V-8) 32=Chevelle 300, 34=Chevelle 300 Deluxe, 36=Malibu, 38=SS 396. The fourth and fifth symbols designates body type: 11=two-door sedan, 17=two-door "flying buttress" sport coupe, 35=four-door six-passenger station wagon, 39=four-door hardtop, 67=two-door convertible and 69=four-door sedan. The sixth symbol designates the model year: 6=1966. The seventh symbol designates the assembly plant location: The seventh symbol indicated assembly plant: A=Atlanta, Georgia; B=Baltimore, Maryland.; F=Flint, Michigan; G=Framingham, Massachusetts.; K=Kansas City, Missouri; Z=Fremont, California The last six symbols are the sequential unit production number at the specific factory. The Fisher Body tag riveted to the top of the cowl on the left side of the car below the hood provides additional vehicle identification information. The Fisher Body STYLE NUMBER (ST) consists of a prefix identifying model year and four or more symbols identifying the series and body style (example: 66-13867 for a 1965 SS 396 convertible, which came with a V-8 only). The BODY NUMBER consists of a prefix designating assembly plant and the sequential unit production number at the specific factory. The TRIM NUMBER (TR) identifies upholstery.

COLORS

(A) Tuxedo Black, (C) Ermine White, (D) Mist Blue Metallic, (E) Danube Blue Metallic, (F) Marina Blue Metallic, (H) Willow Green Metallic, (K) Artesian Turquoise Metallic, (L) Tropic Turquoise Metallic, (M) Aztec Bronze Metallic, (N) Madeira Maroon Metallic, (R) Regal Red, (T) Sandalwood Tan Metallic, (V) Cameo Beige), (W) Chateau Slate Metallic and (Y) Lemonwood Yellow.

ENGINE CODES

Codes appear on the right side of six-cylinder blocks behind the distributor and right front of V-8 engine blocks: (194-cid/120-hp six) AA, AC, AG, AH, AK, AL, AN, AR, AS, AT, AU, AV, AW, AX, AY; (230 cid/140 hp six) CA, CB, CC, CD, BL, BM, BN, BO; (283-cid/195-hp V-8) DA, DB, DE, DF, DK, DI, DJ (283-cid/220-hp V-8) DG, DO, DL, DM; (327-cid/250-hp V-8) EA, EB, EC, EE; (396-cid/325-hp V-8) ED, EH, EK, EM; (396-cid/360-hp V-8) EF, EJ, EL, EN; (396-cid/375-hp V-8) KG.

CHEVELLE 300 — (6-CYL/V-8)

Chevelle 300 models were relatively lacking in ornamentation with series rear fender emblems, bright ventipane frames, bright windshield moldings, bright rear window moldings, an outside rearview mirror, four headlamps with anodized aluminum bezels, grille outline moldings, a rear cove nameplate, front bumper mounted park and turn lights, small hubcaps, single-unit rear lights (with bright bezels) and built-in back-up lights. The interiors were trimmed in pattern cloth and vinyl. A black rubber floor covering was standard, along with all GM safety features, five black sidewall tires and a heater and defroster.

Model Number	Body/Style Number	Body Type & Seating	Factory Price	Shipping Weight	Production Total
CHEVELLE 300 SERIES 131 (6-CYL)					
131	69	4d sedan-6P	$2,202	2,935 lbs.	Note 1
131	11	2d sedan-6P	$2,165	2,695 lbs.	Note 1
CHEVELLE 300 SERIES 132 (V-8)					
132	69	4d sedan-6P	$2,308	3,080 lbs.	Note 1
132	11	2d sedan-6P	$2,271	3,040 lbs.	Note 1

NOTE 1: Individual body style production is not available; see production notes below.

CHEVELLE 300 DELUXE — (6-CYL/V-8)

The Chevelle 300 Deluxe was a slightly upgraded Chevelle 300 with full-length body side moldings, Chevelle 300 Deluxe rear fender nameplates, painted rear quarter reveal moldings and bright tailgate moldings and an emblem on station wagon. A dual-spoke steering wheel with a horn ring was specific to this model, as was the color-keyed upper instrument panel with bright lower panel trim strip. The doors had bright accents on the trim panels and the rear armrests had built-in ashtrays. Cloth-and-vinyl upholstery was featured inside.

Model Number	Body/Style Number	Body Type & Seating	Factory Price	Shipping Weight	Production Total
CHEVELLE 300 DELUXE SERIES 133 (6-CYL)					
133	69	4d sedan-6P	$2,276	2,945 lbs.	Note 1
133	11	2d sedan-6P	$2,239	2,910 lbs.	Note 1
133	35	4d wagon-6P	$2,575	3,210 lbs.	Note 1
CHEVELLE 300 DELUXE SERIES 134 (V-8)					
134	69	4d sedan-6P	$2,362	3,095 lbs.	Note 1
134	11	2d sedan-6P	$2,345	3,060 lbs.	Note 1
134	35	4d wagon-6P	$2,661	3,350 lbs.	Note 1

NOTE 1: Individual body style production is not available; see production notes below.

CHEVELLE MALIBU — (6-CYL/V-8)

Standard equipment for the Chevelle Malibu models started out with the same items found on comparable Chevelle 300 Deluxe models, plus slender body sill, thin wheelhouse moldings, Malibu rear fender nameplates and a hood windsplit molding. An outline surrounded the rear cove and the single-unit rear lights with built-in back-up lamps (vertical light units were used on station wagons). At the center of the rear was a red, white, and blue Chevrolet badge with the bowtie emblem at its center. The Chevelle name was on the edge of the rear deck lid at the center. Malibu station wagons had a full-width ribbed molding, an emblem and a Chevelle nameplate on the tailgate. The Malibu interiors featured plusher cloth-and-vinyl trim combinations (all-vinyl on convertible and station wagon). A distinctive dual-spoke steering wheel was used. Black crackle-finish was used on the instrument panel upper section. Magic-Mirror acrylic lacquer finish, a glove compartment light, a bright-backed rearview mirror, bright roof rails and wall-to-wall deep-twist floor carpeting were advertised as additional Malibu features.

Model Number	Body/Style Number	Body Type & Seating	Factory Price	Shipping Weight	Production Total
CHEVELLE MALIBU SERIES 135 (6-CYL)					
135	69	4d sedan-6P	$2,352	2,960 lbs.	Note 1
135	39	4d sport coupe-6P	$2,458	3,035 lbs.	Note 1
135	17	2d sport coupe-6P	$2,378	2,935 lbs.	Note 1
135	67	2d convertible-6P	$2,586	3,030 lbs.	Note 1
135	35	4d wagon-6P	$2,651	2,651 lbs.	Note 1
CHEVELLE MALIBU SERIES 136 (V-8)					
136	69	4d sedan-6P	$2,458	3,110 lbs.	Note 1
136	39	4d sport coupe-6P	$2,564	3,180 lbs.	Note 1
136	17	2d sport coupe-6P	$2,484	3,075 lbs.	Note 1
136	67	2d convertible-6P	$2,693	3,175 lbs.	Note 1
136	35	4d wagon-6P	$2,756	3,375 lbs.	Note 1

NOTE 1: Individual body style production is not available; see production notes below.

CHEVELLE SS 396 — (V-8)

The Chevelle performance package was no longer the Malibu SS, but simply the Chevelle SS 396. It featured twin simulated air intakes on its hood, a blacked-out grille, wheelhouse moldings, ribbed and color-accented

The flashy 1966 Chevelle SS 396 clocked a 14.66-second quarter mile in one magazine test.

body sill moldings, ribbed and color-accented lower rear fender lower moldings, an SS 396 grille emblem, an SS 396 rear cove emblem and Super Sport script on the rear fenders. Specific mag-style wheel covers were included, as were five nylon red-stripe tires (although white sidewall tires were a no-cost option). The interiors were all-vinyl, with a bench front seat as standard equipment. The interior included all Malibu features (except for color-keyed vinyl-coated cargo floor mats and textured vinyl cargo area sidewalls). Chevelle SS 396 buyers also got a standard 325-hp Turbo-Jet V-8, a special suspension, a fully synchronized three-speed manual transmission and a floor-mounted gear shifter. In a March 1966 six-car comparison road test *Car and Driver* reported that the SS 396 (360-hp sport coupe version) was not the fastest car tested, but "scored very high with us because of its intrinsic balance. It handled very nicely and therefore was a ball to drive. Its engine, which is certainly one of the most advanced designs in the world, has great turbine-like smoothness with tremendous power (and probably more potential than the other cars by a wide margin) plus greater flexibility." It did the quarter mile in 14.66 seconds at 99.88 mph.

Model Number	Body/Style Number	Body Type & Seating	Factory Price	Shipping Weight	Production Total
136	13617	2d sport coupe-6P	$2,276	3,375 lbs.	Note 1
136	13667	2d convertible-6P	$2,964	3,470 lbs.	Note 1

NOTE 1: Individual body style production is not available; see production notes.

PRODUCTION NOTES

NOTE 1 Model-year production of all 1966 Chevelles was 412,155 units.
NOTE 2 Industry statistical breakouts in rounded-off numbers show 111,700 Chevelle sixes and 300,500 Chevelle V-8s were built in 1965.
NOTE 3 Additional statistics record series production, in rounded-off figures (except SS 396), as follows:

Chevelle 300 (6-cyl)	23,300
Chevelle 300 (V-8)	5,300
Total	**28,600**
Chevelle 300 Del. (6-cyl)	27,100
Chevelle 300 (V-8)	10,500
Total	**37,500**
Malibu (6-cyl)	52,300
Malibu (V-8)	189,300
Total	**241,600**
SS 396 (V-8)	72,272

The new Chevelle body style for 1966 had a slight "Coke bottle" shape with the rear fenders bulging upwards.

CHEVELLE

Total	72,272
Wagons (6-cyl)	8,900
Wagons (V-8)	23,000
Total	31,900

NOTE 4 Production by factory was:

Code	Factory	Production	Code	Factory	Production
B	Baltimore	82,132	H	Fremont	48,206
K	Kansas City	100,551	*	Bloomfield	180
A	Atlanta	95,611	G	Framingham	38,111
F	Flint	47,454			

(*) Bloomfield was not actually a factory but an export shipping point for cars actually built at other plants.

ENGINES

CHEVELLE 300, MALIBU, MALIBU SS BASE 194-CID, 120-HP SIX-CYL: Overhead-valve. Cast-iron block. Bore and stroke: 3.562 x 3.25 in. Displacement: 194.4 cid. Compression ratio: 8.5:1. Brake hp: 120 at 4400 rpm. Taxable hp: 36. Torque: 177 lbs.-ft. at 2400 rpm. Seven main bearings. Hydraulic valve lifters. Crankcase capacity: 4 qt. (add 1 qt. for new filter). Cooling system capacity: 11 qt. (add 1 qt. for heater). Carburetor: Rochester one-barrel Model 7023105.

CHEVELLE 300, MALIBU, MALIBU SS OPTIONAL 230-CID, 140-HP SIX-CYL: Overhead-valve. Cast-iron block. Bore and stroke: 3.875 x 3.25 in. Displacement: 230 cid. Compression ratio: 8.5:1. Brake hp: 140 at 4400 rpm. Taxable hp: 36.00. Torque: 220 lbs.-ft. at 1600 rpm. Seven main bearings. Hydraulic valve lifters. Crankcase capacity: 4 qt. (add 1 qt. for new filter). Cooling system capacity: 11 qt. (add 1 qt. for heater). Carburetor: Rochester one-barrel Model 7023105.

CHEVELLE 300, 300 DELUXE, MALIBU BASE 283-CID, 195-HP V-8: Overhead-valve. Cast-iron block and head. Bore and stroke: 3.875 x 3.00 in. Displacement: 283 cid. Compression ratio: 9.25:1. Brake hp: 195 at 4800 rpm. Taxable hp: 48. Torque: 285 lbs.-ft. at 2400. Five main bearings. Hydraulic valve lifters. Crankcase capacity: 4 qt. (add 1 qt. for new filter). Cooling system capacity: 16 qt. (add 1 qt. for heater). Carburetor: Rochester 7024101 two-barrel.

CHEVELLE 300, 300 DELUXE, MALIBU OPTIONAL 283-CID, 220-HP V-8: Overhead-valve. Cast-iron block and head. Bore and stroke: 3.875 x 3.00 in. Displacement: 283 cid. Compression ratio: 9.25:1. Brake hp: 220 at 4800 rpm. Taxable hp: 48. Torque: 295 lbs.-ft. at 3200. Five main bearings. Hydraulic valve lifters. Crankcase capacity: 4 qt. (add 1 qt. for new filter). Cooling system capacity: (Chevy II, Chevelle) 15 qt.; (Chevrolet) 16 qt. (add 1 qt. for heater). Carburetor: Rochester 7025127 four-barrel.

CHEVELLE 300, 300 DELUXE, MALIBU OPTIONAL 327-CID, 275-HP V-8: Overhead-valve. Cast-iron block and head. Bore and stroke: 4.00 x 3.25 in. Dis-

The redesigned 1966 Chevelle was more curvaceous, and the SS 396 packed a punch with its optional 325-, 360- and 375-hp engine choices.

The dual headlights of the 1966 Chevelle were closer together than the previous year. This SS convertible was powered by a 396-cid V-8.

placement: 327 cid. Compression ratio: 10.25:1. Brake hp: 275 at 4800 rpm. Taxable hp: 51.20. Torque: 355 lbs.-ft. at 3200. Five main bearings. Hydraulic valve lifters. Crankcase capacity: 4 qt. (add 1 qt. for new filter). Cooling system capacity: 14 qt. (add 1 qt. for heater). Carburetor: Carburetor: Holley 3876747 or Carter 3876749 four-barrel. Sales code: L30.

CHEVELLE SS 396-CID BASE 325-HP V-8: Overhead-valve. Cast-iron block and head. Bore and stroke: 4.09 x 3.76 in. Displacement: 396 cid. Compression ratio: 10.25:1. Brake hp: 325 at 4800 rpm. Taxable hp: 53.60. Torque: 410 lbs.-ft. at 3200. Five main bearings. Hydraulic valve lifters. Crankcase capacity: 4 qt. (add 1 qt. for new filter). Cooling system capacity: 22 qt. (add 1 qt. for heater). Carburetor: Holley 3874898 or Rochester 7026201 four-barrel. Sales code: L35.

CHEVELLE SS 396-CID OPTIONAL 360-HP V-8: Overhead-valve. Cast-iron block and head. Bore and stroke: 4.09 x 3.76 in. Displacement: 396 cid. Compression ratio: 10.25:1. Brake hp: 360 at 5200 rpm. Taxable hp: 53.60. Torque: 420 lbs.-ft. at 3600. Five main bearings. Hydraulic valve lifters. Crankcase capacity: 4 qt. (add 1 qt. for new filter). Cooling system capacity: 22 qt. (add 1 qt. for heater). Carburetor: Holley 3886087 or Rochester 7026201 four-barrel. Sales code: L34.

CHEVELLE SS 396-CID OPTIONAL 375-HP V-8: Overhead-valve. Cast-iron block and head. Bore and stroke: 4.09 x 3.76 in. Displacement: 396 cid. Compression ratio: 11.0:1. Brake hp: 375 at 5600 rpm. Taxable hp: 53.60. Torque: 415 lbs.-ft. at 3600. Five main bearings. Hydraulic valve lifters. Crankcase capacity: 4 qt. (add 1 qt. for new filter). Cooling system capacity: 22 qt. (add 1 qt. for heater). Carburetor: Holley 3893229 four-barrel. Sales code: L78.

Note: The L78 V-8 option was released at midyear.

CHASSIS

Wheelbase: 115 in. Overall length: (car) 197 in.. (wagon) 197.6 in. Front tread: 58 in. Rear tread: 58 in. Tires: (Chevelle) 6.95 x 14 or 7.35 x 14, (SS 396) 7.75 x 14.

OPTIONS

RPO L77 220-hp V-8 ($52.70). RPO L30 275-hp V-8 ($92,70). RPO L35 325-hp V-8 ($182.95). RPO L79 350-hp V-8 ($190). RPO L34 360-hp V-8 in SS 396 ($105.35); in other Chevelles ($290.55). RPO L78 375-hp V-8 ($236). RPO N10 dual exhaust ($21.10). RPO M13 heavy-duty three-speed manual transmission in SS 396 (no charge. RPO M35 Powerglide transmission in SS 396 ($115.90); in other Chevelles ($194.85). RPO M20 wide-ratio four-speed manual transmission in SS 396 ($105.35); in other Chevelles ($184.35). RPO M21 close-

This 1966 SS had a four-speed and optional floor console.

25

The 396-cid V-8 put the Chevelle SS in the muscle car class.

Robert Genat photo

ratio four-speed manual transmission ($105.35). RPO G80 Positraction rear axle ($36.90). RPO J65 sintered metallic brake linings ($36.90). RPO G66 Superlift rear air shocks ($36.90). RPO F40 special suspension ($4.75). RPO J50 power brakes ($42.15). RPO N40 power steering ($84.30). RPO A31 power windows ($100.10). RPO K30 Cruiser-Master speed control ($76.40). RPO CO8 vinyl roof ($73.75). RPO A51 power front seats ($69.55). RPO A51 Astro bucket front seats ($110.60). RPO C60 Four-Season air conditioning ($356). RPO Z19 Comfort & Convenience group ($21.10). RPO AO1 tinted glass in all windows ($30.55). RPO AO2 tinted windshield ($19.50). RPO V31 front bumper guards ($9.70). RPO V32 rear bumper guards ($9.70). RPO U14 special instrumentation including ammeter, oil pressure gauge, engine coolant temperature gauge and tachometer ($79). RPO N33 Comfortilt steering wheel ($42.15). RPO D55 center console ($47.40). RPO U16 tachometer ($47.40). RPO V74 hazard warning lights ($21.10). RPO U63 AM push-button radio ($57.40). RPO U69 AM/FM push-button radio ($133.80). RPO U80 rear seat speaker ($13.20).

OPTION INSTALLATION RATES

Automatic transmission (65.4 percent). Four-speed manual transmission (17.4 percent). V-8 engine (73.9 percent). Six-cylinder engine (26.1 percent). Radio (71.4 percent). Heater (98.2 percent). Power steering (41.4 percent). Tilt steering (1.4 percent). Power brakes (7.5 percent). Power seat (0.3 percent). Power windows (0.7 percent). Power rear wagon window (2.7 percent). Bucket seats (21.3 percent). White sidewall tires (60.3 percent). Tinted windshield only (42.6 percent). All tinted glass (17.2 percent). Air conditioning (13.6 percent). Dual exhaust (20.9 percent). Positraction (15.2 percent). Full wheel covers (54.0 percent). Power antenna (0.2 percent). Non-glare rearview mirror (4.1 percent). Based on model-year production of 412,680 units.

HISTORICAL FOOTNOTES

E.M. Estes was the chief executive officer of Chevrolet this year, which was the second-best production year in the company's history. Chevelle sales set a new record.

The Chevelle body introduced in 1966 was used again in 1967, but there were styling refinements and trim differences. The forward-thrusting look of the front fenders was toned down a bit by making the front feature line more vertical. The anodized aluminum grille had thicker horizontal members. The dual round headlights moved further apart, with a small space between them showing the hirizontal grille bars. The standard grille had the Chevrolet emblem above it and the Chevelle name was spelled out in chrome letters above the left-hand headlights. The SS 396 grille again had a big SS badge with the numbers 396 below it. The "background"

The 1967 SS 396 convertible came with a price tag of $3,033.

grille moldings got the black-out treatment on the SS 396. Amber-colored front parking lamps were positioned at the outboard ends of a large horizontal slot that ran nearly fully across the front bumper.

The bumper had a front license plate indentation and solid ends. At the rear the "veed" taillights were notched into the fender ends. Ribs molded into the taillight lenses divided them into three stacked segments. Rectangular back-up light lenses were set into the rear bumper on either side of the license plate indentation. The rear panel on base and Malibu models had a thin outline molding. On SS 396s, the panel was finished in flat black and had an "SS" badge in its center.

Naturally, the SS 396 had a special hood with simulated air scoops with bright horizontal louvers. Base 300 models had untrimmed body sides, but other series carried a thin body side molding on the lower feature line. Chevelle, Malibu or Super Sport lettering was placed way back on the rear fender sides. The luxurious-looking Concours Custom station wagon was a new model with a rich wood-grain look and 86 cubic feet of cargo space.

I.D. NUMBERS

VIN embossed on a plate welded to the left front door hinge pillar post facing the driver. The first symbol 1 designates Chevrolet. The second and third symbols designate the series: (six-cylinder) 31=Chevelle 300, 33=Chevelle 300 Deluxe, 35=Malibu, 37=Concours station wagon; (V-8) 32=Chevelle 300, 34=Chevelle 300 Deluxe, 36=Malibu, 38=SS 396 and 38=Concours Estate station wagon. The fourth and fifth symbols designates body type: 11=two-door sedan, 17=two-door "flying buttress" sport coupe, 35=four-door six-passenger station wagon, 39=four-door hardtop, 67=two-door convertible and 69=four-door sedan. The sixth symbol designates the model year: 7=1967. The seventh symbol designates the assembly plant location: The seventh symbol indicated assembly plant: A=Atlanta, Georgia; B=Baltimore, Maryland; G=Framingham, Massachusetts; K=Kansas City, Missouri; Z=Fremont, California. The last six symbols are the sequential unit production number at the specific factory. The Fisher Body tag riveted to the top of the cowl on the left side of the car below the hood provides additional vehicle identification information. The Fisher Body STYLE NUMBER (ST) consists of a prefix identifying model year and four or more symbols identifying the series and body style (example: 67-13835 for a 1967 Concours station wagon with a V-8). The BODY NUMBER consists of a prefix designating assembly plant and the sequential unit production number at the specific factory. The TRIM NUMBER (TR) identifies upholstery.

COLORS

(A) Tuxedo Black, (C) Ermine White, (D) Nantucket Blue, (E) Deepwater Blue, (F) Marina Blue, (G) Granada Gold, (H) Mountain Green, (K) Emerald Turquoise, (L) Tahoe Turquoise, (M) Royal Plum, (N) Madeira Maroon, (R) Bolero Red, (S) Sierra Fawn, (T) Capri Cream and (Y) Butternut Yellow.

ENGINE CODES

Codes appear on the right side of six-cylinder blocks behind the distributor and right front of V-8 engine blocks. Engine codes for 1967 were: (230-cid/140-hp six) CA, CB, CC, CD, BC, BB, BN, BO, BL, BM; (250-cid/155-hp six) CM, CN, CO, CP, CQ, CR, CS and CT; (283-cid/195-hp V-8) DA, DB, DI, DJ, DK, DN and DE; (327/275-hp V-8) EA, EB, EQ, EE and EC; (327-cid/325-hp V-8) EP, ER and ES; (396-cid/325-hp V-8) ED, EF, EH, EM, ET and EV; (396-cid/350-hp V-8) EK, EL, EN, EU and EW; (396-cid/375-hp V-8) EG and EX.

CHEVELLE 300 — (6-CYL/V-8)

All Chevelles had parking and directional signals, windshield bright reveal moldings, bright ventipane frames, bright rear window reveal moldings and back-up lights. Chevelle 300 models had rear fender series iden-

CHEVELLE

tification, single-unit taillights with bright bezels, a chromed outside rearview mirror and Chevelle lettering at the right-hand side of the rear body panel. Chevelle 300 interiors were trimmed in cloth and vinyl and included these features: parking brake and brake system warning light, cigarette lighter, glove compartment lock, lever-type door handles, front door armrests, foam-cushioned front seat, padded sun visors, black rubber floor covering, day/night rearview mirror, four-way hazard flasher system and center dome light.

Model Number	Body/Style Number	Body Type & Seating	Factory Price	Shipping Weight	Production Total
CHEVELLE 300 SERIES 131 (6-CYL)					
131	69	4d sedan-6P	$2,250	2,955 lbs.	Note 1
131	11	2d sedan-6P	$2,221	2,935 lbs.	Note 1
CHEVELLE 300 SERIES 132 (V-8)					
132	69	4d sedan-6P	$2,356	3,090 lbs.	Note 1
132	11	2d sedan-6P	$2,326	3,370 lbs.	Note 1

NOTE 1: Individual body style production is not available; see production notes below.

CHEVELLE 300 DELUXE — (6-CYL/V-8) SERIES 133/134

The slightly embellished Chevelle 300 Deluxe series models featured all Chevelle 300 equipment plus (or instead) bright exterior body sill moldings, rear cove lower trim moldings on the sedan, Chevelle 300 Deluxe rear fender nameplates and a rear cove or tailgate center emblem. Chevelle 300 Deluxe interiors were cloth and vinyl (all-vinyl in station wagon) and the instrument panel had a silver-finished upper accent. The rear armrests had built-in ashtrays, while the floor was covered with color-keyed vinyl-coated rubber. Automatic interior light switches were found on the door jambs. The bodies had "Flush & Dry" rocker panels and inner fenders.

Model Number	Body/Style Number	Body Type & Seating	Factory Price	Shipping Weight	Production Total
CHEVELLE 300 DELUXE SERIES 133 (6-CYL)					
133	69	4d sedan-6P	$2,324	2,980 lbs.	Note 1
133	11	2d sedan-6P	$2,295	2,955 lbs.	Note 1
133	35	4d wagon-6P	$2,619	3,230 lbs.	Note 1
CHEVELLE 300 DELUXE SERIES 134 (V-8)					
134	69	4d sedan-6P	$2,430	3,110 lbs.	Note 1
134	11	2d sedan-6P	$2,400	3,090 lbs.	Note 1
134	35	4d wagon-6P	$2,725	3,360 lbs.	Note 1

NOTE 1: Individual body style production is not available; see production notes below.

MALIBU — (6-CYL/V-8) SERIES 135/136

A nicely appointed Chevelle, the Malibu found exterior distinction by the use of bright lower body side and rear quarter moldings, roof drip cap moldings, bright rear quarter window reveal moldings (on station wagons), Malibu rear fender nameplates, a black-accented rear cove outline panel, single-unit taillights with black-accented bezels and bright horizontal strips, and a Chevelle badge on the rear body panel or tailgate. Station wagons had a tailgate molding. Full wheel covers were also included on the Malibu's standard equipment list. Malibu interiors were plusher than those of Chevelle 300 and 300 Deluxe models and included a specific steering wheel, a walnut-finish upper panel on the instrument panel, an illuminated heater control panel, an electric clock, bright accents on the vinyl sidewalls, bright accents on the door panel trim, bright bases on front armrests, a foam-cushioned rear seat, color-keyed floor carpeting and courtesy lights in the convertible.

Model Number	Body/Style Number	Body Type & Seating	Factory Price	Shipping Weight	Production Total
MALIBU SERIES 135 (6-CYL)					
135	69	4d sedan-6P	$2,400	3,000 lbs.	Note 1

The front end of the 1967 Chevelle got a few modifications, including thicker horizontal grille bars, and a new bumper.

Jerry Heasley photo

The SS grille again had the Chevrolet emblem with the numbers below it.

135	17	2d sport coupe-6P	$2,434	2,980 lbs.	Note 1
135	67	2d conv-6P	$2,637	3,050 lbs.	Note 1
135	35	4d wagon-6P	$2,695	3,260 lbs.	Note 1
135	39	4d sport sedan-6P	$2,506	3,065 lbs.	Note 1
MALIBU SERIES 136 (V-8)					
136	69	4d sedan-6P	$2,506	3,130 lbs.	Note 1
136	17	2d sport coupe-6P	$2,540	3,115 lbs.	Note 1
136	67	2d conv-6P	$2,743	3,185 lbs.	Note 1
136	35	4d wagon-6P	$2,801	3,390 lbs.	Note 1
136	39	4d sport sedan-6P	$2,611	3,200 lbs.	Note 1

NOTE 1: Individual body style production is not available; see production notes below.

CONCOURS CUSTOM — (6-CYL/V-8) SERIES 137/138

The new Concours Custom station wagon was a luxury station wagon of the Chevelle line featuring a special black-accented grille, synthetic wood-grain exterior side and tailgate paneling (with bright outline trim), front and rear wheelhouse moldings, ribbed gray-accented body sill moldings, a tailgate emblem badge for Concours identification and a Concours script on each rear fender. Concours Custom interiors were trimmed in textured vinyl. The passenger floor was carpeted and the cargo load floor had a vinyl coating.

Model Number	Body/Style Number	Body Type & Seating	Factory Price	Shipping Weight	Production Total
CONCOURS CUSTOM SERIES 137 (6-CYL)					
137	35	4d wagon-6P	$2,827	3,270 lbs.	Note 1
CONCOURS CUSTOM SERIES 138 (V-8)					
137	35	4d wagon-6P	$2,933	3,405 lbs.	Note 1

NOTE 1: Individual body style production is not available; see production notes below.

CHEVELLE SS 396 — (V-8) SERIES 138

The Chevelle SS 396 had a youthful flair and was identifiable by these exterior additions or changes from other Chevelles: a special black-accented grille with an SS 396 badge in its center, bright front and rear wheelhouse outline moldings, ribbed gray-accented body sill moldings, color-keyed body side accent stripes, a simulated hood air scoop with a new bright metal horizontal louver, Super Sport rear fender emblems on both sides, a black-painted rear cove panel (with an SS 396 center medallion), five special Red Stripe wide-tread tires, specific full wheel covers, a special three-speed manual transmission with floor-mounted gearshift lever and a 396-cid 325-hp "big-block" V-8 engine. The SS 396 interiors were all-vinyl, with a black-accented upper panel on the instrument board. Bucket seats were a popular option. A 350-hp version of the 396-cid V-8 was a regular production option. The 375-hp version of the 396-cid V-8 was not listed on Chevrolet Motor Division's internal specification sheets, but it was possible to purchase the necessary components from a Chevrolet dealer to convert the 350-hp V-8 to a 375-hp job. The cost of this conversion was $475.80. A "dual-purpose" Turbo-Hydra-Matic 350 transmission was a newly available extra for the SS 396 only. This option allowed shifting gears with an automatic transmission, as well as "shift-less" operation in the "D" range.

Model Number	Body/Style Number	Body Type & Seating	Factory Price	Shipping Weight	Production Total
138	17	2d sport coupe-6P	$2,825	3,415 lbs.	Note 1
138	67	2d convertible-6P	$3,033	3,495 lbs.	Notes 1

NOTE 1: Individual body style production is not available; see production notes.

PRODUCTION NOTES

NOTE 1 Model-year production of all 1967 Chevelles was 369,133 units.
NOTE 2 Industry statistical breakouts in rounded-off numbers show 85,700 Chevelle sixes and 283,400 Chevelle V-8s were built in 1967.
NOTE 3 Additional statistics record series production, in rounded-off figures (except SS 396), as follows:

Chevelle 300 (6-cyl)	19,900
Chevelle 300 (V-8)	4,800
Total	**24,700**
Chevelle 300 Del. (6-cyl)	19,300
Chevelle 300 (V-8)	7,000

CHEVELLE

GM produced 63,000 SS 396 Chevelles for 1967.

Total	26,300
Malibu (6-cyl)	40,600
Malibu (V-8)	187,200
Total	227,800
SS 396 (V-8)	63,000
Total	63,000
Wagons (6-cyl)	5,900
Wagons (V-8)	21,400
Total	27,300

NOTE 4 Production by factory was:

Code	Factory	Production	Code	Factory	Production
B	Baltimore	108,819	Z	Fremont	48,799
K	Kansas City	106,253	*	Bloomfield	120
A	Atlanta	82,622	G	Framingham	22,519

(*) Bloomfield was not actually a factory but an export shipping point for cars actually built at other plants.

NOTE 5 Exactly 12,772 convertibles were built in the 1967 model year, including Chevelle Malibu and Malibu SS models. This figure is included in the rounded-off totals given above There is no SS breakout available.

NOTE 6 Exactly 63,006 Chevelle SS 396 models were built during the 1967 model year. This includes both hardtops and convertibles. All were V-8 powered. No further body style breakouts are available.

NOTE 7 No more than 29,937 Chevelle SS 396 convertibles were built.

ENGINES

CHEVELLE 300, 300 DELUXE, MALIBU BASE SIX-CYL: Inline. Overhead-valve. Cast-iron block. Displacement: 230 cid. Bore and stroke: 3.875 x 3.25 in. Compression ratio: 8.5:1. Brake hp: 140 at 4400 rpm. Seven main bearings. Hydraulic valve lifters. Crankcase capacity: 4 qt. (add 1 qt. for new filter). Cooling system capacity: 12 qt (add 6 qt. for heater). Carburetor: Rochester one-barrel Model 7027003.

CHEVELLE 300, 300 DELUXE, MALIBU OPTIONAL SIX-CYL: Inline. Overhead-valve. Cast-iron block. Displacement: 250 cid. Bore and stroke: 3.875 x 3.53 in. Compression ratio: 8.5:1. Brake hp: 155 at 4200 rpm. Taxable hp: 36. Torque: 235 lbs.-ft. at 1600 rpm. Seven main bearings. Hydraulic valve lifters. Crankcase capacity: 4 qt. (add 1 qt. for new filter). Cooling system capacity: 12 qt (add 6 qt. for heater). Carburetor: Rochester one-barrel Model 7028017.

CHEVELLE 300, 300 DELUXE, MALIBU, CONCOURS BASE V-8: Overhead-valve. Cast-iron block and head. Bore and stroke: 3.875 x 3.00 in. Displacement: 283 cid. Compression ratio: 9.25:1. Brake hp: 195 at 4800 rpm. Taxable hp: 48. Torque: 285 lbs.-ft. at 2400. Five main bearings. Hydraulic valve lifters. Crankcase capacity: 4 qt. (add 1 qt. for new filter). Cooling system capacity: (Chevy II, Chevrolet) 15 qt.; (Chevelle) 16 qt. (add 1 qt. for heater). Carburetor: Rochester 7027101 two-barrel.

CHEVELLE 300, 300 DELUXE, MALIBU, CONCOURS OPTIONAL 327-CID, 275-HP V-8: Overhead-valve. Cast-iron block and head. Bore and stroke: 4.00 x 3.25 in. Displacement: 327 cid. Compression ratio: 10.25:1. Brake hp: 275 at 4800 rpm. Taxable hp: 51.20. Torque: 355 lbs.-ft. at 3200. Five main bearings. Hydraulic valve lifters. Crankcase capacity: 4 qt. (add 1 qt. for new filter). Cooling system capacity: 16 qt. (add 1 qt. for heater). Carburetor: Four-barrel. Sales code: L30.

CHEVELLE 300, 300 DELUXE, MALIBU, CONCOURS OPTIONAL 327-CID, 325-HP V-8: Overhead-valve. Cast-iron block and head. Bore and stroke: 4.00 x 3.25 in. Displacement: 327 cid. Compression ratio: 11.00:1. Brake hp: 325 at 5600 rpm. Taxable hp: 51.20. Torque: 355 lbs.-ft. at 3600. Five main bearings. Hydraulic valve lifters. Crankcase capacity: 4 qt. (add 1 qt. for new filter). Cooling system capacity: 14 qt. (add 1 qt. for heater). Carburetor: Four-barrel. Sales code: L30.

CHEVELLE SS 396 BASE V-8: Overhead-valve. Cast-iron block and head. Bore and stroke: 4.09 x 3.76 in. Displacement: 396 cid. Compression ratio: 10.25:1. Brake hp: 325 at 4800 rpm. Taxable hp: 53.60. Torque:

410 lbs.-ft. at 3200. Five main bearings. Hydraulic valve lifters. Crankcase capacity: 4 qt. (add 1 qt. for new filter). Cooling system capacity: 22 qt. (add 1 qt. for heater). Carburetor: Rochester 7027201 four-barrel. Sales code: L35.

CHEVELLE SS 396-CID, 350-HP OPTIONAL V-8: Overhead-valve. Cast-iron block and head. Bore and stroke: 4.09 x 3.76 in. Displacement: 396 cid. Compression ratio: 10.25:1. Brake hp: 350 at 5200 rpm. Taxable hp: 53.60. Torque: 415 lbs.-ft. at 3400. Five main bearings. Hydraulic valve lifters. Crankcase capacity: 4 qt. (add 1 qt. for new filter). Cooling system capacity: 22 qt. (add 1 qt. for heater). Carburetor: Four-barrel. Sales code: L34.

CHEVELLE SS 396-CID, 375-HP OPTIONAL V-8: Overhead-valve. Cast-iron block and head. Bore and stroke: 4.09 x 3.76 in. Displacement: 396 cid. Compression ratio: 11.00:1. Brake hp: 375 at 5600 rpm. Taxable hp: 53.60. Torque: 415 lbs.-ft. at 3600. Five main bearings. Solid valve lifters. Crankcase capacity: 4 qt. (add 1 qt. for new filter). Cooling system capacity: 23 qt. (add 1 qt. for heater). Carburetor: Four-barrel.

[Note: This engine was not listed in 1967 Chevelle sales literature, but did have a limited installation rate.]

CHASSIS

Wheelbase: 115 in. Overall length: 197 in. Front tread: 58 in. Rear tread: 58 in. Tires: (sport sedan or convertible with 327-cid V-8 and all station wagons) 7.75 x 14; (SS 396) F70 x 14; (other Chevelles) 7.35 x 14.

OPTIONS

Four-Season air conditioning, including 61-amp Delcotron, heavy-duty radiator and temperature-controlled fan and requiring larger tires with some Chevelles ($356). Station wagon rear window air deflector ($19). Air Injection Reactor, requiring closed ventilation system ($44.75). Rear antenna, except station wagons or Chevelles with AM/FM radio ($9.50). Positraction rear axle ($42.15). Special economy or high-performance rear axle ($2.15). Heavy-duty battery ($7.40). Center rear seat belts for cars with standard belts ($6.35). Front and rear Custom Deluxe seat belts ($6.35). Center rear Custom Deluxe seat belts for cars with Custom Deluxe seat belts or Custom Appearance group ($7.90). Standard type shoulder belts, in cars with standard seat belts ($23.20). Custom Deluxe shoulder belts, for cars with Custom Deluxe seat belts or Custom Appearance package ($26.35). Front disc brakes, not available with metallic brakes ($79). Sintered metallic brake linings ($36.90). Front bumper guards ($12.65). Rear bumper guards ($12.65). Electric clock in Chevelle 300 and 300 Deluxe models ($15.80). Heavy-duty clutch, V-8s except SS 396 and cars with cold-air injection ($10.55). Heavy-duty clutch on sixes except 155 hp ($5.30). Rear windshield defroster in sedans and sport coupes ($21.10). Door edge guards, two-door models ($3.20). Door edge guards, four-door models except standard on Custom station wagon ($6.35). 250-cid 155-hp six-cylinder engine ($26.35). 327-cid 325-hp V-8, except SS 396 ($198.05). 327-cid 275-hp V-8 engine, except SS 396 ($92.70). 396-cid 350-hp V-8 engine, SS 396 only ($105.35). Dual exhaust on all Chevelles with the 275-hp engine ($21.10). Temperature-controlled fan, V-8s, standard with air conditioning ($15.80). 42-amp Delcotron generator, not available with air conditioning ($15.80). 61-amp Delcotron generator, standard with air conditioning ($21.10). All windows tinted ($30.55). Tinted windshield only ($21.10). Driver and passenger Strato-Ease headrests, with front bucket seats ($52.70). Driver and passenger Strato-Ease headrests, with standard front bench seat ($42.15). Heater and defroster deletion ($70.70 credit). Tri-volume horn ($13.70). Special instrumentation with ammeter, temperature gauge, oil pressure gauge and tachometer ($79). Ash tray light ($1.60). Courtesy light, all except convertibles ($4.25). Glove box light, Chevelle 300 and 300 Deluxe ($2.65). Luggage light, all except station wagon ($2.65). Underhood light ($2.65). Station wagon luggage rack ($42.15). Twin front and rear floor mats ($10.55). Left-hand outside remote-control mirror ($9.50). Side window moldings, four-door sedans and Malibu station wagons

This 1967 Chevelle SS 396 came in Tahoe Turquoise.

($21.10). Side and rear quarter window molding, Chevelle 300 Deluxe station wagons ($26.35). Two-tone paint ($15.80). Power brakes ($42.15). Four-way power front seat, except with floor-mounted transmission, bucket seats on Chevelle 300 series ($69.55). Power steering ($84.30). Station wagon power tailgate window ($31.60). Power convertible top in white, black or blue ($52.70) Power windows Concours station wagon, Malibus and SS 396 ($100.10). Heavy-duty radiator, except with air conditioning ($10.55). AM/FM push-button radio with front antenna ($133.80). Push-button radio with front antenna ($57.40). AM/FM push-button radio with front antenna ($70.60). AM/FM push-button radio with front antenna and rear speaker ($147). Rear seat speaker ($13.20) Vinyl roof cover, for hardtop models ($73.75). Thick front foam seat cushion, Chevelle 300 and 300 Deluxe ($7.40). Strato bucket seats in sport coupe and convertible ($110.60). Superlift rear shock absorbers ($36.90). Speed and cruise control, V-8s with automatic transmissions ($50.05). Speed warning indicator ($10.55). Deluxe steering wheel in Chevelle 300s ($7.40). Deluxe steering wheel in Chevelle 300 Deluxe ($4.25). Comfort-tilt steering wheel, requires four-speed manual or automatic transmissions ($42.15). Sport styled steering wheel ($31.60). Stereo tape system with four speakers, not available with rear speaker systems ($128.50). Special front and rear suspension ($4.75). Tachometer, for V-8s, standard with special instrumentation group ($47.40). Five 7.35 x 14 four-ply rated white sidewall tires, replacing 7.35 x 14 four-ply rated black sidewall ($31.35). Five 7.75 x 14 four-ply rated black sidewall tires, replacing 7.35 x 14 four-ply rated black sidewall ($14.50). Five 7.75 x 14 four-ply rated white sidewall tires, replacing 7.35 x 14 four-ply rated black sidewall ($45.80). Five F70 x 14 four-ply rated Nylon red stripe tires, replacing 7.35 x 14 four-ply rated black sidewall ($77.60). Five F70 x 14 four-ply rated Nylon white stripe tires, replacing 7.35 x 14 four-ply rated black sidewall ($77.60). Five 7.75 x 14 four-ply rated white sidewall tires, replacing 7.75 x 14 four-ply rated black sidewall ($31.35). Five 7.75 x 14 eight-ply rated black sidewall tires, replacing 7.75 x 14 four-ply rated black sidewall on station wagons only ($45.85). Five 7.75 x 14 eight-ply rated black whitewall tires, replacing 7.75 x 14 four-ply rated black sidewall on station wagons only ($79.20). Five F70 x 14 four-ply rated Nylon red-stripe tires, replacing 7.75 x 14 four-ply rated black sidewall ($63.15). Five F70 x 14 four-ply rated Nylon white stripe tires, replacing 7.75 x 14 four-ply rated black sidewall ($63.15). F70 x 14 four-ply rated white stripe tires on SS 396 in place of red stripe (no cost). Close-ratio four-speed manual transmission for SS 396 ($105.35). Close-ratio four-speed manual transmission for other Chevelles ($184.35). Wide-ratio four-speed manual transmission for SS 396 ($105.35). Wide-ratio four-speed manual transmission for other Chevelles ($184.35). Turbo Hydra-Matic transmission for SS 396 only ($147.45). Special floor-mounted three-speed manual transmission for SS 396 (standard). Special floor-mounted three-speed manual transmission for other Chevelles ($79). Powerglide automatic transmission for six-cylinder Chevelle ($184.35). Powerglide automatic transmission for V-8 Chevelles except SS 396 ($194.85). Powerglide automatic transmission for SS 396 ($115.90). Overdrive transmission with 140-, 155- or 195-hp engines ($115.90). Vinyl interior trim for Chevelle 300 ($5.30). Vinyl interior trim for Malibu sport coupe and sport sedan ($21.10). Deluxe cloth interior trim for Malibu sport sedan ($68.50). Positive crankcase ventilation, standard with 325- and 350-hp engines; on other engines ($5.25). Wheel covers with non-disc brakes ($21.10). Mag-styled wheel covers with non-disc brakes ($73.75). Simulated wire wheel covers with non-disc brakes ($73.75). Appearance group including twin color-keyed front and rear floor mats, front bumper guards and custom deluxe seat belts for Concours Custom station wagon ($29.55). Appearance group including twin color-keyed front and rear floor mats, front bumper guards and custom deluxe seat belts for Chevelle 300 Deluxe and Malibu station wagon with door edge guards ($35.90). Appearance group including twin color-keyed front and rear floor mats, front bumper guards and custom deluxe seat belts for two-door sedans, hardtops and convertibles with door edge and rear bumper guards ($45.40). Appearance group including twin color-keyed front and rear floor mats, front bumper guards and custom deluxe seat belts for four-door sedans and hardtops with door edge and rear bumper guards ($48.55). Auxiliary lighting group includes three or more of courtesy, under hood, ash tray, luggage compartment and glove box lamps for convertible includes items 2, 3 and 4 ($6.90); for Concours and Malibu station wagons includes items 1, 2 and 3 ($8.50); for Malibu sedans and all coupes includes items 1, 2, 3 and 4 ($11.15); for Chevelle 300 Deluxe station wagons includes items 1, 2, 3, and 5 ($11.15); for Chevelle 300 and 300 Deluxe sedans includes all items ($13.80). Foundation group includes push-button radio, clock and extra-thick foam seat cushions ($80.60). Operating convenience group includes remote-control left-hand outside rearview mirror and rear window seat defroster ($30.60). Station wagon convenience group includes luggage carrier, power rear window and rear window air deflector ($92.75).

OPTION INSTALLATION RATES

Automatic transmission (69.5 percent). Four-speed manual transmission (15.2 percent). V-8 engine (77.8 percent). Six-cylinder engine (22.2 percent). AM radio (77.1 percent). Air conditioning (18.6 percent). Power steering (50 percent). Tilt steering (1.6 percent). Power drum brakes (7.9 percent). Power disc brakes (1.3 percent). Power seat (0.2 percent). Power windows (0.7 percent). Power rear wagon window (3.2 percent). Bucket seats (19.7 percent). Vinyl top (17.4 percent). White sidewall tires (56.8 percent). Tinted windshield only (43.8 percent). All tinted glass (20 percent). Dual exhaust (21.7 percent). Positraction (14.4 percent). Full wheel covers (60.4 percent). Cruise control (0.1 percent). AM/FM radio (1.5 percent). Clock (81.3 percent). Based on model-year production of 369,144 units.

HISTORICAL FOOTNOTES

All new Chevrolets appeared in dealer showrooms Sept. 29, 1966. E.M. Estes was the chief executive officer of the company this year.

1968

The 1968 Chevelle received major exterior changes, and had a more rounded, "fastback" body style.

The 1968 Chevelle was heavily restyled. "To say Chevelle is all-new is an understatement," stated the Chevy sales catalog. "It is brilliantly original for '68! Out-of-the-ordinary roof lines, front fenders and taillight arrangements. The latest look in long-hood/short deck styling. Two wheelbases: 112 in. for coupes and convertibles; 116 in. for sedans and wagons. And expansive grille emphasize wider tread."

The "flying buttress" roofline of the Chevelle sport coupe was replaced by a more fastback style and the rear windows had a "veed" appearance (also used on pillared coupes). The four-door Chevelles had a slightly more "formal" looking window treatment. At the front, all models shared a hood that wrapped over the radiator grille and then swept boldly back over the front fenders. The grille had a tight texture of vertical and horizontal members. Chevelle 300s had no grille ornamentation. Deluxe 300s and Malibus had an elongated Chevrolet emblem in the center of the grille. The SS 396 models had appropriate identification badges in the center of the grille. The round-lens headlights were placed in square, hooded chrome housing that edged up into the hood line. There was a small space between the headlights with the grille texture showing through. A bright metal Chevelle script was placed above the left-hand headlights on most models. The front bumper included rectangular openings on each side of the license plate recess and amber, rectangular parking lights below the headlights. All models had front side marker lights. When optional engines were ordered, engine call-outs were added to the side markers lights making them a bit longer.

The rear end featured thin new taillights that wrapped around the body corners with white back-up light lenses incorporated into them if ordered. The rear bumper had a center license plate indentation, but carried no slots or lights in it. A new offering was the Concours Sport Sedan option, which created an upscale four-door hardtop available in only four specific color combinations. There was still a Concous Estate station wagon in its own series. In addition, lower-rung wagons were now given catchy names. The base version was called the Nomad and the one-step-up version was called the Nomad Custom. Inside the Chevelles all ashtray, radio and heater controls were well within the reach of the driver and the ventipanes (vent windows) were operated by cranks. Other trim variations between cars in different series are described below.

I.D. NUMBERS

The VIN is in a new location, stamped on a plate on the top left side of the instrument panel and visible through the windshield. The second and third symbols designate the series: (six-cylinder) 31=Chevelle 300/Nomad, 33=Chevelle 300 Deluxe/Custom Nomad, 35=Malibu, 37=Concours Estate station wagon; (V-8) 32=Chevelle 300/Nomad, 34=Chevelle 300 Deluxe/Custom Nomad, 36=Malibu, 38=SS 396 and 38=Concours Estate station wagon. The fourth and fifth symbols designates body type: 27=two-door pillared coupe, 37=two-door hardtop (sport coupe), 35=four-door six-passenger station wagon, 39=four-door hardtop (sport sedan), 45=four-door three-seat station wagon, 67=two-door convertible and 69=four-door sedan. The sixth symbol

33

designates the model year: 8=1968. The seventh symbol designates the assembly plant location: The seventh symbol indicated assembly plant: A=Atlanta, Georgia; B=Baltimore, Maryland; G=Framingham, Massachusetts; K=Kansas City, Missouri; Z=Fremont, California. The last six symbols are the sequential unit production number at the specific factory. The Fisher body tag riveted to the top of the cowl on the left side of the car below the hood provides additional vehicle identification information. The Fisher Body STYLE NUMBER (ST) consists of a prefix identifying model year and four or more symbols identifying the series and body style (example: 68-13639 for a 1968 Malibu or Concours Sport Sedan with a V-8). The BODY NUMBER consists of a prefix designating assembly plant and the sequential unit production number at the specific factory. The TRIM NUMBER (TR) identifies upholstery.

COLORS

(A) Tuxedo Black, (C) Ermine White, (D) Grotto Blue, (E) Fathom Blue, (F) Island Teal, (G) Ash Gold, (H) Grecian Green, (K) Tripoli Turquoise, (L) Teal Blue, (N) Cordovan Maroon, (P) Seafrost Green, (R) Matador Red, (T) Palomino Ivory, (V) Sequoia Green and (Y) Butternut Yellow.

ENGINE CODES

Codes appear on the right side of six-cylinder blocks behind the distributor and right front of V-8 engine blocks. Engine codes for 1968 were: (230-cid/140-hp six) BA, BB, BC, BD, BF and BH; (250-cid/155-hp six) CM, CN, CQ and CR; (307 cid/200 hp V-8) DA, DB, DE, DF and DN; (327-cid/250-hp V-8) EA, EC, EE and EO; (327-cid/325-hp V-8) EP, ES, EH, EI and EJ; (396-cid/325-hp V-8) EO, EK and ET; (396-cid/350-hp V-8) EF, EL and EU; (396-cid/375-hp V-8) EG.

CHEVELLE 300 — (6-CYL/V-8)

The Chevelle 300 was the base line. Its identifying features included a grille without center ornament, Chevelle script on the front fender sides behind the wheel openings and no rocker panel or lower perimeter moldings. Its standard equipment included a door-operated dome light (*), keyless door locking, a heater and defroster, a suspended accelerator pedal and back-up lights. In addition, standard features for all 1968 Chevelles included a Fisher unisteel-construction body, a three-cross member perimeter frame, Magic Mirror acrylic lacquer finish, inner steel fenders, Flush-and-Dry rocker panels (*), curved side window glass, a long-life exhaust system, Safety-Master self-adjusting brakes, ball-race steering, a single disc dry clutch with positive action diaphragm springs, 14-in. wheels, a full-coil suspension with double-acting hydraulic shock absorbers, an energy-absorbing steering column, seat belts with push-button buckles for all passenger positions, shoulder belts for drivers and front passengers with push-button buckles and convenient stowage provision, except on convertibles (*), Passenger-Guard door locks with deflecting lock buttons on all doors, a four-way hazard warning flasher, a dual master cylinder with warning light, corrosion-resistant brake lines, folding seatbacks with latches, dual-speed windshield wipers, windshield

The 396-cid engine was again offered to Chevelle buyers. It could be had in 325-, 350-, and special order 375-hp versions.

washers, a left-hand outside rearview mirror (*), back-up lights, new front side marker lights, parking lights that illuminated with the headlights, a padded instrument panel, padded sun visors, padded windshield pillars, reduced-glare items (including instrument panel top, inside windshield moldings, horn button, steering wheel hub, windshield wiper arms and wiper blades), an inside day/night mirror with deflecting base, direction signals with a lane-change feature (*), safety armrests, a thick-laminate windshield, soft low-profile window control knobs and coat hooks, energy-absorbing seat backs, yielding door and window handles, an energy-absorbing instrument panel with smooth contoured knobs and levers, tire safety rims, safety door latches and hinges, a uniform-pattern shifter quadrant, a 20-gal. gas tank with secured filler pipe and snag-resistant steering wheel hardware. The Chevelle 300 featured a textured all-vinyl interior available in blue, gold and black. The Chevelle 300 four-door six-passenger station wagon was called the Nomad.

(*) One source indicates these features were not standard on the Chevelle 300, but 1968 Chevelle sales catalog D 49487 indicates they were standard.

Model Number	Body/Style Number	Body Type & Seating	Factory Price	Shipping Weight	Production Total
CHEVELLE 300 SERIES 131 (6-CYL)					
131	11	2d sedan-6P	$2,341	2,988 lbs.	Note 1
131	69	4d Nomad-6P	$2,625	3,350 lbs.	Note 1
CHEVELLE 300 SERIES 132 (V-8)					
132	11	2d sedan-6P	$2,447	3,124 lbs.	Note 1
132	69	4d Nomad-6P	$2,731	3,483 lbs.	Note 1

NOTE 1: Individual body style production is not available; see production notes.

CHEVELLE 300 DELUXE — (6-CYL/V-8) SERIES 133/134

The Chevelle 300 Deluxe represented the one-step-up line. It could be spotted by looking for bright ribbed rocker panel moldings combined with the Chevelle front fender script. It also carried Chevrolet emblems at the center of its grille and rear body panel. Back-up lights were standard equipment, plus everything else included with the base line models. The Chevelle 300 Deluxe offered deluxe fabric-and-vinyl interior trims in gold, bue or black colors, plus all-vinyl choices in the same colors. A sport coupe was available in this series and the 300 Deluxe station wagon was called a Nomad Custom. Two- and four-door sedans were also offered.

Model Number	Body/Style Number	Body Type & Seating	Factory Price	Shipping Weight	Production Total
CHEVELLE 300 DELUXE SERIES 133 (6-CYL)					
133	69	4d sedan-6P	$2,445	3,071 lbs.	Note 1
133	37	2d sport coupe	$2,479	3,036 lbs.	Note 1
133	11	2d coupe-6P	$2,415	3,005 lbs.	Note 1
133	35	4d Cus. Nomad	$2,736	3,409 lbs.	Note 1
CHEVELLE 300 DELUXE SERIES 134 (V-8)					
134	69	4d sedan-6P	$2,550	3,207 lbs.	Note 1
134	37	2d sport coupe	$2,584	3,171 lbs.	Note 1
134	11	2d coupe-6P	$2,521	3,141 lbs.	Note 1
134	35	4d Cus. Nomad	$2,841	3,543 lbs.	Note 1

NOTE 1: Individual body style production is not available; see production notes.

MALIBU — (6-CYL/V-8) SERIES 135/136

Chevrolet advertised that the Malibu blended boldness with sensibility and the copywriters were right. On these models, the front fender script was changed to read "Malibu" and the upper body feature line was pin striped, while the lower perimeter feature line carried a bright molding that extended the sweep of the front fenders to the rear wheel wells. In addition, the rear body panel was outlined with a thin chrome molding. Instead of a Chevrolet emblem in the center of the rear end, the Malbu had a Chevelle script on the right-hand side. Other Malibu extras included Hide-A-Way two-speed windshield wipers, a deluxe three-spoke steering wheel with non-glare metal trim, lighted heater controls and richer interior trims (fabric-and-vinyl in black, blue or gray-green or all-solid-vinyl in gold, black, blue, red or parchment and red). Floor carpeing was standard in the Malibu sport coupe. An added model in the Malibu line was a convertible. While the wagons in other series had names like Nomad, Custom Nomad and Concoyrs Estate, the four-door two-seat wagon in this line was known simply as the Malibu station wagon.

Model Number	Body/Style Number	Body Type & Seating	Factory Price	Shipping Weight	Production Total
MALIBU SERIES 135 (6-CYL)					
135	69	4d sedan-6P	$2,524	3,090 lbs.	Note 1
135	39	4d sport sedan-6P	$2,629	3,165 lbs.	Note 1
135	37	2d sport coupe-6P	$2,558	3,037 lbs.	Note 1
135	67	2d convertible-6P	$2,757	3,115 lbs.	Note 1
135	35	4d wagon-6P	$2,846	3,421 lbs.	Note 1
MALIBU SERIES 136 (V-8)					
136	69	4d sedan-6P	$2,629	3,223 lbs.	Note 1
136	39	4d sport sedan-6P	$2,735	3,298 lbs.	Note 1
136	37	2d sport coupe-6P	$2,663	3,170 lbs.	Note 1
136	67	2d convertible-6P	$2,863	3,245 lbs.	Note 1
136	35	4d wagon-6P	$2,951	3,554 lbs.	Note 1

NOTE 1: Individual body style production is not available; see production notes.

MALIBU CONCOURS SPORT SEDAN (6-CYL/V-8) — SERIES 135/136

Based on its coding, the new Concours sport sedan was not included in the Concours Estate station wagon line, series 138. It was technically an option package for the Malibu version of this body style and therefore part of the series 135/136 Chevelle line. However, this model was so special in 1968 that it deserves separate treatment. Its combination of splendid interior appointments, plus special sound insulation, made it a luxury-level Chevelle. The rich custom fabric interior came in gray-green, gold, blue or black. It also featured upholstered doors with a carpeted lower panel that blended with the color-keyed, wall-to-wall floor carpeting. On the outside it featured special black-accented wheel openings and lower body side moldings. The deep-padded instrument panel had a trim plate with handsome wood-look trim and the deluxe steering wheel sported a special Concours emblem. The rear body panel featured a ribbed trim plate running across it between the taillights. There was also a special bumper with the back-up lights in it. Concours name scripts decorated the body sides and rear deck lid. The Malibu convertible also came with a glass rear window. Convertible tops could be ordered in white, black or blue. A power convertible top was option-

The SS 396 came with red stripe tires, body side moldings, and black trim accents.

CHEVELLE

al. Vinyl tops in black or white could be ordered for Malibu (and SS 396) sport coupes and sport sedans.

Model Number	Body/Style Number	Body Type & Seating	Factory Price	Shipping Weight	Production Total
MALIBU CONCOURS SPORT SEDAN SERIES 135 (6-CYL)					
135	39	4d sport sedan-6P	—	—	Note 1
MALIBU CONCOURS SPORT SEDAN SERIES 136 (V-8)					
136	39	4d sport sedan-6P	—	—	Note 1

NOTE 1: Individual body style production is not available; see production notes.

CONCOURS ESTATE — (6-CYL/V-8) SERIES 137/138

The Concours Custom station wagon was renamed the Concours Estate Wagon. Chevrolet's general sales catalog stated, "The Concours two-seat Estate Wagon lets you load up on luxury. New styling, quality appointments and paneling that looks like hand-rubbed walnut provide a beautiful setting for Chevelle's enlarged 94-cu.-ft. total cargo capacity." In addition to or in place of the equipment used on lower-rung Chevelles, the Concours Estate Wagon featured an all-vinyl interior, a lighted locking glove box, extra-thick foam cushioned seats, simulated walnut side and rear exterior panels, two-speed Hide-A-Way windshield wipers, chrome wheel opening moldings and an oval steering wheel with horn tabs. Other exterior touches included ribbed gray-accented lower body perimeter moldings, a tailgate emblem badge for Concours identification and a Concours script on each front fender. Concours Custom interiors were trimmed in textured vinyl. The passenger floor featured deep-twist carpeting and the cargo load floor had a vinyl coating. The taillights used on wagons were taller than those used on other models and did not run as far onto the rear end.

Model Number	Body/Style Number	Body Type & Seating	Factory Price	Shipping Weight	Production Total
CONCOURS ESTATE WAGON SERIES 137 (6-CYL)					
137	35	4d wagon-6P	$2,978	3,426 lbs.	Note 1
CONCOURS ESTATE WAGON SERIES 138 (V-8)					
137	35	4d wagon-6P	$3,083	3,561 lbs.	Note 1

NOTE 1: Individual body style production is not available; see production notes below.

CHEVELLE SS 396 — (V-8) SERIES 138

"You'll judge both SS 396 sport coupe and convertible the best of the breed," said Chevrolet's 1968 full-line catalog. The Chevelle muscle car again wore an exclusive hood with twin power domes. This year the ornamentation was a smaller section of grille work at the rear of each dome. The heart of the car was the base engine, a 396-cid "big-block" V-8 with 325 hp. Two more powerful versions of this motor were optional. In addition to or in place of the equipment of other models, the SS 396 had a special black grille, a floor-mounted gear shifter, vinyl upholstery (gold, black, blue, red and Parchment-and-black), carpeting, body side moldings, black-accented body trim, SS 396 identification badges, Hide-A-Way windshield wipers and special wide-oval red-stripe or white-stripe tires. Strato bucket seats and a new console were optional. The 325- and 350-hp versions of the 396-cid V-8 were available with a special three-speed Synchromesh transmission as standard equipment. A four-speed manual gearbox and Powerglide or Turbo-Hydra-Matic automatic transmissions were optional. The 375-hp versions, which had to be special ordered, were installed in no more than 2,000 cars. There was a two- to three-month waiting period to get one. On all of these cars, SS badges were seen in the center of the grille, the center of the rear panel and the center of the deluxe three-spoke steering wheel. The SS 396 convertible also came with a glass rear window. Convertible tops could be ordered in white, black or blue. A power convertible top was optional. Vinyl tops in black or white could be ordered for SS 396 sport coupes.

Model Number	Body/Style Number	Body Type & Seating	Factory Price	Shipping Weight	Production Total
138	17	2d sport coupe-6P	$2,899	3,475 lbs.	Note 1
138	67	2d convertible-6P	$3,102	3,551 lbs.	Note 1

NOTE 1: Individual body style production is not available; see production notes.

PRODUCTION NOTES

NOTE 1 Model-year production of all 1967 Chevelles was 422,893 units.
NOTE 2 Industry statistical breakouts in rounded-off numbers show 85,700 Chevelle sixes and 283,400 Chevelle V-8s were built in 1967.
NOTE 3 Additional statistics record series production, in rounded-off figures (except SS 396), as follows:

Chevelle 300 (6-cyl)	9,700
Chevelle 300 (V-8)	2,900
Total	**12,600**
Chevelle 300 Del. (6-cyl)	25,500
Chevelle 300 (V-8)	17,700
Total	**43,200**
Malibu (6-cyl)	33,100
Malibu (V-8)	233,200
Total	**266,300**
SS 396 (V-8)	57,600
Total	**57,600**
Wagons (6-cyl)	10,700
Wagons (V-8)	34,800
Total	**45,500**

NOTE 4 Production by factory was:

Code	Factory	Production	Code	Factory	Production
B	Baltimore	126,137	Z	Fremont	56,022
K	Kansas City	135,732	A	Atlanta	66,282
G	Framingham	38,705			

NOTE 5 Exactly 62,785 Chevelle SS 396 models were built during the 1967 model year. This includes both hardtops and convertibles. All were V-8 powered. No further body style breakouts are available.
NOTE 6 No more than 2,000 Chevelle SS 396 convertibles with the 375-hp V-8 were built.

ENGINES

CHEVELLE 300, 300 DELUXE, MALIBU BASE 230-CID, 140-HP SIX-CYL: Inline. Overhead-valve. Cast-iron block. Displacement: 230 cid. Bore and stroke: 3.875 x 3.25 in. Compression ratio: 8.5:1. Brake hp: 140 at 4400 rpm. Seven main bearings. Hydraulic valve lifters. Crankcase capacity: 4 qt. (add 1 qt. for new filter). Cooling system capacity: 12 qt (add 6 qt. for heater). Carburetor: Rochester one-barrel Model 7027003.

CHEVELLE 300, 300 DELUXE, MALIBU BASE 250-CID, 155-HP SIX-CYL: Inline. Overhead-valve. Cast-iron block. Displacement: 250 cid. Bore and stroke: 3.875 x 3.53 in. Compression ratio: 8.5:1. Brake hp: 155 at 4200 rpm. Taxable hp: 36. Torque: 235 lbs.-ft. at 1600 rpm. Seven main bearings. Hydraulic valve lifters. Crankcase capacity: 4 qt. (add 1 qt. for new filter). Cooling system capacity: 12 qt (add 6 qt. for heater). Carburetor: Rochester one-barrel Model 7028017. Sales code L22.

CHEVELLE 300, 300 DELUXE, MALIBU, NOMAD, CONCOURS BASE 307-CID, 200-HP V-8: Overhead-valve. Cast-iron block and head. Bore and stroke: 3.88 x 3.25 in. Displacement: 307 cid. Compression ratio: 9.00:1. Brake hp: 200 at 4600 rpm. Taxable hp: 48. Torque: 300 lbs.-ft. at 2400. Five main bearings. Hydraulic valve lifters. Crankcase capacity: 4 qt. (add 1 qt. for new filter). Cooling system capacity: 16 qt (add 1 qt. for heater). Carburetor: Rochester 7028101 two-barrel.

CHEVELLE 300, 300 DELUXE, MALIBU, NOMAD, CONCOURS OPTIONAL 327-CID, 250-HP V-8: Overhead-valve. Cast-iron block and head. Bore and stroke: 4.00 x 3.25 in. Displacement: 327 cid. Compression ratio: 8.75:1. Brake hp: 250 at 4800 rpm. Taxable hp: 51.20. Torque: 335 lbs.-ft. at 3200. Five main bearings. Hydraulic valve lifters. Crankcase capacity: 4 qt. (add 1 qt. for new filter). Cooling system capacity: (full-size) 14 qt.; (others) 16 qt. (add 1 qt. for heater). Carburetor: Carburetor: Four-barrel. Sales code L73.

MALIBU, NOMAD, CONCOURS OPTIONAL 327-CID, 275-HP V-8: Overhead-valve. Cast-iron block and head. Bore and stroke: 4.00 x 3.25 in. Displacement: 327 cid. Compression ratio: 10.25:1. Brake hp: 275 at 4800 rpm. Taxable hp: 51.20. Torque: 355 lbs.-ft. at 3200. Five main bearings. Hydraulic valve lifters. Crankcase capacity: 4 qt. (add 1 qt. for new filter). Cooling system capacity: (full-size) 14 qt.; (others) 16 qt. (add 1 qt. for heater). Carburetor: Carburetor: Four-barrel. Sales code: L30.

CHEVELLE 300, 300 DELUXE, MALIBU, NOMAD, CONCOURS OPTIONAL 327-CIDM, 325-HP V-8: Overhead-valve. Cast-iron block and head. Bore and stroke: 4.00 x 3.25 in. Displacement: 327 cid. Compression ratio: 11.00:1. Brake hp: 325 at 5600 rpm. Taxable hp: 51.20. Torque: 355 lbs.-ft. at 3600. Five main bearings. Hydraulic valve lifters. Crankcase capacity: 4 qt. (add 1 qt. for new filter). Cooling system capacity: 14 qt. (add 1 qt. for heater). Carburetor: Carburetor: Four-barrel. Sales code: L79.

CHEVELLE SS 396 BASE V-8: Overhead-valve. Cast-iron block and head. Bore and stroke: 4.09 x 3.76 in. Displacement: 396 cid. Compression ratio: 10.25:1. Brake hp: 325 at 4800 rpm. Taxable hp: 53.60. Torque: 410 lbs.-ft. at 3200. Five main bearings. Hydraulic valve lifters. Crankcase capacity: 4 qt. (add 1 qt. for new filter). Cooling system capacity: 23 qt. (add 1 qt. for heater). Carburetor: Rochester 7028211 four-barrel. Sales code: L35.

CHEVELLE SS 396 OPTIONAL 350-HP V-8: Overhead-valve. Cast-iron block and head. Bore and stroke: 4.09 x 3.76 in. Displacement: 396 cid. Compression ratio: 10.25:1. Brake hp: 350 at 5200 rpm. Taxable hp: 53.60. Torque: 415 lbs.-ft. at 3400. Five main bearings. Hydraulic valve lifters. Crankcase capacity: 4 qt. (add 1 qt. for new filter). Cooling system capacity: 23 qt. (add 1 qt. for heater). Carburetor: Four-barrel. Sales code: L34.

CHEVELLE SS 396 OPTIONAL 375-HP V-8: Overhead-valve. Cast-iron block and head. Bore and stroke: 4.09 x 3.76 in. Displacement: 396 cid. Compression ratio: 11.00:1. Brake hp: 375 at 5600 rpm. Taxable hp: 53.60. Torque: 415 lbs.-ft. at 3600. Five main bearings. Solid valve lifters. Crankcase capacity: 4 qt. (add 1 qt. for new filter). Cooling system capacity: 23 qt. (add 1 qt. for heater). Carburetor: Four-barrel. Sales code L78.

CHEVELLE SS 396 OPTIONAL 375-HP V-8: Overhead-valve. Cast-iron block and head. Bore and stroke: 4.09 x 3.76 in. Displacement: 396 cid. Compression ratio: 11.00:1. Brake hp: 375 at 5600 rpm. Taxable hp: 53.60. Torque: 415 lbs.-ft. at 3600. Five main bearings. Solid valve lifters. Crankcase capacity: 4 qt. (add 1 qt. for new filter). Cooling system capacity: 23 qt. (add 1 qt. for heater). Carburetor: Four-barrel. Sales code L89.

CHASSIS FEATURES

Wheelbase: (two-door) 112 in.; (four-door) 116 in. Overall length: (two-door) 197.1 in. (four-door) 201.1 in. Width: 75.7 in. Height: (sedans 53.3 in. (coupes) 52.7 in; (convertibles) 53.2 in. Front tread: 59 in. Rear tread: 59 in. Gas tank capacity: 20 gal. Tires: (300 car) 7.35 x 14 two-ply/four-ply rated; (300 wagon) 7.75 x 14 two-ply/four-ply rated; (300 Deluxe car) 7.35 x 14 two-ply/four-ply rated; (300 Deluxe wagon) 7.75 x 14 two-ply/four-ply rated; (Malibu car) 7.35 x 14 two-ply/four-ply rated; (Malibu wagon) 7.75 x 14 two-ply/four-ply rated; (SS 396) F70 x 14 special wide-oval red stripe or white stripe.

OPTIONS

C60 Four-Season air conditioning, including 61-amp Delcotron, heavy-duty radiator and temperature-controlled fan and requiring larger tires with some Chevelles ($360.20). C51 Station wagon rear window air deflector ($19). G80 Positraction rear axle ($42.15). AXL1 Special economy or high-performance rear axle ($2.15). T60 heavy-duty battery ($7.40). A51 Standard-type front shoulder belts, in cars with standard seat belts ($23.20). AS1/S5 Standard-type rear shoulder belts, in cars with standard seat belts ($46.40). A39 Custom Deluxe front and rear seat belts, for cars with bucket seats ($7.90). A39 Custom Deluxe front and rear seat belts, for cars with bench front seats ($9.50). A85 Custom Deluxe front shoulder belts, requires Custom Deluxe seat belts ($26.35). A85/S4 Custom Deluxe front and rear shoulder belts, requires Custom Deluxe seat belts ($52.70). V31 Front bumper guards ($15.80). V32 Rear bumper guards ($15.80). V55 Station wagon roof carrier ($44.25). U35 Electric clock in Chevelle 300 and 300 Deluxe models; included with special instrumentation ($15.80). M01 Heavy-duty clutch, V-8s except SS 396 and cars with 155-hp V-8 ($10.55). M01 Heavy-duty clutch on sixes, except 155 hp ($5.30). D55 Console, including electric clock, requires bucket seats ($50.60). C50 Rear windshield defroster, all except convertibles and wagons ($21.10). B93 Door edge guards, two-door models ($4.25). B93 Door edge guards, four-door models except standard on Custom station wagon ($7.40). L22 250-cid 155-hp six-cylinder engine ($26.35). L73 327-cid 250-hp V-8, all except SS 396 ($63.20). L30 327-cid 275-hp V-8 engine, all except SS 396 ($92.70). L79 327-cid 325-hp V-8, all except SS 396 ($198.05). L34 396-cid 350-hp V-8 engine, SS 396 only ($105.35). L78 396-cid 375-hp V-8 SS 396 only ($237). N10 Dual exhaust on all Chevelles with the 275-hp engine ($27.40). K02 Temperature-con-

CHEVELLE

GM cranked out 57,600 of the popular SS 396 Chevelles for 1968.

trolled fan, V-8s, standard witrh air conditioning ($15.80). K79 42-amp Delcotron generator, not available with air conditioning or with C60 ($10.55). K76 61-amp Delcotron generator, with air conditioning ($5.30); without air conditioning ($26.35). A01 All windows tinted ($34.80). A02 Tinted windshield only ($23.20). A81 Driver and passenger headrests, with front Strato bucket seats ($52.70). A82 Driver and passenger headrests, with standard front bench seat ($42.15). U03 Tri-volume horn ($13.70). Special instrumentation with ammeter, temperature gauge, oil pressure gauge and tachometer on Malibu and SS 396 sport coupes and convertibles ($94.80). U46 light monitoring system ($26.35). ZJ19 auxiliary lighting groups with A) ash tray, B) courtesy, C) glove box, D) luggage and E) underhood lights; in Concours and Malibu Wagons includes A, B and E ($8.45); in all convertibles includes A, D and E ($6.85); in Malibu sedans and Sport Coupes and SS 396 Sport Coupe includes A and B ($11.10); in Nomad and Custom Nomad Wagons includes A, B, C and E ($11.10) and in 300, 300 Deluxe includes A, B, C, D and E ($13.70). B37 Twin front and rear floor mats ($10.55). D33 Left-hand outside remote-control mirror ($9.50). B90 Side window moldings in 300 and 300 Deluxe coupes ($21.10). B90 Side window molding, sedans and all station wagons except base Nomad ($26.35). B90 side window moldings and rear quarter window molding for Nomad station wagon ($31.60). Two-tone paint ($21.10). J50 Power drum brakes ($42.15). J50 Power disc front brakes ($100.10). N40 Power steering ($94.80). A33 Station wagon power tailgate window ($31.60). C06 Power convertible top in white, black or blue ($52.70). A31 Power windows Concours, Malibu and SS 396 ($100.10). V01 Heavy-duty radiator, except with air conditioning ($10.55). U63 AM push-button radio with front antenna ($61.10). U69 AM/FM radio with front antenna ($133.80). U69/79 AM/FM radio with front antenna and stereo ($239.15). U57 Stereo tape system with four speakers ($133.80). U80 Rear seat speaker, not available with U79 ($13.20) U73 rear antenna, all except AM/FM and wagons ($9.50). CO81/82 Vinyl roof cover, for hardtop models ($84.30). B55 Thick front foam seat cushion, Chevelle 300 and 300 Deluxe ($7.40). A51 Strato bucket seats in Malibu or SS 396 sport coupe and convertible ($110.60). G66 Superlift rear shock absorbers ($42.15). K30 Speed and cruise control, V-8s with automatic transmissions ($52.70). U15 Speed warning indicator ($10.55). N30 Deluxe steering wheel in Chevelle 300s and Nomads ($7.40). N30 Deluxe steering wheel in Chevelle 300 Deluxe and Nomad Custom ($4.25). N33 Comfortilt steering wheel, requires floor shifter or automatic transmissions ($42.15). N34 Sport styled steering wheel ($31.60). D96 accent striping ($29.50). F40 Special front and rear suspension ($4.75). M22 Close-ratio four-speed manual transmission for SS 396/375 hp ($237). M21 Close-ratio four-speed manual transmission for other SS 396s ($184.35). M20 Wide-ratio four-speed manual transmission for all ($184.35). M40 Turbo Hydra-Matic transmission for SS 396 with 350-hp or 325-hp V-8 only ($237). M13 Special floor-mounted three-speed manual transmission for all except SS 396 ($79 and standard on SS 396). M35 Powerglide automatic transmission for six-cylinder Chevelle ($184.35). M35 Powerglide automatic transmission for V-8 Chevelles, except SS 396 ($194.85). M10 Overdrive transmission with 140-, 155-, 200- or 250-hp engines ($115.90). Vinyl trim interior for 300 series and Malibu sport coupe or sport sedan ($10.55). KD5 Heavy-duty closed engine positive crankcase ventilation system ($6.35). P01 Four bright metal wheel covers ($21.10). N96 Mag-styled wheel covers with non disc brakes ($73.75). N95 Simulated wire wheel covers with non-disc brakes ($73.75). PA2 Mag spoke wheel covers ($73.75). ZJ7 Rallye wheels, including special wheels, hubcaps and trim rings ($31.60). C24 concealed windshield wipers, standard on Malibu, SS 396 and Concours wagons ($19). P1 Appearance group including front bumper guards and front and rear color-keyed floor mats for Concours Estate wagon ($26.35). P1 Appearance group including front bumper guards, door edge guards and front and rear color-keyed floor mats for Nomad, Nomad Custom and Malibu station wagons ($33.75). P1 Appearance group including front and rear bumper guards, door edge guards and front and rear color-keyed floor mats for coupes and convertibles ($46.40). P1 Appearance group including front and rear bumper guards, door edge guards and front and rear color-keyed floor mats for four-door sedans and sport sedans ($49.55). P4 Operating convenience group including electric clock, remote-control left-hand outside rearview mirror and rear window defroster for all models except convertibles and station wagons without U14 special instrumentation ($46.40). P4 Operating convenience group including remote-control left-hand outside rearview mirror and rear window defroster for

Malibu V-8 and SS 396 with U14 special instrumentation ($30.60). P4 Operating convenience group including remote-control left-hand outside rearview mirror for convertibles with U14 special instrumentation ($9.50). P58 Five 7.35 x 14 four-ply rated white sidewall tires, replacing 7.35 x 14 four-ply rated black sidewall ($31.35). Five 7.75 x 14 four-ply rated black sidewall tires, replacing 7.35 x 14 four-ply rated black sidewall ($14.70 or standard on Malibu sport sedan and convertible with 275- or 325-hp V-8s and standard on other 300, 300 Deluxe and Malibu cars with 325-hp V-8). P62 Five 7.75 x 14 four-ply rated white sidewall tires, replacing 7.35 x 14 four-ply rated black sidewall ($46). PW8 Five F70 x 14 four-ply rated Nylon red stripe tires, replacing 7.35 x 14 four-ply rated black sidewall ($69.70). PW7 Five F70 x 14 four-ply rated nylon white-stripe tires, replacing 7.35 x 14 four-ply rated black sidewall ($69.70). P62 Five 7.75 x 14 four-ply rated white sidewall tires, replacing 7.75 x 14 four-ply rated black sidewall ($31.35). PN4 Five 7.75 x 14 eight-ply rated black sidewall tires, replacing 7.75 x 14 four-ply rated black sidewall on station wagons only ($46.25). PN5 Five 7.75 x 14 eight-ply rated black sidewall tires, replacing 7.75 x 14 four-ply rated black sidewall on station wagons only ($79.60). PW8 Five F70 x 14 four-ply rated nylon red stripe tires, replacing 7.75 x 14 four-ply rated black sidewall ($55). PW7 Five F70 x 14 four-ply rated nylon white-stripe tires, replacing 7.75 x 14 four-ply rated black sidewall ($55.05). PW7 Five F70 x 14 four-ply rated white-stripe tires on SS 396 in place of red stripe (no cost)

OPTION INSTALLATION RATES

Automatic transmission (76.5 percent). Four-speed manual transmission (11 percent). V-8 engine (82.2 percent). Six-cylinder engine (17.8 percent). AM radio (17.8 percent). AM radio (79.7 percent). AM-FM radio (3.4 percent). Air conditioning (24.5 percent). Power steering (62.3 percent). Tilt steering (1.6 percent). Power drum brakes (10.1 percent). Power disc brakes (2.8 percent). Power seat (NA percent). Power windows (0.8 percent). Power rear wagon window (3.7 percent). Bucket seats (15.4 percent). Vinyl top (30.6 percent). White sidewall tires (68.8 percent). Tinted windshield only (25.9 percent). All tinted glass (35.2 percent). Dual exhaust (18.8 percent). Positraction (13.0 percent). Full wheel covers (59.8 percent). Cruise control (0.2 percent). Stereo tape player (1.3 percent). Clock (20.1 percent). Based on model year production of 422,880 units.

HISTORICAL FOOTNOTES

The 1968 Chevelle line had its dealer introduction date on September 21, 1967. John Z. Delorean was general manager of Chevrolet Motor Division. The company's new-car sales rose 5.6 percent from 1967 and Chevelle sales set a new all-time high of 417,844 units for the calendar year. Other sporty Chevys setting records this year were the Camaro and the Corvette. Production of the 396-cid Chevy big-block V-8 hit 131,700 engines in the model year. Although not all of these were put in Chevelles. Chevelle production did include 78,300 sixes and 344,600 V-8s in rounded-off numbers. A total of 412,359 new Chevelles were registered in the United States during the calendar year. *Motor Trend* (December 1967) printed an assessment of the SS 396 convertible and stated, "Fifth edition 'super' Chevy still holds all the marbles." Performance figures given in the article were 7.4 to 7.7 seconds for 0 to 60 mph and 15.8 to 16 seconds for the quarter mile, with the lower number applying to stick shift versions and the higher figures for automatics. *Road & Track* (March 1968) road tested the Chevelle 327-cid 275-hp Malibu sport coupe, which it found to be a quiet, comfortable car with good road manners. The magazine described the welll-balanced car as "unpretentious" and said it was "sufficiently impressed" with this bread-and-butter Chevelle. It accelerated from 0 to 60 mph in 9.3 seconds and did the quarter mile in 17.1 seconds with an 82-mph trap speed.

The 1969 Chevelle was a gorgeous update of the 1968 design. I was a food salesman in New Jersey at the time and had a 1969 Mercury Montego sedan as a company car. My friend who worked for the competition had a new blue Malibu sport coupe with silver lower body finish. There was no comparison between the looks of the two cars — the Chevelle had the most eyeball appeal by a long shot. Chevrolet knew it, too. "The '69 Chevelle wishes its rivals a lot of luck," said one Chevy catalog. "They'll need it!"

The aluminum mesh grille of 1968 was replaced with a durable, precision-formed plastic one having 37 "segments" of short moldings stacked six above and six below a bright horizontal molding that carried either a blue Chevy bow tie emblem or "SS" insignia in the center. The entire grille was outlined by a chrome border broken only by the upper edges of the headlights. The headlights were similar to the previous year, but had black finish in the area around the round lenses. The front bumper had a larger air slot opening, which held white, rectangular parking light lenses at either edge of the opening. The rear had taller, segmented taillights that no longer went around the body sides. Instead, small side maker lights were placed at the trailing edge of the rear fender sides. The bumper was solid all across, with no slots or openings for lights. The back-up lights, when ordered, were placed in the center of the lower taillight lens. Trim levels and name badges varied according to series. Engine call-outs were incorporated into the front side marker lights, which sat on each fender, ahead of the wheel openings. Almost all of the Magic Mirror acrylic colors available this season were new for

CHEVELLE

The SS 396 was back in 1969, but as an option rather than a separate series. This car is an ultra-rare SS 396 based on a 300 Deluxe body.

1969. Astro Ventilation — a system that brought outside air into the interior — was made standard equipment on Chevelle sport coupes and convertibles.

Standard engines were the 140-hp Turbo-Thrift 230 in-line six or the 200-hp Turbo-Fire 307 V-8, unless you ordered the SS 396 muscle car, which came with the 325-hp version of the big-block as standard equipment. Chevrolet Easy-Care features found on all Chevelles included long-lasting chassis lubrication, Flush-and-Dry rocker panels, Safety-Master self-adjusting brakes, inner fender well liners (plastic up front), a dual brake master cylinder and corrosion-resistant brake lines. New this year was a single-operation lock system for the ignition, steering wheel and transmission selector. Door lock buttons were relocated closer to the center of the doors for easier access by driver and passengers and two-speed windshield wipers with Hide-A-Way blades and articulated driver-side action were standard on Malibus and optional on 300 Deluxe models. Safety and security features that were standard with all Chevelles included an energy-absorbing steering column, seat belts with push-button buckles for all passengers, shoulder belts with push-button buckles and special storage provisions up front (except convertibles), front seat head restraints, passenger guard door locks, four-way hazard flashers, a brake failure warning light, folding seat back latches, dual-speed wiper/washers, a dual-action safety hood latch, a left-hand outside rearview mirror, back-up lights, front and rear side marker lights, parking lights that illuminated with the headlights, an energy-absorbing instrument panel, padded sun visors, a reduced-glare instrument panel top, reduced-glare inside moldings, a reduced-glare steering wheel hub, a wide inside day/night rearview mirror with deflecting base, directional signals with a lane-change feature, safety armrests, a thick-laminate windshield, soft low-profile knobs and coat hooks, a soft low-profile dome light, padded front seatback tops, smooth-contoured door and window regulators, an ignition key with a buzzer type anti-theft warning, a starter safety switch with all transmissions, safety door latches and hinges, a uniform-pattern gearshift quadrant and a Cargo-Guard luggage compartment.

Several changes were made in Chevrolet's marketing scheme. First, the SS 396 was no longer a separate series, but became the Z25 option, which could be ordered for the Chevelle 300 Deluxe coupe, the Chevelle 300 Deluxe sport coupe, the Malibu sport coupe and the Malibu convertible. It added $347.60 to the price of each of these four cars. Second, the 300 series was dropped, except for the Nomad station wagon. Third, the 300 Deluxe station wagon was now called the Greenbrier. Finally, the Malibu-level wagons were called Concours and Concours Estate models and Estates came only with V-8 power. The Concours sport sedan option introduced in 1968 remained available as a trim upgrade for the Malibu sport sedan.

I.D. NUMBERS

The VIN is stamped on a plate on the top left side of the instrument panel and visible through the windshield. The first symbol 1 designates Chevrolet. The second and third symbols designate the series: (six-cylinder) 31=Chevelle Nomad wagon, 33=Chevelle 300 Deluxe/Greenbrier wagon and 35=Malibu; (V-8) 32=Chevelle Nomad wagon, 34=Chevelle 300 Deluxe/Greenbrier wagon, 36=Malibu and 38=Concours/Estate wagon. The fourth and fifth symbols designates body type: 27=two-door pillared coupe, 37=two-door hardtop (sport coupe), 35=four-door six-passenger station wagon, 36=four-door six-passenger station wagon with dual tailgate, 39=four-door hardtop (sport sedan), 46=four-door three-seat station wagon, 67=two-door convertible and 69=four-door sedan. The sixth symbol designates the model year: 9=1969. The seventh symbol designates the assembly plant location: The seventh symbol indicated assembly plant: A=Atlanta, Georgia; B=Baltimore, Maryland; G=Framingham, Massachusetts; K=Kansas City, Missouri; Z=Fremont, California The last six symbols are the sequential unit production number at the specific factory. The Fisher body tag riveted to the top of the cowl on the left side of the car below the hood provides additional vehicle identification information. The Fisher body STYLE NUMBER (ST) consists of a prefix identifying model year and four or more symbols identifying the series and body style (example: 69-13369 for a 1969 Chevelle 300 Deluxe four-door sedan with a six-cylinder engine). The BODY NUMBER consists of a prefix designating assembly plant and the sequential unit production number at the specific factory. The TRIM NUMBER (TR) identifies upholstery.

COLORS

(10) Tuxedo Black, (40) Butternut Yellow, (50) Dover White, (69) Cortez Silver, (51) Dusk Blue, (52) Garnet Red, (53) Glacier Blue, (55) Azure Turquoise, (57) Fathom Green, (59) Frost Green, (61) Burnished Brown, (63) Champagne, (65) Olympic Gold, (67) Burgundy and (71) LeMans Blue. In addition, cars with the SS 396 option could be ordered in (72) Monaco Orange and (76) Daytona Yellow.

ENGINE CODES

Codes appear on the right side of six-cylinder blocks behind the distributor and right front of V-8 engine blocks. Engine codes for 1969 were: (230-cid/140-hp six) AM, AN, AP, AQ, AR, AS, AU, AT and AV; (250-cid/155-hp six) BB, BC, BD, BE, BF, BH, BK, BW, BI and BJ; (307-cid/200 hp V-8) DA, DC, DD, DE; (350/250-hp V-8) HC, HD, HF; (350-cid/255-hp V-8) HQ, HR and HS; (350-cid/300-hp V-8) HA, HB, HE; (396-cid/325-hp V-8) JA, KF, KG, JV and KI; (396-cid/350-hp V-8) JC, JE and KH and (396-cid/375-hp V-8) JD, JK and KD.

CHEVELLE NOMAD — (6-CYL/V-8) SERIES 131/132

The Nomad station wagon was the only Chevelle left that had less trim than a 300 Deluxe model. Since wagons were merchandised as if they were a line unto themselves, the Nomad was technically the base station wagon, rather than the base Chevelle. Other than Nomad emblems, there was little to distinguish this model.

Model Number	Body/Style Number	Body Type & Seating	Factory Price	Shipping Weight	Production Total
CHEVELLE NOMAD STATION WAGON SERIES 131 (6-CYL)					
131	35	4d nomad-6P	$2,668	3,390 lbs.	Note 1
CHEVELLE NOMAD STATION WAGON SERIES 132 (V-8)					
132	35	4d nomad-6P	$2,758	3,515 lbs.	Note 1

NOTE 1: Individual body style production is not available; see production notes.

CHEVELLE 300 DELUXE — (6-CYL/V-8) SERIES 133/134

The Chevelle 300 Deluxe was technically the base series in the Chevelle line, although the Nomad station wagons actually had plainer trim. In addition to the standard equipment for all Chevelles, as listed above, the Chevelle 300 Deluxe had a heater and defroster. Three tough, yet tasty, cloth-and-vinyl interior trims were available in black, blue or medium green. An all-black all-vinyl trim was optional. Cars in this series had "300" emblems on the front fender sides, behind the wheel opening. The rear panel had a "Chevelle" script on the right-hand side and nothing else other than a bright metal keyhole. Thin rocker panel moldings dressed up the body sides, just below the door break line. Greenbrier station wagons had appropriate exterior and interior trim variations. According to the Chevrolet sales catalog, the Z25 option (SS 396 package) could be ordered for the Chevelle 300 Deluxe coupe or sport coupe. It includ-

The SS 396 option package was available on all Chevelle coupes and Malibu convertibles for 1969.

ed a black accented grille with an "SS" badge in its center, a special hood with twin power blisters, sport wheels, white-lettered wide-oval tires, power front disc brakes, a 396-cid 325-hp V-8 and a special three-speed manual transmission with floor shifter. The "SS" package had a $268.40 dealer cost and added $347.60 to the retail price of the Series 134 coupe or sport coupe.

Model Number	Body/Style Number	Body Type & Seating	Factory Price	Shipping Weight	Production Total
CHEVELLE 300 DELUXE SERIES 133 (6-CYL)					
133	69	4d sedan-6P	$2,488	3,100 lbs.	Note 1
133	37	2d sport coupe	$2,521	3,075 lbs.	Note 1
133	27	2d coupe-6P	$2,458	3,035 lbs.	Note 1
133	46	4d Greenbrier-9P	$2,892	3,615 lbs.	Note 1
133	35/36	4d Greenbrier-6P	$2,779	3,445 lbs.	Note 1
CHEVELLE 300 DELUXE SERIES 134 (V-8)					
134	69	4d sedan-6P	$2,577	3,230 lbs.	Note 1
134	37	2d sport coupe	$2,611	3,205 lbs.	Note 1
134	11	2d coupe-6P	$2,548	3,165 lbs.	Note 1
134	46	4d Greenbrier-9P	$3,024	3,740 lbs.	Note 1
134	35/36	4d Greenbrier-6P	$2,869	3,585 lbs.	Note 1

NOTE 1: Individual body style production is not available; see production notes.

MALIBU — (6-CYL/V-8) SERIES 135/136

This year Chevrolet promoted each Malibu model as if it was a separate type of product. The Malibu sport sedan was highlighted as the family car, while the quickness and beauty of the Malibu sport coupe was emphasized. The convertible's excitement was stressed, while the budget-consciousness of the four-door sedan was spotlighted. The Malibu section of the 1969 Chevelle sales catalog also covered the Concours sedan, which is broken out below. Most of these cars carried "Malibu" block letters just ahead of the rear side marker lights. The rear panel had an anodized bright metal beauty panel running from one side to the other between the taillights. A bright molding ran along the front fender edges and across the lower body feature line and on sport coupes, convertibles and sport sedans the area below this molding was finished in Argent silver. The upper body feature line carried neat double pin striping. Up front the grille had a Chevy bow-tie emblem in its center, unless the SS 396 option was added to the Sport coupe or ragtop. Other Malibu extras included Hide-A-Way two-speed windshield wipers, a deluxe three-spoke steering wheel with non-glare metal trim, lighted heater controls and richer interior trims. Floor carpeting was standard in the Malibu sport coupe. The 1969 Malibu wagons were called Concours models. The SS 396 option (RPO Z25) could be ordered for the Malibu sport coupe or convertible. It substituted a black accented grille with an "SS 396" badge in its center, a special hood with twin power blisters, sport wheels, "SS 396" front fender badges, white-lettered wide-oval tires, power front disc brakes, a 396-cid 325-hp V-8 and a special three-speed manual transmission with floor shifter. The "SS" package also retailed for $347.60 to Malibu buyers. Wider upper body striping was seen on some SS 396 models. The Concours sedan was also, technically, a Malibu, but is covered separately below.

Model Number	Body/Style Number	Body Type & Seating	Factory Price	Shipping Weight	Production Total
MALIBU SERIES 135 (6-CYL)					
135	69	4d sedan-6P	$2,567	3,130 lbs.	Note 1
135	39	4d sport sedan-6P	$2,672	3,205 lbs.	Note 1
135	37	2d sport coupe-6P	$2,601	3,095 lbs.	Note 1
135	67	2d convertible-6P	$2,800	3,175 lbs.	Note 1
135	46	4d Concours-9P	$3,044	3,625 lbs.	Note 1
135	36	4d Concours-6P	$2,931	3,545 lbs.	Note 1
MALIBU SERIES 136 (V-8)					
136	69	4d sedan-6P	$2,657	3,265 lbs.	Note 1
136	39	4d sport sedan-6P	$2,762	3,340 lbs.	Note 1
136	37	2d sport coupe-6P	$2,690	3,230 lbs.	Note 1
136	67	2d convertible-6P	$2,889	3,300 lbs.	Note 1
136	46	4d Concours-9P	$3,134	3,755 lbs.	Note 1
136	35	4d Concours-6P	$3,021	3,685 lbs.	Note 1

NOTE 1: Individual body style production is not available; see production notes.

MALIBU CONCOURS SPORT SEDAN (6-CYL/V-8) — SERIES 135/136

Based on its coding and the 1969 Chevelle sales catalog, the Concours sport sedan was an option package for the Malibu. Said the copywriters, "Start with a Malibu sport sedan. (Quite a start!) Deck it out with special exterior trim and color-accented lower body moldings. Dress it up inside by adding special trim on (the) instrument panel, doors and steering wheel . . . by covering uncommonly comfortable seats with uncommonly fine cloth in black, dark blue or dark green . . . by spreading deep-twist carpeting sill to sill and letting it creep up the door quarter panels and you have the Conours sedan. Possibly the most elegant mid-size car on the road." Concours name scripts were placed on the front fenders behind the wheel opening and on the right-hand side of the rear deck lid. The Concours Sedan package, option Z16, was offered only for the Malibu sport sedan. It had a dealer price of $101.65 and retailed for $131.65. Also included were a steering wheel with a special emblem, a rear panel trim plate, black-accented lower body side and wheel opening moldings and special insulation.

Model Number	Body/Style Number	Body Type & Seating	Factory Price	Shipping Weight	Production Total
MALIBU CONCOURS SPORT SEDAN SERIES 135 (6-CYL)					
135	39	4d sport sedan-6P	$2,804	3,215 lbs.	Note 1
MALIBU CONCOURS SPORT SEDAN SERIES 136 (V-8)					
136	39	4d sport sedan-6P	$2,894	3,350 lbs.	Note 1

NOTE 1: Individual body style production is not available; see production notes.

MALIBU CONCOURS ESTATE — (V-8) SERIES 138

The Concours Estate Wagon featured an all-vinyl interior, a lighted locking glove box, extra-thick foam cushioned seats, simulated walnut side and rear exterior panels, two-speed Hide-A-Way windshield wipers, chrome wheel opening moldings, an oval steering wheel with horn tabs, ribbed color-accented lower body perimeter moldings, a tailgate emblem badge for Concours identification, a Concours script on each front fender and a V-8. Concours Custom interiors were trimmed in textured vinyl. The passenger floor featured deep-twist carpeting and the cargo load floor had a vinyl coating.

Model Number	Body/Style Number	Body Type & Seating	Factory Price	Shipping Weight	Production Total
138	46	4d wagon-9P	$3,266	3,730 lbs.	Note 1
138	35	4d wagon-6P	$3,153	3,680 lbs.	Note 1

NOTE 1: Individual body style production is not available; see production notes.

CHEVELLE SS 396 — (V-8) SERIES 134 or 136

"As if providing seven models in two series weren't selection enough, we take it several steps further," said the 1969 Chevelle sales catalog. "Like turning four models into SS 396s." Then came more details. "SS 396. Say it out loud. Get the feel of it. You'll be hearing it a lot because the SS 396 equipment package is now available on all Chevelle coupes and the Malibu convertible. Includes a choice of 325- or 350-hp Turbo-Jet 396 V-8s. Special three-speed gear box. Power disc brakes. Sport wheels. SS emblems. Twin-domed hood. Beefed-up full coil suspension. Much more that's standard." What Chevy literature didn't mention was that you could also get two 375-hp versions of the 396-cid engine if you really tried. While the new strategy of marketing SS 396 goodies as an option package seems a little confusing today, Chevrolet said it made ordering easier and it probably did, as sales went up.

Model Number	Body/Style Number	Body Type & Seating	Factory Price	Shipping Weight	Production Total
CHEVELLE DELUXE 300 SERIES 134 + RPO Z25 SUPER SPORT 396 OPTION PACKAGE (V-8)					
134	37	2d sport coupe	$2,743	—	Note 1
134	11	2d coupe-6P	$2,680	—	Note 1
MALIBU SERIES 136 + RPO Z25 SUPER SPORT 396 OPTION PACKAGE (V-8)					
136	37	2d sport coupe-6P	$2,822	—	Note 1
136	67	2d convertible-6P	$3,021	—	Note 1

NOTE 1: Individual body style production is not available; see production notes.

PRODUCTION NOTES

NOTE 1 Model-year production of all 1969 Chevelles was 439,611 units.
NOTE 2 Industry statistical breakouts in rounded-off numbers show 47,900 Chevelle sixes and 391,700 Chevelle V-8s were built in 1969.
NOTE 3 Additional statistics record series production, in rounded-off figures (except SS 396), as follows:

Chevelle 300 Del. (6-cyl)	21,000
Chevelle 300 (V-8)	21,000
Total	**42,000**
Malibu (6-cyl)	23,500
Malibu (V-8)	343,600
Total	**367,100**
Wagons (6-cyl)	7,400
Wagons (V-8)	38,500
Total	**45,900**
El Camino (6-cyl)	3,000
Wagons (V-8)	45,400
Total	**48,400**

NOTE 4 Production by factory was:

Code	Factory	Production	Code	Factory	Production
B	Baltimore	103,327	Z	Fremont	53,617
K	Kansas City	158,339	A	Atlanta	56,386
G	Framingham	67,942			

NOTE 5 Exactly 86,307 cars had the Z25 Chevelle SS 396 option installed. All were V-8 powered. No series or body style breakouts are available.

ENGINES

CHEVELLE 300, 300 DELUXE, MALIBU BASE 230-CID, 140-HP SIX-CYL: Inline. Overhead-valve. Cast-iron block. Displacement: 230 cid. Bore and stroke: 3.875 x 3.25 in. Compression ratio: 8.5:1. Brake hp: 140 at 4400 rpm. Seven main bearings. Hydraulic valve lifters. Crankcase capacity: 4 qt. (add 1 qt. for new filter). Cooling system capacity: 12 qt (add 6 qt. for heater). Carburetor: Rochester one-barrel Model 7027003. Available standard with three-speed fully synchronized manual transmission and optional with special fully synchronized three-speed manual transmission, Powerglide automatic transmission or Turbo-Hydra-Matic automatic transmission.

CHEVELLE 300, 300 DELUXE, MALIBU BASE 250-CID, 155-HP SIX-CYL: Inline. Overhead-valve. Cast-iron block. Displacement: 250 cid. Bore and stroke: 3.875 x 3.53 in. Compression ratio: 8.5:1. Brake hp: 155 at 4200 rpm. Taxable hp: 36. Torque: lbs.-ft. 235 at 1600 rpm. Seven main bearings. Hydraulic valve lifters. Crankcase capacity: 4 qt. (add 1 qt. for new filter). Cooling system capacity: 12 qt. (add 6 qt. for heater). Carburetor: Rochester one-barrel Model 7028017. Sales code L22. Available standard with three-speed fully synchronized manual transmission and optional with special fully synchronized three-speed manual transmission, Powerglide automatic transmission or Turbo-Hydra-Matic automatic transmission.

CHEVELLE BASE 307-CID, 200-HP V-8: Overhead-valve. Cast-iron block and head. Bore and stroke: 3.88 x 3.25 in. Displacement: 307 cid. Compression ratio: 9.00:1. Brake hp: 200 at 4600 rpm. Taxable hp: 48. Torque: 300 lbs.-ft. at 2400. Five main bearings. Hydraulic valve lifters. Crankcase capacity: 4 qt. (add 1 qt. for new filter). Cooling system capacity: 16 qt. (add 1 qt. for heater). Carburetor: Two-barrel. Available standard with three-speed fully synchronized manual transmission and optional with special fully synchronized three-speed manual transmission, fully synchronized four-speed manual transmission, Powerglide automatic transmission or Turbo-Hydra-Matic automatic transmission.

CHEVELLE, MALIBU OPTIONAL 350-CID, 255-HP V-8: Overhead-valve. Cast-iron block and head. Bore and stroke: 4.00 x 3.48 in. Displacement: 350 cid. Compression ratio: 9.00:1. Brake hp: 255 at 4800 rpm. Taxable hp: 51.20. Torque: 365 lbs.-ft. at 3200. Five main bearings. Hydraulic valve lifters. Crankcase capacity: 4 qt.

The familiar Chevelle badging could be found above the driver's side headlight.

CHEVELLE

(add 1 qt. for new filter). Cooling system capacity: (full-size) 14 qt.; (others) 15 qt. (add 1 qt. for heater). Carburetor: Four-barrel. Sales code LM1. Available standard with three-speed fully synchronized manual transmission and optional with special fully synchronized three-speed manual transmission, fully synchronized four-speed manual transmission, Powerglide automatic transmission or Turbo-Hydra-Matic automatic transmission.

CHEVELLE, MALIBU OPTIONAL 350-CID, 300-HP V-8: Overhead-valve. Cast-iron block and head. Bore and stroke: 4.00 x 3.48 in. Displacement: 350 cid. Compression ratio: 9.00:1. Brake hp: 300 at 4800 rpm. Taxable hp: 51.20. Torque: 380 lbs.-ft. at 3200. Five main bearings. Hydraulic valve lifters. Crankcase capacity: 4 qt. (add 1 qt. for new filter). Cooling system capacity: (full-size) 14 qt.; (others) 15 qt. (add 1 qt. for heater). Carburetor: Four-barrel. Sales code L48. Available with special fully synchronized three-speed manual transmission, fully synchronized four-speed manual transmission, Powerglide automatic transmission or Turbo-Hydra-Matic automatic transmission.

CHEVELLE SS 396 OPTIONAL 325-HP V-8: Overhead-valve. Cast-iron block and head. Bore and stroke: 4.09 x 3.76 in. Displacement: 396 cid (actually 402 cid). Compression ratio: 10.25:1. Brake hp: 325 at 4800 rpm. Taxable hp: 53.60. Torque: 410 lbs.-ft. at 3200. Five main bearings. Hydraulic valve lifters. Crankcase capacity: 4 qt. (add 1 qt. for new filter). Cooling system capacity: 23 qt. (add 1 qt. for heater). Carburetor: Four-barrel. Sales code L35. Available standard with special fully synchronized three-speed manual transmission, and optional with fully synchronized four-speed manual transmission or Turbo-Hydra-Matic automatic transmission.

CHEVELLE SS 396 OPTIONAL 350-HP V-8: Overhead-valve. Cast-iron block and head. Bore and stroke: 4.09 x 3.76 in. Displacement: 396 cid (actually 402 cid). Compression ratio: 10.25:1. Brake hp: 350 at 5200 rpm. Taxable hp: 53.60. Torque: 415 lbs.-ft. at 3400. Five main bearings. Hydraulic valve lifters. Crankcase capacity: 4 qt. (add 1 qt. for new filter). Cooling system capacity: 23 qt. (add 1 qt. for heater). Carburetor: Four-barrel. Sales code L34. Available standard with special fully synchronized three-speed manual transmission, and optional with fully synchronized four-speed manual transmission or Turbo-Hydra-Matic automatic transmission.

CHEVELLE SS 396 OPTIONAL 375-HP V-8: Overhead-valve. Cast-iron block and head. Bore and stroke: 4.09 x 3.76 in. Displacement: 396 cid (actually 402 cid). Compression ratio: 11.00:1. Brake hp: 375 at 5600 rpm. Taxable hp: 53.60. Torque: 415 lbs.-ft. at 3600. Five main bearings. Hydraulic valve lifters. Crankcase capacity: 4 qt. (add 1 qt. for new filter). Cooling system capacity: 23 qt. (add 1 qt. for heater). Carburetor: Four-barrel. Sales code: L78. Available standard with three-speed fully synchronized manual transmission and optional with special fully synchronized three-speed manual transmission fully synchronized four-speed manual transmission or Turbo-Hydra-Matic automatic transmission.

CHEVELLE SS 396 OPTIONAL 375-HP V-8: Overhead-valve. Cast-iron block. Aluminum head with large valves. Bore and stroke: 4.09 x 3.76 in. Displacement: 396 cid (actually 402 cid). Compression ratio: 11.00:1. Brake hp: 375 at 5600 rpm. Taxable hp: 53.60. Torque: 415 lbs.-ft. at 3600. Five main bearings. Solid valve lifters. Crankcase capacity: 4 qt. (add 1 qt. for new filter). Cooling system capacity: 23 qt. (add 1 qt. for heater). Carburetor: Holley four-barrel carburetor on high-rise aluminum intake manifold. Sales code L78/L89. Available standard with three-speed fully synchronized manual transmission and optional with special fully synchronized three-speed manual transmission fully synchronized four-speed manual transmission or Turbo-Hydra-Matic automatic transmission.

CHEVELLE OPTIONAL V-8 (DRAG RACING ONLY): Overhead-valve. Cast-iron block and head. Bore and stroke: 4.25 x 3.76 in. Displacement: 427 cid. Compression ratio: 10.25:1. Brake hp: 390 at 4800 rpm. Taxable hp: 57.80. Torque: 460 lbs.-ft. at 3600. Five main bearings. Hydraulic valve lifters. Crankcase capacity: 4 qt. (add 1 qt. for new filter). Cooling system capacity: 21 qt. (add 1 qt. for heater). Dual exhaust. Carburetor: Holley 3885067 four-barrel. Sales code: L72. Available standard with three-speed fully synchronized manual transmission and optional with special fully synchronized three-speed manual transmission fully synchronized four-speed manual transmission or Turbo-Hydra-Matic automatic transmission.

CHASSIS FEATURES

Wheelbase: (two-door) 112 in.; (four-door) 116 in. Overall length: (two-door) 197 in. (four-door cars) 201.1 in.; (four-door station wagons) 208 in. Width: 75.7 in. Height: (sedans) 53.5 in. (coupes) 52.7 in. (convertibles) 53.2 in. Front tread: 59 in. Rear tread: 59 in. Gas tank capacity: 20 gal. Tires: (300 Deluxe car) 7.35 x 14 two-ply/four-ply rated; (300 Deluxe wagon) 7.75 x 14 two-ply/four-ply rated; (Malibu car, except Concours sport sedan and convertible) 7.35 x 14 two-ply/four-ply rated; (Concours sport sedan, convertibles and Malibu wagon) 7.75 x 14 two-ply/four-ply rated; (SS 396) F70 x 14 special wide-oval red-stripe or white-stripe. Turn circle: 41 feet. Trunk capacity (sedan) 13.5 cubic feet. Front head room (sedan): 38.5 in. Rear headroom (sedan): 37.1 in. Front legroom (sedan): 42.8 in. Rear legroom (sedan): 35.1 in. Front hip room (sedan): 59.5 in. Rear hip room (sedan): 59.4 in.

OPTIONS

C60 Four-Season air conditioning, including 61-amp Delcotron alternator, heavy-duty radiator and temperature-controlled fan and requiring larger tires with some Chevelles ($376). C51 Station wagon rear window air deflector ($19). ZP5 Appearance group, including front and rear bumper guards, door edge guards, floor mats and visor vanity mirror for two-door Chevelles ($50.65). ZP5 appearance group, including front and rear bumper guards, door edge guards, floor mats and visor vanity mirror for four-door Chevelles ($53.80). G80 Positraction rear axle ($42.15). ZQ8/9 economy, performance or special rear axle ($2.15). T/60 Heavy-duty battery with 396-cid V-8 ($15.80). T/60 Heavy-duty battery without 396-cid V-8 ($8.45). AS1 Standard type front shoulder belts, in convertibles ($23.20). AS5 Standard type rear shoulder belts, in cars with standard seat belts ($23.20). ZK3 Custom Deluxe front shoulder belts for bucket seat cars, except convertibles ($12.15). ZK3 Custom Deluxe

Bucket seats and deluxe interiors were optional in 1969.

front shoulder belts for bench seat cars, except convertibles ($13.70). A39 Custom Deluxe front seat belts, for convertibles with bucket seats ($9). A39 Custom Deluxe front seat belts for convertibles with bench front seats ($10.55). A85 Custom Deluxe front shoulder belts, requires Custom deluxe seat belts for convertibles ($26.35). AS4 Custom Deluxe rear shoulder belts, requires Custom deluxe seat belts ($26.35). J50 power drum brakes ($42.15). J50/52 power front disc brakes ($64.25). V55 Station wagon roof carrier ($52.70). U35 Electric clock in Chevelle 300 and 300 Deluxe models; included with special instrumentation ($15.80). MA6, Heavy-duty 10-in. dual plate clutch, for cars with 300-, 325- or 350-hp V-8s ($47.40). Z16 Concours sport sedan package including luxury cloth seat rim, luxury cloth sidewall trim, a steering wheel emblem, a rear body panel trim plate, black-accented lower body side moldings, black-accented wheel trim opening moldings, a deck lid nameplate and special interior insulation for Malibu sport sedan only ($131.65). D55 Console with courtesy light, not available with standard three-speed manual transmission ($53.75). ZQ1 Décor Group for Nomad and Greenbrier station wagons, includes window moldings and rear fender skirts ($52.70). C50 Rear windshield defroster, all except convertibles and wagons ($22.15). A93 Power door locks for two-door models ($44.80). A93 Power door locks for four-door models ($68.50). L22 250-cid 155-hp six-cylinder engine ($26.35). LM1 350-cid 255-hp V-8 ($68.50). L48 350-cid 300-hp V-8 engine, all except SS 396 ($68.50). L34 396-cid 350-hp V-8 engine, SS 396 only ($121.15). L78 396-cid 375-hp V-8 SS 396 only ($252.80). L78/L89 396-cid 375-hp V-8 with aluminum heads, for SS 396 only ($647.75). N10 Dual exhaust on all Chevelle V-8s with single exhaust ($30.55). K02 Temperature-controlled fan, V-8s, standard with air conditioning ($15.80). K79 42-amp Delcotron generator, not available with air conditioning or with C60 ($10.55). K85 63-amp Delcotron generator, with air conditioning ($5.30); without air conditioning ($26.35). A01 All windows tinted ($36.90).

R93 door edge guards, for two-door Chevelles ($4.25). R93 door edge guards, for four-door Chevelles ($7.40). K05 engine block heater ($10.55). CE1 Headlight washers ($15.80). U05 dual horns ($5.30). U14 Special instrumentation with ammeter, temperature gauge, oil pressure gauge and tachometer on Malibu and SS 396 sport coupes and convertibles ($94.80). U46 light monitoring system ($26.35). ZJ19 auxiliary lighting groups with A) courtesy light, B) glove box light, C) luggage compartment light, D) underhood light, E) mirror map light and F) ash tray light; in Malibu sedans and coupes includes A, C, D, E and F ($16.35), in Malibu convertibles includes C, D, E and F ($12.15), in Chevelle 300 Deluxe includes A, B, C, D, E and F ($19), in Concours and Concours Estate station wagons includes A, D, E and F ($13.70), in Greenbrier and Nomad station wagons includes A, B, C, D, E and F ($16.70). B37 Twin front and rear floor mats ($11.60). D33 Left-hand outside remote-control mirror ($10.55). D34 Visor vanity mirror ($3.20). BX4 upper body side moldings on Chevelle, Concours, Greenbrier and Nomad ($26.35). B90 Window moldings on Chevelle 300 Deluxe coupes ($21.10). B90 Window moldings on Chevelle four-door and station wagon models ($26.35). ZQ2 Operating Convenience group with A) electric clock, B) remote-control left-hand outside rearview mirror and C) rear window defroster; on Chevelles except Malibu sport coupe or convertible includes A, B, C ($48.50), on Malibu sport coupe with special instrumentation includes B, C ($32.70), on Malibu sport coupe without special instrumentation includes A, B, C ($48.50), on Malibu convertible with special instrumentation includes B, C ($43.20), on Malibu convertible without special instrumentation includes A, B, C ($59). Solid color Monaco Orange or Daytona Yellow paint on SS 396 ($42.15). Two-tone paint ($23.20). V01 Heavy-duty radiator ($14.75). U63 AM push-button radio with front antenna ($61.10). U69 AM/FM radio with front antenna ($133.80). U69/79 AM/FM radio with front antenna and stereo ($239.15). U73 Rear antenna, all except AM/FM and wagons ($9.50). CO8 Vinyl roof cover, for hardtop models ($89.55). Z25 SS 396 option package for Chevelle sport coupe or convertible, includes 396-cid 325-hp V-8, black-accented grille, special hood, special ornamentation, special suspension, sport wheels, wide-oval white lettered tires, power disc brakes and special three-speed manual transmission ($37.60). A51 Strato bucket seats in Malibu sport coupe and convertible ($111.15). K30 Speed and cruise control, V-8s with automatic transmissions ($52.70). U15 Speed warning indicator ($10.55). N30 Deluxe steering wheel in Chevelle 300s and Nomads ($7.40). N30 Deluxe steering wheel in Chevelle 300 Deluxe and Nomad Custom ($4.25). N33 Comfortilt steering wheel, requires floor shifter or automatic transmissions ($57.95). U15 speed warning indicator ($11.60). N40 Power steering for all except SS 396 ($100.10). N40 Power steering for SS 396 ($105.35. N33 Comfortilt steering wheel ($45.30). N34 Sport styled steering wheel ($34.80). D96 accent striping for SS 396 only ($26.35). F40 Special front and rear suspension for Chevelle, Concours Estate or Nomad with six or standard V-8 ($16.90); with optional V-8 ($5.30). M20 wide-ratio four-speed manual transmission ($184.80). M22 Close-ratio four-speed

CHEVELLE

This 1969 Chevelle convertible was ordered with the 396-cid V-8 and most of the other available options.

manual transmission ($264). M21 Close-ratio four-speed manual transmission ($184.80). M40 Turbo Hydra-Matic transmission for six-cylinder Chevelles ($190.10). M40 Turbo Hydra-Matic transmission for 375-hp Chevelles ($290.40). M40 Turbo Hydra-Matic transmission for other V-8 Chevelles ($221.80). MC1 Special three-speed manual transmission ($79). M35 Powerglide automatic transmission for six-cylinder Chevelle ($174.25). M10 Overdrive transmission with 140-, 155-, 200- or 250-hp engines ($115.90). Vinyl trim interior for 300 series and Malibu sport coupe or sport sedan ($12.65). KD5 Heavy-duty closed engine positive crankcase ventilation system ($6.35). A33 power tailgate window for station wagons ($34.80). A31 power windows ($100.35). C224 Hide-A-way windshield wipers ($19). P01 Four bright metal wheel covers ($21.10). PA2 Mag spoke wheel covers ($73.75). ZJ7 Rallye wheels, including special wheels, hub caps and trim rings ($31.60). P58 Five 7.35 x 14 four-ply rated white sidewall tires, replacing 7.35 x 14 four-ply rated black sidewall ($31.35). Five 7.75 x 14 four-ply rated black sidewall tires, replacing 7.35 x 14 four-ply rated black sidewall ($14.70 or standard on Malibu sport sedan and convertible with 275- or 325-hp V-8s and standard on other 300, 300 Deluxe and Malibu cars with 325-hp V-8). P62 Five 7.75 x 14 four-ply rated white sidewall tires, replacing 7.35 x 14 four-ply rated black sidewall ($46). PW8 Five F70 x 14 four-ply rated Nylon red-stripe tires, replacing 7.35 x 14 four-ply rated black sidewall ($69.70). PW7 Five F70 x 14 four-ply rated Nylon white-stripe tires, replacing 7.35 x 14 four-ply rated black sidewall ($69.70). P62 Five 7.75 x 14 four-ply rated white sidewall tires, replacing 7.75 x 14 four-ply rated black sidewall ($31.35). PN4 Five 7.75 x 14 eight-ply rated black sidewall tires, replacing 7.75 x 14 four-ply rated black sidewall on station wagons only ($46.25). PN5 Five 7.75 x 14 eight-ply rated black whitewall tires, replacing 7.75 x 14 four-ply rated black sidewall on station wagons only ($79.60). PW8 Five F70 x 14 four-ply rated nylon red-stripe tires, replacing 7.75 x 14 four-ply rated black sidewall ($55). PW7 Five F70 x 14 four-ply rated nylon white-stripe tires, replacing 7.75 x 14 four-ply rated black sidewall ($55.05). PW7 Five F70 x 14 four-ply rated white-stripe tires on SS 396 in place of red stripe (no cost)

OPTION INSTALLATION RATES

Automatic transmission (78.4 percent). Four-speed manual transmission (11.9 percent). Standard V-8 engine (48.7 percent). Optional V-8 engine (40.4 percent). six-cylinder engine (10.9 percent). AM radio (85.1 percent). AM/FM radio (3 percent). Stereo tape (2.5 percent). Air conditioning (34.3 percent). Power steering (72.7 percent). Tilt steering (2.1 percent). Power drum brakes (10.7 percent). Power front disc brakes (22 percent). Power door locks (0.2 percent). Power side windows (0.9 percent). Power tailgate window (5.1 percent). Bucket seats (15.8 percent). Vinyl top (39.8 percent). White sidewall tires (52.6 percent). Tinted windshield only (0.9 percent). All tinted glass (60.5 percent). Dual exhaust (19.8 percent). Positraction (14.5 percent). Optional full wheel covers (49.4 percent). Styled wheels (25 percent). Optional clock (20.1 percent). Station wagon luggage rack (2.6 percent). Based on model year production of 428,827 units.

HISTORICAL FOOTNOTES

The 1969 model year was the third best sales year in Chevrolet history. Retail deliveries of Chevelles rose 4.6 percent over the record set in 1968. Dealer sales of Chevelles in calendar year 1969 were 436,853 units or 5.16 percent of total industry sales. Production of the 396-cid Chevy big-block V-8 hit 170,155 engines in the model year, although not all of these were put in Chevelles. A total of 431,899 new Chevelles were registered in the United States during the calendar year. The Chevelle SS 396 with the 325-hp V-8 and automatic transmission that *Car and Driver* comparison road tested in January 1969 did 0 to 60 mph in 5.8 seconds and covered the quarter mile in 14.41 seconds at 97.35 mph. You could order the SS 396 option for the Chevelle 300 Deluxe two-door coupe over the counter for $3,409 or more than $300 less than a Dodge Super Bee.

1970

In addition to the 454-cid engine, the 1970 Z15 option included bright engine accents, dual exhausts with bright tips, and power front disc brakes.

The more highly sculptured 1970 Chevelle featured a bold-looking frontal treatment with a horizontally split grille opening and dual headlights. The round headlamps were placed in separate chrome housings that were set into body-color panels that ran between the grilles and the front body corners. A new slot-less front bumper "veed" out in the center and incorporated rectangular parking lamps directly below the headlights. The swept-back front fender look was replaced by a front end with a blunter appearance. The upper body feature line ran from about the headlight level to the top of the back bumper. The body panels flared out over the front and rear wheel housings. The front side markers had a twin-slot appearance and were placed low on the front fender, head of the wheel well, just behind the front bumper ends.

The rear side marker, placed just ahead of the rear bumper ends, resembled eight-segment slats stacked on top of each other. At the rear an angular, body-integrated bumper ran high across the rear of the car and housed large rectangular taillights at each end. Coupes and convertibles again featured a 112-in. wheelbase, while sedans and station wagons had a 4-in. longer stance.

This year, the base model was simply called the Chevelle and the Chevelle 300 and Chevelle 300 Deluxe names were dropped. On top was the Malibu. The Super Sport package was merchandised as the SS option and SS 396 and SS 454 versions were available. A wide range of Chevelle station wagons included the Nomad (which was trimmed like the old 300), the deluxe Greenbrier (trimmed like the old 300 Deluxe), the Concours (with Malibu-like trimmings) and the Monte Carlo-like Concours Estate wagon. The 250-cid 155-hp in-line six became the base engine for Chevelles and Malibus. The base engine for the sporty SS was a 396-cid job with an increased 350-hp. Optional engines included 307-, 350-, 396- (actually 402-), 400- and 454-cid V-8s.

I.D. NUMBERS

VIN embossed on the top left-hand side of the instrument panel and visible through the windshield. The first symbol 1 designates Chevrolet. The second symbol indicates series: 3=Chevelle or Monte Carlo. The third symbol indicates the type of engine: odd number=six-cylinder; even number=V-8. The fourth and fifth symbols indicate body style: 36=four-door two-seat station wagon (with dual-action tailgate), 37=two-door notchback/hardtop coupe (sport coupe), 39=four-door notchback/hardtop sedan (sport sedan), 46=four-door three-seat station wagon (with dual-action tailgate), 67=two-door convertible and 69=four-door notchback sedan (pillared). The sixth symbol designates the model year: 0=1970. The seventh symbol designates the assembly plant location: The seventh symbol indicated assembly plant: B=Baltimore, Maryland; F=Flint, Michigan; K=Kansas City, Missouri; L=Van Nuys (Los Angeles) California, and R=Arlington, Texas. The last six symbols are the sequential unit production number at the specific factory. The Fisher body tag riveted to the top of the cowl on the left side of the car below the hood provides additional vehicle identification information. The Fisher body STYLE NUMBER (ST) consists of a prefix identifying model year and four or more symbols identifying the series and body style (example: 70-13369 for a base 1970 Chevelle four-door sedan with a V-8). The BODY NUMBER consists of a prefix designating assembly plant and the sequential unit production number at the specific factory. The TRIM NUMBER (TR) identifies upholstery.

COLORS

(10) classic White, (14) Cortez Silver, (17) Shadow Gray, (19) Tuxedo Black, (25) Astro Turquoise Blue, (28) Fathom Blue, (34) Misty Turquoise, (45) Green Mist, (48) Forest Green, (50) Gobi Beige, (55) Champagne Gold, (58) Autumn Gold, (63) Desert Sand, (75) Cranberry Red and (78) Black Cherry. Engine codes appear on the right side of six-cylinder blocks behind the distributor and right front of V-8 engine blocks. Vinyl tops were available in five colors: AA=White, BB=Black, CC=Dark Blue, HH=Dark Gold and GG=Dark Green.

ENGINE CODES

Engine codes for 1970 were: (250-cid six) CRG, CCH, CCG, CCF, CCM, CCK and CCL; (307-cid V-8) CNC, CND, CNE, CNF, CNG, CNH, CRF; (350/250-hp V-8) CNI, CNN and CNM; (350-cid/300-hp V-8) CNJ, CNK and CRE; (396-cid/350-hp V-8) CTW, CTX and CTZ; (396-cid/375-hp V-8) CTY, CKN, CKO, CKD, CKQ, CKT and CKU; (396-cid/375-hp aluminum cylinder heads) CKP; (400-cid/265-hp) CZX and CRH; (400-cid/330-hp) CKN, CKR and CKS; (454-cid/360-hp) CRN, CGT, CRQ, CRM, CRT, CGU and CRU; (454-cid/450-hp) CRR, CRV and CRX; (454-cid/450-hp aluminum cylinder heads) CRS, CRY and CRW.

CHEVELLE NOMAD — (6-CYL/V-8) SERIES 131/132

The Nomad station wagon was again unique in that it was plainer than even a base 1970 Chevelle passenger car. Since wagons were merchandised as if they were a

A 454-cid engine was available in Chevelles for the first time in 1970.

line unto themselves, the Nomad was technically the base station wagon, rather than the base Chevelle. Other than Nomad emblems, there was little to distinguish this four-door, two-seat wagon.

Model Number	Body/Style Number	Body Type & Seating	Factory Price	Shipping Weight	Production Total
CHEVELLE NOMAD STATION WAGON SERIES 131 (6-CYL)					
131	36	4d Nomad-6P	$2,835	3,615 lbs.	Note 1
CHEVELLE NOMAD STATION WAGON SERIES 132 (V-8)					
132	36	4d Nomad-6P	$2,925	3,718 lbs.	Note 1

NOTE 1: Individual body style production is not available; see production notes below.

CHEVELLE — (6-CYL/V-8) SERIES 133/134

According to some early 1970 Chevelle sales catalogs, Malibu was the base series this year. However, a standard Chevelle series was added to the line at midyear. This series consisted of a two-door sport coupe and a four-door sedan simply called Chevelle. Cars in this line were comparable to the old Deluxe 300 and came with a choice of in-line six-cylinder or V-8 power plants. The comparable wagon (actually grouped with other Chevelle wagons in a separate station wagon catalog) took the Greenbrier name. Standard equipment on these cars included seat belts with push-button buckles for all passenger positions, shoulder belts with push-button buckles for driver and right front passenger in closed cars (not convertibles), two front head rests, an energy-absorbing steering column, passenger guard door locks with forward-mounted lock buttons, safety door latches and hinges, folding seat back latches, an energy-absorbing instrument panel, energy-absorbing front seat back tops, a contoured windshield header (except convertible), a thick-laminate windshield, padded sun visors, safety arm rests, a safety steering wheel, a side-guard door beam structure, a cargo-guard luggage compartment, side marker lights with reflectors, parking lights that illuminate with the headlights, a four-way hazard warning flasher, back-up lights, a lane-change feature in the directional signal controls, a defroster, windshield washers, dual-speed windshield wipers, a vinyl-edged wide-view inside day/night rearview mirror with shatterproof glass and deflecting support, a left-hand outside rearview mirror, bias-belted ply tires with tread wear indicators, a dual brake master cylinder with warning light, a starter safety switch, dual-action safety hood latches, a full-coil-spring suspension, a perimeter frame, an advanced body mounting system, new finned rear brake drums, flush-and-dry rocker panels, double-panel door, hood and deck lid construction, four inner fenders, a heater and defroster, a cigarette lighter, a locking glove box, rubber floor mats, front foam rubber seats and a 155-hp Turbo-Thrift 250-cid six-cylinder engine or a 200-hp Turbo-Fire 307-cid V-8 with three-speed fully synchronized manual transmission. The eight-passenger three-seat Greenbrier station wagon came only with a V-8, while the six-passenger two-seat version was offered with a choice of six-cylinder or V-8 power.

the left-hand side of the lower grille. The Malibu name was spelled out in upper case letters on the front fender sides, behind the wheel housing. All Malibus featured a cigarette lighter, a Delco-Eye battery, Hide-A-Way windshield wipers, a lighted glove box and E78 x 14/B belted bias-ply black sidewall tires. Astro Ventilation was included with coupes and convertibles. Cars with factory radios had an in-the-windshield antenna. The Malibu-style wagons took the Concours name. Standard equipment included seat belts with push-button buckles for all passenger positions, shoulder belts with push-button buckles for driver and right front passenger in closed cars (not convertibles), two front head rests, an energy-absorbing steering column, passenger guard door locks with forward-mounted lock buttons, safety door latches and hinges, folding seat back latches, an energy-absorbing instrument panel, energy-absorbing front seat back tops, a contoured windshield header (except convertible), a thick-laminate windshield, padded sun visors, safety arm rests, a safety steering wheel, a side-guard door beam structure, a cargo-guard luggage compartment, side marker lights with reflectors, parking lights that illuminate with the headlights, a four-way hazard warning flasher, back-up lights, a lane-change feature in the directional signal controls, a defroster, windshield washers, dual-speed windshield wipers, a vinyl-edged wide-view inside day/night rearview mirror with shatterproof glass and deflecting support, a left-hand outside rearview mirror, bias-belted ply tires with tread wear indicators, a dual brake master cylinder with warning light, a starter safety switch, dual-action safety hood latches, a full-coil-spring suspension, a perimeter frame, an advanced body mounting system, new finned rear brake drums, flush-and-dry rocker panels, double-panel

Model Number	Body/Style Number	Body Type & Seating	Factory Price	Shipping Weight	Production Total
CHEVELLE 133 (6-CYL)					
133	69	4d sedan-6P	$2,537	3,196 lbs.	Note 1
133	37	2d sport coupe-6P	$2,572	3,142 lbs.	Note 1
CHEVELLE GREENBRIER 133 (6-CYL)					
133	36	4d wagon-6P	$2,946	3,644 lbs.	Note 1
CHEVELLE 134 (V-8)					
134	69	4d sedan-6P	$2,627	3,312 lbs.	Note 1
134	37	2d sport coupe-6P	$2,662	3,260 lbs.	Note 1
CHEVELLE GREENBRIER 134 (V-8)					
134	36	4d wagon-6P	$3,100	3,748 lbs.	Note 1
134	46	4d wagon-8P	$3,213	3,794 lbs.	Note 1

NOTE 1: Individual body style production is not available; see production notes.
NOTE 2: Some sources and revised sales catalogs list the Malibu series as the base Chevelle line.

MALIBU — (6-CYL/V-8) SERIES 135/136

The Malibu grilles were filled with intersecting horizontal and vertical moldings. There was a blue Chevrolet bow tie emblem at the center of the body-color bar between them and the Chevelle model name was seen on

A total of 3,773 SS 454s were built for 1970.

door, hood and deck lid construction, four inner fenders and a 155-hp Turbo-Thrift 250-cid six-cylinder engine or a 200-hp Turbo-Fire 307-cid V-8 with three-speed fully synchronized manual transmission. Pattern cloth and vinyl interiors came in black, blue, dark green, gold or turquoise (sport sedan or four-door sedan only). All-vinyl trims came in black, blue, saddle, dark green, gold, red or ivory depending on the model selected.

Model Number	Body/Style Number	Body Type & Seating	Factory Price	Shipping Weight	Production Total
MALIBU SERIES 135 (6-CYL)					
135	69	4d sedan-6P	$2,685	$3,221	Note 1
135	39	4d sport sedan-6P	$2,790	$3,302	Note 1
135	37	2d sport coupe-6P	$2,719	$3,197	Note 1
135	67	2d convertible-6P	$2,919	$3,243	Note 1
135	36	4d concours-6P	$3,056	$3,687	Note 1
MALIBU SERIES 136 (V-8)					
136	69	4d sedan-6P	$2,775	$3,330	Note 1
136	39	4d sport sedan-6P	$2,881	$3,409	Note 1
136	37	2d sport coupe-6P	$2,809	$3,307	Note 1
136	67	2d convertible-6P	$3,009	$3,352	Note 1
136	46	4d concours-9P	$3,323	$3,836	Note 1
136	36	4d concours-6P	$3,210	$3,794	Note 1

NOTE 1: Individual body style production is not available; see production notes.

MALIBU CONCOURS ESTATE — (V-8) SERIES 138

The Concours Estate Wagon featured an all-vinyl interior, a lighted locking glove box, extra-thick foam cushioned seats, simulated walnut side and rear exterior panels, two-speed Hide-A-Way windshield wipers, chrome wheel opening moldings, an oval steering wheel with horn tabs, ribbed color-accented lower body perimeter moldings, a tailgate emblem badge for Concours identification, a Concours script on each front fender and a V-8. Concours Custom interiors were trimmed in textured vinyl. The passenger floor featured deep-twist carpeting and the cargo load floor had a vinyl coating.

Model Number	Body/Style Number	Body Type & Seating	Factory Price	Shipping Weight	Production Total
MALIBU CONCOURS ESTATE WAGON SERIES 137 (6-CYL)					
138	46	4d wagon-9P	$3,455	3,880 lbs.	Note 1
138	36	4d wagon-6P	$3,342	3,821 lbs.	Note 1

NOTE 1: Individual body style production is not available; see production notes.

CHEVELLE SS 396 — (V-8) SERIES 136

The Z25 option was available to turn any 1970 Chevelle V-8 sport coupe or convertible into an SS 396. Since these body styles were offered only in the Malibu series, the Malibu became the starting point for the muscular Chevelle. In addition to regular Malibu equipment, the SS 396 featured power front disc brakes, a black-painted grille, wheel opening moldings, a special rear bumper with a resilient black insert, a special domed hood, a special heavy-duty suspension, 14 x 7-in. Sport wheels, F70 x 14 wide-oval white lettered tires, a 396-cid Turbo-Jet 350-hp base V-8 and dual exhausts with bright tips. There were bold SS emblems at the center of the grille, on the front fender sides behind the wheel opening, on the right side of the black finished rear bumper panel and on the center of the special black steering wheel spokes. The Super Sport had its own instrument panel with round gauges. Either a four-speed manual transmission or Turbo-Hydra-Matic transmission was required. An all-vinyl Strato Bucket seat interior was a popular option. So was a center console, a "Cowl Induction" hood, special instrumentation and bright hood-locking pins. The body sill and belt line moldings used on other Malibus were deleted from Super Sports. Sport striping was a $69 option and was initially listed for SS 396s with the standard hood only, although the sales catalog shows a striped car with the Cowl Induction setup. After January 1970, the 396-cid V-8 was actually a 402-cid V-8, although the SS 396 name was still used to promote it.

Model Number	Body/Style Number	Body Type & Seating	Factory Price	Shipping Weight	Production Total
MALIBU SERIES 136 + RPO Z25 SUPER SPORT 396 OPTION PACKAGE (V-8)					
136	37	2d sport coupe-6P	$3,439	—	Note 1
136	67	2d convertible-6P	$3,639	—	Note 1

NOTE 1: Individual body style production is not available; see production notes.
NOTE 2 Prices calculated by adding Malibu model base price, SS 396 option price and required four-speed manual transmission cost. Add $37 to calculate price of a base SS 396 with Turbo-Hydra-Matic.

CHEVELLE SS 454 — (V-8) SERIES 136

Sometime after the start of the 1970 model year, a new Z15 option was released and allowed Malibu V-8 sport coupe or convertible buyers to turn their car into an SS 454. The SS 454 package included bright engine accents, dual exhausts with bright tips, power front disc brakes, a black-painted grille, wheel opening moldings, a special rear bumper with a resilient black insert, a special domed hood, a special heavy-duty suspension, 14 x 7-in. Sport wheels, F70 x 14 wide-oval white lettered tires and a 454-cid Turbo-Jet 360-hp base V-8. There were bold SS emblems at the center of the grille, on the front fender sides behind the wheel opening, on the right side of the black finished rear bumper panel and on the center of the steering wheel spokes. For those interested in ultimate performance, the LS6 option was offered for Malibus with the SS 454 option. This $263.30 package added a version of the 454-cid V-8 that was conservatively rated at 450 hp. Other details of the SS 454 were basically the same as on the SS 396.

Model Number	Body/Style Number	Body Type & Seating	Factory Price	Shipping Weight	Production Total
MALIBU SERIES 136 + RPO Z25 SUPER SPORT 396 OPTION PACKAGE (V-8)					
136	37	2d sport coupe-6P	$3,497	—	Note 1
136	67	2d convertible-6P	$3,697	—	Note 1

NOTE 1: Individual body style production is not available; see production notes below.
NOTE 2 Prices calculated by adding Malibu model base price, SS 396 option price and required four-speed manual transmission cost. Add $37 to calculate price of a base SS 396 with Turbo-Hydra-Matic.

PRODUCTION NOTES

NOTE 1 Model-year production (within U.S.) of all 1970 Chevelles was 394,317 units. Including units made in Canada and imported into the U.S., total production was 442,046 units.
NOTE 2 Industry statistical breakouts in rounded-off numbers (including imports from Canada) show 37,400 Chevelle sixes and 402,900 Chevelle V-8s were built in 1970.
NOTE 3 Additional statistics record series production (including imports from Canada), in rounded-off figures as follows:

Chevelle (6-cyl)	10,700
Chevelle 300 (V-8)	13,200
Total	23,900
Malibu (6-cyl)	21,100
Malibu (V-8)	354,700
Total	375,800
wagons (6-cyl)	5,600

wagons (V-8)		35,000			
Total		40,600			

(*) Malibu figures include Super Sport models.
NOTE 4 Production by factory (U.S.) was:

Code	Factory	Production	Code	Factory	Production
B	Baltimore	66,200	K	Kansas City	100,745
A	Arlington (Tex.)	69,839	V	Van Nuys	54,647
F	Flint (Mich.)	20,387			

Additional 1970 Chevelles were built in Canada.
NOTE 5 Exactly 49,826 cars had the Z25 Chevelle SS 396 option installed. All were V-8 powered. No series or body style breakouts are available.
NOTE 6 Exactly 3,773 cars had the Chevelle SS 454 option installed. All were V-8 powered. No series or body style breakouts are available.
NOTE 7 Exactly 7,511 Chevelle convertibles were built. Some were Malibu and some were Super Sports. No breakouts are available.

ENGINES

CHEVELLE 300, 300 DELUXE, MALIBU BASE 250-CID, 155-HP SIX-CYL: Inline. Overhead valve. Cast iron block. Displacement: 250 cid. Bore and stroke: 3.875 x 3.53 in. Compression ratio: 8.5:1. Brake hp: 155 at 4200 rpm. Taxable hp: 36. Torque: 235 lbs.-ft. at 1600 rpm. Seven main bearings. Hydraulic valve lifters. Crankcase capacity: 4 qt. (add 1 qt. for new filter). Cooling system capacity: 12 qt (add 6 qt. for heater). Carburetor: Rochester one-barrel Model 7028017. Sales code L22. Available standard with three-speed fully synchronized manual transmission and optional with special fully synchronized three-speed manual transmission, Powerglide automatic transmission or Turbo-Hydra-Matic automatic transmission.

MALIBU BASE 307-CID, 200-HP V-8: Overhead-valve. Cast-iron block and head. Bore and stroke: 3.88 x 3.25 in. Displacement: 307 cid. Compression ratio: 9.00:1. Brake hp: 200 at 4600 rpm. Taxable hp: 48. Torque: 300 lbs.-ft. at 2400. Five main bearings. Hydraulic valve lifters. Crankcase capacity: 4 qt. (add 1 qt. for new filter). Cooling system capacity: 14 qt (add 1 qt. for heater). Carburetor: Two-barrel.

CHEVELLE, MALIBU OPTIONAL 350-CID, 250-HP V-8: Overhead-valve. Cast-iron block and head. Bore and stroke: 4.00 x 3.48 in. Displacement: 350 cid. Compression ratio: 9.00:1. Brake hp: 250 at 4800 rpm. Taxable hp: 51.20. Torque: 345 lbs.-ft. at 2800. Five main bearings. Hydraulic valve lifters. Crankcase capacity: 4 qt. (add 1 qt. for new filter). Cooling system capacity: (full-size) 14 qt.; (others) 15 qt. (add 1 qt. for heater). Carburetor: Two-barrel. Sales code: L65 (added midyear).

CHEVELLE, MALIBU OPTIONAL 350-CID, 300-HP V-8: Overhead-valve. Cast-iron block and head. Bore and stroke: 4.00 x 3.48 in. Displacement: 350 cid. Compression ratio: 9.00:1. Brake hp: 300 at 4800 rpm. Taxable hp: 51.20. Torque: 380 lbs.-ft. at 3200. Five main bearings. Hydraulic valve lifters. Crankcase capacity: 4 qt. (add 1 qt. for new filter). Cooling system capacity: (full-size) 14 qt.; (others) 15 qt. (add 1 qt. for heater). Carburetor: Four-barrel. Sales code: L48.

MALIBU OPTIONAL 400-CID, 330-HP V-8: Overhead-valve. Cast-iron block and head. Bore and stroke: 4.13 x 3.76 in. Displacement: 402 cid (400 cid). Compression ratio: 10.25:1. Brake hp: 330 at 4800 rpm. Taxable hp: 54.50. Torque: 410 lbs.-ft. at 3200. Five main bearings. Hydraulic valve lifters. Crankcase capacity: 4 qt. (add 1 qt. for new filter). Cooling system capacity: 22 qt. (add 1 qt. for heater). Carburetor: Four-barrel. Sales code: LS3. (added midyear)

MALIBU OPTIONAL 396-CID, 350-HP V-8: Overhead-valve. Cast-iron block and head. Bore and stroke: 4.13 x 3.76 in. Displacement: 402 cid (396 cid). Compression ratio: 10.25:1. Brake hp: 350 at 5200 rpm. Taxable hp: 54.50. Torque: 415 lbs.-ft. at 3400. Five main bearings. Hydraulic valve lifters. Crankcase capacity: 4 qt. (add 1 qt. for new filter). Cooling system capacity: 22 qt. (add 1 qt. for heater). Carburetor: Four-barrel. Sales code: L34.

CHEVELLE SS 396 OPTIONAL 375-HP V-8: Overhead-valve. Cast-iron block and head. Bore and stroke: 4.09 x 3.76 in. Displacement: 396 cid (actually 402 cid). Compression ratio: 11.00:1. Brake hp: 375 at 5600 rpm. Taxable hp: 53.60. Torque: 415 lbs.-ft. at 3600. Five main bearings. Hydraulic valve lifters. Crankcase capacity: 4 qt. (add 1 qt. for new filter). Cooling system capacity: 23 qt. (add 1 qt. for heater). Carburetor: Four-barrel. Sales code: L78.

CHEVELLE SS 396 OPTIONAL 375-HP V-8: Overhead-valve. Cast-iron block. Aluminum head with large valves. Bore and stroke: 4.09 x 3.76 in. Displacement: 396 cid (actually 402 cid). Compression ratio: 11.00:1. Brake hp: 375 at 5600 rpm. Taxable hp: 53.60. Torque: 415 lbs.-ft. at 3600. Five main bearings. Solid valve lifters. Crankcase capacity: 4 qt. (add 1 qt. for new filter). Cooling system capacity: 23 qt. (add 1 qt. for heater). Carburetor: Holley four-barrel. Sales code: L78/L89.

CHEVELLE SS 454 OPTIONAL 360-HP V-8: Overhead-valve. Cast-iron block and head. Bore and stroke: 4.25 x 4.00 in. Displacement: 454 cid. Compression ratio: 10.25:1. Brake hp: 360 at 4400 rpm. Taxable hp: 57.80. Torque: 500 lbs.-ft. at 3200. Five main bearings. Hydraulic valve lifters. Crankcase capacity: 4 qt. (add 1 qt. for new filter). Cooling system capacity: 22 qt. (add 1 qt. for heater). Dual exhaust. Carburetor: Four-barrel. Sales code: LS5 (added midyear).

CHEVELLE SS 454 OPTIONAL 450-HP V-8: Overhead-valve. Cast-iron block. Bore and stroke: 4.251 x 4.00 in. Displacement: 454 cid. Compression ratio: 11.25:1. Brake hp: 450 at 5600 rpm. Taxable hp: 57.80. Torque: 500 lbs.-ft. at 3600. Five main bearings. Solid valve lifters. High-performance camshaft. Crankcase capacity: 5 qt. (add 1 qt. for filter). Cooling

The cowl-induction hood was part of an option package that included sport striping and locking hook pins.

system capacity: 21 qt. (add 1 qt. for heater). Carburetor: Holley four-barrel. Sales code: LS6 (added midyear).

CHASSIS FEATURES

Wheelbase: (two-door) 112 in.; (four-door) 116 in. Overall length: (two-door) 197.2 in.; (four-door cars) 201.2 in.; (four-door station wagons) 208 in. Width: 75.4 in. Height: (sedans) 53.2 in. (coupes) 52.6 in. Front tread: 59 in. Rear tread: 59 in. Gas tank capacity: 20 gal. Tires: (six) E78 x 14 two-ply/four-ply rated; (V-8) F78 x 14 two-ply/four-ply rated; (station wagon) G78 x 14 two-ply/four-ply rated. Turn circle: 41 feet. Trunk capacity (sedan) 13.5 cubic feet. Front headroom (sedan): 38.5 in. Rear headroom (sedan): 37.1 in. Front legroom (sedan): 42.8 in. Rear leg room (sedan): 35.1 in. Front hip room (sedan): 59.5 in. Rear hip room (sedan): 59.4 in.

OPTIONS

C60 Four-Season air conditioning, including 61-amp Delcotron, heavy-duty radiator and temperature-controlled fan and requiring larger tires with some Chevelles ($376). C51 station wagon rear window air deflector ($19). ZP5 appearance group, including front and rear bumper guards, door edge guards, floor mats and visor vanity mirror for two-door Chevelles; no rear bumper guards on El Camino (on two-doors $34.85; on Concours station wagon $30.60; on other station wagons $38; on four-door cars $53.60). G80 Positraction rear axle (Chevelles $42.15; El Caminos $43.05). YD1 trailering axle ratio ($10.55). ZQ9 performance rear axle on Malibu with 375-hp V-8 and Positraction ($25.30). ZQ9 performance rear axle on El Camino with 375-hp V-8 and Positraction ($25.85). T60 heavy-duty battery in Chevelles with 396-cid V-8 ($15.80). T60 heavy-duty battery in El Caminos with 396-cid V-8 ($16.15). AK1 Custom Deluxe front shoulder belts for bucket seat cars, except convertibles ($12.15). ZK3 Custom Deluxe front shoulder belts for bench seat cars, except El Camino ($13.70). ZK3 Custom Deluxe front shoulder belts for 3-seat station wagons ($16.90). ZK3 Custom Deluxe front shoulder belts for El Camino with bench seat ($9.15). ZK3 Custom Deluxe front shoulder belts for El Camino with bucket seats ($7.55). A39 Custom Deluxe front seat belts, for convertibles with bucket seats ($9.00). A39 Custom Deluxe front seat belts for convertibles with bench front seats ($10.55). A85 Custom Deluxe front shoulder belts, requires Custom deluxe seat belts for convertibles ($26.35). AS4 Custom Deluxe rear shoulder belts, requires Custom deluxe seat belts ($26.35). A85 two front belts for convertible, requires AK1 Custom Deluxe shoulder belts ($26.35) J50 power drum brakes ($42.15). JL2 power front disc brakes ($64.25). V55 adjustable station wagon roof carrier ($52.70). U35 Electric clock in all Chevelle models except El Camino, included with special instrumentation ($15.80). U35 electric clock in El Camino, included with special instrumentation ($16.15). D55 console with courtesy light, not available with standard three-speed manual transmission ($53.75 in Chevelles; $54.90 in El Caminos). C50 rear windshield defroster ($20.85 in coupes and sedans; $29.20 in convertibles and station wagons). AU3 power door locks for two-door models ($44.80). AU3 power door locks for four-door models ($68.50). L65 350-cid 250-hp V-8 engine ($21.10). L48 350-cid 300-hp V-8 engine, all except SS 396 ($68.50). LS3 402-cid 330-hp V-8 engine, all except SS 396 ($162.20). L34 396-cid 350-hp V-8 engine, SS 396 only ($121.15). L78 396-cid 375-hp V-8 engine SS 396 only ($250.00). L78/L89 396-cid 375-hp V-8 with aluminum heads, for SS 396 only ($647.75). LS5 454-cid 360-hp V-8 engine ($191.65). LS6 454-cid 450-hp V-8 engine, for all with SS 454 package ($263.30). NA9 evaporative emission control (on Chevelle $29.20; on El Camino ($30). N10 dual exhaust on all Chevelle V-8s with single exhaust ($30.55). K85 63-amp Delcotron generator, with air conditioning ($5.30); without air conditioning ($26.35). A01 all windows tinted ($36.90). V31/32 front or rear bumper guards ($15.80). B93 door edge guards, for two-door Chevelles ($4.25). R93 door edge guards, for four-door Chevelles ($7.40). K05 engine block heater (Chevelle $10.55; El Camino $10.80). ZL2 cowl-induction hood for Chevelles, includes sport striping on hood of all models, sport striping on the rear deck lid of Malibu models, hood locking pins, an air intake valve at the rear of the hood and a hood-to-air cleaner duct, requires Super Sport packages ($147.45). ZL2 cowl-induction hood for El Camino, includes sport striping on hood of all models, sport striping on the rear deck lid of Malibu models, hood locking pins, an air intake valve at the rear of the hood and a hood-to-air cleaner duct, requires Super Sport packages ($123.75). U14 special instrumentation with ammeter, temperature gauge, oil pressure gauge and tachometer on Malibu and SS 396 sport coupes and convertibles ($94.80). U46 "Vigilite" light monitoring system ($26.35). ZJ19 auxiliary lighting groups with A) courtesy light, B) glove box light, C) luggage compartment light, D) under-hood light, E) mirror map light, F) ash tray light, G) windshield washer monitor light and H) low fuel/check door/seat belt warning lights; in Malibu sedans and coupes includes A, C, D, E and F ($16.35), in Malibu convertibles includes C, D, E, F and G ($21.10), in El Camino Custom includes A, D, E, F and G ($23.15), in El Camino standard includes A, B, D, E, F and G ($25.85), in Concours and Concours Estate station wagons includes A, D, E and F ($22.65), in Greenbrier and Nomad station wagons includes A, B, D, E and F ($25.30). B37 twin front and rear floor mats (Chevelle $11.60; El Camino twin front only $6.50). D33 Left-hand outside remote-control mirror (Chevelle $10.55, El Camino $10.80). D34 visor vanity mirror (Chevelle $3.20, El Camino $3.25). B90 window moldings on Chevelle Concours and Concours Estate four-door and station wagon models ($26.35). B90 window moldings on Chevelle Nomad and Greenbrier station wagon models ($31.60). B90 window moldings on Malibu four-door sedan ($26.35). ZQ2 Operating Convenience group with A) electric clock, B) remote-control left-hand outside rearview mirror, C) rear window defroster and D) headlight delay system; on Chevelle sedans includes A, B, C ($52.70), on Malibu sport coupe with special instrumentation includes B, C ($36.90), on Malibu sport coupe without special instrumentation includes A, B, C ($52.70), on Malibu convertible with special instrumentation includes B, C ($47.45), on Malibu convertible without special instrumentation includes A, B, C

The front end of the '70 Chevelle featured a horizontal split grille and dual headlights.

($63.25); on Chevelle station wagons includes A, B and D ($63.25). Two-tone paint ($23.20). V01 heavy-duty radiator ($14.75). U63 AM push-button radio with front antenna (Chevelle $61.10, El Camino $62.45). U69 AM/FM radio with front antenna (Chevelle $133.80, El Camino $136.70). U79 AM/FM radio with front antenna and stereo, all except El Camino ($239.15). UM1 AM radio with stereo tape deck, for all except El Camino ($194.85). UM2 AM/FM radio with stereo tape deck for all except El Camino ($372.85). U80 rear seat speaker, not available in El Camino or with stereo ($13.20). Vinyl roof ($94.80). U73 rear antenna, all except AM/FM and wagons ($9.50). CO8 Vinyl roof cover, for hardtop models ($89.55). Z25 SS 396 option package for Chevelle sport coupe or convertible, includes 396-cid 350-hp Turbo-Jet V-8, black-accented grille, a special rear bumper with black insert, a special domed hood, special ornamentation, wheel opening moldings, special suspension, sport wheels, wide-oval white-lettered tires, power front disc brakes, dual exhaust with bright tips and special three-speed manual transmission ($445.55). Z25 SS 396 option package with L78 engine for Chevelle sport coupe or convertible, includes 396-cid 375-hp Turbo-Jet V-8, black-accented grille, a special rear bumper with black insert, a special domed hood, special ornamentation, wheel opening moldings, special suspension, sport wheels, wide-oval white-lettered tires, power front disc brakes, dual exhaust with bright tips and special three-speed manual transmission ($656.20). Z25 SS 396 option package with L78/L89 engine with aluminum cylinder heads for Chevelle sport coupe or convertible, includes 396-cid 375-hp Turbo-Jet V-8, black-accented grille, a special rear bumper with black insert, a special domed hood, special ornamentation, wheel opening moldings, special suspension, sport wheels, wide-oval white-lettered tires, power front disc brakes, dual exhaust with bright tips and special three-speed manual transmission ($840.50). Z25 SS 396 option package for El Camino, includes 396-cid 350-hp Turbo-Jet V-8, black-accented grille, a special rear bumper with black insert, a special domed hood, special ornamentation, wheel opening moldings, special suspension, sport wheels, wide-oval white-lettered tires, power front disc brakes, dual exhaust with bright tips and special three-speed manual transmission ($455.15). Z25 SS 396 option package with L78 engine for El Camino, includes 396-cid 375-hp Turbo-Jet V-8, black-accented grille, a special rear bumper with black insert, a special domed hood, special ornamentation, wheel opening moldings, special suspension, sport wheels, wide-oval white-lettered tires, power front disc brakes, dual exhaust with bright tips and special three-speed manual transmission ($670.35). Z25 SS 396 option package with L78/L89 engine with aluminum cylinder heads for Chevelle sport coupe or convertible, includes 396-cid 375-hp Turbo-Jet V-8, black-accented grille, a special rear bumper with black insert, a special domed hood, special ornamentation, wheel opening moldings, special suspension, sport wheels, wide-oval white-lettered tires, power front disc brakes, dual exhaust with bright tips and special three-speed manual transmission ($858.65). Electric seat back latch ($23.70). A51 Strato bucket seats in Malibu sport coupe and convertible ($121.15). K30 speed and cruise control, V-8s with automatic transmissions ($57.95). N40 power steering for all except SS 396 ($100.10). N40 power steering for SS 396 (Chevelle $105.35, El Camino with SS 396 $102.25, El Camino without SS 396 $107.60). N33 Comfortilt steering wheel (Chevelle

$45.30, El Camino $46.30). Cushioned rim steering wheel (Chevelle $34.80, El Camino $35.55). N34 Sport styled steering wheel ($34.80). D96 sport striping for SS 396 only, standard with ZL2 (Chevelle $68.50, El Camino $43.05). F40 Special front and rear suspension for Chevelle, Concours Estate or Nomad with six or standard V-8 ($16.90); for El Camino V-8 ($17.25). Power convertible top ($52.70). M20 wide-ratio four-speed manual transmission (Chevelle $184.80, El Camino $189). M21 Close-ratio four-speed manual transmission (Chevelle $184.80, El Camino $189). M40 Turbo Hydra-Matic transmission for six-cylinder Chevelles ($190.10). M40 Turbo Hydra-Matic transmission for 375-hp Chevelles ($290.40). M40 Turbo Hydra-Matic transmission for other V-8 Chevelles ($221.80). M35 Powerglide automatic transmission for six-cylinder Chevelle ($174.25). Vinyl trim interior for 300 series and Malibu sport coupe or sport sedan ($12.65). A33 power tailgate window for station wagons ($34.80). A31 power windows ($105.35). PO1 Four bright metal wheel covers (Chevelle $21.10, El Camino $21.55). ZJ7 Rallye wheels, including special wheels, hubcaps and trim rings (Chevelle $35.85, El Camino $36). PO6 wheel trim rings with standard hubcaps, not available with SS 396 (Chevelle $21.10, El Camino $21.55). PL3 five E78-14/B white-stripe tires replacing five E78-14/B black sidewall tires on Malibu six ($26.05). PX5 five F78-14/B black sidewall tires replacing five E78-14/B black sidewall tires on Malibu six ($15.20). PX6 five F78-14/B white stripe tires replacing five E78 x 14/B black sidewall tires on Malibu six ($43.30). PY4 five F70-14/B white stripe tires replacing five E78 x 14/B black sidewall tires on Malibu six ($65.70). PL4 five F70-14/B white lettered tires replacing five E78-14/B black sidewall tires on Malibu six ($65.45). PX6 five F78-14/B white stripe tires replacing five F78-14/B black sidewall tires on Malibu V-8 ($28.10). PY4 five F70-14/B white stripe tires replacing five F78-14/B black sidewall tires on Malibu V-8 ($50.50). PL4 five F70-14/B white lettered tires replacing five F78-14/B black sidewall tires on Malibu V-8 ($50.50). PY4 five F70-14/B white stripe tires replacing PL4-SS 396 option (no cost). PX6 five F78-14/B white stripe tires replacing five F78-14/B black sidewall tires on El Camino V-8 ($28.55). PY4 five F70-14/B white stripe tires replacing five F78-14/B black sidewall tires on El Camino V-8 ($51.40). PL4 five F70-14/B white lettered tires replacing five F78-14/B black sidewall tires on El Camino V-8 ($51.05).

OPTIONS (MIDYEAR CHANGES)

ZQ9 performance rear axle on Malibu with standard V-8, M40 transmission required ($10.55). ZQ9 performance rear axle on Malibu with 450-hp V-8, G80 required ($25.30). YD1 trailering axle ratio for Chevelles with 250- or 300-hp V-8, M40 and F40 required ($10.55). MA6 heavy-duty clutch (price not available). L65 350-cid 250-hp Turbo Fire V-8 ($21.10). L48 350-cid 300-hp Turbo Fire V-8 ($68.50). LS3 400/402-cid 330-hp Turbo Jet V-8 ($162.20). LS6 454-cid 450-hp Turbo Jet V-8 for all with SS 454 package ($263.30). A01 Soft Ray tinted glass for all windows ($36.90). ZL2 Cowl Induction hood, for all with SS 396 package required ($147.45). U14 special instrumentation for V-8 sport coupes ($84.30). B90 side window molding for four-door sedan ($26.35). Vinyl roof covering for all models ($94.80). K30 speed and cruise control for V-8 models, M40 and J50 required ($57.85). F41 Special Performance suspension for Chevelles with the 330-hp V-8 ($29.50). M22 four-speed close-ratio manual transmission ($221.80). M20 wide-range four-speed manual transmission ($184.80). M21 close-range four-speed manual transmission ($184.80). M40 Turbo Hydra-Matic transmission with 330-, 350-hp SS 396 and 360-hp SS 454 ($221.80). M40 Turbo Hydra-Matic transmission with 450-hp SS 454 ($290.40). Interior trim ($12.65). PO6 wheel trim rings and standard hubcaps for all except SS 396 ($21.10). A31 power windows, Malibus only ($105.35). CD3 finger tip windshield wiper control, for Malibu, Concours and Concours Estate ($19). ZJ9 auxiliary lighting package ($27.95). Z15 SS 454 package includes 454-cid 360-hp Turbo-Jet V-8, bright engine accents, a black-painted grille, a special rear bumper with black insert, a special domed hood, special ornamentation, wheel opening moldings, special suspension, sport wheels, F70-14 wide-oval white lettered tires, heavy-duty battery, power front disc brakes and dual exhaust with bright tips for Malibu V-8 sport coupe or convertible with M40 or four-speed manual transmission ($503.45).

OPTION INSTALLATION RATES

Automatic transmission (85.6 percent). Four-speed manual transmission (9.9 percent). Standard V-8 engine (44.9 percent). Optional V-8 engine (48.6 percent). 6-cylinder engine (6.5 percent). AM radio (89.6 percent). AM/FM radio (3.9 percent). Stereo tape (4.5 percent). Air conditioning (45.7 percent). Power steering (82.5 percent). Tilt steering (3.2 percent). Power drum brakes (9.1 percent). Power front disc brakes (31.6 percent).

The 1970 Chevelle came with either a base 250-cid six or a 307-cid, 200-hp V-8, like this one.

Power door locks (1 percent). Power side windows (1.2 percent). Power tailgate window (5.6 percent). Bucket seats (16.9 percent). Vinyl top (38.2 percent). White sidewall tires (83.1 percent). Tinted windshield only (1.9 percent). All tinted glass (68.8 percent). Dual exhaust (17.4 percent). Positraction (10.9 percent). Optional full wheel covers (49.4 percent). Styled wheels (25.7 percent). Optional clock (13.4 percent). Station wagon luggage rack (3 percent). Cruise control (0.1 percent). Based on model year production of 442,046 units.

HISTORICAL FOOTNOTES

The 1970 Chevelle line had its dealer introduction date on September 18, 1969. John Z. Delorean was general manager of Chevrolet Motor Division. The 1970 model year was one of the worst in Chevrolet history. Calendar-year sales of Chevelles dropped to 379,859 units from 436,853 the previous 12 months. Calendar-year registrations were 346,714 Chevelle passenger cars versus 389,103 the prior year and 34,340 station wagons versus 42,796 the previous year. The Chevelle SS 396 with the 325-hp V-8 and automatic transmission that Car and Driver comparison road tested in January 1969 did 0 to 60 mph in 5.8 seconds and covered the quarter mile in 14.41 seconds at 97.35 mph. The magazine noted that you could order the SS 396 option for the Chevelle 300 Deluxe two-door coupe over the counter for $3,409 or more than $300 less than a Dodge Super Bee. *Motor Trend*, in October 1968, stated, "The newest Chevelle SS 396 performs like the best of the sporty cars in both handling and power. Suspension has been reworked to eliminate much of the understeer and add neutrality." By 1970, the U.S.-Canada Free Trade Agreement signed in 1965 was having a large effect on the automobile industry and cross-border shipments topped 1,138,000 units. Among the cars that General Motors exported to the U.S. from Canada was the Chevelle. This affected record keeping in that some production records include Chevelles built in Canada for the U.S. market, while other do not. For this reason, you may find different Chevelle production numbers in different books or you may find numbers broken out in different ways that do not add up to the same total production.

The intermediate Chevrolet series for 1971 included two Chevelles, four Malibus and seven Nomad, Greenbrier, Concours and Concours Estate station wagons with dual-action tailgates. All models featured a new grille that did away with the body-colored horizontal center divider used the previous year. The new grille had a chrome horizontal center divider separating upper and lower sections that had a more integrated look. The upper and lower sections still had four thin, bright horizontal moldings (as in 1970), but the number of vertical moldings was cut from 23 to nine. Also, the bow tie used at the center of the standard grille changed from blue in color to chrome. New single round headlamps set in bright, square housings replaced the twin, separated headlights of 1970 models. There was a new front bumper. The new front parking and signal lights were stacked, twin-segment units that wrapped around the corners of the body.

On Malibu, the model name still decorated the sides of the front fenders behind the wheel opening, but the chrome block letters were less spaced out than before. A new rear bumper with built-in taillights was seen. Full-flow ventilation was now standard on all two-door models. All Chevelles featured a new sealed side terminal Energizer battery. Included at no extra cost on Malibus were Hide-A-Way windshield wipers and Malibu convertibles had a power-operated folding top. New interior colors and trims and a redesigned steering wheel were seen inside Chevelles. There were also new, softer instrument panel knobs.

The '71 Super Sport package came in two versions called the Chevelle SS and the Chevelle SS 454. A glance at the engine call-outs under the SS logos on the grille, fenders and bumper told you which you were looking at. Base engine in the SS was a 245-hp version of the 350-cid small-block V-8 and a 270-hp "Corvette" version was optional. You could also get a 400-cid 300-hp Turbo-Jet big-block V-8 (which was promoted as an SS 396, but actually displaced 402 cubic in). With the SS 454 package, 365 hp was standard and 425 hp was on tap at additional cost.

Totally new was a stripped-down muscle car called the "Heavy Chevy." This came as a sports coupe only and was promoted as a car that could save enthusiasts from the high insurance rates being charged to Chevelle Super Sport owners.

I.D. NUMBERS

VIN embossed on the top left-hand side of the instrument panel and visible through the windshield. The first symbol 1 designates Chevrolet. The second symbol indicates series: 3=Chevelle or Monte Carlo. The third symbol indicates the type of engine: odd number=six-cylinder; even number=V-8. The fourth and fifth symbols indicate body style: 36=four-door two-seat station wagon with dual-action tailgate, 37=two-door notchback/hardtop coupe (sport coupe), 39=four-door notchback/hardtop sedan (sport sedan), 46=four-door three-seat station wagon with dual-action tailgate, 67=two-door convertible and 69=four-door notchback sedan (pillared). The sixth symbol designates the model year: 1=1971. The seventh symbol designates the assembly plant location: B=Baltimore, Maryland; K=Leeds, Missouri; L=Van Nuys (Los Angeles) California, and R=Arlington, Texas. The

Chevelle

The 1971 Chevelles that had cowl-induction hoods, like this SS 454, came with either black or white stripes.

last six symbols are the sequential unit production number at the specific factory. The Fisher body tag riveted to the top of the cowl on the left side of the car below the hood provides additional vehicle identification information. The Fisher Body STYLE NUMBER (ST) consists of a prefix identifying model year and four or more symbols identifying the series and body style (example: 71-13336 for a 1971 Greenbrier station wagon with an inline six-cylinder engine). The BODY NUMBER consists of a prefix designating assembly plant and the sequential unit production number at the specific factory. The TRIM NUMBER (TR) identifies upholstery.

COLORS

(11) Antique White, (13) Nevada Silver, (19) Tuxedo Black, (24) Ascot Blue, (26) Mulsanne Blue, (42) Cottonwood Green, (43) Lime Green, (49) Antique Gold, (52) Sunflower Yellow, (53) Placer Gold, (61) Sandalwood, (62) Burnt Orange, (67) Classic Copper, (75) Cranberry Red and (78) Rosewood. Vinyl tops were available in five colors: AA=White, BB=Black, CC=Dark Blue, FF=Dark Brown and GG=Dark Green.

ENGINE CODES

Codes appear on the right side of six-cylinder blocks behind the distributor and right front of V-8 engine blocks. Engine codes for 1971 were: (250-cid six) CAG, CAB, CAA; (307-cid V-8) CCA and CCB; (350/245-hp V-8) CGA, CGB and CGC; (350-cid/270-hp V-8) CGK, CGL, CJD and CJJ; (396-cid/300-hp V-8) CLP, CLB, CLL, CLR and CLS; (454-cid/365-hp) CPA, CPG and CPD and (454-cid/425-hp) CPP, CPR and CPZ.

CHEVELLE NOMAD — (6-CYL/V-8) SERIES 131/132

The Nomad station wagon was again unique in that it was plainer than even a base 1971 Chevelle passenger car. Since wagons were merchandised as if they were a line unto themselves, the Nomad was technically the base station wagon, rather than the base Chevelle. Other than Nomad emblems, there was little to distinguish this four-door, two-seat wagon. Standard equipment on all Chevelles included seat belts with push-button buckles for all passenger positions, shoulder belts with push-button buckles for driver and right front passenger (except convertibles), two front seat head restraints, an energy-absorbing steering column, passenger-guard door locks with forward-mounted lock buttons, safety door latches and hinges, folding seat back latches, an energy-absorbing padded instrument panel, padded front seat back tops, a contoured windshield header (except convertibles), a thick-laminate windshield, padded sun visors,

The 1971 SS 454 package came with a 365-hp engine, but a 425-hp version was also available.

safety armrests, a safety steering wheel, side-guard door beams, a cargo guard luggage compartment, side marker lights and reflectors (front side marker lights flash with directional signals), parking lights that illuminate with the headlights, a four-way hazard warning flasher, back-up lights, a lane-change feature in the direction signal control, a windshield defroster, windshield washers, dual-speed windshield wipers, a wide-view day/night inside rearview mirror (vinyl-edged with shatter-resistant glass and a deflecting support), an inside-the-windshield radio antenna (when a radio was ordered), a left-hand outside rearview mirror, a dual master cylinder brake system with warning light, a dual-action safety hood latch, an anti-theft ignition key warning buzzer and an anti-theft steering column lock. Nomads also came with a dual-action tailgate, a concealed storage compartment, all-vinyl upholstery, a vinyl-coated textured metal cargo floor and G78-14/B bias-belted black sidewall tires, flush-and-dry rocker panels, cigarette lighter, a locking glove box, carpeting, a foam front seat and a 250-cid, 145-hp inline six-cylinder engine or a 307-cid 200-hp V-8.

Model Number	Body/Style Number	Body Type & Seating	Factory Price	Shipping Weight	Production Total
CHEVELLE NOMAD STATION WAGON SERIES 131 (6-CYL)					
131	36	4d Nomad-6P	$2,997	3,632 lbs.	Note 1
CHEVELLE NOMAD STATION WAGON SERIES 132 (V-8)					
132	36	4d Nomad-6P	$3,097	3,746 lbs.	Note 1

NOTE 1: Individual body style production is not available; see production notes.

CHEVELLE — (6-CYL/V-8) SERIES 133/134

The base Chevelle series consisted of two-door hardtops and four-door sedans arranged in two lines: six and V-8. These cars had no fender names or bright rocker panel moldings. The comparable wagon (actually grouped with other Chevelle wagons in a separate station wagon catalog) took the Greenbrier name. Standard equipment on all Chevelles included seat belts with push-button buckles for all passenger positions, shoulder belts with push-button buckles for driver and right front passenger (except convertibles), two front seat head restraints, an energy-absorbing steering column, passenger-guard door locks with forward-mounted lock buttons, safety door latches and hinges, folding seat back latches, an energy-absorbing padded instrument panel, padded front seat back tops, a contoured windshield header (except convertibles), a thick-laminate windshield, padded sun visors, safety armrests, a safety steering wheel, side-guard door beams, a cargo guard luggage compartment, side marker lights and reflectors (front side marker lights flash with directional signals), parking lights that illuminate with the headlights, a four-way hazard warning flasher, back-up lights, a lane-change feature in the direction signal control, a windshield defroster, windshield washers, dual-speed windshield wipers, a wide-view day/night inside rearview mirror (vinyl-edged with shatter-resistant glass and a deflecting support), a left-hand outside rearview mirror, a dual master cylinder brake system with warning light, a dual-action safety hood latch, an anti-theft ignition key warning buzzer and an anti-theft steering column lock. Base models also came with a cigarette lighter, a locking glove box, color-keyed vinyl-coated rubber floor mats, a foam front seat and a 250-cid 145-hp inline six-cylinder engine or a 307-cid 200-hp V-8. A three-speed manual transmission with column-mounted gearshift controls was standard. All forward gears were fully synchronized. The standard cloth-and-vinyl interior was available in black, dark blue or dark jade. An all-vinyl interior was available only in black. With all interiors the doors and sidewalls were trimmed in matching vinyl panels. Greenbrier station wagons came only with V-8 power and featured the following standard equipment: a dual-action tailgate, a concealed storage compartment, all-vinyl upholstery, a vinyl-coated textured metal cargo floor, G78-14/B bias-belted black sidewall tires, flush-and-dry rocker panels, a cigarette lighter, a locking glove box, floor carpeting, a foam front seat and a 307-cid, 200-hp V-8. Three-seat station wagons also included a rear-facing third seat and a power-operated tailgate window.

Model Number	Body/Style Number	Body Type & Seating	Factory Price	Shipping Weight	Production Total
CHEVELLE 133 (6-CYL)					
133	69	4d sedan-6P	$2,677	3,210 lbs.	Note 1
133	37	2d sport coupe-6P	$2,712	3,166 lbs.	Note 1
CHEVELLE 134 (V-8)					
134	69	4d sedan-6P	$2,773	3,338 lbs.	Note 1
134	37	2d sport coupe-6P	$2,807	3,296 lbs.	Note 1
CHEVELLE GREENBRIER STATION WAGON 134 (V-8)					
134	36	4d wagon-6P	$3,228	3,820 lbs.	Note 1
134	46	4d wagon-8P	$3,340	3,882 lbs.	Note 1

NOTE 1: Individual body style production is not available; see production notes.

MALIBU — (6-CYL/V-8) SERIES 135/136

All Malibus featured a cigarette lighter, Hide-A-Way windshield wipers, a lighted glove box and E78-14/B belted bias-ply black sidewall tires. Astro Ventilation was included with coupes and convertibles. Cars with factory radios had an in-the-windshield antenna. New wheel opening moldings and wide body sill moldings were also seen on cars in this line. The Malibu-style wagons took the Concours name. Standard equipment with all body styles included seat belts with push-button buckles for all passenger positions, shoulder belts with push-button buckles for driver and right front passenger in closed cars (not convertibles), two front head rests, an energy-absorbing steering column, passenger guard door locks with forward-mounted lock buttons, safety door latches and hinges, folding seat back latches, an energy-absorbing instrument panel, energy-absorbing front seat back tops, a contoured windshield header (except convertible), a thick-laminate windshield, padded sun visors, safety arm rests, a safety steering wheel, a side-guard door beam structure, a cargo-guard luggage compartment, side marker lights with reflectors, parking lights that illuminate with the headlights, a four-way hazard warning flasher, back-up lights, a lane-change feature in the directional signal controls, a defroster, windshield washers, dual-speed windshield wipers, a vinyl-edged wide-view inside day/night rearview mirror with shatterproof glass and deflecting support, a left-hand outside rearview mirror, bias-belted ply tires with tread wear indicators, a dual brake master cylinder with warning light, a starter safety switch, dual-action safety hood latches, a full-coil-spring suspension, a perimeter frame, an advanced body mounting system, new finned rear brake drums, flush-and-dry rocker panels, double-panel door, hood and deck lid construction, four inner fenders and a 145-hp Turbo-Thrift 250-cid six-cylinder engine or a 200-hp Turbo-Fire 307-cid V-8 with three-speed fully synchronized manual transmission. Convertibles also came with courtesy lights. Newly designed standard cloth-and-vinyl interiors were available in black, dark blue or dark jade green for sport coupe, sport sedan and four-door sedan models. In addition, a Sandalwood interior was available for sport coupe and sport sedan models. Convertibles offered a standard all-vinyl interior in black, dark jade or dark saddle. All-vinyl interiors for Malibu sport coupes came in black, dark jade, sandalwood or dark saddle; for Malibu sport sedans in black, dark blue, dark jade or Sandalwood; and for four-door Sedans in black, Sandalwood or dark saddle. An all-vinyl Strato-bucket seat interior for sport coupe and convertible models came in black, dark jade or dark saddle. With all Malibu interiors the doors and sidewalls were styled in matching vinyl panels to complement the seat trim. The floors were covered with durable, color-keyed, deep-twist carpeting. Only two Malibu body styles — the four-door sedan and the two-door sport coupe — were available with six-cylinder power. Concours station wagons came only with V-8 power and featured the following standard equipment: Hide-A-Way windshield wipers, power front disc/rear drum brakes, a lighted locking glove box, a dual-action tailgate, a concealed storage compartment, all-vinyl upholstery, a vinyl-coated textured metal cargo floor, G78-14/B bias-belted black sidewall tires, flush-and-dry rocker panels, a cigarette lighter, floor carpeting, a foam front seat and a 307-cid 200-hp V-8. Three-seat station wagons also included a rear-facing third seat and a power-operated tailgate window.

Model Number	Body/Style Number	Body Type & Seating	Factory Price	Shipping Weight	Production Total
MALIBU SERIES 135 (6-CYL)					
135	69	4d sedan-6P	$2,851	3,250 lbs.	Note 1
135	37	2d sport coupe-6P	$2,885	3,212 lbs.	Note 1
MALIBU SERIES 136 (V-8)					
136	69	4d sedan-6P	$2,947	3,380 lbs.	Note 1
136	39	4d sport sedan-6P	$3,052	3,450 lbs.	Note 1
136	37	2d sport coupe-6P	$2,980	3,342 lbs.	Note 1
136	67	2d convertible-6P	$3,260	3,908 lbs.	Note 1
136	36	4d Concours-6P	$3,337	3,864 lbs.	Note 1
136	46	4d Concours-9P	$3,450	3,836 lbs.	Note 1

NOTE 1: Individual body-style production is not available; see production notes.

MALIBU CONCOURS ESTATE WAGON (V-8) — SERIES 138

Concours Estate station wagons came only with V-8 power and featured the following standard equipment: door edge guards, wood-grained body side paneling, a wood-grained rear body panel, Hide-A-Way windshield wipers, power front disc/rear drum brakes, a lighted locking glove box, a dual-action tailgate, a concealed storage compartment, all-vinyl upholstery, a vinyl-coated textured metal cargo floor, G78-14/B bias-belted black sidewall tires, flush-and-dry rocker panels, a cigarette lighter, floor carpeting, a foam front seat and a 307-cid 200-hp V-8. Three-seat station wagons also included a rear-facing third seat and a power-operated tailgate window.

Model Number	Body/Style Number	Body Type & Seating	Factory Price	Shipping Weight	Production Total
MALIBU CONCOURS ESTATE WAGON SERIES 137 (6-CYL)					
138	36	4d wagon-6P	$3,514	3,892 lbs.	Note 1
138	46	4d wagon-9P	$3,626	3,944 lbs.	Note 1

NOTE 1: Individual body style production is not available; see production notes.

HEAVY CHEVY — (V-8) — VF3 OPTION

The Heavy Chevy package was a midyear option for any 1971 Chevelle sport coupe with V-8 power that didn't have the optional SS equipment package. It had a dealer cost of $112.50 and retailed for $142.20. Ingredients of the package included a black-accented grille, special body side striping, "Heavy Chevy" decals for the hood, front fenders and rear deck, a special domed hood with locking pins and 14 x 6-in. Rallye wheels (with bright lug nuts and center caps). Buyers had a choice of black or white stripes, except with a vinyl roof or when a black or white painted roof was specified. Like Plymouth's Road Runner, Pontiac's "The Judge" version of the GTO and Ford's Falcon Torino, the Heavy Chevy was aimed at budget-priced super car buyers. Although it looked like a real muscle car, its 350-cid 200-hp base engine did not command the same insurance premiums as larger big-block V-8s. Only 6,727 cars were fitted with this package, but it is not known if all the cars were of one series or if both Chevelle and Malibu versions were ordered. The list below shows the base prices of the sport coupe in both series, with the retail price of the YF3 package added. The Heavy Chevy was also available with 245-, 270- and 300-hp V-8s.

Model Number	Body/Style Number	Body Type & Seating	Factory Price	Shipping Weight	Production Total
CHEVELLE HEAVY CHEVY MODEL 13337 + VF3 OPTION (V-8)					
134	37	2d sport coupe-6P	$2,804	3,260 lbs.	See text above
CHEVELLE MALIBU HEAVY CHEVY MODEL 13537 + VF3 OPTION (V-8)					
136	37	2d sport coupe-6P	$2,951	3,307 lbs.	See text above

MALIBU SS OPTION — (V-8) SERIES 136 + Z15 OPTION

This year the Super Sport package became Regular Production Option (RPO) Z15 and it was now specifically available only for Malibu models and El Caminos (which are covered separately in this book) with V-8 engines. In addition to regular Malibu equipment, the SS 396 featured power front disc brakes, a black-painted grille, wheel opening moldings, a special domed hood with locking pins, a remote-controlled Sport-style left-hand outside rearview mirror, a special heavy-duty Sport suspension, 15 x 7-in. wheels with bright lug nuts, special wheel center caps, wheel trim rings and F60-15 wide-oval white lettered tires. There were bold SS emblems at the center of the grille, on the front fender sides behind the wheel opening and on the right side of the black finished rear. The Super Sport also its own instrument panel with function symbols. Newly designed standard cloth-and-vinyl interiors were available in black, dark blue, dark jade green or sandalwood for sport coupes. Convertibles offered a standard all-vinyl interior in black, dark jade or dark saddle. All-vinyl interiors for sport coupes came in black, dark jade, Sandalwood or dark Saddle. An all-vinyl Strato-bucket seat interior was optional for sport coupe and convertible models in black, dark jade or dark saddle. With all Super Sports the doors and sidewalls were styled in matching vinyl panels to complement the seat trim. The floors were covered with durable, color-keyed, deep-twist carpeting. The SS package had a dealer cost of $282.44 and a retail price of $357.05. It was a bit more expensive on El Caminos.

Model Number	Body/Style Number	Body Type & Seating	Factory Price	Shipping Weight	Production Total
MALIBU SS OPTION — SERIES 136 + RPO Z15 SS OPTION PACKAGE (V-8)					
136	37	2d sport coupe-6P	$3,337	3,407 lbs.	Note 1
136	67	2d convertible-6P	$3,617	3,452 lbs.	Note 1

NOTE 1: Individual body style production is not available; see production notes.
NOTE 2 Prices calculated by adding Malibu model base price and SS option price.

MALIBU SS 454 OPTION — SERIES 136 + RPO Z15 OPTION + LS5 OR LS6 OPTION

The 1971 Z15 option allowed Malibu V-8 sport coupe or convertible buyers to turn their car into a Super Sport. They could then add the LS5 to make the car an SS 454. And if they wanted to go even faster, after midyear they could pay more to get the 425-hp LS6 engine option. This was actually a de-tuned version of the previous LS6 and was one of just two Chevrolet engines made in 1971 to have a compression ratio higher than 8.5:1. A new cylinder head and redesigned camshaft allowed Chevrolet to maintain the engine's 425-hp rating despite its having a lower compression ratio than it did in 1970.

Model Number	Body/Style Number	Body Type & Seating	Factory Price	Shipping Weight	Production Total
MALIBU SS 454 OPTION — SERIES 136 + RPO Z15 SUPER SPORT OPTION PACKAGE + LS5 V-8					
136	37	2d sport coupe-6P	$3,443	3,407 lbs.	Note 1
136	67	2d convertible-6P	$3,645	3,452 lbs.	Note 1
MALIBU SS 454 OPTION — SERIES 136 + RPO Z15 SUPER SPORT OPTION PACKAGE + LS6 V-8					
136	37	2d sport coupe-6P	—	—	Note 1
136	67	2d convertible-6P	—	—	Note 1

NOTE 1: Individual body style production is not available; see production notes.
NOTE 3 Prices calculated by adding Malibu model base prices, SS option price and retail price of extra-cost V-8.
NOTE 4 Price of the LS6 not available in source material.

PRODUCTION NOTES

NOTE 1 Model-year production (within U.S.) of all 1971 Chevelles was 327,159 units, including 23,417 six-cylinder models and 303,742 V-8 models.

NOTE 2 Additional statistics record series production (in the U.S.), in rounded-off figures as follows:

Chevelle (6-cyl)	11,500
Chevelle 300 (V-8)	24,100
Total	35,600
Malibu (6-cyl)	9,100
Malibu (V-8)	240,200
Total	249,300
Wagons (6-cyl)	2,800
Wagons (V-8)	39,500
Total	42,300

(*) Malibu figures include Super Sport models.

NOTE 3 Production by factory (United States) was:

Code	Factory	Production	Code	Factory	Production
B	Baltimore	100,800	K	Leeds (Mo.)	77,790
R	Arlington (Tex.)	99,675	L	Van Nuys (LA)	48,892

Additional 1971 Chevelles were built in Canada.

NOTE 4 Exactly 6,727 cars had the YF3 Heavy Chevy option installed. All were V-8 powered. No series breakouts are available.

NOTE 5 The SS equipment package was added to approximately 80,000 cars of which 19,992 were Malibu SS 454s. No body style breakouts are available. No breakout of LS5 and LS6 production is available.

NOTE 6 Exactly 5,089 Malibu convertibles were built. Some were Malibu and some were Super Sports. No breakouts are available.

ENGINES

CHEVELLE BASE SIX-CYL: Inline. Overhead-valve.

CHEVELLE

Cast-iron block. Displacement: 250 cid. Bore and stroke: 3.875 x 3.53 in. Compression ratio: 8.5:1. Brake hp: 145 at 4200 rpm. Net brake hp: 110 at 3800 rpm. Taxable hp: 36. Torque: 230 lbs.-ft. at 1600 rpm. Seven main bearings. Hydraulic valve lifters. Crankcase capacity: 4 qt. (add 1 qt. for new filter). Cooling system capacity: 12 qt (add 6 qt. for heater). Carburetor: Rochester one-barrel Model 7028017. Sales code L22. Available standard with three-speed fully synchronized manual transmission and Powerglide automatic transmission.

CHEVELLE BASE V-8: Overhead-valve. Cast-iron block and head. Bore and stroke: 3.88 x 3.25 in. Displacement: 307 cid. Compression ratio: 8.50:1. Gross brake hp: 200 at 4600 rpm. Net brake hp: 140 at 4400 rpm. Taxable hp: 48.0. Gross torque: 300 lbs.-ft. at 2400. Net torque. 235 lbs.-ft. at 2400 rpm. Five main bearings. Hydraulic valve lifters. Crankcase capacity: 4 qt. (add 1 qt. for new filter). Cooling system capacity: (Camaro) 14 qt.; (Chevelle, Monte Carlo) 15 qt.; (add 1 qt. for heater). Carburetor: Two-barrel. Available with three-speed manual, Powerglide automatic or Turbo-Hydra-Matic transmission.

CHEVELLE OPTIONAL 350-CID, 245-HP V-8: Overhead-valve. Cast-iron block and head. Bore and stroke: 4.00 x 3.48 in. Displacement: 350 cid. Compression ratio: 8.50:1. Gross brake hp: 245 at 4800 rpm. Net brake hp: 165 at 4000 rpm. Taxable hp: 51.20. Gross torque: 350 lbs.-ft. at 2800. Net torque: 280 lbs.-ft. at 2400 rpm. Five main bearings. Hydraulic valve lifters. Crankcase capacity: 4 qt. (add 1 qt. for new filter). Cooling system capacity: (full-size) 14 qt.; (others) 15 qt. (add 1 qt. for heater). Carburetor: Two-barrel. Sales code L65. Available with four-speed manual or Turbo-Hydra-Matic transmission.

CHEVELLE OPTIONAL 350-CID, 270-HP V-8: Overhead-valve. Cast-iron block and head. Bore and stroke: 4.00 x 3.48 in. Displacement: 350 cid. Compression ratio: 8.50:1. Gross brake hp: 270 at 4800 rpm. Net brake hp: 210 at 4400 rpm. Taxable hp: 51.20. Gross torque: 360 lbs.-ft. at 3200. Net torque: 300 lbs.-ft. at 2800 rpm. Five main bearings. Hydraulic valve lifters. Crankcase capacity: 4 qt. (add 1 qt. for new filter). Cooling system capacity: (full-size) 14 qt.; (others) 15 qt. (add 1 qt. for heater). Carburetor: Four-barrel. Sales code L48. Available with three-speed manual transmission with floor shift, four-speed manual transmission or Turbo-Hydra-Matic automatic transmission.

CHEVELLE OPTIONAL 400-CID, 300-HP V-8: Overhead-valve. Cast-iron block and head. Bore and stroke: 4.13 x 3.76 in. Displacement: 402 cid (400 cid). Compression ratio: 8.50:1. Gross brake hp: 300 at 4800 rpm. Net brake hp: 260 at 4400 rpm. Taxable hp: 54.50. Gross torque: 400 lbs.-ft. at 3200. Net torque. lbs.-ft. 345 at 3200 rpm. Five main bearings. Hydraulic valve lifters. Crankcase capacity: 4 qt. (add 1 qt. for new filter). Cooling system capacity: 22 qt. (add 1 qt. for heater). Carburetor: Four-barrel. Sales code LS3. Promoted as SS 396. Available with special three-speed manual transmission with floor shift, four-speed manual transmission or Turbo-Hydra-Matic automatic transmission.

CHEVELLE OPTIONAL 454-CID, 285-HP V-8: Overhead-valve. Cast-iron block and head. Bore and stroke: 4.25 x 4.00 in. Displacement: 454 cid. Compression ratio: 8.50:1. Gross brake hp: 365 at 4800 rpm. Net brake hp: 285 at 4000 rpm. Taxable hp: 57.80. Gross torque: 465 lbs.-ft. at 3200. Net torque. 390 lbs.-ft. at 3200 rpm. Five main bearings. Hydraulic valve lifters. Crankcase capacity: 4 qt. (add 1 qt. for new filter). Cooling system capacity: 21 qt. (add 1 qt. for heater). Dual exhaust. Carburetor: Four-barrel. Sales code LS5. Available with special four-speed manual transmission or Turbo-Hydra-Matic automatic transmission.

CHEVELLE OPTIONAL 454-CID, 425-HP V-8: Overhead-valve. Cast-iron block and head. Bore and stroke: 4.25 x 4.00 in. Displacement: 454 cid. Compression ratio: 9.00:1. Gross brake hp: 425 at 5600 rpm. Net brake hp: 325 at 5600 rpm. Taxable hp: 57.80. Gross torque: 475 lbs.-ft. at 4000. Net torque. 390 lbs.-ft. at 3600 rpm. Five main bearings. Hydraulic valve lifters. Crankcase capacity: 4 qt. (add 1 qt. for new filter). Cooling system capacity: 21 qt. (add 1 qt. for heater). Dual exhaust. Carburetor: Four-barrel. Sales code LS6. Available with special four-speed manual transmission or Turbo-Hydra-Matic automatic transmission.

CHASSIS FEATURES

Wheelbase: (two-door) 112 in.; (four-door) 116 in. Overall length: (two-door) 197.5 in. (four-door cars) 201.5 in.; (four-door station wagons) 208.3 in.; Width: 75.4 in. Height: (sedans) 53.3 in.; (coupes) 52.7 in.; (convertible) 52.9 in. Front tread: 60 in. Rear tread: 59.9 in. Gas tank capacity: 20 gal. Tires: (six) E78 x 14 two-ply/four-ply rated; (V-8) E78 x 14 two-ply/four-ply rated; (station wagon) G78 x 14 two-ply/four-ply rated. Turn circle: 41 ft. Trunk capacity (sedan) 13.5 cubic feet. Front headroom (sedan): 38.5 in. Rear headroom (sedan): 37.1 in. Front legroom (sedan): 42.8 in. Rear legroom (sedan): 35.1 in. Front hip room (sedan): 59.5 in. Rear hip room (sedan): 59.4 in.

OPTIONS

C60 Four-Season air conditioning, including 61-amp Delcotron generator, heavy-duty radiator and temperature-controlled fan and requiring larger tires with some Chevelles (Chevelle $407.60; El Camino $411.05). C51 station wagon rear window air deflector ($21.10). G80 Positraction rear axle (Chevelles $46.35; El Caminos $45.20). YD1 trailering axle ratio ($12.65). ZQ9 performance rear axle on Malibu with standard V-8 and Positraction ($12.65). T60 heavy-duty 80-amp battery (Chevelle $15.60; El Camino $16.15). AK1 Custom Deluxe front shoulder belts for bench seat cars, except El Camino ($16.90). AK1 Custom Deluxe front shoulder belts for coupe with bucket seats ($15.30). AK1 Custom Deluxe front shoulder belts for 3-seat station wagons ($20.05). AK1 Custom Deluxe front shoulder belts for 2-seat station wagons ($16.90). AK1 Custom Deluxe front shoulder belts for El Camino with bench seat ($12.40). AK1 Custom Deluxe front shoulder belts for El Camino with bucket seats ($10.80). A39 Custom Deluxe front seat belts, for convertibles with bucket seats ($13.20). A39 Custom Deluxe front seat belts for convertibles with bench front seats ($14.75). A85 Custom Deluxe front shoulder belts, requires Custom deluxe seat belts for convertibles with bench seats ($26.35). AS4 Custom Deluxe rear shoulder belts, for all except El Camino requires Custom deluxe seat belts ($26.35). V55 adjustable station wagon roof carrier ($57.95). U35 Electric clock in all Chevelle models except El Camino, included with special instrumentation ($16.90). U35 Electric clock in El Camino, included with special instrumentation ($17.25). D55 Console with courtesy light, not available with standard three-speed manual transmission ($59 in Chevelles; $60.30 in El Caminos). C50 Rear windshield defroster ($31.60 in coupes and sedans; $36.90 in convertibles and station wagons). AU3 power door locks for two-door models ($44.80). AU3 power door locks for four-door models ($68.50). L65 350-cid 245-hp V-8 engine, except El Camino ($26.35). L48 350-cid 270-hp V-8 engine (Chevelle $73.75; El Camino $75.35). LS3 402-cid 300-hp V-8 engine in Chevelle and Malibu with E78 x 14 tires or Super Sport package ($172.75). LS3 402-cid 300-hp V-8 engine in El Camino with F78 x 14 tires or Super Sport package ($176.50). LS3 402-cid 300-hp V-8 engine in Chevelle station wagons ($172.75). LS5 454-cid 365-hp V-8 engine in Chevelle or Malibu with Super Sport equipment, heavy-duty battery and Sport suspension ($279.10). LS5 454-cid 365-hp V-8 engine in El Camino with Super Sport equipment, heavy-duty battery and Sport suspension ($285.15). LS6 454-cid 365-hp V-8 engine in Chevelle or Malibu with Super Sport equipment, heavy-duty battery and Sport suspension ($290.40). LS6 454-cid 365-hp V-8 engine in El Camino with Super Sport equipment, heavy-duty battery and Sport suspension ($296.50). K85 63-amp Delcotron generator for Chevelles, with air conditioning ($5.30); without air conditioning ($26.35). K85 63-amp Delcotron generator for El Caminos, with air conditioning ($5.40); without air conditioning ($26.90). A01 All windows tinted ($43.20). V30 front and rear bumper guards ($31.60). V30 front bumper guards (Chevelle wagons $15.80; El Caminos $16.15). B93 door edge guards, for two-door Chevelles, except El Camino ($6.35). B93 door edge guards, for four-door Chevelles ($9.50). B93 door edge guards, for El Camino ($6.50). ZL2 cowl-induction hood for Chevelles, includes sport striping on hood, air intake valve at rear of hood, sport striping on the rear deck lid of Malibu models (with choice of white or black stripes) and a hood-to-air cleaner duct, requires Super Sport package and 365-hp engine ($158). ZL2 cowl-induction hood for El Camino, includes sport striping on hood, air intake valve at rear of hood, sport striping on the rear deck lid of Malibu models (with choice of white or black stripes) and a hood-to-air cleaner duct, requires Super Sport package and 365-hp engine ($134.50). U14 Special instrumentation with ammeter, temperature gauge, oil pressure gauge and tachometer on Malibu and SS 396 sport coupes and convertibles (Chevelle and Malibu two-doors $94.80; El Camino Custom $102.25). ZJ9 auxiliary lighting groups with A) ashtray light, B) courtesy light, C) glove box light, D) luggage compartment light, E) underhood light, F) Mirror map light and G) warning lights; in Chevelle includes A, B, C, D, E and F ($21.10), in Malibu convertibles includes A, D, E and F ($15.80), in Malibus except convertibles includes A, B, D, E and F ($15.80), in El Camino Custom includes A, B, E and F ($18.85), in El Camino standard includes A, B, C, E and F ($21.55), in Concours and Concours Estate station wagons includes A, B, E and F ($18.45), in Greenbrier and Nomad station wagons includes A, B, C, E and F ($21.10). B37 twin front and rear floor mats (Chevelle $12.65; El Camino twin front only $7.00). B37 color-keyed front and rear floor mats (Chevelle $12.65; El Camino $7). D33 left-hand outside remote-control mirror (Chevelle $12.65, El Camino $12.95). D34 visor vanity mirror (Chevelle $3.20, El Camino $3.25). B90 window moldings on Chevelle Concours and Concours Estate four-door and station wagon models ($26.35). B90 window moldings on Chevelle Nomad and Greenbrier station wagon models ($31.60). B90 window moldings on Malibu four-door sedan ($26.35). B90 window moldings on El Camino, not available on El Camino Custom ($21.55). Two-tone paint with bright metal outline moldings ($31.60). J50 power drum brakes (Chevelle $47.40; El Camino $48.45). JL2 power disc brakes (Chevelle $69.55; El Camino $71.05). AU3 power door locks system, on two-door models, except El Camino ($46.35). AU3 power door locks system, on four-door models ($70.60). AU3 power door locks system on El Camino ($47.35). N40 power steering (Chevelle $115.90; El Camino $113). A33 power tailgate window on mid-size two-seat station wagons ($34.80). V01 Heavy-duty radiator with six-cylinder engine (Chevelle $14.75; El Camino $15.10). V01 heavy-duty radiator with V-8 engine (Chevelle $21.10; El Camino $21.55). U63 AM push-button radio with front antenna (Chevelle $66.40, El Camino $67.80). U69 AM/FM radio with front antenna (Chevelle $139.05, El Camino $142.05). U79 AM/FM radio with front antenna and stereo, all except El Camino ($239.10). UM1 AM radio with stereo tape deck, for all except El Camino ($200.15). UM2 AM/FM radio with setero tape deck for all except El Camino ($372.85). U80 rear seat speaker, not available in El Camino or with stereo ($15.80). Vinyl roof (Chevelle $94.80; El Camino $64.60). K30 cruise control, requires power brakes and Turbo-Hydra-Matic transmission (Chevelle $63.20; El Camino $64.60). N33 Comfortilt steering, requires automatic transmission (Chevelle $45.35; El Camino $46.30). NK2 Custom black four-spoke steering wheel, not available with N33 (Chevelle $15.80; El Camino $16.15). NK4 black four-spoke Sport steering wheel (Chevelle $15.80; El Camino $16.15). D88 Malibu sport striping package includes sport striping on hood, Sport striping on rear deck lid with choice of either black or white stripes available on sport coupe, except with vinyl top covering or white or black painted roof ($79 or standard with ZL2 option). D88 El Camino sport striping package includes sport striping on hood with choice of either black or white stripes available, except with vinyl top covering or white or black painted roof ($53.80 or standard with ZL2 option). F40 heavy-duty front and rear suspension with special springs and matching shocks, includes 2,700-lb. capacity rear springs on El Camino, not available on Malibu with SS equipment or El Camino with 365-hp engine (Chevelle $17.95; El Camino Custom $18.30). F41 Sport suspension with special front and rear stabilizers, matching rear shocks and rear axle control arms, standard with SS equipment ($30.35). M40 Turbo-Hydra-Matic transmission for Chevelle with 245- or 270-hp V-8 ($216.50). M40 Turbo-Hydra-Matic transmission for El Camino with 200-, 245-

or 270-hp engines ($221.40). M40 Turbo-Hydra-Matic transmission for Chevelles with 300- or 365-hp V-8s ($237.60). M40 Turbo-Hydra-Matic transmission for El Caminos with 300- or 365-hp V-8s ($243.00). M35 Powerglide automatic transmission for six-cylinder Chevelle ($179.55). M35 Powerglide automatic transmission for Chevelle 307-cid V-8 ($190.10). M35 Powerglide automatic transmission for six-cylinder El Camino ($183.60). M35 Powerglide automatic transmission for El Camino V-8 ($194.40). M20 wide-range four-speed manual transmission for Chevelles with 245-, 270- or 300-hp V-8s ($195.40). M20 wide-range four-speed manual transmission for El Caminos with 245-, 270- or 300-hp V-8s ($199.80). M22 special close-ratio four-speed manual transmission for Chevelles with 365-hp V-8 ($237.60). M22 special close-ratio four-speed manual transmission for El Camino with 365-hp V-8 ($243). M11 floor-mounted three-speed manual transmission for Chevelles with 270-hp V-8 ($132). M11 floor-mounted three-speed manual transmission for El Caminos with 270-hp V-8 ($135). MC1 floor-mounted three-speed manual transmission for Chevelles with 300-hp V-8 ($132). MC1 floor-mounted three-speed manual transmission for El Camino s with 300-hp V-8 ($135). Trim interior for Chevelles and Malibus, except convertible, with vinyl bench seats ($19). A51 Strato-bucket vinyl seats for Malibu Sport Coupe or convertible ($136.95). A51 Strato-bucket cloth or vinyl seats for El Camino Custom ($139.90). P01 bright metal wheel covers (Chevelle $26.35; El Camino $26.90). P02 custom wheel covers, not available with SS equipment or special performance package (Chevelle $84.30; El Camino $86.10). ZJ7 Rally wheels, including special wheels, hubcaps and trim rings, not available with SS equipment (Chevelle $45.30, El Camino $46.30). ZP5 Appearance Guard group with A) front and rear bumper guards, B) door edge guards, C) color-keyed front and rear floor mats and D) visor-vanity mirror; on Concours Estate including A, C and D ($31.65); on other station wagons including A, B, C and D ($41.15); on four-door Chevelles including A, B, C and D ($56.95); on two-door Chevelles including A, B, C and D ($53.80); on El Camino including A, B, C and D ($32.90). ZQ2 Operating Convenience group with A) Electric clock, B) Rear window defroster, C) Headlight delay system and D) Remote-contol left-hand outside rearview mirror, on sedans includes A, B, D ($61.15), on sport coupe with special instrumentation includes B, D ($44.25), on sport coupe without special instrumentation includes A, B, D ($61.15), on Malibu SS sport coupe with special instrumentation includes B ($31.60), on Malibu SS sport coupe without special instrumentation includes A, B ($48.50), on Malibu convertible with spe-

This SS 454 was resplendid in Sunflower Yellow with black stripes on the hood and deck lid.

The all-vinyl interior was available in black for 1971.

cial instrumentation includes B, D ($49.55), on Malibu convertible without special instrumentation includes A, B, D ($66.45); on Malibu SS convertible with special instrumentation includes B ($36.90), on Malibu SS convertible without special instrumentation includes A, B ($53.80);on Chevelle station wagons includes A, B and D ($66.45); on El Camino without special instrumentation or SS equipment includes A and D ($30.20); on El Camino with special instrumentation without SS equipment includes D ($12.95); on El Camino without special instrumentation with SS equipment includes A ($17.25). Z15 SS equipment package includes power front disc rear drum brakes, a black-finished grille, a special domed hood with locking pins, a remote-control left-hand outside Sport rearview mirror, an SS grille emblem, an SS fender emblem, an SS steering wheel, Sport suspension, 15 x 7-in. wheels with bright lug nuts, special center caps and trim rings, F60 x 15 white lettered tires and function symbols on instrument panel knobs for Malibu sport coupe or convertible with optional V-8 ($357.05). Z15 SS equipment package includes power front disc rear drum brakes, a black-finished grille, a special domed hood with locking pins, a remote-control left-hand outside non-Sport rearview mirror, an SS grille emblem, an SS fender emblem, an SS steering wheel, Sport suspension, 15 x 7-in. wheels with bright lug nuts, special center caps and trim rings, F60 x 15 white letter tires and function symbols on instrument panel knobs for El Camino Custom with optional V-8 ($364.80). PL3 five E78 x 14/B white stripe tires replacing five E78-14/B black sidewall tires ($28.15). PX5 five F78-14/B black sidewall tires replacing five E78-14/B black sidewall tires on Malibu without 300-hp engine ($17.95). PX5 five F78-14/B black sidewall tires replacing five E78-14/B black sidewall tires on Malibu with 300-hp engine, includes 14 x 6-in. wheels ($23.20). PX6 five F78-14/B white stripe tires replacing five E78-14/B black sidewall tires on Malibu without 300-hp engine ($48.10). PX6 five F78-14/B white stripe tires replacing five E78-14/B black sidewall tires on Malibu with 300-hp engine, includes 14 x 6-in. wheels ($53.35). PL3 five E78-14/B white stripe tires replacing five E78-14/B black sidewall tires on El Camino ($26.50). PX5 five F78-14/B black sidewall tires replacing five E78-14/B black sidewall tires on El Camino without 300-hp engine ($18.10). PX5 five F78-14/B black sidewall tires replacing five E78-14/B black sidewall tires on El Camino with 300-hp engine, includes 14 x 6-in. wheels ($23.50). PX6 five F78-14/B white stripe tires replacing five E78-14/B black sidewall tires on El Camino without 300-hp engine ($46.65). PX6 five F78-14/B white stripe tires replacing five E78-14/B black sidewall tires on El Camino with 300-hp engine, includes 14 x 6-in. wheels ($52.00). PK2 five G78-14/B white-stripe belted tires replacing five G78-14/B black sidewall tires on station wagons ($32.30). PM5 five G78-14/D bias-belted black sidewall tires replacing five G78-14/B black sidewall tires on station wagons ($45.30). PM6 five G78-14/D bias-belted white stripe tires replacing five G78-14/B black sidewall tires on station wagons ($77.15).

OPTIONS (MIDYEAR CHANGES)

ZQ9 performance rear axle on Malibu with 425-hp V-8, includes heavy-duty radiator ($33.75). ZQ9 performance rear axle on El Camino with 425-hp V-8, includes heavy-duty radiator ($34.45). J55 heavy-duty brakes for station wagons ($19). LS6 454-cid 425-hp Turbo Jet V-8 for Chevelle with Malibu SS equipment package and heavy-duty battery, including special four-speed manual transmission or Turbo-Hydra-Matic transmission (price unknown). LS6 454-cid 425-hp Turbo Jet V-8 for El Camino with SS equipment package and heavy-duty battery, including special four-speed manual transmission or Turbo-Hydra-Matic transmission (price unknown). F40 Special front and rear suspension for El Camino, includes 2,700-lb. rear springs ($18.30). ZQ2 Operating Convenience group with A) electric clock, B) rear window defroster, C) headlight delay system and D) remote-control left-hand outside rearview mirror, on station wagons includes A, B, D ($66.45). VF3 Heavy Chevy package for Chevelle V-8 coupes, includes black-accented grille, special side striping, "Heavy Chevy" hood decal, "Heavy Chevy" front fender decal, "Heavy Chevy" rear deck lid decal, special domed hood with locking pins and 14 x 6-in. Rallye-type wheels with bright lug nuts and center caps ($142.20). M40 Turbo-Hydra-Matic transmission with 425-hp V-8 (Chevelle $306.26, El Camino $313.20).

OPTION INSTALLATION RATES

Automatic transmission (93.7 percent). Four-speed manual transmission (3.2 percent). Standard V-8 engine (49.3 percent). Optional V-8 engine (44.1 percent). six-cylinder engine (6.6 percent). AM radio (89.5 percent). AM/FM radio (6.4 percent). Stereo tape (4.1 percent). Air conditioning (55.3 percent). Power steering (90.5 percent). Tilt steering (4.1 percent). Power drum brakes (32.9 percent). Power front disc brakes (22.1 percent). Power door locks (1.2 percent). Power side windows (7.6 percent). Bucket seats (10.3 percent). Vinyl top (35.5 percent). White sidewall tires (81.8 percent). Tinted windshield only (1.4 percent). All tinted glass (73.9 percent). Dual exhaust (4.2 percent). Positraction (6.5 percent). Optional full wheel covers (54 percent). Styled wheels (24 percent). Optional clock (11.1 percent). Cruise control (1 percent). Based on model-year production of 327,159 units.

HISTORICAL FOOTNOTES

The 1970 Chevelle line had its dealer introduction date on September 29, 1970. John Z. Delorean was general manager of Chevrolet Motor Division during the 1971 model year. Chevrolet became the first automaker to break the 3,000,000 barrier for combined sales of passenger cars and trucks in the United States. Calendar year sales of Chevelles rose to 399,510 units from 379,859 the previous 12 months. That represented a 4.6 percent share of total U.S. auto sales, Calendar-year registrations were 335,378 Chevelle passenger cars versus 346,714 the prior year and 44,776 station wagons versus 34,340 the previous year. The new Heavy Chevy Coupe was available with the 200-, 245-, 270- and 300-hp V-8s. A typical 0 to 60 mph time for the 200-hp version with Turbo-Hydra-Matic transmission was 10.5 seconds.

The 1972 Chevelles, this one is an SS coupe, were the last to use the body style that originated in 1968.

Two Chevelles, four Malibus and Nomad, Greenbrier, Concours and Concours Estate station wagons made up the modestly changed 1972 Chevelle model lineup. These were the last Chevelles to use the basic body design that had been introduced back in 1968 and they had very few innovations in either styling or technology. There was a good reason for this. According to a mid-1972 *Hot Rod* magazine article, Chevrolet's original plan was to bring out an all-new Chevelle for the 1972 model year to compete with Ford's new-for-1972 Torino. However, the redesign was delayed for a year for two reasons. The first was the midyear introduction of a new Camaro, which tapped the division's creative resources. The second was General Motors chief Ed Cole's decision to re-engineer all 1971 GM cars to operate on leaded gas, which became a top-priority job for Chevy engineers.

This pushed the all-new Chevelle into the 1973 model year and led to the 1971 model being carried over into 1972 with just a few small changes. A wider grille and new single-unit front parking lamps characterized the front-end appearance. The grille had a new texture with prominent horizontal bars and was divided horizontally by two wider, bright metal moldings that gave it a tri-level look. The front parking lamps were still notched into the fender caps, but now had a larger, one-piece, square-shaped plastic lens decorated with thin horizontal lines. The lenses wrapped around the body corners to serve double duty as side marker lights. A new molding treatment with some trim levels included a stainless-steel spear at mid-body height running only between the front and rear wheel openings. The rear end was virtually the same as in 1971. An SS option for Malibu V-8 sport coupes and convertibles combined Sport wheels, power front disc/rear drum brakes, and a black-accented grille with a special domed hood and white-lettered tires. It could now be ordered for any Chevelle V-8, including

1972

those with the base 307-cid motor. The Heavy Chevy option was also carried over with virtually no changes. The Concours Estate station wagon had new wood-grain body panels.

I.D. NUMBERS (LATE 1972)

VIN embossed on the top left-hand side of the instrument panel and visible through the windshield. The first symbol 1 designates Chevrolet. The second symbol indicates series: C=Chevelle, El Camino or Greenbrier; D=Malibu, Custom El Camino or Concours; H=Concours Estate. The third and fourth symbols indicate body style: 36=four-door two-seat station wagon with dual-action tailgate, 37=two-door notchback/hardtop coupe (sport coupe), 39=four-door notchback/hardtop sedan (sport sedan), 46=four-door three-seat station wagon with dual-action tailgate, 67=two-door convertible and 69=four-door notchback sedan (pillared). The fifth symbol indicates engine (net horsepower): D=250-cid 110-hp inline six-cylinder; F=307-cid 130-hp V-8, H=350-cid 165-hp V-8, J=350-cid 175-hp V-8, U=402-cid (Turbo-Jet) 240-hp V-8 with dual exhausts and W=454-cid 270-hp V-8 with dual exhausts. The sixth symbol designates the model year: 2=1972. The seventh symbol designates the assembly plant location: B=Baltimore, Maryland; K=Leeds, Missouri; L=Van Nuys (Los Angeles) California, and R=Arlington, Texas. The last six symbols are the sequential unit production number at the specific factory. The Fisher body tag riveted to the top of the cowl on the left side of the car below the hood provides additional vehicle identification information. The Fisher body STYLE NUMBER (ST) consists of a prefix identifying model year and four or more symbols identifying the series and body style (example: 72-1D67 for a 1972 Malibu convertible with a V-8 engine). The BODY NUMBER consists of a prefix designating assembly plant and the sequential unit production number at the specific factory. The TRIM NUMBER (TR) identifies upholstery.

COLORS

(11) Antique White, (14) Pewter Silver, (18) Dusk Gray Poly, (19) Tuxedo Black, (24) Ascot Blue Poly, (25) Mediterranean Blue Poly, (26) Mulsanne Blue, (28) Fathom Blue Poly, (36) Spring Green Poly, (43) Gulf Green Poly, (46) Oasis Green Poly, (48) Sequoia Green Poly, (50) Covert Tan, (53) Placer Gold Poly, (54) Desert Gold Poly, (56) Cream Yellow, (57) Golden Brown Poly, (58) Turin Tan, (62) Driftwood, (63) Mohave Gold Poly, (65) Orange Flame Poly, (68) Midnight Bronze Poly, (69) Agean Brown and (75) Cranberry Red. Vinyl tops were available in five colors: AA=White, BB=Black, DD=Blue, GG=Green and TT=Covert Tan convertible tops came in black or white.

ENGINE CODES

Codes appear on the right side of six-cylinder blocks behind the distributor and right front of V-8 engine blocks. Engine codes for 1972 were: (250-cid six) CDM, CDL, CBJ, CBG, CSD, CBA, CBK, CBD and CAH; (307-cid V-8) CKG, CKH, CAY, CAZ and CMA; (350-cid two-barrel V-8) CKA, CTL, CSH, CDA, CMD, CAR and CDB; (350-cid four-barrel V-8) CKK, CKD, CDG, CDD and CKB; (402/396-cid V-8) CLA, CLB, CTA and CTB; (400-cid V-8) CLS, CTJ and CTH; (454-cid V-8) CPA, CPD, CRX and CRW. [Note: In some reference sources the 1971-style model numbers appear and may have been used early in the model year].

CHEVELLE NOMAD — (6-CYL/V-8) SERIES 1B

The Nomad was the lowest-rung Chevelle for 1972. Other than Nomad emblems, there was little to distinguish this four-door, two-seat wagon. Standard equipment on all Chevelles included seat belts with push-button buckles for all passenger positions, shoulder belts with push-button buckles for driver and right front passenger (except convertibles), two front seat head restraints, an energy-absorbing steering column, passenger-guard door locks with forward-mounted lock buttons, safety door latches and hinges, folding seat back latches, an energy-absorbing padded instrument panel, padded front seat back tops, a contoured windshield header (except convertibles), a thick-laminate windshield, padded sun visors, safety armrests, a safety steering wheel, side-guard door beams, a cargo guard luggage compartment, side marker lights and reflectors (front side marker lights flash with directional signals), parking lights that illuminate with the headlights, a four-way hazard warning flasher, back-up lights, a lane-change feature in the direction signal control, a windshield defroster, windshield washers, dual-speed windshield wipers, a wide-view day/night inside rearview mirror (vinyl-edged with shatter-resistant glass and a deflecting support), an inside-the-windshield radio antenna (when a radio was ordered), a left-hand outside rearview mirror, a dual master cylinder brake system with warning light, a dual-action safety hood latch, an anti-theft ignition key warning buzzer and an anti-theft steering column lock. Nomads also came with a dual-action tailgate, a concealed storage compartment, all-vinyl upholstery, a vinyl-coated textured metal cargo floor and G78-14/B bias-belted black sidewall tires, flush-and-dry rocker panels, cigarette lighter, a locking glove box, carpeting, a foam front seat and a 250-cid in-line six-cylinder engine with 100 net brake hp or a 307-cid two-barrel V-8 with 130 net brake hp. The Nomad was the only 1972 Chevelle station wagon available with a six-cylinder engine.

Model Number	Body/Style Number	Body Type & Seating	Factory Price	Shipping Weight	Production Total
CHEVELLE NOMAD STATION WAGON SERIES 1B (6-CYL)					
1B	36	4d Nomad-6P	$2,926	3,605 lbs.	Note 1
CHEVELLE NOMAD STATION WAGON SERIES 1B (V-8)					
1B	36	4d Nomad-6P	$3,016	3,732 lbs.	Note 1

NOTE 1: Individual body style production is not available; see production notes.

CHEVELLE — (6-CYL/V-8) — SERIES 1C

The base Chevelle series consisted of two-door hardtops and four-door sedans arranged in two car-lines, six and V-8. These cars had no fender names or bright rocker panel moldings. The comparable wagon (actually grouped with other Chevelle wagons in a separate station wagon catalog) took the Greenbrier name. Standard equipment on all Chevelles included seat belts with push-button buckles for all passenger positions, shoulder belts with push-button buckles for driver and right front passenger (except convertibles), two front seat head restraints, an energy-absorbing steering column, passenger-guard door locks with forward-mounted lock buttons, safety door latches and hinges, folding seat back latches, an energy-absorbing padded instrument panel, padded front seat back tops, a contoured windshield header (except convertibles), a thick-laminate windshield, padded sun visors, safety armrests, a safety steering wheel, side-guard door beams, a cargo guard luggage compartment, side marker lights and reflectors (front side marker lights flash with directional signals), parking lights that illuminate with the headlights, a four-way hazard warning flasher, back-up lights, a lane-change feature in the direction signal control, a windshield defroster, windshield washers, dual-speed windshield wipers, a wide-view day/night inside rearview mirror (vinyl-edged with shatter-resistant glass and a deflecting support), a left-hand outside rearview mirror, a dual master cylinder brake system with warning light, a dual-action safety hood latch, an anti-theft ignition key warning buzzer and an anti-theft steering column lock. Base models also came with a cigarette lighter, a locking glove box, color-keyed vinyl-coated rubber floor mats, a foam front seat and the 250-cid inline six or 307-cid V-8. A three-speed manual transmission with column-mounted gearshift controls was standard. All forward gears were fully synchronized. Greenbrier station wagons came only with V-8 power and featured the following standard equipment: a dual-action tailgate, a concealed storage compartment, all-vinyl upholstery, a vinyl-coated textured metal cargo floor, G78-14/B bias-belted black sidewall tires, flush-and-dry rocker panels, a cigarette lighter, a locking glove box, floor carpeting, a foam front seat and a 307-cid V-8. Three-seat station wagons also included a rear-facing third seat and a power-operated tailgate window.

Model Number	Body/Style Number	Body Type & Seating	Factory Price	Shipping Weight	Production Total
CHEVELLE 1C (6-CYL)					
1C	69	4d sedan-6P	$2,636	3,204 lbs.	Note 1
1C	37	2d sport coupe-6P	$2,669	3,172 lbs.	Note 1
CHEVELLE 1C (V-8)					
1C	69	4d sedan-6P	$2,726	3,332 lbs.	Note 1
1C	37	2d sport coupe-6P	$2,759	3,300 lbs.	Note 1
CHEVELLE GREENBRIER STATION WAGON 1C (V-8)					
1C	36	4d wagon-6P	$3,140	3,814 lbs.	Note 1
1C	46	4d wagon-8P	$3,247	3,870 lbs.	Note 1

NOTE 1: Individual body style production is not available; see production notes.

MALIBU — (6-CYL/V-8) — SERIES 1D

All Malibus featured a cigarette lighter, Hide-A-Way windshield wipers, a lighted glove box and E78-14/B belted bias-ply black sidewall tires. Astro Ventilation was included with coupes and convertibles. Cars with factory radios had an in-the-windshield antenna. New wheel opening moldings and wide body sill moldings were also seen on cars in this line. The Malibu-style wagons took the Concours name. Standard equipment with all body styles included seat belts with push-button buckles for all passenger positions, shoulder belts with push-button buckles for driver and right front passenger in closed cars (not convertibles), two front head rests, an energy-absorbing steering column, passenger guard door locks with forward-mounted lock buttons, safety door latches and hinges, folding seat back latches, an energy-absorbing instrument panel, energy-absorbing front seat back tops, a contoured windshield header (except convertible), a thick-laminate windshield, padded sun visors, safety arm rests, a safety steering wheel, a side-guard door beam structure, a cargo-guard luggage compartment, side marker lights with reflectors, parking lights that illuminate with the headlights, a four-way hazard warning flasher, back-up lights, a lane-change feature in the directional signal controls, a defroster, windshield washers, dual-speed windshield wipers, a vinyl-edged wide-view inside day/night rearview mirror with shatterproof glass and deflecting support, a left-hand outside rearview mirror, bias-belted ply tires with tread wear indicators, a dual brake master cylinder with warning light, a starter safety switch, dual-action safety hood latches, a full-coil-spring suspension, a perimeter frame, an advanced body mounting system, new finned rear brake drums, flush-and-dry rocker panels, double-panel door, hood and deck lid construction and four inner fenders. The 250-cid six-cylinder engine was available in the Malibu sport coupe or four-door sedan only. The base 307-cid V-8 was optional in these models and standard in convertibles and sport sedans. A three-speed fully synchronized manual transmission was also standard. Convertibles came with courtesy lights. Concours station wagons came only with V-8 power and featured the following standard equipment: Hide-A-Way windshield wipers, power front disc/rear drum brakes, a lighted locking glove box, a dual-action tailgate, a concealed storage compartment, all-vinyl upholstery, a vinyl-coated textured metal cargo floor, G78-14/B bias-belted black sidewall tires, flush-and-dry rocker panels, a cigarette lighter, floor carpeting, a foam front seat and the 307-cid V-8. Three-seat station wagons also included a rear-facing third seat and a power-operated tailgate window.

Model Number	Body/Style Number	Body Type & Seating	Factory Price	Shipping Weight	Production Total
MALIBU SERIES 1D (6-CYL)					
1D	69	4d sedan-6P	$2,801	3,240 lbs.	Note 1
1D	37	2d sport coupe-6P	$2,833	3,194 lbs.	Note 1
MALIBU SERIES 1D (V-8)					
1D	69	4d sedan-6P	$2,891	3,371 lbs.	Note 1
1D	39	4d sport sedan-6P	$2,991	3,438 lbs.	Note 1
1D	37	2d sport coupe-6P	$2,923	3,327 lbs.	Note 1
1D	67	2d convertible-6P	$3,187	3,379 lbs.	Note 1
CONCOURS SERIES 1D (V-8)					
1D	36	4d Concours-6P	$3,244	3,857 lbs.	Note 1
1D	46	4d Concours-9P	$3,351	3,909 lbs.	Note 1

NOTE 1: Individual body style production is not available; see production notes.

MALIBU CONCOURS ESTATE WAGON (V-8) — SERIES 1H

Concours Estate station wagons came only with V-8 power and featured the following standard equipment: door edge guards, wood-grained body side paneling, a wood-grained rear body panel, Hide-A-Way windshield wipers, power front disc/rear drum brakes, a lighted locking glove box, a dual-action tailgate, a concealed storage compartment, all-vinyl upholstery, a vinyl-coated textured metal cargo floor, G78-14/B bias-belted black sidewall tires, flush-and-dry rocker panels, a cigarette lighter, floor carpeting, a foam front seat and a 307-cid 200-hp V-8. Three-seat station wagons also included a rear-facing third seat and a power-operated tailgate window.

Model Number	Body/Style Number	Body Type & Seating	Factory Price	Shipping Weight	Production Total
1H	36	4d wagon-6P	$3,431	3,887 lbs.	Note 1
1H	46	4d wagon-9P	$3,538	3,943 lbs.	Note 1

NOTE 1: Individual body style production is not available; see production notes below.

HEAVY CHEVY — (V-8) — YF3/YF8 OPTION

The Heavy Chevy package was a midyear option for any Chevelle sport coupe. It had a dealer cost of $107.64 and retailed for $138. Ingredients of the package included a black-accented grille, special body side striping, "Heavy Chevy" decals for the hood, front fenders and rear deck, a special domed hood with locking pins and 14 x 6-in. Rallye wheels (with bright lug nuts and center caps). Buyers had a choice of black or white stripes. Only 6,727 cars were fitted with this package, but it is not known if all the cars were of one series or if both Chevelle and Malibu versions were ordered. The list below shows the base prices of the sport coupe in both series, with the retail price of the YF3/YF8 package added.

Model Number	Body/Style Number	Body Type & Seating	Factory Price	Shipping Weight	Production Total
CHEVELLE HEAVY CHEVY MODEL 1C + VF3/VF8 OPTION (V-8)					
1C	37	2d sport coupe-6P	$2,897	3,300 lbs.	Note 1
CHEVELLE MALIBU HEAVY CHEVY 1D + VF3/VF8 OPTION (V-8)					
1D	37	2d sport coupe-6P	$3,061	3,327 lbs.	Note 1

MALIBU SS OPTION — (V-8) SERIES 1D + Z15 OPTION

This year the Super Sport package became Regular Production Option (RPO) Z15 and it was now specifically available only for Malibu sport coupes and convertibles. In addition to regular Malibu equipment, the SS 396 featured power front disc brakes, a black-finished grille, a special domed hood with locking pins, a special heavy-duty Sport suspension, 15 x 7-in. wheels with bright lug nuts, special wheel center caps, wheel trim rings and F60 x 15 wide-oval white lettered tires. There were bold SS emblems at the center of the grille, on the front fender sides behind the wheel opening and on the right side of the black finished rear. The SS package had a dealer cost of $270.66 and a retail price of $350.15.

Model Number	Body/Style Number	Body Type & Seating	Factory Price	Shipping Weight	Production Total
1D	37	2d sport coupe-6P	$3,273	3,407 lbs.	Note 1
1D	67	2d convertible-6P	$3,537	3,452 lbs.	Note 1

NOTE 1: Individual body-style production is not available; see production notes.
NOTE 1 Prices calculated by adding Malibu model base price and SS option price.

MALIBU SS 454 OPTION — SERIES 1D + RPO Z15 OPTION + LS5 OPTION

The Z15 option allowed Malibu V-8 sport coupe or convertible buyers to turn their car into a Super Sport. They could then add the LS5 to make the car an SS 454. The 1972 LS5 version of the 454-cid came only with 270 net hp. Dual exhausts were extra. A cowl induction hood was again optional.

Model Number	Body/Style Number	Body Type & Seating	Factory Price	Shipping Weight	Production Total
1D	37	2d sport coupe-6P	$3,545	3,407 lbs.	Note 1
1D	67	2d convertible-6P	$3,809	3,452 lbs.	Note 1

NOTE 1: Individual body style production is not available; see production notes below.
NOTE 2: Prices calculated by adding Malibu model base prices, SS option price and retail price of LS5 V-8.

PRODUCTION NOTES

NOTE 1 Model-year production (within U.S.) of all 1972 Chevelles was 393,695 units including 25,065 six-cylinder models and 368,630 V-8 models.
NOTE 2 Additional statistics record series production (in the U.S.), in rounded-off figures as follows:

Chevelle (6-cyl)	13,800
Chevelle 300 (V-8)	35,600
Total	**49,400**
Malibu (6-cyl)	8,400
Malibu (V-8)	281,700
Total	**290,100**
Wagons (6-cyl)	3,000
Wagons (V-8)	51,400
Total	**54,400**

(*) Malibu figures include Super Sport optioned models.

NOTE 3 Production by factory (U.S.) was:

Code	Factory	Production	Code	Factory	Production
B	Baltimore	130,574	K	Leeds (Mo.)	90,075
R	Arlington (Tex.)	88,247	L	Van Nuys (LA)	48,924

NOTE 4 Exactly 24,946 cars had the SS option. All were V-8 powered. No body style breakout is available.
NOTE 5 Exactly 5,333 of the SS-optioned cars were Malibu SS 454s. All were V-8 powered. No body style breakout is available.
NOTE 6 Exactly 4,853 Malibu convertibles were built. Some were Malibu and some were Malibu SS models. No breakouts are available.

ENGINES

CHEVELLE BASE 250-CID, 145-HP SIX-CYL: Inline. Overhead-valve. Cast-iron block. Displacement: 250 cid. Bore and stroke: 3.875 x 3.53 in. Compression ratio: 8.5:1. Brake hp: 145 at 4200 rpm. Net brake hp: 110 at 3800 rpm. Taxable hp: 36. Torque: 230 lbs.-ft. at 1600 rpm. Seven main bearings. Hydraulic valve lifters. Crankcase capacity: 4 qt. (add 1 qt. for new filter). Cooling system capacity: 12 qt (add 6 qt. for heater). Carburetor: Rochester one-barrel Model 7028017. Sales code L22. Available standard with three-speed fully synchronized manual transmission and Powerglide automatic transmission.

CHEVELLE BASE 307-CID, 130-HP V-8: Overhead-valve. Cast-iron block and head. Bore and stroke: 3.88 x 3.25 in. Displacement: 307 cid. Compression ratio: 8.50:1. Net brake hp: 130 at 4000 rpm. Taxable hp: 48. Net torque. 230 lbs.-ft. at 2400 rpm. Five main bearings. Hydraulic valve lifters. Crankcase capacity: 4 qt. (add 1 qt. for new filter). Cooling system capacity: 14 qt.; (add 1 qt. for heater). Carburetor: Two-barrel.

CHEVELLE OPTIONAL 350-CID, 165-HP V-8: Overhead-valve. Cast-iron block and head. Bore and stroke: 4.00 x 3.48 in. Displacement: 350 cid. Compression ratio: 8.50:1. Net brake hp: 165 at 4000 rpm. Taxable hp: 51.20. Net torque: 280 lbs.-ft. at 2400 rpm. Five main bearings. Hydraulic valve lifters. Crankcase capacity: 4 qt. (add 1 qt. for new filter). Cooling system capacity: 15 qt. (add 1 qt. for heater). Sales code L65. Carburetor: Two-barrel.

CHEVELLE OPTIONAL 350-CID, 175-HP V-8: Overhead-valve. Cast-iron block and head. Bore and stroke: 4.00 x 3.48 in. Displacement: 350 cid. Compression ratio: 8.50:1. Net brake hp: 175 at 4000 rpm. Taxable hp: 51.20. Net torque: 280 lbs.-ft. at 2400 rpm. Five

This immaculate '72 SS convertible came with a small-block V-8. The SS option could be ordered on any Chevelle V-8.

main bearings. Hydraulic valve lifters. Crankcase capacity: 4 qt. (add 1 qt. for new filter). Cooling system capacity: 15 qt. (add 1 qt. for heater). Sales code: L48. Carburetor: Four-barrel.

CHEVELLE AND MALIBU SS OPTIONAL 396-CID, 240-HP V-8: Overhead-valve. Cast-iron block and head. Bore and stroke: 4.126 x 3.76 in. Displacement: 402 cid (a.k.a. 396 cid). Compression ratio: 8.50:1. Net brake hp: 240 at 4400 rpm. Taxable hp: 54.50. Net torque: 345 lbs.-ft. at 3200 rpm. Five main bearings. Hydraulic valve lifters. Crankcase capacity: 4 qt. (add 1 qt. for new filter). Cooling system capacity: 22 qt. (add 1 qt. for heater). Sales code LS3. Carburetor: Four-barrel.

CHEVELLE MALIBU SS OPTIONAL 454-CID, 270-HP V-8: Overhead-valve. Cast-iron block and head. Bore and stroke: 4.251 x 4.00 in. Displacement: 454 cid. Compression ratio: 8.50:1. Net brake hp: 270 at 4000 rpm. Taxable hp: 57.80. Net torque. 390 lbs.-ft. at 3200 rpm. Five main bearings. Hydraulic valve lifters. Crankcase capacity: 4 qt. (add 1 qt. for new filter). Cooling system capacity: 22 qt. (add 1 qt. for heater). Dual exhaust. Sales code: LS5. Carburetor: Four-barrel.

CHASSIS FEATURES

Wheelbase: (two-door) 112 in; (four-door) 116 in. Overall length: (two-door) 197.5 in; (four-door cars) 201.5 in; (four-door station wagons) 208.3 in. Width: 75.4 in. Height: (sedans) 53.3 in; (coupes) 52.7 in; (convertible) 52.9 in. Front tread: 60 in. Rear tread: 59.9 in. Gas tank capacity: 20 gal. Tires: (six) E78 x 14 two-ply/four-ply rated; (V-8) E78 x 14 two-ply/four-ply rated; (station wagon) G78 x 14 two-ply/four-ply rated. Turn circle: 41 feet. Trunk capacity (sedan) 13.5 cubic feet. Front headroom (sedan): 38.5 in. Rear headroom (sedan): 37.1 in. Front legroom (sedan): 42.8 in. Rear legroom (sedan): 35.1 in. Front hip room (sedan): 59.5 in. Rear hip room (sedan): 59.4 in.

OPTIONS

C60 Four-Season air conditioning, including 61-amp Delcotron generator, heavy-duty radiator and temperature-controlled fan and requiring larger tires with some Chevelles ($397.60). C51 station wagon rear window air deflector ($21). G80 Positraction rear axle (Chevelles $45). ZQ9 performance rear axle on Malibu with standard V-8 and Positraction ($12). YD1 trailering axle ratio with 350-cid V-8s or 402-cid V-8, required heavy-duty suspension and Positraction ($12). Y60 heavy-duty 80-amp battery ($15). A39 Custom Deluxe front seat belts, for convertibles with bucket seats ($12.50). A39 Custom Deluxe front seat belts for convertibles with bench front seats ($14.00). AK1 Custom Deluxe color-keyed seat belts with bench seat and two front shoulder belts for coupes, sedans and two-seat station wagons ($16). AK1 Custom Deluxe color-keyed seat belts with bucket seats and two front shoulder belts for coupes ($14.50). AK1 Custom Deluxe color-keyed seat belts with bench seats and two front shoulder belts for three-seat station wagons ($19). A85 Custom Deluxe front shoulder belts, requires Custom deluxe seat belts for convertibles with bench seats ($26). V30 front and rear bumper guards ($31). V30 front bumper guards only, for station wagons ($15). YF5 California assembly line emissions test released to conform to California registration requirements, not available with 240- or 270-hp V-8s ($15). V55 adjustable station wagon roof carrier ($6). U35 Electric clock in all Chevelle models except El Camino, included with special instrumentation ($16). D55 Console with floor-mounted shift, rear seat courtesy light and luggage compartment light, bucket seats and optional transmission required ($57). C50 rear windshield defroster ($31). AU3 power door locks for two-door models ($44.80). AU3 power door locks for four-door models ($68.50). L65 350-cid two-barrel V-8 engine, except El Camino ($26). L48 350-cid four-barrel V-8 engine (Chevelle $72). LS3 402-cid V-8 engine in Chevelle and Malibu with E78 x 14 tires or Super Sport package and mid-size station wagons ($168). LS5 454-cid V-8 engine in Chevelle or Malibu with Super Sport equipment, heavy-duty battery and Sport suspension ($272). K85 63-amp Delcotron generator for Chevelles, with air conditioning ($5); without air conditioning ($26). A01 all windows tinted ($42). ZL2/YF8 cowl-induction hood for Chevelle or Malibu, includes white or black striping

1972

($154). U14 special instrumentation package for Chevelle or Malibu coupes and convertibles ($82). ZJ9 auxiliary lighting groups with A) ashtray light, B) courtesy light, C) glove box light, D) luggage compartment light, E) underhood light and F) mirror map light; in Chevelle includes A, B, C, D, E and F ($23.50), in Malibu convertibles includes A, D, E and F ($15), in Malibu except convertibles includes A, B, D, E and F ($21), in Concours and Concours Estate station wagons includes A, B, E and F ($17.50), in Greenbrier and Nomad station wagons includes A, B, C, E and F ($21). B37 twin front and rear floor mats ($12). D33 Left-hand outside remote-control mirror ($12). D34 visor vanity mirror (Chevelle $3). B90 window moldings on Chevelle Concours and Concours Estate four-door and station wagon models ($26.35). B90 window moldings (on Chevelle and Malibu sedans $26; on Concours and Concours Estate wagons $26. Two-tone paint with bright metal outline moldings ($31). J50 power drum brakes (Chevelle $46). JL2 power disc brakes ($68). AU3 power door locks system, on two-door models ($45). AU3 power door locks system, on four-door models ($69). N40 power steering ($113). A33 power tailgate window on mid-size two-seat station wagons ($34). V01 heavy-duty radiator with six-cylinder engine ($14). V01 heavy-duty radiator with V-8 engine ($21). U63 AM push-button radio with front antenna ($65). U69 AM/FM radio with front antenna ($135). U79 AM/FM radio with front antenna and stereo, all except El Camino ($233). UM1 AM radio with stereo tape deck ($195). UM2 AM/FM radio with setero tape deck ($363). U80 rear seat speaker ($15). Vinyl roof ($92). K30 cruise control, requires power brakes and Turbo-Hydra-Matic transmission ($62). N33 Comfortilt steering, requires automatic transmission ($44). NK2 Custom black four-spoke steering wheel, not available with N33 ($15). NK4 black four-spoke sport steering wheel ($15). D88 Malibu sport striping package includes sport striping on hood, sport striping on rear deck lid with choice of either black or white stripes available on sport coupe, except with vinyl top covering or white or black painted roof ($77). F40 special front and rear suspension ($17). F41 Sport suspension for Chevelle/Malibu with 240-hp V-8 ($30). BB/AA power convertible top (no cost). M40 Turbo-Hydra-Matic transmission for Chevelle with 165- or 175-hp V-8 ($210). M40 Turbo-Hydra-Matic transmission for Chevelles with 165-, 175- or 240-hp V-8 ($231). M35 Powerglide automatic transmission for six-cylinder Chevelle ($174). M20 wide-range four-speed manual transmission for for Chevelles with 165-, 175- or 240-hp V-8 ($190). M22 special close-ratio four-speed manual transmission ($231). M11 floor-mounted three-speed manual transmission for Chevelles with 165-hp or 175-hp V-8 ($128). MC1 floor-mounted three-speed manual transmission for Chevelles with 240-hp V-8 ($128). A51 vinyl bench seat for Chevelles, except convertible and standard with station wagon ($18). A51 Strato-bucket cloth or vinyl ($133). F01 bright metal wheel covers (26). F02 Custom wheel covers, not available with SS equipment or special performance package ($82). ZJ7 Rallye wheels, including special wheels, hubcaps and trim rings, not available with SS equipment ($44). ZP5 Appearance Guard group with A) front and rear bumper guards, B) door edge guards, C) color-keyed front and rear floor mats and D) visor-vanity mirror; on Concours Estate including A, C and D ($30); on other station wagons including A, B, C and D ($39); on four-door Chevelles including A, B, C and D ($55) and on two-door Chevelles including A, B, C and D ($52). ZQ2 Operating Convenience group with A) electric clock, B) rear window defroster, C) day/night rearview mirror and D) remote-control left-hand outside rearview mirror, on sedans includes A, B, D ($59), on sport coupe with special instrumentation includes B, D ($43), on sport coupe without special instrumentation includes A, B, D ($59), on Malibu SS sport coupe with special instrumentation includes B ($31), on Malibu SS sport coupe without spe-

To turn the 1972 Chevelle into an SS 454, buyers had to purchase the Z15 SS option, then add the LS5 option.

cial instrumentation includes A, B ($47), on Malibu convertible with special instrumentation includes A, B, D ($36), on Malibu convertible without special instrumentation includes A, B, D ($64); on Malibu SS convertible with special instrumentation includes B ($36.90), on Malibu SS convertible without special instrumentation includes A, B ($53.80). Z15 SS equipment package includes power front disc rear drum brakes, a black-finished grille, a special domed hood with locking pins, a remote-control left-hand outside Sport rearview mirror, an SS grille emblem, an SS fender emblem, an SS steering wheel, Sport suspension, 15 x 7-in. wheels with bright lug nuts, special center caps and trim rings, F60 x 15 white lettered tires and function symbols on instrument panel knobs for Malibu sport coupe or convertible with optional V-8 ($350). Specific tire options not listed in source material, but similar to 1971 in content with slightly lower prices.

OPTION INSTALLATION RATES

Automatic transmission (94.8 percent). Four-speed manual transmission (2.5 percent). Standard V-8 engine (38.5 percent). Optional V-8 engine (56.3 percent). six-cylinder engine (5.2 percent). AM radio (86.3 percent). AM/FM radio (7.3 percent). Stereo radio (0.9 percent). Stereo tape (4.3 percent). Air conditioning (62.8 percent). Power steering (92.9 percent). Tilt steering (5 percent). Power drum brakes (42.4 percent). Power front disc brakes (30.2 percent). Power door locks (1.7 percent). All power windows (8.9 percent). Bucket seats (9.8 percent). Vinyl top (44.6 percent). White sidewall tires (87.5 percent). Tinted windshield only (1.8 percent). All tinted glass (78.7 percent). Dual exhaust (3 percent). Positraction (6.4 percent). Optional full wheel covers (49.8 percent). Styled wheels (30.1 percent). Optional clock (11.2 percent). Cruise control (1.9 percent). Based on partial model year production of 357,820 units in the United States only.

HISTORICAL FOOTNOTES

The 1972 Chevelle line had its dealer introduction date on September 23, 1971. John Z. Delorean was general manager of Chevrolet Motor Division at the beginning of the 1972 model year, although F.J. McDonald would soon become the next in line to hold the title. The company had its best sales year ever, up to this point in time, in 1972. Total sales for the calendar year came to 3,188,911 cars and trucks. Calendar-year sales of Chevelles, however, fell slightly to 374,448 cars from 399,510 the previous 12 months. That represented a 4 percent share of total U.S. auto sales, Calendar-year registrations were 298,028 Chevelle passenger cars versus 335,378 the prior year and 45,972 station wagons versus 44,776 the previous year. Despite some damaging strikes, Chevrolet's model-year production hit 2,281,578 cars, the highest since 1965. For all intents and purposes, 1972 was the final year that the Chevelle SS was a true high-performance car. The LS6 V-8 was no longer an official engine option, although enthusiasts could still buy over-the-counter parts and assemble one.

For its 10th birthday, Chevrolet gave its popular mid-size Chevelle new looks, a bit more length and cleaner exhaust, but held over some of its potential to be optioned into a high-performance car. As pointed out in an article titled "Exposing the '73 Chevelle" in a mid-1972 issue of Hot Rod magazine, Chevrolet had more than the usual amount of time to redesign the 1973 Chevelle, because it was originally planned as a 1972 model. However, the rushed birth of the second-generation Camaro and GM's early changeover to no-lead-compatible engines interrupted development of the new Chevelle and made the schedule tight, even though an extra year was taken to get the project done. "There's very little chance of mistaking the '73 Chevelle for anything but a Chevrolet," said Hot Rod. "The tail end carries a hint of the '65 and '66 Impala, and now that the Impala has grown quite a bit, chances are good of the Chevelle taking some of its market."

The Chevelle continued to use a perimeter frame with separate body construction. All Chevelles had the same stance. The wheelbase for coupes was 112 in. and the wheelbase for sedans and wagons was 116 in. There was no convertible and the true two-door hardtop, which Chevy called a sport coupe, was gone as well. In its place was new "Colonnade" styling that met the latest federal vehicle rollover standards. There were pillars separating the front and rear side glass on all models, although the deluxe models had "hardtop-like" door glass with no upper window retention. The cars were also a bit taller than the previous models and about 5 in. longer overall. Passenger models had coil springs at all four corners. All models had impact-resistant front bumpers and were said to be substantially improved in roadability, comfort and styling. Engine availability included a de-tuned version of the 250-cid inline six, a base 307-cid V-8 and two versions of the 350-cid V-8. According to Hot Rod, around mid-1972, Chevrolet was attempting to get the 402- and 454-cid engines certified for California emissions and was having difficulties cleaning up the low-range operation of both big-block V-8s, especially at idle. Ultimately, the 454 was approved as a Chevelle option. The base series was called the Chevelle Deluxe, the one-step-up line used the Malibu name and at the top of the heap was the V-8-only Laguna series. Station wagon offerings included the Deluxe, Malibu, Malibu Estate, Laguna and Laguna Estate, with all offering two- or three-seat configurations. Only the Deluxe two-seat wagon came with a six.

I.D. NUMBERS

VIN embossed on the top left-hand side of the instrument panel and visible through the windshield. The first symbol 1 designates Chevrolet. The second symbol indicates series: C=Chevelle deluxe; D=Chevelle Malibu; E=Chevelle Laguna; G=Chevelle Malibu Estate; H=Laguna Estate. The third and fourth symbols indicate body style: 29=four-door pillared hardtop sedan, 37=two-door pillared hardtop coupe, 35=four-door station wagon and 35/AQ4=four-door station wagon with optional third seat. The fifth symbol indicates engine (net horsepower): D=250-cid 100-hp inline six-cylinder; F=307-cid 115-hp V-8, H=350-cid 145-hp V-8, K=350-cid 175-hp V-8 and X or Y=454-cid 245-hp V-8. The sixth symbol designates the model year: 3=1973. The seventh symbol designates the assembly plant location: B=Baltimore, Maryland; K=Leeds, Missouri; Z=Fremont, California, and R=Arlington, Texas. The last six symbols are the sequential unit production number at the specific factory. The Fisher body tag riveted to the top of the cowl on the left side of the car below the hood provides additional vehicle identification information. The Fisher body STYLE NUMBER (ST) consists of a prefix identifying model year and four or more symbols identifying the series and body style (example: 73-1E37 for a 1973 Laguna Colonnade coupe with a V-8 engine). The BODY NUMBER consists of a prefix designating assembly plant and the sequential unit production number at the specific factory. The TRIM NUMBER (TR) identifies upholstery.

COLORS

(11) Antique White, (19) Tuxedo Black, (24) Light Blue Poly, (26) Dark Blue Poly, (29) Midnight Blue Poly, (42) Dark Green Poly, (44) Light Green Poly, (46) Green-Gold Poly, (48) Midnight Green, (51) Light Yellow, (56) Chamois, (60) Light Copper Poly, (64) Silver Poly, (66) Taupe Poly, (68) Dark Brown Poly, (74) Dark Red Poly, (75) Medium Red Poly, (81) Beige, (86) Bright Orange and (97) Medium Orange. Vinyl tops were available in five colors: AA=White, BB=Black, DD=Medium Blue, FF=Chamois, GG=Medium Green, HH=Dark Red and TT=Light Neutral. Convertible tops came in black or white.

ENGINE CODES

Codes appear on the right side of six-cylinder blocks behind the distributor and right front of V-8 engine blocks. Engine codes for 1973 were: (250-cid six) CCK, CBD, CCA, CCB, CCC and CCD; (307-cid V-8) CHD, CHA, CHB, CHC and CMA; (350 two-barrel V-8) CKM, CKR, CKA, CKL, CKB, CKC and CKK; (350-cid four-barrel V-8) CKH, CKD and CKJ; (454 cid V-8) CWC, CWD, CWR, CWA and CWB.

CHEVELLE DELUXE — (6-CYL/V-8) SERIES 1C

Standard equipment on all 1973 Chevelles included a double-panel steel acoustical roof, seat belts with push-button buckles for all passenger positions, shoulder belts with push-button buckles for driver and right front passenger, two front seat head restraints, an energy-absorbing steering column, passenger-guard door locks, safety door latches and hinges, folding seat back latches, an energy-absorbing padded instrument panel, padded front

The Chevelle redesign originally planned for 1972 finally arrived in 1973 with an elongated body style and the elimination of the convertible and two-door hardtop coupe.

seat back tops, a contoured windshield header, a thick-laminate windshield, padded sun visors, safety armrests, a safety steering wheel, side-guard door beams, a cargo guard luggage compartment, side marker lights and reflectors (front side marker lights flash with directional signals), parking lights that illuminate with the headlights, a flow-through power ventilation system, and inside hood release, a four-way hazard warning flasher, back-up lights, a lane-change feature in the direction signal control, a windshield defroster, windshield washers, dual-speed Hide-A-Way windshield wipers, a wide-view day/night inside rearview mirror (vinyl-edged with shatter-resistant glass and a deflecting support), an inside-the-windshield radio antenna (when a radio was ordered), a cigarette lighter, a left-hand outside rearview mirror, a dual master cylinder manual front disc/rear drum brake system with warning light, a dual-action safety hood latch, an anti-theft ignition key warning buzzer, an anti-theft steering column lock, a windshield radio antenna, full-foam seats, color-keyed vinyl coated rubber flooring, a Delcotron generator, a 250-cid inline six-cylinder engine with 100 net brake hp or a 307-cid two-barrel V-8 with 115 net brake hp and E78-14/B black sidewall bias-belted tires (sixes) or G78-14/B black sidewall bias-belted tires (V-8s). The Chevelle Deluxe station wagon also had a hatchback tailgate with a fixed rear window, a "door ajar" warning light, power front disc/rear drum brakes, full-foam front and rear seats, front and rear armrests, a hidden stowage compartment, and H78-14/B bias-belted black sidewall tires.

Model Number	Body/Style Number	Body Type & Seating	Factory Price	Shipping Weight	Production Total
CHEVELLE DELUXE SERIES 1C (6-CYL)					
1C	29	4d Colonnade-6P	$2,719	3,435 lbs.	Note 1
1C	37	2d Colonnade-6P	$2,743	3,423 lbs.	Note 1
CHEVELLE DELUXE STATION WAGON SERIES 1C (V-8)					
1C	35	4d wagon-6P	$3,106	3,849 lbs.	Note 1
CHEVELLE DELUXE SERIES 1C (V-8)					
1C	29	4d Colonnade-6P	$2,835	3,585 lbs.	Note 1
1C	37	2d Colonnade-6P	$2,860	3,580 lbs.	Note 1
CHEVELLE DELUXE STATION WAGON SERIES 1C (V-8)					
1C	35	4d wagon-6P	$3,198	4,006 lbs.	Note 1
1C	35/AQ4	4d wagon-8P	$3,331	4,054 lbs.	Note 1

NOTE 1: Individual body style production is not available; see production notes.

CHEVELLE MALIBU — (6-CYL/V-8) SERIES 1D

Standard equipment on all 1973 Chevelles included a double-panel steel acoustical roof, seat belts with push-button buckles for all passenger positions, shoulder belts with push-button buckles for driver and right front passenger, two front seat head restraints, an energy-absorbing steering column, passenger-guard door locks, safety door latches and hinges, folding seat back latches, an energy-absorbing padded instrument panel, padded front seat back tops, a contoured windshield header, a thick-laminate windshield, padded sun visors, safety armrests, a safety steering wheel, side-guard door beams, a cargo guard luggage compartment, side marker lights and reflectors (front side marker lights flash with directional signals), parking lights that illuminate with the headlights, a flow-through power ventilation system, and inside hood release, a four-way hazard warning flasher, back-up lights, a lane-change feature in the direction signal control, a windshield defroster, windshield washers, dual-speed Hide-A-Way windshield wipers, a wide-view day/night inside rearview mirror (vinyl-edged with shatter-resistant glass and a deflecting support), an inside-the-windshield radio antenna (when a radio was ordered), a cigarette lighter, a left-hand outside rearview mirror, a dual master cylinder front disc/rear drum brake system with warning light, a dual-action safety hood latch, an anti-theft ignition key warning buzzer, an anti-theft steering column lock, a windshield radio antenna, full-foam seats, color-keyed vinyl coated rubber flooring, a Delcotron generator, a 250-cid inline six-cylinder engine with 100 net brake hp or a 307-cid two-barrel V-8 with 115 net brake hp and E78-14/B black sidewall bias-belted tires (sixes) or G78-14/B black sidewall bias-belted tires (V-8s). In addition to or in place of the above equipment, Chevelle Malibus also featured floor carpeting, a lighted glove box, pattern cloth-and-vinyl seat trim, bright body side moldings, bright rocker panel moldings, bright roof drip moldings, bright wheel opening moldings and a deluxe front seat with a center armrest. The Chevelle Malibu station wagon also had full floor carpeting, a hatchback tailgate with a fixed rear window, a "door ajar" warning light, power front disc/rear drum brakes, full-foam front and rear seats, front and rear armrests, a hidden stowage compartment, a glove box light and H78-14/B bias-belted black sidewall tires. Three-seat wagons also included swing-out rear quarter windows ad a power tailgate switch.

Model Number	Body/Style Number	Body Type & Seating	Factory Price	Shipping Weight	Production Total
CHEVELLE MALIBU SERIES 1D (6-CYL)					
1D	29	4d Colonnade-6P	$2,871	3,477 lbs.	Note 1
1D	37	2d Colonnade-6P	$2,894	3,430 lbs.	Note 1
CHEVELLE MALIBU SERIES 1D (V-8)					
1D	29	4d Colonnade-6P	$2,835	3,585 lbs.	Note 1
1D	37	2d Colonnade-6P	$2,860	3,580 lbs.	Note 1
CHEVELLE MALIBU STATION WAGON SERIES 1D (V-8)					
1D	35	4d sagon-6P	$3,290	4,027 lbs.	Note 1
1D	35/AQ4	4d wagon-8P	$3,423	4,075 lbs.	Note 1

NOTE 1: Individual body style production is not available; see production notes.

CHEVELLE MALIBU SS — (V-8) SERIES 1D + A15

Chevrolet continued to list a Super Sport equipment package on its 1973 options list. The package was coded RPO A15 and was available for the Malibu Colonnade coupe and the station wagon. In addition to or in place of the standard Malibu equipment listed above, the SS equipment package included a black-finished grille with an SS emblem, a remote-control left-hand outside Sport style rearview mirror, a manual right-hand Sport style outside rearview mirror, SS fender emblems, SS door trim, and SS steering wheel, an SS emblem above the rear bumper, bright roof drip moldings, lower body side and wheel opening stripes keyed to the body color, black-accented taillight frames, a special instrument cluster, special front and rear stabilizer bars, 14 x 7-in. Rally wheels with special center caps and trim rings and G70-14 white letter tires. The cost of the SS equipment package was $243 and the prices given below represent the price of the standard-equipped Malibu model plus $243.

1973

Model Number	Body/Style Number	Body Type & Seating	Factory Price	Shipping Weight	Production Total
CHEVELLE MALIBU SERIES 1D + A15 (V-8)					
1D	37	2d Colonnade-6P	$3,103	3,580 lbs.	Note 1
CHEVELLE MALIBU STATION WAGON SERIES 1D + A15 (V-8)					
1D	35	4d wagon-6P	$3,533	4,027 lbs.	Note 1

NOTE 1: Individual body style production is not available; see production notes.

CHEVELLE MALIBU ESTATE — (V-8) SERIES 1G

Standard equipment on all 1973 Chevelles included a double-panel steel acoustical roof, seat belts with push-button buckles for all passenger positions, shoulder belts with push-button buckles for driver and right front passenger, two front seat head restraints, an energy-absorbing steering column, passenger-guard door locks, safety door latches and hinges, folding seat back latches, an energy-absorbing padded instrument panel, padded front seat back tops, a contoured windshield header, a thick-laminate windshield, padded sun visors, safety armrests, a safety steering wheel, side-guard door beams, a cargo guard luggage compartment, side marker lights and reflectors (front side marker lights flash with directional signals), parking lights that illuminate with the headlights, a flow-through power ventilation system, and inside hood release, a four-way hazard warning flasher, back-up lights, a lane-change feature in the direction signal control, a windshield defroster, windshield washers, dual-speed Hide-A-Way windshield wipers, a wide-view day/night inside rearview mirror (vinyl-edged with shatter-resistant glass and a deflecting support), an inside-the-windshield radio antenna (when a radio was ordered), a cigarette lighter, a left-hand outside rearview mirror, a dual master cylinder front disc/rear drum brake system with warning light, a dual-action safety hood latch, an anti-theft ignition key warning buzzer, an anti-theft steering column lock, a windshield radio antenna, full-foam seats, color-keyed vinyl coated rubber flooring, a Delcotron generator, a 250-cid inline six-cylinder engine with 100 net brake hp or a 307-cid two-barrel V-8 with 115 net brake hp and E78-14/B black sidewall bias-belted tires (sixes) or G78-14/B black sidewall bias-belted tires (V-8s). In addition to or in place of the above equipment, the Chevelle Malibu Estate also featured floor carpeting, a lighted glove box, wood grained body side panels, bright rocker panel moldings, bright roof drip moldings, bright wheel opening moldings, a deluxe front seat with a center armrest, full floor carpeting, a hatchback tailgate with a fixed rear window, a "door ajar" warning light, power front disc/rear drum brakes, full-foam front and rear seats, front and rear armrests, a hidden stowage compartment, a glove box light and H78-14/B bias-belted black sidewall tires. Three-seat versions also included swing-out rear quarter windows ad a power tailgate switch.

Model Number	Body/Style Number	Body Type & Seating	Factory Price	Shipping Weight	Production Total
1G	35	4d wagon-6P	$3,475	4,032 lbs.	Note 1
1G	35/AQ4	4d wagon-8P	$3,608	4,080 lbs.	Note 1

NOTE 1: Individual body style production is not available; see production notes.

CHEVELLE LAGUNA — (V-8) SERIES 1E

Chevrolet boasted about the European flair of the distinctive Laguna. The top-of-the line Chevelle was available as a Colonnade coupe, a Colonnade sedan and a four-door station wagon. The latter came with a choice of six- or eight-passenger seating. The Laguna featured a chrome die-cast grille with a distinctive grid pattern insert, horizontal center bars and built-in parking lights. It had a resilient body-color front end and bumper impact strips, its own circular taillights, special interior fabrics, a special steering wheel, wood-grain vinyl interior accents, front door map pockets. Like all 1973 Chevelles, the Laguna included a double-panel steel acoustical roof, seat belts with push-button buckles for all passenger positions, shoulder belts with push-button buckles for driver and right front passenger, two front seat head restraints, an energy-absorbing steering column, passenger-guard door locks, safety door latches and hinges, folding seat back latches, an energy-absorbing padded instrument panel, padded front seat back tops, a contoured windshield header, a thick-laminate windshield, padded sun visors, safety armrests, a safety steering wheel, side-guard door beams, a cargo guard luggage compartment, side marker lights and reflectors (front side marker lights flash with directional signals), parking lights that illuminate with the headlights, a flow-through power ventilation system, and inside hood release, a four-way hazard warning flasher, back-up lights, a lane-change feature in the direction signal control, a windshield defroster, windshield washers, dual-speed Hide-A-Way windshield wipers, a wide-view day/night inside rearview mirror (vinyl-edged with shatter-resistant glass and a deflecting support), an inside-the-windshield radio antenna (when a radio was ordered), a cigarette lighter, a left-hand outside rearview mirror, a dual master cylinder front disc/rear drum brake system with warning light, a dual-action safety hood latch, an anti-theft ignition key warning buzzer, an anti-theft steering column lock, a windshield radio antenna, full-foam seats, color-keyed vinyl coated rubber flooring, a Delcotron generator, a 250-cid inline six-cylinder engine with 100 net brake hp or a 307-cid two-barrel V-8 with 115 net brake hp and E78-14/B black sidewall bias-belted tires (sixes) or G78-14/B black sidewall bias-belted tires (V-8s). In addition to or in place of the above equipment, the Chevelle Laguna station wagon also featured floor carpeting, a lighted glove box, bright body side moldings, bright rocker panel moldings, bright roof drip moldings, bright wheel opening moldings, a deluxe front seat with a center armrest, full floor carpeting, a hatchback tailgate with a fixed rear window, a "door ajar" warning light, power front disc/rear drum brakes, full-foam front and rear seats, front and rear armrests, a hidden stowage compartment, a glove box light and H78-14/B bias-belted black sidewall tires. Three-seat versions also included swing-out rear quarter windows and a power tailgate switch.

Model Number	Body/Style Number	Body Type & Seating	Factory Price	Shipping Weight	Production Total
CHEVELLE LAGUNA SERIES 1E (V-8)					
1E	29	4d Colonnade-6P	$3,179	3,627 lbs.	Note 1
1E	37	2d Colonnade-6P	$3,203	3,678 lbs.	Note 1
CHEVELLE LAGUNA STATION WAGON SERIES 1E (V-8)					
1E	35	4d wagon-6P	$3,483	4,110 lbs.	Note 1
1E	35/AQ4	4d wagon-8P	$3,616	4,158 lbs.	Note 1

NOTE 1: Individual body style production is not available; see production notes.

CHEVELLE LAGUNA ESTATE WAGON (V-8) — SERIES 1H

All 1973 Chevelles came with a double-panel steel acoustical roof, seat belts with push-button buckles for all passenger positions, shoulder belts with push-button buckles for driver and right front passenger, two front seat head restraints, an energy-absorbing steering column, passenger-guard door locks, safety door latches and hinges, folding seat back latches, an energy-absorbing padded instrument panel, padded front seat back tops, a contoured windshield header, a thick-laminate windshield, padded sun visors, safety armrests, a safety steering wheel, side-guard door beams, a cargo guard luggage compartment, side marker lights and reflectors (front side marker lights flash with directional signals), parking lights that illuminate with the headlights, a flow-through power ventilation system, and inside hood release, a four-way hazard warning flasher, back-up lights, a lane-change feature in the direction signal control, a windshield defroster, windshield washers, dual-speed Hide-A-Way windshield wipers, a wide-view day/night inside rearview mirror (vinyl-edged with shatter-resistant glass and a deflecting support), an inside-the-windshield radio antenna (when a radio was ordered), a cigarette lighter, a left-hand outside rearview mirror, a dual master cylinder front disc/rear drum brake system with warning light, a dual-action safety hood latch, an anti-theft ignition key warning buzzer, an anti-theft steering column lock, a windshield radio antenna, full-foam seats, color-keyed vinyl coated rubber flooring, a Delcotron generator, a 250-cid in-line six-cylinder engine with 100 net brake hp or a 307-cid two-barrel V-8 with 115 net brake hp and E78-14/B black sidewall bias-belted tires (sixes) or G78-14/B black sidewall bias-belted tires (V-8s). In addition to or in place of the above equipment, the Chevelle Laguna station wagon also featured floor carpeting, a lighted glove box, bright body side moldings, bright rocker panel moldings, bright roof drip moldings, bright wheel opening moldings, a deluxe front seat with a center armrest, full floor carpeting, a hatchback tailgate with a fixed rear window, a "door ajar" warning light, power front disc/rear drum brakes, full-foam front and rear seats, front and rear armrests, a hidden stowage compartment, a glove box light and H78-14/B bias-belted black sidewall tires. Three-seat versions also included swing-out rear quarter windows ad a power tailgate switch. In addition to or in place of the above equipment, the Chevelle Laguna Estate also featured floor carpeting, a lighted glove box, wood-grained body side panels, bright rocker panel moldings, bright roof drip moldings, bright wheel opening moldings, a deluxe front seat with a center armrest, full floor carpeting, a hatchback tailgate with a fixed rear window, a "door ajar" warning light, power front disc/rear drum brakes, full-foam front and rear seats, front and rear armrests, a hidden stowage compartment, a glove box light and H78-14/B bias-belted black sidewall tires. Three-seat versions also included swing-out rear quarter windows ad a power tailgate switch.

Model Number	Body/Style Number	Body Type & Seating	Factory Price	Shipping Weight	Production Total
LAGUNA ESTATE WAGON SERIES 1H (6-CYL)					
1H	36	4d wagon-6P	$3,662	4,141 lbs.	Note 1
1H	46	4d wagon-9P	$3,795	4,189 lbs.	Note 1

NOTE 1: Individual body-style production is not available; see production notes.

PRODUCTION NOTES

NOTE 1 Model-year production (within U.S.) of all 1973 Chevelles was 386,752 units, including 19,138 six-cylinder models and 367,614 V-8 models.
NOTE 1 Additional statistics record series production (in the U.S.) as follows:

Chevelle (6-cyl)	11,575
Chevelle (V-8)	30,547
Total	42,122
Malibu (6-cyl)	5,693
Malibu (V-8)	223,793
Total	229,486
Laguna (V-8)	56,036
Total	56,036
Wagons (6-cyl)	1,870
Wagons (V-8)	57,238
Total	59,108

(*) Malibu figures include Super Sport optioned models.

NOTE 3 Production by factory (United States) was:

Code	Factory	Production	Code	Factory	Production
B	Baltimore	139,953	K	Leeds (Mo.)	102,197
R	Arlington (Tex.)	52,058	Z	Fremont (Cal.)	34,325

ENGINES

CHEVELLE BASE 350-CID, 100-HP SIX-CYL: Inline. Overhead-valve. Cast-iron block. Displacement: 250 cid. Bore and stroke: 3.875 x 3.53 in.. Compression ratio: 8.25:1. Net brake hp: 100 at 3800 rpm. Taxable hp: 36. Torque: 175 lbs.-ft. at 1600 rpm. Seven main bearings. Hydraulic valve lifters. Crankcase capacity: 4 qt. (add 1 qt. for new filter). Cooling system capacity: 12 qt. (add 6 qt. for heater). Carburetor: Rochester one-barrel Model 7028017. Sales code L22.

CHEVELLE BASE 307-CID, 115-HP V-8: Overhead valve. Cast-iron block and head. Bore and stroke: 3.88 x 3.25 in. Displacement: 307 cid. Compression ratio: 8.50:1. Net brake hp: 115 at 4000 rpm. Taxable hp: 48. Net torque. 205 lbs.-ft. at 2000 rpm. Five main bearings. Hydraulic valve lifters. Crankcase capacity: 4 qt. (add 1 qt. for new filter). Cooling system capacity: 15 qt. (add 1 qt. for heater). Carburetor: Two-barrel.

LAGUNA AND LAGUNA ESTATE BASE 350-CID, 145-HP V-8; (OPTIONAL OTHER CHEVELLES): Overhead-valve. Cast-iron block and head. Bore and stroke: 4.00 x 3.48 in. Displacement: 350 cid. Compression ratio: 8.50:1. Net brake hp: 145 at 4000 rpm. Taxable hp: 51.20. Net torque: 255 lbs.-ft. at 2400 rpm. Five main bearings. Hydraulic valve lifters. Crankcase capacity: 4 qt. (add 1 qt. for new filter). Cooling system capacity: (Nova) 17 qt.; (Chevrolet) 16 qt. (others) 15 qt. (add 1 qt. for heater). Carburetor: Two-barrel. Sales code L65.

CHEVELLE OPTIONAL 350-CID, 175-HP V-8: Overhead-valve. Cast-iron block and head. Bore and stroke: 4.00 x 3.48 in. Displacement: 350 cid. Compression ratio: 8.50:1. Net brake hp: 175 at 4000 rpm. Taxable hp: 51.20. Net torque: 270 lbs.-ft. at 2400 rpm. Five main bearings. Hydraulic valve lifters. Crankcase capacity: 4 qt. (add 1 qt. for new filter). Cooling system capacity: (Nova) 17 qt.; (Chevrolet) 16 qt. (others) 15 qt. (add 1 qt. for heater). Carburetor: Four-barrel. Sales code L48.

CHEVELLE OPTIONAL 454-CID, 245-HP V-8:

Overhead-valve. Cast-iron block and head. Bore and stroke: 4.25 x 4.00 in. Displacement: 454 cid. Compression ratio: 8.50:1. Net brake hp: 245 at 4000 rpm. Taxable hp: 57.80. Net torque: 375 lbs.-ft. at 2800 rpm. Five main bearings. Hydraulic valve lifters. Crankcase capacity: 4 qt. (add 1 qt. for new filter). Cooling system capacity: (Chevelle, Monte Carlo) 22 qt.; (Chevrolet) 23 qt. (add 1 qt. for heater). Dual exhaust. Carburetor: Four-barrel. Sales code LS5.

CHASSIS FEATURES

Wheelbase: (two-door) 112 in.; (four-door) 116 in. Overall length: (two-door) 202.9 in.; (four-door cars) 206.9 in.; (four-door station wagons) 213.3 in. Width: 76.6 in. Height: (sedans) 53.8 in.; (coupes) 53.1 in.; (wagon) 55.7 in. Front tread: 60 in. Rear tread: 59.9 in. Gas tank capacity: 20 gal. Tires: (six) E78 x 14 two-ply/four-ply rated; (V-8) G78 x 14 two-ply/four-ply rated; (station wagon) H78 x 14 two-ply/four-ply rated.

OPTIONS

C60 Four-Season air conditioning, including 61-amp Delcotron generator, heavy-duty radiator and temperature-controlled fan for Chevelle six-cylinder ($461). C60 Four-Season air conditioning, including 61-amp Delcotron generator, heavy-duty radiator and temperature-controlled fan and requiring larger tires with some Chevelles, not available with 454 with dual exhausts ($412). C51 station wagon rear window air deflector ($21). G80 Positraction rear axle (Chevelles $45). G94 special axle ratio ($12). YD1 trailering axle ratio ($12). UA1 heavy-duty 80-amp battery ($14). AK1 Custom Deluxe color-keyed seat belts with bench seat and two front shoulder belts for coupes, sedans and two-seat station wagons ($13.50). AN7 Strato-bucket swivel seats. V30 front and rear bumper guards ($31). V30 front bumper guards only, for station wagons ($15). YF5 California assembly line emissions test released to conform to California registration requirements ($20). D55 Console with floor-mounted shift, rear seat courtesy light and luggage compartment light, bucket seats and optional transmission required ($59). C50 rear windshield defroster for passenger car ($33). C50 rear windshield defroster for station wagon ($38). U35 electric clock ($17). L65 350-cid two-barrel V-8 engine ($30). L48 350-cid four-barrel V-8 engine ($76). LS5 454-cid V-8 ($273). K76 61-amp Delcotron generator ($26). A01 All windows tinted ($43). U14 special instrumentation package ($88). V55 station wagon luggage carrier ($61). D33 left-hand remote-control outside rearview mirror ($13). B84 bright body side moldings ($32.50). J50 power drum brakes, standard on station wagons ($49). JL2 power disc brakes ($71). AU3 power door locks system, on two-door models ($47). AU3 power door locks system, on four-door models ($71). A42 six-way power bench seat ($103). ZJ9 auxiliary lighting groups with A) ash tray light, B) courtesy light, C) glove box light, D) luggage compartment light, E) under-hood light, F) mirror map light and G) dome reading lamp, in Chevelle includes A, B, C, D, E, F and G ($31), in Malibu convertibles includes A, C, D, E, F and G ($27.50), in Malibu two-seat station wagons includes A, B, C, D, E, F and G ($31), in Malibu Estate and Laguna Estate three-seat station wagons includes A, B, E and

The SS package for 1973 included an SS steering wheel, special instrument cluster, and remote-control driver's side Sport mirror. This car also had an optional swivel driver's seat.

F ($17.50). B37 twin front and rear floor mats ($12). D33 left-hand outside remote-control mirror ($12). D34 visor vanity mirror ($3). D35 remote-control Sport style left-hand outside rearview mirror ($26). B84 body side moldings, not available with SS equipment package ($33). Two-tone paint with bright metal outline moldings ($31). N40 power steering ($113). A31 power windows, coupes ($75). A31 power windows, sedans and wagons ($103). CA1 electric sky roof ($325). A33 power tailgate window on station wagons ($34). AU6 power station wagon tailgate release ($14). V01 heavy-duty radiator with V-8 engine ($21). U63 AM push-button radio with front antenna ($65). U69 AM/FM radio with front antenna ($135). U59 AM/FM stereo radio ($233). UM1 AM radio with stereo tape deck ($195). UM2 AM/FM radio with setero tape deck ($363). U80 rear seat speaker ($15). C08 vinyl roof ($92). AN7 swing-out Strato bucket seats in Laguna ($97). AN7 swing-out Strato bucket seats in other Chevelles ($133). K30 cruise control, requires power brakes and Turbo-Hydra-Matic transmission ($62). N35 Comfortilt steering, requires automatic transmission ($44). F40 special front and rear suspension ($17). M40 Turbo-Hydra-Matic transmission for Chevelle without 454-cid V-8 ($210). F40 special front and rear suspension ($17). M40 Turbo-Hydra-Matic transmission for Chevelle with 454-cid V-8 ($231). M21 close-ratio four-speed manual transmission ($190). Vinyl bench

CHEVELLE

seats in coupes and sedans ($18 and standard in station wagons). P01 bright metal wheel covers ($26). N95 wire wheel covers ($82). ZJ7 Rallye wheels, including special wheels, hub caps and trim rings ($44). PE1 Turbine I wheels ($84.50-$110). A20 swing-out rear side windows on station wagons ($40). A15 Super Sport equipment package ($243). Specific tire options not available, but similar to 1974.

OPTION INSTALLATION RATES

Automatic transmission (96.9 percent). Four-speed manual transmission (0.8 percent). Standard V-8 engine (27.1 percent). Optional V-8 engine (67.9 percent). six-cylinder engine (5 percent). AM radio (74.7 percent). AM/FM radio (10.1 percent). Stereo radio (1.5 percent). Stereo tape (5.1 percent). Air conditioning (66.2 percent). Power steering (96.4 percent). Tilt steering (9.2 percent). Power drum brakes (10 percent). Power front disc brakes (21 percent). Power door locks (2.1 percent). All power windows (8.9 percent). Sun roof (0.3 percent). Bucket seats (12.3 percent). Vinyl top (44.6 percent). Tinted windshield only (2.8 percent). All tinted glass (72.8 percent). Dual exhaust (11.2 percent). Positraction (4.5 percent). Standard wheel covers (15.1 percent). Optional full wheel covers (55.6 percent). Styled wheels (9.2 percent). Optional clock (15.5 percent). Cruise control (1.9 percent). Power rear window defogger (9.9 percent). Remote-control side-view mirror (41 percent). Based on partial model-year production of 386,752 units in the United States only.

HISTORICAL FOOTNOTES

The 1973 Chevelle line had its dealer introduction date on September 21, 1972. F.J. McDonald was general manager of Chevrolet Motor Division. Total sales included 2,334,135 cars and trucks. Calendar-year sales of Chevelles dropped to 264,594 cars from 374,448 the previous 12 months. The Chevelle contributed a 3.8 percent share of total U.S. auto sales, Calendar-year registrations were 312,420 Chevelle passenger cars versus 320,400 the prior year and 52,463 station wagons versus 49,994 the previous year.

The Laguna became the Laguna Type S-3 for 1974. This one is a Colonnade hardtop coupe.

Chevrolet introduced its 1974 mid-size lineup on September 20, 1973. A handsome new grille characterized the base Malibu models and was also used on the new Malibu Classics, which were considered to be top-of-the-line offerings. It had a neo-classic look that resembled a widened Mercedes-Benz grille. Against a background of fine vertical and horizontal bars the designers place two horizontal moldings that divided the grille into three segments and a single vertical center molding that split the three segments into six. The grille no longer extended below the taillights, which were round-lens units set into bright square housings with rounded corners.

The Laguna became the single-model Laguna Type S-3, which continued to feature a distinctive grille that was fully surrounded by a body-color front panel. It had thin horizontal and vertical members in a wider texture than the standard grille. Square parking lamps sat on either end of a prominent horizontal center bar that had a "Laguna Type S-3" badge at its middle. The round tail lamps of 1973 were replaced with basically rectangular units on either side at the rear. The 1973 rear bumper, which rose up over the license plate at its center, was replaced with a straight-across style for 1974. This year the license plate was housed in the rear body panel, above the center of the bumper.

The 307-cid V-8 was dropped, but a 400-cid V-8

1974

The 1974 Chevelles, this is a Malibu coupe, were recognizable by their stylish new grille assembly.

returned. In addition, buyers could get the inline six, two de-tuned 350-cid V-8s or a 454-cid "big-block" V-8 with 245 hp.

I.D. NUMBERS

VIN embossed on the top left-hand side of the instrument panel and visible through the windshield. The first symbol 1 designates Chevrolet. The second symbol indicates series: C=Malibu, D=Malibu Classic, E=Laguna Type S-3 and G=Malibu Classic Estate. The third and fourth symbols indicate body style: 29=four-door pillared hardtop sedan, 37=two-door pillared hardtop coupe and 35=four-door station wagon. The fifth symbol indicates engine (net hp): D=250-cid 100-hp inline six-cylinder, H=350-cid 145-hp V-8, L=350-cid 160-hp V-8, R=400-cid 180-hp V-8, U=400-cid 180-hp V-8 and Y=454-cid 235-hp V-8. The sixth symbol designates the model year: 4=1974. The seventh symbol designates the assembly plant location: B=Baltimore, Maryland, D=Doraville, Georgia, K=Leeds, Missouri, Z=Fremont, California, R=Arlington, Texas and 1=Oshawa, Canada. The last six symbols are the sequential unit production number at the specific factory. The Fisher body tag riveted to the top of the cowl on the left side of the car below the hood provides additional vehicle identification information. The Fisher Body STYLE NUMBER (ST) consists of a prefix identifying model year and four or more symbols identifying the series and body style (example: 74-1E37 for a 1974 Laguna Type S-3 Colonnade coupe with a V-8 engine). The BODY NUMBER consists of a prefix designating assembly plant and the sequential unit production number at the specific factory. The TRIM NUMBER (TR) identifies upholstery.

COLORS

(11) Antique White, (19) Tuxedo Black, (24) Light Blue Poly, (26) Bright Blue Poly, (29) Midnight Blue Poly, (36) Aqua Blue Poly, (40) Lime-Yellow, (44) Medium Green Poly, (46) Bright Green Poly, (49) Medium Dark Green Poly, (50) Cream Beige, (51) Bright Yellow, (53) Bright Gold Poly, (55) Sandstone, (59) Golden Brown Poly, (64) Silver Poly, (66) Bronze Poly, (68) Dark Brown Poly, (69) Dark Taupe Poly, (74) Medium Red Poly, (75) Medium Red and (86) Bright Orange. Vinyl tops were available in: AA=White, BB=Black, DD=Medium Blue, EE=Cream Beige, FF=Brown, GG=Medium Green, HH=Dark Red, LL=Russet, RR=Medium Saddle and WW=Silver Taupe.

CHEVELLE

ENGINE CODES

Codes appear on the right side of six-cylinder blocks behind the distributor and right front of V-8 engine blocks. Engine codes for 1974 were: (250-cid 100-hp six) CCX, CCR and CCW; (350-cid 145-hp V-8 two-barrel V-8) CMC and CMR; (350-cid 160-hp four-barrel V-8) CKH and CKD; (400-cid 150-hp V-8) CSU, CSX and CTA; (400-cid 180-hp V-8) CTC; (454-cid 235-hp V-8) CWA, CWX, CWD, CXM, CXR and CXS.

CHEVELLE MALIBU — (6-CYL/V-8) SERIES 1C

Standard equipment on 1974 Malibus included all federally mandated safety features and anti-pollution equipment, a flow-through power ventilation system, a double-panel steel acoustical roof, an inside hood latch release, manual front disc brakes, side marker lights and reflectors, a defroster, dual speed windshield wipers, a windshield washer system, an inside day/night rearview mirror, a left-hand outside rearview mirror, a 100-hp six-cylinder engine or a two-barrel 350-cid V-8, E78-14/B black sidewall bias-belted tires on sixes or G78-14/B black sidewall bias-belted tires on V-8s, full foam seats, color-keyed vinyl coated rubber flooring, a cigar lighter, Hide-A-Way wipers, a windshield antenna (when an optional radio was ordered) and a Delcotron generator. Malibu station wagons had, in addition to or instead of the above equipment, a base V-8 engine, a hatchback tailgate with fixed rear window and a "door ajar" warning light, power front disc/rear drum brakes, full-foam seats front and rear, front and rear armrests, a hidden stowage compartment and H78-14/B bias-belted black sidewall tires. Three-seat wagons also had swing-out rear quarter windows and a power tailgate switch.

Model Number	Body/Style Number	Body Type & Seating	Factory Price	Shipping Weight	Production Total
CHEVELLE MALIBU SERIES 1C (6-CYL)					
1C	29	4d Colonnade-6P	$3,049	3,638 lbs.	Note 1
1C	37	2d Colonnade-6P	$3,054	3,573 lbs.	Note 1
CHEVELLE MALIBU SERIES 1C (V-8)					
1C	29	4d Colonnade-6P	$3,340	3,788 lbs.	Note 1
1C	37	2d Colonnade-6P	$3,345	3,723 lbs.	Note 1
CHEVELLE MALIBU STATION WAGON SERIES 1C (V-8)					
1C	35	4d wagon-6P	$3,701	4,191 lbs.	Note 1
1C	35/AQ4	4d wagon-8P	$3,834	4,223 lbs.	Note 1

NOTE 1: Individual body style production is not available; see production notes below.

CHEVELLE MALIBU CLASSIC (6-CYL/V-8) — SERIES 1D

The Malibu Classic line was considered the top-rung series for mid-sized 1974 Chevrolets. A new die-cast metal grille set this trim level apart. A new offering in this series was the Colonnade Coupe with a high-styled landau roof treatment. This featured a smaller rear quarter window than the regular Colonnade coupe. Standard equipment on all 1974 Malibus included all federally mandated safety features and anti-pollution equipment, a flow-through power ventilation system, a double-panel steel acoustical roof, an inside hood latch release, manual front disc brakes, side marker lights and reflectors, a defroster, dual speed windshield wipers, a windshield washer system, an inside day/night rearview mirror, a left-hand outside rearview mirror, a 100-hp six-cylinder engine or a two-barrel 350-cid V-8, E78-14/B black sidewall bias-belted tires on sixes or G78-14/B black sidewall bias-belted tires on V-8s, full foam seats, color-keyed vinyl coated rubber flooring, a cigar lighter, Hide-A-Way wipers, a windshield antenna (when an optional radio was ordered) and a Delcotron generator. In addition to or in place of the above, the Malibu Classic models featured floor carpeting, a lighted glove box, mixed pattern cloth-and-vinyl upholstery, bright body side moldings, bright roof drip moldings, bright wheel opening moldings and a deluxe front seat with armrest. All 1974 Malibu station wagons had, in addition to or instead of the standard Malibu equipment, a base V-8 engine, a hatchback tailgate with fixed rear window and a "door ajar" warning light, power front disc/rear drum brakes, full-foam seats front and rear, front and rear armrests, a hidden stowage compartment and H78-14/B bias-belted black sidewall tires. Malibu Classic station wagons also had bumper parking lights, bright radiator grille outline moldings, bright lower body sill moldings and bright hubcaps. All three-seat wagons added swing-out rear quarter windows and a power tailgate switch.

Model Number	Body/Style Number	Body Type & Seating	Factory Price	Shipping Weight	Production Total
CHEVELLE MALIBU CLASSIC SERIES 1D (6-CYL)					
1D	29	4d Colonnade-6P	$3,304	3,695 lbs.	Note 1
1D	37	2d Colonnade-6P	$3,307	3,609 lbs.	Note 1
1D	37	2d Landau-6P	$3,518	3,609 lbs.	Note 1
CHEVELLE MALIBU CLASSIC SERIES 1D (V-8)					
1D	29	4d Colonnade-6P	$3,595	3,845 lbs.	Note 1
1D	37	2d Colonnade-6P	$3,598	3,759 lbs.	Note 1
1D	37	2d Landau-6P	$3,800	3,759 lbs.	Note 1
CHEVELLE MALIBU CLASSIC STATION WAGON SERIES 1D (V-8)					
1D	35	4d wagon-6P	$4,118	4,283 lbs.	Note 1
1D	35/AQ4	4d wagon-8P	$4,251	4,315 lbs.	Note 1

NOTE 1: Individual body style production not available; see production notes.

CHEVELLE MALIBU CLASSIC ESTATE (V-8) — SERIES 1D

The Malibu Classic Estate was a richer version of the Malibu Classic station wagon which had the characteristic exterior wood-grain paneling to set it apart from its siblings. Its equipment list started with the features that were standard on all 1974 mid-sized Chevrolets, such as federally mandated safety features and anti-pollution equipment, a flow-through power ventilation system, a double-panel steel acoustical roof, an inside hood latch release, manual front disc brakes, side marker lights and reflectors, a defroster, dual speed windshield wipers, a windshield washer system, an inside day/night rearview mirror, a left-hand outside rearview mirror, a 100-hp six-cylinder engine or a two-barrel 350-cid V-8, E78-14/B black sidewall bias-belted tires on sixes or G78-14/B black sidewall bias-belted tires on V-8s, full foam seats, color-keyed vinyl coated rubber flooring, a cigar lighter, Hide-A-Way wipers, a windshield antenna (when an optional radio was ordered) and a Delcotron generator. It also included the Malibu Classic array such as floor carpeting, a lighted glove box, mixed pattern cloth-and-vinyl upholstery, bright body side moldings, bright roof drip moldings, bright wheel opening moldings and a deluxe front seat with armrest. Like all 1974 Malibu station wagons it also had a base V-8 engine, a hatchback tailgate with fixed rear window and a "door ajar" warning light, power front disc/rear drum brakes, full-foam seats front and rear, front and rear armrests, a hidden stowage compartment and H78-14/B bias-belted black sidewall tires. In addition, Malibu Classic station wagon features like bumper parking lights, bright radiator grille outline moldings, bright lower body sill moldings and bright hubcaps were standard. Naturally, this top-of-the-line hauler had richer interior appointments and that wood-look exterior trim. It was available in a three-seat version that included swing-out rear quarter windows and a power tailgate switch.

Model Number	Body/Style Number	Body Type & Seating	Factory Price	Shipping Weight	Production Total
1G	35	4d wagon-6P	$4,291	4,306 lbs.	Note 1
1G	35/AQ4	4d wagon-8P	$4,424	4,338 lbs.	Note 1

NOTE 1: Individual body style production is not available; see production notes.

CHEVELLE LAGUNA TYPE S-3 — (V-8) SERIES 1E

The Euro-styled Laguna became the Laguna Type S-3 high-performance Colonnade coupe in 1974. Sedan and station wagons using the Laguna name were dropped and the coupe was given a much sportier look than it had in 1973. The Laguna Type S-3 standard equipment list now included a handling package, a vinyl top, opera windows, sporty body side tape stripes and contrasting finish along the lower body sides. The special front end featured a molded body-color urethane front panel surrounding a chrome die-cast grille with a distinctive grid pattern insert. A horizontal center bars ran between the built-in parking lights and carried a Laguna Type S-3 badge in its center. Other Laguna Type S-3 equipment included bumper impact strips, new horizontal rectangular taillights, special interior fabrics, a special steering wheel, wood-grain vinyl interior accents, front door map pockets. Like all 1974 mid-sized Chevrolets, the Laguna Type S-3 had all federally mandated safety features and anti-pollution equipment, a flow-through power ventilation system, a double-panel steel acoustical roof, an inside hood latch release, manual front disc brakes, side marker lights and reflectors, a defroster, dual speed windshield wipers, a windshield washer system, an inside day/night rearview mirror, a left-hand outside rearview mirror, full foam seats, a cigar lighter, Hide-A-Way wipers, a windshield antenna (when an optional radio was ordered) and a Delcotron generator. A 350-cid two-barrel V-8 engine was standard, along with GR70-15/B steel-belted radial tires.

Model Number	Body/Style Number	Body Type & Seating	Factory Price	Shipping Weight	Production Total
1E	37	2d Colonnade-6P	$3,723	3,951 lbs.	21,902

PRODUCTION NOTES

NOTE 1 Model-year production of all 1974 Chevelles was 362,492 units including 36,128 six-cylinder models and 326,364 V-8 models.

NOTE 1 Additional statistics record series production as follows:

Malibu (6-cyl)	27,188
Malibu (V-8)	64,424
Total	91,612
Malibu Classic (6-cyl)	8,940
Malibu (V-8)	195,930
Total	204,870
Laguna (V-8)	21,902
Total	21,902
Wagons (V-8)	44,108
Total	44,108

NOTE 3 Production by factory (United States only) was:

Code	Factory	Production	Code	Factory	Production
B	Baltimore	148,001	D	Doraville, Ga.	26,426
K	Leeds (Mo.)	34,146	R	Arlington (Tex.)	50,879
Z	Fremont (Cal.)	32,306			

ENGINES

CHEVELLE BASE 250-CID, 100-HP SIX-CYL: Inline. Overhead-valve. Cast-iron block. Displacement: 250 cid. Bore and stroke: 3.875 x 3.53 in. Compression ratio: 8.25:1. Net brake hp: 100 at 3800 rpm. Taxable hp: 36. Torque: 175 lbs.-ft. at 1600 rpm. Seven main bearings. Hydraulic valve lifters. Crankcase capacity: 4 qt. (add 1 qt. for new filter). Cooling system capacity: 12 qt (add 6 qt. for heater). Carburetor: Rochester one-barrel Model 7028017. Sales code L22.

CHEVELLE BASE 350-CID, 145-HP V-8: Overhead-valve. Cast-iron block and head. Bore and stroke: 4.00 x 3.48 in. Displacement: 350 cid. Compression ratio: 8.50:1. Net brake hp: 145 at 3600 rpm. Taxable hp: 51.20. Net torque: 250 lbs.-ft. at 2200 rpm. Five main bearings. Hydraulic valve lifters. Crankcase capacity: 4 qt. (add 1 qt. for new filter). Cooling system capacity with heater: 18 qt. Carburetor: Two-barrel. Sales code L65.

CHEVELLE OPTIONAL 400-CID, 150-HP V-8: Overhead valve. Cast-iron block and head. Bore and stroke: 4.13 x 3.75 in. Displacement: 400 cid. Compression ratio: 8.50:1. Net brake hp: 150 at 3200 rpm. Taxable hp: 54.40. Net torque. 295 lbs.-ft. at 2000 rpm. Five main bearings. Hydraulic valve lifters. Crankcase capacity: 4 qt. (add 1 qt. for new filter). Cooling system capacity with heater: (Chevrolet) 16 qt.; (others) 18 qt. Carburetor: Two-barrel. Sales code LF6.

CHEVELLE OPTIONAL 350-CID, 160-HP V-8: Overhead-valve. Cast-iron block and head. Bore and stroke: 4.00 x 3.48 in. Displacement: 350 cid. Compression ratio: 8.50:1. Net brake hp: 160 at 3800 rpm. Taxable hp: 51.20. Net torque: 250 lbs.-ft. at 2400 rpm. Five main bearings. Hydraulic valve lifters. Crankcase capacity: 4 qt. (add 1 qt. for new filter). Cooling system capacity with heater: (Chevrolet) 16 qt.; (Others) 18 qt. Carburetor: Four-barrel. Sales code: LM1.

CHEVELLE OPTIONAL 400-CID, 180-HP V-8: Overhead-valve. Cast-iron block and head. Bore and stroke: 4.13 x 3.75 in. Displacement: 400 cid. Compression ratio: 8.50:1. Net brake hp: 180 at 3800 rpm. Taxable hp: 54.40. Net torque: 290 lbs.-ft. at 2400 rpm. Five main bearings. Hydraulic valve lifters. Crankcase capacity: 4 qt. (add 1 qt. for new filter). Cooling system capacity with heater: 16.5 qt. Carburetor: Four-barrel. Sales code LT4.

CHEVELLE OPTIONAL 454 V-8: Overhead-valve. Cast-iron block and head. Bore and stroke: 4.25 x 4.00 in. Displacement: 454 cid. Compression ratio: 8.50:1. Net brake hp: 235 at 4000 rpm. Taxable hp: 57.80. Net torque. 360 lbs.-ft. at 2800 rpm. Five main bearings. Hydraulic valve lifters. Crankcase capacity: 5 qt. (add 1 qt. for new filter). Cooling system capacity with heater: 23 qt. Dual exhaust. Carburetor: Four-barrel. Sales code LS4.

CHASSIS FEATURES

Wheelbase: (two-door) 112 in.; (four-door) 116 in. Overall length: (two-door) 202.9 in. (four-door cars) 206.9 in.; (four-door station wagons) 213.3 in. Width: 76.6 in. Height: (sedans) 53.8 in. (coupes) 53.1 in. (wagon) 55.7 in. Front tread: 60 in. Rear tread: 59.9 in. Gas tank capacity: 20 gal. Tires: (six) E78 x 14 two-ply/four-ply rated; (V-8) G78 x 14 two-ply/four-ply rated; (station wagon) H78 x 14 two-ply/four-ply rated.

OPTIONS

C60 Four-Season air conditioning, including 61-amp Delcotron generator, heavy-duty radiator and temperature-controlled fan for Chevelle six-cylinder ($461). C60 Four-Season air conditioning, including 61-amp Delcotron generator, heavy-duty radiator and temperature-controlled fan and requiring larger tires with some Chevelles, not available with 454 with dual exhausts ($412). C51 station wagon rear window air deflector ($21). G80 Positraction rear axle (Chevelles $45). G94 special axle ratio ($12). YD1 trailering axle ratio ($12). UA1 heavy-duty 80-amp battery ($14). AK1 Custom Deluxe color-keyed seat belts with bench seat and two front shoulder belts for coupes, sedans and two-seat station wagons ($13.50). V30 front and rear bumper guards ($31). V30 front bumper guards only, for station wagons ($15). YF5 California assembly line emissions test released to conform to California registration requirements ($20). D55 Console with floor-mounted shift, rear seat courtesy light and luggage compartment light, bucket seats and optional transmission required ($59). C50 rear windshield defroster for passenger car ($33). C50 rear windshield defroster for station wagon ($38). U35 electric clock ($17). L65 350-cid two-barrel V-8 engine ($30). L48 350-cid four-barrel V-8 engine ($76). LS5 454-cid V-8 ($273). K76 61-amp Delcotron generator ($26). A01 All windows tinted ($43). U14 special instrumentation package ($88). V55 station wagon luggage carrier ($61). D33 left-hand remote-control outside rearview mirror ($13). B84 bright body side moldings ($32.50). J50 power drum brakes, standard on station wagons ($49). JL2 power disc brakes ($71). AN7 Strato-bucket swivel seats. AU3 power door locks system, on two-door models ($47). AU3 power door locks system, on four-door models ($71). A42 six-way power bench seat ($103). ZJ9 auxiliary lighting groups with A) ash tray light, B) courtesy light, C) glove box light, D) luggage compartment light, E) under hood light, F) mirror map light and G) dome reading lamp, in Chevelle includes A, B, C, D, E, F and G ($31), in Malibu convertibles includes A, C, D, E, F and G ($27.50), in Malibu two-seat station wagons includes A, B, C, D, E, F and G ($31), in Malibu Estate and Laguna Estate three-seat station wagons includes A, B, E and F ($17.50). B37 twin front and rear floor mats ($12). D33 left-hand outside remote-control mirror ($12). D34 visor vanity mirror ($3). D35 remote-control Sport style left-hand outside rearview mirror ($26). B84 body side moldings, not available with SS equipment package)$33). Two-tone paint with bright metal outline moldings ($31). N40 power steering ($113). A31 power windows, coupes ($75). A31 power windows, sedans and wagons ($103). CA1 electric sky roof ($325). A33 power tailgate window on station wagons ($34). AU6 power station wagon tailgate release ($14). V01 heavy-duty radiator with V-8 engine ($21). U63 AM push-button radio with front antenna ($65). U69 AM/FM radio with front antenna ($135). U59 AM/FM stereo radio ($233). UM1 AM radio with stereo tape deck ($195). UM2 AM/FM radio with setero tape deck ($363). U80 rear seat speaker ($15). C08 vinyl roof ($92). AN7 swing-out Strato bucket seats in Laguna ($97). AN7 swing-out Strato bucket seats in other Chevelles ($133). K30 cruise control, requires power brakes and Turbo-Hydra-Matic transmission ($62). N35 Comfortilt steering, requires automatic transmission ($44). F40 special front and rear suspension ($17). M40 Turbo-Hydra-Matic transmission for Chevelle without 454-cid V-8 ($210). F40 special front and rear suspension ($17). M40 Turbo-Hydra-Matic

The Malibu, Malibu Classic, and Laguna Type S-3 line for 1974.

transmission for Chevelle with 454-cid V-8 ($231). M21 close-ratio four-speed manual transmission ($190). Vinyl bench seats in coupes and sedans ($18 and standard in station wagons). P01 bright metal wheel covers ($26). N95 wire wheel covers ($82). ZJ7 Rally wheels, including special wheels, hubcaps and trim rings ($44). PE1 Turbine I wheels ($84.50-$110). A20 swing-out rear side windows on station wagons ($40). QEH E78-14/B white-stripe bias-ply tires replacing E78-14/B black sidewall bias-ply tires on six-cylinder Malibu ($28). QGL G78-14/B white stripe bias-ply tires replacing E78 x 14/B black sidewall bias-ply tires on six-cylinder Malibu ($66.75). QGL G78-14/B white stripe bias-ply tires replacing G78-14/B black sidewall bias-ply tires on Malibu V-8 passenger cars ($32). QGF G70-14/B white-stripe bias-ply tires replacing G78-14/B black sidewall bias-ply tires on Malibu V-8 passenger cars ($61.75). QHF H78-14/B white-stripe bias-ply tires replacing G78-14/B black sidewall bias-ply tires on Malibu V-8 passenger cars ($58.65). QHE H78-14/B black sidewall bias-ply tires replacing G78-14/B black sidewall bias-ply tires on Malibu V-8 passenger cars ($24.65). QDR GR78-15/B white-stripe steel-belted radial tires replacing G78-14/B black sidewall bias-ply tires on Malibu V-8 passenger cars ($134.10). QRN GR70-15/B black sidewall steel-belted radial tires replacing G78-14/B black sidewall bias-ply tires on Malibu V-8 passenger cars ($143.15). QRV HR70-15/B black sidewall steel-belted radial tires replacing G78-14/B black sidewall bias-ply tires on Malibu V-8 passenger cars ($168.80). QRM GR70-15/B white sidewall steel-belted radial tires replacing G78-14/B black sidewall bias-ply tires on Malibu V-8 passenger cars ($175.15). QQZ HR70-15/B white sidewall steel-belted radial tires replacing G78-14/B black sidewall bias-ply tires on Malibu V-8 passenger cars ($203.80). QRZ GR70-15/B white letter steel-belted radial tires replacing G78-14/B black sidewall bias-ply tires on Malibu V-8 passenger cars ($188.15). QRV HR70-15/B black sidewall steel-belted radial tires replacing GR70-15/B black sidewall radial tires on Laguna Type S-3 ($24.85). QRM GR70-15/B white sidewall steel-belted radial tires replacing GR70-15/B black sidewall radial tires on Laguna Type S-3 ($32.00). QQZ HR70-15/B white sidewall steel-belted radial tires replacing GR70-15/B black sidewall radial tires on Laguna Type S-3 ($59.85). QRZ GR70-15/B white letter steel-belted radial tires replacing GR70-15/B black sidewall radial tires on Laguna Type S-3 ($45.00). QHF H78-14/B white stripe bias-ply tires replacing H78 x 14/B black sidewall bias-ply tires on Malibu V-8 station wagon ($35). QEL HR78-15/B white-stripe steel-belted radial tires replacing H78-14/B black sidewall bias-ply tires on Malibu V-8 station wagon ($151). QRV H70-15/B black sidewall steel-belted radial tires replacing H78-14/B black sidewall bias-ply tires on Malibu V-8 station wagon ($143.95). QQZ H70-15/B white sidewall steel-belted radial tires replacing H78-14/B black sidewall bias-ply tires on Malibu V-8 station wagon ($178.95).

OPTION INSTALLATION RATES

Automatic transmission (97.1 percent). Four-speed manual transmission (0.1 percent). Standard V-8 engine (72 percent). Optional V-8 engine (18 percent). six-cylinder engine (10 percent). AM radio (71.4 percent). AM/FM monaural radio (10.5 percent). AM/FM stereo radio (1.9 percent). Stereo tape (4.5 percent). Air conditioning (70.3 percent). Power steering (97.8 percent). Tilt steering (12.1 percent). Manual disc brakes (10.3 percent). Power front disc brakes (89.7 percent). Power door locks (2.9 percent). Power windows (2.6 percent). Sun roof (0.3 percent). Bucket seats (12.4 percent). Power seats (0.7 percent). Vinyl top (50.9 percent). Tinted windshield only (3.0 percent). All tinted glass (77.3 percent). Dual exhaust (0.8 percent). Positraction (2.6 percent). Standard wheel covers (13.7 percent). Optional full wheel covers (68.1 percent). Styled wheels (4.5 percent). Steel-belted radial tires (14.4 percent). Optional clock (21.7 percent). Rear window defogger (16.7 percent). Remote-control side-view mirror (45.1 percent). Based on partial model-year production of 362,495 units in the U.S. and Canada.

HISTORICAL FOOTNOTES

The 1974 Chevelle line had its dealer introduction date on September 20, 1973. F.J. McDonald was general manager of Chevrolet Motor Division. Calendar year sales of Chevelles was 345,591 units which equaled 4.6 percent of total U.S. auto sales. That compared to 369,594 sales and a 3.8 share of market in calendar-year 1973. Model-year U.S. dealer sales actually crept up to 362,052 units against 358,906 in 1973. The drop in calendar-year sales was largely attributable to the energy crisis that struck the United States in the early months of 1974. The fuel shortage and gas station lines swung many Malibu buyers towards six-cylinder cars. Calendar-year registrations were 290,618 Malibu and Laguna Type S-3 passenger cars and 42,787 Malibu station wagons versus 312,420 Chevelle passenger cars and 52,463 Chevelle station wagons the previous season. By 1975, Robert L. Lund would assume the role of Chevrolet general manager.

New styling — at the front end of the Malibu Classic and the rear end of other models — was the most obvious change in the 1975 mid-size Chevrolets. There were other revisions to the engine offerings, ride quality and handling. Net horsepower ratings for some V-8 engines climbed, while others stayed the same or dropped. The standard 250-cid inline six-cylinder engine was revamped to provide better operating efficiency, fuel economy and performance. All Malibus featured a High Energy Ignition (HEI) system and a catalytic converter.

CHEVELLE

The 1975 Chevelle Malibu line received yet another new front end treatment, in addition to some changes in the power train options.

The Laguna Type S-3, which wasn't reintroduced until February 1975, featured a new "soft" front-end design. The three series and 17 models available in 1974 were carried over into 1975 without change.

I.D. NUMBERS

VIN embossed on the top left-hand side of the instrument panel and visible through the windshield. The first symbol 1 designates Chevrolet. The second symbol indicates series: C=Malibu, D=Malibu Classic, E=Laguna Type S-3 and G=Malibu Classic Estate. The third and fourth symbols indicate body style: 29=four-door pillared hardtop sedan, 37=two-door pillared hardtop coupe, 35=four-door station wagon and 80=El Camino. The fifth symbol indicates engine (net horsepower): D=250-cid 105-hp inline six-cylinder, H=350-cid 145-hp V-8, L=350-cid 165-hp V-8, U=400-cid 175-hp V-8 and Y=454-cid 215-hp V-8. The sixth symbol designates the model year: 5=1975. The seventh symbol designates the assembly plant location: B=Baltimore, Maryland, D=Doraville, Georgia, Z=Fremont, California, R=Arlington, Texas and 1=Oshawa, Canada. The last six symbols are the sequential unit production number at the specific factory. The Fisher body tag riveted to the top of the cowl on the left side of the car below the hood provides additional vehicle identification information. The Fisher Body STYLE NUMBER (ST) consists of a prefix identifying model year and four or more symbols identifying the series and body style (example: 75-1E37 for a 1975 Laguna Type S-3 Colonnade coupe with a V-8 engine). The BODY NUMBER consists of a prefix designating assembly plant and the sequential unit production number at the specific factory. The TRIM NUMBER (TR) identifies upholstery.

COLORS

(10) White, (11) Antique White, (13) Silver poly, (15) Light Graystone, (16) Medium Graystone Poly, (19) Black, (21) Silver Blue Poly, (24) Medium Blue, (26) Bright Blue Poly, (29) Midnight Blue Poly, (44) Medium Green, (45) Light Green Poly, (49) Dark Green Poly, (50) Cream Beige, (51) Bright Yellow, (55) Sandstone, (58) Dark Sandstone Poly, (59) Dark Brown Poly, (63) Light Saddle, (64) Persimmon Poly, (66) Bronze Poly, (72) Medium Red, (74) Dark Red Poly, (75) Light Red, (79) Burgundy Poly and (80) Orange. Vinyl tops were available in: AA=White, BB=Black, DD=Dark Blue, FF=Dark Brown, GG=Medium Green, HH=Dark Red, RR=Red, TT=Sandstone and WW=Metallic Silver.

ENGINE CODES

Codes appear on the right side of six-cylinder blocks behind the distributor and right front of V-8 engine blocks. Engine codes for 1975 were: (250-cid 105-hp six) CJJ, CJU, CJL and CJZ; (350-cid 145-hp V-8 two-barrel V-8) CMJ and CMU; (350-cid 165-hp four-barrel V-8) CMM and CMH; (400-cid 175-hp V-8) CTU, CTX, CSB and CSM; (454-cid 215-hp V-8) CXW.

1975

CHEVELLE MALIBU — (6-CYL/V-8) SERIES 1C

Malibus had a Mercedes-like grille with nine vertical members forming 10 segments. Each segment was filled with thinner, criss-crossing, bright vertical and horizontal moldings that had a screen-like texture. There were no body side moldings, rocker panel moldings or wheel lip moldings. The rear featured horizontal, rectangular taillights. The lenses were somewhat longer and narrower, with nearly square back-up lights added at the inboard end. Standard equipment included all federally mandated safety features and anti-pollution equipment, a flow-through power ventilation system, a double-panel steel acoustical roof, an inside hood latch release, manual front disc brakes, side marker lights and reflectors, a defroster, dual speed windshield wipers, a windshield washer system, an inside day/night rearview mirror, FR78-15/B black sidewall steel-belted radial tires on passenger cars, full foam seats, color-keyed vinyl coated rubber flooring, a cigar lighter, Hide-A-Way wipers, a windshield antenna (when an optional radio was ordered) and a Delcotron generator. Malibu station wagons had, in addition to or instead of the above equipment, a base 350-cid two-barrel V-8 engine, a hatchback tailgate with fixed rear window and a "door ajar" warning light, power front disc/rear drum brakes, full-foam seats front and rear, front and rear armrests, a hidden stowage compartment and HR78-15/B steel-belted radial black sidewall tires. Three-seat wagons also had swing-out rear quarter windows and a power tailgate switch.

Model Number	Body/Style Number	Body Type & Seating	Factory Price	Shipping Weight	Production Total
CHEVELLE MALIBU SERIES 1C (6-CYL)					
1C	29	4d Colonnade-6P	$3,402	3,713 lbs.	Note 1
1C	37	2d Colonnade-6P	$3,407	3,642 lbs.	Note 1
CHEVELLE MALIBU SERIES 1C (V-8)					
1C	29	4d Colonnade-6P	$3,652	3,833 lbs.	Note 1
1C	37	2d Colonnade-6P	$3,657	3,762 lbs.	Note 1
CHEVELLE MALIBU STATION WAGON SERIES 1C (V-8)					
1C	35	4d Wagon-6P	$4,318	4,207 lbs.	Note 1
1C	35/AQ4	4d Wagon-8P	$4,463	4,239 lbs.	Note 1

NOTE 1: Individual body style production is not available; see production notes.

CHEVELLE MALIBU CLASSIC (6-CYL/V-8) — SERIES 1D

Malibu Classic models had the same basic grille as other Chevelles, but the screen-like background texture was finished in flat black. This made the nine vertical members stand out more prominently. There was also a stand-up hood ornament, rocker panel moldings and wheel lip moldings. The rear featured horizontal, rectangular taillights similar to those on other models, but the rectangular panel housing the taillights and center license plate indentation featured satin silver finish and held a "Malibu Classic" chrome script on the right-hand side. A vinyl-clad rear quarter roof treatment, opera windows and body side moldings (mainly on the doors) characterized the Landau coupe model. Standard equipment on all Malibus included all federally-mandated safety features and anti-pollution equipment, a flow-through power ventilation system, a double-panel steel acoustical roof, an inside hood latch release, manual front disc brakes, side marker lights and reflectors, a defroster,

☐ Malibu Classic Landau Coupe

☐ Malibu Classic Coupe

☐ Malibu Classic Sedan

☐ Laguna Type S-3 Coupe

☐ Malibu Coupe

☐ Malibu Sedan

Six models of Malibus and Malibu Classics were offered for 1975.

83

dual speed windshield wipers, a windshield washer system, an inside day/night rearview mirror, a left-hand outside rearview mirror, a 105-hp six-cylinder engine or a two-barrel 350-cid V-8, FR78-15/B black sidewall steel-belted radial tires, full foam seats, a cigar lighter, Hide-A-Way wipers, a windshield antenna (when an optional radio was ordered) and a Delcotron generator. In addition to or in place of the above, the Malibu Classic models featured floor carpeting, a lighted glove box, mixed pattern cloth-and-vinyl upholstery, bright roof drip moldings, bright wheel opening moldings and a deluxe front seat with armrest. All 1975 Malibu station wagons had, in addition to or instead of the standard Malibu equipment, a base V-8 engine, a hatchback tailgate with fixed rear window and a "door ajar" warning light, power front disc/rear drum brakes, full-foam seats front and rear, front and rear armrests, a hidden stowage compartment and H78-15/B bias-belted black sidewall tires. Malibu Classic station wagons also had bumper parking lights, bright radiator grille outline moldings, bright lower body sill moldings and bright hub caps. All three-seat wagons added swing-out rear quarter windows and a power tailgate switch.

Model Number	Body/Style Number	Body Type & Seating	Factory Price	Shipping Weight	Production Total
CHEVELLE MALIBU CLASSIC SERIES 1D (6-CYL)					
1D	29	4d Colonnade-6P	$3,695	3,778 lbs.	Note 1
1D	37	2d Colonnade-6P	$3,698	3,681 lbs.	Note 1
1D	37	2d Landau-6P	$3,930	3,681 lbs.	Note 1
CHEVELLE MALIBU CLASSIC SERIES 1D (V-8)					
1D	29	4d Colonnade-6P	$3,945	3,898 lbs.	Note 1
1D	37	2d Colonnade-6P	$3,948	3,801 lbs.	Note 1
1D	37	2d Landau-6P	$4,180	3,801 lbs.	Note 1
CHEVELLE MALIBU CLASSIC STATION WAGON SERIES 1D (V-8)					
1D	35	4d wagon-6P	$4,556	4,275 lbs.	Note 1
1D	35/AQ4	4d wagon-8P	$4,701	4,309 lbs.	Note 1

NOTE 1: Individual body style production is not available; see production notes.

CHEVELLE MALIBU CLASSIC ESTATE (V-8) — SERIES 1D

Wood-grained exterior panels decorated the front and rear fender sides and all doors of the Malibu Classic Estate station wagon. Its equipment list started with the features that were standard on all 1975 mid-sized Chevrolets, such as federally mandated safety features and anti-pollution equipment, a flow-through power ventilation system, a double-panel steel acoustical roof, an inside hood latch release, manual front disc brakes, side marker lights and reflectors, a defroster, dual speed windshield wipers, a windshield washer system, an inside day/night rearview mirror, a left-hand outside rearview mirror, a two-barrel 350-cid V-8, HR78-15/B black sidewall steel-belted radial tires, full foam seats, color-keyed vinyl coated rubber flooring, a cigar lighter, Hide-A-Way wipers, a windshield antenna (when an optional radio was ordered) and a Delcotron generator. It also included the Malibu Classic array such as floor carpeting, a lighted glove box, mixed pattern cloth-and-vinyl upholstery, bright body side moldings, bright roof drip moldings, bright wheel opening moldings and a deluxe front seat with armrest. Like all 1975 Malibu station wagons it also had a base V-8 engine, a hatchback tailgate with fixed rear window and a "door ajar" warning light, power front disc/rear drum brakes, full-foam seats front and rear, front and rear armrests, and a hidden stowage compartment. In addition, Malibu Classic station wagon features like bumper parking lights, bright radiator grille outline moldings, bright lower body sill moldings and bright hubcaps were standard. Naturally, this top-of-the-line hauler also had slightly richer interior appointments. It was available in a three-seat version that included swing-out rear quarter windows and a power tailgate switch.

Model Number	Body/Style Number	Body Type & Seating	Factory Price	Shipping Weight	Production Total
1G	35	4d wagon-6P	$4,748	4,301 lbs.	Note 1
1G	35/AQ4	4d wagon-8P	$4,893	4,334 lbs.	Note 1

NOTE 1: Individual body style production is not available; see production notes.

CHEVELLE LAGUNA TYPE S-3 — (V-8) SERIES 1E

The Laguna Type S-3 was actually dropped at the start of the 1975 model year and then reinstated at midyear. It had a totally different urethane-clad front end over an impact-resistant bumper structure. Louvered opera windows were also new for the sporty model. The grille sloped backwards and was divided by body-colored members both horizontally and vertically. This formed four large rectangular slots with screen-textured inserts. The parking lights were incorporated at the outboard ends of the upper slot, while the left-hand edge of the lower slot held a "Laguna Type S-3" badge. Headlights used on the Type S-3 were a bit different with a kind of protruding "lip" at their lower end. It also featured a special slotted valance panel below the front bumper with unique end pieces. The Type S-3 came in only six colors with specific body striping and half-vinyl roofs on the options list. It included Rally wheel rims and a radial-tuned suspension. Other Laguna Type S-3 equipment included Type S-3 fender badges, bumper impact strips, special interior fabrics, a special steering wheel, wood grain vinyl interior accents and front door map pockets. Like all 1975 mid-sized Chevrolets, the Laguna Type S-3 had all federally mandated safety features and anti-pollution equipment, a flow-through power ventilation system, a double-panel steel acoustical roof, an inside hood latch release, manual front disc brakes, side marker lights and reflectors, a defroster, dual speed windshield wipers, a windshield washer system, an inside day/night rearview mirror, a left-hand outside rearview mirror, full foam seats, a cigar lighter, Hide-A-Way wipers, a windshield antenna (when an optional radio was ordered) and a Delcotron generator. A 350-cid two-barrel V-8 engine was standard, along with GR70-15/B steel-belted radial tires.

Model Number	Body/Style Number	Body Type & Seating	Factory Price	Shipping Weight	Production Total
1E	37	2d Colonnade-6P	$4,113	3,908 lbs.	6,714

PRODUCTION NOTES

NOTE 1 Model-year production (United States only) of all 1975 Chevelles was 247,281 units including 25,648 six-cylinder models and 221,633 V-8 models.
NOTE 2 Additional statistics record series production (U.S. only) as follows:

Malibu (6-cyl)	21,804
Malibu (V-8)	41,726
Total	**63,530**
Malibu Classic (6-cyl)	3,844

Malibu (V-8)	127,611				
Total	131,455				
Laguna (V-8)	6,714				
Total	6,714				
Wagons (V-8)	45,582				
Total	45,582				

NOTE 3 Production by factory (U.S. only) was:

Code	Factory	Production	Code	Factory	Production
B	Baltimore	119,974	D	Doraville (Ga.)	50,142
R	Arlington (Tex.)	77,114	Z	Fremont (Cal.)	35,135

ENGINES

CHEVELLE BASE SIX-CYL: Inline. Overhead-valve. Cast-iron block. Displacement: 250 cid. Bore and stroke: 3.875 x 3.53 in. Compression ratio: 8.25:1. Net brake hp: 105 at 3800 rpm. Taxable hp: 36. Torque: 185 lbs.-ft. at 1200 rpm. Seven main bearings. Hydraulic valve lifters. Crankcase capacity: 4 qt. (add 1 qt. for new filter). Cooling system capacity: 12 qt (add 6 qt. for heater). Carburetor: Rochester one-barrel Model 7028017. Sales code L22.

CHEVELLE BASE 350 V-8: Overhead-valve. Cast-iron block and head. Bore and stroke: 4.00 x 3.48 in. Displacement: 350 cid. Compression ratio: 8.50:1. Net brake hp: 145 at 3800 rpm. Taxable hp: 51.20. Net torque: 250 lbs.-ft. at 2200 rpm. Five main bearings. Hydraulic valve lifters. Crankcase capacity: 4 qt. (add 1 qt. for new filter). Cooling system capacity with heater: 16 qt. Carburetor: Two-barrel. Sales code: L65.

CHEVELLE OPTIONAL 350-CID, 165-HP V-8: Overhead-valve. Cast-iron block and head. Bore and stroke: 4.00 x 3.48 in. Displacement: 350 cid. Compression ratio: 8.50:1. Net brake hp: 165 at 3800 rpm. Taxable hp: 51.20. Net torque: 260 lbs.-ft. at 2400 rpm. Five main bearings. Hydraulic valve lifters. Crankcase capacity: 4 qt. (add 1 qt. for new filter). Cooling system capacity with heater: 16 qt. Carburetor: Four-barrel. Sales code: LM1.

CHEVELLE OPTIONAL 400-CID, 175-HP V-8: Overhead-valve. Cast-iron block and head. Bore and stroke: 4.13 x 3.75 in. Displacement: 400 cid. Compression ratio: 8.50:1. Net brake hp: 175 at 3600 rpm. Taxable hp: 54.40. Net torque: 305 lbs.-ft. at 2000 rpm. Five main bearings. Hydraulic valve lifters. Crankcase capacity: 4 qt. (add 1 qt. for new filter). Cooling system capacity with heater: 16 qt. Carburetor: Four-barrel. Sales code: LT1.

CHEVELLE OPTIONAL 454-CID, 215-HP V-8: Overhead-valve. Cast-iron block and head. Bore and stroke: 4.25 x 4.00 in. Displacement: 454 cid. Compression ratio: 8.15:1. Net brake hp: 215 at 4000 rpm. Taxable hp: 57.80. Net torque: 350 lbs.-ft. at 2400 rpm. Five main bearings. Hydraulic valve lifters. Crankcase capacity: 5 qt. (add 1 qt. for new filter). Cooling system capacity with heater: 24 qt. Dual exhaust. Carburetor: Four-barrel. Sales code: LS4.

CHASSIS FEATURES

Wheelbase: (two-door) 112 in; (four-door) 116 in. Overall length: (two-door) 205.3 in; (four-door cars) 209.3 in; (four-door station wagons) 215.2 in. Width: 76.6 in. Height: (sedans) 54 in; (coupes) 53.1 in; (wagon) 55.6 in. Tires: (cars) GR78 x 15 steel-belted radial; (station wagon) HR78 x 14 steel-belted radial.

OPTIONS

A01 tinted body glass. A02 tinted windshield. A20 station wagon swing-out rear quarter window. A31 electric power windows. A42 six-way power front bench seat ($113). A52 front bench seat. A65 split front bench seat. A90 electric trunk lid release. AG7 6-way power driver's seat ($113). AK1 Deluxe seat belts and shoulder harness. AN7 Strato-bucket swivel front seats. AQ4 station wagon rear-facing third seat. AT8 50-50 split bench front seat. AU3 power door locks. AU6 electric tailgate release. B37 front and rear floor mats. B44 station wagon load floor carpeting. B48 deluxe luggage compartment rim. B80 roof drip molding. B84 body side moldings. B93 door edge guards. B96 wheel opening moldings. BW2 exterior ornamentation. BX8 two-tone paint with outline moldings. C08 soft padded roof cover. C09 vinyl roof ($96). C50 electric rear window defroster and defogger. C51 station wagon rear window air deflector. C60 All-Weather air conditioning. CA1 electric sky roof ($350). CB1 exterior soft trim cover. CB4 landau top. CB7 forward half-vinyl roof. CD4 pulse-type windshield wipers. D24 litter container. D33 remote-control left-hand outside rearview mirror. D34 visor vanity mirror. D35 remote-control Custom style left-hand outside rearview mirror. D55 front center console. D68 dual Sport mirrors. D91 front end paint stripe. D99 special two-tone paint. DF3 remote-control right-hand outside rearview mirror. F40 heavy-duty front and rear suspension. FE8 radial tuned suspension. G80 Positraction rear axle. G92 3.08:1 ratio rear axle. G95 3.55:1 differential carrier ratio. J50 power brakes. K05 engine block heater. K30 emission control delete. K75 emission control delete. K76 61-amp. Delcotron generator. L22 250-cid in-line six-cylinder engine (standard). L65 350-cid two-barrel V-8 (standard V-8; standard in Laguna Type S-3 and station wagons at no extra cost). LM1 350-cid four-barrel regular-fuel V-8. LT4 400-cid four-barrel V-8. LS4 454-cid four-barrel V-8 ($340 in station wagons; car price unavailable). M15 three-speed manual transmission (standard). M38 three-speed automatic transmission. M40 three-speed Turbo-Hydra-Matic transmission. N31 Sport style steering wheel. N33 tilt steering. N41 variable-ratio power steering. N95 simulated wire wheel covers. P01 wheel covers. PA3 special wheel covers. PE2 15 x 7-in. custom wheels ($46). QBW FR78-15/B white stripe steel-belted radial tires. QBU FR78-15/B black sidewall steel-belted radial tires. QBX GR70-15/B black sidewall steel-belted radial tires. QCF GR78-15/B black sidewall steel-belted radial tires. QCN HR70-15/B white stripe steel-belted radial tires. QCP HR70-15/B black sidewall steel-belted radial tires. QCV HR70-15/B raised white letter steel-belted radial tires. QCX GR70-15/B white stripe steel-belted radial tires. QCY GR70-15/B white letter steel-belted radial tires. QDR GR78-15/B white stripe steel-belted radial tires. QDU HR78-15/B white sidewall steel-belted radial tires. QEL HR78-15/B white stripe steel-belted radial tires. QGK G78-14/B black sidewall tires. QGL G78x 14/B white-stripe tires. QHE H78-14/B black sidewall tires. QHF H78-14/B white stripe tires. QRM GR70-15/B white stripe steel-belted radial tires. U05 dual

CHEVELLE

horns. U14 special instrumentation. U18 export type speedometer. U35 electric clock. U58 AM-FM stereo radio ($233). U63 push-button radio. U69 AM/FM push-button radio. U76 windshield antenna. U80 auxiliary radio speaker. UA1 heavy-duty battery. UF7 gauge package. UM1 AM push-button radio and tape player. UM2 AM/FM push-button radio and tape player ($363). V01 heavy-duty radiator. V30 bumper guards. V55 station wagon luggage rack ($65). VE5 bumper impact strip. YA2 Estate wagon package. YB5 general processing order. YF5 California emissions. YJ9 exterior décor package. Z95 regular fuel engine equipment. ZJ7 special wheel treatment with hubcaps and trim rings. ZJ9 auxiliary lighting group.

OPTION INSTALLATION RATES

Automatic transmission (98.6 percent). Standard V-8 engine (80.7 percent). Optional V-8 engine (8.4 percent). 6-cylinder engine (10.9 percent). AM radio (67.4 percent). AM/FM monaural radio (11.6 percent). AM/FM stereo radio (2 percent). Stereo tape (3.6 percent). Air conditioning (74.5 percent). Power steering (98.8 percent). Tilt steering (14.7 percent). Manual disc brakes (7.4 percent). Power front disc brakes (92.6 percent). Power door locks (5 percent). Power windows (4.1 percent). Sun roof (0.2 percent). Cruise control (8.9 percent). Bucket seats (6.1 percent). Power seats (4.8 percent). Reclining seats (7.1 percent). Vinyl top (28.7 percent). Tinted windshield only (3.9 percent). All tinted glass (78 percent). Dual exhaust (0.1 percent). Positraction (2.7 percent). Standard wheel covers (5.6 percent). Optional full wheel covers (64.8 percent). Standard styled wheels (2.7 percent). Optional styled wheels (10.3 percent). Steel-belted radial tires (98.5 percent). Standard clock (2.7 percent). Optional clock (18.8 percent). Rear window defogger (18.2 percent). Remote-control sideview mirror (51.2 percent). Based on model year production of 283,313 units in the United States and Canada.

HISTORICAL FOOTNOTES

The 1975 Chevelle line had its dealer introduction date on September 27, 1974, and the Laguna Type S-3 was reintroduced at the Chicago Auto Show on Feb. 22, 1975, and appeared in Chevy showrooms around April. Robert L. Lund was Chevrolet general manager. The company's total output of 1,686,062 cars was the lowest on record since 1970. Calendar-year sales of Chevelles was 285,726 units which equaled 4 percent of total U.S. auto sales. That compared to 345.591 sales and a 4.6 percent share of market in calendar-year 1974. Model year U.S. dealer sales dropped to 276,079 units against 362,052 in 1974. The trends towards more six-cylinder Chevelles continued among buyers of 1975 models. Calendar-year registrations were 232,030 passenger cars and 44,176 station wagons versus 290,618 passenger cars and 42,787 station wagons the previous season. The slope-nosed 1975 Laguna Type S-3 had a successful season in NASCAR stock-car racing and Cale Yarborough used such a car to capture the NASCAR Winston Cup titles in 1976 and 1977.

Two Chevelle series were offered for 1976, plus — for the last time — the sportier Laguna Type S-3. Malibu sported an Argent Silver grille and single headlamps with bright bezels. A new lightweight chrome grille, stacked dual rectangular headlights and a new front bumper greatly changed the appearance of Malibu Classics up front.

A 250-cid in-line six or an all-new 305-cid base V-8 powered Malibu. The 305-cid engine was promoted as being cleaner burning and more economical than the 350-cid V-8. It had the same stroke as the 350 combined with a smaller 3.74-in. bore. The 350-cid V-8 returned in two-barrel and four-barrel versions and the 400-cid V-8 was back in one four-barrel version. The 454-cid V-8 did not reappear. Transmissions were a three-speed manual and Turbo-Hydra-Matic. All Chevelles except the basic six-cylinder Malibu models had power brakes as standard equipment.

I.D. NUMBERS

VIN embossed on the top left-hand side of the instrument panel and visible through the windshield. The first symbol 1 designates Chevrolet. The second symbol indicates series: C=Malibu, D=Malibu Classic, E=Laguna Type S-3 and G=Malibu Classic Estate. The third and fourth symbols indicate body style: 29=four-door pillared hardtop sedan, 37=two-door pillared hardtop coupe, 35=four-door station wagon and 80=El Camino. The fifth symbol indicates engine (net horsepower): D=250-cid 105-hp inline six-cylinder, Q=305-cid 140-hp V-8, V=350-cid 145-hp V-8, L=350-cid 165-hp V-8 and U=400-cid 175-hp V-8. The sixth symbol designates the model year: 6=1976. The seventh symbol designates the assembly plant location: B=Baltimore, Maryland, D=Doraville, Georgia, Z=Fremont, California, R=Arlington, Texas and 1=Oshawa, Canada. The last six symbols are the sequential unit production number at the specific factory. The Fisher body tag riveted to the top of the cowl on the left side of the car below the hood provides additional vehicle identification information. The Fisher body STYLE NUMBER (ST) consists of a prefix identifying model year and four or more symbols identifying the series and body style (example: 76-1E37 for a 1976 Laguna Type S-3 Colonnade coupe with a V-8 engine). The BODY NUMBER consists of a prefix designating assembly plant and the sequential unit production num-

1976

The Malibu Classic Coupe demonstrated the new stacked-headlight look for 1976.

ber at the specific factory. The TRIM NUMBER (TR) identifies upholstery.

COLORS

(10) Classic White, (11) Antique White, (13) Silver poly, (16) Medium Gray Poly, (19) Black, (21) Light Blue, (28) Light Blue Poly, (35) Dark Blue Poly, (36) Firethorn Poly, (37) Mahogany Poly, (40) Lime Poly, (45) Lime Green, (49) Dark Green Poly, (50) Cream, (51) Bright Yellow, (57) Cream Gold, (65) Buckskin, (66) Burnt Orange, (67) Medium Saddle Poly, (72) Medium Red, (75) Light Red and (76) Medium Orange. Engine codes appear on the right side of six-cylinder blocks behind the distributor and right front of V-8 engine blocks. Engine codes for 1976 were: (250-cid 105-hp six) CCF, CCD and CCC; (305-cid 140-hp two-barrel V-8) CPB, (350-cid 145-hp two-barrel V-8) CMJ and CLF; (350-cid 165-hp four-barrel V-8) CMN, CUF and CMH; (400-cid 175-hp V-8) CSX, CSB, CSF, CSA, CSW, CTU, CTX and CSM. Vinyl tops were available in: 11T=White, 13T=Silver, 19T=Black, 35T=Dark Blue, 36F=Firethorn, 37T=Mahogany and 65T=Buckskin.

CHEVELLE MALIBU — (6-CYL/V-8) SERIES 1C

Base Malibus came in coupe, sedan or wagon form with a new mesh-pattern Argent Silver grille. They had single headlamps with bright bezels on each side and looked. Overall, much like the 1975 models. Standard equipment included all federally-mandated safety features and anti-pollution equipment, a flow-through power ventilation system, a double-panel steel acoustical roof, an inside hood latch release, manual front disc brakes, side marker lights and reflectors, a defroster, dual speed windshield wipers, a windshield washer system, an inside day/night rearview mirror, FR78 x 15/B black sidewall steel-belted radial tires on passenger cars, full foam seats, cut-pile carpeting, a cigar lighter, Hide-A-Way wipers, a windshield antenna (when an optional radio was ordered), a Delcotron generator, the 250-cid six-cylinder engine and three-speed manual transmission. Chevelle V-8s had the standard 305-cid V-8 and Turbo-Hydra-Matic transmission. Malibu station wagons had, in addition to or instead of the above equipment, a base 350-cid two-barrel V-8 engine, a hatchback tailgate with fixed rear window and a "door ajar" warning light, power front disc/rear drum brakes, full-foam seats front and rear, front and rear armrests, a hidden stowage compartment and HR78 x 15/B steel-belted radial black sidewall tires. Three-seat wagons also had swing-out rear quarter windows and a power tailgate switch.

Model Number	Body/Style Number	Body Type & Seating	Factory Price	Shipping Weight	Production Total
CHEVELLE MALIBU SERIES 1C (6-CYL)					
1C	29	4d Colonnade-6P	$3,671	3,729 lbs.	Note 1
1C	37	2d Colonnade-6P	$3,636	3,650 lbs.	Note 1
CHEVELLE MALIBU SERIES 1C (V-8)					
1C	29	4d Colonnade-6P	$4,201	3,834 lbs.	Note 1
1C	37	2d Colonnade-6P	$4,166	3,755 lbs.	Note 1
CHEVELLE MALIBU STATION WAGON SERIES 1C (V-8)					
1C	35	4d wagon-6P	$4,543	4,238 lbs.	Note 1
1C	35/AQ4	4d wagon-8P	$4,686	4,268 lbs.	Note 1

NOTE 1: Individual body style production is not available; see production notes.

CHEVELLE MALIBU CLASSIC (6-CYL/V-8) — SERIES 1D

The Malibu Classic's restyled front end displayed new

87

stacked, rectangular headlights, a lightweight diamond-pattern grille with a "Malibu Classic" script in the lower left-hand corner and a stand-up hood ornament. Standard equipment on all Malibus included all federally-mandated safety features and anti-pollution equipment, a flow-through power ventilation system, a double-panel steel acoustical roof, an inside hood latch release, manual front disc brakes, side marker lights and reflectors, a defroster, dual speed windshield wipers, a windshield washer system, an inside day/night rearview mirror, a left-hand outside rearview mirror, a 105-hp six-cylinder engine or a two-barrel 305-cid V-8, FR78-15/B black sidewall steel-belted radial tires, full foam seats, carpeting, a cigar lighter, Hide-A-Way wipers, a windshield antenna (when an optional radio was ordered) and a Delcotron generator. In addition to or in place of the above, the Malibu Classic models featured a lighted glove box, mixed pattern cloth-and-vinyl upholstery, bright roof drip moldings, bright wheel opening moldings, a deluxe front seat with an armrest and larger taillight lenses. All 1976 Malibu station wagons had, in addition to or instead of the standard Malibu equipment, a base 350-cid V-8 engine, a hatchback tailgate with fixed rear window and a "door ajar" warning light, power front disc/rear drum brakes, full-foam seats front and rear, front and rear armrests, a hidden stowage compartment and H78-15/B bias-belted black sidewall tires. Malibu Classic station wagons also had bumper parking lights, bright radiator grille outline moldings, bright lower body sill moldings and bright hubcaps. All eight-passenger wagons added a rear-facing third seat, swing-out rear quarter windows and a power tailgate switch.

Model Number	Body/Style Number	Body Type & Seating	Factory Price	Shipping Weight	Production Total
CHEVELLE MALIBU CLASSIC SERIES 1D (6-CYL)					
1D	29	4d Colonnade-6P	$4,196	3,827 lbs.	Note 1
1D	37	2d Colonnade-6P	$3,926	3,688 lbs.	Note 1
1D	37	2d Landau-6P	$4,124	3,688 lbs.	Note 1
CHEVELLE MALIBU CLASSIC SERIES 1D (V-8)					
1D	29	4d Colonnade-6P	$4,490	3,932 lbs.	Note 1
1D	37	2d Colonnade-6P	$4,455	3,793 lbs.	Note 1
1D	37	2d Landau-6P	$4,640	3,801 lbs.	Note 1
CHEVELLE MALIBU CLASSIC STATION WAGON SERIES 1D (V-8)					
1D	35	4d wagon-6P	$4,776	4,300 lbs.	Note 1
1D	35/AQ4	4d wagon-8P	$4,919	4,330 lbs.	Note 1

NOTE 1: Individual body style production is not available; see production notes.

CHEVELLE MALIBU CLASSIC ESTATE (V-8) SERIES 1D

Wood-grained exterior panels decorated the front and rear fender sides and all doors of the Malibu Classic Estate station wagon. Its equipment list started with the features that were standard on all 1976 mid-sized Chevrolets, such as federally mandated safety features and anti-pollution equipment, a flow-through power ventilation system, a double-panel steel acoustical roof, an inside hood latch release, manual front disc brakes, side marker lights and reflectors, a defroster, dual speed windshield wipers, a windshield washer system, an inside day/night rearview mirror, a left-hand outside rearview mirror, a two-barrel 350-cid V-8, HR78-15/B black sidewall steel-belted radial tires, full foam seats, color-keyed vinyl coated rubber flooring, a cigar lighter, Hide-A-Way wipers, a windshield antenna (when an optional radio was ordered) and a Delcotron generator. It also included the Malibu Classic array, such as a lighted glove box, mixed pattern cloth-and-vinyl upholstery, bright body side moldings, bright roof drip moldings, bright wheel opening moldings and a deluxe front seat with armrest. Like all 1976 Malibu station wagons it also had a base 350-cid V-8 engine, a hatchback tailgate with fixed rear window and a "door ajar" warning light, power front disc/rear drum brakes, full-foam seats front and rear, front and rear armrests, and a hidden stowage compartment. In addition, Malibu Classic station wagon features like bumper parking lights, bright radiator grille outline moldings, bright lower body sill moldings, bright hubcaps and richer interior appointments were standard. It was available in a three-seat version that included a rear-facing third seat, swing-out rear quarter windows and a power tailgate switch.

Model Number	Body/Style Number	Body Type & Seating	Factory Price	Shipping Weight	Production Total
1G	35	4d wagon-6P	$4,971	4,326 lbs.	Note 1
1G	35/AQ4	4d wagon-8P	$5,114	4,356 lbs.	Note 1

NOTE 1: Individual body style production is not available; see production notes.

CHEVELLE LAGUNA TYPE S-3 — (V-8) SERIES 1E

Very few changes were apparent on the Model E37 Laguna Type S-3 in its last season. The slope-nose styling was used again. The grille angled backwards and was divided by body-colored members both horizontally and vertically. This formed four large rectangular slots with wide screen-textured inserts. The parking lights were incorporated at the outboard ends of the upper slot, while the left-hand edge of the lower slot held a "Laguna Type S-3" badge. Headlights used on the Type S-3 were a bit different with a kind of protruding "lip" at their lower end. It also featured a special slotted valance panel below the front bumper with unique end pieces. The "opera windows" in the rear quarter of the roof were decorated with louvers and the rear body panel was done in "blackout" style with a "Laguna Type S-3" badge between the center license plate recess and the right-hand taillight. Standard Type S-3 equipment included Rallye wheel rims, dual Sport mirrors (left-hand remote-control), a radial-tuned suspension (with large-diameter stabilizer bars and re-valved shocks), Type S-3 fender badges, color-keyed bumper impact strips, special interior fabrics, a special steering wheel, a round-dial instrument panel with wood grain vinyl accents and front door map pockets. The Laguna Type S-3 was not available in the following colors: Light Blue Poly, Cream, Medium Saddle Poly, Dark Green Poly, Medium Red, Buckskin and Cream Gold. Laguna interiors were trimmed in sport cloth-and-vinyl in Black or Buckskin, or in all-vinyl Black, Buckskin, Blue or Mahogany, or in Black, Lime or Mahogany with White accents. Like all 1976 mid-sized Chevrolets, the Laguna Type S-3 had all federally mandated safety features and anti-pollution equipment, a flow-through power ventilation system, a double-panel steel acoustical roof, an inside hood latch release, manual front disc brakes, side marker lights and reflectors, a defroster, dual speed windshield wipers, a windshield washer system, an inside day/night rearview mirror, a left-hand outside rearview mirror, full foam seats, a cigar

1976

lighter, Hide-A-Way wipers, a windshield antenna (when an optional radio was ordered) and a Delcotron generator. The 305-cid two-barrel V-8 engine was standard, along with GR78-15/B steel-belted radial tires.

Model Number	Body/Style Number	Body Type Seating	Factory Price	Shipping Weight	Production Total
1E	37	2d Colonnade-6P	$4,621	3,978 lbs.	8,236

NOTE 1: The figure of 8,236 represents U.S. model-year production total.

NOTE 2: Some source show Laguna Type S-3 production as 9,100, which may be North American production total including units built in Canada.

PRODUCTION NOTES

NOTE 1 Model year production (United States only) of all 1975 Chevelles was 307,970. This agrees with reported production totals by factory, but does not agree with figures in Note 2 below, which total 307, 949. The difference cannot be explained using our sources.

NOTE 2 Additional statistics record series production (U.S. only) as follows:

Malibu (6-cyl)	22,457
Malibu (V-8)	39,038
Total	**61,495**
Malibu Classic (6-cyl)	9,614
Malibu (V-8)	163,882
Total	**173,496**
Laguna (V-8)	8,236
Total	**8,236**
Wagons (V-8)	64,722
Total	**64,722**

NOTE 3 Production by factory (U.S. only) was:

Code	Factory	Production	Code	Factory	Production
B	Baltimore	136,693	D	Doraville (Ga.)	65,146
R	Arlington (Tex.)	66,236	Z	Fremont (Cal.)	39,895

ENGINES

CHEVELLE BASE SIX-CYL: Inline. Overhead-valve. Cast-iron block. Displacement: 250 cid. Bore and stroke: 3.875 x 3.53 in. Compression ratio: 8.25:1. Net brake hp: 105 at 3800 rpm. Taxable hp: 36. Torque: 185 lbs.-ft. at 1200 rpm. Seven main bearings. Hydraulic valve lifters. Crankcase capacity: 4 qt. (add 1 qt. for new filter). Cooling system capacity: 12 qt. (add 6 qt. for heater). Carburetor: Rochester one-barrel. Sales code L22.

CHEVELLE (CARS) BASE V-8: Overhead-valve. Cast-iron block and head. Bore and stroke: 4.00 x 3.48 in. Displacement: 305 cid. Compression ratio: 8.50:1. Net brake hp: 140 at 3800 rpm. Taxable hp: 44.66. Net torque: 245 lbs.-ft. at 2000 rpm. Five main bearings. Hydraulic valve lifters. Crankcase capacity: 4 qt. (add 1 qt. for new filter). Cooling system capacity with heater: 16 qt. Carburetor: Two-barrel. Sales code: LG3.

CHEVELLE (WAGON) BASE V-8; CHEVELLE (CARS) OPTIONAL 350-CID, 145-HP V-8: Overhead-valve. Cast-iron block and head. Bore and stroke: 4.00 x 3.48 in. Displacement: 350 cid. Compression ratio: 8.50:1. Net brake hp: 145 at 3800 rpm. Taxable hp: 51.20. Net torque: 250 lbs.-ft. at 2200 rpm. Five main bearings. Hydraulic valve lifters. Crankcase capacity: 4 qt. (add 1 qt. for new filter). Cooling system capacity with heater: 16 qt. Carburetor: Two-barrel. Sales code L65.

CHEVELLE OPTIONAL 350-CID, 165-HP V-8: Overhead-valve. Cast-iron block and head. Bore and stroke: 4.00 x 3.48 in. Displacement: 350 cid. Compression ratio: 8.50:1. Net brake hp: 165 at 3800 rpm. Taxable hp: 51.20. Net torque: 260 lbs.-ft. at 2400 rpm. Five main bearings. Hydraulic valve lifters. Crankcase capacity: 4 qt. (add 1 qt. for new filter). Cooling system capacity with heater: 16 qt. Carburetor: Four-barrel. Sales code: LM1.

CHEVELLE OPTIONAL 400-CID, 175-HP V-8: Overhead-valve. Cast-iron block and head. Bore and stroke: 4.13 x 3.75 in. Displacement: 400 cid. Compression ratio: 8.50:1. Net brake hp: 175 at 3600 rpm. Taxable hp: 54.40. Net torque: 305 lbs.-ft. at 2000 rpm. Five main bearings. Hydraulic valve lifters. Crankcase capacity: 4 qt. (add 1 qt. for new filter). Cooling system capacity with heater 16 qt. Carburetor: Four-barrel. Sales code LT4.

CHASSIS FEATURES

Wheelbase: (two-door) 112 in; (four-door) 116 in. Overall length: (two-door) 205.7 in; (four-door cars) 209.7 in; (four-door station wagons) 215.2 in. Width: (cars) 76.9 in; (wagons) 76.8 in. Height: (sedans) 54 in; (coupes) 53.3 in; (wagon) 55.7 in. Tires: (six-cylinder cars) FR78-15 steel-belted radial; (V-8 cars) GR78-15/B; (station wagon) HR78-14 steel-belted radial.

OPTIONS

A01 tinted body glass ($49). A02 tinted windshield. A20 station wagon swing-out rear quarter window. A31 electric power windows (coupes $99, four-doors $140). A42 six-way power front bench seat. A65 split-back front bench seat. A90 electric release lock ($20). AG7 power seats ($124). AK1 Deluxe seat belts and shoulder harness ($14-20). AN7 Strato-bucket swiveling front bucket seats. AQ4 station wagon rear-facing third seat. AU3 power door locks. AU6 electric tailgate release. B37 front and rear floor mats ($15). B44 station wagon load floor carpeting. B48 deluxe luggage compartment rim. B80 roof drip moldings ($16). B84 body side moldings ($38). B93 door edge guards. B96 wheel opening moldings. BX8 two-tone paint with outline moldings ($40). CA1 sky roof ($370). C50 electric rear window defroster and defogger ($77). C51 station wagon rear window air deflector ($23). C60 manual air conditioning ($452-$479). CB7 forward vinyl roof ($109). CD4 pulse-type windshield wipers. D24 litter container. D33 remote-control left-hand outside rearview mirror. D34 visor vanity mirror ($4). D35 remote-control Custom style left-hand outside rearview mirror ($14). D55 front center console ($71). D68 dual Sport mirrors ($27). D91 special two-tone paint. FE8 radial tuned suspension ($27). F40 heavy-duty suspension ($18). G80 Positraction rear axle ($51). G92 3.08:1 ratio rear axle ($13). G95 3.55:1 differential carrier ratio ($13). J50 power brakes ($58). K05 engine block heater. K30 Cruise-Master speed control ($73). K76 61-amp Delcotron generator ($27). L22 250-cid in-line six-cylinder engine (standard). LG3 305-cid two-barrel V-8. L65 350-cid two-barrel V-8 (standard V-8; standard in station wagons at no extra cost, $30 in coupes and sedans). LM1 350-cid four-barrel regular-fuel V-8 ($55 in wagons and $85 otherwise). LT4 400-cid four-barrel V-8. M15 three-speed manual transmission (standard). M38 three-speed automatic transmission ($260 in sixes). N31 custom style steering wheel ($52). N33 tilt steering ($52). N41 variable-ratio power steering

Chevelle

The Laguna Type S-3 was largely unchanged for 1976 and came with a standard 305-cid V-8.

($136). N65 stowaway spare wheel and tire. N95 simulated wire wheel covers ($59-89). P01 wheel covers. QBW FR78-15/B white stripe steel-belted radial tires. QBU FR78-15/B black sidewall steel-belted radial tires ($43-51). QBX GR70-15/B black sidewall steel-belted radial tires ($73-91). QCF GR78-15/B black sidewall steel-belted radial tires ($30-37). QCX GR70-15/B white stripe steel-belted radial tires. QCY GR70-15/B white letter steel-belted radial tires. QDR GR78-15/B white stripe steel-belted radial tires. QDU HR78-15/B white sidewall steel-belted radial tires. QEL HR78-15/B white stripe steel-belted radial tires. QGK G78-14/B black sidewall tires. QGL G78-14/B white stripe tires. QHE H78-14/B black sidewall tires. QHF H78-14/B white stripe tires. U05 dual horns ($6). U35 electric clock ($19). U58 AM-FM stereo radio ($226). U63 push-button radio ($75). U69 AM/FM push-button radio ($137). U76 windshield antenna ($16). U80 auxiliary radio speaker ($21). UA1 heavy-duty battery. UF7 gauge package ($92). UM1 AM push-button radio and tape player ($209). UM2 AM/FM push-button radio and tape player ($324). V01 heavy-duty radiator ($25-$34). V30 bumper guards ($36). V55 station wagon luggage rack ($68). V78 certificate of compliance plate delete. VE5 bumper impact strip. Deluxe bumpers on base Malibu ($29). YF5 California emissions. YJ9 exterior décor package. Z03 Landau equipment package. Z49 mandatory Canadian base equipment mod. ZJ7 special wheel treatment with hub caps and trim rings ($35-60). ZJ9 auxiliary lighting group ($21-41). Econominder gauge package ($45). Sport striping ($8). Knit or Sport cloth seats in wagons ($20). Litter container ($6).

OPTION INSTALLATION RATES

Automatic transmission (99.1 percent). Standard V-8 engine (55.5 percent). Optional V-8 engine (33.6 percent). 6-cylinder engine (10.9 percent). AM radio (59.7 percent). AM/FM monaural radio (13.8 percent). AM/FM stereo radio (4.5 percent). Stereo tape (4.4 percent). Manual air conditioning (80.6 percent). Power steering (99.4 percent). Tilt steering (18.7 percent). Manual disc brakes (2.3 percent). Power front disc brakes (97.7 percent). Power door locks (8.3 percent). Power windows (5.2 percent). Cruise control (14.5 percent). Bucket seats (5.7 percent). Power seats (1.6 percent). Vinyl top (26.5 percent). Tinted windshield only (3.5 percent). All tinted glass (82 percent). Positraction (3.2 percent). Standard wheel covers (4.7 percent). Optional full wheel covers (60.6 percent). Standard styled wheels (17 percent). Optional styled wheels (10.3 percent). Steel-belted radial tires (99.3 percent). Standard clock (2.7 percent). Optional clock (21.9 percent). Rear window defogger (19.6 percent). Remote-control left-hand side-view mirror (58 percent). Remote-control right-hand side-view mirror (4.3 percent). Based on model-year production of 333,243 units in the United States and Canada.

HISTORICAL FOOTNOTES

The 1976 Chevelle line had its dealer introduction date on October 7, 1975. Robert D. Lund was Chevrolet general manager. The company's total output of 2,077,119 was a much-needed gain over the 1975 figure. Calendar-year sales of Chevelles was 334,267 for a 3.9 percent share of the total market. This compared to 285,726 units and 4.0 percent of total U.S. auto sales the previous calendar year. Model-year U.S. dealer sales were 333,759 (a 21.1 percent gain) against 276,079 units in 1975. While Chevrolet was gaining unit sales, its share of General Motors total sales declined to 42.6 percent, since Oldsmobile Division's popular Cutlass was changing overall corporate sales trends. Calendar-year registrations climbed to 262,310 passenger cars and 62,560 station wagons versus 232,030 cars and 44,176 wagons the previous season. The slope-nosed 1976 Laguna Type S-3 had a successful season in NASCAR stock-car racing with Cale Yarborough capturing the NASCAR Winston Cup titles behind the wheel of such a car.

1977

With several station wagon options available, the Chevelle Malibu was evolving into more of a family hauler by 1977.

Chevelles had minor revisions to their front and rear end styling this year, plus some suspension changes. The top-of-the-line Malibu Classic got another new grille with a vertical theme and new taillights. Coupes continued to be built off a 112-in. wheelbase platform while sedans and station wagons had 116-in. stances. Only three engines were offered in 1977, but all had five more horsepower than their 1976 counterparts.

I.D. NUMBERS

VIN embossed on the top left-hand side of the instrument panel and visible through the windshield. The first symbol 1 designates Chevrolet. The second symbol indicates series: C=Malibu, D=Malibu Classic. The third and fourth symbols indicate body style: 29=four-door pillared hardtop sedan, 37=two-door pillared hardtop coupe and 35=four-door station wagon. The fifth symbol indicates engine (net hp): D=250-cid 110-hp inline six-cylinder, Q=305-cid 145-hp V-8, V=350-cid 170-hp V-8. The sixth symbol designates the model year: 7=1977. The seventh symbol designates the assembly plant location: B=Baltimore, Maryland, D=Doraville, Georgia, Z=Fremont, California, R=Arlington, Texas and 1=Oshawa, Canada. The last six symbols are the sequential unit production number at the specific factory. The Fisher body tag riveted to the top of the cowl on the left side of the car below the hood provides additional vehicle identification information. The Fisher body STYLE NUMBER (ST) consists of a prefix identifying model year and four or more symbols identifying the series and body style (example: 77-1AD29 for a 1977 Malibu Classic four-door sport sedan). The BODY NUMBER consists of a pre-

CHEVELLE

fix designating assembly plant and the sequential unit production number at the specific factory. The TRIM NUMBER (TR) identifies upholstery.

COLORS

(11) Antique White, (13) Silver poly, (16) Medium Gray Poly, (19) Black, (21) Light Blue, (22) Light Blue Poly, (29) Dark Blue Poly, (32) Light Lime, (36) Firethorn Poly, (38) Dark Aqua Poly, (44) Medium Green Poly, (50) Cream Gold, (51) Bright Yellow, (61) Light Buckskin, (63) Buckskin Poly, (69) Brown Poly, (72) Red, (75) Light Red, (78) Orange Poly and (85) Medium Blue. Vinyl tops were available in: 11T=White, 13T=Silver, 19T=Black, 22T=Light Blue, 36T=Firethorn, 44T=Medium Green and 61T=Light Buckskin.

ENGINE CODES

Codes appear on the right side of six-cylinder blocks behind the distributor and right front of V-8 engine blocks. Engine codes for 1977 were: (250-cid 110-hp six) CCC, CCD, CCF, CGA and 7SB; (305-cid 145-hp two-barrel V-8) CRA and CRF; 350-cid 170-hp four-barrel V-8) CMF, CKH, CKM, CKR, CHA, CHB, CHX and CKK.

CHEVELLE MALIBU — SERIES 1C SIX/V-8

Chevelle dropped down to two series for 1977: Malibu and Malibu Classic. Two-door coupe, four-door sedan and station wagon bodies (two or three seat) were offered in both. The Laguna coupe and Malibu Classic Estate wagon were gone. Both series had new grilles and six-section tail lamps this year. The Malibu had a mesh pattern grille with many wide rectangles and single round headlights. A script was in the grille's lower corner (driver's side). Small horizontal rectangular parking lamps were again inset in the bumper. The Malibu coupe's rear side windows got "coach" style glass this year. Malibu station wagons had a standard 305-cid (5.0-liter) V-8. The base engine for other bodies was the 250-cid in-line six. Standard equipment on base Malibu included seat belts with push-button buckles for all positions, two front combination seat and inertia-reel shoulder belts for driver (with reminder light and buzzer) and right front passenger, an energy-absorbing steering column, a safety steering wheel, passenger guard door locks, safety door latches and hinges, folding seat back latches, an energy-absorbing padded instrument panel, padded front seat backs, a contoured windshield header, a thick-laminate windshields, safety armrests, side marker lights and reflectors, parking lamps that illuminate with the headlamps, a four-way hazard warning flasher, directional signals with a lane-change feature, back-up lights, a defroster, dual-speed windshield wipers with washers, a vinyl-edged wide-view day/night inside rearview mirror with shatterproof glass and a deflecting support, a left-hand outside rearview mirror, a dual master brake cylinder with warning light, a starter safety switch, a dual-action safety hood latch, an ignition-key reminder buzzer, a steering column lock, a full-coil suspension with computer-selected springs, a perimeter frame, a cushioned body-mounting system, a High-Energy ignition system, a catalytic converter, six-month or 7,500-mile chassis lubrication, front disc/rear drum brakes with finned rear aluminum brake drums, a Delcotron generator, a solid-state regulator, a sealed side-terminal battery, a 22-gallon fuel tank, Magic-Mirror acrylic exterior finish, Hide-A-Way windshield wipers, an inside hood release, a cigarette lighter, illuminated instrument panel controls, new sport cloth-and-vinyl upholstery in black, blue or buckskin and wall-to-wall nylon cut-pile carpeting.

Model Number	Body/Style Number	Body Type & Seating	Factory Price	Shipping Weight	Production Total
CHEVELLE MALIBU SERIES 1C (6-CYL)					
1C	29	4d Colonnade-6P	$3,935	3,628 lbs.	Note 1
1C	37	2d Colonnade-6P	$3,885	3,551 lbs.	Note 1
CHEVELLE MALIBU SERIES 1C (V-8)					
1C	29	4d Colonnade-6P	$4,055	3,727 lbs.	Note 1
1C	37	2d Colonnade-6P	$4,005	3,650 lbs.	Note 1
CHEVELLE MALIBU STATION WAGON SERIES 1C (V-8)					
1C	35	4d wagon-6P	$4,734	4,139 lbs.	Note 1
1C	35/AQ4	4d wagon-8P	$4,877	4,169 lbs.	Note 1

NOTE 1: Individual body style production is not available; see production notes.

CHEVELLE MALIBU CLASSIC SERIES 1D — SIX/V-8

The Malibu Classic grille showed a vertical theme with many narrow bars. As in 1976, Malibu Classics also had stacked rectangular headlamps. A chrome "Malibu Classic" script was placed in the lower left-hand corner of the grille. Small horizontal rectangular parking lamps were again inset in the bumper. Standard equipment on base Malibu included seat belts with push-button buckles for all positions, two front combination seat and inertia-reel shoulder belts for driver (with reminder light and buzzer) and right front passenger, an energy-absorbing steering column, a safety steering wheel, passenger guard door locks, safety door latches and hinges, folding seat back latches, an energy-absorbing padded instrument panel, padded front seat backs, a contoured windshield header, a thick-laminate windshields, safety armrests, side marker lights and reflectors, parking lamps that illuminate with the headlamps, a four-way hazard warning flasher, directional signals with a lane-change feature, back-up lights, a defroster, dual-speed windshield wipers with washers, a vinyl-edged wide-view day/night inside rearview mirror with shatterproof glass and a deflecting support, a left-hand outside rearview mirror, a dual master brake cylinder with warning light, a starter safety switch, a dual-action safety hood latch, an ignition-key reminder buzzer, a steering column lock, a full-coil suspension with computer-selected springs, a perimeter frame, a cushioned body-mounting system, a High-Energy ignition system, a catalytic converter, six-month or 7,500-mile chassis lubrication, front disc/rear drum brakes with finned rear aluminum brake drums, a Delcotron generator, a solid-state regulator, a sealed side-terminal battery, a 22-gallon fuel tank, Magic-Mirror acrylic exterior finish, Hide-A-Way windshield wipers, an inside hood release, a cigarette lighter, illuminated instrument panel controls, a colored-keyed instrument cluster with wood grained accents, knit cloth-and-vinyl upholstery in blue, green or Firethorn (or buckskin in coupes only) and wall-to-wall plush cut-pile carpeting. The Malibu Classic coupe's rear side windows got "coach" style glass this year and the Malibu Classic tail lamps had fancier bright work that reached toward the license plate. Its rocker panels also wore wide bright moldings. The Malibu Classic station wagon had a 350-cid (5.7-liter) V-8 with a four-barrel carburetor. Base engine for other body styles was the 250-cid inline six. A three-speed manual transmission was standard on six-cylinder models except the Malibu Classic sedan, which had Turbo-Hydra-Matic. Station wagons also had the same automatic transmission, plus power brakes and steering. FR78-15/B fiberglass-belted radial tires (HR78-15/B steel-belted radials on station wagons). The Classic Landau added a vinyl roof, dual horns, dual sport mirrors (left-hand remote-controlled), deluxe front and rear bumpers and full wheel covers. Coupes rode a 112-in. wheelbase and sedans and wagons had the 116-in. stance.

Model Number	Body/Style Number	Body Type & Seating	Factory Price	Shipping Weight	Production Total
CHEVELLE MALIBU CLASSIC SERIES 1D (6-CYL)					
1D	29	4d Colonnade-6P	$4,475	3,725 lbs.	Note 1
1D	37	2d Colonnade-6P	$4,125	3,599 lbs.	Note 1
1D	37	2d Landau-6P	$4,353	3,688 lbs.	Note 1
CHEVELLE MALIBU CLASSIC SERIES 1D (V-8)					
1D	29	4d Colonnade-6P	$4,595	3,824 lbs.	Note 1
1D	37	2d Colonnade-6P	$4,245	3,698 lbs.	Note 1
1D	37	2d Landau-6P	$4,473	3,801 lbs.	Note 1
CHEVELLE MALIBU CLASSIC STATION WAGON SERIES 1D (V-8)					
1D	35	4d wagon-6P	$5,065	4,233 lbs.	Note 1
1D	35/AQ4	4d wagon-8P	$5,208	4,263 lbs.	Note 1

NOTE 1: Individual body style production is not available; see production notes.

PRODUCTION NOTES

NOTE 1 Model-year production (U.S. only) of all 1977 Chevelles was 374,749. This does not agree with figures in Note 2 or Note 3 below. Note 2 figures total 328,216. Note 3 figures total 291,995. The differences cannot be explained using our sources.

NOTE 2 Additional statistics record series production (United States only) as follows:

Malibu (6-cyl)	24,076
Malibu (V-8)	43,781
Total	**67,857**
Malibu Classic (6-cyl)	7,765
Malibu (V-8)	179,965
Total	**187,730**
Wagons (V-8)	72,629
Total	**72,629**

NOTE 3 Production by factory (U.S. only) was:

Code	Factory	Production	Code	Factory	Production
B	Baltimore	114,154	D	Doraville (Ga.)	44,126
R	Arlington (Tex.)	27,641	Z	Fremont (Cal.)	43,841
L	Leeds, Mo.	62,193			

NOTE 4 Total production including units made in Canada for the U.S. market was 411,038.

ENGINES

CHEVELLE BASE six-CYL: Inline. Overhead-valve. Cast-iron block. Displacement: 250 cid. Bore and stroke: 3.875 x 3.53 in. Compression ratio: 8.25:1. Net brake hp: 110 at 3800 rpm. Taxable hp: 36. Torque: 185 lbs.-ft. at 1200 rpm. Seven main bearings. Hydraulic valve lifters. Crankcase capacity: 4 qt. (add 1 qt. for new filter). Cooling system capacity: 12 qt (add 6 qt. for heater). Carburetor: Rochester one-barrel. Sales code L22.

CHEVELLE BASE V-8: Overhead-valve. Cast-iron block and head. Bore and stroke: 3.74 x 3.48 in. Displacement: 305 cid (5.0 liters). Compression ratio: 8.5:1. Net brake hp: 145 at 3800 rpm. Taxable hp: 44.66. Net torque: 245 lbs.-ft. at 2400 rpm. Five main bearings. Hydraulic valve lifters. Carburetor: Rochester 2GC two-barrel. VIN Code: U.

Note: There was no extra cost for the 5.0-liter V-8 in the Malibu station wagon.

CHEVELLE OPTIONAL 350-CID, 170-HP V-8: Overhead-valve. Cast-iron block and head. Bore and stroke: 4.00 x 3.48 in. Displacement: 350-cid (5.7 liters). Compression ratio: 8.5:1. Net brake hp: 170 at 3800 rpm. Taxable hp: 51.20. Net torque: 270 lbs.-ft. at 2400 rpm. Five main bearings. Hydraulic valve lifters. Carburetor: Rochester M4MC four-barrel. VIN Code: L.

CHASSIS DATA

Wheelbase: (two-door) 112 in; (four-door) 116 in Overall length: (two-door) 205.7 in; (four-door) 209.7 in; (wagon) 215.4 in. Height: (two-door) 53.4 in; (four-door) 54.1 in; (wagon) 55.8 in. Width: 76.9 in. Front tread: 61.5 in; Rear tread: 60.7 in. Front headroom: (sedan) 37.9 in; (coupe) 37.2 in. Rear headroom: (sedan) 37.3 in; (coupe) 36.7 in. Front hip room: (sedan) 54.7 in; (coupe) 51.8 in. Rear hip room: (sedan) 57.8 in; (coupe) 52.7 in. Front shoulder room: (sedan) 59.6 in; (coupe) 59.6 in. Rear shoulder room: (sedan) 58.9; (coupe) 58 in. Front legroom: (sedan) 42.1 in; (coupe) 42.1 in. Rear legroom: (sedan) 36.9 in; (coupe) 32.9 in. Usable luggage space: (sedan) 15.3 cubic feet; (coupe) 15.3 cubic feet. Standard tires: (car) FR78-15/B fiberglass-belted radials; (wagon) HR78-15/B steel-belted radials. Transmission: Three-speed manual transmission with column shift) standard. Gear ratios: (1st) 3.11:1; (2nd) 1.84:1; (3rd) 1.00:1; (rev) 3.22:1. Automatic gear ratios: (1st) 2.52:1; (2nd) 1.52:1; (3rd) 1.00:1; (rev) 1.94:1. Standard final drive ratio: (Six-cylinder) 2.73:1; (V-8) 2.56:1. Steering: re-circulating ball. Brakes: Front disc, rear drum. Ignition: Electronic. Fuel tank: 22 gal.

OPTIONS

Engines: 305-cid V-8 ($120). 350-cid V-8 (Cars $210; Wagons $90). Turbo-Hydra-matic transmission ($282). Positraction axle ($54). Highway axle ratio ($13). Performance axle ratio ($13-$14). Power brakes: ($61). Power steering: ($146). F40 heavy-duty suspension ($19). F41 sport suspension ($36). Heavy-duty radiator ($27-$37). Heavy-duty 61-amp alternator ($29). Heavy-duty battery ($16-$17). California emission system ($70). High altitude emission system ($22). Estate station wagon equipment ($185). Air conditioning ($478-$507). Rear defogger, forced-air ($48). Electric rear window defogger ($82). Cruise-master speed control ($80). Tinted glass ($54). Comfortilt steering wheel ($57). Six-way power seat ($137). Power windows ($108-$151). Power door locks ($68-$96). Power trunk release ($18). Station wagon power tailgate release ($22). Electric clock ($20). Econominder gauge package ($47). Intermittent wipers ($30). Auxiliary lighting ($22-$44). Dual horns ($6). Remote-control driver's mirror ($15). Twin sport mirrors, left-hand remote control ($30). Twin remote sport mirrors ($21-$51). Visor vanity mirror ($4). Lighted visor mirror ($28). AM radio ($72). AM/FM radio ($137). AM/FM stereo radio ($226). Stereo tape player w/AM radio ($209). Stereo tape player with AM/FM stereo radio ($324). Rear speaker ($23). Windshield antenna ($17, included with radios). Electric sky roof ($394). Vinyl roof ($111). Exterior decor package

($20-$54). Two-tone paint ($43). Two-seat station wagon swing-out rear windows ($52). Body side moldings ($40). Door edge guards ($8-$12). Station wagon rear window air deflector ($26). Station wagon roof carrier ($71). Bumper rub strips ($32). Front and rear bumper guards (cars $39; wagons $20). Front center console ($75). Bench or notch back bench seat with sport cloth or vinyl ($20). Vinyl Strato-bucket swiveling front seats ($109-$129). Litter container ($6). Station wagon load-floor carpeting ($45). Front and rear color-keyed floor mats ($16). Deluxe seat belts ($16-$22). Rallye wheels ($38-$65). Full wheel covers ($33). Sport wheel covers ($48-$81). FR78-15/B fiberglass-belted white sidewall ($33-$41). FR78-15/B steel-belted black sidewall ($35-$45). FR78-15/B steel-belted white sidewall ($68-$86). GR78-15/B steel-belted black sidewall ($56-$71). GR78-15/B steel-belted white sidewall ($90-$114). HR78-15/B steel-belted black sidewall ($110). HR78-15/B steel-belted white sidewall ($157); HR78-15/B steel-belted white sidewall on Chevelle wagon ($47). GR70-15/B steel-belted black sidewall ($74-$93). GR70-15/B steel-belted white sidewall ($119-$150). Stow-away spare (no extra charge).

OPTION INSTALLATION RATES

Automatic transmission (98.7 percent). Standard V-8 engine (22.1 percent). Optional V-8 engine (68.2 percent). Six-cylinder engine (9.7 percent). AM radio (53 percent). AM/FM monaural radio (15 percent). AM/FM stereo radio (5 percent). Stereo tape (4 percent). Manual air conditioning (80.6 percent). Power steering (99.3 percent). Tilt steering (21.9 percent). Manual disc brakes (2.6 percent). Power front disc brakes (97.4 percent). Power door locks (4.1 percent). Power windows (5.7 percent). Cruise control (17 percent). Bucket seats (5 percent). Power seats (1 percent). Vinyl top (23 percent). Tinted windshield only (2.2 percent). All tinted glass (83.8 percent). Positraction (3 percent). Standard wheel covers (4 percent). Optional full wheel covers (63 percent). Standard styled wheels (18 percent). Optional styled wheels (18 percent). Steel-belted radial tires (96.1 percent). Fiberglass-belted radial tires (3.4 percent). Optional clock (25 percent). Rear window defogger (20 percent). Remote-control left-hand sideview mirror (61 percent). Remote-control right-hand sideview mirror (3 percent). Based on model-year production of 328,216 units in the United States and Canada.

HISTORICAL FOOTNOTES

The 1977 Chevelle line had its dealer introduction date on September 30, 1976. Robert D. Lund was Chevrolet general manager. The company's total output of 2,154,893 was another increase. Calendar-year sales of Chevelle Malibu was 296,193 for a 3.3 percent share of the total market. This compared to 334,267 units and 3.9 percent of total U.S. auto sales the previous calendar year. Model-year U.S. dealer sales were 298,605 against 333,759 units in 1975. Calendar-year registrations fell to 286,911 versus 324,870 the previous season. Once again, Cale Yarborough captured the NASCAR Winston Cup championship with his Chevelle Malibu racing car.

Malibu
1978-1983

Malibu

1978

The Chevelle name disappeared from the Chevrolet line in 1978. The mid-size offerings were now simply called Malibus and Malibu Classics.

By 1978, mid-size Chevrolets were no longer called Chevelles. "The 1978 Malibu from Chevrolet" said the year's sales catalog. Full-size Chevrolets had been downsized in 1977 and the mid-size (A-body) Malibu got the same treatment this year. Chevrolet cleverly promoted the redesigned intermediates as "good news for here and now" to emphasize their modern flavor and in-step-with-the-times smaller size. These all-new Malibus and Malibu Classics were a foot shorter and 500-800 lbs. lighter than equivalent 1977 models.

In spite of this, they boasted more interior head and leg room, front and rear, and a larger trunk. The base engine was a thrifty V-6. Compared to 1977 models, the '78s were easier to park and more maneuverable in city traffic. They retained full-frame construction. Other selling features included a standard front stabilizer bar, extensive corrosion-resisting treatments, 14 noise-insulating body mounts (for a quieter ride) and double-panel doors, hood and deck lid construction.

I.D. NUMBERS

VIN embossed on the top left-hand side of the instrument panel and visible through the windshield. The first symbol 1 designates Chevrolet. The second symbol indicates series: T=Malibu, W=Malibu Classic. The third and fourth symbols indicate body style: 19=four-door sedan, 27=two-door notchback coupe, 35=four-door station wagon and 80=El Camino. The fifth symbol indicates engine (net horsepower): M=RPO L26 200-cid 94-hp V-6, A=RPO LD5 231-cid 105-hp V-6 (California), U=RPO LG3 305-cid 145-hp V-8 and L=RPO LM1 350-cid 170-hp V-8. The sixth symbol designates the model year: 8=1978. The seventh symbol designates the assembly plant location: B=Baltimore, Maryland, D=Doraville, Georgia, Z=Fremont, California, R=Arlington, Texas, L=Leeds, Missouri, and 1=Oshawa, Canada. The last six symbols are the sequential unit production number at the specific factory. The Fisher body tag riveted to the top of the cowl on the left side of the car below the hood provides additional vehicle identification information. The Fisher Body STYLE NUMBER (ST) consists of a prefix identifying model year and four or more symbols identifying the series and body style (example: 78-1AW27 for a 1978 Malibu Classic two-door notchback coupe). The BODY NUMBER consists of a prefix designating assembly plant and the sequential unit production number at the specific factory. The TRIM NUMBER (TR) identifies upholstery.

COLORS

(11) Antique White, (15) Silver poly, (16) Gray Poly, (19) Black, (21) Pastel Blue, (22) Light Blue Poly, (24)

Ultramarine Blue, (29) Dark Blue Poly, (34) Orange, (44) Medium Green Poly, (45) Dark Green Poly, (48) Dark Blue Green Poly, (51) Bright Yellow, (56) Gold Poly, (61) Camel Beige, (63) Camel Tan Poly, (67) Safron Poly, (69) Dark Camel Poly, (77) Carmine Poly, (79) Dark Carmine Poly. Vinyl tops were available in: 11T=White, 15T=Silver Poly, 19T=Black, 22T=Light Blue Poly, 44T=Medium Green Poly, 61T=Camel Beige and 79T Dark Carmine Poly.

ENGINE CODES

Codes appear on the right side of six-cylinder blocks behind the distributor and right-hand side of V-8 engine blocks. Engine codes for 1978 were: (200-cid two-barrel V-8) CWA and CWB; (231-cid two-barrel V-6) DH, EA and OK; (305-cid V-8) CRW, CRX, CRH, C4D, CRY, CRZ, CER and DAF; (350-cid V-8) CMD, CMA, CMB and CMC.

MALIBU — SERIES 1A — V-6/V-8

These Malibus looked like small versions of the big Chevy with their clean, somewhat angular lines. The grille was a chrome rectangle with an "egg crate" style insert and a six-sided badge at the center of the upper surround. The headlamps were large, rectangular units set in an even larger bright housing that canted backwards at each corner, on the bottom. The parking lamps were positioned vertically between the grille and the headlamps, with amber-colored side-marker lamps and directionals at the outboard ends. The front body sides had a curvature to them and were angled forward at the front and at the rear. The rear end featured triple rectangular-segment taillights with the outboard segments notched into the body sides to serve as side marker lights. The inboard rectangular segments had a smaller white rectangular lens in the center to serve as back-up lights. In the center of the rear panel, between the taillights, was a license plate recess. The back bumper dipped down a little under the license plate recess. The front bumper was of a simple, straight-across design. Both bumpers had black rubber impact strips. Bumper guards were optional. The station wagon had a different rear bumper with large, rectangular, single-unit taillights near each corner and square back-up light lenses built into them. These new-size Malibu were 12 1/2 to 22 in. shorter than their 1977 counterparts and narrower, too, but just as tall. Slimmer doors and the reduced body side curvature helped keep interior space ample. By providing broad glass areas, the Chevrolet designers improved visibility. The rear armrests in sedans and station wagons were now recessed into the back door trim panels so that the door glass was fixed, rather than movable. Somehow, the newly shrunken Malibu managed to offer more interior and luggage space. Shell-type seats helped add headroom and legroom. Coupes lost 550 lbs. and wagons were close to half a ton lighter. Both coupes and sedans had bright roof drip moldings and wheel covers. Sedans had large pivoting quarter vent windows. A Chevrolet block-letter nameplate was on the lower right side of the rear deck lid. Malibu The standard power plant was a new 200-cid (3.3-liter) V-6 derived from the popular small-block V-8. The new engine had a cast-iron block and cylinder heads, a new "Dual Jet" carburetor and a lightweight aluminum intake manifold. New dynamic balancing was supposed to ensure a smooth-running power plant. Cars sold in California were required to use a 231-cid V-6 in place of the 3.3-liter engine. The standard transmission was a three-speed manual type, except in California, where the otherwise optional Turbo-Hydra-Matic transmission was mandatory. An optional 305-cid (5.0-liter) V-8 could have either a four-speed manual or automatic transmission. Station wagons in high-altitude areas had to have a 350-cid V-8 with a four-barrel carburetor. A new vertical-style instrument panel, mounted well forward, helped to enhance the spaciousness of the interior. A separate module held the radio controls, heater controls and instruments. Plug-in components and a swing-down glove compartment made behind-the-dash servicing easier. The headlight dimmer switch was moved to the turn-signal lever. A new ventilation system delivered outside air under all driving conditions, whether power assisted or ram vented. Sedans and station wagons had standard swing-out rear vent windows. Drivers had a delta-spoke soft vinyl steering wheel. Station wagons had a much wider cargo opening than before, plus a split tailgate instead of the previous swing-up version. As in full-size wagons, storage compartments were in the rear quarter trim panels, just inside the tailgate. The new Malibu still used a full perimeter type frame to keep their "big car" ride. The chassis featured coil springs all around, a single-piece propeller shaft, lower rear axle ratios, relay-type steering and front disc, rear drum brakes. The new fuel tank held 17.5 gallons. Malibu rode on radial-ply tires on 14-in. wheels. All had a modular mini-enersorber bumper system. A new temporary spare tire saved 15 lbs. and allowed greater trunk space. Fourteen tuned rubber body mounts helped keep road noise down. Standard equipment included self-adjusting front disc brakes with wear indicators, a High Energy Ignition system, a Freedom side-terminal battery, a dual-mode ventilation system with picture windows, full carpeting, radial tires, new interior styling with a delta-spoked soft-vinyl steering wheel, a fully inflated compact spare tire, rectangular headlights with chrome-plated bezels, bright windshield and rear window reveal moldings, bright belt side and roof drip moldings, a bright left-hand outside rearview mirror, extensive corrosion-resisting treatments, triple wraparound taillights on coupes and sedans, full wheel covers and wheel opening moldings on station wagons, visible ball-joint wear indicators, a front stabilizer bar, a Delcotron generator, a coolant recovery system, seat belts with push-button buckle releases for all passengers, two combination seat and inertia reel shoulder belts for driver and right front passenger (with reminder light and buzzer), an energy-absorbing steering column, passenger guard door locks, safety door latches with stamped steel hinges, folding seatback latches, an energy-absorbing padded instrument panel, padded front seat back tops, a contoured windshield header, a thick laminate windshield, safety armrests, a safety steering wheel, side marker lights and reflectors, parking lights that illuminate with the headlamps, four-way hazard flashers, back-up lights, directional signals with a lane-change feature, a defroster, dual-speed windshield wipers, windshield washers, a wide-view day/night inside rearview mirror with vinyl edging and a deflecting sup-

Malibu

The 1978 Malibus came in two- and four-door versions, with a base V-6 and optional 305- and 350-cid V-8s.

port, a left-hand outside rearview mirror, a dual master cylinder brake system with warning light, a starter safety switch, a dual-action safety hood latch, an ignition key reminder buzzer, a steering column lock and P185/75R14 fiberglass-belted radial tires (P195/75R14 on station wagons). In addition to 14 solid colors, five custom two-tone combinations were optional: dark blue and light blue metallic, gold and light camel, carmine and dark carmine metallic, green and light green metallic and silver with medium gray accenting. The Malibu passenger cars offered soft cloth bench seats in black, blue, green or camel, while station wagons featured all-vinyl bench seats in blue, camel or carmine. The station wagon's easy-to-operate two-piece tailgate opened from the top or from the top and bottom. The top was like a hatch window and the bottom was like a tailgate.

Model Number	Body/Style Number	Body Type & Seating	Factory Price	Shipping Weight	Production Total
MALIBU SERIES 1T (V-6)					
1T	27	2d sport coupe-6P	$4,204	3,001 lbs.	Note 1
1T	19	4d sedan-6P	$4,279	3,006 lbs.	Note 1
1T	35	4d wagon-6P	$4,516	3,169 lbs.	Note 1
MALIBU SERIES 1T (V-8)					
1T	27	2d sport coupe-6P	$4,394	3,138 lbs.	Note 1
1T	19	4d sedan-6P	$4,469	3,143 lbs.	Note 1
1T	35	4d wagon-6P	$4,706	3,350 lbs.	Note 1

MALIBU CLASSSIC — SERIES 1W V-6/V-8

Standard equipment on Malibu Classics included Malibu Classic logos on the rear body sides, just ahead of the side-marker lights, a 50-50 front bench seat with folding center armrest, wheel opening moldings on all models, dual horns, self-adjusting front disc brakes with wear indicators, a High Energy Ignition system, a Freedom side-terminal battery, a dual-mode ventilation system with picture windows, full carpeting, radial tires, new interior styling with a delta-spoked soft-vinyl steering wheel, a fully inflated compact spare tire, rectangular headlights with chrome-plated bezels, bright windshield and rear window reveal moldings, bright belt side and roof drip moldings, a bright left-hand outside rearview mirror, extensive corrosion-resisting treatments, triple wraparound taillights on coupes and sedans, full wheel covers, visible ball-joint wear indicators, a front stabilizer bar, a Delcotron generator, a coolant recovery system, seat belts with push-button buckle releases for all passengers, two combination seat and inertia reel shoulder belts for driver and right front passenger (with reminder light and buzzer), an energy-absorbing steering column, passenger guard door locks, safety door latches with stamped steel hinges, folding seatback latches, an energy-absorbing padded instrument panel, padded front seat back tops, a contoured windshield header, a thick laminate windshield, safety armrests, a safety steering wheel, side marker lights and reflectors, parking lights that illuminate with the headlamps, four-way hazard flashers, back-up lights, directional signals with a lane-change feature, a defroster, dual-speed windshield wipers, windshield washers, a wide-view day/night inside rearview mirror with vinyl edging and a deflecting support, a left-hand outside rearview mirror, a dual master cylinder brake system with warning light, a starter safety switch, a dual-action safety hood latch, an ignition key reminder buzzer, a steering column lock and P185/75R14 fiberglass-belted radial tires (P195/75R14 on station wagons). In addition to 14 solid colors, five custom two-tone combinations were optional: dark blue and light blue metallic, gold and light camel, carmine and dark carmine metallic, green and light green metallic and silver with medium gray accenting. The Malibu Classic passenger cars offered knit cloth or all vinyl bench seats in black, blue, green, camel or carmine. Station wagons featured all-vinyl or Sport cloth bench seats in black, blue, camel or carmine. The station wagon's easy-to-operate two-piece tailgate opened from the top or from the top and bottom. The top was like a hatch window and the bottom was like a tailgate. A Malibu Classic Landau coupe was available, as was an Estate option with wood-grain exterior paneling for the Malibu Classic wagon. The Malibu Classic Landau had an elk-grain vinyl half top, bright-edged black side pillar trim, body side pin striping, sport wheel covers and special Landau identification.

Model Number	Body/Style Number	Body Type & Seating	Factory Price	Shipping Weight	Production Total
MALIBU CLASSIC SERIES 1W (V-6)					
1W	27	2d sport coupe-6P	$4,461	3,031 lbs.	Note 1
1W	27 + Z03	2d Landau coupe	$4,684	—	Note 1

1W	19	4d sedan-6P	$4,561	3,039 lbs.	Note 1
1W	35	4d wagon-6P	$4,714	3,196 lbs.	Note 1
MALIBU CLASSIC SERIES 1W (V-8)					
1W	27	2d sport coupe-6P	$4,651	3,167 lbs.	Note 1
1W	27 + Z03	2d Landau coupe	$4,874	—	Note 1
1W	19	4d sedan-6P	$4,651	3,175 lbs.	Note 1
1W	35	4d wagon-6P	$4,904	3,377 lbs.	Note 1

PRODUCTION NOTES

NOTE 1 Model-year production (North American production for the U.S. market) of all 1978 Malibu was 358,636.

NOTE 2 Model-year production by series and body style was as follows:

Malibu		Malibu Classic		Total
sedan	44,426	sedan	102,967	
station wagon	30,850	station wagon	63,152	
sport coupe	27,089	sport coupe	60,992	
Landau coupe		29,160		
	102,365		256,271	=358,636

NOTE 3 Additional statistics record series production (North American production for the U.S. market) as follows:

Malibu (V-6)	45,600	Malibu (V-8)	25,915	Total	71,515
Malibu Classic (V-6)	68,504	Malibu (V-8)	124,615	Total	193,119
wagons (V-6)	28,765	wagons (V-8)	65,237	Total	94,002

NOTE 4 Production by factory (U.S. only) was:

Code	Factory	Production	Code	Factory	Production
B	Baltimore	97,394	D	Doraville (Ga.)	50,977
R	Arlington (Tex.)	38,932	Z	Fremont (Cal.)	30,152
L	Leeds, (Mo.)	106,078			

NOTE 5 In 1978, only 8,930 Malibus had the 231-cid V-6 and only 802 had the 350 V-8 (code LM1).

ENGINES

MALIBU BASE V-6 (FEDERAL): Overhead-valve V-6. Cast-iron block and head. Displacement: 200 cid (3.3 liters). Bore & stroke: 3.50 x 3.48 in. Compression ratio: 8.2:1. Brake hp: 95 at 3800 rpm Torque: 160 lbs.-ft. at 2000 rpm Four main bearings. Hydraulic valve lifters. Carburetor: Rochester 2GC two-barrel. Sales Code: L26. VIN code: M.

MALIBU BASE V-6 (CALIFORNIA): Overhead-valve V-6. Cast-iron block and head. Displacement: 231 cid (3.8 liters). Bore & stroke: 3.80 x 3.40 in. Compression ratio: 8.0:1. Brake hp: 105 at 3400 rpm Torque: 185 lbs.-ft. at 2000 rpm Four main bearings. Hydraulic valve lifters. Carburetor: Rochester 2GE two-barrel. Sales Code: LD5. VIN code: A.

MALIBU BASE V-8: Overhead-valve. Cast-iron block and head. Bore and stroke: 3.74 x 3.48 in. Displacement: 305 cid (5.0 liters). Compression ratio: 8.4:1. Net brake hp: 145 at 3800 rpm. Taxable hp: 44.66. Net torque: 245 lbs.-ft. at 2400 rpm. Five main bearings. Hydraulic valve lifters. Carburetor: Rochester 2GC two-barrel. Sales Code: LG3. VIN code: U.

MALIBU OPTIONAL V-8 Overhead-valve. Cast-iron block and head. Bore and stroke: 4.00 x 3.48 in. Displacement: 350 cid (5.7 liters). Compression ratio: 8.2:1. Net brake hp: 170 at 3800 rpm. Taxable hp: 51.20. Net torque: 270 lbs.-ft. at 2400 rpm. Five main bearings. Hydraulic valve lifters. Carburetor: Rochester M4MC four-barrel. Sales Code: LM1. VIN code: L.

CHASSIS DATA

Wheelbase: 108.1 in. Overall length: (coupe and sedan) 192.7 in. (wagon) 193.4 in. Height: (coupe) 53.3 inches; (sedan) 54.2 in. (wagon) 54.5 in. Width: (coupe and sedan) 71.5 in. (wagon) 71.2 in. Front tread: 58.5 in. Rear tread: 57.8 in. Standard tires: (coupe and sedan) P185/75R14 fiberglass belted; (wagon) P195/75R14 fiberglass belted. Front headroom: (sedan) 38.7 in.; (coupe) 37.8 in.; (wagon) 38.7 in. Front legroom: (sedan) 42.8 in.; (coupe) 42.8 in.; (wagon) 42.8 in. Front shoulder room: (sedan) 57.3 in.; (coupe) 56.8 in.; (wagon) 57.3 in. Front hip room: (sedan) 52.2 in. (coupe) 51.7 in.; (wagon) 52.2 in. Rear headroom: (sedan) 37.7 in.; (coupe) 37.2 in.; (wagon) 38.8 in. Rear legroom: (sedan) 38 in.; (coupe) 35.1 in.; (wagon) 35.9 in. Rear shoulder room: (sedan) 57.1 in.; (coupe) 55.6 in.; (wagon) 57.1 in. Rear hip room: (sedan) 55.6 in.; (coupe) 54.5 in.; (wagon) 55.6 in. Transmission: Three-speed manual transmission (floor shift) standard with V-6. Gear ratios: (1st) 3.50:1; (2nd) 1.81:1; (3rd) 1.00:1; (rev) 3.62:1. Four-speed floor shift optional on Malibu with 5.0-liter V-8: (1st) 2.85:1; (2nd) 2.02:1; (3rd) 1.35:1; (4th) 1.00:1; (rev) 2.85:1. Gear ratios: (1st) 2.52:1; (2nd) 1.52:1; (3rd) 1.00:1; (rev) 1.94:1 except Malibu V-6 (1st) 2.74:1; (2nd) 1.57:1; (3rd) 1.00:1; (rev) 2.07:1. Standard final drive ratio: (Malibu) 2.73:1 except 2.29:1 with V-8; (Malibu wagon) 2.41:1. Brakes: Front disc, rear drum. Fuel tank: (coupe and sedan) 17.5 gal.; (station wagon) 18 gal.

OPTIONS

Engines: 231-cid V-6 ($40). 305-cid V-8 ($190). 350-cid V-8: in station wagon ($305). Four-speed manual shift: ($125). Turbo-Hydra-Matic: ($307). Positraction axle: ($60). Performance axle ratio ($14-$17). Power brakes: ($69). Power steering: ($152). F40 heavy-duty suspension for coupe and sedan ($9-$33). F41 sport suspension: for coupe and sedan ($38). Heavy-duty radiator ($29-$31). Heavy-duty 61-amp. alternator ($31). Heavy-duty battery ($17-$18). California emission system ($75). High altitude emission system ($33). Estate equipment package for Malibu station wagon ($235). Quiet sound group ($46). Security package for station wagon ($35). Air conditioning: ($544). Forced-air rear window defogger ($51). Electric rear window defogger ($92). Cruise-master speed control ($90). Tinted glass ($62). Comfortilt steering wheel ($69). Six-way power seat ($151). Power windows ($124-$172). Power door locks ($74-$112). Power trunk release ($21). Electric clock ($21). Special instrumentation ($118). Gauge package ($53). Intermittent wipers ($32). Auxiliary lighting ($28-$52). Dome reading light ($16). Dual horns on base Malibu ($7). Remote-control driver's mirror ($16). Twin sport mirrors, left-hand remote controlled ($33). Twin remote sport mirrors ($57). Visor vanity mirror ($4). Lighted visor mirror ($37). AM radio ($77-$79). AM/FM radio ($149). AM/FM stereo radio ($229). Stereo tape player with AM radio Malibu/Monte ($233). Stereo tape player with AM/FM stereo radio ($328). Rear speaker ($24). Dual front speakers ($20). Windshield antenna, included with radios ($25). Power antenna ($45). Power sky roof ($499). Vinyl roof ($116). Two-tone paint ($62-$110). Deluxe body side moldings ($53). Door edge guards ($11-$18). Wheel opening moldings ($21). window reveal moldings ($41). Body side pin striping ($48). Rear window air deflector on station wagon ($28). Station wagon roof carrier ($85). Bumper rub strips ($36). Front and rear bumper guards for Malibu ($40). Console ($80). Vinyl bench seat for coupe and sedan ($24). Vinyl bucket seats ($110). Knit cloth 50/50 seating in Malibu coupe or sedan ($164). Vinyl 50/50 seating in Malibu coupe or sedan ($188); in Malibu station wagon ($164). Litter container: ($6). Color-keyed mats ($20). Deluxe seatbelts ($19-$21). Deluxe trunk trim ($41). Custom styled wheels ($41-$78), but standard on Malibu Landau coupe. Full wheel covers Malibu coupe or sedan ($37). Sport wheel covers, silver or gold: $49-$86). Wire wheel covers ($60-$146). P185/75R14 fiberglass-belted white sidewall for Malibu coupe or sedan ($37). P195/75R14 steel-belted radial white sidewall for Malibu coupe or sedan ($96); for Malibu station wagon ($78). P205/75R14 steel-belted radial white sidewall: for Malibu coupe or sedan ($148). P195/75R14 fiberglass-belted white sidewall for Malibu station wagon ($39). P205/75R14 steel-belted radial white letter for Malibu coupe or sedan ($160).

OPTION INSTALLATION RATES

Automatic transmission (97.8 percent). Four-speed manual transmission (0.5 percent). Optional V-8 engine (60.2 percent). Six-cylinder engine (39.8 percent). AM radio (54.2 percent). AM/FM monaural radio (16.10 percent). AM 8-track (3.7 percent). AM/FM stereo radio (11.9 percent). AM/FM stereo 8-track (11.8 percent). Manual air conditioning (80.4 percent). Power steering (99.2 percent). Tilt steering (25.5 percent). Manual disc brakes (2.7 percent). Power front disc brakes (99.8 percent). Power door locks (9.9 percent). Power windows (8.6 percent). Cruise control (20.3 percent). Bucket seats (2.7 percent). Power seats (2.8 percent). Vinyl top (15.1 percent). Tinted windshield only (2.4 percent). All tinted glass (82.8 percent). Positraction (3.6 percent). Standard wheel covers (60.3 percent). Optional full wheel covers (21.7 percent). Styled steel wheels (12.5 percent). Optional styled wheels (18 percent). Steel-belted radial tires (72 percent). Fiberglass-belted radial tires (28 percent). Optional clock (29.2 percent). Forced-air rear window defogger (8 percent). Electric rear window defogger (19.8 percent). Remote-control left-hand sideview mirror (63.5 percent). Remote-control right-hand sideview mirror (2.4 percent). Based on model-year production of 358,636 units in the U.S. and Canada (North American production for the U.S. market).

HISTORICAL FOOTNOTES

The 1978 Malibu line had its dealer introduction date on October 6, 1977. Robert D. Lund was Chevrolet general manager. The company's total output of 2,346,103 was up 9.8 percent from 1977's 2,135,942. Calendar-year sales of Malibu was 374,124 for a 4 percent share of the total market. This compared to 296.193 units and 3.3 percent of total U.S. auto sales the previous calendar year. Model-year U.S. dealer sales were 2,342,035. Calendar-year registrations rose to 366,196 versus 286,911 the previous season. Taken together, the new Malibu and new Monte Carlo raised sales of Chevy intermediates to 711,730 units, a 4.9 percent increase.

Model-year production of the 1979 Malibu lineup was 42,147. Shown here is a four-door Malibu Classic Sedan in two-tone black and silver.

A new grille and new taillights were some visible attractions on the 1979 Malibu and Malibu Classic models. These cars represented Chevrolet Motor Division's "regular" intermediate offerings and were available in coupe, sedan and station wagon body styles. The Malibu Classic offered a Landau coupe model option. The 3.3-liter V-6 remained the standard engine for both series, but an optional 4.4-liter "small-block" V-8 bridged the gap between two V-6s and a larger V-8. Special Equipment Order police vehicles were also built on the Malibu platform. These were designed to replace Nova-based police cars. All Malibu and Malibu Classic models benefited from engine advancements such as new exhaust gas re-circulation (EGR) systems and new cold-trapped spark control systems.

I.D. NUMBERS

VIN embossed on the top left-hand side of the instrument panel and visible through the windshield. The first symbol 1 designates Chevrolet. The second symbol indicates series: T=Malibu, W=Malibu Classic. The third and fourth symbols indicate body style: 19=four-door sedan, 27=two-door notchback coupe, 35=four-door station wagon and 80=El Camino. The fifth symbol indicates engine (net horsepower): M=RPO L26 200-cid 94-hp V-6, A=RPO LD5 231-cid 105-hp V-6 (California), J=RPO L39 267-cid 125-hp V-8, H=RPO LG4 305-cid 155-hp V-8 and L=RPO LM1 350-cid 170-hp V-8. The sixth symbol designates the model year: 9=1979. The seventh symbol designates the assembly plant location: B=Baltimore, Maryland, D=Doraville, Georgia, Z=Fremont, California, R=Arlington, Texas, K=Leeds, Missouri, and 1=Oshawa, Canada. The last six symbols are the sequential unit production number at the specific factory. The Fisher body tag riveted to the top of the cowl on the left side of the car below the hood provides additional vehicle identification information. The Fisher Body STYLE NUMBER (ST) consists of a prefix identifying model year and four or more symbols identifying the series and body style (example: 79-1AW27 for a 1979 Malibu Classic two-door notchback coupe). The BODY NUMBER consists of a prefix designating assembly plant and the sequential unit production number at the specific factory. The TRIM NUMBER (TR) identifies upholstery.

COLORS

(11) Antique White, (15) Silver Poly, (16) Gray Poly, (19) Black, (21) Pastel Blue, (22) Light Blue Poly, (24) Bright Blue Poly, (29) Dark Blue Poly, (40) Pastel Green, (44) Medium Green Poly, (51) Bright Yellow, (54) Light Yellow, (61) Medium Beige, (63) Camel Poly, (69) Dark Brown Poly, (75) Red, (77) Carmine Poly, (79) Dark Carmine Poly and (85) Medium Blue Poly two-tone. Vinyl tops were available in: 11T=White, 15T=Silver Poly, 19T=Black, 22T=Light Blue Poly, 40T Pastel Green, 61T=Medium Beige and 79T Dark Carmine Poly.

ENGINE CODES

Engine codes appear on the right side of six-cylinder blocks behind the distributor and right-hand side of V-8 engine blocks. Engine codes for 1979 were: (200-cid two-barrel V-8) DHB and DHA; (231-cid two-barrel V-6) RB, NJ, RW, NH, NC, RJ, NE, RM, NT, NU, SJ and SO; (267-cid two-barrel V-8) DMB, DMD, DMH, DMA, DMC, DMM, DMF and DMR; (305-cid four-barrel V-8) DTF, DTX, DNT, DNW, DNS, DTS, DTA, DTB, DTH, DTJ, DWA, DWB, DTU and DNY; (350-cid four-barrel V-8) DUF, DUJ, DUH and DRX.

MALIBU — SERIES 1A — V-6/V-8

Buyers may have been promised "a fresh new slice of apple pie," but the mid-size Chevrolets didn't change much in 1979. Both Malibu and Malibu Classic models — now in their second season with a downsized format — had a new checkered-look, horizontally divided grille and new taillights. The grille was actually in four horizontal sections. Each of the four sections was divided into two rows. The parking lamps and single rectangular headlamps were structured as in 1978. In addition to the base 200-cid (3.3-liter) V-6, there was an optional 267-cid (4.4-liter) V-8, an optional 305-cid (5.0-liter) V-8 and a 350-cid (5.7-liter) V-8. A total of 849 Malibus were built with the power sky roof option, 8,300 had an F41 Sport suspension and 1,903 carried an MM4 four-speed transmission. Standard equipment included the 200-cid V-6, a three-speed manual transmission, a High Energy ignition system, a front stabilizer bar, a heater/defroster, concealed windshield wipers, an inside day/night rearview mirror, an inside hood release and a locking glove compartment.

Model Number	Body/Style Number	Body Type & Seating	Factory Price	Shipping Weight	Production Total
MALIBU SERIES 1T (V-6)					
1T	27	2d sport coupe-6P	$4,398	2,983 lbs.	Note 1
1T	19	4d sedan-6P	$4,498	2,988 lbs.	Note 1
1T	35	4d wagon-6P	$4,745	3,155 lbs.	Note 1
MALIBU SERIES 1T (V-8)					
1T	27	2d sport coupe-6P	$4,588	3,111 lbs.	Note 1
1T	19	4d sedan-6P	$4,688	3,116 lbs.	Note 1
1T	35	4d wagon-6P	$4,935	3,297 lbs.	Note 1

MALIBU CLASSSIC — SERIES 1W V-6/V-8

Standard equipment on all Malibu models included the 200-cid V-6, a three-speed manual transmission, a High Energy ignition system, a front stabilizer bar, a heater/defroster, concealed windshield wipers, an inside day/night rearview mirror, an inside hood release and a locking glove compartment. The Malibu Classics added dual horns and a special acoustical package. Malibu Classic models now carried an identifying script on their dashboards. The special Malibu Classic Landau coupe had a vinyl roof and silver sport wheel covers. Malibu Classic station wagons had power brakes, wheel opening moldings and full wheel covers.

Model Number	Body/Style Number	Body Type & Seating	Factory Price	Shipping Weight	Production Total
MALIBU CLASSIC SERIES 1W (V-6)					
1W	27	2d sport coupe-6P	$4,676	3,017 lbs.	Note 1
1W	27 + Z03	2d Landau coupe	$4,915	—	Note 1
1W	19	4d sedan-6P	$4,801	3,024 lbs.	Note 1
1W	35	4d wagon-6P	$4,955	3,183 lbs.	Note 1
MALIBU CLASSIC SERIES 1W (V-8)					
1W	27	2d sport coupe-6P	$4,866	3,145 lbs.	Note 1
1W	27 + Z03	2d Landau coupe	$5,105	—	Note 1
1W	19	4d sedan-6P	$4,991	3,152 lbs.	Note 1
1W	35	4d wagon-6P	$5,145	3,325 lbs.	Note 1

PRODUCTION NOTES

NOTE 1 Model-year production (U.S.) of all 1979 Malibu was 377,788 units.
NOTE 2 Model-year production (North American) was 412,147.
NOTE 3 Model-year production by series and body style was as follows:

Malibu		Malibu Classic		Total
sedan	59,674	sedan	104,222	163,896
wagon	50,344	wagon	70,095	120,439
sport coupe	41,848	sport coupe	60,751	102,599
Landau coupe	25,213			25,213
	151,866		260,281	= 412,147

NOTE 4 Additional statistics record series production (North American production for the U.S. market) as follows:

Malibu (V-6)	63,637	Malibu (V-8)	37,885	Total 101,522
Malibu Classic (V-6)	52,054	Malibu (V-8)	138,132	Total 190,186
Wagons (V-6)	33,329	wagons (V-8)	87,110	Total 120,439

NOTE 5 Production by factory (U.S. only) was:

Code	Factory	Production	Code	Factory	Production
B	Baltimore	108,497	D	Doraville, (Ga.)	61,318
R	Arlington (Tex.)	41,275	Z	Fremont (Cal.)	34,911
K	Leeds, (Mo.)	131,787			

ENGINES

MALIBU BASE V-6 (FEDERAL): Overhead-valve. Cast-iron block and head. Displacement: 200 cid (3.3 liters). Bore & stroke: 3.50 x 3.48 in. Compression ratio: 8.2:1. Brake hp: 95 at 3800 rpm Torque: 160 lbs.-ft. at 2000 rpm. Four main bearings. Hydraulic valve lifters. Carburetor: Rochester 2GC two-barrel. Sales Code: L26. VIN code: M.

MALIBU BASE V-6 (CALIFORNIA): Overhead-valve. Cast-iron block and head. Displacement: 231 cid (3.8 liters). Bore & stroke: 3.80 x 3.40 in. Compression ratio: 8.0:1. Brake hp: 105 at 3400 rpm Torque: 185 lbs.-ft. at 2000 rpm Four main bearings. Hydraulic valve lifters. Carburetor: Rochester 2GE two-barrel. Sales Code: LD5. VIN code: A.

MALIBU BASE V-8: Overhead-valve. Cast-iron block and head. Bore and stroke: 3.50 x 3.48 in. Displacement: 267 cid (4.4 liters). Compression ratio: 8.2:1. Brake hp: 125 at 3800 rpm. Taxable hp: 39.20. Net torque: 215 lbs.-ft. at 2400 rpm. Five main bearings. Hydraulic valve lifters. Carburetor: Rochester M2MC two-barrel. VIN Code: J.

MALIBU OPTIONAL V-8: Overhead-valve. Cast-iron block and head. Bore and stroke: 3.74 x 3.48 in. Displacement: 305 cid (5.0 liters). Compression ratio: 8.4:1. Brake hp: 155 at 4000 rpm. Taxable hp: 44.66. Net torque: 235 lbs.-ft. at 2400 rpm. Five main bearings. Hydraulic valve lifters. Carburetor: Rochester M4MC four-barrel. VIN Code: H.

MALIBU WAGON OPTIONAL V-8: Overhead-valve. Cast-iron block and head. Bore and stroke: 4.00 x 3.48 in. Displacement: 350 cid (5.7 liters). Compression ratio: 8.2:1. Brake hp: 165-170 at 3800 rpm. Taxable hp: 51.20. Net torque: 260-270 lbs.-ft. at 2400 rpm. Five main bearings. Hydraulic valve lifters. Carburetor: Rochester M4MC four-barrel. VIN Code: L.

CHASSIS DATA

Wheelbase: 108.1 in. Overall length: (coupe and sedan) 192.7 in.; (wagon) 193.4 in.. Height: (coupe) 53.3 in.; (sedan) 54.2 in.; (wagon) 54.5 in. Width: (coupe and sedan) 71.5 in.; (wagon) 71.2 in. Front tread: 58.5 in. Rear tread: 57.8 in. Standard tires: (coupe and sedan) P185/75R14 fiberglass belted; (Wagon) P195/75R14 fiberglass belted. Front headroom: (sedan) 38.7 in.; (coupe) 37.8 in.; (wagon) 38.7 in. Front legroom: (sedan) 42.8 in.; (coupe) 42.8 in.; (wagon) 42.8 in.. Front shoulder room: (sedan) 57.3 in.; (coupe) 56.8 in.; (wagon) 57.3 in. Front hip room: (sedan) 52.2 in.; (coupe) 51.7 in.; (wagon) 52.2 in. Rear head room: (sedan) 37.7 in.; (coupe) 37.2 in.; (wagon) 38.8 in. Rear leg room: (sedan) 38 in.; (coupe) 35.1 in.; (wagon) 35.9 in. Rear shoulder room: (sedan) 57.1 in; (coupe) 55.6 in.; (wagon) 57.1 in. Rear hip room: (sedan) 55.6 in.; (coupe) 54.5 in.; (wagon) 55.6 in. Transmission: Three-speed manual transmission (floor shift) standard with V-6. Gear ratios: (1st) 3.50:1; (2nd) 1.81:1; (3rd) 1.00:1; (rev) 3.62:1. Four-speed floor shift optional on Malibu with 5.0-liter V-8: (1st) 2.85:1; (2nd) 2.02:1; (3rd) 1.35:1; (4th) 1.00:1; (rev) 2.85:1. Gear ratios: (1st) 2.52:1; (2nd) 1.52:1; (3rd) 1.00:1; (rev) 1.94:1 except Malibu V-6 (1st) 2.74:1; (2nd) 1.57:1; (3rd) 1.00:1; (Rev) 2.07:1. Standard final drive ratio: (Malibu) 2.73:1 except 2.29:1 with V-8; (Malibu wagon) 2.41:1. Brakes: Front disc, rear drum. Fuel tank: (coupe and sedan) 17.5 gal.; (station wagon) 18 gal. Transmission: Three-speed manual transmission standard with base V-6. Gear ratios: (1st) 3.50:1; (2nd) 1.89:1; (3rd) 1.00:1; (rev) 3.62:1. Four-speed floor shift optional: (1st) 2.85:1; (2nd) 2.02:1; (3rd) 1.35:1; (4th) 1.00:1; (rev) 2.85:1. Four-speed floor shift optional with Malibu 267-cid V-8: (1st) 3.11:1; (2nd) 2.20:1; (3rd) 1.47:1; (4th) 1.00:1; (rev) 3.11:1. Three-speed Turbo-Hydra-Matic transmission optional. Gear ratios: (1st) 2.52:1; (2nd) 1.52:1; (3rd) 1.00:1; (rev) 1.93:1 except some Malibu V-6 ratios: (1st) 2.74:1; (2nd) 1.57:1; (3rd) 1.00:1; (rev) 2.07:1. Standard final drive ratio: (V-6) 2.73:1; (V-8) 2.29:1 or 2.73:1 with automatic transmission; (station wagon with V-8) 2.56:1 or 2.41:1. Steering: recirculating ball. Brakes: Front disc/rear drum. Fuel tank: 18.1 gal.

OPTIONS

A01 all tinted glass ($70). A02 tinted windshield. A31 power windows with electric control ($132-$187). A42 six-way power seat adjuster ($163). A90 electric trunk release ($24). AG1 60/40 driver's seat with six-way power seat adjuster. AK1 deluxe seat belts and shoulder harness ($21-$23). AU3 power door locks ($80-$120). AU6 El Camino electric tailgate release ($25). AV3 El Camino pickup box tie downs. AX9 El Camino right rear cargo door latch. B32 front floor mats. B37 front and rear color-keyed floor mats ($23). B48 deluxe station wagon load floor carpet trim ($70). Deluxe luggage compartment trim ($43). B90 side window moldings ($41). B93 door edge guards ($13-$21). B96 wheel opening moldings ($23). BS1 Quiet sound group acoustical insulation ($51). BW2 deluxe exterior body moldings ($53). BX3 station wagon wood-grained side panels ($258). BX8 front fender and body moldings ($15-$37). B2H Olympic Eurosport striping package ($48). B3W advance price sheet. C49 electric rear window defogger ($99). C50 forced air rear window defogger ($55). C51 station wagon rear window air deflector ($30). C60 manual air conditioning ($562). C95 dome and reading lamp ($20). CA1 electric sliding steel sky roof ($529). CD4 pulse-type windshield wipers and washers. D24 litter container ($8). D33 remote-control left-hand outside rearview mirror ($18). D34 visor vanity mirror ($5). D35 custom outside rearview mirror. D55 front seat center console ($80). Vinyl bench seat in Malibu coupe or sedan ($26). Sport cloth bench seat in Malibu (no charge). Knit cloth bench seat in Malbu station wagons ($28). Vinyl bucket seats in Malibu coupes and sedans ($85). Knit cloth 50/50 seating in Malibu coupe or sedan ($172). Knit cloth 50/50 bench seating in Malibu station wagon ($198). Vinyl 50/50 seating in Malibu coupes or sedans ($198). Vinyl 50/50 seating in Malibu station wagons ($172). D64 lighted visor mirror ($40). D68 dual Sport-style rearview mirrors ($43-$68). D73 hand rail. D84 custom two-tone paint. D85 body side lower accent stripes. D91 special two-tone paint. F40 heavy-duty front and rear suspension ($22). F41 special front and rear heavy-duty Sport suspension ($41). G80 Positraction rear axle ($65). G92 performance ratio rear axle ($18). J50 vacuum power brake ($76). K05 engine block heater. K30 Cruise-Master speed control ($103). K81 63-amp Delcotron generator ($5-$33). K97 80-amp Delcotron generator. L26 200-cid V-6 engine. L39 267-cid V-8 engine ($190). LD5 231-cid V-6 engine ($40). LG4 305-cid V-8 engine ($295). LM1 350-cid V-8 engine in station wagon ($360). MM3 three-speed manual transmission (no cost). MM4 four-speed manual transmission ($135). MX1 Turbo-Hydra-Matic automatic transmission ($335). N23 22-gal. fuel tank. N33 Comfort-Tilt steering wheel ($75). N41 variable-ratio power steering ($163). N95 simulated wire wheel covers with locks ($65-$160). NA5 federal emissions system. P01 deluxe wheel trim cover ($43). P40 export tire equipment. PB2 silver or gold ABA plastic sport wheel trim covers ($52-$95). QFK P205/70R14B steel belted radial tires with white stripe ($149). QFV P205-70R14B steel-belted radial tires with raised white letters. QFZ P195/75R14B steel-belted radial tires with white stripes. QJY P205/75R14B steel belted radial tires with white stripe. QKL P205-75R14B steel-belted radial tires with raised white letters. QKP P185/75R14B fiberglass-belted radial black sidewall tires. QKQ P185/75R14B fiberglass-belted radial tires with white stripes ($40-$41). QKR P195/75R14B fiberglass-belted radial black sidewall tires. QKS P195/75R14B fiberglass-belted radial tires with white stripes ($83-$102). T72 two rectangular export-type left-hand headlights. T84 rectangular export-type right-hand headlight. T85 rectangular export-type left-hand headlight. T90 export-type signal light and marker lamp. TR9 lamp group. U05 dual horns ($9). U14 special instrumentation gauge package with tachometer ($125). U18 export speedometer. U35 electric clock ($23). U58 AM/FM push-button stereo ($232) U63 AM push-button radio ($82-$85). U69 AM/FM push-button radio ($158). U75 power antenna ($47). U76 windshield antenna included with all radios ($27). U80 auxiliary rear radio speaker ($25). UA1 heavy-duty battery ($19-$21). UF7 gauge package without tachometer ($57). UM1 AM push-button radio and tape player ($244-$248). UM2 AM/FM push-button radio and tape player ($335). UN3 AM/FM stereo cassette radio less clock ($341). UP5 AM/FM monaural CB radio ($489). UP6 AM/FM stereo CB radio ($570). UX6 dual front in-dash speakers ($21). UY8 AM/FM stereo radio with digital clock ($395). V01 heavy-duty radiator ($31-$33). V30 front and rear bumper guards ($46). V31 front bumper guard. V55 station wagon roof top luggage carrier ($90). V78 less certificate of compliance plate. VE5 front and rear bumper impact strips ($41). YC8 demo option drive. YF5 California emission requirement ($83). YG6 El Camino Royal Sierra Bonanza package A. YG7 El Camino Royal Sierra Bonanza package B. YG8 El Camino Royal Sierra Bonanza package C. YJ7 demo drive. Z03 Landau Coupe equipment package. Z15 El Camino SS package. Z49 mandatory Canadian base equipment modifications. ZJ7 special hub caps and trim rings ($47-$90). ZN7 color-keyed Ralley-style spare wheel. Vinyl roof ($116). Style trim package with two-tone paint ($120-$160).

OPTION INSTALLATION RATES

Automatic transmission (97.9 percent). Four-speed manual transmission (0.5 percent). V-8 engine (63.8 percent). V-6 engine (36.2 percent). AM radio (52.1 percent). AM/FM monaural radio (15.1 percent). AM 8-track (0.6 percent). AM/FM stereo radio (6.8 percent). AM/FM stereo 8-track (2.6 percent). Manual air conditioning (80.3 percent). Power steering (99.4 percent). Tilt steering (23.2 percent). Manual disc brakes (1.4 percent). Power front disc brakes (98.6 percent). Power door locks (8.5 percent). Power windows (6.8 percent). Cruise control (19.6 percent). Bucket seats (2.5 percent). Power seats (3.1 percent). Vinyl top (10.6 percent). Tinted windshield only (2.5 percent). All tinted glass (82.2 percent). Standard wheel covers (52.5 percent). Optional full wheel covers (27.1 percent). Styled steel wheels (13.5 percent). Steel-belted radial tires (70.2 percent). Fiberglass-belted radial tires (29.8 percent). Optional regular clock (24.6 percent). Optional digital clock (0.1 percent). Forced-air rear window defogger (5.9 percent). Electric rear window defogger (28.5 percent). Remote-control left-hand side-view mirror (60.9 percent). Remote-control right-hand side-view mirror (2.5 percent). Positraction limited-slip differential (3.8 percent). Sky roof (0.2 percent). Based on model-year production of 412,147 units in the United States and Canada (North American production for the U.S. market).

HISTORICAL FOOTNOTES

Robert D. Lund was Chevrolet general manager in 1979. The Chevrolet Division passed the 100 million mark in vehicles produced during the model year and announced that the milestone included 78.5 million cars and 24.2 million trucks. The company's total model-year output of 2,412,378 cars was up from 1978's total of 2,239,873. Calendar-year sales of Malibu was 344,233 for a 4.1 percent share of the total market. This compared to 374,124 units and 4 percent of total U.S. auto sales the previous calendar year. Model-year U.S. dealer sales rose to 362,103 versus 356.070 the year before. Calendar-year registrations rose to 243,699 cars and 93,142 station wagons compared with 269,780 cars and 96,416 wagons in 1978.

MALIBU

The 1980 Malibu sport coupe came with a starting price of $5,133.

"You could get better gas mileage. You could get more room," said an advertisement for the 1980 Chevrolet Malibu. "But you'd have to get two cars." The latest Malibu was one fine machine and Chevy billed it as "a trim and maneuverable car on the outside, a roomy and comfortable car on the inside." Ad copywriters stressed that the sedan had more room than any other intermediate, plus it averaged 20 mpg and got 26 mpg on the highway. A brighter, vertical-emphasis grille, larger headlights, larger side marker lamps and a new 3.8-liter standard V-6 were the year's major revisions. The windshield washer system worked more precisely and rally wheels were a new option. The base V-6 and optional 5.0-liter V-8 could be had with a new automatic transmission with a "lock-up" torque converter.

I.D. NUMBERS

VIN embossed on the top left-hand side of the instrument panel and visible through the windshield. The first symbol 1 designates Chevrolet. The second symbol indicates series: T=Malibu, W=Malibu Classic. The third and fourth symbols indicate body style: 19=four-door sedan, 27=two-door notchback coupe and 35=four-door station wagon. The fifth symbol indicates engine (net horsepower): K=RPO LC3 229-cid 110-hp V-6, A=RPO LD5 231-cid 110-hp V-6 (California), J=RPO L39 267-cid 115-hp V-8 and H=RPO LG4 305-cid 150-hp V-8. The sixth symbol designates the model year: A=1980. The seventh symbol designates the assembly plant location: B=Baltimore, Maryland, D=Doraville, Georgia, Z=Fremont, California, R=Arlington, Texas, K=Leeds, Missouri and 1=Oshawa, Canada. The last six symbols are the sequential unit production number at the specific factory. The Fisher body tag riveted to the top of the cowl on the left side of the car below the hood provides additional vehicle identification information. The Fisher body STYLE NUMBER (ST) consists of a prefix identifying model-year and four or more symbols identifying the series and body style (example: 80-1AW27 for a 1980 Malibu Classic two-door notchback coupe). The BODY NUMBER consists of a prefix designating assembly plant and the sequential unit production number at the specific factory. The TRIM NUMBER (TR) identifies upholstery.

COLORS

(11) Antique White, (15) Silver Poly, (16) Gray Poly, (19) Black, (21) Light Blue Poly, (22) Medium Blue Poly, (24) Bright Blue Poly, (29) Dark Blue Poly, (40) Lime Green, (44) Dark Green Poly, (50) Yellow, (51) Bright Yellow, (56) Yellow, (57) Gold Poly, (59) Beige, (63) Camel Poly, (67) Dark Brown Poly, (69) Medium Camel Poly, (72) Red, (75) Claret Poly, (76) Dark Claret Poly, (77) Cinnabar, (79) Red Orange, (80) Rust Poly, (84) Charcoal Poly and (85) Vapor Gray. Vinyl tops were available in: 11T=White, 19T=Black, 21T=Light Blue Poly, 44T Dark Green, 63T=Camel Poly, 76T=Dark Claret and 85T=Gray.

ENGINE CODES

Engine codes appear on the right side of V-6 cylinder blocks behind the distributor and right-hand side of V-8 engine blocks. Engine codes for 1980 were: (229-cid two-barrel V-6) DHB and DHA; (229-cid two-barrel V-6) CLA, CLB and CRC; (231-cid two-barrel V-6) OV, OW, OP and OR; (267-cid two-barrel V-8) CPA, CPB, CPM and CPR; (305-cid four-barrel V-8) CEA, CER, CEC, CMF, CMC, CMD and CMN; (350-cid four-barrel V-8) CHB.

MALIBU — SERIES 1T — V-6/V-8

Though similar to the previous edition, Malibu sported a brighter, lightweight grille for 1980. It was made up of narrow vertical bars divided by two subdued horizontal bars. A Chevrolet nameplate was in the lower left-hand corner of the grille. On base Malibus, a red badge was imbedded in the front of the hood at the center. The single rectangular headlights, parking lights and side marker lights all grew larger. There was a Malibu script at the lower rear of the body side above the side marker lamp. Plain body sides were standard. Deluxe body side moldings with color-coordinated vinyl inserts and wheel opening moldings were optional, but often shown in catalog art and advertisements. At the rear were three-segment wraparound taillights. The outer segments were red and wrapped around the body corners to serve as side marker lamps. The center segments were white back-up lights and the inner segments were red. A license plate recess was in the center. Plain chrome bumpers were standard equipment, though most sales catalog photos show optional black-rubber-faced bumper guards and bumper rub strips. The Malibu had a new 229-cid (3.8-liter) base V-6. A 267-cid (4.4-liter) V-8 and a 305-cid (5.0-liter) V-8 were optional. Malibu station wagons carried the 305-cid V-8 as standard equipment. The 350-cid was out of the Malibu sales catalog, though still offered for the El Camino. A three-speed manual transmission with floor shift control was standard and a rare four-on-the-floor option was installed in only 202 Malibus. The automatic was an extra-cost item in all models. Malibu standard equipment included an all-welded Fisher body, double-panel doors, hood and deck lid, seat belts with push-button buckles for all passenger positions, two front combination seat and inertia reel shoulder belts, a driver's belt reminder light and buzzer, an energy-absorbing steering column, passenger guard door locks, safety door latches, stamped steel door hinges, folding seat back latches, an energy-absorbing padded instrument panel, padded front seat back tops, a laminated windshield, safety armrests, side marker lights and reflectors, parking lamps that illuminate with the headlights, four-way hazard warning flashers, back-up lights, directional signals with a lane-change feature, a defroster, dual-speed windshield wipers, a windshield defroster, a vinyl-edged wide-view inside mirror with shatter-resistant glass and a deflecting support, a left-hand outside rearview mirror, a dual master cylinder brake system with a warning light, a starter safety switch, a dual-action safety hood latch, an anti-theft ignition key reminder buzzer, an anti-theft steering column lock, the 229-cid 3.8-liter V-6 (231-cid in cars sold in California), a High-Energy ignition system, a three-speed manual floor shift, a full-coil suspension, a front stabilizer bar, P185/75R14 fiberglass-belted radial-ply tires, power front disc/rear drum brakes, windshield and back window reveal moldings, roof drip moldings, a cigar lighter, a Delco Freedom battery, extensive corrosion-resisting measures and a locking glove box. Malibu station wagons had P195/75R14 tires.

Model Number	Body/Style Number	Body Type & Seating	Factory Price	Shipping Weight	Production Total
MALIBU SERIES 1T (V-6)					
1T	27	2d sport coupe-6P	$5,133	2,996 lbs.	Note 1
1T	19	4d sedan-6P	$5,246	3,001 lbs.	Note 1
1T	35	4d wagon-6P	$5,402	3,141 lbs.	Note 1
MALIBU SERIES 1T (V-8)					
1T	27	2d sport coupe-6P	$5,313	3,117 lbs.	Note 1
1T	19	4d sedan-6P	$5,426	3,122 lbs.	Note 1
1T	35	4d wagon-6P	$5,582	3,261 lbs.	Note 1

MALIBU CLASSIC — SERIES 1W V-6/V-8

"Sure you want everything that makes Malibu such an outstanding value," stated the 1980 Chevrolet Malibu sales catalog. "But maybe you'd also like some flourishes to go with it. Then have them, savor them, with the 1980 Malibu Classic." Like the base Malibu, the upscale Classic version had a Chevrolet nameplate in the lower left-hand corner of the grille, but its hood ornament was a stand-up type. Wide rocker panel moldings, wheel opening moldings, full wheel covers, an ash tray light, courtesy lights, a glove box light, added sound insulation and extra padding in the one-piece cloth headliner were standard. Deluxe body side moldings, bumper rub strips and bumper guards, while seen in many catalog photos, were optional. The rear end treatment was similar to that of the base Malibu, but with more bright moldings and other highlights. Engine and transmission offerings were the same as for Malibu. Malibu Classic standard equipment also included an all-welded Fisher body, double-panel doors, hood and deck lid, seat belts with push-button buckles for all passenger positions, two front combination seat and inertia reel shoulder belts, a driver's belt reminder light and buzzer, an energy-absorbing steering column, passenger guard door locks, safety door latches, stamped steel door hinges, folding seat back latches, an energy-absorbing padded instrument panel, padded front seat back tops, a laminated windshield, safety armrests, side marker lights and reflectors, parking lamps that illuminate with the headlights, four-way hazard warning flashers, back-up lights, directional signals with a lane-change feature, a defroster, dual-speed windshield wipers, a windshield defroster, a vinyl-edged wide-view inside mirror with shatter-resistant glass and a deflecting support, a left-hand outside rearview mirror, a dual master cylinder brake system with a warning light, a starter safety switch, a dual-action safety hood latch, an anti-theft ignition key reminder buzzer, an anti-theft steering column lock, the 229-cid 3.8-liter V-6 (231-cid in cars sold in California), a High-Energy ignition system, a three-speed manual floor shift, a full-coil suspension, a front stabilizer bar, P185/75R14 fiberglass-belted radial-ply tires (P195/75R14 on wagons), power front disc/rear drum brakes, windshield and back window reveal moldings, roof drip moldings, a cigar lighter, a Delco Freedom battery, extensive corrosion-resisting measures, a locking glove box, bright deck lid moldings, bright end cap moldings and dual horns. Standard features of the Malibu Classic Landau coupe included a smartly angled roof with a vinyl cover over the rear portion (set off by bright roof moldings), non-deluxe body side moldings, rear pin striping and sport wheel covers.

Model Number	Body/Style Number	Body Type & Seating	Factory Price	Shipping Weight	Production Total
MALIBU CLASSIC SERIES 1W (V-6)					
1W	27	2d sport coupe-6P	$5,439	3,027 lbs.	Note 1
1W	27 + Z03	2d Landau Coupe	$5,688	—	Note 1
1W	19	4d sedan-6P	$5,567	3,031 lbs.	Note 1

MALIBU

1W	35	4d wagon-6P	$5,654	3,167 lbs.	Note 1
MALIBU CLASSIC SERIES 1W (V-8)					
1W	27	2d sport coupe-6P	$5,619	3,148 lbs.	Note 1
1W	27 + Z03	2d Landau coupe	$5,868	—	note 1
1W	19	4d sedan-6P	$5,747	3,152 lbs.	Note 1
1W	35	4d wagon-6P	$5,834	3,387 lbs.	Note 1

PRODUCTION NOTES

NOTE 1 Model-year production (U.S.) of all 1980 Malibus was 231,895 units.
NOTE 2 Model-year production (North American) was 278,350.
NOTE 3 Model-year production by series and body style was as follows:

Malibu		Malibu Classic		Total
sedan	67,696	sedan	77,938	145,634
wagon	30,794	wagon	35,730	66,524
sport coupe	28,425	sport coupe	28,425	56,850
Landau coupe		9,342		9,342
	126,915		151,435	=278,350

NOTE 4 Additional statistics record series production (North American production for the U.S. market) as follows:

Malibu (V-6)	76,025	Malibu (V-8)	20,096	Total 96,121
Malibu Classic (V-6)	75,958	Malibu (V-8)	39,747	Total 115,705
wagons (V-6)	39,917	wagons (V-8)	26,607	Total 66,524

NOTE 5 Production by factory (U.S. only) was:

Code	Factory	Production	Code	Factory	Production
B	Baltimore	64,151	D	Doraville, (Ga.)	45,387
R	Arlington (Tex.)	36,886	Z	Fremont (Cal.)	9,847
K	Leeds (Mo.)	75,624			

ENGINES

MALIBU BASE V-6 (FEDERAL): Overhead-valve V-6. Cast-iron block and head. Displacement: 229 cid (3.8 liters). Bore & stroke: 3.74 x 3.48 in. Compression ratio: 8.6:1. Brake hp: 115 at 4000 rpm. Torque: 175 lbs.-ft. at 2000 rpm. Four main bearings. Hydraulic valve lifters. Carburetor: Rochester two-barrel M2ME. Sales Code: LC3. VIN code: K.

MALIBU BASE V-6 (CALIFORNIA): Overhead-valve V-6. Cast-iron block and head. Displacement: 231 cid (3.8 liters). Bore & stroke: 3.80 x 3.40 in. Compression ratio: 8.0:1. Brake hp: 110 at 3800 rpm Torque: 190 lbs.-ft. at 2000 rpm Four main bearings. Hydraulic valve lifters. Carburetor: Rochester M2ME two-barrel. Sales Code: LD5. VIN code: A.

MALIBU BASE V-8: Overhead-valve. Cast-iron block and head. Bore and stroke: 3.50 x 3.48 in. Displacement: 267 cid (4.4 liters). Compression ratio: 8.3:1. Net brake hp: 120 at 3600 rpm. Taxable hp: 39.20. Net torque: 215 at 2000 rpm. Five main bearings. Hydraulic valve lifters. Carburetor: Rochester M2ME two-barrel. VIN Code: J.

MALIBU OPTIONAL V-8: Overhead-valve. Cast-iron block and head. Bore and stroke: 3.74 x 3.48 in. Displacement: 305 cid (5.0 liters). Compression ratio: 8.6:1. Net brake hp: 155 at 4000 rpm. Taxable hp: 44.66. Net torque: 240 lbs.-ft. at 1600 rpm. Five main bearings. Hydraulic valve lifters. Carburetor: Rochester M4ME four-barrel. VIN Code: H.

CHASSIS DATA

Wheelbase: 108.1 in. Overall length: (car) 192.7 in. (station wagon) 193.4 in. Height: (coupe) 53.3 in.; (sedan) 54.2 in.; (station wagon) 54.5 inches. Width: (car) 71.5 in.; (station wagon) 71.2 in. Front tread: 58.5 in. Rear tread: 57.8 in. Tires: (car) P185/75R14/B fiberglass-belted radial; (station wagon) P195/75R14/B fiberglass-belted radial. Transmission: Three-speed manual floor shift transmission standard with Malibu V-6. Gear ratios: (1st) 3.50:1; (2nd) 1.89:1; (3rd) 1.00:1; (rev) 3.62:1. Four-speed floor shift optional on Camaro/Malibu 305-cid V-8: Gear ratios: (1st) 2.85:1; (2nd) 2.02:1; (3rd) 1.35:1; (4th) 1.00:1; (rev) 2.85:1. Three-speed Turbo-Hydra-Matic optional: Gear ratios: (1st) 2.52:1; (2nd) 1.52:1; (3rd) 1.00:1; (rev) 1.93:1; Malibu 267-cid V-6 gear ratios: (1st) 2.74:1; (2nd) 1.57:1; (3rd) 1.00:1; (rev) 2.07:1. Standard final drive ratio: (V-6) 2.73:1; (V-8) 2.29:1; (Station wagon V-8) 2.41:1. Steering: recirculating ball. Front suspension: Control arms, coil springs and stabilizer bar. Rear suspension: Rigid axle, lower trailing radius arms, upper oblique torque arms and coil springs. Brakes: Front disc/rear drum. Body construction: Separate body and perimeter box frame. Fuel tank: (car) 18.1 gal.; (wagon) 18.2 gal.

OPTIONS

A01 all tinted glass ($75). A02 tinted windshield. A26 United Kingdom and European Glazing Window. A31 power windows with electric control ($143-$202). AG9 six-way power seat adjuster ($175). A90 electric trunk release ($26). AG1 60/40 driver's seat with six-way power seat adjuster. AU3 power door locks ($93-$132). AU6 El Camino electric tailgate release ($27). AV3 El Camino pickup box tie downs. AW9 station wagon quarter stow and luggage compartment security group ($40). B32 front floor mats. B37 front and rear color-keyed floor mats ($25). B39 load floor carpet ($75). B90 side window moldings ($47). B93 door edge guards ($14-$22). B96 wheel opening moldings ($25). B3W advance price sheet. BS1 Quiet sound group acoustical insulation ($55). BW2 deluxe body molding exterior decoration ($57). BX3 station wagon wood-grained side panels ($276). BX8 front fender and body moldings. C49 electric rear window defogger ($107). C50 forced air rear window defogger ($59). C51 station wagon rear window air deflector ($32). C60 manual air conditioning ($601). CD4 pulse-type windshield wipers and washers. D33 remote-control left-hand outside rearview mirror ($18). D35 custom outside rearview mirror. D55 front seat center console ($86). Vinyl bench seat in Malibu coupe or sedan ($28). Vinyl bucket seats in Malibu coupes and sedans ($91). Cloth 50/50 seating in Malibu coupe or sedan ($186-$244). Knit cloth 50/50 bench seating in Malibu station wagon ($244). Vinyl 50/50 seating in Malibu coupes or sedans ($212-$244). Custom vinyl bench seat in Malibu station wagons ($64). D64 lighted visor mirror. D68 dual sport-style rearview mirrors ($46). Dual sport-style remote-control rearview mirrors ($48-$73). D73 pickup box hand rail. D84 custom two-tone paint ($72-$123). D85 body side lower accent stripes ($51). D91 special two-tone paint. F40 heavy-duty front and rear suspension ($24). F41 special front and rear heavy-duty sport suspension ($45). G80 Positraction rear axle ($69). G92 performance ratio rear axle ($19). K05 engine block heater. K30 Cruise-Master speed control ($81). K73 70-amp. Delcotron generator. K81 63-amp Delcotron generator ($5-$33). LC3 229-cid V-6 engine (standard Federal engine). L39 267-cid V-8 engine ($180). LD5 231-cid V-6 engine (standard California engine). LG4 305-cid V-8 engine ($295). LM1 350-cid V-8 engine in El Camino ($360). MM3 three-speed manual transmission (standard). MM4 four-speed manual transmission ($144). MX1 Turbo-Hydra-Matic automatic transmission ($358). N23 22-gal. fuel tank. N33 Comfort-Tilt steering wheel ($78). N41 variable-ratio power steering ($174). N95 simulated wire wheel covers with locks ($69-$171). NA5 federal emissions system. P01 deluxe wheel trim cover ($56-$102). P40 export tire equipment. PB2 silver or gold ABS plastic sport wheel trim covers ($52-$95). QFK P205/70R14B steel-belted radial tires with white stripe ($171). QFV P205/70R14B steel-belted radial tires with raised white letters. QFZ P195/75R14B steel-belted radial tires with white stripes ($119). QJY P205/75R14B steel-belted radial tires with white stripe. QJZ P205/75R14B steel-belted radial tires with white stripe. QKL P205-75R14B steel-belted radial tires with raised white letters. QKP P185/75R14B steel-belted radial black sidewall tires. QKQ P185-75R14B fiberglass-belted radial tires with white stripes ($45). QKR P195-75R14B fiberglass-belted radial black sidewall tires. QKS P195-75R14B fiberglass-belted radial tires with white stripes ($48). T72 two rectangular export-type left-hand headlights. T84 rectangular export-type right-hand headlight. T90 export-type signal light and marker lamp. TR9 lamp group. U05 dual horns ($10). U14 special instrumentation gauge package with tachometer ($134). U18 export speedometer. U35 electric clock ($25). U58 AM/FM push-button stereo ($192). U63 AM push-button radio ($97). U69 AM/FM push-button radio ($153). U75 power antenna ($51). U76 windshield antenna included with all radios ($27). U80 auxiliary rear radio speaker ($25). U92 front dual and RR dual speakers. UA1 heavy-duty battery ($21). UF7 gauge package with clock ($66). UM1 AM push-button radio and tape player ($249). UM2 AM/FM push-button radio and tape player. UN3 AM/FM stereo cassette radio less clock ($285). UP5 AM/FM monaural CB radio ($473). UP6 AM/FM stereo CB radio ($525). UX6 dual front in-dash speakers ($23). Dual front and rear speakers ($43). UY8 AM/FM stereo radio with digital clock ($353). V08 heavy-duty radiator ($33). V30 front and rear bumper guards ($48). V55 station wagon roof top luggage carrier ($96). V78 less certificate of compliance plate. VE5 front and rear bumper impact strips ($44). YC8 demo option drive. YF5 California emission requirement ($85). ZJZ special hub caps and trim rings ($46). Z03 Landau coupe equipment. Z15 El Camino SS package. Z16 El Camino Black Knight sport décor package. Z49 mandatory Canadian base equipment model. ZJ7 special wheel package with hub cap and trim rings ($50-$96). Auxiliary lighting ($33-$60). Vinyl roof ($124).

OPTION INSTALLATION RATES

Automatic transmission (97.8 percent). Four-speed manual transmission (0.1 percent). V-8 engine (31.1 percent). V-6 engine (68.9 percent). AM radio (29.5 percent). AM/FM monaural radio (13.1 percent). AM/FM monaural CB radio (0.1 percent). AM 8-track (0.6 percent). AM/FM stereo radio (21.7 percent). AM/FM stereo 8-track (7.4 percent). AM/FM stereo cassette (3.7 percent). AM/FM stereo CB (0.3 percent). Manual air conditioning (80.4 percent). Power steering (99.7 percent). Tilt steering (20 percent). Power front disc brakes (100 percent). Power door locks (8.4 percent). Power windows (6 percent). Cruise control (20.8 percent). Bucket seats (2 percent). Power seats (1.9 percent). Vinyl top (6.5 percent). Tinted windshield only (2.2 percent). All tinted glass (83.6 percent). Wheel covers (80.7 percent). Styled steel wheels (10.9 percent). Steel-belted radial tires (64.2 percent). Fiberglass-belted radial tires (35.8 percent). Optional regular clock (19.8 percent). Optional digital clock (0.1 percent). Forced-air rear window defogger (4.1 percent). Electric rear window defogger (35.4 percent). Remote-control left-hand side-view mirror (58.1 percent). Remote-control right-hand side-view mirror (2.7 percent). Positraction limited-slip differential (3.3 percent). Based on model-year production of 278,350 units in the U.S. and Canada (North American production for the U.S. market).

HISTORICAL FOOTNOTES

Robert D. Lund was Chevrolet general manager in 1980. While remaining the top dog on the GM ladder, Chevrolet felt the downturn in U.S. auto sales in 1980. Calendar-year sales of Malibus was down 23.6 percent to 267,732 units for a 4.1 percent share of the total market. This compared to 344,233 units and 4.1 percent of total U.S. auto sales the previous calendar year. Model-year U.S. dealer sales fell to 267,767 compared to 362,103 the year before. Calendar-year registrations rose to 200,790 cars and 61,815 station wagons compared with 243,699 cars and 93,142 station wagons in 1979.

The Malibu intermediates were relatively unchanged in 1981, other than a minor grille redesign dominated by prominent horizontal elements. The four-door sedan also had a restyled roof line. The major mechanical change was the adoption of General Motors' CCC (Computer Command Control) system for engine management, particularly of exhaust emission control by electronic means.

The base 3.8-liter V-6 with a two-barrel carburetor was available with a three-speed manual or automatic transmission. Only the automatic gearbox was offered with the optional 4.4-liter (267-cid) and 5.0-liter (305-cid) V-8s. The latter engine, with a four-barrel carburetor, was offered in station wagons and all cars sold in California. Higher-pressure radial tires were standard for improved fuel economy.

Malibu

One of the only cosmetic changes to the Malibu line for 1981 was a new roofline for the four-door sedan.

I.D. NUMBERS

VIN embossed on the top left-hand side of the instrument panel and visible through the windshield. The VIN system changed this year. The first designates the country of origin: 1=United States and 2=Canada. The second symbol indentifies the manufacturer: G=General Motors. The third symbol indicates the make: 1=Chevrolet. The fourth symbol indicates the type of restraint system: A=non-passive/manual seat belts; B=passive/automatic seat belts and C=passive/inflatable. The fifth symbol indicates the car line/series: T=Malibu and W=Malibu Classic. The sixth and seventh symbols indicate body type: 27=two-door notchback coupe, 35=four-door station wagon and 69=four-door notchback sedan. The eighth symbol indicates engine (net horsepower): K=RPO LC3 229-cid 110-hp V-6, A=RPO LD5 231-cid 110-hp V-6 (California), J=RPO L39 267-cid 115-hp V-8 and H=RPO LG4 305-cid 150-hp V-8. The ninth symbol is a check digit. The 10th symbol designates the model year: B=1981. The seventh symbol designates the assembly plant location: B=Baltimore, Maryland, D=Doraville, Georgia, Z=Fremont, California, R=Arlington, Texas, K=Leeds, Missouri. and 1=Oshawa, Canada. The last six symbols are the sequential unit production number at the specific factory. The Fisher body tag riveted to the top of the cowl on the left side of the car below the hood provides additional vehicle identification information. The Fisher body STYLE NUMBER (ST) consists of four or more symbols identifying the series and body style (example: 1AW27 for a 1981 Malibu Classic two-door notchback coupe). The BODY NUMBER consists of a prefix designating assembly plant and the sequential unit production number at the specific factory. The TRIM NUMBER (TR) identifies upholstery.

COLORS

(11) Antique White, (16) Silver Poly, (19) Black, (20) Bright Blue Poly; (21) Light Blue Poly, (22) Medium Blue Poly, (29) Dark Blue Poly, (35) Pastel Waxberry, (36) Light Waxberry Poly, (37) Medium Waxberry Poly, (45) Light Jadestone Poly, (47) Dark Jadestone Poly, (48) Dark Green Poly, (51) Bright Yellow, (54) Gold Poly, (56) Yellow, (57) Citrus Orange Poly, (58) Orange Poly, (63) Pastel Sandstone, (67) Dark Brown Poly, (68) Medium Sandstone Poly, (69) Dark Sandstone Poly, (72) Light Maple Poly, (75) Spectra Red, (77) Dark Maple Poly and (84) Charcoal Poly. Vinyl tops were available in: 11T=White, 19T=Black, 29T=Dark Blue Poly, 36T=Light waxberry Poly, 45T=Light Jadestone Poly, 63T=Pastel Sandstone Poly, 64T=Doeskin, 77T=Dark Maple and 85T=Medium Slate Poly.

ENGINE CODES

Codes appear on the right side of V-6 cylinder blocks behind the distributor and right-hand side of V-8 engine blocks. Engine codes for 1981 were: (229-cid two-barrel V-6) DAA, DAB, DAC, DAD, DAH, DAJ, DAK, D7A and D7B; (231-cid two-barrel V-6) NA, NB, NC, ND, NF, NL, LZ, RA, RB, NJ, RK, RL, RC, RD, NZ and NK; (267-cid two-barrel V-8) DFA, DFC, DFD, DFF, DFH, DBA, D8C, D8D, D8F, D8H and DFK; (305-cid four-barrel V-8) DHA, DHB, DHC, DHD, DKH, DHF, DHH, DHK, DHJ, DHZ, DKB, D6A, D6B, D6C, D6D, DHU and DKF; (350-cid four-barrel El Camino V-8) DMA, DMC, DMD, D5A, D5B, DMB, DMF and DMH.

MALIBU — SERIES 1T — V-6/V-8

Although the mid-size Malibu didn't change drastically this year, it got several appearance alterations. The four-door sedan (now marketed as a "sport sedan") got a dramatically restyled, squarish formal roof line and back window section. (The profile looked similar to that of the 1980 Buick Century.) The new grille with prominent horizontal bars had bright upper and lower moldings that extended the full width of the front end. Malibus also had new headlamp bezels and triple-unit taillights and side marker lenses. The Argent Silver taillight bezels had black accents and the optional full wheel covers were restyled. A revised dashboard featured a new glossy-black appliqué. Also new were high-pressure easy-roll tires, a Delco maintenance-free Freedom II battery and a jack that lifted the car from the side. The Malibu front end held single rectangular headlamps. A Chevrolet nameplate appeared on the lower part of the grille, on the driver's side, as well as on the deck lid, on the passenger side. Malibu nameplates adorned the rear quarter panels. Classic Landau coupes had a "Landau" emblem on the "B" pillar. The base Malibu had an ornament with a Chevrolet crest. Cloth and vinyl interiors came in Camel, Champagne, Dark Blue, Jade or Maroon and the custom interiors was also available in Beige. Power steering was now standard. As before, the base Malibu came in coupe, sedan or station wagon forms. Halogen headlamps were a new option. Malibu standard equipment included an all-welded Fisher body, double-panel doors, hood and deck lid, seat belts with push-button buckles for all passenger positions, two front combination seat and inertia reel shoulder belts, a driver's belt reminder light and buzzer, an energy-absorbing steering column, passenger guard door locks, safety door latches, stamped steel door hinges, folding seat back latches, an energy-absorbing padded instrument panel, padded front seat back tops, a laminated windshield, safety armrests, side marker lights and reflectors, parking lamps that illuminate with the headlights, four-way hazard warning flashers, back-up lights, directional signals with a lane-change feature, a defroster, dual-speed windshield wipers, a windshield defroster, a vinyl-edged wide-view inside mirror with shatter-resistant glass and a deflecting support, a left-hand outside rearview mirror, a dual master cylinder brake system with a warning light, a starter safety switch, a dual-action safety hood latch, an anti-theft ignition key reminder buzzer, an anti-theft steering column lock, the 229-cid 3.8-liter V-6 (231-cid in cars sold in California), a High-Energy ignition system, a three-speed manual transmission, a full-coil suspension, a front stabilizer bar, P185/75R14 fiberglass-belted radial-ply tires, power front disc/rear drum brakes, windshield and back window reveal moldings, roof drip moldings, a cigar lighter, a Delco Freedom battery, extensive corrosion-resisting measures and a locking glove box. Malibu station wagons had P195/75R14 tires.

Model Number	Body/Style Number	Body Type & Seating	Factory Price	Shipping Weight	Production Total
MALIBU SERIES 1T (V-6)					
1T	27	2d sport coupe-6P	$6,498	3,037 lbs.	Note 1
1T	19	4d sedan-6P	$6,614	3,028 lbs.	Note 1
1T	35	4d wagon-6P	$6,792	3,201 lbs.	Note 1
MALIBU SERIES 1T (V-8)					
1T	27	2d sport coupe-6P	$6,548	3,199 lbs.	Note 1
1T	19	4d sedan-6P	$6,664	3,194 lbs.	Note 1
1T	35	4d wagon-6P	$6,842	3,369 lbs.	Note 1

MALIBU CLASSIC — SERIES 1W V-6/V-8

Malibu Classic standard equipment also included an all-welded Fisher body, double-panel doors, hood and deck lid, seat belts with push-button buckles for all passenger positions, two front combination seat and inertia reel shoulder belts, a driver's belt reminder light and buzzer, an energy-absorbing steering column, passenger guard door locks, safety door latches, stamped steel door hinges, folding seat back latches, an energy-absorbing padded instrument panel, padded front seat back tops, a laminated windshield, safety armrests, side marker lights and reflectors, parking lamps that illuminate with the headlights, four-way hazard warning flashers, back-up lights, directional signals with a lane-change feature, a defroster, dual-speed windshield wipers, a windshield defroster, a vinyl-edged wide-view inside mirror with shatter-resistant glass and a deflecting support, a left-hand outside rearview mirror, a dual master cylinder brake system with a warning light, a starter safety switch, a dual-action safety hood latch, an anti-theft ignition key reminder buzzer, an anti-theft steering column lock, the 229-cid 3.8-liter V-6 (231-cid in cars sold in California), a High-Energy ignition system, a three-speed manual floor shift, a full-coil suspension, a front stabilizer bar, P185/75R14 fiberglass-belted radial-ply tires (P195/75R14 on wagons), power front disc/rear drum brakes, windshield and back window reveal moldings, roof drip moldings, a cigar lighter, a Delco Freedom battery, extensive corrosion-resisting measures, a locking glove box, bright deck lid moldings, bright end cap moldings and dual horns. In addition, Malibu Classic models had a stand-up hood ornament, dual horns, side window reveal moldings (except coupes) and front door-pull straps. Standard features of the Malibu Classic Landau coupe included a smartly angled roof with a vinyl cover over the rear portion (set off by bright roof moldings), non-deluxe body side moldings, rear pin striping and silver sport wheel covers. Station wagons included wheel opening moldings. Cloth upholstery was standard in coupes and sedans and vinyl upholstery was standard in station wagons.

Model Number	Body/Style Number	Body Type & Seating	Factory Price	Shipping Weight	Production Total
MALIBU CLASSIC SERIES 1W (V-6)					
1W	27	2d sport coupe-6P	$6,828	3,065 lbs.	Note 1
1W	27 + Z03	2d Landau coupe	$7,092	—	Note 1
1W	19	4d sedan-6P	$6,961	3,059 lbs.	Note 1
1W	35	4d wagon-6P	$7,069	3,222 lbs.	Note 1
MALIBU CLASSIC SERIES 1W (V-8)					
1W	27	2d sport coupe-6P	$6,878	3,227 lbs.	Note 1
1W	27 + Z03	2d Landau coupe	$7,142	—	Note 1
1W	19	4d sedan-6P	$7,011	3,225 lbs.	Note 1
1W	35	4d wagon-6P	$7,119	3,390 lbs.	Note 1

PRODUCTION NOTES

NOTE 1 Model-year production (U.S.) of all 1981 Malibus was 226,727 units.
NOTE 2 Model-year production (North American) was 242,447.
NOTE 3 Model-year production by series and body style was as follows:

Malibu		Malibu Classic		Total
sedan	60,643	sedan	80,908	141,551
wagon	29,387	station wagon	36,798	66,185
sport coupe	15,834	sport coupe	14,255	30,089
Landau coupe	4,622		4,622	
	105,864		136,583	= 242,447

NOTE 4 Additional statistics record series production (North American production for the U.S. market) as follows:

Malibu (V-6)	64,826	Malibu (V-8)	11,651	Total 76,477
Malibu Classic (V-6)	81,460	Malibu (V-8)	18,325	Total 99,785
wagons (V-6)	49,240	wagons (V-8)	16,945	Total 66,185

NOTE 5 Production by factory (U.S. only) was:

Code	Factory	Production	Code	Factory	Production
B	Baltimore	39,023	D	Doraville (Ga.)	91,880
R	Arlington (Tex.)	23,312	Z	Fremont (Cal.)	19,439
K	Leeds (Mo.)	53,073			

ENGINES

MALIBU BASE V-6 (FEDERAL): Overhead-valve V-6. Cast-iron block and head. Displacement: 229 cid (3.8

liters). Bore & stroke: 3.74 x 3.48 in. Compression ratio: 8.6:1. Brake hp: 110 at 4200 rpm. Torque: 170 lbs.-ft. at 2000 rpm. Four main bearings. Hydraulic valve lifters. Carburetor: Rochester two-barrel 2ME. Sales Code: LC3. VIN code: K.

MALIBU BASE V-6 (CALIFORNIA): Overhead-valve V-6. Cast-iron block and head. Displacement: 231 cid (3.8 liters). Bore & stroke: 3.80 x 3.40 in. Compression ratio: 8.0:1. Brake horsepower: 110 at 3800 rpm Torque: 190 lbs.-ft. at 1600 rpm Four main bearings. Hydraulic valve lifters. Carburetor: Rochester E2ME two-barrel. Sales Code: LD5. VIN code: A.

MALIBU BASE V-8: Overhead-valve. Cast-iron block and head. Bore and stroke: 3.50 x 3.48 in. Displacement: 267 cid (4.4 liters). Compression ratio: 8.3:1. Net brake hp: 115 at 4000 rpm. Taxable hp: 39.20. Net torque: 200 lbs.-ft. at 2400 rpm. Five main bearings. Hydraulic valve lifters. Carburetor: Rochester 2ME two-barrel. VIN Code: J.

MALIBU OPTIONAL V-8: Overhead-valve. Cast-iron block and head. Bore and stroke: 3.74 x 3.48 in. Displacement: 305 cid (5.0 liters). Compression ratio: 8.6:1. Net brake hp: 150 at 3800 rpm. Taxable hp: 44.66. Net torque: 240 lbs.-ft. at 2400 rpm. Five main bearings. Hydraulic valve lifters. Carburetor: Rochester 4ME four-barrel. VIN Code: H.

CHASSIS DATA

Wheelbase: 108.1 in. Overall length: (car) 192.7 in.; (station wagon) 193.4 in. Height: (coupe) 55.7 inches; (sedan) 55.7 in.; (station wagon) 55.8 in. Width: (car) 72.3 in.; (station wagon) 71.9 in. Front tread: 58.5 in. Rear tread: 57.8 in. Tires: (car) P185/75R14/B steel-belted radial; (Station wagon) P195/75R14/B steel-belted radial. Transmission: Three-speed manual floor shift transmission standard with Malibu V-6. Gear ratios: (1st) 3.50:1; (2nd) 1.89:1; (3rd) 1.00:1; (Rev) 3.62:1. Four-speed floor shift optional on Malibu 305-cid V-8: Gear ratios: (1st) 2.85:1; (2nd) 2.02:1; (3rd) 1.35:1; (4th) 1.00:1; (rev) 2.85:1. Three-speed Turbo-Hydra-Matic optional: Gear ratios: (1st) 2.52:1; (2nd) 1.52:1; (3rd) 1.00:1; (rev) 1.93:1; Malibu 267-cid V-6 gear ratios: (1st) 2.74:1; (2nd) 1.57:1; (3rd) 1.00:1; (rev) 2.07:1. Standard final drive ratio: (V-6) 2.73:1; (V-8) 2.29:1; (station wagon V-8) 2.41:1. Steering: recirculating ball. Front suspension: Control arms, coil springs and stabilizer bar. Rear suspension: Rigid axle, lower trailing radius arms, upper oblique torque arms and coil springs. Brakes: Front disc/rear drum. Body construction: Separate body and perimeter box frame. Fuel tank: (car) 18.1 gal.; (station wagon) 18.2 gal.

OPTIONS

A01 all tinted glass ($75). A02 tinted windshield. A26 United Kingdom and European Glazing Window. A31 power windows with electric control ($195). A32 electric front door window ($140). AG9 six-way power seat adjuster ($173). AU3 power door locks ($93-$132). AU6 El Camino electric tailgate release ($27). AV3 El Camino pickup box tie downs. AW9 station wagon quarter stow and luggage compartment security group ($39). B32 front floor mats. B37 front and rear color-keyed floor mats ($25). B39 load floor carpet ($74). B90 side window moldings ($44). B93 door edge guards ($13-$21). B96 wheel opening moldings ($25). B3W advance price sheet. BS1 Quiet sound group acoustical insulation ($54). BW2 deluxe body molding exterior decoration ($53). BX3 station wagon wood-grained side panels ($271). BX8 front fender and body moldings. C09 vinyl padded full top roof ($115-$124). C49 electric rear window defogger ($107). C51 station wagon rear window air deflector ($32). C60 manual air conditioning ($585). CB4 vinyl padded Landau top ($171). CD4 pulse-type windshield wipers and washers ($41). D28 outside RR rearview mirror. D33 remote-control left-hand outside rearview mirror ($19). D35 custom outside rearview mirror ($47). D36 10-inch tilting export-type inside rearview mirror. D55 front seat center console ($86). D68 dual Sport-style rearview mirrors ($73). D73 pickup box hand rail. D84 custom two-tone paint ($71-$121). D85 body side lower accent stripes ($50). D91 special two-tone paint. F40 heavy-duty front and rear suspension ($23). F41 special front and rear heavy-duty sport suspension ($43). G80 Positraction rear axle ($67). G92 performance ratio rear axle ($19). K05 engine block heater. K35 Cruise and speed control with resume ($132). K73 70-amp. Delcotron generator ($11-$45). K81 63-amp Delcotron generator ($6-$34). LC3 229-cid V-6 engine (standard federal engine). L39 267-cid V-8 engine ($50). LD5 231-cid V-6 engine (standard California engine). LG4 305-cid V-8 engine ($50). LM1 350-cid V-8 engine in El Camino ($360). MM3 three-speed manual transmission (standard). MM4 four-speed manual transmission ($141). MX1 Turbo-Hydra-Matic automatic transmission ($349). Full wheel covers ($46). N23 22-gal. fuel tank. N33 Tilt steering wheel ($81). N41 variable-ratio power steering ($172). N95 simulated wire wheel covers with locks ($80-$135). NM5 non-closed loop emission system on Canadian cars. NM8 leaded gas emissions modification. P01 Deluxe wheel trim cover ($56-$102). P41 export tire equipment. P42 self-sealing tire. PB2 gold or silver ABS plastic Sport wheel trim covers ($55-$101). QFW P195/75R14B radial tires with white stripe ($125). QXX P205/75R14B radial black sidewall tires. QXY P205/75R14B radial tires with white stripes ($183). QXZ P205/75R14B radial tires with raised white letters. QYA P205/70R14B radial black sidewall tires. QYB P205/75R14B radial tires with white stripes. QYC P205/75R14B radial tires with raised white letters. QYD P185/75R14B radial black sidewall tires. QYE P185/75R14B radial tires with white stripes ($48). QYF P195/75R14B radial black sidewall tires. QYG P195/75R14B radial tires with white stripes. T72 two rectangular export-type left-hand headlights. T84 rectangular export-type right-hand headlight. T90 export-type signal light and marker lamp. TR9 lamp group ($33-$59). TT4 tungsten quartz halogen headlights ($36). U05 dual horns ($10). U14 special instrumentation gauge package ($80). U18 export speedometer. U35 electric clock ($23). U58 AM/FM push-button stereo ($178). U63 AM push-button radio ($90). U69 AM/FM push-button radio ($142). U75 power antenna ($47). U76 windshield antenna included with all radios ($25). U80 auxiliary rear radio speaker ($19). U81 dual rear radio speakers. UA1 heavy-duty battery ($20). UF7 gauge package, except tachometer. UM2 AM/FM push-button radio and tape player ($252). UN3 AM/FM stereo cassette radio less clock. UP6 AM/FM stereo CB radio ($487). V08 heavy-duty radiator ($34-$61). V30 front and rear bumper guards ($48). V55 station wagon roof top luggage carrier ($95). V78 less certificate of compliance plate. V84 government export orders, U.S. vehicles. VB1 Japanese shipping label. VC3 U.S. Territory shipping label. VC4 Puerto Rico shipping label. VC5 price label, non-Japan. VE5 front and rear bumper impact strips ($43). YC8 demo option drive. YF5 California emission requirement ($85). YJ7 demo drive. Z03 Landau Coupe equipment. Z15 El Camino SS package. Z16 El Camino Black Knight sport décor package. Z49 mandatory Canadian base equipment model. ZJ1 two-tone custom interior. ZJ2 custom exterior moldings. ZJ3 Chevy's '81 Value Bonus package. ZJ4 Chevy's '81 Value Bonus package. ZJ7 special wheel package with hubcap and trim rings ($49-$95). ZL6 Chevy's '81 Value Bonus package phase II. ZL7 Chevy's '81 Value Bonus package phase II. ZL8 Chevy's '81 Value Bonus package phase II. ZL9 Chevy's '81 Value Bonus package phase II. Cloth 55/45 seating ($181-$241).

OPTION INSTALLATION RATES

Automatic transmission (98.9 percent). V-8 engine (19.3 percent). V-6 engine (80.7 percent). AM radio (44 percent). AM/FM monaural radio (14.1 percent). AM/FM stereo radio (16.0 percent). AM/FM stereo 8-track (0.9 percent). AM/FM stereo cassette (2.5 percent). AM/FM stereo CB (0.1 percent). Manual air conditioning (85.8 percent). Power steering (100 percent). Tilt steering (30.2 percent). Power front disc brakes (100 percent). Power door locks (11.6 percent). Power windows (8.5 percent). Cruise control (31.6 percent). Bucket seats (1.7 percent). Power seats (3.0 percent). Vinyl top (6.5 percent). Tinted windshield only (3.2 percent). All tinted glass (86.7 percent). Wheel covers (80.2 percent). Styled steel wheels (13 percent). Steel-belted radial tires (62.9 percent). Fiberglass-belted radial tires (35.0 percent). Optional regular clock (22.3 percent). Electric rear window defogger (39.7 percent). Remote-control left-hand side-view mirror (65.8 percent). Remote-control right-hand side-view mirror (3.2 percent). Positraction limited-slip differential (3 percent). Vinyl roof ($6.6). Based on model year production of 242,447 units in the United States and Canada (North American production for the U.S. market).

HISTORICAL FOOTNOTES

Robert D. Lund was Chevrolet general manager at the start of the 1981 model year and Robert C. Stempel moved into the same position by 1982. An anticipated turnaround in Chevrolet sales failed to materialize and the Malibu experienced a 12.9 percent drop in popularity. Calendar year sales of Malibus fell to 211,133 units for a 3.4 percent share of the total market. Model-year U.S. dealer sales fell to 242,856. Calendar-year registrations declined to 153,396 cars and 56,126 station wagons.

The Malibu was again available only as a four-door sedan or station wagon for 1982.

The Malibu adopted a Caprice-styled grille and dual rectangular headlamps in 1982. It continued to be available only in four-door sport sedan and station wagon models. The Malibu gained diesel power through the optional 5.7-liter (350-cid) V-8 or the new 4.3-liter (260-cid) V-6 engine. Chevrolet carried over the gas engine lineup from 1981, including the standard 3.8-liter (229-cid) V-6 and optional 4.4-liter (267-cid) V-8 and 5.0-liter (305-cid) V-8. The fact that Malibu now wore a grille similar to full-size models helped fuel rumors that the big Chevrolets were doomed. However, the reports of their imminent demise proved premature.

MALIBU

I.D. NUMBERS

VIN embossed on the top left-hand side of the instrument panel and visible through the windshield. The first designates the country of origin: 1=United States. The second symbol identifies the manufacturer: G=General Motors. The third symbol indicates the make: 1=Chevrolet. The fourth symbol indicates the type of restraint system: A=non-passive/manual seat belts; B=passive/automatic seat belts and C=passive/inflatable. The fifth symbol indicates the car line/series: W=Malibu Classic. The sixth and seventh symbols indicate body type: 35=four-door station wagon, 69=four-door notchback sedan and 80=El Camino. The eighth symbol indicates engine (net horsepower): K=RPO LC3 229-cid 110-hp V-6, A=RPO LD5 231-cid 110-hp V-6 (California), J=RPO L39 267-cid 115-hp V-8, H=RPO LG4 305-cid 145-hp V-8, V=RPO LT6 260-cid 85-hp diesel V-6 and N=RPO LF9 350-cid 105-hp diesel V-8. The ninth symbol is a check digit. The 10th symbol designates the model year: C=1982. The seventh symbol designates the assembly plant location: B=Baltimore, Maryland, and R=Arlington, Texas. The last six symbols are the sequential unit production number at the specific factory. The Fisher body tag riveted to the top of the cowl on the left side of the car below the hood provides additional vehicle identification information. The Fisher body STYLE NUMBER (ST) consists of four or more symbols identifying the series and body style (example: 1AW69 for a 1982 Malibu Classic four-door sedan). The BODY NUMBER consists of a prefix designating assembly plant and the sequential unit production number at the specific factory. The TRIM NUMBER (TR) identifies upholstery.

COLORS

(11) Antique White, (16) Silver Poly, (19) Black, (21) Light Blue Poly, (22) Bright Blue Poly, (29) Dark Blue Poly, (45) Light Jadestone Poly, (49) Dark Jadestone Poly, (55) Goldwing Poly, (57) Marigold, (63) Pastel Sandstone, (67) Dark Goldwing Poly, (68) Medium Sandstone Poly, (72) Light Redwood Poly, (74) Autumn Maple, (75) Spectra Red, (77) Dark Redwood Poly, (78) Dark Claret Poly, (80) Slate Gray, (84) Charcoal Poly, (85) Medium Slate Firemist and (88) Dark Brown Firemist. Vinyl tops were available in: 11T=White, 19T=Black, 29T=Dark Blue Poly, 36T=Light waxberry Poly, 45T=Light Jadestone Poly, 63T=Pastel Sandstone Poly, 64T=Doeskin, 77T=Dark Maple and 85T=Medium Slate Poly.

ENGINE CODES

Codes appear on the right side of V-6 cylinder blocks behind the distributor and right-hand side of V-8 engine blocks. Engine codes for 1982 were: (229-cid two-barrel V-6) CCA, CCH, CCM, CCR, CCC, CCK, CCN, CCS and CCF; (231-cid two-barrel V-6) ML and MG; (260-cid diesel V-6) UAA, UAD and UAJ; (267-cid two-barrel V-8) CDB, CDJ, C4S, C4U, CDC, C4N, C4T, C4W, CDD and C4R; (305-cid four-barrel V-8) CFA, CFH, CFZ, C2T, CFB, CFR, CRA, C2U, CFC, CFT, C2R, C2W, CFD, CFW, C2S, C2X, CFF and CFY; (350-cid diesel V-8) VAB, VAM, VAW, VBB, VAC, VAN, VAX, VBC, VAD, VAP, VAY, VBP, VAK, VAS, VAZ, VB4, VAL, VAU, VBA and VBW.

MALIBU CLASSIC — SERIES 1W V-6/V-8

There was no Malibu this year, only a Malibu Classic. Two-door models were also dropped and all production was now quartered in two U.S. factories, Baltimore and Arlington. The 1982 Malibu Classic had a distinctive crosshatch grille similar to that seen on the Caprice. It was flanked by quad rectangular headlamps that stood over horizontal quad park/signal lamps. A dozen body colors were available in combination with either cloth or vinyl interiors. A four-door sport sedan and four-door station wagon were the only models. The base engine was the 229-cid (3.8-liter) V-6, but Malibu Classics could also be ordered with either of two gas V-8s, a 4.3-liter diesel V-6 or the big 5.7-liter diesel V-8 from Oldsmobile. The smaller diesel — which arrived late in the model year — was the first V-6 version offered in a Chevrolet and was actually produced by Oldsmobile. It had roller hydraulic valve lifters, a serpentine belt system, a venturi-shaped pre-chamber and a torque-pulse compensator for smoother power flow. The diesel had aluminum cylinder heads and an aluminum intake manifold, water outlet and oil pump body. Standard equipment included a redesigned grille with quad rectangular headlights, a notchback bench seat with folding center armrest, automatic transmission, low-drag front disc brakes, an improved windshield washer system, power front disc/rear drum brakes with disc brake audible wear sensors, power steering, a Delcotron generator with built-in solid-state regulator, steel bumpers with high-strength reinforcements, visible ball-joint wear indicators, a coolant recovery system, fiberglass-belted radial-ply tires with high-pressure recommendations, an early fuel evaporation system, a full-coil suspension system with computer-selected springs and a front stabilizer bar, dual horns, double-panel door, hood and deck lid (or tailgate) construction, a special sound package, extensive anti-corrosion treatments, a dual-mode flow-through ventilation system, Hide-A-Way dual-speed electric windshield wipers, front and rear inner fenders for corrosion protection, color-keyed seat and shoulder belts, a compact spare tire, full wheel covers, a side-lift frame jack, a notchback front seat with molded full-foam seat construction, a foam-backed cloth headliner, color-keyed cut-pile carpeting, a day/night rearview mirror, a color-keyed steering column and steering wheel, a glove compartment lock and light, vinyl door pull straps, GM Computer Command Control engine management system, manual lap/shoulder belts with push-button buckles for driver and right front passenger, a safety belt audible warning system, manual lap belts with push-button buckles for rear passengers and center front, an energy-absorbing steering column, passenger guard door locks, safety door latches, stamped steel door hinges, folding seatback latches, an energy-absorbing instrument panel, energy-absorbing front seat back tops, a laminated windshield, tempered side and rear glass, safety armrests, identification symbols for controls and displays, side marker lights and reflectors, parking lights that illuminate with the headlights, four-way hazard warning flashers, back-up lights, a lane-change feature in the directional lights, a defroster, dual-speed windshield wiper/washers, a vinyl-edged inside rearview mirror, a left-hand outside rearview mirror, a dual master cylinder brake system with warning light, a starter safety switch, dual-action safety hood latches, an audible anti-theft ignition key reminder, an anti-theft steering lock, an inside hood release, dual horns, a front stabilizer bar, full wheel covers and a stand-up hood ornament. Malibu Classic bodies displayed a bright wide upper grille molding, bright back window and windshield reveal moldings, bright sill and roof drip moldings and wide wheel opening moldings. The redesigned circular instrumentation was similar to the Monte Carlo's. Inside were a cigar lighter, a dome light and a day/night mirror. Sedans also had bright deck lid and end cap moldings, plus black-accented bright taillight trim.

Model Number	Body/Style Number	Body Type & Seating	Factory Price	Shipping Weight	Production Total
MALIBU CLASSIC SERIES 1W (V-6)					
1W	69	4d sedan-6P	$8,137	3,097 lbs.	Note 1
1W	35	4d wagon-6P	$8,265	3,247 lbs.	Note 1
MALIBU CLASSIC SERIES 1W (V-8)					
1W	69	4d sedan-6P	$8,207	3,228 lbs.	Note 1
1W	35	4d wagon-6P	$8,335	3,387 lbs.	Note 1

PRODUCTION NOTES

NOTE 1 Model-year production (U.S.) of all 1982 Malibus was 116,125 units. This was also the North American production total, since no Malibus were built in Canada this year.

NOTE 2 Model year production by series and body style was as follows:

Malibu Classic
sedan   70,793
station wagon   45,332
Total   116,125

NOTE 3 Additional statistics record series production (North American production for the U.S. market) as follows:

Malibu Classic (V-6)	54,265	Malibu Classic (V-8)	16,258	Total 70,793
Classic wagon (V-6)	31,190	Classic wagons (V-8)	14,142	Total 45,332

NOTE 4 Production by factory (U.S. only) was:

Code	Factory	Production
B	Baltimore	56,887
R	Arlington (Tex.)	59,238

ENGINES

MALIBU BASE V-6: 90-degree, overhead-valve V-6. Cast-iron block and head. Bore and stroke: 3.74 x 3.48 in. Displacement: 229 cid (3.8 liters). Compression ratio: 8.6:1. Brake hp: 110 at 4200 rpm. Torque: 170 lbs.-ft. at 2000 rpm. Four main bearings. Hydraulic valve lifters. Carburetor: Rochester two-barrel E2ME. VIN Code: K.

MALIBU OPTIONAL DIESEL V-6: 90-degree, overhead-valve V-6. Cast-iron block and aluminum head. Displacement: 262 cid. (4.3 liters). Bore and stroke: 4.057 x 3.385 in. Compression ratio: 22.5:1. Brake hp: 85 at 3600 rpm. Torque: 165 lbs.-ft. at 1600 rpm. Four main bearings. Hydraulic valve lifters. Fuel injection. VIN Code: V.

MALIBU OPTIONAL DIESEL V-8: Overhead-valve. Cast-iron block and head. Bore and stroke: 4.057 x 3.385 in. Displacement: 350 cid (5.7 liters). Compression ratio: 22.5:1. Net brake hp: 105 at 3200 rpm. Taxable hp: 51.20. Net torque: 200 lbs.-ft. at 1600 rpm. Five main bearings. Hydraulic valve lifters. Induction system: fuel injection. Olds-built. VIN Code: N.

MALIBU OPTIONAL V-8 Overhead-valve. Cast-iron block and head. Bore and stroke: 3.50 x 3.48 in. Displacement: 267 cid (4.4 liters). Compression ratio: 8.3:1. Net brake hp: 115 at 4000 rpm. Taxable hp: 39.20. Net brake hp: 120 at 3600 rpm. Net torque: 205 lbs.-ft. at 2400 rpm. Five main bearings. Hydraulic valve lifters. Carburetor: Rochester E2ME two-barrel. VIN Code: J.

MALIBU OPTIONAL V-8 Overhead-valve. Cast-iron block and head. Bore and stroke: 3.74 x 3.48 in. Displacement: 305 cid (5.0 liters). Compression ratio: 8.6:1. Net brake hp: 145 at 4000 rpm. Taxable hp: 44.66. Net torque: 240 lbs.-ft. at 2000 rpm. Five main bearings. Hydraulic valve lifters. Carburetor: Rochester E4ME four-barrel. VIN Code: H.

CHASSIS DATA

Wheelbase: 108.1 in. Overall length: (car) 192.7 in.; (station wagon) 193.3 in. Height: (sedan) 55.7 in.; (station wagon) 55.8 in. Width: (car) 72.3 in.; (station wagon) 71.9 in. Front tread: 58.5 in. Rear tread: 57.8 in. Tires: (car) P185/75R14/B steel-belted radial; (station wagon) P195/75R14/B steel-belted radial. Transmission: Three-speed Turbo-Hydra-Matic standard: Gear ratios: (1st) 2.52:1; (2nd) 1.52:1; (3rd) 1.00:1; (rev) 1.93:1; Malibu Classic 267-cid V-6 gear ratios: (1st) 2.74:1; (2nd) 1.57:1; (3rd) 1.00:1; (rev) 2.07:1 except Malibu Classic diesel V-6: (1st) 2.74:1; (2nd) 1.57:1; (3rd) 1.00:1; (rev) 2.07:1. Standard final drive ratio: (Malibu Classic V-6 sedan) 2.41:1; (Malibu Classic V-8 sedan) 2.29:1; (Malibu Classic V-6 station wagon) 2.73:1, (Malibu Classic 267-cid V-8 station wagon) 2.41:1 or (Malibu Classic station wagon with 305-cid V-8) 2.73:1. Steering: recirculating ball. Front suspension: Control arms, coil springs and stabilizer bar. Rear suspension: Rigid axle, lower trailing radius arms, upper oblique torque arms and coil springs. Brakes: Front disc/rear drum. Body construction: Separate body and perimeter box frame. Fuel tank: (car) 18.1 gal.; (station wagon) 18.2 gal.

OPTIONS

A01 all tinted glass ($105). A02 tinted windshield. A26 United Kingdom and European Glazing Window. A31 power windows with electric control ($255). A32 electric front door window. AG9 six-way power seat adjuster. AU3 power door locks ($170). AU6 El Camino electric tailgate release ($40). AV3 El Camino pickup box tie downs. AV9 Japanese export seating requirements. AW9 station wagon quarter stow and luggage compartment security group. B32 front floor mats. B37 front and rear color-keyed floor mats. B39 load floor carpet ($84). B93 door edge guards ($15-$25). BW2 deluxe body molding exterior decoration ($57). BX3 station wagon wood-grained side panels ($307). BX8 front fender and body moldings. C49 electric rear window defogger ($135). C51 station wagon rear window air deflector ($36). C60 manual air conditioning ($725). CD4 pulse-type windshield wipers and washers. D33 remote-control left-hand outside rearview mirror ($22). D35 custom outside rearview mirrors ($59). D73 pickup box hand rail. D84 custom two-tone paint ($138). D85 body side lower accent stripes. F40 heavy-duty front and rear suspension ($26). F41 special front and rear heavy-duty sport suspension ($49). G80 Positraction rear axle ($80). G84 high-altitude rear axle ratio. G92 performance ratio rear axle ($21). GH2 2.29:1 rear axle ratio.

Malibu

GM7 2.39:1 rear axle ratio. GM8 2.56:1 rear axle ratio. GU1 2.41:1 rear axle ratio. GU2 2.73:1 rear axle ratio. GU3 2.93:1 rear axle ratio. GU4 3.08:1 rear axle ratio. GU5 3.23:1 rear axle ratio. GW9 2.93:1 rear axle ratio. JE1 European export brake system. K05 engine block heater. K35 Cruise and speed control with resume . K73 70-amp. Delcotron generator. LC3 229-cid V-6 engine (standard Federal engine). L39 267-cid V-8 engine ($70). LD5 231-cid V-6 engine (standard California engine). LF9 350-cid diesel V-8 ($825). LG4 305-cid V-8 engine in station wagon ($70). LT6 4.3-liter diesel V-6. MX1 Turbo-Hydra-Matic automatic transmission. N18 simulated wire wheel covers. N23 22-gal. fuel tank. N33 Tilt steering wheel ($105). N81 full-size spare radial tire. N95 simulated wire wheel covers with locks ($190). NA6 alternate requirements emission system. NM5 Non-closed loop emission system on Canadian cars. NM8 leaded gas emissions modification. P41 export tire equipment. P42 self-sealing tire. QVJ P195/75R14 steel-belted white stripe radial tires. QVT P205/75R14B steel-belted radial tires with white stripe. QXW P195/75R14B steel-belted radial tires with white stripe. QXX P205/75R14B steel-belted radial black sidewall tires. QXY P205-75R14B steel-belted radial tires with white stripe. QXZ P205/75R14B steel-belted radial tires with raised white letters. QYD P185/75R14B radial black sidewall tires. QYE P185/75R14B radial tires with white stripes. QYF P195/75R14B radial black sidewall tires. QYG P195/75R14B radial tires with white stripes. T84 rectangular export-type right-hand headlight. T90 export-type signal light and marker lamp. TR9 lamp group ($49-$56). TT5 tungsten quartz halogen headlights. U14 special instrumentation gauge package ($95). U18 export speedometer. U35 electric clock ($35). U58 AM/FM push-button stereo ($198). U63 AM push-button radio ($112). U69 AM/FM push-button radio ($171). U73 fixed antenna ($41). U75 power antenna ($60). U76 windshield antenna included with all radios. U81 dual rear radio speakers. UA1 heavy-duty battery ($25). UF7 gauge package, except tachometer. UM2 AM/FM push-button radio and tape player. UN3 AM/FM stereo cassette radio less clock ($298). V08 heavy-duty radiator ($40-$70). V10 cold climate package. V30 front and rear bumper guards ($50). VC3 U.S. Territory shipping label. VC4 Puerto Rico shipping label. VE5 front and rear bumper impact strips ($50). YC8 demo option drive. Z15 El Camino SS package. Z16 El Camino Black Knight sport décor package. Z49 mandatory Canadian base equipment model. ZJ1 two-tone custom interior. ZJ2 custom exterior moldings. ZJ7 special wheel package with hub cap and trim rings. Dual horns ($12). Side window reveal moldings ($35). Wheel opening moldings ($30). Rocker panel moldings ($25). Body pin striping ($57). Station wagon roof carrier ($125).

OPTION INSTALLATION RATES

Automatic transmission (100 percent). V-8 engine (22.3 percent). Diesel V-6 engine (4.1 percent). V-6 gas engine (73 percent). Diesel V-6 engine (0.6 percent). AM radio (34.8 percent). AM/FM monaural radio (13.1 percent). AM/FM stereo radio (31.8 percent). AM/FM stereo 8-track (0.7 percent). AM/FM stereo cassette (5.3 percent). Manual air conditioning (87.7 percent). Power steering (100 percent). Tilt steering (40.7 percent). Power front disc brakes (100 percent). Power door locks (16.5 percent). Power windows (10.7 percent). Cruise control (47.1 percent). Bucket seats (1.2 percent). All tinted glass (91.2 percent). Styled steel wheels (17.7 percent). Steel-belted radial tires (65.1 percent). Fiberglass-belted radial tires (34.9 percent). Optional regular clock (29.1 percent). Electric rear window defogger (50.3 percent). Remote-control left-hand side-view mirror (76.7 percent). Positraction limited-slip differential (3.4 percent). Based on model year production of 116,125 units in the United States and Canada (North American production for the U.S. market).

HISTORICAL FOOTNOTES

Robert C. Stempel was Chevrolet general manager in 1982. Stempel stressed the need to get Chevrolet back into the low-to-middle end of the pricing spectrum and initiated a marketing program aimed at stealing customers from Ford, Chrysler and imported car buyers. Unfortunately, this didn't work when market trends shifted. Chevrolet had started to emphasize small, fuel-efficient models just when interest in larger, higher-performance cars was revived. As a result, the Malibu lost a lot of ground and its model-year sales at U.S. dealerships dropped to 121,206 units. Calendar-year registrations declined to 64,998 cars and 42,766 station wagons.

Slated for extinction after 1983, the rear-wheel-drive, six-passenger Malibu was merchandised in a new, single series that appealed to economy-minded buyers. Carry-over offerings were similar to 1982 in body style and power train, except that the 305-cid engine now became the base V-8 and the 267-cid V-8 was dropped.

I.D. NUMBERS

VIN embossed on the top left-hand side of the instrument panel and visible through the windshield. The first designates the country of origin: 1=United States. The second symbol identifies the manufacturer: G=General Motors. The third symbol indicates the make: 1=Chevrolet. The fourth symbol indicates the type of restraint system: A=non-passive/manual seat belts; B=passive/automatic seat belts and C=passive/inflatable. The fifth symbol indicates the car line/series: W=Malibu Classic. The sixth and seventh symbols indicate body type: 35=four-

GM built 117,426 Malibus for the 1983 model year — the last time the Chevelle/Malibu line was built until it was revived in 1997.

door station wagon and 69=four-door notchback sedan. The eighth symbol indicates engine (net hp): 9=RPO LC3 229-cid 115-hp V-6, A=RPO LD5 231-cid 110-hp V-6 (California), H=RPO LG4 305-cid 150-hp V-8, V=RPO LT6 260-cid 85-hp diesel V-6 and N=RPO LF9 350-cid 125-hp diesel V-8. The ninth symbol is a check digit. The 10th symbol designates the model year: D=1983. The seventh symbol designates the assembly plant location: B=Baltimore, Maryland, and R=Arlington, Texas. The last six symbols are the sequential unit production number at the specific factory. The Fisher body tag riveted to the top of the cowl on the left side of the car below the hood provides additional vehicle identification information. The Fisher Body STYLE NUMBER (ST) consists of four or more symbols identifying the series and body style (example: 1AW69 for a 1983 Malibu Classic four-door sedan). The BODY NUMBER consists of a prefix designating assembly plant and the sequential unit production number at the specific factory. The TRIM NUMBER (TR) identifies upholstery.

COLORS

(11) White, (15) Silver Sand Poly, (19) Black, (22) Light Blue Poly, (27) Medium Dark Royal Blue Poly, (42) Light Grayfern Poly, (48) Dark Grayfern Poly, (60) Light Sand Gray, (62) Light Briar Brown Poly, (67) Dark Briar Brown Poly, (75) Spectra Red and (78) Dark Autumn Maple Poly. Vinyl tops were available in: 11T=White, 19T=Black, 27T=Medium Dark Royal Blue, 42T=Light Grayfern, 60T Light Sand Gray, 67T Dark Briar Brown, 78T=Dark Autumn Maple and 91T=Light Flax Poly.

ENGINE CODES

Codes appear on the right side of V-6 cylinder blocks behind the distributor and right-hand side of V-8 engine blocks. Engine codes for 1982 were: (229-cid two-barrel V-6) DBA, DBB and DBC; (231-cid two-barrel V-6) NL, ND, NG, NH and NJ; (260-cid diesel V-6) UKA, UKB, UKC, UKJ and UKK; (305-cid four-barrel V-8) DDB, DDJ, DDK, DGN, D5F, DDD, D5B, D5H, DDF, DDN, D5C and DDH; (350-cid diesel V-8) VLB, VKZ and VLA.

MALIBU — SERIES 1W — V-6/V-8

This would be the final season for the rear-drive six-passenger Malibu, whose family-carrying duties were being taken over by the front-drive Celebrity. Base engine was the 229-cid (3.8-liter) V-6, with V-6 and V-8 diesels available as well as the 305-cid gas V-8. Only two bodies were offered: four-door sedan and four-door wagon. The Malibu Classic nameplate was dropped (replaced by the luxury CL option), so only one series remained this year to stress economy. Notchback bench or 55/45 split front seats with fold-down armrests came in cloth or vinyl. Several trim items were added to the option list, including rocker panel and wheel opening moldings. Malibu's standard equipment included power brakes and steering, automatic transmission, a locking glove compartment, a cigar lighter, a dome light, a compact spare tire, a front stabilizer bar, two-speed wiper/washers, power (low-drag) front disc/rear drum brakes with disc brake audible wear sensors, a Delcotron generator with built-in solid-state regulator, steel bumpers with high-strength reinforcements, visible ball-joint wear indicators, a coolant recovery system, fiberglass-belted radial-ply tires with high-pressure recommendations, an early fuel evaporation system, a full-coil suspension system with computer-selected springs and a front stabilizer bar, dual horns, double-panel door, hood and deck lid (or tailgate) construction, a special sound package, extensive anti-corrosion treatments, a dual-mode flow-through ventilation system, Hide-A-Way dual-speed electric windshield wipers, front and rear inner fenders for corrosion protection, color-keyed seat and shoulder belts, a compact spare tire, full wheel covers, a side-lift frame jack, a notchback front seat with molded full-foam seat construction, a foam-backed cloth headliner, color-keyed cut-pile carpeting, a day/night rearview mirror, a color-keyed steering column and steering wheel, a glove compartment lock and light, vinyl door pull straps, GM Computer Command Control engine management system, manual lap/shoulder belts with push-button buckles for driver and right front passenger, a safety belt audible warning system, manual lap belts with push-button buckles for rear passengers and center front, an energy-absorbing steering column, passenger guard door locks, safety door latches, stamped steel door hinges, folding seatback latches, an energy-absorbing instrument panel, energy-absorbing front seat back tops, a laminated windshield, tempered side and rear glass, safety armrests, identification symbols for controls and displays, side marker lights and reflectors, parking lights that illuminate with the headlights, four-

MALIBU

way hazard warning flashers, back-up lights, a lane-change feature in the directional lights, a defroster, dual-speed windshield wiper/washers, a vinyl-edged inside rearview mirror, a left-hand outside rearview mirror, a dual master cylinder brake system with warning light, a starter safety switch, dual-action safety hood latches, an audible anti-theft ignition key reminder, an anti-theft steering lock, an inside hood release, dual horns, a front stabilizer bar, full wheel covers and a stand-up hood ornament. Malibu Classic bodies displayed a bright wide upper grille molding, bright back window and windshield reveal moldings, bright sill and roof drip moldings and wide wheel opening moldings. Sedans also had bright deck lid and end cap moldings, plus black-accented bright taillight trim. The Malibu bodies held bright sill, rear window and windshield reveal, roof drip and belt moldings.

Model Number	Body/Style Number	Body Type & Seating	Factory Price	Shipping Weight	Production Total
MALIBU SERIES 1W (V-6)					
1W	69	4d sedan-6P	$8,084	3,106 lbs.	Note 1
1W	35	4d wagon-6P	$8,217	3,249 lbs.	Note 1
MALIBU SERIES 1W (V-8)					
1W	69	4d sedan-6P	$8,309	3,214 lbs.	Note 1
1W	35	4d wagon-6P	$8,442	3,376 lbs.	Note 1

PRODUCTION NOTES

NOTE 1 Model-year production (U.S.) of all 1983 Malibus was 117,426 units. This was also the North American production total, since no Malibu were built in Canada this year.

NOTE 2 Model-year production by series and body style was as follows:

Malibu
- sedan — 61,534
- station wagon — 55,892
- Total — 116,125

NOTE 3 Additional statistics record series production (North American production for the U.S. market) as follows:

Malibu sedan (V-6)	44,948	Malibu sedan (V-8)	16,586	Total	61,534
Malibu wagon (V-6)	39,549	Malibu wagon (V-8)	16,343	Total	55,892

NOTE 4 Production by factory (U.S. only) was:

Code	Factory	Production
B	Baltimore	23,835
R	Arlington (Tex.)	93,591

ENGINES

MALIBU BASE V-6 90-degree, overhead-valve V-6. Cast-iron block and head. Bore and stroke: 3.74 x 3.48 in. Displacement: 229-cid (3.8 liters). Compression ratio: 8.6:1. Brake hp: 110 at 4000 rpm. Torque: 190 lbs.-ft at 1600 rpm. Four main bearings. Hydraulic valve lifters. Carburetor: two-barrel Rochester E2ME. VIN Code: K or 9.

(**NOTE** California models used a Buick 231-cid V-6.)

MALIBU OPTIONAL DIESEL V-6 90-degree, overhead-valve V-6. Cast-iron block and head. Bore and stroke: 4.057 x 3.385 in. Displacement: 262-cid (4.3 liters). Compression ratio: 22.8:1. Brake hp: 85 at 3600 rpm. Torque: 165 lbs.-ft. at 1600 rpm. Four main bearings. Hydraulic valve lifters. Fuel injection. VIN Code: T or V.

MALIBU OPTIONAL V-8: 90-degree, overhead-valve. Cast-iron block and head. Bore and stroke: 3.74 x 3.48 in. Displacement: 305-cid (5.0 liters). Compression ratio: 8.6:1. Brake hp: 150 at 4000 rpm. Torque: 240 lbs.-ft. at 2400 rpm. Five main bearings. Hydraulic valve lifters. Carburetor: four-barrel Rochester E4ME. VIN Code: H.

MALIBU OPTIONAL DIESEL V-8: 90-degree, overhead-valve V-8. Cast-iron block and head. Bore and stroke: 4.057 x 3.385 in. Displacement: 350-cid (5.7 liters). Compression ratio: 22.5:1. Brake hp: 105 at 3200 rpm. Torque: 200 lbs.-ft. at 1600 rpm. Five main bearings. Hydraulic valve lifters. Fuel injection. Olds-built. VIN Code: N.

CHASSIS DATA

Wheelbase: 108.1 in. Overall length: (car) 192.7 in.; (station wagon) 193.3 in. Height: (sedan) 55.7 in.; (station wagon) 55.8 in. Width: (car) 72.3 in.; (station wagon) 71.9 in. Front tread: 58.5 in. Rear tread: 57.8 in. Tires: (car) P185/75R14/B steel-belted radial; (station wagon) P195/75R14/B steel-belted radial. Transmission: Three-speed Turbo-Hydra-Matic standard: Gear ratios: (1st) 2.52:1; (2nd) 1.52:1; (3rd) 1.00:1; (rev) 1.93:1; Malibu 267-cid V-6 gear ratios: (1st) 2.74:1; (2nd) 1.57:1; (3rd) 1.00:1; (rev) 2.07:1 except Malibu diesel V-6: (1st) 2.74:1; (2nd) 1.57:1; (3rd) 1.00:1; (rev) 2.07:1. Standard final drive ratio: (Malibu V-6 sedan) 2.41:1; (Malibu V-8 Sedan) 2.29:1; (Malibu V-6 station wagon) 2.73:1, (Malibu 267-cid V-8 station wagon) 2.41:1 or (Malibu station wagon with 305-cid V-8) 2.73:1. Steering: recirculating ball. Front suspension: Control arms, coil springs and stabilizer bar. Rear suspension: Rigid axle, lower trailing radius arms, upper oblique torque arms and coil springs. Brakes: Front disc/rear drum. Body construction: Separate body and perimeter box frame. Fuel tank: (car) 18.1 gal.; (station wagon) 18.2 gal.

OPTIONS

A01 all tinted glass ($105). A02 tinted windshield. A26 United Kingdom and European Glazing Window. A31 power windows with electric control ($255). A32 electric front door window. AG9 six-way power seat adjuster. AU3 power door locks ($170). AW9 station wagon quarter stow and luggage compartment security group. B37 front and rear color-keyed floor mats. B39 load floor carpet ($84). B93 door edge guards ($15-$25). BS1 acoustical insulation. BW2 Deluxe body molding exterior decoration ($57). BX3 station wagon wood-grained side panels ($307). BX8 front fender and body moldings. B2L fleet early order option. B3W preliminary price information. B6W fleet A/C incentive program. C49 electric rear window defogger ($135). C51 station wagon rear window air deflector ($36). C60 manual air conditioning ($725). CD4 pulse-type windshield wipers and washers. D33 remote-control left-hand outside rearview mirror ($22). D35 custom outside rearview mirrors ($59). D73 pickup box hand rail. D84 custom two-tone paint ($138). D85 body side lower accent stripes. DG8 export breakaway mirror. F40 heavy-duty front and rear suspension ($26). G80 Positraction rear axle ($95). G84 high-altitude rear axle ratio. G92 performance ratio rear axle ($21). GH2 2.29:1 rear axle ratio. GM7 2.39:1 rear axle ratio. GM8 2.56:1 rear axle ratio. GM8 2.56:1 rear axle ratio. GT4 3.73:1 rear axle ratio. GU1 2.41:1 rear axle ratio. GU2 2.73:1 rear axle ratio. GU3 2.93:1 rear axle ratio. GU4 3.08:1 rear axle ratio. GU5 3.23:1 rear axle ratio. GU6 3.42:1 rear axle ratio. GW9 2.93:1 rear axle ratio. JE1 European export brake system. K05 engine block heater. K35 Cruise and speed control with resume. K64 78-amp. Delcotron generator. LC3 229-cid V-6 engine (standard federal engine). LD5 231-cid V-6 engine (standard California engine). LF9 350-cid diesel V-8 ($700). LG4 305-cid V-8 engine ($225). LT6 4.3-liter diesel V-6 ($500). MX1 Turbo-Hydra-Matic automatic transmission (standard). N18 simulated wire wheel covers. N23 22-gal. fuel tank. N33 tilt steering wheel ($105). N81 full-size spare radial tire. N95 simulated wire wheel covers with locks ($190). NA6 alternate requirements emission system. NM5 non-closed loop emission system on Canadian cars. NM8 leaded gas emissions modification. P01 deluxe wheel trim covers. P41 export tire equipment. PB2 ABS plastic wheel trim covers. QVJ P195/75R14 steel-belted white stripe radial tires. QVT P205/75R14B steel-belted radial tires with white stripe. QXX P205/75R14B steel-belted radial black sidewall tires. QYD P185/75R14B radial black sidewall tires. QYE P185/75R14B radial tires with white stripes. QYF P195/75R14B radial black sidewall tires. QYG P195/75R14B radial tires with white stripes. T90 export-type signal light and marker lamp. TR9 lamp group ($49-$56). TT5 tungsten quartz halogen headlights. U05 dual A note horn. U14 special instrumentation gauge package ($95). U18 export speedometer. U35 electric clock ($35). U58 AM/FM push-button stereo ($198). U63 AM push-button radio ($112). U69 AM/FM push-button radio ($171). U73 fixed antenna ($41). U81 dual rear radio speakers. UA1 heavy-duty battery ($25). UN3 AM/FM stereo cassette radio less clock ($298). V08 heavy-duty radiator ($40-$70). V10 cold climate package ($99). V30 front and rear bumper guards ($50). V55 roof luggage carrier. V78 less certificate of compliance plate. VC3 U.S. Territory shipping label. VC4 Puerto Rico shipping label. VC5 export shipping label. VE5 front and rear bumper impact strips ($50). YF5 California emission requirements. Z49 mandatory Canadian base equipment model. ZJ7 special wheel package with hub cap and trim rings.

OPTION INSTALLATION RATES

Automatic transmission (100 percent). V-8 gas engine (27.4 percent). Diesel V-6 engine (0.2 percent). V-6 gas engine (71.8 percent). Diesel V-8 engine (0.6 percent). AM radio (32.3 percent). AM/FM monaural radio (9.8 percent). AM/FM stereo radio (32.9 percent). AM/FM stereo cassette (6 percent). Manual air conditioning (84.7 percent). Power steering (100 percent). Tilt steering (34.3 percent). Power front disc brakes (100 percent). Power door locks (16.5 percent). Power windows (7.9 percent). Cruise control (38.8 percent). Power seat (0.1 percent). Reclining seat (1.9 percent). All tinted glass (84.9 percent). Styled steel wheels (16.1 percent). Steel-belted radial tires (55.1 percent). Fiberglass-belted radial tires (44.9 percent). Optional regular clock (25.9 percent). Electric rear window defogger (54.4 percent). Remote-control left-hand side-view mirror (79.2 percent). Positraction limited-slip differential (4.1 percent). Based on model year production of 117,426 units in the U.S. and Canada (North American production for the U.S. market).

HISTORICAL FOOTNOTES

Robert D. Burger was Chevrolet general manager in 1983. Model-year sales at U.S. dealerships dropped to 107,761 units. Calendar-year registrations declined to 43,992 cars and 41,505 station wagons.

El Camino
1964-1987

1964

The front end of the 1964 El Camino featured twin round headlights and segmented grille with vertical and horizontal moldings.

Returning after a four-year hiatus in 1964 was the El Camino, which Chevrolet described as a "personal pickup." Built on the mid-size Chevelle's 115-inch wheelbase, the El Camino was available with many passenger-car options. It came with two trim levels.

The grille featured 10 main segments, with the eight nearest the center formed by seven vertical moldings and crisscrossing horizontal molding. The dual, round headlights were housed in the outer segments with the grille texture around them and rounded outer ends. Amber-colored, rectangular front parking lights were housed in the otherwise solid front bumper.

The El Camino came with either a base 120-hp six-cylinder or 195-hp V-8. Also available were optional 220-, 250-, 300-, and 365-hp V-8s.

I.D. NUMBERS

VIN embossed on a plate welded to the left front door hinge pillar post facing the driver. The first symbol designates the model year: 4=1964. The second and third symbols designate the series: (6-cylinder) 53=Regular El Camino, 55=Deluxe El Camino; (V-8) 54=Regular El Camino, 56=Deluxe El Camino. The fourth and fifth symbols designates body type: 80=two-door three-passenger sedan pickup. The sixth symbol designates the assembly plant location: A=Atlanta, Georgia, B=Baltimore, Maryland, G=Framingham, Massachusetts, H=Fremont, California, K=Kansas City, Missouri, and L=Los Angeles. The last six symbols are the sequential unit production number at the specific factory. The Fisher body tag riveted to the top of the cowl on the left side of the car below the hood provides additional vehicle identification information. The Fisher body STYLE NUMBER (ST) consists of a prefix identifying model year and four or more symbols identifying the series and body style (example: 64-13480 for a V-8-powered 1964 El Camino or 64-13680 for a V-8-powered 1964 El Camino Custom. The BODY NUMBER consists of a prefix designating assembly plant and the sequential unit production number at the specific factory (example: B 100001 is the first

EL CAMINO

car built at the Baltimore factory). The TRIM NUMBER (TR) identifies upholstery. Interior colors of fawn, aqua and red were available on specific models with specific exterior paint colors.

COLORS

(900) Tuxedo Black, (905) Meadow Green Metallic, (908) Bahama Green Metallic, (912) Silver Blue Metallic, (916) Daytona Blue Metallic, (918) Azure Aqua Metallic, (919) Aqua Lagoon Metallic, (920) Almond Fawn Metallic, (922) Ember Red, (932) Saddle Tan, (936) Ermine White, (938) Desert Beige, (940) Satin Silver and (948) Palomar Red Metallic. Interior colors of fawn, aqua and red were available on specific models with specific exterior paint colors.

ENGINE CODES

Codes appear on the right side of six-cylinder blocks behind the distributor and right front of V-8 engine blocks: (194-cid/120-hp six) GH, GJ, KC, KD, G, GB, GF, GG, GK, GL, GM, GN, K, KB, KJ and KH; (283-cid/220-hp V-8) JG, JH; (327-cid/250-hp V-8) JQ, JT and SR; (327-cid/300-hp V-8) JR, SS.

EL CAMINO — MODEL A/SERIES 53-54 SIX/V-8

El Caminos in the 53 (six-cylinder) and 54 (V-8) series were the base models, with trim and appointments comparable to a Chevelle 300. The base level El Camino had no body side moldings. A long, thin rectangular badge with the El Camino name decorated the trailing edge of the rear fenders. The Chevrolet name was spelled out in chrome letters on the edge of the hood and drop-down tailgate and the Chevelle name was spelled out on the front fender tips. Standard equipment included a sturdy all-welded rugged steel frame with welded torque-box design, metal inner front fender liners, a long-life exhaust system, high-level ventilation through dual vents in the front cowl side panels with individual knob controls for each, push-button outside door handles, an inside rearview mirror, an enclosed steering column, a rheostat-controlled lighted instrument cluster (with a dial speedometer, fuel gauge, oil pressure indicator light, engine temperature indicator light and generator indicator light), a five-position ignition switch, direction signal indicators, an ash tray, a radio speaker grille in top of the instrument panel, a locking glove box, a counter-balanced hood and rear deck lid, a diaphragm-spring type single dry disc clutch with two facings, Safety-Master self-adjusting brakes, 14-in. wheels with tubeless tires, a 54-plate 44-amp-hour 12-volt battery, a high-output heater and defroster, foam front seat cushions, dual interior sun visors, an easy-care vinyl headlining, electric windshield wipers, a color-keyed steering wheel with horn ring, an automatic cigarette lighter, a key-locking glove compartment, front seat belts and five black sidewall tires. The vinyl seats inside El Camino came in three colors, fawn, aqua and red. The vinyl-coated rubber floor mats were color-keyed and featured an attractive spatter design. Other quality interior details included a half-circle steering wheel horn ring, padded armrests front and rear and dual rear ashtrays. Color-keyed all-vinyl seats and sidewall trim were available in almond fawn, lagoon aqua or ember red for base models.

Model Number	Body/Style Number	Body Type & Seating	Factory Price	Shipping Weight	Production Total
EL CAMINO SERIES 53 (6-CYL)					
53	80	pickup	$2,267	2,935 lbs.	Note 1
EL CAMINO SERIES 54 (V-8)					
54	80	pickup	$2,367	2,935 lbs.	Note 1

EL CAMINO CUSTOM MODEL A/SERIES 55-56 — SIX/V-8

El Caminos in the 55 (six-cylinder) and 56 (V-8) series were the custom models, with upscale trim and appointments. The El Camino Custom had no body side moldings, but carried bright rocker panel moldings, bright wheel opening moldings, bright load box moldings, chrome window and windshield frames and a chrome windsplit molding on the center of the hood. A long, thin rectangular badge with the El Camino name decorated the trailing edge of the rear fenders. The Chevrolet name was spelled out in chrome letters on the edge of the hood and drop-down tailgate and the Chevelle name was spelled out on the front fender tips. Standard equipment included a sturdy all-welded rugged steel frame with welded torque-box design, metal inner front fender liners, a long-life exhaust system, high-level ventilation through dual vents in the front cowl side panels with individual knob controls for each, push-button outside door handles, an inside rearview mirror, an enclosed steering column, a rheostat-controlled lighted instrument cluster (with a dial speedometer, fuel gauge, oil pressure indicator light, engine temperature indicator light and generator indicator light), a five-position ignition switch, direction signal indicators, an ash tray, a radio speaker grille in top of the instrument panel, a locking glove box, a counter-balanced hood and rear deck lid, a diaphragm-spring type single dry disc clutch with two facings, Safety-Master self-adjusting brakes, 14-in. wheels with tubeless tires, a 54-plate 44-amp-hour 12-volt battery, a high-output heater and defroster, foam front seat cushions, dual interior sun visors, an easy-care vinyl headlining, electric windshield wipers, a color-keyed steering wheel with horn ring, an automatic cigarette lighter, a key-locking glove compartment, front seat belts and five black sidewall tires. The vinyl seats inside El Camino came in two colors, aqua and red. The vinyl-coated rubber floor mats were color-keyed and featured an attractive spatter design. Other quality interior details included a half-circle steering wheel horn ring, padded armrests front and rear and dual rear ashtrays. Color-keyed all-vinyl seats and sidewall trim were available in almond fawn, lagoon aqua or ember red for base models. El Camino Customs also featured color-keyed pattern cloth and leather-grain vinyl upholstery in fawn, aqua or red. They had deep-twist floor carpeting, deluxe door lock and door window handles, a bright glove compartment facing, a two-tone steering wheel and an electric clock.

Model Number	Body/Style Number	Body Type & Seating	Factory Price	Shipping Weight	Production Total
EL CAMINO SERIES 55 (6-CYL)					
55	80	custom pickup	$2,342	2,935 lbs.	Note 1
EL CAMINO SERIES 56 (V-8)					
56	80	custom pickup	$2,442	—	Note 1

NOTE 1: Total El Camino production was 36,615.

ENGINES

EL CAMINO BASE 194-CID, 120-HP SIX-CYL: Overhead-valve. Cast-iron block. Bore and stroke: 3.562 x 3.25 in. Displacement: 194.4 cid. Compression ratio: 8.5:1. Brake hp: 120 at 4400 rpm. Taxable hp: 36. Torque: 177 lbs.-ft. at 2400 rpm. Seven main bearings. Hydraulic valve lifters. Crankcase capacity: 4 qt. (add 1 qt. for new filter). Cooling system capacity: 10.5 qt. (add 1 qt. for heater). Carburetor: Rochester one-barrel Model 7023105. Three-speed manual transmission standard; three-speed overdrive and Powerglide transmissions optional.

EL CAMINO BASE 283-CID, 195-HP V-8: Overhead-valve. Cast-iron block and head. Bore and stroke: 3.875 x 3.00 in. Displacement: 283 cid. Compression ratio: 9.25:1. Brake hp: 195 at 4800 rpm. Taxable hp: 48. Torque: 285 lbs.-ft. at 2400. Five main bearings. Hydraulic valve lifters. Crankcase capacity: 4 qt. (add 1 qt. for new filter). Cooling system capacity: 16 qt. (add 1 qt. for heater). Carburetor: Rochester 7024101 two-barrel. Three-speed manual transmission standard; three-speed overdrive and Powerglide transmissions optional.

EL CAMINO OPTIONAL 283-CID, 220-HP V-8: Overhead-valve. Cast-iron block and head. Bore and stroke: 3.875 x 3.00 in. Displacement: 283 cid. Compression ratio: 9.25:1. Brake hp: 220 at 4800 rpm. Taxable hp: 48. Torque: 295 lbs.-ft. at 3200. Five main bearings. Hydraulic valve lifters. Crankcase capacity: 4 qt. (add 1 qt. for new filter). Cooling system capacity: 16 qt. (add 1 qt. for heater). Carburetor: Rochester 7024024 four-barrel. Three-speed manual transmission standard; three-speed overdrive, four-speed manual and Powerglide transmissions optional.

EL CAMINO OPTIONAL 327-CID, 250-HP V-8: Overhead-valve. Cast-iron block and head. Bore and stroke: 4.00 x 3.25 in. Displacement: 327 cid. Compression ratio: 10.50:1. Brake hp: 250 at 4400 rpm. Taxable hp: 51.20. Torque: 350 lbs.-ft. at 2800. Five main bearings. Hydraulic valve lifters. Crankcase capacity: 4 qt. (add 1 qt. for new filter). Cooling system capacity: 15 qt. (add 1 qt. for heater). Carburetor: (Chevelle) Rochester 7024125 four-barrel. Three-speed manual transmission standard; three-speed all-synchromesh, four-speed manual and Powerglide transmissions optional.

EL CAMINO OPTIONAL 327-CID, 300-HP V-8: Overhead-valve. Cast-iron block and head. Bore and stroke: 4.00 x 3.25 in. Displacement: 327 cid. Compression ratio: 10.50:1. Brake hp: 300 at 5000 rpm. Taxable hp: 51.20. Torque: 360 lbs.-ft. at 3200. Five main bearings. Hydraulic valve lifters. Crankcase capacity: 4 qt. (add 1 qt. for new filter). Cooling system capacity: 15 qt. (add 1 qt. for heater). Dual exhaust. Carburetor: Carter 3826004 four-barrel. Three-speed manual transmission standard; three-speed all-synchromesh, four-speed manual and Powerglide transmissions optional.

EL CAMINO OPTIONAL 327-CID, 365-HP V-8: Overhead-valve. Cast-iron block and head. Bore and stroke: 4.00 x 3.25 in. Displacement: 327 cid. Compression ratio: 11.00:1. Brake hp: 365 at 6200 rpm. Taxable hp: 51.20. Torque: 350 lbs.-ft. at 4000. Five main bearings. Hydraulic valve lifters. Crankcase capacity: 4 qt. (add 1 qt. for new filter). Cooling system capacity: 15 qt. (add 1 qt. for heater). Dual exhaust. Carburetor: Holley 3858399 four-barrel. Three-speed manual transmission standard; three-speed all-synchromesh and four-speed manual transmissions optional.

CHASSIS

Wheelbase: 115 in. Overall length: 198 1/4 in. Front tread: 58 in. Rear tread: 58 in. Tires: 7.00 x 14 in. Standard transmission: Chevrolet three-speed manual transmission (Borg-Warner heavy-duty three-speed optional).

This Custom El Camino was decked out in Silver Blue.

Column-mounted gear shift lever. Single-plate, dry-disc clutch. Base rear axle: 3.08:1. Brake linings: 9 1/2 x 2 1/2 in. Kelsey-Hayes pressed steel wheels. The El Camino shared a heavy-duty suspension system with Chevelle station wagons. The El Camino had an outside width of 73 1/4 in. The pickup box inside width was 59 3/4 in. behind the cab, and 64 3/4 in. near the tailgate. There was 46 in between the wheel housings. The bed of the box was 78 1/2 in. long. The tailgate measured 55 1/2 in. x 23 in. With the bed-level tailgate lowered, the overall bed length was 101.6 in. This box was larger than the one used on full-size 1959-1960 El Caminos.

OPTIONS

283-cid 220-hp V-8 engine. 327-cid 250-hp Turbo-Fire V-8 engine. Overdrive transmission. Four-speed synchromesh transmission. Powerglide transmission with six-cylinder engine. Powerglide transmission with V-8 engines. Power brakes. Power steering. Power windows. 3.36:1 ratio rear axle. Positraction rear axle. 66-plate 70-amp.-hr. heavy-duty battery. Metallic brake linings. Heavy-duty front and rear suspension. Temperature-controlled fan for 195-hp V-8 (included with Four Season air conditioner or optional V-8). 42-amp Delcotron generator. 55-amp Delcotron generator (included with air conditioning). 62-amp Delcotron generator. 62-amp Delcotron generator for use with air conditioner. Car-to-trailer plug-in electrical harness. Heavy-duty radiator. Electric tachometer. Speed and Cruise Control. Four Season air conditioning (includes 55-amp Delcotron generator, heavy-duty radiator, and temperature-controlled fan. Soft-Ray tinted glass (all windows). Soft-Ray tinted glass in windshield only. Padded instrument panel. Driver and passenger seat belts, Custom, Custom Deluxe or Custom Deluxe with retractors. Bucket seats for models 13580 and 13680 only. Compass with integral battery and switch. Clock. Type A Comfort and Convenience equipment including outside rear view mirror, inside non-glare mirror, two-speed electric wiper/washer system for 13380 and 13560 models or 13480 and 13680 models. Type B Comfort and Convenience equipment including remote-control outside rear view mirror, inside non-glare mirror, two-speed electric wiper/washer system for 13380 and 13560 models or 13480 and 13680 models. Front bumper guard. Rear bumper guard. Low "D" note horn to supplement standard horn. Simulated wood trim steering wheel. AM/FM push-button radio. AM manual radio. AM push-button radio. Full wheel covers.

The base six-cylinder 1964 Custom El Camino came with a base sticker price of $2,267. The base V-8 model was $100 more. Buyers could also upgrade to 283- and 327-cid V-8s.

Simulated wire wheel covers. 7.35 x 14 4-ply white sidewall tires. 7.75 x 14 4-ply black sidewall tires. 7.75 x 14 4-ply white sidewall tires. 7.75 x 14 8-ply black sidewall tires. For prices of many El Camino options cross-reference with 1964 Chevelle options list.

(**Note:** For prices of many El Camino options cross-reference with 1964 Chevelle options list.)

HISTORICAL FOOTNOTES

Dealer introductions of new Chevrolet cars occurred on Sept. 28, 1964. Semon E. Knudsen remained as general manager of Chevrolet Division. El Camino output reached 36,615 units.

The 1965 El Camino came in a base and custom version. This base model was painted Ermine White.

The intermediate-sized El Camino had a new vehicle-wide lattice-type silver-anodized radiator grille with new central emblem and bright moldings. It had a finer pattern and heavier horizontal center bar. Chevrolet's red, white and blue emblem was in the bar's mid-section. A massive new chrome wraparound front bumper was slotted. The front parking lamps were relocated into long, horizontal slots. Newly styled front fenders featured new engine emblems in front of the wheel openings. A newly styled hood featured Chevrolet lettering along its lip.

Built on the mid-size Chevelle's 115-in. wheelbase, the El Camino was available with many passenger-car options. The low, sleek lines of the sedan-pickup were accented by curved side windows. All models had new rear quarter panel El Camino nameplates, bright body side lower moldings with black paint fill, chrome hubcaps, and bright vent window frames and posts. Bright moldings also adorned the pickup box and the roof.

I.D. NUMBERS

VIN embossed on a plate welded to the left front door hinge pillar post facing the driver. The first symbol 1 designates Chevrolet. The second and third symbols designate the series: (six-cylinder) 33=Deluxe El Camino, 35=Custom El Camino; (V-8) 34=Deluxe El Camino, 36=Custom El Camino. The fourth and fifth symbols designates body type: 80=two-door sedan pickup. The sixth symbol designates the model year: 5=1965. The seventh symbol designates the assembly plant location: A=Atlanta, Georgia, B=Baltimore, Maryland, G=Framingham, Massachusetts, H=Fremont, California and K=Kansas City, Missouri. The last six symbols are the sequential unit production number at the specific factory. The Fisher body tag riveted to the top of the cowl on the left side of the car below the hood provides additional vehicle identification information. The Fisher Body STYLE NUMBER (ST) consists of a prefix identifying model year and four or more symbols identifying the series and body style (example: 65-13480 for a V-8-powered 1965 Deluxe El Camino). The BODY NUMBER consists of a prefix designating assembly plant and the sequential unit production number at the specific factory (example: B 100001 is the first car built at the Baltimore factory). The TRIM NUMBER (TR) identifies

EL CAMINO

The 1965 El Camino had a few cosmetic modifications, including a new grille, a redesigned hood, and different badging.

upholstery. Interior colors of fawn, turquoise or red were available with specific exterior paint colors.

COLORS

(A) Tuxedo Black, (C) Ermine White, (D) Mist Blue, (E) Danube Blue, (H) Willow Green, (J) Cypress Green, (K) Artesian Turquoise, (L) Tahitian Turquoise, (N) Madeira Maroon, (P) Evening Orchard, ® Regal Red, (S) Sierra Tan, (V) Cameo Beige and (Y) Crocus Yellow. Interior colors of fawn, turquoise or red were available with specific exterior paint colors.

ENGINE CODES

Codes appear on the right side of six-cylinder blocks behind the distributor and right front of V-8 engine blocks: (194-cid/120-hp six) AA, AC, AG, AH, AK, AL, AN, AR; (230-cid/140-hp six) BK, BN, BY, BZ, CA, CB, CC, CD; (283-cid/195-hp V-8) DA, DB, DE; (283-cid/220-hp V-8) DG, DH; (327-cid/250-hp V-8) EA, EE; (327-cid/300-hp V-8) ED, EF; (327-cid/350-hp V-8) EC, ED; (396-cid/375-hp V-8) IX.

EL CAMINO — SERIES 33/34 — SIX/V-8

El Caminos came with two trim levels. El Caminos in the 53 (six-cylinder) and 54 (V-8) series were the base models, with trim and appointments comparable to the Chevelle 300. Color-keyed all-vinyl seats and sidewall trim were featured as standard equipment, along with an instrument cluster trim plate, steering wheel hub emblem, chrome door hardware, and two-key locking system. The standard interior also included an embossed vinyl headliner, dual sun visors, left- and right-hand arm rests, color-keyed vinyl floor mats, a cigar lighter, a dome lamp with door jamb switches, a horn ring, a lockable glove compartment, seat belts, and foam seat cushions. Fawn, aqua, or red interior trims were available according to the exterior finish color. All models had an all-steel perimeter frame with 12 body mounting points, box-section roof pillars, headers, and rails, a heavily ribbed underbody, a double-wall cowl, flush-and-dry rocker panels, protective inner fender skirts, and six-month/6,000-mile chassis lubrication. The 1964-1967 El Camino style pickup box was used again. It featured rigid double-panel all-steel construction, a tailgate, and an all-steel box floor. There was an emblem and Chevrolet lettering in the center of the tailgate. The inside width of the pickup box was 59 3/4 in. behind the cab and 64 3/4 in near the tailgate. There was 46 in. between the wheel housings. The bed of the box was 78 1/2 in. long. The tailgate measured 55 1/2 in. x 23 in. With the bed-level tailgate lowered, the overall bed length was 101.6 in. At the rear was a massive chrome wraparound bumper with new integral back-up lamp provisions, plus bright rear roof peak, rear window, and tailgate moldings. Under the hood, El Camino buyers could get standard or optional six-cylinder engines, plus a standard 283-cid V-8 or choice of two optional 327-cid Turbo-Fire V-8s. All engines had automatic chokes, overhead valves, full-flow oil filters, four-quart oil changes, Delcotron AC generators, a 54-plate battery, a positive crankcase ventilation system, and 6,000-mile/60-day oil change intervals. New engine features included oil-wetted paper air cleaner elements for V-8s and new oil pumps with thicker flanges for sixes.

Model Number	Body/Style Number	Body Type & Seating	Factory Price	Shipping Weight	Production Total
EL CAMINO SERIES 33 (6-CYL)					
33	80	pickup	$2,272	2,925 lbs.	Note 1
EL CAMINO SERIES 34 (V-8)					
34	80	pickup	$2,380	3,060 lbs.	Note 1

EL CAMINO CUSTOM — SERIES 35/36 SIX/V-8

Custom El Caminos in the 55 (six-cylinder) and 56 (V-8) Custom series had trim and appointments comparable to the Chevelle Malibu. Custom El Caminos also had a new bright body sill molding, front and rear wheel opening moldings, a roof drip gutter molding, windshield pillar moldings, bright door frame moldings and a chrome hood wind split molding. Customs featured color-keyed pattern cloth and leather-grain vinyl upholstery with bright back rest trim plates, plus luxury carpeting, a bright glove box door trim plate and light, and a two-tone steering wheel and an electric clock. A new vinyl bucket seat option included a vinyl spare wheel and tire cover and wheel trim disks. Other new options were an AM/FM radio and simulated wire wheels covers.

Model Number	Body/Style Number	Body Type & Seating	Factory Price	Shipping Weight	Production Total
EL CAMINO CUSTOM SERIES 33 (6-CYL)					
35	80	Custom pickup	$2,353	2,935 lbs.	Note 1
EL CAMINO CUSTOM SERIES 34 (V-8)					
36	80	Custom pickup	$2,461	3,060 lbs.	Note 1

NOTE 1: Total El Camino production was 36,316.

The 1965 El Camino was marketed as a do-everything vehicle.

ENGINES

EL CAMINO BASE SIX-CYL: Overhead-valve. Cast-iron block. Bore and stroke: 3.562 x 3.25 in. Displacement: 194.4 cid. Compression ratio: 8.5:1. Brake hp: 120 at 4400 rpm. Taxable hp: 36. Torque: 177 lbs.-ft. at 2400 rpm. Seven main bearings. Hydraulic valve lifters. Crankcase capacity: 4 qt. (add 1 qt. for new filter). Cooling system capacity: 11 qt. (add 1 qt. for heater). Carburetor: Rochester one-barrel Model 7023105. Three-speed manual transmission standard, overdrive and Powerglide transmissions optional.

EL CAMINO OPTIONAL SIX-CYL: Overhead-valve. Cast-iron block. Bore and stroke: 3.875 x 3.25 in. Displacement: 230 cid. Compression ratio: 8.5:1. Brake hp: 140 at 4400 rpm. Taxable hp: 36. Torque: 220 at 1600 rpm. Seven main bearings. Hydraulic valve lifters. Crankcase capacity: 4 qt. (add 1 qt. for new filter). Cooling system capacity: 11 qt. (add 1 qt. for heater). Carburetor: Rochester one-barrel Model 7023105. Three-speed manual transmission standard, overdrive and Powerglide transmissions optional.

EL CAMINO BASE V-8: Overhead-valve. Cast-iron block and head. Bore and stroke: 3.875 x 3.00 in. Displacement: 283 cid. Compression ratio: 9.25:1. Brake hp: 195 at 4800 rpm. Taxable hp: 48. Torque: 285 lbs.-ft. at 2400. Five main bearings. Hydraulic valve lifters. Crankcase capacity: 4 qt. (add 1 qt. for new filter). Cooling system capacity: 16 qt. (add 1 qt. for heater). Carburetor: Rochester 7024101 two-barrel. Three-speed manual transmission standard, four-speed manual, overdrive and Powerglide transmissions optional.

EL CAMINO OPTIONAL V-8: Overhead-valve. Cast-iron block and head. Bore and stroke: 4.00 x 3.25 in Displacement: 327 cid. Compression ratio: 10.50:1. Brake hp: 250 at 4400 rpm. Taxable hp: 51.20. Torque: 350 lbs.-ft. at 2800. Five main bearings. Hydraulic valve lifters. Crankcase capacity: 4 qt. (add 1 qt. for new filter). Cooling system capacity: 15 qt. (add 1 qt. for heater). Carburetor: Rochester 7024125 four-barrel. Three-speed manual transmission standard, four-speed manual and Powerglide transmissions optional.

EL CAMINO OPTIONAL V-8: Overhead-valve. Cast-iron block and head. Bore and stroke: 4.00 x 3.25 in Displacement: 327 cid. Compression ratio: 10.50:1. Brake hp: 300 at 5000 rpm. Taxable hp: 51.20. Torque: 360 lbs.-ft. at 3200. Five main bearings. Hydraulic valve lifters. Crankcase capacity: 4 qt. (add 1 qt. for new filter). Cooling system capacity: 15 qt. (add 1 qt. for heater). Carburetor: Rochester 7024125 four-barrel. Four-speed manual and Powerglide transmissions optional.

NOTE: Engine and transmission data according to *Chevrolet Sales Digest '65* (CC-64-9).

CHASSIS

Wheelbase: 115 in Overall length: 201.3 in Overall width: 73.2 in. Loaded overall height: 54.1 in. Tailgate opening at floor: 55.5 in. Tailgate to ground (open and loaded): 15.1 in. Box length at floor with tailgate open: 101.5 in. Box length at floor with tailgate closed: 78.5 in. Floor width between wheel housings: 46 in. Box capacity: 38.5 cu.-ft. Front tread: 58 in. Rear tread: 58 in. Tires: 7.35 x 14 in GVW rating: 4,200 lb. Chevrolet three-speed manual transmission (Borg-Warner heavy-duty three-speed optional). Column-mounted gear shift lever. Single-plate, dry-disc clutch. Base rear axles: 3.08:1. Four-wheel hydraulic, drum brakes. Brake linings: 9 1/2 x 2 1/2 in. Kelsey-Hayes pressed steel wheels.

OPTIONS

230-cid/140-hp Turbo-Thrift six-cylinder engine for 13380 and 13580 models. 327-cid/250-hp Turbo-Fire V-8 engine for 13480 and 13680 models. 327-cid/300-hp Turbo-Fire V-8 for 13480 and 13680 models. Overdrive transmission. Four-speed synchromesh transmission. Powerglide transmission with six-cylinder engine. Powerglide transmission with V-8 engines. Power brakes. Power steering. Power windows. 3.36:1 ratio rear axle. Positraction rear axle. 66-plate 70-amp.-hr. heavy-duty battery. Metallic brake linings. Heavy-duty front and rear suspension. Temperature-controlled fan for 195-hp V-8 (included with Four Season air conditioner or optional V-8). 42-amp Delcotron generator. 55-amp Delcotron generator (included with air conditioning). 62-amp Delcotron generator. 62-amp Delcotron generator for use with air conditioner. Car-to-trailer plug-in electrical harness. Heavy-duty radiator. Electric tachometer. Speed and Cruise Control. Four Season air conditioning (includes 55-amp Delcotron generator, heavy-duty radiator, and temperature-controlled fan. Soft-Ray tinted glass (all windows). Soft-Ray tinted glass in windshield only. Padded instrument panel. Driver and passenger seat belts, Custom, Custom Deluxe or Custom Deluxe with retractors. Bucket seats for models 13580 and 13680 only. Compass with integral battery and switch. Clock. Type A Comfort and Convenience equipment including outside rear view mirror, inside non-glare mirror, two-speed electric wiper/washer system for 13380 and 13560 models or 13480 and 13680 models. Type B Comfort and Convenience equipment including remote-control outside rear view mirror, inside non-glare mirror, two-speed electric wiper/washer system for 13380 and 13560 models or 13480 and 13680 models. Front bumper guard. Rear bumper guard. Low "D" note horn to supplement standard horn. Simulated wood trim steering wheel. AM/FM push-button radio. AM manual radio. AM push-button radio. Full wheel covers. Simulated wire wheel covers. 7.35 x 14 four-ply white sidewall tires. 7.75 x 14 four-ply black sidewall tires. 7.75 x 14 four-ply white sidewall tires. 7.75 x 14 8-ply black sidewall tires.

(Note: For prices of many El Camino options cross-reference with 1965 Chevelle options list.)

HISTORICAL FOOTNOTES

Chevrolet showcased the Turbo Titan III, a gas turbine-powered experimental truck, in 1965. Chevy called it the "Truck of Tomorrow." The 1965 Chevrolet commercial vehicles were advertised as "work power" trucks. This was an all-time record season for America's number one truck maker and the first in which registrations broke the 500,000 level. Chevrolet claimed that by the end of 1965 there were 4,751,127 Chevrolet trucks operating in the U.S.

1966

The 1966 El Camino received a redesigned body with a more sloping front end, new parking light configuration, new grille and wraparound fenders.

An all-new Chevelle body was used for the El Camino, although the pickup box was unchanged. It had a slanted front end. The front fenders had a wraparound design. A new grille was lower and wider. It had multiple horizontal blades and wider-spaced vertical blades with a Chevrolet emblem in its center. There were two slots inside the bumper that were shorter and wider than in 1968.

Following the Chevelle's every-other-year pattern, the parking lights were moved to a position inside the bumper slots below the headlamps. There was a new dashboard and new hubcaps, too. Redesigned full wheel covers had a spoked, rather than finned, look.

I.D. NUMBERS

VIN embossed on a plate welded to the left front door hinge pillar post facing the driver. The first symbol 1 designates Chevrolet. The second and third symbols designate the series: (6-cylinder) 33=Deluxe El Camino, 35=Custom El Camino; (V-8) 34=Deluxe El Camino, 36=Custom El Camino. The fourth and fifth symbols designates body type: 80=two-door sedan pickup. The sixth symbol designates the model year: 6=1966. The seventh symbol designates the assembly plant location: The seventh symbol indicated assembly plant: A=Atlanta, Georgia; B=Baltimore, Maryland; F=Flint, Michigan; G=Framingham, Massachusetts; K=Kansas City, Missouri; Z=Fremont, California. The last six symbols are the sequential unit production number at the specific factory. The Fisher body tag riveted to the top of the cowl on the left side of the car below the hood provides additional vehicle identification information. The Fisher body STYLE NUMBER (ST) consists of a prefix identifying model year and four or more symbols identifying the series and body style (example: 66-13480 for a V-8-powered 1966 Deluxe El Camino). The BODY NUMBER consists of a prefix designating assembly plant and the sequential unit production number at the specific factory. The TRIM NUMBER (TR) identifies upholstery.

COLORS

(A) Tuxedo Black, (C) Ermine White, (D) Mist Blue Metallic, (E) Danube Blue Metallic, (F) Marina Blue Metallic, (H) Willow Green Metallic, (K) Artesian

Turquoise Metallic, (L) Tropic Turquoise Metallic, (M) Aztec Bronze Metallic, (N) Madeira Maroon Metallic, (R) Regal Red, (T) Sandalwood Tan Metallic, (V) Cameo Beige), (W) Chateau Slate Metallic and (Y) Lemonwood Yellow.

ENGINE CODES

Codes appear on the right side of six-cylinder blocks behind the distributor and right front of V-8 engine blocks: (194-cid/120-hp six) AA, AC, AG, AH, AK, AL, AN, AR, AS, AT, AU, AV, AW, AX, AY; (230-cid/140-hp six) CA, CB, CC, CD, BL, BM, BN, BO; (283-cid/195-hp V-8) DA, DB, DE, DF, DK, Dl, DJ (283-cid/220-hp V-8) DG, DO, DL, DM; (327-cid/275-hp V-8) EA, EB, EC, EE; (396-cid/325-hp V-8) ED, EH, EK, EM; (396-cid/360-hp V-8) EF, EJ, EL, EN.

EL CAMINO — SERIES 33/34 — SIX/V-8

There were engine designation badges on the front fender, El Camino nameplates on the rear fenders, and a tailgate with a bright latch and Chevrolet lettering. Even the standard model had bright windshield frames and a chrome hood wind split molding. The El Camino Custom added bright side and rear window frames, moldings on the upper edge of the pickup box and wide rocker panel moldings with rear quarter panel extensions. There was no official Super Sport option this year, although the 396-cid V-8 was available as a separate option. The standard interior trims were fawn (beige), blue or red vinyl. Custom interiors came with still richer all-vinyl trims in black, fawn or red. Bucket seats were optional. The pickup box inside width was 59 3/4 in. behind the cab and 64 3/4 in. near the tailgate. There was 46 in. between the wheel housings. The bed of the box was 78 1/2 in. long. The tailgate measured 55 1/2 in. x 23 in. With the bed-level tailgate lowered, the overall bed length was 101.6 in.

Model Number	Body/Style Number	Body Type & Seating	Factory Price	Shipping Weight	Production Total
EL CAMINO SERIES 33 (6-CYL)					
33	80	pickup	$2,318	2,930 lbs.	Note 1
EL CAMINO SERIES 34 (V-8)					
34	80	pickup	$2,426	3,075 lbs.	Note 1

EL CAMINO CUSTOM — SERIES 35/36 SIX/V-8

Custom El Caminos in the 55 (six-cylinder) and 56 (V-8) Custom series had trim and appointments comparable to the Chevelle Malibu. Custom El Caminos also had a new bright body sill molding, front and rear wheel opening moldings, a roof drip gutter molding, windshield pillar moldings, bright door frame moldings and a chrome hood wind split molding. Customs featured color-keyed pattern cloth and leather-grain vinyl upholstery with bright back rest trim plates, plus luxury carpeting, a bright glove box door trim plate and light, and a two-tone steering wheel and an electric clock.

Model Number	Body/Style Number	Body Type & Seating	Factory Price	Shipping Weight	Production Total
EL CAMINO CUSTOM SERIES 33 (6-CYL)					
35	80	Custom pickup	$2,396	2,930 lbs.	Note 1
EL CAMINO CUSTOM SERIES 34 (V-8)					
36	80	Custom pickup	$2,504	3,075 lbs.	Note 1

NOTE 1 Total El Camino production was 35,119.

ENGINES

EL CAMINO BASE SIX-CYL: Overhead-valve. Cast-iron block. Bore and stroke: 3.562 x 3.25 in. Displacement: 194.4 cid. Compression ratio: 8.5:1. Brake hp: 120 at 4400 rpm. Taxable hp: 36. Torque: 177 lbs.-ft. at 2400 rpm. Seven main bearings. Hydraulic valve lifters. Crankcase capacity: 4 qt. (add 1 qt. for new filter). Cooling system capacity: 11 qt. (add 1 qt. for heater). Carburetor: Rochester one-barrel Model 7023105.

EL CAMINO OPTIONAL SIX-CYL: Overhead-valve. Cast-iron block. Bore and stroke: 3.875 x 3.25 in. Displacement: 230 cid. Compression ratio: 8.5:1. Brake hp: 140 at 4400 rpm. Taxable hp: 36. Torque: 220 lbs.-ft. at 1600 rpm. Seven main bearings. Hydraulic valve lifters. Crankcase capacity: 4 qt. (add 1 qt. for new filter). Cooling system capacity: 11 qt. (add 1 qt. for heater). Carburetor: Rochester one-barrel Model 7023105.

EL CAMINO BASE 283-CID, 195-HP V-8: Overhead-valve. Cast-iron block and head. Bore and stroke: 3.875 x 3.00 in. Displacement: 283 cid. Compression ratio: 9.25:1. Brake hp: 195 at 4800 rpm. Taxable hp: 48. Torque: 285 lbs.-ft. at 2400. Five main bearings. Hydraulic valve lifters. Crankcase capacity: 4 qt. (add 1 qt. for new filter). Cooling system capacity: 16 qt. (add 1 qt. for heater). Carburetor: Rochester 7024101 two-barrel.

EL CAMINO OPTIONAL 283-CID, 220-HP V-8: Overhead-valve. Cast-iron block and head. Bore and stroke: 3.875 x 3.00 in. Displacement: 283 cid. Compression ratio: 9.25:1. Brake hp: 220 at 4800 rpm. Taxable hp: 48. Torque: 295 lbs.-ft. at 3200. Five main bearings. Hydraulic valve lifters. Crankcase capacity: 4 qt. (add 1 qt. for new filter). Cooling system capacity: (Chevy II, Chevelle) 15 qt.; (Chevrolet) 16 qt. (add 1 qt. for heater). Carburetor: Rochester 7025127 four-barrel.

EL CAMINO OPTIONAL 327-CID, 275-HP V-8: Overhead-valve. Cast-iron block and head. Bore and stroke: 4.00 x 3.25 in. Displacement: 327 cid. Compression ratio: 10.25:1. Brake hp: 275 at 4800 rpm. Taxable hp: 51.20. Torque: 355 lbs.-ft. at 3200. Five main bearings. Hydraulic valve lifters. Crankcase capacity: 4 qt. (add 1 qt. for new filter). Cooling system capacity: 14 qt. (add 1 qt. for heater). Carburetor: Carburetor: Holley 3876747 or Carter 3876749 four-barrel. Sales code: L30.

EL CAMINO BASE 396-CID, 325-HP V-8: Overhead-valve. Cast-iron block and head. Bore and stroke: 4.09 x 3.76 in. Displacement: 396 cid. Compression ratio: 10.25:1. Brake hp: 325 at 4800 rpm. Taxable hp: 53.60. Torque: 410 lbs.-ft. at 3200. Five main bearings. Hydraulic valve lifters. Crankcase capacity: 4 qt. (add 1 qt. for new filter). Cooling system capacity: 22 qt. (add 1 qt. for heater). Carburetor: Holley 3874898 or Rochester 7026201 four-barrel. Sales code: L35.

EL CAMINO OPTIONAL 396-CID, 360-HP V-8

Overhead-valve. Cast-iron block and head. Bore and stroke: 4.09 x 3.76 in. Displacement: 396 cid. Compression ratio: 10.25:1. Brake hp: 360 at 5200 rpm. Taxable hp: 53.60. Torque: 420 lbs.-ft. at 3600. Five main bearings. Hydraulic valve lifters. Crankcase capacity: 4 qt. a 1 qt. for new filter). Cooling system capacity: 22 qt. (add 1 qt. for heater). Carburetor: Holley 3886087 or

1966

There were seven engine choices for the 1966 El Camino, including a pair of 396-cid V-8s. The most powerful model was rated at 360 hp.

Rochester 7026201 four-barrel. Sales code: L34.

CHASSIS

Wheelbase: 115 in. Overall length: 197 in. Front tread: 58 in. Rear tread: 58 in. Tires: 7.35 x 14 in. Gross vehicle weight: 4,300 lbs. Chevrolet three-speed manual transmission (Borg-Warner heavy-duty three-speed optional). Base rear axles: 3.08:1. Four-wheel hydraulic, drum brakes. Brake linings: 9 1/2 x 2 1/2-in. Kelsey-Hayes pressed steel wheels.

OPTIONS

Oil bath air cleaner. No-Spin rear axle. Heavy-duty battery. Two-tone paint. Heavy-duty cooling. Heavy-duty front shocks. Heavy-duty rear shocks. Heavy-duty three-speed transmission. Four-speed transmission. Turbo-Hydramatic transmission (with V-8). Powerglide transmission (with six). Engine, 230 High-Torque six. Engine, 283-cid V-8 ($108). Engine, 327-cid/250-275 hp. Power steering ($86). Engine, 396 cid/325 hp. Engine, 396 cid/360 hp. Engine, 396 cid/375 hp. Full wheel discs. Custom interior. Bucket seats (Custom). Power windows. 3.36:1 ratio rear axle. Positraction rear axle. 66-plate 70-amp.-hr. heavy-duty battery. Metallic brake linings. Heavy-duty front and rear suspension. Temperature-controlled fan for 195-hp V-8 (included with Four Season air conditioner or optional V-8). 42-amp Delcotron generator. 55-amp Delcotron generator (included with air conditioning). 62-amp Delcotron generator. 62-ampere Delcotron generator for use with air conditioner. Car-to-trailer plug-in electrical harness. Heavy-duty radiator. Electric tachometer. Speed and Cruise Control. Four Season air conditioning (includes 55-amp Delcotron generator, heavy-duty radiator, and temperature-controlled fan. Soft-Ray tinted glass (all windows). Soft-Ray tinted glass in windshield only. Padded instrument panel. Driver and passenger seat belts, Custom, Custom Deluxe or Custom Deluxe with retractors. Bucket seats for models 13580 and 13680 only. Compass with integral battery and switch. Clock. Type A Comfort and Convenience equipment including outside rear view mirror, inside non-glare mirror, two-speed electric wiper/washer system for 13380 and 13560 models or 13480 and 13680 models. Type B Comfort and Convenience equipment including remote-controlled outside rear view mirror, inside non-glare mirror, two-speed electric wiper/washer system for 13380 and 13560 models or 13480 and 13680 models. Front bumper guard. Rear bumper guard. Low "D" note horn to supplement standard horn. Simulated wood trim steering wheel. AM/FM push-button radio. AM manual radio. AM push-button radio. Full wheel covers. Simulated wire wheel covers. 7.35 x 14 four-ply white sidewall tires. 7.75 x 14 four-ply black sidewall tires. 7.75 x 14 four-ply white sidewall tires. 7.75 x 14 eight-ply black sidewall tires. For prices of many El Camino options cross-reference with 1966 Chevelle options list.

HISTORICAL

Model-year production (all El Camino) was 35,119. Chevy clinched its 10 millionth truck sale this season.

EL CAMINO

There were virtually no changes in El Camino styling between 1966 and 1967. New options included disc brakes, air pollution equipment in California and front head rests.

I.D. NUMBERS

VIN embossed on a plate welded to the left front door hinge pillar post facing the driver. The first symbol 1 designates Chevrolet. The second and third symbols designate the series: (six-cylinder) 33=Deluxe El Camino, 35=Custom El Camino; (V-8) 34=Deluxe El Camino, 36=Custom El Camino. The fourth and fifth symbols designates body type: 80=two-door sedan pickup. The sixth symbol designates the model year: 7=1967. The seventh symbol designates the assembly plant location: The seventh symbol indicated assembly plant: A=Atlanta, Georgia; B=Baltimore, Maryland; G=Framingham, Massachusetts; K=Kansas City, Missouri; Z=Fremont, California. The last six symbols are the sequential unit production number at the specific factory. The Fisher body tag riveted to the top of the cowl on the left side of the car below the hood provides additional vehicle identification information. The Fisher body STYLE NUMBER (ST) consists of a prefix identifying model year and four or more symbols identifying the series and body style (example: 66-13480 for a V-8-powered 1966 Deluxe El Camino). The BODY NUMBER consists of a prefix designating assembly plant and the sequential unit production number at the specific factory. The TRIM NUMBER (TR) identifies upholstery.

COLORS

(A) Tuxedo Black, (C) Ermine White, (D) Nantucket Blue, (E) Deepwater Blue, (F) Marina Blue, (G) Granada Gold, (H) Mountain Green, (K) Emerald Turquoise, (L) Tahoe Turquoise, (M) Royal Plum, (N) Madiera Maroon, (R) Bolero Red, (S) Sierra Fawn, (T) Capri Cream and (Y) Butternut Yellow.

ENGINE CODES

(230-cid/140-hp six) CA, CB, CC, CD, BC, BB, BN, BO, BL, BM; (250-cid/155 hp six) CM, CN, CO, CP, CQ, CR, CS and CT; (283-cid/195-hp V-8) DA, DB, DI, DJ, DK, DN and DE; (327/275-hp V-8) EA, EB, EQ, EE and EC; (327-cid/325-hp V-8) EP, ER and ES; (396-cid/325-hp V-8) ED, EF, EH, EM, ET and EV; (396-cid/350-hp V-8) EK, EL, EN, EU and EW; (396-cid/375-hp V-8) EG and EX.

EL CAMINO — SERIES 33/34 — SIX/V-8

The last of the first-generation El Caminos had a new radiator grille, front bumpers, fenders and hood, plus restyled wraparound taillights. The front fenders had more of a vertical downward curve. The grille again had horizontal and vertical elements, but the horizontal moldings were brighter and wider and stood out more. The widest molding, just below the hood lip, had a satin finished look and a Chevrolet emblem in its center. Dual headlamps were used. There was one wide horizontal slot, and the parking lamps were in other openings at either end. At the rear, the three-slot-styled taillights wrapped around the body corners. An El Camino script decorated the rear fenders. The front fender, just behind the headlamps, had an engine call-out. It was a shield with a 250 on top for sixes, a V with flags for 283 V-8s, a V with flags and 327 numbers for a bigger V-8, and an open-center V with flags and a Turbo-Jet 396 plaque for the biggest V-8, a high-performance big-block engine. Chevelle 300-style all-vinyl upholstery, with all-vinyl embossed side panels, door arm rests and vinyl-coated color-keyed floor mats was standard. Exterior body colors were: Tuxedo Black, Ermine White, Nantucket Blue, Deepwater Blue, Marina Blue, Granada Gold, Mountain Green, Emerald Turquoise, Tahoe Turquoise, Royal Plum, Madiera Maroon, Bolero Red, Sierra Fawn, Capri Cream, and Butternut Yellow. The 1964 type pickup box was also in its last appearance. It was 59 3/4 in. wide behind the cab and 64 3/4 in. wide near the tailgate. There was 46 in. between the wheel housings. The bed of the box was 78 1/2 in. long. The tailgate measured 55 1/2 x 23 in. With the bed-level tailgate lowered, the overall bed length was 101.6 in.

Model Number	Body/Style Number	Body Type & Seating	Factory Price	Shipping Weight	Production Total
EL CAMINO SERIES 33 (6-CYL)					
33	80	pickup	$2,389	2,970 lbs.	Note 1
EL CAMINO SERIES 34 (V-8)					
34	80	pickup	$2,613	3,193 lbs.	Note 1

EL CAMINO CUSTOM — SERIES 35/36 SIX/V-8

The Custom models had a thin chrome molding along the lower body feature line, a rear wood-grained beauty panel between two moldings running across the tailgate and hubcaps with Chevrolet bow ties. This was the first year for an official SS 396 "model," although it was an option rather than a series. The SS 396 featured a blacked-out grille with SS emblems at its center. The Custom interior added horizontal pleats embossed into the vinyl seat coverings and door panels with horizontal ribs. Bucket seats were available in Customs, including those with the SS 396 option.

Model Number	Body/Style Number	Body Type & Seating	Factory Price	Shipping Weight	Production Total
EL CAMINO CUSTOM SERIES 33 (6-CYL)					
35	80	Custom pickup	$2,467	3,100 lbs.	Note 1
EL CAMINO CUSTOM SERIES 34 (V-8)					
36	80	Custom pickup	$2,694	3,210 lbs.	Note 1

NOTE 1 Total El Camino production was 34,830

Aside from a few extra options, the 1967 El Camino was identical to the previous year's model.

ENGINES

EL CAMINO BASE 230-CID, 140-HP SIX-CYL: Inline. Overhead-valve. Cast-iron block. Displacement: 230 cid. Bore and stroke: 3.875 x 3.25 in. Compression ratio: 8.5:1. Brake hp: 140 lbs.-ft. at 4400 rpm. Seven main bearings. Hydraulic valve lifters. Crankcase capacity: 4 qt. (add 1 qt. for new filter). Cooling system capacity: 12 qt (add 6 qt. for heater). Carburetor: Rochester one-barrel Model 7027003.

EL CAMINO BASE 250-CID, 155-HP SIX-CYL Inline. Overhead-valve. Cast-iron block. Displacement: 250 cid. Bore and stroke: 3.875 x 3.53 in. Compression ratio: 8.5:1. Brake hp: 155 at 4200 rpm. Taxable hp: 36. Torque: 235 lbs.-ft. at 1600 rpm. Seven main bearings. Hydraulic valve lifters. Crankcase capacity: 4 qt. (add 1 qt. for new filter). Cooling system capacity: 12 qt. (add 6 qt. for heater). Carburetor: Rochester one-barrel Model 7028017. Sales code: L22.

EL CAMINO BASE 283-CID, 195-HP V-8: Overhead-valve. Cast-iron block and head. Bore and stroke: 3.875 x 3.00 in. Displacement: 283 cid. Compression ratio: 9.25:1. Brake hp: 195 at 4800 rpm. Taxable hp: 48. Torque: 285 lbs.-ft. at 2400. Five main bearings. Hydraulic valve lifters. Crankcase capacity: 4 qt. (add 1 qt. for new filter). Cooling system capacity: (Chevy II, Chevrolet) 15 qt.; (Chevelle) 16 qt. (add 1 qt. for heater). Carburetor: Rochester 7027101 two-barrel.

EL CAMINO OPTIONAL 327-CID, 275-HP V-8 Overhead-valve. Cast-iron block and head. Bore and stroke: 4.00 x 3.25 in. Displacement: 327 cid. Compression ratio: 10.25:1. Brake hp: 275 at 4800 rpm. Taxable hp: 51.20. Torque: 355 ft.-lbs. at 3200. Five main bearings. Hydraulic valve lifters. Crankcase capacity: 4 qt. (add 1 qt. for new filter). Cooling system capacity: 16 qt. (add 1 qt. for heater). Carburetor: Carburetor: Four-barrel. Sales code: L30.

EL CAMINO OPTIONAL 327-CID, 325-HP V-8 Overhead-valve. Cast-iron block and head. Bore and stroke: 4.00 x 3.25 in. Displacement: 327 cid. Compression ratio: 11.00:1. Brake hp: 325 at 5600 rpm. Taxable hp: 51.20. Torque: 355 lbs.-ft. at 3600. Five main bearings. Hydraulic valve lifters. Crankcase capacity: 4 qt. (add 1 qt. for new filter). Cooling system capacity: 14 qt. (add 1 qt. for heater). Carburetor: Carburetor: Four-barrel. Sales code: L79.

EL CAMINO OPTIONAL 396-CID, 325-HP V-8: Overhead-valve. Cast-iron block and head. Bore and stroke: 4.09 x 3.76 in. Displacement: 396 cid. Compression ratio: 10.25:1. Brake hp: 325 at 4800 rpm. Taxable hp: 53.60. Torque: 410 lbs.-ft. at 3200. Five main bearings. Hydraulic valve lifters. Crankcase capacity: 4 qt. (add 1 qt. for new filter). Cooling system capacity: 22 qt. (add 1 qt. for heater). Carburetor: Rochester 7027201 four-barrel. Sales code: L35.

EL CAMINO OPTIONAL 396-CID, 350-HP V-8: Overhead-valve. Cast-iron block and head. Bore and stroke: 4.09 x 3.76 in. Displacement: 396 cid. Compression ratio: 10.25:1. Brake hp: 350 at 5200 rpm. Taxable hp: 53.60. Torque: 415 lbs.-ft. at 3400. Five main bearings. Hydraulic valve lifters. Crankcase capacity: 4 qt. (add 1 qt. for new filter). Cooling system capacity: 22 qt. (add 1 qt. for heater). Carburetor: Four-barrel. Sales code: L34.

CHASSIS

Wheelbase: 115 in. Overall length: 197 in. Front tread: 58 in. Rear tread: 58 in. Tires: 7.35 x 14 in. Gross vehicle weight: 4,300 lb. Chevrolet three-speed manual transmission (Borg-Warner heavy-duty three-speed optional). Column-mounted gearshift lever. Single-plate, dry-disc clutch. Rear axle: semi-floating. Base rear axles: 3.08:1. Four-wheel hydraulic, drum brakes. Brake linings: 9 1/2 x 2 1/2 in. Kelsey-Hayes pressed steel wheels.

OPTIONS

Four-Season air conditioning, including 61-amp Delcotron, heavy-duty radiator and temperature-controlled fan ($363.70). Air Injection Reactor, requiring closed ventilation system ($44.75). Rear antenna, except station wagons or with AM/FM radio ($9.50). Positraction rear axle ($43.05). Special economy or high-performance rear axle ($2.15). Heavy-duty battery ($7.40). Front and Custom Deluxe seat belts ($6.35). Standard type shoulder belts, with standard seat belts ($23.20). Custom Deluxe shoulder belts, Custom Deluxe seat belts or Custom Appearance package ($26.35). Front disc brakes, not available with metallic brakes ($80.70). Sintered metallic brake linings ($36.90). Front bumper guards ($12.65). Rear bumper guards ($12.65). Electric clock ($15.80). Heavy-duty clutch, V-8s except SS 396 and cars with cold-air injection ($10.55). Heavy-duty clutch on sixes except 155 hp ($5.30). Door edge guards, two-door models ($3.20). 250-cid 155-hp six-cylinder engine ($26.35). 327-cid 325-hp V-8, except SS 396 ($198.05). 327-cid 275-hp V-8 engine, except SS 396 ($92.70). 396-cid 325-hp V-8 engine, SS 396 only ($182.95). 396-cid 350-hp V-8 engine, SS 396 only ($290.55). Dual exhaust with the 275-hp engine ($21.10). Temperature-controlled fan, V-8s, standard with air conditioning ($15.80). 42-amp Delcotron generator, not available with air conditioning ($15.80). 61-amp Delcotron generator, standard with air conditioning ($21.10). All windows tinted ($30.55). Tinted windshield only ($21.10). Driver and passenger Strato-Ease headrests, with front bucket seats ($52.70). Driver and passenger Strato-Ease headrests, with standard front bench seat ($42.15). Heater and defroster deletion ($70.70 credit). Tri-volume horn ($13.70). Special instrumentation with ammeter, temperature gauge, oil pressure gauge and tachometer ($79). Ash tray light ($1.60). Courtesy light, all except convertibles ($4.25). Glove box light, El Camino Deluxe ($2.65). Under-hood light ($2.65). Twin front and rear floor mats ($10.55). Left-hand outside remote-control mirror ($9.50). Two-tone paint ($15.80). Power brakes ($43.05). Four-way power front seat, except with floor mounted transmission, bucket seats on on El Camino Deluxe ($69.55). Power steering ($86.10). Power windows ($100.10). Heavy-duty radiator, except with air conditioning ($10.55). AM radio ($58.65). AM/FM push-button radio with front antenna ($133.80). Push-button radio with front antenna ($57.40). AM/FM push-button radio with front antenna ($70.60). AM/FM push-button radio with front antenna and speaker ($147). Vinyl roof cover ($73.75). Thick front foam seat cushion, Chevelle 300 and 300 Deluxe ($7.40). Strato bucket seats ($113). Superlift rear shock absorbers ($36.90). Speed and cruise control, V-8s with automatic transmissions ($50.05). Speed warning indi-

The 1967 El Camino was available in either standard or custom versions and came with a total of seven different engine choices.

cator ($10.55). Deluxe steering wheel in El Camino Deluxe ($7.40). Deluxe steering wheel in El Camino Deluxe ($4.25). Comfortilt steering wheel, requires four-speed manual or automatic transmissions ($42.15). Sport styled steering wheel ($31.60). Stereo tape system with four speakers, not available with rear speaker systems ($128.50). Special front and rear suspension ($4.75). Tachometer, for V-8s, standard with special instrumentation group ($47.40). Close-ratio four-speed manual transmission for SS 396 ($105.35). Close-ratio four-speed manual transmission for other El Caminos ($184.35). Wide-ratio four-speed manual transmission for SS 396 ($105.35). Wide-ratio four-speed manual transmission for other El Caminos ($184.35). Turbo Hydra-Matic transmission for SS 396 only ($231.35). Special floor-mounted three-speed manual transmission for SS 396 (standard). Special floor-mounted three-speed manual transmission for other El Caminos ($79). Powerglide automatic transmission for six-cylinder El Camino ($194.85). Powerglide automatic transmission for V-8 El Camino except SS 396 ($194.85). Powerglide automatic transmission for SS 396 ($115.90). Overdrive transmission with 140-, 155- or 195-hp engines ($115.90). Positive crankcase ventilation, standard with 325- and 350-hp engines; on other engines ($5.25). Wheel covers with non-disc brakes ($21.10). Mag-styled wheel covers with non-disc brakes ($73.75). Simulated wire wheel covers with non disc brakes ($73.75). Appearance group with door edge and rear bumper guards ($45.40). Foundation group includes push-button radio, clock and extra-thick foam seat cushions ($80.60). Operating convenience group includes remote-controlled left-hand outside rearview mirror and rear window seat defroster ($30.60). F70 x 14 wide oval tires ($64.10).

HISTORICAL FOOTNOTES

Introduced Sept. 11, 1966. The 1967 El Camino was extensively restyled. R.M. O'Connor was assistant general sales manager, truck & fleet sales, for Chevrolet Motor Division. The July 1967 issue of *Motor Trend* included an article called "Tres Chevelles" that included a road test of the El Camino with the 396-cid, 325-hp V-8. It did 0 to 60 mph in 7.4 seconds and covered the quarter mile in 15.7 seconds at 90 mph.

The 1968 El Camino was 10 in. longer and had different box dimensions than previous editions.

EL CAMINO

For 1968, the El Camino was totally restyled. The cab had a more streamlined "flying buttress" rear roofline. A new 116-in. wheelbase, the same used for Chevelle four-door sedans and station wagons, was featured. Overall length grew from 197 in. (1964-1967) to 207 in. (1968-1972).

The new pickup box, which would be used through 1972, had different dimensions than the earlier one. Outside width increased to 75 1/2 in. Inside width behind the cab was down slightly to 59 in. Inside width near the tailgate remained at 64 1/2 in. The width between the wheel housings fell to 44 in. The bottom bed length increased slightly to 79 1/4 in. However, tailgate measurements changed to 54 1/2 x 22 1/2 in., so lowering the tailgate added slightly less extra load length.

This was the first year for a Super Sport (SS) version of the El Camino.

I.D. NUMBERS

VIN embossed on a plate welded to the left front door hinge pillar post facing the driver. The first symbol 1 designates Chevrolet. The second and third symbols designate the series: (six-cylinder) 33=Deluxe El Camino, 35=Custom El Camino; (V-8) 34=Deluxe El Camino, 36=Custom El Camino, 38=El Camino SS-396. The fourth and fifth symbols designates body type: 80=two-door sedan pickup. The sixth symbol designates the model year: 8=1968. The seventh symbol designates the assembly plant location: The seventh symbol indicated assembly plant: A=Atlanta, Georgia; B=Baltimore, Maryland; G=Framingham, Massachusetts; K=Kansas City, Missouri; Z=Fremont, California. The last six symbols are the sequential unit production number at the specific factory. The Fisher body tag riveted to the top of the cowl on the left side of the car below the hood provides additional vehicle identification information. The Fisher body STYLE NUMBER (ST) consists of a prefix identifying model year and four or more symbols identifying the series and body style (example: 68-13480 for a V-8-powered 1968 Deluxe El Camino). The BODY NUMBER consists of a prefix designating assembly plant and the sequential unit production number at the specific factory. The TRIM NUMBER (TR) identifies upholstery.

COLORS

(A) Tuxedo Black, (C) Ermine White, (D) Grotto Blue, (E) Fathom Blue, (F) Island Teal, (G) Ash Gold, (H) Grecian Green, (K) Tripoli Turquoise, (L) Teal Blue, (N) Cordovan Maroon, (P) Seafrost Green, (R) Matador Red, (T) Palomino Ivory, (V) Sequoia Green and (Y) Butternut Yellow.

ENGINE CODES

Engine codes appear on the right side of six-cylinder blocks behind the distributor and right front of V-8 engine blocks. Engine codes for 1968 were: (230-cid/140-hp six) BA, BB, BC, BD, BF and BH; (250-cid/155-hp six) CM, CN, CQ and CR; (307-cid/200-hp V-8) DA, DB, DE, DF and DN; (327/250-hp V-8) EA, EC, EE and EO; (327-cid/325-hp V-8) EP, ES, EH, EI and EJ; (396-cid/325-hp V-8) EO, EK and ET; (396-cid/350-hp V-8) EF, EL and EU.

EL CAMINO — SERIES 33/34 — SIX/V-8

The new El Camino front end was patterned along the lines of the 1968 Chevelle passenger cars. Features included a front bumper that was slotted behind the license plate only. The parking lights were relocated to the ends of the bumper. Two headlamps on each side were set into squarish, bright metal housings. A fine, screen-like mesh grille ran the full width of the front. It had a horizontal Chevrolet badge in its center. All El Caminos had front side markers with the engine's cubic in. displacement on the front marker bezel. The base model had a chrome front bumper, a Chevrolet grille badge, chrome-framed side marker lamps, an El Camino rear fender script, a bright tailgate latch and a chrome Chevrolet script on the right-hand side of the tailgate. Rear side markers were optional, at least late in the model-year. Hide-Away headlamps were optional, too.

Model Number	Body/Style Number	Body Type & Seating	Factory Price	Shipping Weight	Production Total
EL CAMINO SERIES 33 (6-CYL)					
33	80	pickup	$2,505	3,206 lbs.	Note 1
EL CAMINO SERIES 34 (V-8)					
34	80	pickup	$2,615	3,350 lbs.	Note 1

EL CAMINO CUSTOM — SERIES 35/36 SIX/V-8

All El Caminos had front side markers with the engine's cubic-inch displacement on the front marker bezel. The base model had a chrome front bumper, a Chevrolet grille badge, chrome-framed side marker lamps, an El Camino rear fender script, a bright tailgate latch, and a chrome Chevrolet script on the right-hand side of the tailgate. Added on El Camino Customs were bright window frames, pickup box upper edge moldings, rear body corner moldings, and wide rocker panel accent moldings.

Model Number	Body/Style Number	Body Type & Seating	Factory Price	Shipping Weight	Production Total
EL CAMINO CUSTOM SERIES 33 (6-CYL)					
35	80	Custom pickup	$2,585	3,223 lbs.	Note 1
EL CAMINO CUSTOM SERIES 34 (V-8)					
36	80	Custom pickup	$2,695	3,367 lbs.	Note 1

EL CAMINO SS-396 — SERIES 38 — V-8

The SS 396 was a distinct model-option this year. On SS 396 versions, the grille was blacked out and an SS grille center badge was added. This option also included a special power dome hood, fat Wide-Oval tires on 6-in. JK rims, black-out lower body perimeter finish, chrome moldings on lower body feature lines, special styled wheels, and SS tailgate moldings. The 396-cid/325-hp engine was standard. A 350-hp version of the big-block with a high-lift camshaft and dual exhausts was optional at extra cost and body accent striping was available, at extra cost, for SS 396s only.

Model Number	Body/Style Number	Body Type & Seating	Factory Price	Shipping Weight	Production Total
EL CAMINO CUSTOM SERIES 38 (V-8)					
38	80	SS 396 pickup	$3,184	—	Note 1

NOTE 1 Total El Camino production was 41,791.

ENGINES

EL CAMINO BASE 230-CID, 140-HP SIX-CYL:

Inline. Overhead-valve. Cast-iron block. Displacement: 230 cid. Bore and stroke: 3.875 x 3.25 in. Compression ratio: 8.5:1. Brake hp: 140 at 4400 rpm. Seven main bearings. Hydraulic valve lifters. Crankcase capacity: 4 qt. (add 1 qt. for new filter). Cooling system capacity: 12 qt. (add 6 qt. for heater). Carburetor: Rochester one-barrel Model 7027003.

EL CAMINO BASE 250-CID, 155-HP SIX-CYL: Inline. Overhead-valve. Cast-iron block. Displacement: 250 cid. Bore and stroke: 3.875 x 3.53 in. Compression ratio: 8.5:1. Brake hp: 155 at 4200 rpm. Taxable hp: 36. Torque: 235 lbs.-ft. at 1600 rpm. Seven main bearings. Hydraulic valve lifters. Crankcase capacity: 4 qt. (add 1 qt. for new filter). Cooling system capacity: 12 qt. (add 6 qt. for heater). Carburetor: Rochester one-barrel Model 7028017. Sales code L22.

EL CAMINO BASE 307-CID, 200-HP V-8: Overhead-valve. Cast-iron block and head. Bore and stroke: 3.88 x 3.25 in. Displacement: 307 cid. Compression ratio: 9.00:1. Brake hp: 200 at 4600 rpm. Taxable hp: 48. Torque: 300 lbs.-ft. at 2400. Five main bearings. Hydraulic valve lifters. Crankcase capacity: 4 qt. (add 1 qt. for new filter). Cooling system capacity: 16 qt. (add 1 qt. for heater). Carburetor: Rochester 7028101 two-barrel.

EL CAMINO OPTIONAL 327-CID, 250-HP V-8: Overhead-valve. Cast-iron block and head. Bore and stroke: 4.00 x 3.25 in. Displacement: 327 cid. Compression ratio: 8.75:1. Brake hp: 250 at 4800 rpm. Taxable hp: 51.20. Torque: 335 lbs.-ft. at 3200. Five main bearings. Hydraulic valve lifters. Crankcase capacity: 4 qt. (add 1 qt. for new filter). Cooling system capacity: (full-size) 14 qt.; (others) 16 qt. (add 1 qt. for heater). Carburetor: Carburetor: Four-barrel. Sales code L73.

EL CAMINO OPTIONAL 327-CID, 275-HP V-8: Overhead-valve. Cast-iron block and head. Bore and stroke: 4.00 x 3.25 in. Displacement: 327 cid. Compression ratio: 10.25:1. Brake hp: 275 at 4800 rpm. Taxable hp: 51.20. Torque: 355 lbs.-ft. at 3200. Five main bearings. Hydraulic valve lifters. Crankcase capacity: 4 qt. (add 1 qt. for new filter). Cooling system capacity: (full-size) 14 qt.; (others) 16 qt. (add 1 qt. for heater). Carburetor: Carburetor: Four-barrel. Sales code: L30.

EL CAMINO OPTIONAL 327-CID, 325-HP V-8: Overhead-valve. Cast-iron block and head. Bore and stroke: 4.00 x 3.25 in. Displacement: 327 cid. Compression ratio: 11.00:1. Brake hp: 325 at 5600 rpm. Taxable hp: 51.20. Torque: 355 lbs.-ft. at 3600. Five main bearings. Hydraulic valve lifters. Crankcase capacity: 4 qt. (add 1 qt. for new filter). Cooling system capacity: 14 qt. (add 1 qt. for heater). Carburetor: Four-barrel. Sales code: L79.

EL CAMINO SS 396 BASE 325-HP V-8: Overhead-valve. Cast-iron block and head. Bore and stroke: 4.09 x 3.76 in. Displacement: 396 cid. Compression ratio: 10.25:1. Brake hp: 325 at 4800 rpm. Taxable hp: 53.60. Torque: 410 lbs.-ft. at 3200. Five main bearings. Hydraulic valve lifters. Crankcase capacity: 4 qt. (add 1 qt. for new filter). Cooling system capacity: 23 qt. (add 1 qt. for heater). Carburetor: Rochester 7028211 four-barrel. Sales code: L35.

EL CAMINO OPTIONAL 396-CID, 350-HP V-8: Overhead-valve. Cast-iron block and head. Bore and stroke: 4.09 x 3.76 in. Displacement: 396 cid. Compression ratio: 10.25:1. Brake hp: 350 at 5200 rpm. Taxable hp: 53.60. Torque: 415 lbs.-ft. at 3400. Five main bearings. Hydraulic valve lifters. Crankcase capacity: 4 qt. (add 1 qt. for new filter). Cooling system capacity: 23 qt. (add 1 qt. for heater). Carburetor: Four-barrel. Sales code: L34.

CHASSIS

Wheelbase: 116 in. Overall length: 206 in. Front tread: 59 in. Rear tread: 59 in. Tires: 7.35 x 14 in. Gross vehicle weight: 4,300 lbs. Standard transmission: Chevrolet three-speed manual (Borg-Warner heavy-duty three-speed optional). Type transmission: 3F/1R. Column-mounted gearshift lever. Single-plate, dry-disc clutch. Rear axle: Semi-floating. Base rear axles: 3.08:1. Brakes: Four-wheel hydraulic drums. Brake linings: 9 1/2 x 2 1/2 in. Kelsey-Hayes pressed steel wheels.

OPTIONS

C60 Four-Season air conditioning, including 61-amp Delcotron, heavy-duty radiator and temperature-controlled fan ($360.20). G80 Positraction rear axle ($42.15). AXL1 special economy or high-performance rear axle ($2.15). T60 heavy-duty battery ($7.40). A51 standard type front shoulder belts, in cars with standard seat belts ($23.20). A85 Custom Deluxe front shoulder belts, requires Custom Deluxe seat belts ($26.35). V31 Front bumper guards ($15.80). V32 Rear bumper guards ($15.80). U35 electric clock in Chevelle 300 and 300 Deluxe models; included with special instrumentation ($15.80). M01 heavy-duty clutch, V-8s except SS 396 and cars with 155-hp V-8 ($10.55). M01 heavy-duty clutch on sixes except 155 hp ($5.30). D55 console, including electric clock, requires bucket seats ($50.60). B93 door edge guards, two-door models ($4.25). L22 250-cid 155-hp six-cylinder engine ($26.35). L73 327-cid 250-hp V-8, all except SS 396 ($63.20). L30 327-cid 275-hp V-8 engine, all except SS 396 ($92.70). L79 327-cid 325-hp V-8, all except SS 396 ($198.05). N10 dual exhaust on all Chevelles with the 275-hp engine ($27.40). K02 temperature-controlled fan, V-8s, standard with air conditioning ($15.80). K79 42-amp Delcotron generator, not available with air conditioning or with C60 ($10.55). K76 61-amp Delcotron generator, with air conditioning ($5.30); without air conditioning ($26.35). A01 all windows tinted ($34.80). A02 tinted windshield only ($23.20). A81 driver and passenger headrests, with front Strato bucket seats ($52.70). A82 driver and passenger headrests, with standard front bench seat ($42.15). U03 tri-volume horn ($13.70). special instrumentation with ammeter, temperature gauge, oil pressure gauge and tachometer on Malibu Custom and SS 396 ($94.80). U46 light monitoring system ($26.35). ZJ19 auxiliary lighting groups with A) ash tray, B) courtesy, C) glove box, D) luggage and E) under-hood lights includes A, B and E ($8.45). D33 left-hand outside remote-control mirror ($9.50). B90 side window moldings ($21.10). Two-tone paint ($21.10). J50 power drum brakes ($42.15). J50 power disc front brakes ($100.10). N40 power steering ($94.80). A31 power windows ($100.10). V01 Heavy-duty radiator, except with air conditioning ($10.55). U63 AM push-button radio with front antenna ($61.10). U69 AM/FM radio with front antenna ($133.80). U69/79 AM/FM radio with front antenna and stereo ($239.15). U57 stereo tape system with four speakers ($133.80). U80 rear seat speaker, not available with U79 ($13.20) U73 rear antenna, all except AM/FM and wagons ($9.50). CO81/82 vinyl roof cover, for hardtop models ($84.30). B55 Thick front foam seat cushion, El Camino Deluxe ($7.40). A51 Strato bucket seats in Malibu or SS 396 sport coupe and convertible ($110.60). G66 Superlift rear shock absorbers ($42.15). K30 speed and cruise control, V-8s with automatic transmissions ($52.70). U15 speed warning indicator ($10.55). N30 Deluxe steering wheel in base El Camino ($7.40). N30 Deluxe steering wheel in El Camino Custom ($4.25). N33 Comfortilt steering wheel, requires floor shifter or automatic transmissions ($42.15). N34 Sport styled steering wheel ($31.60). D96 accent striping ($29.50). F40 special front and rear suspension ($4.75). M21 Close-ratio four-speed manual transmission for SS 396 ($184.35). M20 wide-ratio four-speed manual transmission for all ($184.35). M40 Turbo Hydra-Matic transmission for SS 396 with 350-hp or 325-hp V-8 only ($237). M13 special floor-mounted three-speed manual transmission for all except SS 396 ($79 and standard on SS 396). M35 Powerglide automatic transmission for six-cylinder El Camino ($184.35). M35 Powerglide automatic transmission for V-8 El Caminos except SS 396 ($194.85). M10 overdrive transmission with 140-, 155-, 200- or 250-hp engines ($115.90). KD5 heavy-duty closed engine positive crankcase ventilation system ($6.35). P01 four bright metal wheel covers ($21.10). N96 Mag-styled wheel covers with non-disc brakes ($73.75). N95 simulated wire wheel covers with non disc brakes ($73.75). PA2 Mag spoke wheel covers ($73.75). ZJ7 Rallye wheels, including special wheels, hubcaps, and trim rings ($31.60). C24 concealed windshield wipers, standard on El Camino Custom ($19). P4 operating convenience group including electric clock, remote-controlled left-hand outside rearview mirror and rear window defroster for all models except convertibles and station wagons without U14 special instrumentation ($46.40). P4 operating convenience group including remote-control left-hand outside rearview mirror and rear window defroster for El Camino Custom V-8 and SS 396 with U14 special instrumentation ($30.60).

HISTORICAL FOOTNOTES

Chevrolet celebrated its 50th year of truck manufacturing in 1968. Special Anniversary Gold with off-white paint was optional on some models. Record sales and production marked Chevrolet's truck operations this season. Dealers delivered 843,990 trucks of all sizes. This was the first year that production of V-8-powered Chevrolet trucks outpaced production of sixes. T.L. Pritchett, assistant general sales manager, was head of the truck division.

The 396-cid, 325-hp V-8 was standard in the 1969 El Camino SS. The El Camino line had a few exterior revisions, including a slightly different grille.

For 1969, the El Camino had a mild, but handsome, facelift. A new fine-finned grille insert was dominated by bright horizontal molding at its top, center and bottom. The center molding had a Chevrolet badge in the middle. The center bumper slot was also larger.

Following an every-other-year Chevelle tradition, the parking lamps were moved back inside the slot, which was widened just enough to accommodate the lenses. At the rear, all El Caminos had large back-up lamps set into the tailgate on either side of the Chevrolet nameplate in the center. The rear bumper indentations filled by back-up lamps on passenger cars had red reflectors on the sedan-pickup.

I.D. NUMBERS

The VIN is stamped on a plate on the top left side of the instrument panel and visible through the windshield. The first symbol 1 designates Chevrolet. The second and third symbols designate the series: (six-cylinder) 33=Deluxe El Camino, 35=Custom El Camino; (V-8) 34=Deluxe El Camino, 36=Custom El Camino. The fourth and fifth symbols designate body type: 80=two-door sedan pickup. The sixth symbol designates the model year: 9=1969. The seventh symbol designates the assembly plant location: The seventh symbol indicated assembly plant: A=Atlanta, Georgia; B=Baltimore, Maryland; G=Framingham, Massachusetts; K=Kansas City, Missouri; Z=Fremont, California. The last six symbols are the sequential unit production number at the specific factory. The Fisher body tag riveted to the top of the cowl on the left side of the car below the hood provides additional vehicle identification information. The Fisher Body STYLE NUMBER (ST) consists of a prefix identifying model year and four or more symbols identifying the series and body style (example: 69-13480 for a V-8-powered 1969 Deluxe El Camino). The BODY NUMBER consists of a prefix designating assembly plant and the sequential unit production number at the specific factory. The TRIM NUMBER (TR) identifies upholstery.

COLORS

(10) Tuxedo Black, (40) Butternut Yellow, (50) Dover White, (51) Dusk Blue Metallic, (52) Garnet Red, (53) Glacier Blue Metallic, (55) Azure Turquoise Metallic, (59) Frost Green Metallic, (61) Burnished Brown Metallic, (63) Champagne Metallic and (65) Olympic Gold Metallic.

ENGINE CODES

Codes appear on the right side of six-cylinder blocks behind the distributor and right front of V-8 engine blocks. Engine codes for 1968 were: (230-cid/140-hp six) AM, AN, AO, AP, AQ, AR, AS, AU, At and AV; (250-cid/155-hp six) BB, BC, BD, BE, BF, BH, BK, BW, BI and BJ; (307-cid/200-hp V-8) DA, DC, DD, DE, FS and FT; (350/250-hp V-8) HC, HD, and HF; (350-cid/300-hp V-8) HA, HB and HE; (396-cid/325-hp V-8) JA, KG, KHJV and KI; (396-cid/350-hp V-8) JC and KB, (396-cid/375-hp V-8) JD, KF and KD; (402-cid/325-hp V-8) CJA and CJK; (402-cid/350-hp V-8) CJC and CJD and (402-cid/375-hp V-8) CKF, CKG and CKH.

EL CAMINO — SERIES 33/34 — SIX/V-8

Accenting base models was a Chevrolet script on the left fender top, front side marker engine call-outs, rear side marker lamps, rear fender El Camino nameplates, bright windshield frames, a bright tailgate latch, a Chevrolet nameplate on tailgate and narrow rocker panel moldings. The pickup box, used through 1972, had an outside width of 75 1/2 in. Inside width behind the cab was 59 in. Inside width near the tailgate was 64 1/2 in. The width between the wheel housings was 44 in. The bottom bed length measured 79 1/4 in. Tailgate measurements were 54 1/2 x 22 1/2 in.

Model Number	Body/Style Number	Body Type & Seating	Factory Price	Shipping Weight	Production Total
EL CAMINO SERIES 33 (6-CYL)					
33	80	pickup	$2,552	3,206 lbs.	Note 1
EL CAMINO SERIES 34 (V-8)					
34	80	pickup	$2,642	3,216 lbs.	Note 1

EL CAMINO CUSTOM — SERIES 35/36 SIX/V-8

Custom models had bright window frames, pickup box upper edge moldings, rear body corner moldings, two moldings across the tailgate at taillight top and bottom height, a bright rear window frame, bright moldings on lower body feature line and silver anodized lower body perimeter finish.

Model Number	Body/Style Number	Body Type & Seating	Factory Price	Shipping Weight	Production Total
EL CAMINO CUSTOM SERIES 35 (6-CYL)					
35	80	Custom pickup	$2,632	3,219 lbs.	Note 1
EL CAMINO CUSTOM SERIES 36 (V-8)					
36	80	Custom pickup	$2,723	3,248 lbs.	Note 1

EL CAMINO SS — SERIES 34/36 + Z25 V-8

The SS 396 reverted to an option this year. On SS 396 El Caminos, the grille had black-out finish. The grille center and middle of the tailgate had SS 396 badges. The engine call-outs on the front side marker lamp housings said Turbo-Jet 396. This option also included a special power dome hood, fat G70 x 14 red stripe tires on 14 x 7-in. rims, black-out style lower body perimeter finish, chrome moldings on the lower body feature line, special styled wheels, suspension upgrades, power disc brakes, wheel opening moldings, and SS tailgate moldings. The 396-cid 325-hp engine with chrome accents was standard. A 350-hp version of the big-block with a high-lift camshaft and dual exhausts was optional at extra cost. The "flying buttress" roofline was retained.

Model Number	Body/Style Number	Body Type & Seating	Factory Price	Shipping Weight	Production Total
EL CAMINO SS SERIES 34 +Z25 (V-8)					
34	80	SS 396 pickup	$3,012	—	Note 1
EL CAMINO CUSTOM SS SERIES 36 + Z25 (V-8)					
36	80	SS 396 pickup	$3,093	—	Note 1

NOTE 1 Total El Camino production was 48,385.

ENGINES

EL CAMINO BASE 230-CID, 140-HP SIX-CYL: Inline. Overhead-valve. Cast-iron block. Displacement: 230 cid. Bore and stroke: 3.875 x 3.25 in. Compression ratio: 8.5:1. Brake hp: 140 at 4400 rpm. Seven main bearings. Hydraulic valve lifters. Crankcase capacity: 4 qt. (add 1 qt. for new filter). Cooling system capacity: 12 qt (add 6 qt. for heater). Carburetor: Rochester one-barrel Model 7027003.

EL CAMINO BASE 250-CID, 155-HP SIX-CYL: Inline. Overhead-valve. Cast-iron block. Displacement: 250 cid. Bore and stroke: 3.875 x 3.53 in. Compression ratio: 8.5:1. Brake hp: 155 at 4200 rpm. Taxable hp: 36. Torque: 235 lbs.-ft. at 1600 rpm. Seven main bearings. Hydraulic valve lifters. Crankcase capacity: 4 qt. (add 1 qt. for new filter). Cooling system capacity: 12 qt. (add 6 qt. for heater). Carburetor: Rochester one-barrel Model 7028017. Sales code L22.

EL CAMINO BASE 307-CID, 200-HP V-8: Overhead-valve. Cast-iron block and head. Bore and stroke: 3.88 x 3.25 in. Displacement: 307 cid. Compression ratio: 9.00:1. Brake hp: 200 at 4600 rpm. Taxable hp: 48 Torque: 300 lbs.-ft. at 2400. Five main bearings. Hydraulic valve lifters. Crankcase capacity: 4 qt. (add 1 qt. for new filter). Cooling system capacity: 16 qt (add 1 qt. for heater). Carburetor: Rochester 7028101 two-barrel.

EL CAMINO OPTIONAL 350-CID, 250-HP V-8: Overhead-valve. Cast-iron block and head. Bore and stroke: 4.00 x 3.48 in. Displacement: 350 cid. Compression ratio: 9.00:1. Brake hp: 250 at 4800 rpm. Taxable hp: 51.20. Torque: 345 lbs.-ft. at 2800. Five main bearings. Hydraulic valve lifters. Crankcase capacity: 4 qt. (add 1 qt. for new filter). Cooling system capacity: 15 qt. (add 1 qt. for heater). Carburetor: Two-barrel.

EL CAMINO OPTIONAL 350-CID, 255-HP V-8: Overhead-valve. Cast-iron block and head. Bore and stroke: 4.00 x 3.48 in. Displacement: 350 cid. Compression ratio: 9.00:1. Brake hp: 255 at 4800 rpm. Taxable hp: 51.20. Torque: 365 lbs.-ft. at 3200. Five main bearings. Hydraulic valve lifters. Crankcase capacity: 4 qt. (add 1 qt. for new filter). Cooling system capacity: (full-size) 14 qt.; (others) 15 qt. (add 1 qt. for heater). Carburetor: Four-barrel.

EL CAMINO OPTIONAL 350-CID, 300-HP V-8: Overhead-valve. Cast-iron block and head. Bore and stroke: 4.00 x 3.48 in. Displacement: 350 cid. Compression ratio: 10.25:1. Brake hp: 300 at 4800 rpm. Taxable hp: 51.20. Torque: 380 lbs.-ft. at 3200. Five main bearings. Hydraulic valve lifters. Crankcase capacity: 4 qt. (add 1 qt. for new filter). Cooling system capacity: 15 qt. (add 1 qt. for heater). Carburetor: Four-barrel.

EL CAMINO OPTIONAL 396-CID, 325-HP V-8: Overhead-valve. Cast-iron block and head. Bore and stroke: 4.09 x 3.76 in. Displacement: 396 cid. Compression ratio: 10.25:1. Brake hp: 325 at 4800 rpm. Taxable hp: 53.60. Torque: 410 lbs.-ft. at 3200. Five main bearings. Hydraulic valve lifters. Crankcase capacity: 4 qt. (add 1 qt. for new filter). Cooling system capacity: 23 qt. (add 1 qt. for heater). Carburetor: Four-barrel.

EL CAMINO OPTIONAL 396-CID, 350-HP V-8: Overhead-valve. Cast-iron block and head. Bore and stroke: 4.09 x 3.76 in. Displacement: 396 cid. Compression ratio: 10.25:1. Brake hp: 350 at 5200 rpm. Taxable hp: 53.60. Torque: 415 lbs.-ft. at 3400. Five main bearings. Hydraulic valve lifters. Crankcase capacity: 4 qt. (add 1 qt. for new filter). Cooling system capacity: 23 qt. (add 1 qt. for heater). Carburetor: Four-barrel.

EL CAMINO OPTIONAL 396-CID, 375-HP V-8: Overhead-valve. Cast-iron block and head. Bore and stroke: 4.09 x 3.76 in. Displacement: 396 cid. Compression ratio: 11.00:1. Brake hp: 375 at 5600 rpm. Taxable hp: 53.60. Torque: 415 lbs.-ft. at 3600. Five main bearings. Hydraulic valve lifters. Crankcase capacity: 4 qt. (add 1 qt. for new filter). Cooling system capacity: 23 qt. (add 1 qt. for heater). Carburetor: Four-barrel. Sales code: L78.

EL CAMINO OPTIONAL 396-CID, 375-HP V-8: Overhead-valve. Cast-iron block. Aluminum head with large valves. Bore and stroke: 4.09 x 3.76 in. Displacement: 396 cid (actually 402 cid). Compression ratio: 11.00:1. Brake hp: 375 at 5600 rpm. Taxable hp: 53.60. Torque: 415 at 3600. Five main bearings. Solid valve lifters. Crankcase capacity: 4 qt. (add 1 qt. for new fil-

Bench seats were still standard for the 1969 El Camino. Astro bucket seats were an option.

ter). Cooling system capacity: 23 qt. (add 1 qt. for heater). Carburetor: Holley four-barrel carburetor on high-rise aluminum intake manifold. Sales code L78/L89.

CHASSIS

Wheelbase: 116 in. Overall length: 201 in. Front tread: 59 in. Rear tread: 59 in. Tires: 7.35 x 14 in. Gross vehicle weight: 4,300 lb. Standard transmission: Chevrolet three-speed manual 3F/1R. Column-mounted gearshift lever. Single-plate, dry-disc clutch. Rear axle: (1/2-ton) semi-floating. Base rear axles: (El Camino) 3.08:1. Brakes: Four-wheel hydraulic, drum brakes. Brake linings: 9 1/2 x 2 1/2-in. Kelsey-Hayes pressed steel wheels.

OPTIONS

A01 tinted body glass. A02 tinted windshield. A31 electric windows. A39 front and rear seat belts with retractors. A42 four-way electric front seat control. A51 Astro bucket seats. A85 front shoulder belts. A93 power door locks. AR1 less head restraint. AS5 driver's adjustable seat back. B37 floor mats. B90 door edge and window frame moldings. B93 door edge guards. BX4 upper body side moldings. C08 vinyl top. C24 special windshield wiper. C60 all-weather air conditioning. C75 automatic temperature control. CE1 headlamp washer. D33 remote-control driver's mirror. D34 visor-vanity mirror. D55 front compartment floor console. D96 wide body side paint stripe. F40 heavy-duty suspension. F41 special performance suspension. G76 3.36:1 ratio axle. G80 Positraction. G82 4.56:1 ratio axle. G84 4.10:1 ratio axle. G92 3.08:1 ratio axle. G94 3.31:1 ratio axle. G96 3.55:1 ratio axle. G97 2.37:1 ratio axle. GT1 2.56:1 ratio axle. H01 3.07:1 ratio axle. H05 3.73:1 ratio axle. J50 power brakes. J52 front disc brakes. K02 fan drive. K05 engine block heater. K79 42-amp. Delcotron. K85 63-amp. Delcotron. KD5 heavy-duty closed crankcase ventilation. L22 250-cid six. L34 high-performance 396-cid V-8. L35 396-cid V-8. L48 350-cid four-barrel V-8. L65 350-cid two-barrel V-8. L78 396-cid special high-performance V-8. L89 aluminum cylinder heads. LM1 350-cid regular-fuel four-barrel V-8. M20 4-speed manual transmission. M21 four-speed close-ratio transmission. M22 heavy-duty four-speed manual transmission. M35 Powerglide automatic transmission. M38 three-speed automatic transmission. M40 three-speed automatic transmission. MC1 heavy-duty three-speed manual transmission. N10 dual exhaust. N33 tilt steering. N34 wood-grained plastic steering wheel. N40 power steering. N95 simulated wire wheel covers. N96 simulated mag-style wheel covers. NC8 chambered exhaust system. P01 wheel trim covers. P06 wheel trim ring. P58 7.35 x 14 four-ply-rated white sidewall tires. P62 7.75 x 14 four-ply-rated white sidewall tires. P77 8.25 x 14 four-ply-rated white sidewall tires. PA2 simulated mag-style wheels. PK2 G78 x 14 four-ply-rated bias-belted white sidewall tires. PK4 G70 x 14 four-ply-rated red stripe tires. PL5 F70 x 14 four-ply-rated white letter tires. PN5 7.75 x 14 8-ply-rated white sidewall tires. PQ7 8.25 x 14 four-ply-rated white sidewall tires. PR3 8.25 x 14 four-ply-rated white sidewall tires. PW7 F70 x 14 4-ply rated white sidewall tires. PW8 F70 x 14 four-ply-rated red stripe tires. PX6 F78 x 14 four-ply-rated bias-belted white sidewall tires. PX8 G70 x 14 four-ply-rated bias-belted white sidewall tires. PX9 G70 x 14 four-ply-rated white stripe tires. PY4 F70 x 14 four-ply-rated bias-belted white stripe tires. PY5 F70 x 14 four-ply-rated bias-belted red stripe tires. PY7 G60 x 14 four-ply-rated bias-belted red stripe tires. T60 heavy-duty battery. U05 dual horn. U14 instrument panel gauges. U15 speed warning indicator. U26 under-hood lamp. U27 glove compartment lamp. U28 ash tray lamp. U29 instrument panel courtesy lamp. U35 electric clock. U46 lamp monitoring. U57 tape player. U63 push-button radio. U69 AM/FM push-button radio. U80 auxiliary speaker. UF1 map lamp. V01 heavy-duty radiator. V31 front bumper guard. V32 rear bumper guard. V75 traction compound and dispenser. Z25 SS 396 package. ZJ7 special hub caps and trim rings. ZJ9 auxiliary lighting group. ZK3 deluxe seat belts and front shoulder harness. 796 vinyl coated trim. 959 two-tone color combination.

HISTORICAL FOOTNOTES

In 1969, Chevrolet became a full-line truck-maker sharing GMC's heavy over-the-road product line with Chevrolet nameplates.

The 1970 El Camino had a blunter, heftier front end replacing the 1968-1969 wrap-over look. The dual headlamps were placed in square bezels outside the grille. A cross-hatch pattern grille insert was divided into four sections by wider chrome cross-bars. There was a bow tie in the center. Following the every-other-year pattern used since 1964, the rectangular parking lights were moved from inside the bumper air slot to the outer ends of the bumper.

At the rear, all El Caminos had large back-up lamps set into the tailgate, on either side of the Chevrolet nameplate in the center. The rear bumper indentations filled by back-up lamps on passenger cars had red reflectors on the sedan-pickup.

I.D. NUMBERS

The VIN is stamped on a plate on the top left side of the instrument panel and visible through the windshield. The first symbol 1 designates Chevrolet. The second and third symbols designate the series: (six-cylinder)

El Camino

The 1970 El Camino had yet another new grille and front-end design. This immaculate car is an SS 454.

33=Deluxe El Camino, 35=Custom El Camino; (V-8) 34=Deluxe El Camino, 36=Custom El Camino. The fourth and fifth symbols designate body type: 80=two-door sedan pickup. The sixth symbol designates the model year: 0=1970. The seventh symbol designates the assembly plant location: The seventh symbol indicated assembly plant: A=Atlanta/Lakewood, Georgia; B=Baltimore, Maryland; F=Flint, Michigan; K-=Kansas City/Leeds, Missouri; L=Los Angles/Van Nuys, California; R=Arlington, Texas and 1-Oshawa, Canada. The last six symbols are the sequential unit production number at the specific factory. The Fisher body tag riveted to the top of the cowl on the left side of the car below the hood provides additional vehicle identification information. The Fisher body STYLE NUMBER (ST) consists of a prefix identifying model year and four or more symbols identifying the series and body style (example: 70-13680 for a V-8-powered 1970 Custom El Camino). The BODY NUMBER consists of a prefix designating assembly plant and the sequential unit production number at the specific factory. The TRIM NUMBER (TR) identifies upholstery.

COLORS

(10) Classic White, (14) Cortez Silver Metallic, (17) Shadow Gray Silver Metallic, (19) Tuxedo Black, (25) Astro Turquoise Silver Metallic, (28) Fathom Blue Silver Metallic, (34) Misty Turquoise Silver Metallic, (45) Green Mist Silver Metallic, (48) Forest Green Silver Metallic, (50) Gobi Beige, (55) Champagne Gold Silver Metallic, (58) Autumn Gold Silver Metallic, (63) Desert Sand Silver Metallic, (75) Cranberry Red and (78) Black Cherry Silver Metallic. Vinyl tops were available in five colors: AA=White, BB=Black, CC=Dark Blue, HH=Dark Gold and GG=Dark Green.

ENGINE CODES

Codes appear on the right side of six-cylinder blocks behind the distributor and right front of V-8 engine blocks. Engine codes for 1970 were: (250-cid six) CRG, CCH, CCG, CCF, CCM, CCK and CCL; (307-cid V-8) CNC, CND, CNE, CNF, CNG, CNH, CRF; (350/250 hp V-8) CNI, CNN and CNM; (350-cid/300-hp V-8) CNJ, CNK and CRE; (396-cid/350-hp V-8) CTW, CTX and CTZ;

(396-cid/375-hp V-8) CTY, CKN, CKO, CKD, CKQ, CKT and CKU; (396-cid/375-hp aluminum cylinder heads) CKP; (400-cid/265-hp) CZX and CRH; (400-cid/330-hp) CKN, CKR and CKS; (454-cid/360-hp) CRN, CGT, CRQ, CRM, CRT, CGU and CRU; (454-cid/450-hp) CRR, CRV and CRX; (454-cid/450-hp aluminum cylinder heads) CRS, CRY and CRW.

EL CAMINO — SERIES 33/34 — SIX/V-8

Regular El Caminos featured a new dash with a wide rectangular-shaped speedometer and gauges. Accenting base models was a Chevrolet script on the upper left grille section, El Camino nameplates and engine plaques above the feature line behind the front wheel openings, bright tailgate latch, and Chevrolet nameplate on tailgate. The pickup box, used through 1972, had an outside width of 75 1/2 in. Inside width behind the cab was 59 in. Inside width near the tailgate was 64 1/2 in. The width between the wheel housings was 44 in. The bottom bed length measured 79 1/4 in. Tailgate measurements were 54 1/2 x 22 1/2 in.

Model Number	Body/Style Number	Body Type & Seating	Factory Price	Shipping Weight	Production Total
EL CAMINO SERIES 33 (6-CYL)					
33	80	pickup	$2,676	3,302 lbs.	Note 1
EL CAMINO SERIES 34 (V-8)					
34	80	pickup	$2,770	3,418 lbs.	Note 1

EL CAMINO CUSTOM — SERIES 35/36 SIX/V-8

Custom El Camino models had lower body side and wheel opening moldings, silver anodized lower body perimeter finish, pickup box edge and rear body corner moldings, moldings running across the tailgate at top and bottom of tail lamps and a contrasting rear beauty panel with Chevrolet nameplate. There was an SS 396 option (RPO Z25). In midyear, the 396 cid engine was actually enlarged to 402 cid, though the well-known SS 396 name was still used in sales promotion. About the same time (January, 1970) a new SS 454 option was released. Technically, it came in RPO Z15/LS5 and RPO Z15/LS6 versions. The first had a high-lift camshaft and 10.25:1 compression for 360 hp. The second had a special camshaft and 11.25:1 compression to produce 450 hp. A cowl-induction hood was available for SS models at $124. A popular option was the hood racing stripes, which were $43 extra. Super Sports included a black-accented grille with SS grille badges, special hood with locking pins, styled wheels, suspension upgrades, power disc brakes, wheel opening moldings, and SS tailgate emblems. The lower body perimeter was also blacked-out. The flying buttress roofline was retained for all El Caminos. The pickup box, used through 1972, had an outside width of 75 1/2 in. Inside width behind the cab was 59 in. Inside width near the tailgate was 64 1/2 in.

Model Number	Body/Style Number	Body Type & Seating	Factory Price	Shipping Weight	Production Total
EL CAMINO CUSTOM SERIES 35 (6-CYL)					
35	80	Custom pickup	$2,760	3,324 lbs.	Note 1
EL CAMINO CUSTOM SERIES 36 (V-8)					
36	80	Custom pickup	$2,850	3,442 lbs.	Note 1

EL CAMINO SS 396 — SERIES 34/36 + Z25 — V-8

There was an El Camino SS 396 option (RPO Z25) in 1970. The 396-cid engine was actually 402 cid, though the well-known SS 396 name was still used in sales promotion. A cowl-induction hood was available for SS models at $124. A popular option was the hood racing stripes, which were $43 extra. Super Sports included a black-accented grille with SS grille badges, special hood with locking pins, styled wheels, suspension upgrades, power disc brakes, wheel opening moldings and SS tail-

The SS 454 was the top dog in the Chevelle lineup for 1970. Buyers could get a 360- or 450-hp engine.

EL CAMINO

gate emblems. The lower body perimeter was also blacked out.

Model Number	Body/Style Number	Body Type & Seating	Factory Price	Shipping Weight	Production Total
EL CAMINO SS 396 SERIES 34 + Z25 (V-8)					
34	80	pickup	$3,225	—	Note 1
EL CAMINO CUSTOM SS 396 SERIES 36 + Z25 (V-8)					
36	80	Custom pickup	$3,305	—	Note 1

EL CAMINO SS 454 — SERIES 34/36 + Z15 — V-8

Around January, 1970, a new SS 454 option was released. Technically, it came in RPO Z15/LS5 and RPO Z15/LS6 versions. The first had a high-lift camshaft and 10.25:1 compression for 360 hp. The second had a special camshaft and 11.25:1 compression to produce 450 hp. A cowl-induction hood was available and a popular option was the hood racing stripes. SS 454s also had the black-accented grille with SS grille badges, special hood with locking pins, styled wheels, suspension upgrades, power disc brakes, wheel opening moldings and SS tailgate emblems. The lower body perimeter was blacked-out.

Model Number	Body/Style Number	Body Type & Seating	Factory Price	Shipping Weight	Production Total
EL CAMINO SS 454 SERIES 34 + Z15 (V-8)					
34	80	pickup	—	—	Note 1
EL CAMINO CUSTOM SS 454 SERIES 36 + Z15 (V-8)					
36	80	Custom pickup	—	—	Note 1

NOTE 1 Total El Camino production was 47,707.

ENGINES

EL CAMINO BASE 250-CID, 155-HP SIX-CYL: Inline. Overhead-valve. Cast-iron block. Displacement: 250 cid. Bore and stroke: 3.875 x 3.53 in. Compression ratio: 8.5:1. Brake hp: 155 at 4200 rpm. Taxable hp: 36. Torque: 235 lbs.-ft. at 1600 rpm. Seven main bearings. Hydraulic valve lifters. Crankcase capacity: 4 qt. (add 1 qt. for new filter). Cooling system capacity: 12 qt. (add 6 qt. for heater). Carburetor: Rochester one-barrel Model 7028017. Sales code L22. Available standard with three-speed fully synchronized manual transmission and optional with special fully synchronized three-speed manual transmission, Powerglide automatic transmission or Turbo-Hydra-Matic automatic transmission.

EL CAMINO BASE 307-CID, 200-HP V-8: Overhead-valve. Cast-iron block and head. Bore and stroke: 3.88 x 3.25 in. Displacement: 307 cid. Compression ratio: 9.00:1. Brake hp: 200 at 4600 rpm. Taxable hp: 48. Torque: 300 lbs.-ft. at 2400. Five main bearings. Hydraulic valve lifters. Crankcase capacity: 4 qt. (add 1 qt. for new filter). Cooling system capacity: 14 qt (add 1 qt. for heater). Carburetor: Two-barrel.

EL CAMINO OPTIONAL 350-CID, 250-HP V-8: Overhead-valve. Cast-iron block and head. Bore and stroke: 4.00 x 3.48 in. Displacement: 350 cid. Compression ratio: 9.00:1. Brake hp: 250 at 4800 rpm. Taxable hp: 51.20. Torque: 345 lbs.-ft. at 2800. Five main bearings. Hydraulic valve lifters. Crankcase capacity: 4 qt. (add 1 qt. for new filter). Cooling system capacity: 15 qt. (add 1 qt. for heater). Carburetor: Two-barrel. Sales code: L65 (added midyear).

EL CAMINO OPTIONAL 350-CID, 300-HP V-8: Overhead-valve. Cast-iron block and head. Bore and

The cowl-induction hood was a $124 option.

The SS badges were found right behind the front wheel wells.

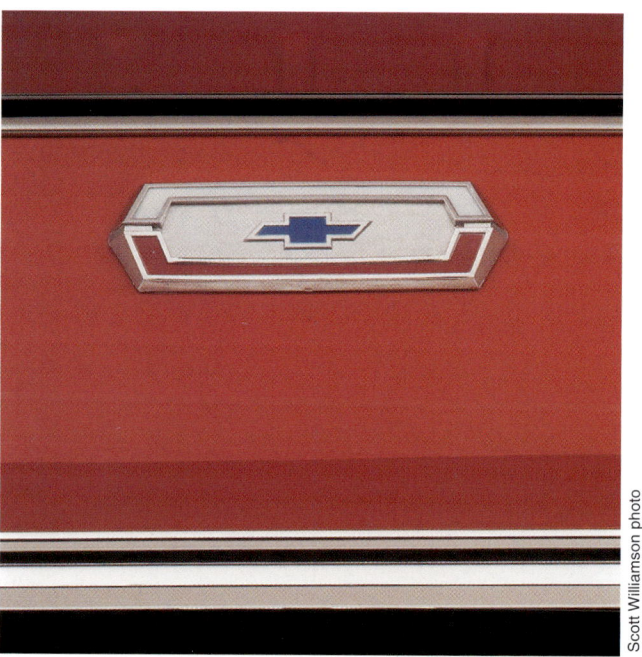

The tailgate sported the Cherolet bow-tie emblem and wide moldings.

The SS 454 had two engine options. The Z15/LS6 version produced 450 hp.

stroke: 4.00 x 3.48 in. Displacement: 350 cid. Compression ratio: 9.00:1. Brake hp: 300 at 4800 rpm. Taxable hp: 51.20. Torque: 380 lbs.-ft. at 3200. Five main bearings. Hydraulic valve lifters. Crankcase capacity: 4 qt. (add 1 qt. for new filter). Cooling system capacity: 15 qt. (add 1 qt. for heater). Carburetor: Four-barrel. Sales code: L48.

EL CAMINO OPTIONAL 396-CID, 330-HP V-8: Overhead-valve. Cast-iron block and head. Bore and stroke: 4.13 x 3.76 in. Displacement: 402 cid (400 cid). Compression ratio: 10.25:1. Brake hp: 330 at 4800 rpm. Taxable hp: 54.50. Torque: 410 lbs.-ft. at 3200. Five main bearings. Hydraulic valve lifters. Crankcase capacity: 4 qt. (add 1 qt. for new filter). Cooling system capacity: 22 qt. (add 1 qt. for heater). Carburetor: Four-barrel. Sales code: LS3 (added midyear).

EL CAMINO OPTIONAL 396-CID, 350-HP V-8: Overhead-valve. Cast-iron block and head. Bore and stroke: 4.13 x 3.76 in. Displacement: 402 cid (396 cid). Compression ratio: 10.25:1. Brake hp: 350 at 5200 rpm. Taxable hp: 54.50. Torque: 415 lbs.-ft. at 3400. Five main bearings. Hydraulic valve lifters. Crankcase capacity: 4 qt. (add 1 qt. for new filter). Cooling system capacity: 22 qt. (add 1 qt. for heater). Carburetor: Four-barrel. Sales code: L34.

EL CAMINO OPTIONAL 396-CID, 375-HP V-8: Overhead-valve. Cast-iron block and head. Bore and stroke: 4.09 x 3.76 in. Displacement: 396 cid (actually 402 cid). Compression ratio: 11.00:1. Brake hp: 375 at 5600 rpm. Taxable hp: 53.60. Torque: 415 lbs.-ft. at 3600. Five main bearings. Hydraulic valve lifters. Crankcase capacity: 4 qt. (add 1 qt. for new filter). Cooling system capacity: 23 qt. (add 1 qt. for heater). Carburetor: Four-barrel. Sales code: L78.

EL CAMINO OPTIONAL 396-CID, 375-HP V-8: Overhead-valve. Cast-iron block. Aluminum head with large valves. Bore and stroke: 4.09 x 3.76 in. Displacement: 396 cid (actually 402 cid). Compression ratio: 11.00:1. Brake hp: 375 at 5600 rpm. Taxable hp: 53.60. Torque: 415 lbs.-ft. at 3600. Five main bearings. Solid valve lifters. Crankcase capacity: 4 qt. (add 1 qt. for new filter). Cooling system capacity: 23 qt. (add 1 qt. for heater). Carburetor: Holley four-barrel. Sales code: L78/L89.

EL CAMINO OPTIONAL 454-CID, 360-HP V-8: Overhead-valve. Cast-iron block and head. Bore and stroke: 4.25 x 4.00 in. Displacement: 454 cid. Compression ratio: 10.25:1. Brake hp: 360 at 4400 rpm. Taxable hp: 57.80. Torque: 500 lbs.-ft. at 3200. Five main bearings. Hydraulic valve lifters. Crankcase capacity: 4 qt. (add 1 qt. for new filter). Cooling system capacity: 22 qt. (add 1 qt. for heater). Dual exhaust. Carburetor: Four-barrel. Sales code: LS5 (added midyear).

EL CAMINO OPTIONAL 454-CID, 450-HP V-8: Overhead-valve. Cast-iron block. Bore and stroke: 4.251 x 4.00 in. Displacement: 454 cid. Compression ratio: 11:25:1. Brake hp: 450 at 5600 rpm. Taxable hp: 57.80. Torque: 500 lbs.-ft. at 3600 rpm. Five main bearings. Solid valve lifters. High-performance camshaft. Crankcase capacity: 5 qt. (add 1 qt. for filter). Cooling system capacity: 21 qt. (add 1 qt. for heater). Carburetor: Holley four-barrel. Sales code: LS6 (added midyear).

CHASSIS

Wheelbase: 116 in. Overall length: 206.8 in. Height: 54.4 in. Front tread: 60.2 in. Rear tread: 59.2 in. Tires: F78 x 14. Gross vehicle weight: 4,100 lbs. Chevrolet manual transmission standard. Type of transmission: 3F/1R. Column-mounted gear shift lever standard. Clutch: Single-plate, dry-disc type. Rear axle: (semi-floating). Base rear axles: 3.08:1. Brakes: Four-wheel hydraulic, front disc/rear drum. Kelsey-Hayes pressed steel wheels.

OPTIONS

A01 tinted body glass. A02 tinted windshield. A31 electric windows. A39 front and rear seat belts with retractors. A41 four-way power seat. A42 Four-way electric front seat control. A46 power driver's bucket seat. A51 Astro bucket seats. A85 front shoulder belts. AK1 deluxe safety belts. AU3 power door locks. B37 floor mats. B85 belt reveal molding. B90 door edge and window frame moldings. B93 door edge guards. C08 vinyl top. C60 all-weather air conditioning. C75 automatic temperature control. CD2 windshield washer fluid level monitor. CD3 electro-tip windshield wiper control. D33 remote-control driver's mirror. D34 visor-vanity mirror. D55 front compartment floor console. D88 Super Sport striping. F40 heavy-duty suspension. F41 special performance suspension. G67 level-control rear shock absorbers. G80 Positraction. J50 power brakes. J52 front disc brakes. K05 engine block heater. K30 speed and cruise control. K85 63-amp. Delcotron. L48 350-cid four-barrel V-8. L65 350-cid two-barrel V-8. L78 396-cid special high-performance V-8. L89 aluminum cylinder heads. LF6 400-cid two-barrel V-8. LS3 400-cid four-barrel V-8. LS6 special high-performance 454-cid four-barrel V-8. M20 four-speed manual transmission. M21 four-speed close-ratio transmission. M22 heavy-duty four-speed manual transmission. M35 Powerglide automatic transmission. M38 three-speed automatic transmission. M40 three-speed automatic transmission. N10 dual exhaust. N33 tilt steering. N40 power steering. NA9 California evaporative emission controls. NK1 cushioned-rim steering wheel. P01 wheel trim covers. P02 simulated wire wheel covers. P06 wheel trim rings. P90 G70-15B white stripe tires. P91 G70-15B glass-belted red stripe tires. PA3 special wheel covers. PK2 G78-14 B glass-belted white stripe tires. PL3 E78-14 B glass-belted white

El Camino

stripe tires. PL4 F70-14 B glass-belted white stripe tires. PM6 G78-14 B glass-belted white stripe tires. PU8 G78-15 B glass-belted white stripe tires. PX6 F78-14 B glass-belted white stripe tires. PY4 F70-14 B glass-belted white stripe tires. PY5 F70-14 B glass-belted white red tires. PY7 G70-14 B glass-belted white red tires. T60 heavy-duty battery. U14 instrument panel gauges. U35 electric clock. U46 lamp monitoring. U63 push-button radio. U69 AM/FM push-button radio. U76 windshield antenna. U79 stereo radio. U80 auxiliary speaker. UM1 AM push-button radio and tape player. UM2 AM-FM push-button radio and tape player. V01 heavy-duty radiator. V31 front bumper guard. V32 rear bumper guard. YD1 trailering rear axle ratio. Z15 SS 454 package. Z25 SS 396 package. ZJ7 special hub caps and trim rings. ZJ9 auxiliary lighting group. ZL2 special ducted hood air system. ZQ9 performance ratio rear axle. 795 vinyl coated trim. 961-7 two-tone color combination.

HISTORICAL

September 18, 1969 was the introduction date for 1970 El Caminos.

The 1970 Chevelle options list included four-way electric bucket seats, power driver's seat, automatic temperature control, and other assorted goodies.

The 1971 El Camino, this one has the SS option, was recognizable by its new "ice cube tray" grille insert and bow tie in the center.

The El Camino models had a new look due to the use of single-unit Power Beam headlamps in square bezels. The grille had an "ice cube tray" insert and Chevrolet bow tie in its center. The front parking lamps were double-deck rectangles that angled around the body corners to double as side marker lights. El Camino nameplates and designation badges were mounted on the front fender sides, behind the wheel opening. The rear end appearance had hardly any changes. For the first time, the front bumper had no air slots or parking lamps in it. The Custom model now came only with a V-8 engine.

I.D. NUMBERS

The VIN is stamped on a plate on the top left side of the instrument panel and visible through the windshield. The first symbol 1 designates Chevrolet. The second and third symbols designate the series: (six-cylinder) 33=Deluxe El Camino, 35=Custom El Camino; (V-8) 36=Custom El Camino. The fourth and fifth symbols designate body type: 80=two-door sedan pickup. The sixth symbol designates the model year: 1=1971. The seventh symbol designates the assembly plant location: The seventh symbol indicated assembly plant: B=Baltimore, Maryland; F=Flint, Michigan; K-=Kansas City/Leeds, Missouri; L=Los Angles/Van Nuys, California; R=Arlington, Texas and 1-Oshawa, Canada. The last six symbols are the sequential unit production number at the specific factory. The Fisher body tag riveted to the top of the cowl on the left side of the car below the hood provides additional vehicle identification information. The Fisher Body STYLE NUMBER (ST) consists of a prefix identifying model year and four or more symbols identifying the series and body style (example: 71-13680 for a V-8-powered 1971 Custom El Camino). The BODY NUMBER consists of a prefix designating assembly plant and the sequential unit production number at the specific factory. The TRIM NUMBER (TR) identifies upholstery.

COLORS

(11) Antique White, (13) Nevada Silver Metallic, (19) Tuxedo Black, (24) Ascot Blue Metallic, (26) Mulsanne Blue Metallic, (42) Cottonwood Green Metallic, (43) Lime Green Metallic, (49) Antique Green Metallic, (52) Sunflower Yellow, (53) Placer Gold, (61) Sandalwood, (62) Burnt Orange, (67) Classic Copper, (75) Cranberry Red and (78) Rosewood.

ENGINE CODES

Codes appear on the right side of six-cylinder blocks behind the distributor and right front of V-8 engine blocks. Engine codes for 1971 were: (250-cid six) CAG, CAB, CAA; (307-cid V-8) CCA and CCB; (350-cid/245-hp V-8) CGA, CGB and CGC; (350-cid/270-hp V-8) CGK, CGL, CJD and CJJ; (396-cid/300-hp V-8) CLP, CLB, CLL, CLR and CLS; (454-cid/365-hp) CPA, CPG and CPD and (454-cid/425-hp) CPP, CPR and CPZ. Vinyl tops were available in five colors: AA=White, BB=Black, CC=Dark Blue, FF=Dark Brown and GG=Dark Green.

EL CAMINO — SERIES 33/34 — SIX/V-8

Standard models had bright windshield frames, back-up lights on the tailgate, and a base six-cylinder engine. A plain cloth and vinyl interior was standard. The colors were black, dark blue, dark jade green and sandalwood. The pickup box, used through 1972, had an outside width of 75 1/2 in. The inside width behind the cab was 59 in. and the inside width near the tailgate was 64 1/2 in. The width between the wheel housings was 44 in. The bottom bed length measured 79 1/4 in. Tailgate measurements were 54 1/2 x 22 1/2 in.

Model Number	Body/Style Number	Body Type & Seating	Factory Price	Shipping Weight	Production Total
EL CAMINO SERIES 33 (6-CYL)					
33	80	pickup	$2,886	3,302 lbs.	Note 1
EL CAMINO SERIES 34 (V-8)					
34	80	pickup	$2,983	3,418 lbs.	Note 1

EL CAMINO CUSTOM — SERIES 36 V-8

Customs added a V-8 as base engine, body side moldings, wheelhouse moldings, pickup box rim moldings, rear body corner moldings, two moldings on the tailgate, and silver anodized lower body perimeter. The Custom interior had vinyl seats with ribbed insert panels, color-keyed carpeting and imitation wood-grain trim. It came in black, light sandalwood, antique saddle knit-vinyl, dark saddle, dark blue or antique dark jade.

Model Number	Body/Style Number	Body Type & Seating	Factory Price	Shipping Weight	Production Total
EL CAMINO CUSTOM SERIES 36 (V-8)					
36	80	Custom pickup	$3,069	3,442 lbs.	Note 1

EL CAMINO CUSTOM SS 454 SERIES 36 + Z15 — V-8

Super Sport equipment (RPO Z15) was available for all Custom models with V-8s other than the base 307-cid V-8. You could get an SS 350, SS 396 (it actually had a 402-cid V-8), or SS 454. The basic SS package was $365 extra and the engine selections were separate options. The performance and appearance package included a black-accented grille with SS emblems, SS badges behind the front wheel cutouts, sport suspension, power front disc brakes, domed hood with lock pins, and 15 x 7 sport wheels with F60 x 15 raised white letter tires. By the end of the year, the 454-cid V-8 replaced the 396-cid V-8 completely.

Model Number	Body/Style Number	Body Type & Seating	Factory Price	Shipping Weight	Production Total
EL CAMINO CUSTOM SS 454 SERIES 36 + Z15 (V-8)					
34	80	pickup	—	—	Note 1

NOTE 1: Total El Camino production was 41,606.

ENGINES

EL CAMINO BASE SIX-CYL: Inline. Overhead-valve. Cast-iron block. Displacement: 250 cid. Bore and stroke: 3.875 x 3.53 in. Compression ratio: 8.5:1. Brake hp: 145 at 4200 rpm. Net brake hp: 110 at 3800 rpm. Taxable hp: 36. Torque: 230 lbs.-ft. at 1600 rpm. Seven main bearings. Hydraulic valve lifters. Crankcase capacity: 4 qt. (add 1 qt. for new filter). Cooling system capacity: 12 qt. (add 6 qt. for heater). Carburetor: Rochester one-barrel Model 7028017. Sales code L22. Available standard with three-speed fully synchronized manual transmission and Powerglide automatic transmission.

EL CAMINO BASE 307-CID, 140-HP V-8: Overhead-valve. Cast-iron block and head. Bore and stroke:

3.88 x 3.25 in. Displacement: 307 cid. Compression ratio: 8.50:1. Gross brake hp: 200 at 4600 rpm. Net brake hp: 140 at 4400 rpm. Taxable hp: 48.0. Gross torque: 300 lbs.-ft. at 2400. Net torque. 235 lbs.-ft. at 2400 rpm. Five main bearings. Hydraulic valve lifters. Crankcase capacity: 4 qt. (add 1 qt. for new filter). Cooling system capacity: 15 qt. (add 1 qt. for heater). Carburetor: Two-barrel. Available with three-speed manual, Powerglide automatic or Turbo-Hydra-Matic transmission.

EL CAMINO OPTIONAL 350-CID, 165-HP V-8: Overhead-valve. Cast-iron block and head. Bore and stroke: 4.00 x 3.48 in. Displacement: 350 cid. Compression ratio: 8.50:1. Gross brake hp: 245 at 4800 rpm. Net brake hp: 165 at 4000 rpm. Taxable hp: 51.20. Gross torque: 350 lbs.-ft. at 2800. Net torque: 280 lbs.-ft. at 2400 rpm. Five main bearings. Hydraulic valve lifters. Crankcase capacity: 4 qt. (add 1 qt. for new filter). Cooling system capacity: 15 qt. (add 1 qt. for heater). Carburetor: Two-barrel. Sales code L65. Available with four-speed manual or Turbo-Hydra-Matic transmission.

EL CAMINO OPTIONAL 350-CID, 270-HP V-8: Overhead-valve. Cast-iron block and head. Bore and stroke: 4.00 x 3.48 in. Displacement: 350 cid. Compression ratio: 8.50:1. Gross brake hp: 270 at 4800 rpm. Net brake hp: 210 at 4400 rpm. Taxable hp: 51.20. Gross torque: 360 lbs.-ft. at 3200. Net torque: 300 lbs.-ft. at 2800 rpm. Five main bearings. Hydraulic valve lifters. Crankcase capacity: 4 qt. (add 1 qt. for new filter). Cooling system capacity: (full-size) 14 qt.; (others) 15 qt. (add 1 qt. for heater). Carburetor: Four-barrel. Sales code L48. Available with three-speed manual transmission with floor shift, four-speed manual transmission or Turbo-Hydra-Matic automatic transmission.

EL CAMINO OPTIONAL 402-CID, 300-HP V-8: Overhead-valve. Cast-iron block and head. Bore and stroke: 4.13 x 3.76 in. Displacement: 402 cid (400 cid). Compression ratio: 8.50:1. Gross brake hp: 300 at 4800 rpm. Net brake hp: 260 at 4400 rpm. Taxable hp: 54.50. Gross torque: 400 lbs.-ft. at 3200. Net torque. 345 lbs.-ft. at 3200 rpm. Five main bearings. Hydraulic valve lifters. Crankcase capacity: 4 qt. (add 1 qt. for new filter). Cooling system capacity: 22 qt. (add 1 qt. for heater). Carburetor: Four-barrel. Sales code LS3. Promoted as SS 396. Available with special three-speed manual transmission with floor shift, four-speed manual transmission or Turbo-Hydra-Matic automatic transmission.

EL CAMINO OPTIONAL 454-CID, 365-HP V-8: Overhead-valve. Cast-iron block and head. Bore and stroke: 4.25 x 4.00 in. Displacement: 454 cid. Compression ratio: 8.50:1. Gross brake hp: 365 at 4800 rpm. Net brake hp: 285 at 4000 rpm. Taxable hp: 57.80. Gross torque: 465 lbs.-ft. at 3200. Net torque. 390 lbs.-ft. at 3200 rpm. Five main bearings. Hydraulic valve lifters. Crankcase capacity: 4 qt. (add 1 qt. for new filter). Cooling system capacity: 21 qt. (add 1 qt. for heater). Dual exhaust. Carburetor: Four-barrel. Sales code LS5. Available with special four-speed manual transmission or Turbo-Hydra-Matic automatic transmission.

EL CAMINO OPTIONAL 454-CID, 425-HP V-8: Overhead-valve. Cast-iron block and head. Bore and stroke: 4.25 x 4.00 in. Displacement: 454 cid. Compression ratio: 9.00:1. Gross brake hp: 425 at 5600 rpm. Net brake hp: 325 at 5600 rpm. Taxable hp: 57.80. Gross

Vinyl tops were available in five colors on the 1971 El Camino.

torque: 475 lbs.-ft. at 4000. Net torque: 390 lbs.-ft. at 3600 rpm. Five main bearings. Hydraulic valve lifters. Crankcase capacity: 4 qt. (add 1 qt. for new filter). Cooling system capacity: 21 qt. (add 1 qt. for heater). Dual exhaust. Carburetor: Four-barrel. Sales code LS6. Available with special four-speed manual transmission or Turbo-Hydra-Matic automatic transmission

CHASSIS

Wheelbase: 116 in. Overall length: 206.8 in. Height: 54.4 in. Front tread: 60.2. Rear tread: 59.2 in. Tires: E78 x 14B. Gross vehicle weight: 4,100 lbs. Saginaw manual, fully synchronized, transmission. Speeds: 3F/1R. Column-mounted gearshift lever. Single-plate dry-disc clutch (six-cylinder) or coil spring single-dry-plate (V-8). Rear axle: semi-floating. Hydraulic, four-wheel brakes. Kelsey-Hayes pressed steel wheels.

OPTIONS

A01 tinted body glass. A02 tinted windshield. A31 electric windows. A39 front and rear seat belts with retractors. A41 four-way power seat. A42 six-way electric front seat control. A46 power driver's bucket seat. A51 Astro bucket seats. A85 front shoulder belts. AK1 deluxe safety belts. AU3 power door locks. B37 floor mats. B85 belt reveal molding. B90 door edge and window frame moldings. B93 door edge guards. C08 vinyl top. C60 all-weather air conditioning. C75 automatic temperature control. D33 remote-control driver's mirror. D34 visor-vanity mirror. D55 front compartment floor console. D88 Super Sport striping. F40 heavy-duty suspension. F41 special performance suspension. G67 level-control rear shock absorbers. G80 Positraction. J50 power brakes. J52 front disc brakes. JL2 front disc brakes. K85 63-amp. Delcotron. L48 350-cid four-barrel V-8. L65 350-cid two-barrel V-8. L78 396-cid special high-performance V-8. LS3 402-cid four-barrel V-8. LS5 454-cid four-barrel V-8. M11 floor shifter. M20 four-speed manual transmission. M22 heavy-duty four-speed manual transmission. M35 Powerglide automatic transmission. M38 three-speed automatic transmission. M40 three-speed automatic transmission. MC1 heavy-duty three-speed manual transmission. N33 tilt steering. N40 power steering. NK2 Deluxe vinyl steering wheel. NK4 sport steering wheel. P01 wheel trim covers. P02 simulated wire wheel covers. P90 G70-15B white stripe tires. PA3 special wheel covers. PK2 G78-14B glass-belted white stripe tires. PL3 E78-14B glass-belted white stripe tires. PM6 G78-14B glass-belted white stripe tires. PM7 F60-15B glass-belted white-letter tires. PU8 G78-15B glass-belted white stripe tires. PX6 F78-14B glass-belted white stripe tires. T60 heavy-duty battery. U14 instrument panel gauges. U35 electric clock. U63 push-button radio. U69 AM/FM push-button radio. U76 windshield antenna. U79 stereo radio. U80 auxiliary speaker. UM1 AM push-button radio and tape player. UM2 AM-FM push-button radio and tape player. V01 heavy-duty radiator. V30 bumper guards. YD1 trailering rear axle ratio. Z15 SS 454 package. ZJ7 special hubcaps and trim rings ZJ9 auxiliary lighting group. ZL2 special ducted hood air system. ZQ9 performance ratio rear axle.

HISTORICAL

Production start-up date 1971 models was Aug. 21, 1970. They hit the showrooms one month and eight days later (Sept. 29, 1970). All 1971 Chevrolet truck engines were modified to operate on unleaded gasoline. Front disc brakes were standard on all conventional light-duty models. A big recovery from strike-year 1970 made this a banner season. Several Chevrolet factories ran six days a week, all year, to keep up with demand. A.T. Olson was assistant general sales manager of the Chevrolet truck division. The division also started producing a new, badge-engineered version of the El Camino that was sold as the GMC Sprint.

Larger, one-piece corner lights were seen on the El Camino. They bent around the body corners to double as side markers. The grille had a cross-hatch pattern, but four horizontal moldings with bright finish stood out the most. They split the grille into three horizontal segments. The center bow tie emblem of 1971 was replaced with Chevrolet letters at the left-hand side of the lower grille segment. El Camino nameplates and designation badges were mounted on the front fender sides, behind the wheel opening. The rear end appearance had hardly any changes. The front bumper had no air slots or parking lamps in it.

I.D. NUMBERS

The VIN is stamped on a plate on the top left side of the instrument panel and visible through the windshield. The first symbol 1 designates Chevrolet. The second symbol designate the series: C=El Camino and D=Custom El Camino. The third and fourth symbols designate body type: 80=two-door sedan pickup. The fifth symbol designates the engine: D=250-cid in-line one-barrel six-cylinder; F=307-cid two-barrel V-8, H=350-cid two-barrel V-8, J=350-cid four-barrel V-8, U=402-cid four-barrel V-08 and W=454-cid four-barrel V-8. The sixth symbol designates the model year: 2=1972. The seventh symbol indicated assembly plant: B=Baltimore, Maryland; F=Flint, Michigan; K-=Kansas City/Leeds, Missouri; L=Los Angles/Van Nuys, California; R=Arlington, Texas and 1-Oshawa, Canada. The last six symbols are the sequential unit production number at the specific factory. The Fisher body tag riveted to the top of the cowl on the left side of the car below the hood provides additional vehicle identification information. The Fisher body STYLE NUMBER (ST) consists of a prefix identifying

EL CAMINO

The Super Sport package (RPO Z15) was available on all 1972 El Camino Custom models except the base 307-cid V-8. This SS 454 was ordered with a white vinyl top.

model year and more symbols identifying the series and body style (example: 72-1D80 for a 1972 Custom El Camino). The BODY NUMBER consists of a prefix designating assembly plant and the sequential unit production number at the specific factory. The TRIM NUMBER (TR) identifies upholstery

COLORS

(11) Antique White, (14) Pewter Silver, (18) Dusk Gray Poly, (19) Tuxedo Black, (24) Ascot Blue Poly, (25) Mediterranean Blue Poly, (26) Mulsanne Blue, (28) Fathom Blue Poly, (36) Spring Green Poly, (43) Gulf Green Poly, (46) Oasis Green Poly, (48) Sequoia Green Poly, (50) Covert Tan, (53) Placer Gold Poly, (54) Desert Gold Poly, (56) Cream Yellow, (57) Golden Brown Poly, (58) Turin Tan, (62) Driftwood, (63) Mohave Gold Poly, (65) Orange Flame Poly, (68) Midnight Bronze Poly, (69) Agean Brown and (75) Cranberry Red. Vinyl tops were available in five colors: AA=White, BB=Black, DD=Blue, GG=Green and TT=Covert Tan.

ENGINE CODES

Codes appear on the right side of six-cylinder blocks behind the distributor and right front of V-8 engine blocks. Engine codes for 1972 were: (250-cid six) CDM, CDL, CBJ, CBG, CSD, CBA, CBK, CBD and CAH; (307-cid V-8) CKG, CKH, CAY, CAZ and CMA; (350-cid two-barrel V-8) CKA, CTL, CSH, CDA, CMD, CAR and CDB; (350-cid four-barrel V-8) CKK, CKD, CDG, CDD and CKB; (402/396-cid V-8) CLA, CLB, CTA and CTB; (400-cid V-8) CLS, CTJ and CTH; (454-cid V-8) CPA, CPD, CRX and CRW.

EL CAMINO — SERIES C — SIX/V-8

Standard models had bright windshield frames, back-up lights on the tailgate and a base six-cylinder engine. The pickup box still had an outside width of 75 1/2 in. Inside width behind the cab was 59 in. Inside width near the tailgate was 64 1/2 in. The width between the wheel housings was 44 in. El Camino interiors came in black, antique covert tan vinyl and cloth-and-vinyl combinations, as well as Pinta fabric combinations. The "flying buttress" roofline was retained for all El Caminos The bottom bed length measured 79 1/4 in. Tailgate measurements were 54 1/2 x 22 1/2 in. This was the last year for this El Camino pickup box. An unusual dealer option costing about $65 extra was a "Flame Chevy '73" decal kit.

Model Number	Body/Style Number	Body Type & Seating	Factory Price	Shipping Weight	Production Total
EL CAMINO SERIES C (6-CYL)					
33	80	pickup	$2,790	3,302 lbs.	Note 1
EL CAMINO SERIES C (V-8)					
34	80	pickup	$2,880	3,418 lbs.	Note 1

EL CAMINO CUSTOM — SERIES D SIX/V-8

El Camino Customs added a V-8 as base engine, all bright window frames, body side moldings, wheel house moldings, pickup box rim moldings, rear body corner moldings, two moldings on the tailgate and a silver anodized lower body perimeter.

Model Number	Body/Style Number	Body Type & Seating	Factory Price	Shipping Weight	Production Total
EL CAMINO CUSTOM SERIES D (V-8)					
36	80	Custom pickup	$2,960	$3,442	Note 1

EL CAMINO CUSTOM SS — SERIES D SIX/V-8

Super Sport equipment (RPO Z15) was available for all Custom models with V-8s other than the base 307-cid V-8. You could get an SS 350, SS 396 (actually a 402-cid engine) or SS 454. The basic SS (Super Sport) package cost less than last year. It was a $350 option. The engine selected by the buyer was a separate option. The basic SS package included a black-accented grille with SS badges, cowl badges, hood locking pins, styled wheels, special vertically pleated door panels, round instrument panel gauges, sport suspension, power front disc brakes, and 15 x 7 Sport wheels with F60 x 15 raised white-letter tires. The 396-cid engine was gone, although the 402-cid V-8-powered trucks were promoted as SS 396 models.

Model Number	Body/Style Number	Body Type & Seating	Factory Price	Shipping Weight	Production Total
EL CAMINO CUSTOM SERIES D (V-8)					
36	80	Custom pickup	$3,310	—	Note 1

NOTE 1 Total El Camino production was 57,147.

ENGINES

EL CAMINO BASE 250-CID, 110-HP SIX-CYL: Inline. Overhead-valve. Cast-iron block. Displacement: 250 cid. Bore and stroke: 3.875 x 3.53 in. Compression ratio: 8.5:1. Brake hp: 145 at 4200 rpm. Net brake hp: 110 at 3800 rpm. Taxable hp: 36. Torque: 230 lbs.-ft. at 1600 rpm. Seven main bearings. Hydraulic valve lifters. Crankcase capacity: 4 qt. (add 1 qt. for new filter). Cooling system capacity: 12 qt (add 6 qt. for heater). Carburetor: Rochester one-barrel Model 7028017. Sales code L22. Available standard with three-speed fully synchronized manual transmission and Powerglide automatic transmission.

EL CAMINO BASE 307-CID, 130-HP V-8: Overhead-valve. Cast-iron block and head. Bore and stroke: 3.88 x 3.25 in. Displacement: 307 cid. Compression ratio: 8.50:1. Net brake hp: 130 at 4000 rpm. Taxable hp: 48. Net torque. 230 lbs.-ft. at 2400 rpm. Five main bearings. Hydraulic valve lifters. Crankcase capacity: 4 qt. (add 1 qt. for new filter). Cooling system capacity: 14 qt.; (add 1 qt. for heater). Carburetor: Two-barrel.

EL CAMINO OPTIONAL 350-CID, 165-HP V-8: Overhead-valve. Cast-iron block and head. Bore and stroke: 4.00 x 3.48 in. Displacement: 350 cid. Compression ratio: 8.50:1. Net brake hp: 165 at 4000 rpm. Taxable hp: 51.20. Net torque: 280 lbs.-ft. at 2400 rpm. Five main bearings. Hydraulic valve lifters. Crankcase capacity: 4 qt. (add 1 qt. for new filter). Cooling system capacity: 15 qt. (add 1 qt. for heater). Sales code L65. Carburetor: Two-barrel.

EL CAMINO OPTIONAL V-8 350-CID, 175-HP V-8: Overhead-valve. Cast-iron block and head. Bore and stroke: 4.00 x 3.48 in. Displacement: 350 cid. Compression ratio: 8.50:1. Net brake hp: 175 at 4000 rpm. Taxable hp: 51.20. Net torque: 280 lbs.-ft. at 2400 rpm. Five main bearings. Hydraulic valve lifters. Crankcase capacity: 4 qt. (add 1 qt. for new filter). Cooling system capacity: 15 qt. (add 1 qt. for heater). Sales code: L48. Carburetor: Four-barrel.

EL CAMINO OPTIONAL V-8 396-CID, 240-HP V-8: Overhead-valve. Cast-iron block and head. Bore and

Bucket seats remained an option for the 1972 El Caminos.

stroke: 4.126 x 3.76 in. Displacement: 402 cid (a.k.a. 396 cid). Compression ratio: 8.50:1. Net brake hp: 240 at 4400 rpm. Taxable hp: 54.50. Net torque: 345 lbs.-ft. at 3200 rpm. Five main bearings. Hydraulic valve lifters. Crankcase capacity: 4 qt. (add 1 qt. for new filter). Cooling system capacity: 22 qt. (add 1 qt. for heater). Sales code LS3. Carburetor: Four-barrel.

EL CAMINO SS 454 OPTIONAL 454-CID, 270-HP V-8: Overhead-valve. Cast-iron block and head. Bore and stroke: 4.251 x 4.00 in. Displacement: 454 cid. Compression ratio: 8.50:1. Net brake hp: 270 at 4000 rpm. Taxable hp: 57.80. Net torque: 390 lbs.-ft. at 3200 rpm. Five main bearings. Hydraulic valve lifters. Crankcase capacity: 4 qt. (add 1 qt. for new filter). Cooling system capacity: 22 qt. (add 1 qt. for heater). Dual exhaust. Sales code: LS5. Carburetor: Four-barrel.

CHASSIS

Wheelbase: 116 in. Overall length: 206.8 in. Height: 54.4 in. Front tread: 60.2 in. Rear tread: 59.2 in. Tires: E78-14B. Transmission: Three-speed synchromesh. Gears: 3F/1R. Column-mounted gearshift lever. Single-plate, dry-disc clutch (250-cid engine), coil-spring single-dry-plate (307/350/402/454-cid engines). Rear axle: semi-floating. Hydraulic four-wheel brakes. Kelsey-Hayes pressed steel wheels.

OPTIONS

A01 tinted body glass. A02 tinted windshield. A31 electric windows. A39 front and rear seat belts with retractors. A41 four-way power seat. A42 six-way electric front seat control. A46 power driver's bucket seat. A51 Astro bucket seats. A85 front shoulder belts. AK1 deluxe safety belts. AU3 power door locks. B37 floor mats. B84 body side moldings. B85 belt reveal molding. B90 door edge and window frame moldings. B93 door edge guards. C08 vinyl top. C60 all-weather air conditioning. C75 automatic temperature control. D33

EL CAMINO

remote-control driver's mirror. D34 visor-vanity mirror. D55 front compartment floor console. D88 Super Sport striping. F40 heavy-duty suspension. F41 special performance suspension. G67 level-control rear shock absorbers. G80 Positraction. J50 power brakes. JL2 front disc brakes. K30 speed and cruise control. K85 63-amp. Delcotron. L48 350-cid four-barrel V-8. L65 350-cid two-barrel V-8. LS3 402-cid four-barrel V-8. LS5 454-cid four-barrel V-8. M11 floor shifter. M20 four-speed manual transmission. M22 heavy-duty four-speed manual transmission. M35 Powerglide automatic transmission. M38 three-speed automatic transmission. M40 three-speed automatic transmission. MC1 heavy-duty three-speed manual transmission. N33 tilt steering. N40 power steering. NK2 deluxe vinyl steering wheel. NK4 sport steering wheel. P01 wheel trim covers. P02 simulated wire wheel covers. P90 G70-15B white stripe tires. PA3 special wheel covers. PK2 G78-14B glass-belted white stripe tires. PL3 E78-14B glass-belted white stripe tires. PM6 G78-14B glass-belted white stripe tires. PM7 F60-15B glass-belted white-letter tires. PU8 G78-15 B glass-belted white stripe tires. PX6 F78-14B glass-belted white stripe tires. T60 heavy-duty battery. U14 instrument panel gauges. U35 electric clock. U63 push-button radio. U69 AM/FM push-button radio. U76 windshield antenna. U79 stereo radio. U80 auxiliary speaker. UM1 AM push-button radio and tape player. UM2 AM-FM push-button radio and tape player. V01 heavy-duty radiator. V30 bumper guards. YD1 trailering rear axle ratio. YF5 California assembly line emissions test. Z15 SS 454 package. ZJ7 special hubcaps and trim rings. ZJ9 auxiliary lighting group. ZL2 special ducted hood air system. ZQ9 performance ratio rear axle.

HISTORICAL FOOTNOTES

Introduced Sept. 21, 1971. Calendar-year registrations: (Nova Sportvan) 16,839. (others) 774,871, including 165,829 Chevy Van/El Caminos/Blazer/Vega/LUV. Calendar-year registrations by weight class: (6,000 lbs. and less) 539,242. During 1972, Chevrolet predicted that it would have its first 1 million unit truck year in 1973. A.T. Olson was assistant general sales manager, the top spot in the truck division.

The redesigned 1973 El Camino was slightly taller, 5 in. longer, and boasted a few stylish upgrades, including optional swivel bucket seats.

The El Camino received its first new body since 1968. Chevrolet gave its popular sedan-pickup, based on the mid-size Chevelle, new looks, a bit more length and cleaner exhaust. The SS 454 high-performance option was carried over. The trucks were a bit taller than the previous models and about 5 in longer overall. All models had impact-resistant front bumpers and were said to be substantially improved in roadability, comfort and styling.

Engine choices included a de-tuned version of the 250-cid in-line six, a base 307-cid V-8 and two versions of the 350-cid V-8. The base series was called the El Camino and was comparable to the Chevelle Deluxe. The one-step-up line was called the El Camino Custom and was comparable to a Malibu passenger car. The SS 454 option was available for the El Camino Custom. Estate and Conquista packages were offered, too. Since these are all collectible we are looking at each as a separate model-option below.

I.D. NUMBERS

VIN embossed on the top left-hand side of the instrument panel and visible through the windshield. The first symbol 1 designates Chevrolet. The second symbol indicates series: C=El Camino; D=El Camino Custom. The third and fourth symbols indicate body style: 80=two-door pickup delivery. The fifth symbol indicates engine (net horsepower): D=250-cid 100-hp inline six-cylinder; F=307-cid 115-hp V-8, H=350-cid 145-hp V-8, K=350-cid 175-hp V-8 and Y=454-cid 245-hp V-8. The sixth symbol designates the model year: 3=1973. The seventh symbol designates the assembly plant location: B=Baltimore, Maryland; K=Leeds, Missouri; Z=Fremont, California, R=Arlington, Texas, 1=Oshawa, Canada. The last six symbols are the sequential unit production number at the specific factory. The Fisher body tag riveted to the top of the cowl on the left side of the car below the hood provides additional vehicle identification information. The Fisher Body STYLE NUMBER (ST) consists of a prefix identifying model year and four or more symbols identifying the series and body style (example: 73-1D80 for a 1973 El Camino Custom). The BODY NUMBER consists of a prefix designating assembly plant and the sequential unit production number at the specific factory. The TRIM NUMBER (TR) identifies upholstery.

COLORS

(11) Antique White, (19) Tuxedo Black, (23) Medium Blue, (24) Light Blue Metallic, (26) Dark Blue Metallic, (29) Midnight Blue Metallic, (42) Dark Green Metallic, (44) Light Green Metallic, (46) Green-Gold Metallic, (48) Midnight Green, (51) Light Yellow, (56) Chamois, (60) Light Copper Metallic, (64) Silver Metallic, (66) Taupe Metallic, (68) Dark Brown Metallic, (74) Dark Red Metallic, (75) Medium Red Metallic, (81) Beige, (86) Bright Orange and (97) Medium Orange. Vinyl tops were available in five colors: AA=White, BB=Black, DD=Medium Blue, FF=Chamois, GG=Medium Green, HH=Dark Red and TT=Light Neutral. Convertible tops came in black or white.

ENGINE CODES

Codes appear on the right side of six-cylinder blocks behind the distributor and right front of V-8 engine blocks. Engine codes for 1973 were: (250-cid six) CCK, CBD, CCA, CCB, CCC and CCD; (307 cid V-8) CHD, CHA, CHB, CHC and CMA; (350 two-barrel V-8) CKM, CKR, CKA, CKL, CKB, CKC and CKK; (350-cid four-barrel V-8) CKH, CKD and CKJ; (454 cid V-8) CWC, CWD, CWR, CWA and CWB.

EL CAMINO — SERIES C — 6-CYL/V-8

Standard equipment on all 1973 El Caminos included a bright El Camino nameplate on the left-hand grille panel, a bright Chevrolet grille center emblem, bright back window reveal moldings, a bright El Camino nameplate on the lower right-hand side of the tailgate, chrome front and rear bumpers, bright door lock handles, bright door lock cylinder covers, bright El Camino nameplates on the front fender sides, a bright grille outer edge molding, a bright headlight bezel bead, a bright hood molding, bright hub caps, a bright left-hand outside rearview mirror, bright body side, tailgate, drip rail and wheel opening moldings, bright windshield reveal moldings, side doors with a lift-bar latch release and key lock cylinders, a rear tailgate with a single-handle double-latch mechanism, safety glass (in windshield, back glass and side windows), an Argent Silver plastic grid grille insert, instrument panel knobs marked with function symbols, back-up lights, two single-lens front park/turn lights, two Class A rear lamps with tail/stop/signal and side marker functions, two Power-Beam headlights, a single rear license plate light, win front and rear side marker lights, a single D note horn, steel side door guard beams, a mechanical jack and wheel lug nut wrench, partial under body and full wheel well undercoating, body-color steel wheels, two-speed electric windshield wipers with hideaway wipers and arms, left- and right-hand cowl air vents with individual controls, dual armrests, bright seat back latch and adjuster knobs, bright window regulator knobs, a cigarette lighter, color-coordinated upholstery with black trim, a door-actuated dome lamp, push-button door locks, closed-cell rubber door seals, color-keyed vinyl covered rubber floor mats, a speedometer, an odometer, a fuel gauge, directional signals with a lane-change feature, a hazard warning, a heater and defroster, warning lights (for generator, oil pressure, temperature, brake-on, directionals and headlight high beams), a fiberglass-filled plastic instrument panel, sound deadening insulation, a 12-in. inside rearview mirror, full-width seats with textured all-vinyl trim, seat and shoulder safety belts, a black-grained plastic steering wheel with soft rim and brushed chrome insert with the Chevrolet name, dual sun shades, side door opening scuff plates and floor mat retainers, a spare tire carrier behind the driver seating position, a lockable steering column, vinyl door trim panels with bright trim, vinyl-coated cowl side panels, a vinyl-coated headliner, an ignition key warning buzzer, bright metal window regulators, padded windshield pillars, a 250-cid in-line six-cylinder engine, three-speed manual transmission and G78-14B black sidewall tires.

Model Number	Body/Style Number	Body Type & Seating	Factory Price	Shipping Weight	Production Total
EL CAMINO SERIES C (6-CYL)					
C	80	pickup	$2,860	3,525 lbs.	Note 1
EL CAMINO SERIES C (V-8)					
C	80	pickup	$2,976	3,625 lbs.	Note 1

EL CAMINO CONQUISTA — SERIES C 6-CYL/V-8

Late in the model year the Conquista trim option was released for the El Camino. This was initially considered a "special edition" model. In addition to base El Camino features, the Conquista package included extra front fender, body side moldings and tailgate moldings that set off a special two-tone paint scheme. The hood and a stripe extending down the body sides and around the tailgate were finished in one color. The top of the cab, the upper portion of the pickup box and the entire lower body perimeter were finished in a second contrasting color. The Conquista package was promoted in a two-page advertisement in the August 1973 issue of *Hot Rod* magazine. The price of this package was not listed in our regular sources, probably because it arrived late in the year.

Model Number	Body/Style Number	Body Type & Seating	Factory Price	Shipping Weight	Production Total
EL CAMINO SERIES C (6-CYL)					
C	80	pickup	—	—	Note 1
EL CAMINO SERIES C (V-8)					
C	80	pickup	—	—	Note 1

EL CAMINO CUSTOM — SERIES D V-8

In addition to standard El Camino equipment, the El Camino Custom included a 307-cid V-8 engine, lower body sill moldings, color-keyed carpeting, a choice of Black or Light Neutral color interior trim, a deluxe vinyl-coated headliner, an instrument with a panel crown pad and dull paint finish, an inside rearview mirror with black finish on the back and mirror support and a full-width seat with custom vinyl trim.

Model Number	Body/Style Number	Body Type & Seating	Factory Price	Shipping Weight	Production Total
D	80	Pickup	$3,038	3,635 lbs.	Note 1

EL CAMINO CUSTOM CONQUISTA SERIES D — 6-CYL/V-8

The late-in-the-year Conquista trim option was also available for the El Camino Custom. This combined the special Conquista trim and two-tone paint finish with the extra features characteristic of an El Camino Custom model.

Model Number	Body/Style Number	Body Type & Seating	Factory Price	Shipping Weight	Production Total
D	80	pickup	—	—	Note 1

EL CAMINO CUSTOM ESTATE SERIES D + YA2 — V-8

Accentuating the appearance of the El Camino Custom, which was essentially that of the Chevelle Malibu, was a new Estate trim package. It consisted of full body side and tailgate accents with a wood-grain vinyl trim. Chrome scripts calling out the "Estate" name were located on the front fenders below the El Camino nameplates. Also included were special vinyl-covered pattern door trim panels. The price of the Estate package was $161.

Model Number	Body/Style Number	Body Type & Seating	Factory Price	Shipping Weight	Production Total
D	80	pickup	$3,199	—	Note 1

EL CAMINO CUSTOM SS — SERIES D + YA2 — V-8

Chevrolet continued to list a Super Sport equipment package for the 1973 El Camino. In addition to or in place of the standard El Camino Custom equipment listed above, the SS equipment package included a black-finished grille with an SS emblem, a remote-control left-hand outside Sport style rearview mirror, a manual right-hand Sport style outside rearview mirror, SS fender emblems, SS door trim, and SS steering wheel, an SS emblem above the rear bumper, bright roof drip moldings, lower body side and wheel opening stripes keyed to the body color, black-accented taillight frames, a special instrument cluster, special front and rear stabilizer bars, 14 x 7-in. Rallye wheels with special center caps and trim rings and G70 x 14 white letter tires. The cost of the SS equipment package was $280 and the prices given below represent the price of the standard-equipped Custom El Camino model plus $280.

Model Number	Body/Style Number	Body Type & Seating	Factory Price	Shipping Weight	Production Total
D	80	pickup	$3,318	—	Note 1

NOTE 1 Total El Camino production was 64,987.

ENGINES

EL CAMINO BASE 250-CID, 100-HP SIX-CYL: Inline. Overhead-valve. Cast-iron block. Displacement: 250 cid. Bore and stroke: 3.875 x 3.53 in. Compression ratio: 8.25:1. Net brake hp: 100 at 3800 rpm. Taxable hp: 36. Torque: 175 at 1600 rpm. Seven main bearings. Hydraulic valve lifters. Crankcase capacity: 4 qt. (add 1 qt. for new filter). Cooling system capacity: 12 qt (add 6 qt. for heater). Carburetor: Rochester one-barrel Model 7028017. Sales code L22.

EL CAMINO BASE 307-CID, 115-HP V-8: Overhead-valve. Cast-iron block and head. Bore and stroke: 3.88 x 3.25 in. Displacement: 307 cid. Compression ratio: 8.50:1. Net brake hp: 115 at 4000 rpm. Taxable hp: 48. Net torque. 205 lbs.-ft. at 2000 rpm. Five main bearings. Hydraulic valve lifters. Crankcase capacity: 4 qt. (add 1 qt. for new filter). Cooling system capacity: 15 qt.; (add 1 qt. for heater). Carburetor: Two-barrel.

EL CAMINO OPTIONAL 350-CID, 145-HP V-8: Overhead-valve. Cast-iron block and head. Bore and stroke: 4.00 x 3.48 in. Displacement: 350 cid. Compression ratio: 8.50:1. Net brake hp: 145 at 4000 rpm. Taxable hp: 51.20. Net torque: 255 lbs.-ft. at 2400 rpm. Five main bearings. Hydraulic valve lifters. Crankcase capacity: 4 qt. (add 1 qt. for new filter). Cooling system capacity: (Nova) 17 qt.; (Chevrolet) 16 qt. (others) 15 qt. (add 1 qt. for heater). Carburetor: Two-barrel. Sales code L65.

EL CAMINO OPTIONAL V-8: Overhead-valve. Cast-iron block and head. Bore and stroke: 4.00 x 3.48 in. Displacement: 350 cid. Compression ratio: 8.50:1. Net brake hp: 175 at 4000 rpm. Taxable hp: 51.20. Net torque: 270 lbs.-ft. at 2400 rpm. Five main bearings. Hydraulic valve lifters. Crankcase capacity: 4 qt. (add 1 qt. for new filter). Cooling system capacity: (Nova) 17 qt.; (Chevrolet) 16 qt. (others) 15 qt. (add 1 qt. for heater). Carburetor: Four-barrel. Sales code L48.

EL CAMINO OPTIONAL V-8: Overhead-valve. Cast-iron block and head. Bore and stroke: 4.25 x 4.00 in. Displacement: 454 cid. Compression ratio: 8.50:1. Net brake hp: 245 at 4000 rpm. Taxable hp: 57.80. Net torque. 375 lbs.-ft. at 2800 rpm. Five main bearings. Hydraulic valve lifters. Crankcase capacity: 4 qt. (add 1 qt. for new filter). Cooling system capacity: (Chevelle, Monte Carlo) 22 qt.; (Chevrolet) 23 qt. (add 1 qt. for heater). Dual exhaust. Carburetor: Four-barrel. Sales code LS5.

CHASSIS

Wheelbase: 116 in. Overall length: 216.25 in. Height: 54 in. Overall width: 76.75 in. Front tread: 58.5 in. Rear tread: 57.8 in. Load floor length 80.75 in. Cargo box length from back of cab to top of tailgate: 71.50 in. Cargo box height: 13.50 in. Bed width between rear wheel housings: 45.25 in. Maximum bed width: 58.50 in. Tires: G78-14B. Transmission: Three-speed synchromesh. Gears: 3F/1R. Column-mounted gearshift lever. Single-plate, dry-disc clutch (250-cid engine), coil-spring single-dry-plate (307/350/454-cid engines). Rear axle: semi-floating. Hydraulic four-wheel brakes. Kelsey-Hayes pressed steel wheels. (Note: The measurements given above are the basic specifications for all 1973-1975 El Camino models, but there may have been minor variations in some measurements from year to year).

OPTIONS

A01 tinted body glass. A02 tinted windshield. A31 electric windows. A42 six-way electric front seat control. AK1 deluxe safety belts. AN7 swivel front seat. AU3 power door locks. B37 floor mats. B80 roof drip moldings. B84 body side moldings. B93 door edge guards. B96 wheel opening moldings. C08 vinyl top. C60 all-weather air conditioning. D33 remote-control driver's mirror. D34 visor-vanity mirror. D35 custom remote-control left-hand outside rearview mirror. D55 front compartment floor console. F40 heavy-duty suspension. G80 Positraction. J50 power brakes. K30 speed and cruise control. K76 61-amp Delcotron. K85 63-amp. Delcotron. L48 350-cid four-barrel V-8. L65 350-cid two-barrel V-8. LS4 454-cid four-barrel V-8. M20 4-speed manual transmission. M21 close-ratio four-speed manual transmission. M38 three-speed automatic transmission. M40 three-speed automatic transmission. N33 tilt steering. N40 power steering. N95 simulated wire wheel cover. P01 wheel trim covers. PA3 special wheel covers. PE1 14 x 7 turbine wheels. PE2 15 x 7 custom wheels. T60 heavy-duty battery. QEH E78-14B white stripe tires. QGF G70-14B white-letter tires. QGL G78-14B white stripe tires. QGT G78-15B white stripe tires. QHF H78-14B white stripe tires. QRM GR70-15 steel-belted radial tires. U14 instrument panel gauges. U35 electric clock. U58 AM/FM stereo. U63 push-button radio. U69 AM/FM push-button radio. U76 windshield antenna. U80 auxiliary speaker. UM1 AM push-button radio and tape player. UM2 AM-FM push-button radio and tape player. V01 heavy-duty radiator. V30 bumper guards. VE5 bumper impact strip. YA2 El Camino Estate package. YD1 trailering rear axle ratio. YA7 California assembly line emissions test. YJ9 exterior décor package. Z15 SS 454 package. ZJ7 special hubcaps and trim rings. ZJ9 auxiliary lighting group. ZQ9 performance ratio rear axle.

OPTION INSTALLATION RATES

Automatic transmission (93.2 percent). Power brakes (93.3 percent). Disc brakes (100 percent). Power steering (96.1 percent). AM radio (78 percent). AM/FM stereo radio (16.6 percent). V-8 engine 350-cid or less (93.5 percent). V-8 engine over 350-cid (6.5 percent). Air conditioning (67.8 percent). Positraction (17.9 percent). Tinted glass (81.6 percent). Wheel covers (61.5 percent). Interior trim package (57.4 percent).

HISTORICAL FOOTNOTES

The 1973 Chevrolets went on sale on September 21, 1972. A.T. Olson was assistant general sales manager of Chevrolet's truck division for 1973. J.T. Riley was merchandising manager for light- and medium-duty trucks. Chevrolet had its sights set on its first 1 million truck sales year in 1973 and hit it. Total sales was a record 1,013,860 units. The milestone millionth vehicle rolled off the assembly line on December 19, 1973. Retail deliveries for 1973 totaled 1,055,273, wiping out the previous record for a calendar year set by Ford in 1972. For the second calendar year in a row, Chevrolet sold more trucks than it produced, which lowered dealer inventories.

Chevrolet introduced its 1974 mid-size lineup on September 20, 1973. A handsome new grille characterized the base El Camino models and the new El Camino Classic model, which was the top-of-the-line offering. The grille resembled a widened Mercedes-Benz grille. Against a background of fine vertical and horizontal bars the designers place two horizontal moldings that divided the grille into three segments and a single vertical center molding that split the three segments into six. The grille no longer extended below the taillights, which were round-lens units set into bright square housings with rounded corners.

I.D. NUMBERS

VIN embossed on the top left-hand side of the instrument panel and visible through the windshield. The first symbol 1 designates Chevrolet. The second symbol indicates series: C=El Camino; D=El Camino Classic. The third and fourth symbols indicate body style: 80=two-door pickup delivery. The fifth symbol indicates engine (net hp): D=250-cid 100-hp inline six-cylinder, H=350-cid 145-hp V-8, L=350-cid 160-hp V-8, R=400-cid 180-hp V-8, U=400-cid 180-hp V-8 and Y=454-cid 235-hp V-8. The sixth symbol designates the model year: 4=1974. The seventh symbol designates the assembly plant loca-

EL CAMINO

The Conquista package, which was mainly a two-tone paint scheme, was avialable on both the El Camino and El Camino Classic.

tion: B=Baltimore, Maryland, D=Doraville, Georgia, K=Leeds, Missouri, Z=Fremont, California, R=Arlington, Texas and 1=Oshawa, Canada. The last six symbols are the sequential unit production number at the specific factory. The Fisher body tag riveted to the top of the cowl on the left side of the car below the hood provides additional vehicle identification information. The Fisher body STYLE NUMBER (ST) consists of a prefix identifying model year and four or more symbols identifying the series and body style (example: 74-1D80 for a 1974 El Camino Classic V-8). The BODY NUMBER consists of a prefix designating assembly plant and the sequential unit production number at the specific factory. The TRIM NUMBER (TR) identifies upholstery.

COLORS

(11) Antique White, (19) Tuxedo Black, (24) Light Blue Poly, (26) Bright Blue Poly, (29) Midnight Blue Poly, (36) Aqua Blue Poly, (40) Lime-Yellow, (44) Medium Green Poly, (46) Bright Green Poly, (49) Medium Dark Green Poly, (50) Cream Beige, (51) Bright Yellow, (53) Bright Gold Poly, (55) Sandstone, (59) Golden Brown Poly, (64) Silver Poly, (66) Bronze Poly, (68) Dark Brown Poly, (69) Dark Taupe Poly, (74) Medium Red Poly, (75) Medium Red and (86) Bright Orange. Vinyl tops were available in: AA=White, BB=Black, DD=Medium Blue, EE=Cream Beige, FF=Brown, GG=Medium Green, HH=Dark Red, LL=Russet, RR=Medium Saddle and WW=Silver Taupe.

ENGINE CODES

Codes appear on the right side of six-cylinder blocks behind the distributor and right front of V-8 engine blocks. Codes for 1974 were: (250-cid/100-hp six) CCX, CCR and CCW; (350-cid/145-hp V-8 two-barrel V-8) CMC and CMR; (350-cid/160-hp four-barrel V-8) CKH and CKD; (400-cid/150-hp V-8) CSU, CSX and CTA; (400-cid/180-hp V-8) CTC; (454-cid 235-hp V-8) CWA, CWX, CWD, CXM, CXR and CXS.

EL CAMINO — SERIES C — 6-CYL/V-8

Standard equipment on base El Caminos included a bright El Camino nameplate on the left-hand grille panel, a bright Chevrolet grille center emblem, bright back window reveal moldings, a bright El Camino nameplate on the lower right-hand side of the tailgate, chrome front and rear bumpers, bright door lock handles, bright door lock cylinder covers, bright El Camino nameplates on the front fender sides, a bright grille outer edge molding, a bright headlight bezel bead, a bright hood molding, bright hubcaps, a bright left-hand outside rearview mirror, bright body side, tailgate, drip rail and wheel opening moldings, bright windshield reveal moldings, side doors with a lift-bar latch release and key lock cylinders, a rear tailgate with a single-handle double latch mechanism, safety glass (in windshield, back glass and side windows), an Argent Silver plastic grid grille insert, instrument panel knobs marked with function symbols, back-up lights, two single-lens front park/turn lights, two class A rear lamps with tail/stop/signal and side marker functions, two Power-Beam headlights, a single rear license plate light, front and rear side marker lights, a single D note horn, steel side door guard beams, a mechanical jack and wheel lug nut wrench, partial under body and full-wheel well undercoating, body-color steel wheels, two-speed electric windshield wipers with hideaway wipers and arms, left- and right-hand cowl air vents with individual controls, dual armrests, bright seat back latch and adjuster knobs, bright window regulator knobs, a cigarette lighter, color-coordinated upholstery with black trim, a door-actuated dome lamp, push-button door locks, closed-cell rubber door seals, color-keyed vinyl covered rubber floor mats, a speedometer, an odometer, a fuel gauge, directional signals with a lane-change feature, a hazard warning, a heater and defroster, warning lights (for generator, oil pressure, temperature, brake-on, directionals and headlight high beams), a fiberglass-filled plastic instrument panel, sound deadening insulation, a 12-in. inside rearview mirror, full-width seats with textured all-vinyl trim, seat and shoulder safety belts, a black-grained plastic steering wheel with soft rim and brushed chrome insert with the Chevrolet name, dual sun shades, side door opening scuff plates and floor mat retainers, a spare tire carrier behind the driver seating position, a lockable steering column, vinyl door trim panels with bright trim, vinyl-coated cowl side panels, a vinyl-coated headliner, an ignition key warning buzzer, bright metal window regulators, padded windshield pillars, a 250-cid in-line six-cylinder engine, three-speed manual transmission and G78 x 14B black sidewall tires.

Model Number	Body/Style Number	Body Type & Seating	Factory Price	Shipping Weight	Production Total
EL CAMINO SERIES C (V-8)					
C	80	pickup	$3,139	3,817 lbs.	Note 1

EL CAMINO CONQUISTA — SERIES C SIX-CYL/V-8

In addition to base El Camino features, the Conquista package included extra front fender, body side moldings and tailgate moldings that set off a special two-tone paint scheme. The hood and a stripe extending down the body sides and around the tailgate were finished in one color. The top of the cab, the upper portion of the pickup box and the entire lower body perimeter were finished in a second contrasting color.

Model Number	Body/Style Number	Body Type & Seating	Factory Price	Shipping Weight	Production Total
EL CAMINO SERIES C (6-CYL)					
C	80	pickup	—	—	Note 1
EL CAMINO SERIES C (V-8)					
C	80	pickup	—	—	Note 1

EL CAMINO CLASSIC — SERIES D V-8

In addition to standard El Camino equipment, the El Camino Classic featured a bright lower body sill molding, a full-width Classic seat with fold-down center arm rest,

The SS option package cost $280 for 1974. Another $273 could get a buyer the 454-cid engine.

Classic door panel trim, a deluxe vinyl-coated headliner and a black-finished inside rearview mirror.

Model Number	Body/Style Number	Body Type & Seating	Factory Price	Shipping Weight	Production Total
D	80	pickup	$3,277	3,832 lbs.	Note 1

EL CAMINO CLASSIC CONQUISTA SERIES D — 6-CYL/V-8

The Conquista trim option was also available for the El Camino Classic. This combined the special Conquista trim and two-tone paint finish with the extra features characteristic of an El Camino Classic model.

Model Number	Body/Style Number	Body Type & Seating	Factory Price	Shipping Weight	Production Total
D	80	pickup	—	—	Note 1

EL CAMINO CLASSIC ESTATE SERIES D + YA2 — V-8

Available to accentuate the appearance of the El Camino Classic, which was essentially that of the Malibu Classic, was the Estate trim package. It consisted of full body side and tailgate accents with a wood-grain vinyl trim. Chrome scripts calling out the "Estate" name were located on the front fenders below the El Camino nameplates. Also included were special vinyl-covered pattern door trim panels. The price of the 1974 Estate package was $131.

Model Number	Body/Style Number	Body Type & Seating	Factory Price	Shipping Weight	Production Total
D	80	pickup	$3,408	—	Note 1

EL CAMINO CLASSIC SS SERIES D + Z03 — V-8

In addition to or in place of the standard El Camino Classic equipment listed above, the SS equipment package included a black-finished grille with an SS emblem, a remote-control left-hand outside Sport style rearview mirror, a manual right-hand Sport style outside rearview mirror, SS fender emblems, SS door trim, and SS steering wheel, an SS emblem above the rear bumper, bright roof drip moldings, lower body side and wheel opening stripes keyed to the body color, black-accented taillight frames, a special instrument cluster, special front and rear stabilizer bars, 14 x 7-in. Rallye wheels with special center caps and trim rings and G70 x 14 white letter tires. The cost of the SS equipment package was $280 and the prices given below represent the price of the standard-equipped El Camino Classic model plus $250. If you wanted to turn your El Camino SS into an El Camino SS 454, the big engine was another $273 extra.

Model Number	Body/Style Number	Body Type & Seating	Factory Price	Shipping Weight	Production Total
D	80	pickup	$3,527	—	Note 1

NOTE 1 Total El Camino production was 51,223.
NOTE 2 Total El Camino production of 33,620 units included 4,543 El Caminos with the SS equipment package.

ENGINES

EL CAMINO BASE 250-CID, 100-HP SIX-CYL: Inline. Overhead-valve. Cast-iron block. Displacement: 250 cid. Bore and stroke: 3.875 x 3.53 in. Compression ratio: 8.25:1. Net brake hp: 100 at 3800 rpm. Taxable hp: 36. Torque: 175 lbs.-ft. at 1600 rpm. Seven main bearings. Hydraulic valve lifters. Crankcase capacity: 4 qt. (add 1 qt. for new filter). Cooling system capacity: 12 qt (add 6 qt. for heater). Carburetor: Rochester one-barrel Model 7028017. Sales code L22.

EL CAMINO BASE 350-CID, 145-HP V-8: Overhead-valve. Cast-iron block and head. Bore and stroke: 4.00 x 3.48 in. Displacement: 350 cid. Compression ratio: 8.50:1. Net brake hp: 145 at 3600 rpm. Taxable hp: 51.20. Net torque: 250 lbs.-ft. at 2200 rpm. Five main bearings. Hydraulic valve lifters. Crankcase capacity: 4 qt. (add 1 qt. for new filter). Cooling system capacity with heater: 18 qt. Carburetor: Two-barrel. Sales code L65.

EL CAMINO OPTIONAL 400-CID, 150-HP V-8: Overhead-valve. Cast-iron block and head. Bore and stroke: 4.13 x 3.75 in. Displacement: 400 cid. Compression ratio: 8.50:1. Net brake hp: 150 at 3200 rpm. Taxable hp: 54.40. Net torque: 295 lbs.-ft. at 2000 rpm. Five main bearings. Hydraulic valve lifters. Crankcase capacity: 4 qt. (add 1 qt. for new filter). Cooling system capacity with heater: (Chevrolet) 16 qt.; (others) 18 qt. Carburetor: Two-barrel. Sales code LF6.

EL CAMINO OPTIONAL 350-CID, 160-HP V-8: Overhead-valve. Cast-iron block and head. Bore and stroke: 4.00 x 3.48 in. Displacement: 350 cid. Compression ratio: 8.50:1. Net brake hp: 160 at 3800 rpm. Taxable hp: 51.20. Net torque: 250 lbs.-ft. at 2400 rpm. Five main bearings. Hydraulic valve lifters. Crankcase capacity: 4 qt. (add 1 qt. for new filter). Cooling system capacity with heater: (Chevrolet) 16 qt.; (others) 18 qt. Carburetor: Four-barrel. Sales code LM1.

EL CAMINO OPTIONAL 400-CID, 180-HP V-8: Overhead-valve. Cast-iron block and head. Bore and stroke: 4.13 x 3.75 in. Displacement: 400 cid. Compression ratio: 8.50:1. Net brake hp: 180 at 3800 rpm. Taxable hp: 54.40. Net torque: 290 lbs.-ft. at 2400 rpm. Five main bearings. Hydraulic valve lifters. Crankcase capacity: 4 qt. (add 1 qt. for new filter). Cooling system capacity with heater: 16.5 qt. Carburetor: Four-barrel. Sales code LT4.

EL CAMINO OPTIONAL 454-CID, 235-HP V-8: Overhead-valve. Cast-iron block and head. Bore and stroke: 4.25 x 4.00 in. Displacement: 454 cid. Compression ratio: 8.50:1. Net brake hp: 235 at 4000 rpm. Taxable hp: 57.80. Net torque: 360 lbs.-ft. at 2800 rpm. Five main bearings. Hydraulic valve lifters. Crankcase capacity: 5 qt. (add 1 qt. for new filter). Cooling system capacity with heater: 23 qt. Dual exhaust. Carburetor: Four-barrel. Sales code LS4.

CHASSIS

Wheelbase: 116 in. Overall length: 216.25 in. Height: 54 in. Overall width: 76.75 in. Front tread: 58.5 in. Rear tread: 57.8 in. Load floor length 80.75 in. Cargo box length from back of cab to top of tailgate: 71.50 in. Cargo box height: 13.50 in. Bed width between rear wheel housings: 45.25 in. Maximum bed width: 58.50 in. Tires: G78 x 14B. Transmission: Three-speed synchromesh. Gears: 3F/1R. Column-mounted gearshift lever. Single-plate, dry-disc clutch (250-cid engine), coil-spring single-dry-plate (307/350/454-cid engines). Rear axle: semi-floating. Hydraulic four-wheel brakes. Kelsey-Hayes pressed steel wheels.

(**Note**: The measurements given above are the basic specifications for all 1973-1975 El Camino models, but there may have been minor variations in some measurements from year to year).

OPTIONS

A01 tinted body glass. A02 tinted windshield. A31 electric windows. A42 six-way electric front seat control. AK1 deluxe safety belts. AN7 Strato-bucket swivel front seat. AU3 power door locks. B37 floor mats. B80 roof drip moldings. B84 body side moldings. B93 door edge guards. B96 wheel opening moldings. BX8 moldings and two-tone paint. BZH interim equipment change. BZM delete power steering. C08 vinyl top. C60 all-weather air conditioning. CB1 exterior soft trim cover. D24 litter container. D33 remote-control driver's mirror. D34 visor-vanity mirror. D35 Classic remote-control left-hand outside rearview mirror. D55 front compartment floor console. D91 front end paint stripe. F40 heavy-duty suspension. G80 Positraction. G92 3.08:1 rear axle. G95 3.55:1 rear axle. J50 power brakes. K30 speed and cruise control. K76 61-amp Delcotron. L22 250-cid six-cylinder engine. L65 350-cid two-barrel V-8. L90 low-compression six-cylinder engine for export. LF6 400-cid two-barrel V-8. LT4 400-cid four-barrel V-8. LM1 350-cid four-barrel V-8. LS4 454-cid four-barrel V-8. M21 close-ratio 4-speed manual transmission. M38 three-speed automatic transmission. M40 three-speed automatic transmission. N31 Sport-style steering wheel. N33 tilt steering. N41 variable-ratio power steering. N65 space saver spare tire. N95 simulated wire wheel cover. P01 wheel trim covers. PA3 special wheel covers. PE1 14 x 7 turbine wheels. PE2 15 x 7-in. Classic wheels. QDR GR78-15B steel-belted radial tires. QEH E78-14B white stripe tires. QEL HR78-15B steel-belted radial tires. QGF G70-14B white letter tires. QGK G78-14B glass-belted tires. QGL G78-14B white stripe tires. QHE H78-14 glass-belted tires. QHF H78-14B glass-belted white-stripe tires. QQZ HR70-15B steel-belted radial tires. QRM GR70-15 steel-belted radial tires. QRN GR70-15 steel-belted radial tires. QRV HR70-15B steel-belted radial tires. QRZ GR70-15B steel-belted radial tires. U05 dual horns. U14 instrument panel gauges. U35 electric clock. U58 AM/FM stereo. U63 push-button radio. U69 AM/FM push-button radio. U76 windshield antenna. U80 auxiliary speaker. UA1 heavy-duty battery. UM1 AM push-button radio and tape player. UM2 AM-FM push-button radio and tape player. V01 heavy-duty radiator. V30 bumper guards. VE5 bumper impact strip. YA2 El Camino Estate package. YD1 trailering rear axle ratio. YJ9 exterior décor package. Z03 SS equipment package. Z15 SS 454 package. ZJ7 special hubcaps and trim rings. ZJ9 auxiliary lighting group.

OPTION INSTALLATION RATES

Automatic transmission (95.8 percent). Power front disc brakes (100 percent). Power steering (97.3 percent). AM radio (77.5 percent). AM/FM stereo radio (16.4 percent). V-8 engine 350-cid or less (66.4 percent). V-8 engine over 350-cid (33.1 percent). Air conditioning (72.4 percent). Positraction (9.9 percent). Tinted glass (90.9 percent). Steel-belted radial tires (16.8 percent). Wheel covers (70.3 percent). Interior trim package (44.5 percent). Exterior trim package (44.5 percent).

HISTORICAL

J.T. Riley became assistant general sales manager for Chevrolet trucks in 1974. L.P. Schinzing took over as merchandising manager for light- and medium-duty trucks. Chevrolet scored its second-best truck sales year in history with 885,362 units.

The 1975 El Camino continued the basic 1974 look, but it had a slightly revised grille that was vertically segmented with nine prominent members. There was now a built-in license plate holder at the center of the bumper. There were revisions to the engine offerings, ride quality and handling. Net horsepower ratings for some V-8 engines climbed, while others stayed the same or dropped. The standard 250-cid in-line six-cylinder engine was revamped to provide better operating efficiency, fuel economy and performance.

All six-cylinder and V-8 engines featured a High Energy Ignition (HEI) system and a catalytic converter. Routine maintenance intervals were extended as follows: (oil changes) 1974 was four months or 6,000 miles and 1975 was six months or 7,500 miles; (oil filter) 1974 was first 600 miles and every 12,000 thereafter and 1975 was first 7,500 miles and every 15,000 miles thereafter; (spark plugs) 1974 was every 6,000 miles and 1975 was every 22,500 miles; (chassis lubrication) 1974 was every four months or 6,000 miles and 1975 was every six months or 7,500 miles.

I.D. NUMBERS

VIN embossed on the top left-hand side of the instrument panel and visible through the windshield. The first symbol 1 designates Chevrolet. The second symbol indicates series: C=El Camino; D=El Camino Classic. The third and fourth symbols indicate body style: 80=two-door pickup delivery. The fifth symbol indicates engine (net hp): D=250-cid 105-hp inline six-cylinder, H=350-cid 145-hp V-8, L=350-cid 165-hp V-8, U=400-cid 175-hp V-8 and Y=454-cid 215-hp V-8. The sixth symbol designates the model year: 5=1975. The seventh symbol designates the assembly plant location: B=Baltimore, Maryland, D=Doraville, Georgia, Z=Fremont, California, R=Arlington, Texas and 1=Oshawa, Canada. The last six

EL CAMINO

The 1975 El Camino Classic featured a variety of trim and molding upgrades. It came with a base 350-cid V-8 and a starting price of $3,966.

symbols are the sequential unit production number at the specific factory. The Fisher body tag riveted to the top of the cowl on the left side of the car below the hood provides additional vehicle identification information. The Fisher body STYLE NUMBER (ST) consists of a prefix identifying model year and four or more symbols identifying the series and body style (example: 75-1D80 for a 1975 El Camino Classic V-8). The BODY NUMBER consists of a prefix designating assembly plant and the sequential unit production number at the specific factory. The TRIM NUMBER (TR) identifies upholstery.

COLORS

(10) White, (11) Antique White, (13) Silver poly, (15) Light Graystone, (16) Medium Graystone Poly, (19) Black, (21) Silver Blue Poly, (24) Medium Blue, (26) Bright Blue Poly, (29) Midnight Blue Poly, (44) Medium Green, (45) Light Green Poly, (49) Dark Green Poly, (50) Cream Beige, (51) Bright Yellow, (55) Sandstone, (58) Dark Sandstone Poly, (59) Dark Brown Poly, (63) Light Saddle, (64) Persimmon Poly, (66) Bronze Poly, (72) Medium Red, (74) Dark Red Poly, (75) Light Red, (79) Burgundy Poly and (80) Orange. Vinyl tops were available in: AA=White, BB=Black, DD=Dark Blue, FF=Dark Brown, GG=Medium Green, HH=Dark Red, RR=Red, TT=Sandstone and WW=Metallic Silver.

ENGINE CODES

Codes appear on the right side of six-cylinder blocks behind the distributor and right front of V-8 engine blocks. Engine codes for 1975 were: (250-cid/105-hp six) CJJ, CJU, CJL and CJZ; (350-cid/145-hp V-8 two-barrel V-8) CMJ and CMU; (350-cid/165-hp four-barrel V-8) CMM and CMH; (400-cid/175-hp V-8) CTU, CTX, CSB and CSM; (454-cid/215-hp V-8) CXW.

EL CAMINO — SERIES C — 6-CYL/V-8

Standard equipment on base El Caminos included a bright El Camino nameplate on the left-hand grille panel, a bright Chevrolet grille center emblem, bright back window reveal moldings, a bright El Camino nameplate on the lower right-hand side of the tailgate, chrome front and rear bumpers with a hydraulic/pneumatic impact cushioning system, bright door lock handles, bright door lock cylinder covers, bright El Camino nameplates on the front fender sides, a bright grille outer edge molding, a bright headlight bezel bead, a bright hood molding, bright hub caps, a bright left-hand outside rearview mirror, bright body side, tailgate, drip rail and wheel opening moldings, bright windshield reveal moldings, side doors with a lift-bar latch release and key lock cylinders, a rear tailgate with a single-handle double latch mechanism, safety glass (in windshield, back glass and side windows), an Argent Silver plastic grid grille insert, instrument panel knobs marked with function symbols, back-up lights, two single-lens front park/turn lights, two class A rear lamps with tail/stop/signal and side marker functions, two Power-Beam headlights, a single rear license plate light, win front and rear side marker lights, a single D note horn, steel side door guard beams, a mechanical jack and wheel lug nut wrench, partial under body and full wheel well undercoating, body-color steel wheels, two-speed electric windshield wipers with hideaway wipers and arms, left- and right-hand cowl air vents with individual controls, dual armrests, bright seat back latch and adjuster knobs, bright window regulator knobs, a cigarette lighter, color-coordinated upholstery with black trim, a door-actuated dome lamp, push-button door locks, closed-cell rubber door seals, color-keyed vinyl covered rubber floor mats, a speedometer, an odometer, a fuel gauge, directional signals with a lane-change feature, a hazard warning, a heater and defroster, warning lights (for generator, oil pressure, temperature, brake-on, directionals and headlight high beams), a fiberglass-filled plastic instrument panel, sound deadening insulation, a 12-in. inside rearview mirror, seat and shoulder safety belts, a black-grained plastic steering wheel with soft rim and brushed chrome insert with the Chevrolet name, dual sun shades, side door opening scuff plates and floor mat retainers, a spare tire carrier behind the passenger seating position, a lockable steering column, vinyl door trim panels with bright trim, vinyl-coated cowl side panels, a vinyl-coated headliner, an ignition key warning buzzer, bright metal window regulators, padded windshield pillars, a 250-cid in-line six-cylinder engine, three-speed manual transmission, G78-14B black sidewall tires, front disc/rear drum brakes with disc brake lining sensors, a concealed storage compartment for tools and small items behind the driver's seat, front suspension ball joint wear indicators, tough double-walled body panel construction, a full-coil spring suspension, air-adjustable shock absorbers, an integrated voltage regulator, a catalytic converter, a new durable aluminized muffler and a Delco sealed side terminal battery. The standard El Camino interior featured a full-width foam-cushioned seat in either fabric-and-vinyl or all-vinyl combinations with matching vinyl door panels, side panels and headliners, plus a carpeted floor color-keyed to trim selections.

Model Number	Body/Style Number	Body Type & Seating	Factory Price	Shipping Weight	Production Total
EL CAMINO SERIES C (6-CYL)					
C	80	pickup	$3,716	—	Note 1
EL CAMINO SERIES C (V-8)					
C	80	pickup	$3,966	3,748 lbs.	Note 1

EL CAMINO CONQUISTA — SERIES C SIX-CYL/V-8

In addition to base El Camino features, the Conquista package included special two-tone paint, special bright moldings separating the colors, bright wheel opening moldings, bright lower body sill moldings and bright roof drip rails. The price for the Conquista package in 1975 was $128.

Model Number	Body/Style Number	Body Type & Seating	Factory Price	Shipping Weight	Production Total
EL CAMINO SERIES C (6-CYL)					
C	80	pickup	$3,844	—	Note 1
EL CAMINO SERIES C (V-8)					
C	80	pickup	$4,094	—	Note 1

EL CAMINO CLASSIC — SERIES D V-8

In addition to standard El Camino equipment, the El Camino Classic featured a bright lower body sill molding, a full-width custom seat with fold-down center arm rest, a padded instrument panel, special door panel trim, a deluxe vinyl-coated headliner and a black-finished

SS interior with available bucket seats

The all-vinyl SS interior is shown here with special swivel bucket seats you can order. The seats pivot up to 90 degrees, have built-in headrests. Full-foam cushioned, the seats are contoured for comfort and can be adjusted forward or backward.

El Camino buyers could again order their trucks with vinyl swivel bucket seats for 1975.

inside rearview mirror. A wide selection of upholstery fabrics and color-keyed vinyl accents was available.

Model Number	Body/Style Number	Body Type & Seating	Factory Price	Shipping Weight	Production Total
D	80	pickup	$3,966	3,821 lbs.	Note 1

EL CAMINO CLASSIC CONQUISTA SERIES D — 6-CYL/V-8

The Conquista trim option was also available for the El Camino Classic. This combined the special Conquista trim and two-tone paint finish with the extra features characteristic of an El Camino Classic model.

Model Number	Body/Style Number	Body Type & Seating	Factory Price	Shipping Weight	Production Total
D	80	pickup	$4,094	—	Note 1

EL CAMINO CLASSIC ESTATE SERIES D + YA2 — V-8

Buyers could give their 1974 El Camino even more elegance by ordering the Estate package. It featured full body side and tailgate accents in "Mozambique" woodgrain vinyl trim, plus bright body, wheel opening and roof drip rail moldings. The price of the 1975 Estate package was $157.

Model Number	Body/Style Number	Body Type & Seating	Factory Price	Shipping Weight	Production Total
D	80	pickup	$4,123	—	Note 1

EL CAMINO CLASSIC SS SERIES D + Z03 — V-8

This sporty package for V-8 models included special pattern and custom vinyl seat trim, matching right- and left-hand outside rearview mirrors, black or white body striping, 15 x 7-in. Rallye wheels, GR70-15 white-lettered steel-belted radial tires and SS emblems. The all-vinyl SS interior featured full-foam bucket seats. Shown in the sales catalog were the optional special swivel bucket seats that had built-in headrests and pivoted up to 90 degrees. They were contoured for comfort and could be adjusted forward or backward. The price of the SS equipment package was $215. A 400-cid V-8 was $113 additional and the 454-cid V-8 was $340 additional.

Model Number	Body/Style Number	Body Type & Seating	Factory Price	Shipping Weight	Production Total
D	80	pickup	$4,181	—	Note 1

NOTE 1 Total El Camino production was 33,620.
NOTE 2 Total El Camino production of 33,620 units included 3,521 El Caminos with the SS equipment package.

ENGINES

EL CAMINO BASE 250-CID, 105-HP SIX-CYL: Inline. Overhead-valve. Cast-iron block. Displacement: 250-cid. Bore and stroke: 3.875 x 3.53 in. Compression ratio: 8.25:1. Net brake hp: 105 at 3800 rpm. Taxable hp: 36. Torque: 185 lbs.-ft. at 1200 rpm. Seven main bearings. Hydraulic valve lifters. Crankcase capacity: 4 qt. (add 1 qt. for new filter). Cooling system capacity: 12 qt (add 6 qt. for heater). Carburetor: Rochester one-barrel Model 7028017. Sales code L22.

EL CAMINO BASE 350-CID, 145-HP V-8 Overhead-valve. Cast-iron block and head. Bore and stroke: 4.00 x 3.48 in. Displacement: 350 cid. Compression ratio: 8.50:1. Net brake hp: 145 at 3800 rpm. Taxable hp: 51.20. Net torque: 250 lbs.-ft. at 2200 rpm. Five main bearings. Hydraulic valve lifters. Crankcase capacity: 4 qt. (add 1 qt. for new filter). Cooling system capacity with heater: 16 qt. Carburetor: Two-barrel. Sales code: L65.

EL CAMINO OPTIONAL 350-CID, 165-HP V-8: Overhead-valve. Cast-iron block and head. Bore and stroke: 4.00 x 3.48 in. Displacement: 350 cid. Compression ratio: 8.50:1. Net brake hp: 165 at 3800 rpm. Taxable hp: 51.20. Net torque: 260 lbs.-ft. at 2400 rpm. Five main bearings. Hydraulic valve lifters. Crankcase capacity: 4 qt. (add 1 qt. for new filter). Cooling system capacity with heater: 16 qt. Carburetor: Four-barrel. Sales code: LM1.

EL CAMINO OPTIONAL 400-CID, 175 HP V-8: Overhead-valve. Cast-iron block and head. Bore and stroke: 4.13 x 3.75 in. Displacement: 400 cid. Compression ratio: 8.50:1. Net brake hp: 175 at 3600 rpm. Taxable hp: 54.40. Net torque: 305 lbs.-ft. at 2000 rpm. Five main bearings. Hydraulic valve lifters. Crankcase capacity: 4 qt. (add 1 qt. for new filter). Cooling system capacity with heater: 16 qt. Carburetor: Four-barrel. Sales code: LT1.

EL CAMINO OPTIONAL 454-CID, 215-HP V-8: Overhead-valve. Cast-iron block and head. Bore and stroke: 4.25 x 4.00 in. Displacement: 454 cid. Compression ratio: 8.15:1. Net brake hp: 215 at 4000 rpm. Taxable hp: 57.80. Net torque: 350 lbs.-ft. at 2400 rpm. Five main bearings. Hydraulic valve lifters. Crankcase capacity: 5 qt. (add 1 qt. for new filter). Cooling system capacity with heater: 24 qt. Dual exhaust. Carburetor: Four-barrel. Sales code: LS4.

CHASSIS

Wheelbase: 116 in. Overall length: 216.25 in. Height: 54 in. Overall width: 76.75 in. Front tread: 58.5 in. Rear tread: 57.8 in. Load floor length 80.75 in. Cargo box length from back of cab to top of tailgate: 71.50 in. Cargo box height: 13.50 in. Bed width between rear wheel housings: 45.25 in. Maximum bed width: 58.50 in. Tires: G78-14B. Transmission: Three-speed synchromesh. Gears: 3F/1R. Column-mounted gearshift lever. Single-plate, dry-disc clutch (250-cid engine), coil-spring single-dry-plate (307/350/454-cid engines). Rear axle: semi-floating. Hydraulic four-wheel brakes. Kelsey-Hayes pressed steel wheels.

(**Note**: The measurements given above are the basic specifications for all 1973-1975 El Camino models, but there may have been minor variations in some measurements from year to year.)

OPTIONS

A01 tinted body glass. A02 tinted windshield. A31 electric windows. A42 six-way electric front seat control. A52 front bench seat. A65 front bench seat with split seat belts. AK1 deluxe safety belts. AG7 six-way power passenger seat. AN7 Strato-bucket swivel front seat. AT8 50/50 front bench seat. AU3 power door locks. AV3 pickup box tie downs. B37 floor mats. B80 roof drip moldings. B84 body side moldings. B93 door edge guards. B96 wheel opening moldings. BW2 exterior ornamentation.

BX8 moldings and two-tone paint. C08 exterior soft trim roof cover. C09 vinyl roof. C60 all-weather air conditioning. CB1 exterior soft trim cover. CD4 pulse type windshield wipers. D24 litter container. D33 remote-control driver's mirror. D34 visor-vanity mirror. D35 Classic remote-control left-hand outside rearview mirror. D55 front compartment floor console. D68 dual sport-style exterior rearview mirrors. D91 front end paint stripe. D99 special two-tone paint. DF3 remote-control right-hand outside rearview mirror. F40 heavy-duty suspension. FE8 radial tuned suspension. G80 Positraction. G92 3.08:1 rear axle. G95 3.55:1 rear axle. J50 power brakes. K05 engine block heater. K30 speed and cruise control. K72 emission control delete. K75 emission control delete. K76 61-amp Delcotron. L22 250-cid six-cylinder engine. L65 350-cid two-barrel V-8. LM1 350-cid four-barrel V-8. LT4 400-cid four-barrel V-8. LS4 454-cid four-barrel V-8. M15 three-speed manual transmission. M38 three-speed automatic transmission. M40 three-speed automatic transmission. N31 Sport style steering wheel. N33 tilt steering. N41 variable-ratio power steering. N95 simulated wire wheel cover. P01 wheel trim covers. PA3 special wheel covers. PE2 15 x 7 custom wheels. QBW FR78-15B steel-belted radial white-stripe tires. QBU FR78-15B steel-belted radial black sidewall tires. QBX GR70-15B steel-belted radial black sidewall tires. QCF GR78-15B steel-belted radial black sidewall tires. QCN HR70-15B steel-belted radial white stripe tires. QCP HR70-15B steel-belted radial black sidewall tires. QCV HR70-15B steel-belted radial white-letter tires. QCX GR70-15B steel-belted radial white stripe tires. QCY GR70-15B steel-belted radial white-letter tires. QDR GR78-15B steel-belted radial white stripe tires. QDU HR78-15B steel-belted radial white sidewall tires. QEL HR78-15B steel-belted radial white stripe tires. QGK G78-14B bias-belted black sidewall tires. QGL G78-14B bias-belted white stripe tires. QHE H78-14B bias-belted black sidewall tires. QHF H78-14B bias-belted white sidewall tires. QRM GR70-15B steel-belted white stripe tires. U05 dual horns. U14 instrument panel gauges. U18 export speedometer. U35 electric clock. U58 AM/FM stereo. U63 push-button radio. U69 AM/FM push-button radio. U76 windshield antenna. U80 auxiliary speaker. UA1 heavy-duty battery. UF7 gauges package. UM1 AM push-button radio and tape player. UM2 AM-FM push-button radio and tape player. V01 heavy-duty radiator. V30 bumper guards. VE5 bumper impact strip. YA2 El Camino Estate package. YB5 general processing option. YF5 California emissions certification. YJ9 exterior décor package. Z03 SS package. Z15 SS 454 package. Z95 regular fuel engine equipment. ZJ7 special hubcaps and trim rings. ZJ9 auxiliary lighting group.

OPTION INSTALLATION RATES

Automatic transmission (97.8 percent). Manual disc brakes (5.2 percent). Power front disc brakes (94.8 percent). Power steering (98.6 percent). AM radio (71 percent). V-8 engine 350-cid or less (76.2 percent). V-8 engine over 350-cid (19.5 percent). Six-cylinder engine (4.4 percent). Air conditioning (56.7 percent). Positraction (9.7 percent). Tinted glass (68.5 percent). Steel-belted radial tires (99.7 percent). Wheel covers (57 percent). Interior trim package (92 percent). Exterior trim package (92 percent). Adjustable steering column (27.6 percent). Cruise control (20.2 percent).

HISTORICAL

J.T. Riley remained assistant general sales manager for Chevrolet trucks in 1975. L.P. Schinzing also remained as merchandising manager for light- and medium-duty trucks. This was a year in which pickup truck sales plummeted, even as the sales of vans skyrocketed. Total model-year sales of trucks fell to 796,412 units from 975,257 in 1974. Overall truck production at Chevrolet Motor Division dropped by 15 percent.

This year the headlights and grille of the standard El Camino and El Camino Classic looked different from each other. A blue Chevrolet bow tie emblem was seen at the center of the standard grille, and a gold bow tie graced the Classic grille. When the Super Sport equipment package was ordered, the Chevrolet bow tie changed to red and an "SS" badge was used at the right-hand lower corner of the Classic-style grille. The 454-cid V-8 engine option was dropped. Also gone was the El Camino Estate option with its wood-grained exterior body panels.

I.D. NUMBERS

VIN embossed on the top left-hand side of the instrument panel and visible through the windshield. The first symbol 1 designates Chevrolet. The second symbol indicates series: C=El Camino; D=El Camino Classic. The third and fourth symbols indicate body style: 80=two-door pickup delivery. The fifth symbol indicates engine (net hp): D=250-cid 105-hp inline six-cylinder, L=350-cid 165-hp V-8, Q=305-cid 140-hp V-8, U=400-cid 175-hp V-8 and V=350-cid 145-hp V-8. The sixth symbol designates the model year: 6=1976. The seventh symbol designates the assembly plant location: B=Baltimore, Maryland, D=Doraville, Georgia, Z=Fremont, California, R=Arlington, Texas and 1=Oshawa, Canada. The last six symbols are the sequential unit production number at the specific factory. The Fisher body tag riveted to the top of the cowl on the left side of the car below the hood provides additional vehicle identification information. The Fisher body STYLE NUMBER (ST) consists of a prefix identifying model year and four or more symbols

EL CAMINO

El Camino Classics came with a starting price of $4,468 in 1976.

identifying the series and body style (example: 76-1D80 for a 1976 El Camino Classic V-8). The BODY NUMBER consists of a prefix designating assembly plant and the sequential unit production number at the specific factory. The TRIM NUMBER (TR) identifies upholstery.

COLORS

(10) Classic White, (11) Antique White, (13) Silver poly, (16) Medium Gray Poly, (19) Black, (21) Light Blue, (28) Light Blue Poly, (35) Dark Blue Poly, (36) Firethorn Poly, (37) Mahogany Poly, (40) Lime Poly, (45) Lime Green, (49) Dark Green Poly, (50) Cream, (51) Bright Yellow, (57) Cream Gold, (65) Buckskin, (66) Burnt Orange, (67) Medium Saddle Poly, (72) Medium Red, (75) Light Red and (76) Medium Orange. Vinyl tops were available in: 11T=White, 13T=Silver, 19T=Black, 35T=Dark Blue, 36F=Firethorn, 37T=Mahogany and 65T=Buckskin.

ENGINE CODES

Codes appear on the right side of six-cylinder blocks behind the distributor and right front of V-8 engine blocks. Engine codes for 1976 were: (250-cid/105-hp six) CCF, CCD and CCC; (305-cid/140-hp two-barrel V-8) CPB, (350-cid/145-hp two-barrel V-8) CMJ and CLF; (350-cid/165-hp four-barrel V-8) CMN, CUF and CMH; (400-cid/175-hp V-8) CSX, CSB, CSF, CSA, CSW, CTU, CTX and CSM.

EL CAMINO — SERIES C — 6-CYL/V-8

The base El Camino featured single round headlights in square bright-metal housings and its grille was of the wide "Mercedes-Benz" style grille with a delicate crosshatch of vertical and horizontal bars. There were seven wide-spaced vertical members and 11 horizontal members with tighter spacing. Standard equipment on base El Caminos included a bright Chevrolet grille center emblem, bright back window reveal moldings, a bright El Camino nameplate on the lower right-hand side of the tailgate, chrome front and rear bumpers with a hydraulic/pneumatic impact cushioning system, bright door lock handles, bright door lock cylinder covers, bright El Camino nameplates on the front fender sides, a bright grille outer edge molding, a bright headlight bezel bead, a bright hood molding, bright hub caps, a bright left-hand outside rearview mirror, bright body side, tailgate, drip rail and wheel opening moldings, bright windshield reveal moldings, side doors with a lift-bar latch release and key lock cylinders, a rear tailgate with a single-handle double latch mechanism, safety glass (in windshield, back glass and side windows), an Argent Silver plastic grid grille insert, instrument panel knobs marked with function symbols, back-up lights, two single-lens front park/turn lights, two Class A rear lamps with tail/stop/signal and side marker functions, two Power-Beam headlights, a single rear license plate light, win front and rear side marker lights, a single D note horn, steel side door guard beams, a mechanical jack and wheel lug nut wrench, partial under body and full wheel well undercoating, body-color steel wheels, two-speed electric windshield wipers with hideaway wipers and arms, left- and right-hand cowl air vents with individual controls, dual armrests, bright seat back latch and adjuster knobs, bright window regulator knobs, a cigarette lighter, color-coordinated upholstery with black trim, a door-actuated dome lamp, push-button door locks, closed-cell rubber door seals, color-keyed vinyl covered rubber floor mats, a speedometer, an odometer, a fuel gauge, directional signals with a lane-change feature, a hazard warning, a heater and defroster, warning lights (for generator, oil pressure, temperature, brake-on, directionals and headlight high beams), a fiberglass-filled plastic instrument panel, sound deadening insulation, a 12-in. inside rearview mirror, seat and shoulder safety belts, a black-grained plastic steering wheel with soft rim and brushed chrome insert with the Chevrolet name, dual sun shades, side door opening scuff plates and floor mat retainers, a spare tire carrier behind the passenger seating position, a lockable steering column, vinyl door trim panels with bright trim, vinyl-coated cowl side panels, a vinyl-coated headliner, an ignition key warning buzzer, bright metal window regulators, padded windshield pillars, a 250-cid inline six-cylinder engine, three-speed manual transmission, G78-14B black sidewall tires, front disc/rear drum brakes with disc brake lining sensors, a concealed storage compartment for tools and small items behind the driver's seat, front suspension ball joint wear indicators, tough double-walled body panel construction, a full-coil spring suspension, air-adjustable shock absorbers, an integrated voltage regulator, a catalytic converter, a new durable aluminized muffler and a Delco sealed side terminal battery. The standard El Camino interior featured a full-width foam-cushioned seat upholstered in textured all-vinyl trim with color-coordinated vinyl door panels, side panels and headliners, plus a carpeted floor color-keyed to trim selections. Both doors had full-depth armrests.

Model Number	Body/Style Number	Body Type & Seating	Factory Price	Shipping Weight	Production Total
EL CAMINO SERIES C (6-CYL)					
C	80	pickup	$4,083	—	Note 1
EL CAMINO SERIES C (V-8)					
C	80	pickup	$4,333	3,791 lbs.	Note 1

EL CAMINO CONQUISTA — SERIES C 6-CYL/V-8

In addition to base El Camino features, the Conquista package included special two-tone paint, special bright moldings separating the colors, bright wheel opening moldings, bright lower body sill moldings and bright roof drip rails. The price for the Conquista package in 1976 was $128.

Model Number	Body/Style Number	Body Type & Seating	Factory Price	Shipping Weight	Production Total
EL CAMINO SERIES C (6-CYL)					
C	80	pickup	$4,211	—	Note 1
EL CAMINO SERIES C (V-8)					
C	80	pickup	$4,461	—	Note 1

EL CAMINO CLASSIC — SERIES D V-8

The El Camino Classic now had its own front-end treatment. The headlights featured two square units at each end stacked on top of each other. The grille insert was a diagonal wire mesh design. The Chevy bow tie at the center of the grille was gold. In addition to standard El Camino equipment, the El Camino Classic featured a bright wide lower rocker panel molding, bright wheel opening moldings, bright body side moldings and bright drip rails. A full-width custom seat with fold-down center armrest was standard and bucket seats were available at extra cost. The El Camino Classic also had a padded instrument panel, smart looking door panel trim, a deluxe vinyl-coated headliner and a black-finished inside rearview mirror.

Model Number	Body/Style Number	Body Type & Seating	Factory Price	Shipping Weight	Production Total
EL CAMINO CLASSIC — SERIES D — V-8					
D	80	pickup	$4,468	3,821 lbs.	Note 1

EL CAMINO CLASSIC CONQUISTA SERIES D — 6-CYL/V-8

The Conquista trim option was also available for the El Camino Classic. This combined the special Conquista trim and two-tone paint finish with the extra features characteristic of an El Camino Classic model.

Model Number	Body/Style Number	Body Type & Seating	Factory Price	Shipping Weight	Production Total
EL CAMINO CLASSIC CONQUISTA — SERIES D — V-8					
D	80	pickup	$4,596	—	Note 1

EL CAMINO CLASSIC SS SERIES D + Z03 — V-8

The 1976 El Camino SS had the Classic style front end with dual stacked headlights and a diagonal-mesh grille. The Chevy bow tie in the center of the grille was red, but an SS badge was added near the lower driver's side. This sporty package for V-8 models included matching right- and left-hand outside rearview mirrors, black or white body striping, 15 x 7-in. Rallye wheels, GR70-15 steel-belted radial tires with raised white letters and SS identification on the fenders and tailgate, as well as the grille. The interior featured full-foam seats (swivel bucket seats were optional) and door trim panels in a special vinyl-covered pattern. You could get an SS 305, SS 350 or SS 400 in 1976, but not an SS 454. The SS equipment package cost $226, the 350-cid V-8 was $30 and the 400-cid V-8 was $148 extra.

Model Number	Body/Style Number	Body Type & Seating	Factory Price	Shipping Weight	Production Total
EL CAMINO CLASSIC SS — SERIES D + Z03 — V-8					
D	80	pickup	$4,694	—	Note 1

NOTE 1 Total El Camino production was 44,890.
NOTE 2 Total El Camino production of 44,890 units included 5,163 El Caminos with the SS equipment package.

ENGINES

EL CAMINO BASE 250-CID, 105-HP SIX-CYL: Inline. Overhead-valve. Cast-iron block. Displacement: 250-cid. Bore and stroke: 3.875 x 3.53 in. Compression ratio: 8.25:1. Net brake hp: 105 at 3800 rpm. Taxable hp: 36. Torque: 185 lbs.-ft. at 1200 rpm. Seven main bearings. Hydraulic valve lifters. Crankcase capacity: 4 qt. (add 1 qt. for new filter). Cooling system capacity: 12 qt (add 6 qt. for heater). Carburetor: Rochester one-barrel. Sales code L22.

EL CAMINO BASE 305-CID, 140-HP V-8: Overhead-valve. Cast-iron block and head. Bore and stroke: 4.00 x 3.48 in. Displacement: 305 cid. Compression ratio: 8.50:1. Net brake hp: 140 at 3800 rpm. Taxable hp: 44.66. Net torque: 245 lbs.-ft. at 2000 rpm. Five main bearings. Hydraulic valve lifters. Crankcase capacity: 4 qt. (add 1 qt. for new filter). Cooling system capacity with heater: 16 qt. Carburetor: Two-barrel. Sales code: LG3.

EL CAMINO OPTIONAL 350-CID, 145-HP V-8: Overhead-valve. Cast-iron block and head. Bore and stroke: 4.00 x 3.48 in. Displacement: 350 cid. Compression ratio: 8.50:1. Net brake hp: 145 at 3800 rpm. Taxable hp: 51.20. Net torque: 250 lbs.-ft. at 2200 rpm. Five main bearings. Hydraulic valve lifters. Crankcase capacity: 4 qt. (add 1 qt. for new filter). Cooling system capacity with heater: 16 qt. Carburetor: Two-barrel. Sales code L65.

EL CAMINO OPTIONAL 350-CID, 165-HP V-8: Overhead-valve. Cast-iron block and head. Bore and stroke: 4.00 x 3.48 in. Displacement: 350 cid. Compression ratio: 8.50:1. Net brake hp: 165 at 3800 rpm. Taxable hp: 51.20. Net torque: 260 lbs.-ft. at 2400 rpm. Five

EL CAMINO

main bearings. Hydraulic valve lifters. Crankcase capacity: 4 qt. (add 1 qt. for new filter). Cooling system capacity with heater: 16 qt. Carburetor: Four-barrel. Sales code: LM1.

EL CAMINO OPTIONAL V-8 400-CID, 175-HP V-8: Overhead-valve. Cast-iron block and head. Bore and stroke: 4.13 x 3.75 in. Displacement: 400 cid. Compression ratio: 8.50:1. Net brake hp: 175 at 3600 rpm. Taxable hp: 54.40. Net torque. 305 lbs.-ft. at 2000 rpm. Five main bearings. Hydraulic valve lifters. Crankcase capacity: 4 qt. (add 1 qt. for new filter). Cooling system capacity with heater 16 qt. Carburetor: Four-barrel. Sales code LT4.

CHASSIS

Wheelbase: 116 in. Overall length: 213.25 in. Height: 54 in. Overall width: 76.75 in. Front tread: 58.5 in. Rear tread: 57.8 in. Load floor length 80.75 in. Cargo box length from back of cab to top of tailgate: 71.50 in. Cargo box height: 13.50 in. Bed width between rear wheel housings: 45.25 in. Maximum bed width: 58.50 in. Tires: G78-14B. Transmission: Three-speed synchromesh. Gears: 3F/1R. Column-mounted gearshift lever. Single-plate, dry-disc clutch (250-cid engine), coil-spring single-dry-plate (307/350/454-cid engines). Rear axle: semi-floating. Hydraulic four-wheel brakes. Kelsey-Hayes pressed steel wheels.

(**NOTE:** The measurements given above are the basic specifications for all 1976-1977 El Camino models, but there may have been minor variations in some measurements from year to year).

OPTIONS

A01 tinted body glass. A02 tinted windshield. A31 electric windows. A42 six-way electric front seat control. A65 front bench seat with split seat backs. AK1 deluxe safety belts. AN7 swivel front seat. AU3 power door locks. AV3 pickup box tie downs. B37 floor mats. B80 roof drip moldings. B84 body side moldings. B93 door edge guards. B96 wheel opening moldings. BX8 moldings and two-tone paint. C60 all-weather air conditioning. CD4 pulse type windshield wipers. D24 litter container. D33 remote-control driver's mirror. D34 visor-vanity mirror. D35 Classic remote-control left-hand outside rearview mirror. D55 front compartment floor console. D64 visor mirror. D68 dual sport-style exterior rearview mirrors. D73 pickup box handrail. D91 special two-tone paint. FE8 radial tuned suspension. F40 heavy-duty front and rear suspension. G80 Positraction. G92 3.08:1 rear axle. G95 3.55:1 rear axle. J50 power brakes. K05 engine block heater. K30 speed and cruise control. K76 61-amp Delcotron. L22 250-cid six-cylinder engine. L65 350-cid two-barrel V-8. LG3 305-cid two-barrel V-8. LM1 350-cid four-barrel V-8. LT4 400-cid four-barrel V-8. M15 three-speed manual transmission. M38 three-speed automatic transmission. N31 sport style steering wheel. N33 tilt steering. N41 variable-ratio power steering. N65 stow-away spare tire and wheel. N95 simulated wire wheel cover. P01 wheel trim covers. QBW FR78-15B steel-belted radial white stripe tires. QBU FR78-15B steel-belted radial black sidewall tires. QBX GR70-15B steel-belted radial black sidewall tires. QCF GR78-15B steel-belted radial black sidewall tires. QCX GR70-15B steel-belted radial white stripe tires. QCY GR70-15B steel-belted radial white letter tires. QDR GR78-15B steel-belted radial white stripe tires. QDU HR78-15B steel-belted radial white sidewall tires. QEL HR78-15B steel-belted radial white stripe tires. QGK G78-14B bias-belted black sidewall tires. QGL G78-14B bias-belted white stripe tires. QHE H78-14B bias-belted black sidewall tires. QHF H78-14B bias-belted white sidewall tires. U05 dual horns. U35 electric clock. U58 AM/FM stereo. U63 push-button radio. U69 AM/FM push-button radio. U76 windshield antenna. U80 auxiliary speaker. UA1 heavy-duty battery. UF7 gauges package. UM1 AM push-button radio and tape player. UM2 AM-FM push-button radio and tape player. V01 heavy-duty radiator. V30 bumper guards. V78 less certificate of compliance plate. VE5 bumper impact strip. YF5 California emissions certification. YJ9 exterior décor package. Z03 SS package. Z15 SS 454 package. Z49 mandatory Canadian base equipment modifications. ZJ7 special hubcaps and trim rings. ZJ9 auxiliary lighting group.

The 1976 El Caminos had a different front end than the Classics and SS models. The standard El Camino had single headlights, while the other two had two stacked rectangular lights.

OPTION INSTALLATION RATES

Automatic transmission (97.6 percent). Power front disc brakes (100 percent). Power steering (99 percent). AM radio (56.3 percent). AM/FM radio (17 percent). Stereo (13 percent). V-8 engine 350-cid or less (77.4 percent). V-8 engine over 350-cid (17.5 percent). Six-cylinder engine (5.1 percent). Air conditioning (80.1 percent). Positraction (9.3 percent). Tinted glass (91.4 percent). Steel-belted radial tires (99.6 percent). Wheel covers (40.9 percent). Styled wheels (51.3 percent). Interior trim package (83.7 percent). Exterior trim package (1.8 percent). Adjustable steering column (47.9 percent). Cruise control (22.4 percent). Bumper guards (46.6 percent). Bucket seats (9.7 percent).

HISTORICAL FOOTNOTES

J.T. Riley remained assistant general sales manager for Chevrolet trucks in 1976. L.P. Schinzing was again merchandising manager for light- and medium-duty trucks. For the 1976 model year, Chevrolet dealers delivered a record 1,045,169 trucks to customers, breaking the previous all-time record set back in 1973. El Camino model-year sales were 43,595 units compared to 33,022 the previous season.

As usual, Chevrolet designers updated the front end of the El Camino for the new model year. And as in 1976, the base and Classic models each had distinctive front end looks. Only three engines were offered this year, the 250-cid in-line six-cylinder, the 305-cid V-8 (which was not available in California) and the 350-cid four-barrel V-8.

Exterior color offerings were revised and the interval for changing the automatic transmission fluid and filter was extended to every 60,000 miles. In addition to the base, El Camino and El Camino Classic, there was an SS option for the Classic and a Conquista trim package.

I.D. NUMBERS

VIN embossed on the top left-hand side of the instrument panel and visible through the windshield. The first symbol 1 designates Chevrolet. The second symbol indicates series: C=El Camino; D=El Camino Classic. The third and fourth symbols indicate body style: 80=two-door pickup delivery. The fifth symbol indicates engine (net hp): D=250-cid 110-hp inline six-cylinder, Q=305-cid 145-hp V-8, V=350-cid 170-hp V-8. The sixth symbol designates the model year: 7=1977. The seventh symbol designates the assembly plant location: D=Doraville, Georgia, and R=Arlington, Texas. The last six symbols are the sequential unit production number at the specific factory. The Fisher body tag riveted to the top of the cowl on the left side of the car below the hood provides additional vehicle identification information. The Fisher body STYLE NUMBER (ST) consists of a prefix identifying model year and four or more symbols identifying the series and body style (example: 77-1D80 for a 1977 El Camino Classic V-8). The BODY NUMBER consists of a prefix designating assembly plant and the sequential unit production number at the specific factory. The TRIM NUMBER (TR) identifies upholstery.

COLORS

(11) Antique White, (13) Silver Poly, (16) Medium Gray Poly, (19) Black, (21) Light Blue, (22) Light Blue Poly, (29) Dark Blue Poly, (32) Light Lime, (36) Firethorn Poly, (38) Dark Aqua Poly, (44) Medium Green Poly, (50) Cream Gold, (51) Bright Yellow, (61) Light Buckskin, (63) Buckskin Poly, (69) Brown Poly, (72) Red, (75) Light Red, (78) Orange Poly and (85) Medium Blue. Vinyl tops were available in: 11T=White, 13T=Silver, 19T=Black, 22T=Light Blue, 36T=Firethorn, 44T=Medium Green and 61T=Light Buckskin.

ENGINE CODES

Codes appear on the right side of six-cylinder blocks behind the distributor and right front of V-8 engine blocks. Engine codes for 1977 were: (250-cid/110-hp six) CCC, CCD, CCF, CGA and 7SB; (305-cid/145-hp two-barrel V-8) CRA and CRF; 350-cid/170-hp four-barrel V-8) CMF, CKH, CKM, CKR, CHA, CHB, CHX and CKK.

EL CAMINO — SERIES C — 6-CYL/V-8

The base El Camino had a new cross-hatched grille. It consisted of 11 thin horizontal members and seven thin vertical members, plus a slightly wider vertical center bar carrying a red or gold Chevrolet bow tie badge. A bold front bumper set off the front end. Both the grille and bumper were designed to emphasize the El Camino's wide stance and to complement its long, low profile. Frameless door glass and thin roof pillars added grace to the sleek roofline. Standard equipment on base El Caminos included a bright Chevrolet grille center emblem, bright back window reveal moldings, a bright El Camino nameplate on the lower right-hand side of the tailgate, chrome front and rear bumpers with a hydraulic/pneumatic impact cushioning system, bright door lock handles, bright door lock cylinder covers, bright El Camino nameplates on the front fender sides, a bright grille outer edge molding, a bright headlight bezel bead, a bright hood molding, bright hub caps, a bright left-hand outside rearview mirror, bright body side, tailgate, drip rail and wheel opening moldings, bright windshield reveal moldings, side doors with a lift-bar latch release and key lock cylinders, a rear tailgate with a single-handle double latch mechanism, safety glass (in windshield, back glass and side windows), an Argent Silver plastic grid grille insert, instrument panel knobs marked with function symbols, back-up lights, two single-lens front park/turn lights, two Class A rear lamps with tail/stop/signal and side marker functions, two

El Camino

The 1977 El Camino lineup was largely unchanged from the previous year, and only three engines were offered: 250-cid inline six, 305-cid V-8 and 350-cid four-barrel V-8.

Power-Beam headlights, a single rear license plate light, win front and rear side marker lights, a single D note horn, steel side door guard beams, a mechanical jack and wheel lug nut wrench, partial under body and full wheel well undercoating, body-color steel wheels, two-speed electric windshield wipers with hideaway wipers and arms, left- and right-hand cowl air vents with individual controls, dual armrests, bright seat back latch and adjuster knobs, bright window regulator knobs, a cigarette lighter, color-coordinated upholstery with black trim, a door-actuated dome lamp, push-button door locks, closed-cell rubber door seals, color-keyed vinyl covered rubber floor mats, a speedometer, an odometer, a fuel gauge, directional signals with a lane-change feature, a hazard warning, a heater and defroster, warning lights (for generator, oil pressure, temperature, brake-on, directionals and headlight high beams), a fiberglass-filled plastic instrument panel, sound deadening insulation, a 12-in. inside rearview mirror, seat and shoulder safety belts, a black grained plastic steering wheel with soft rim and brushed chrome insert with the Chevrolet name, dual sun shades, side door opening scuff plates and floor mat retainers, a spare tire carrier behind the passenger seating position, a lockable steering column, vinyl door trim panels with bright trim, vinyl-coated cowl side panels, a vinyl-coated headliner, an ignition key warning buzzer, bright metal window regulators, padded windshield pillars, a 250-cid in-line six-cylinder engine, three-speed manual transmission, G78-14B black sidewall tires, front disc/rear drum brakes with disc brake lining sensors, a concealed storage compartment for tools and small items behind the driver's seat, front suspension ball joint wear indicators, tough double-walled body panel construction, a full-coil spring suspension, air-adjustable shock absorbers, an integrated voltage regulator, a catalytic converter, a new durable aluminized muffler and a Delco sealed side terminal battery. The standard El Camino interior featured a full-width foam-cushioned seat upholstered in textured all-vinyl trim with color-coordinated vinyl door panels, side panels and headliners, plus a carpeted floor color-keyed to trim selections. Both doors had full-depth armrests.

Model Number	Body/Style Number	Body Type & Seating	Factory Price	Shipping Weight	Production Total
EL CAMINO SERIES C (6-CYL)					
C	80	pickup	$4,148	—	Note 1
EL CAMINO SERIES C (305-CID V-8)					
C	80	pickup	$4,268	3,797 lbs.	Note 1

EL CAMINO CONQUISTA — SERIES C
6-CYL/V-8

In addition to base El Camino features, the Conquista package included special two-tone paint, special bright moldings separating the colors, bright wheel opening moldings, bright lower body sill moldings and bright roof drip rails. This year the Conquista package cost $138.

Model Number	Body/Style Number	Body Type & Seating	Factory Price	Shipping Weight	Production Total
EL CAMINO SERIES C (6-CYL)					
C	80	pickup	$4,286	—	Note 1
EL CAMINO SERIES C (V-8)					
C	80	pickup	$4,406	—	Note 1

EL CAMINO CLASSIC — SERIES D
V-8

A new formal grille combined with the El Camino Classic's stacked rectangular headlights to give it a look of elegance. The grille had 21 thin, vertical blades on each side of a slightly thicker vertical center divider that carried the Chevrolet bow tie emblem. In addition to standard El Camino equipment, the El Camino Classic featured a bright, wide, lower rocker panel molding, bright wheel opening moldings, bright body side moldings, bright drip rails and bright front fender nameplates with the word Classic below the El Camino front fender nameplates. A full-width custom seat with fold-down center armrest was standard and bucket seats were available at extra cost. The El Camino Classic also had a padded instrument panel, smart-looking door panel trim, a deluxe vinyl-coated headliner and a black-finished inside rearview mirror.

Model Number	Body/Style Number	Body Type & Seating	Factory Price	Shipping Weight	Production Total
D	80	pickup	$4,403	3,763 lbs.	Note 1

EL CAMINO CLASSIC CONQUISTA
SERIES D — 6-CYL/V-8

The Conquista trim option was also available for the El Camino Classic. This combined the special Conquista trim and two-tone paint finish with the extra features characteristic of an El Camino Classic model.

Model Number	Body/Style Number	Body Type & Seating	Factory Price	Shipping Weight	Production Total
D	80	pickup	$4,541	—	Note 1

EL CAMINO CLASSIC SS
SERIES D + Z03 — V-8

The 1977 El Camino SS had the Classic style front end with dual stacked headlights and a formal vertical-elements grille. The Chevy bow tie was in the center of the grille, but an SS badge was added near the lower driver's side. This sporty package for V-8 models included matching right- and left-hand outside rearview mirrors, black or white body striping, 15 x 7-inch Rallye wheels, GR70-15 steel-belted radial tires with raised white letters and SS identification on the fenders and tailgate, as well as the grille. The interior featured full-foam seats (swivel bucket seats were optional) and door trim panels in a special vinyl-covered pattern. You could get an SS 305 or SS 350 in 1977, but not an SS 400. This year the SS package sold for $244.

Model Number	Body/Style Number	Body Type & Seating	Factory Price	Shipping Weight	Production Total
D	80	pickup	$4,647	—	Note 1

NOTE 1 Total El Camino production was 54,321.
NOTE 2 Total El Camino production of 54,321 units included 5,226 El Caminos with the SS equipment package.

ENGINES

EL CAMINO BASE 250-CID, 110-HP SIX-CYL: Inline. Overhead-valve. Cast-iron block. Displacement: 250 cid. Bore and stroke: 3.875 x 3.53 in. Compression ratio: 8.25:1. Net brake hp: 110 at 3800 rpm. Taxable hp: 36. Torque: 185 lbs-ft. at 1200 rpm. Seven main bearings. Hydraulic valve lifters. Crankcase capacity: 4 qt. (add 1 qt. for new filter). Cooling system capacity: 12 qt (add 6 qt. for heater). Carburetor: Rochester one-barrel. Sales code L22.

EL CAMINO BASE 305-CID, 145-HP V-8: Overhead-valve. Cast-iron block and head. Bore and stroke: 3.74 x 3.48 in. Displacement: 305 cid (5.0 liters). Compression ratio: 8.5:1. Net brake hp: 145 at 3800 rpm. Taxable hp: 44.66. Net torque: 245 lbs.-ft. at 2400 rpm. Five main bearings. Hydraulic valve lifters. Carburetor: Rochester 2GC two-barrel. VIN Code: U.

EL CAMINO OPTIONAL 350-CID, 170-HP V-8: Overhead-valve. Cast-iron block and head. Bore and stroke: 4.00 x 3.48 in. Displacement: 350 cid (5.7 liters). Compression ratio: 8.5:1. Net brake hp: 170 at 3800 rpm. Taxable hp: 51.20. Net torque: 270 lbs.-ft. at 2400 rpm. Five main bearings. Hydraulic valve lifters. Carburetor: Rochester M4MC four-barrel. VIN Code: L.

CHASSIS

Wheelbase: 116 in. Overall length: 213.25 in. Height: 54 in. Overall width: 76.75 in. Front tread: 58.5 in. Rear tread: 57.8 in. Load floor length 80.75 in. Cargo box length from back of cab to top of tailgate: 71.50 in. Cargo box height: 13.50 in. Bed width between rear wheel housings: 45.25 in. Maximum bed width: 58.50 in. Tires: G78-14B. Transmission: Three-speed synchromesh. Gears: 3F/1R. Column-mounted gearshift lever. Single-plate, dry-disc clutch (250-cid engine), coil-spring single-dry-plate (307/350/454-cid engines). Rear axle: semi-floating. Hydraulic four-wheel brakes. Kelsey-Hayes pressed steel wheels.

(**NOTE:** The measurements given above are the basic specifications for all 1976-1977 El Camino models, but there may have been minor variations in some measurements from year to year).

OPTIONS

A01 tinted body glass ($54). A02 tinted windshield. A31 electric windows ($108). A42 six-way electric front seat control ($137). A65 front bench seat with split seat backs. AK1 deluxe safety belts. AN7 swivel front seat ($129). AU3 power door locks. AV3 pickup box tie downs ($14). B32 front floor mats. B80 roof drip moldings. B84 body side moldings. B93 door edge guards. B96 wheel opening moldings. BX8 moldings and two-tone paint ($138). C60 all-weather air conditioning ($499). CD4 pulse type windshield wipers. D24 litter container. D33 remote-control driver's mirror. D34 visor-vanity mirror. D35 Classic remote-control left-hand outside rearview mirror. D55 front compartment floor console. D64 visor mirror. D68 dual sport-style exterior rearview mirrors. D73 pickup box handrail ($68). D91 special two-tone paint. F40 heavy-duty front and rear suspension. F41 special heavy-duty suspension front and rear. G80 Positraction. G92 3.08:1 rear axle ($14). G95 3.55:1 rear axle ($14). J50 power brakes. K05 engine block heater. K30 speed and cruise control ($80). K76 61-amp Delcotron. L22 250-cid six-cylinder engine. LG3 305-cid two-barrel V-8 ($120). LM1 350-cid four-barrel V-8 ($210). M15 three-speed manual transmission. M38 three-speed automatic transmission ($282). N33 tilt steering. N41 variable-ratio power steering ($146). N65 stowaway spare tire and wheel. NA6 alternative emissions requirements. P01 wheel trim covers. PB2 ABS plastic wheel trim covers. QBU FR78-15B steel-belted radial black sidewall tires. QBW FR78-15B steel-belted radial white stripe tires. QBX GR70-15B steel-belted radial black sidewall tires. QCF GR78-15B steel-belted radial black sidewall tires. QCX GR70-15B steel-belted radial white stripe tires. QCY GR70-15B steel-belted radial white letter tires. QDR GR78-15B steel-belted radial white stripe tires. QDU HR78-15B steel-belted radial white sidewall tires. QEL HR78-15B steel-belted radial white stripe tires. QGK G78-14B bias-belted black sidewall tires. QGL G78-14B bias-belted white stripe tires. QHE H78-14B bias-belted black sidewall tires. QHF H78-14B bias-belted white sidewall tires. QKM FR78-15B glass-belted radial black sidewall tires. QKN FR78-15B glass-belted radial white stripe tires. T59 conventional battery. U05 dual horns. U35 electric clock. U58 AM/FM stereo. U63 push-button radio ($72). U69 AM/FM push-button radio ($137). U76 windshield antenna. U80 auxiliary speaker. UA1 heavy-duty battery. UF7 gauges package. UM1 AM push-button radio and stereo tape player ($209). UM2 AM-FM push-button radio and stereo tape player ($324). V01 heavy-duty radiator ($29). V30 bumper guards. V31 front bumper guard. VE5 bumper impact strip. YC8 demo option drive. YF5 California emissions certification. YG6 Royal Sierra Bonanza package A. YG7 Royal Sierra Bonanza package B. YG8 Royal Sierra Bonanza package C. YJ9 exterior décor package. YM6 export headrest. Z03 Landau equipment. Z15 SS package ($244). Z49 mandatory Canadian base equipment modifications. ZJ7 special hubcaps and trim rings. ZJ9 auxiliary lighting group.

OPTION INSTALLATION RATES

Automatic transmission (96.8 percent). Six-cylinder engine (3.2 percent). V-8 engine 350-cid or less (96.8 percent). Power front disc brakes (100 percent). Power steering (99.5 percent). Positraction (9.1 percent). Styled wheels (67.6 percent). Wheel covers (25.5 percent). AM radio (56.3 percent). Rear bumper (100 percent). Front bumper guards (52.1 percent). Exterior trim package (1.1 percent). Bucket seats (8.8 percent). Tinted glass (94.4 percent). Air conditioning (85.2 percent). Adjustable steering column (65.2 percent). Cruise control (39.4 percent). AM radio (44.5 percent). AM/FM radio (20.1 percent). Stereo (16.9 percent). Steel-belted radial tires (99.7 percent).

HISTORICAL

The new Chevrolets were introduced September 30, 1976. D.A. Bouchard was general sales manager for Chevrolet trucks in 1977. R.L. Higginbotham was merchandising manager for light- and medium-duty trucks. For the 1977 model year, Chevrolet dealers delivered a record 1,122,769 commercial vehicles. El Camino model-year sales were 50,189 units compared to 43,595 the previous season.

Full-size Chevrolets had been downsized in 1977 and the mid-size cars got the same treatment this year. The old Chevelle became the Malibu and the old Chevelle Malibu became the Malibu Classic. The sedan-pickup versions retained the El Camino Classic name this year. The Conquista and SS options were carried over and joined by a new Royal Knight package.

According to Chevrolet, divisional truck engineers felt that a complete downsizing of the 1978 El Camino Classic to the 108-in. wheelbase used under the new Malibu would have compromised the car-based pickup's already limited cargo capacity. Instead, the new El Camino Classic's wheelbase was made about an inch *longer* than the old one, but the body was several in shorter and the weight was reduced by 200-300 lbs. Interior head and leg room increased.

The base engine was a thrifty V-6. Full-frame construction was retained. Other selling features included a standard front stabilizer bar, extensive corrosion-resisting treatments, 14 noise-insulating body mounts (for a quieter ride) and double-panel doors, hood and deck lid construction.

I.D. NUMBERS

VIN embossed on the top left-hand side of the instrument panel and visible through the windshield. The first symbol 1 designates Chevrolet. The second symbol indicates series: W=El Camino. The third and fourth symbols indicate body style: 80=El Camino. The fifth symbol indicates engine (net hp): M=RPO L26 200-cid 94-hp V-6, A=RPO LD5 231-cid 105-hp V-6 (California), U=RPO LG3 305-cid 145-hp V-8 and L=RPO LM1 350-cid 170-hp V-8. The sixth symbol designates the model year: 8=1978. The seventh symbol designates the assembly plant location: B=Baltimore, Maryland, D=Doraville, Georgia, Z=Fremont, California, R=Arlington, Texas, L=Leeds, Missouri. and 1=Oshawa, Canada. The last six symbols are the sequential unit production number at

The 1978 El Camino was slightly smaller overall than the previous year, but still had an 800-lb. load capacity.

the specific factory. The Fisher body tag riveted to the top of the cowl on the left side of the car below the hood provides additional vehicle identification information. The Fisher body STYLE NUMBER (ST) consists of a prefix identifying model year and four or more symbols identifying the series and body style (example: 78-1AW for a 1978 El Camino). The BODY NUMBER consists of a prefix designating assembly plant and the sequential unit production number at the specific factory. The TRIM NUMBER (TR) identifies upholstery.

COLORS

(11) Antique White, (15) Silver poly, (16) Gray Poly, (19) Black, (21) Pastel Blue, (22) Light Blue Poly, (24) Ultramarine Blue, (29) Dark Blue Poly, (34) Orange, (44) Medium Green Poly, (45) Dark Green Poly, (48) Dark Blue Green Poly, (51) Bright Yellow, (56) Gold Poly, (61) Camel Beige, (63) Camel Tan Poly, (67) Safron Poly, (69) Dark Camel Poly, (77) Carmine Poly, (79) Dark Carmine Poly. Vinyl tops were available in: 11T=White, 15T=Silver Poly, 19T=Black, 22T=Light Blue Poly, 44T=Medium Green Poly, 61T=Camel Beige and 79T Dark Carmine Poly.

ENGINE CODES

Codes appear on the right side of six-cylinder blocks behind the distributor and right-hand side of V-8 engine blocks. Engine codes for 1978 were: (200-cid two-barrel V-8) CWA and CWB; (231-cid two-barrel V-6) DH, EA and OK; (305-cid V-8) CRW, CRX, CRH, C4D, CRY, CRZ, CER and DAF; (350-cid V-8) CMD, CMA, CMB and CMC.

EL CAMINO CLASSIC — SERIES W V-6/V-8

Sitting on a 117.1-in. wheelbase, the new El Camino Classic reflected the model's most extensive redesign since 1964. Overall length was reduced to 201.6 in. or 11.7 in. less than in 1977. Key styling features included a sweeping roofline with small side quarter windows, a wraparound rear window and single rectangular headlights. Despite the reduction in curb weight, load capacity remained at 800 lbs. The standard 3.3-liter V-6 was a derivative of the small-block Chevy V-8. It weighed almost 80 lbs. less than the in-line six it replaced. A second V-6, with a 3.8-liter displacement, was mandatory for trucks sold in California. The new El Camino pickup box was 79.5 in. long, 45 in. wide between the wheel housings and 59.1 in. wide above the wheel housings. The radiator grille was a chrome rectangle with an "eggcrate" style insert and a six-sided badge at the center of the upper surround. The headlamps were large, rectangular units set in an even larger bright housing that canted backwards at each corner, on the bottom. The parking lamps were positioned vertically between the grille and the headlamps, with amber-colored side marker lamps and directionals at the outboard ends. The front body sides had a curvature to them and angled forward at the front and at the rear. The rear end featured a drop-down tailgate with a chrome-rimmed license plate recess in its center and a bright Chevrolet bow tie logo above the recess. The rectangular taillights were placed in the rear bumper. Separate rectangular side markers were placed on the body sides, just ahead of the wraparound bumper corners. The front bumper was of a simple, straight-across design. Black rubber impact strips and bumper guards were optional. A new vertical-style instrument panel, mounted well forward, helped to enhance the spaciousness of the interior. A separate module held the radio controls, heater controls and instruments. Plug-in components and a swing-down glove compartment made behind-the-dash servicing easier. The headlight dimmer switch was moved to the turn-signal lever. A new ventilation system delivered outside air under all driving conditions, whether power assisted or ram vented. The chassis featured coil springs all around, a single-piece propeller shaft, lower rear axle ratios, relay-type steering and front disc, rear drum brakes. The new fuel tank held 17.5 gallons. The El Camino rode on radial-ply tires on 14-in. wheels. Standard equipment included self-adjusting front disc brakes with wear indicators, a High Energy Ignition system, a Freedom side-terminal battery, a dual-mode ventilation system, full carpeting, radial tires, new interior styling with a delta-spoked soft vinyl steering wheel, a fully inflated compact spare tire, rectangular headlights with chrome-plated bezels, bright windshield and rear window reveal moldings, bright belt side and roof drip moldings, a bright left-hand outside rearview mirror, extensive corrosion-resisting treatments, full wheel covers, wheel opening moldings, visible ball-joint wear indicators, a front stabilizer bar, a Delcotron generator, a coolant recovery system, seat belts with push-button buckle releases for all passengers, two combination seat and inertia reel shoulder belts for driver and passenger (with reminder light and buzzer), an energy-absorbing steering column, passenger guard door locks, safety door latches with stamped steel hinges, an energy-absorbing padded instrument panel, a contoured windshield header, a thick laminate windshield, safety armrests, a safety steering wheel, side marker lights and reflectors, parking lights that illuminate with the headlamps, four-way hazard flashers, back-up lights, directional signals with a lane-change feature, a defroster, dual speed windshield wipers, windshield washers, a wide-view day/night inside rearview mirror with vinyl edging and a deflecting support, a left-hand outside rearview mirror, a dual master cylinder brake system with warning light, a starter safety switch, a dual-action safety hood latch, an ignition key reminder buzzer and a steering column lock. Standard interior trim included a 4-in.-thick, foam-cushioned 50/50 seat with a handy split back. All controls were easily accessible in the trim rectangular instrument cluster. For added convenience, Chevy offered an optional split-back bench seat with fold-down center armrest. Options included a six-way power driver's seat or Strato bucket seats (with or without a center console and optional integral shift lever.

For 1978, the El Camino received a larger wheelbase, a few cosmetic changes, and a new V-6 engine.

Model Number	Body/Style Number	Body Type & Seating	Factory Price	Shipping Weight	Production Total
EL CAMINO CLASSIC SERIES W (V-6)					
W	80	pickup	$4,653	—	Note 1
EL CAMINO CLASSIC SERIES W (305-CID V-8)					
W	80	pickup	$4,843	3,076 lbs.	Note 1

EL CAMINO CLASSIC SS SERIES W + Z15 — V-8

In addition to the features of the base El Camino, the El Camino Super Sport (SS) came with a large front air dam, matching sport mirrors, a special black paint treatment around the grille openings, a choice of accent colors on the lower body, decal stripes to accent the paint-break lines, Rallye wheels painted to match the lower body color, black quarter window moldings and Supper Sport identification.

Model Number	Body/Style Number	Body Type & Seating	Factory Price	Shipping Weight	Production Total
W	80	Pickup	$5,022	3,076 lbs.	Note 1

MODEL OPTIONS

CONQUISTA PACKAGE: The El Camino Conquista package was highlighted by a striking molding and paint treatment. The basic body color appeared on the roof, the upper portion of the pickup box, the lower body sides and on the tailgate. The center section of the body side, the hood and the lower portion of the tailgate were set off by a special accent color. Also featured were bright paint break moldings along the upper side of the pickup box and tailgate, bright moldings along the lower body sides and wheel house moldings. A Conquista decal was placed on the tailgate.

ROYAL KNIGHT PACKAGE: Released after the start of the model year, the Royal Knight package featured a distinctive exterior décor treatment for the El Camino Super Sport only. Most apparent was a large, bold hood decal. Other ingredients of the option included color-keyed side striping, a large front air dam, matching sport mirrors and rally wheels. The "Royal Knight" name appeared on the fenders as a decal.

NOTE 1: Total El Camino Classic production was 54,286.

ENGINES

EL CAMINO BASE 200-CID, 95-HP V-6 (FEDERAL): Overhead-valve. Cast-iron block and head. Displacement: 200 cid (3.3 liters). Bore & stroke: 3.50 x 3.48 in. Compression ratio: 8.2:1. Brake hp: 95 at 3800 rpm Torque: 160 lbs.-ft. at 2000 rpm Four main bearings. Hydraulic valve lifters. Carburetor: Rochester 2GC two-barrel. Sales Code: L26. VIN code: M.

EL CAMINO BASE 231-CID, 105-HP V-6 (CALIFORNIA): Overhead-valve V-6. Cast-iron block and head. Displacement: 231 cid (3.8 liters). Bore & stroke: 3.80 x 3.40 in. Compression ratio: 8.0:1. Brake hp: 105 at 3400 rpm Torque: 185 lbs.-ft. at 2000 rpm Four main bearings. Hydraulic valve lifters. Carburetor: Rochester 2GE two-barrel. Sales Code: LD5. VIN code: A.

EL CAMINO BASE 305-CID, 145-HP V-8: Overhead-valve. Cast-iron block and head. Bore and stroke: 3.74 x 3.48 in. Displacement: 305 cid (5.0 liters). Compression ratio: 8.4:1. Net brake hp: 145 at 3800 rpm. Taxable hp: 44.66. Net torque: 245 lbs.-ft. at 2400 rpm. Five main bearings. Hydraulic valve lifters. Carburetor: Rochester 2GC two-barrel. Sales Code: LG3. VIN code: U.

EL CAMINO OPTIONAL V-8: Overhead-valve. Cast-iron block and head. Bore and stroke: 4.00 x 3.48 in. Displacement: 350 cid (5.7 liters). Compression ratio: 8.2:1. Net brake hp: 170 at 3800 rpm. Taxable hp: 51.20. Net torque: 270 lbs.-ft. at 2400 rpm. Five main bearings. Hydraulic valve lifters. Carburetor: Rochester M4MC four-barrel. Sales Code: LM1. VIN code: L.

CHASSIS

Wheelbase: 117.1 in. Overall length: 201.60 in. Height: 53.8 in. Front tread: 58.5 in. Rear tread: 57.8 in. Cargo box length from back of cab to top of tailgate: 79.5 in. Bed width between rear wheel housings: 45 in. Bed width above rear wheel housings: 59.5 in. Tires: G78-14B. Transmission: Three-speed synchromesh. Gears: 3F/1R. Column-mounted gearshift lever. Single-plate, dry-disc clutch (with V-6). Rear axle: semi-floating. Hydraulic four-wheel brakes. Kelsey-Hayes pressed steel wheels.

OPTIONS

A01 tinted body glass. A02 tinted windshield. A31 electric windows. AG7 Six-way electric 50/50 front seat control. AK1 deluxe safety belts. AU3 power door locks. AV3 pickup box tie downs. B32 front floor mats. B90 side window moldings. B93 door edge guards. B96 wheel opening moldings. BS1 acoustical insulation. BW2 deluxe body molding exterior ornamentation. BX8 moldings and two-tone paint. BW3 advance price sheet. C60 all-weather air conditioning. C95 ASM dome and reading lamp. CD4 pulse type windshield wipers. D24 litter container. D33 remote-control driver's mirror. D34 visor-vanity mirror. D35 Classic remote-control left-hand outside rearview mirror. D55 front compartment floor console. D64 visor mirror. D68 dual Sport-style exterior rearview mirrors. D73 pickup box handrail. D84 custom two-tone paint. D85 lower body side accent stripe. D91 special two-tone paint. F40 heavy-duty front and rear suspension. F41 special heavy-duty suspension front and rear. G80 Positraction. G92 3.08:1 rear axle. J50 power brakes. K05 engine block heater. K30 speed and cruise control. K76 61-amp Delcotron. K97 80-amp Delcotron. L26 200-cid V-6 engine. LD5 231-cid V-6 engine. LG3 305-cid two-barrel V-8. LM1 350-cid four-barrel V-8. MM3 three-speed manual transmission. MM4 four-speed manual transmission. MX1 automatic transmission. N23 22-gallon fuel tank. N33 tilt steering. N41 variable-ratio power steering. N95 simulated wire wheel covers. NA6 alternative emissions requirements. P01 wheel trim covers. PB2 ABS plastic wheel trim covers. QFZ P195-75R steel-belted radial white sidewall tires. QKH P205-75R steel-belted radial black sidewall tires. QKJ P205-75R steel-belted radial white sidewall tires. QKK P205-75R steel-belted radial white letter tires. QKP P185-75R steel-belted radial black sidewall tires. QKQ P185-75R steel-belted radial white stripe tires. QKR P195-75R steel-belted radial black sidewall tires. QKP P195-75R steel-belted radial white stripe tires. T59 conventional battery. U05 dual horns. U14 gauge package. U35 electric clock. U58 AM/FM stereo. U63 push-button radio. U69

AM/FM push-button radio. U75 power antenna. U76 windshield antenna. U80 auxiliary speaker. UA1 heavy-duty battery. UF7 gauges package. UM1 AM push-button radio and stereo tape player. UM2 AM-FM push-button radio and stereo tape player. V01 heavy-duty radiator. V30 bumper guards. VE5 bumper impact strip. Y57 demo drive. YC8 demo option drive. YJ6 economy décor package. Z03 Landau equipment. Z15 SS package. Z16 Royal Knight. Z49 mandatory Canadian base equipment modifications. ZJ7 special hubcaps and trim rings. ZJ9 auxiliary lighting group.

OPTION INSTALLATION RATES

V-8 engine under 350 cid (47.6 percent). V-8 engine 350 cid or more (40.2 percent). V-6 (12.2 percent. Automatic transmission (94.9 percent. Four-speed transmission (3.3 percent). Power front disc brakes (99.1 percent). Manual front disc brakes (0.1 percent). Power steering (99.4 percent). Steel-belted radial tires (100 percent). Positraction (9.0 percent). Styled wheels (73.9 percent). Standard wheel covers (16.8 percent). Optional wheel covers (9.3 percent). Regular bumpers (100 percent). Front bumper guards (46.1 percent). Rear bumper guards (46.1 percent). Exterior trim package (39.9 percent). Two-tone paint (62.1) percent. Exterior striping (22.2 percent). Bucket seats (9.6 percent). Tinted glass (93.7 percent). Air conditioning (83.7 percent). Cruise control (41.3 percent). Adjustable steering column (66.5 percent. Power windows (17.5 percent). Power door locks (15 percent). AM radio (39.6 percent). AM/FM radio (21.5 percent). Stereo (21.3 percent). Tape player (8.4 percent).

HISTORICAL

D.A. Bouchard was general sales manager for Chevrolet trucks. R.L. Higginbotham was merchandising manager for light- and medium-duty trucks. For the 1978 calendar year, Chevrolet built a record 1,215,995 commercial vehicles. El Camino model-year sales were 50,155 units compared to 50,189 the previous season. The new El Camino handily outsold the Ford Ranchero, which was in its next-to-last appearance in 1978.

For 1979, El Caminos featured a new "Mercedes" style grille with eight distinct horizontal segments formed by bright metal moldings. The moldings ran horizontally, three across, with a thin one down the center. The grille was surrounded by a chrome molding which was thicker on the top, where a six-sided red badge held a gold Chevy bow tie emblem. The grille was flanked by large, single rectangular headlamps with the upright parking lamps notched into the body corners. A new technical option was a 267-cid V-8, although it wasn't available in California.

I.D. NUMBERS

VIN embossed on the top left-hand side of the instrument panel and visible through the windshield. The first symbol 1 designates Chevrolet. The second symbol indicates series: W=El Camino. The third and fourth symbols indicate body style: 80=El Camino. The fifth symbol indicates engine (net hp): M=RPO L26 200-cid 94-hp V-6, A=RPO LD5 231-cid 105-hp V-6 (California), J=RPO L39 267-cid 125-hp V-8, H=RPO LG4 305-cid 155-hp V-8 and L=RPO LM1 350-cid 170-hp V-8. The sixth symbol designates the model year: 9=1979. The seventh symbol designates the assembly plant location: B=Baltimore, Maryland, D=Doraville, Georgia, Z=Fremont, California, R=Arlington, Texas, K=Leeds, Missouri. and 1=Oshawa, Canada. The last six symbols are the sequential unit production number at the specific factory. The Fisher body tag riveted to the top of the cowl on the left side of the car below the hood provides additional vehicle identification information. The Fisher body STYLE NUMBER (ST) consists of a prefix identifying model year and four or more symbols identifying the series and body style (example: 79-1AW for a 1979 El Camino). The BODY NUMBER consists of a prefix designating assembly plant and the sequential unit production number at the specific factory. The TRIM NUMBER (TR) identifies upholstery.

COLORS

(11) Antique White, (15) Silver Poly, (16) Gray Poly, (19) Black, (21) Pastel Blue, (22) Light Blue Poly, (24) Bright Blue Poly, (29) Dark Blue Poly, (40) Pastel Green, (44) Medium Green Poly, (51) Bright Yellow, (54) Light Yellow, (61) Medium Beige, (63) Camel Poly, (69) Dark Brown Poly, (75) Red, (77) Carmine Poly, (79) Dark Carmine Poly and (85) Medium Blue Poly two-tone. Vinyl tops were available in: 11T=White, 15T=Silver Poly, 19T=Black, 22T=Light Blue Poly, 40T=Pastel Green, 61T=Medium Beige and 79T=Dark Carmine Poly.

ENGINE CODES

Codes appear on the right side of six-cylinder blocks behind the distributor and right-hand side of V-8 engine blocks. Engine codes for 1979 were: (200-cid two-barrel V-8) DHB and DHA; (231-cid two-barrel V-6) RB, NJ, RW, NH, NC, RJ, NE, RM, NT, NU, SJ and SO; (267-cid two-barrel V-8) DMB, DMD, DMH, DMA, DMC, DMM, DMF and DMR; (305-cid four-barrel V-8) DTF, DTX, DNT, DNW, DNS, DTS, DTA, DTB, DTH, DTJ, DWA, DWB, DTU and DNY; (350-cid four-barrel V-8) DUF, DUJ, DUH and DRX.

EL CAMINO — SERIES W — V-6/V-8

"Chevy El Camino has the style, comfort and luxury of a fine passenger car, plus the hard-working ability of a tough Chevy truck," said the 1979 El Camino sales catalog. "Out back there are 35.5 cubic feet of ribbed steel

The Royal Knight package for 1979 helped dress up the El Camino SS with a distinctive paint and decal scheme.

cargo space, with a payload up to 800 lbs." The base model came with an impressive array of standard equipment features including a 3.3-liter V-6 (not available in California), frameless door glass and thin roof pillars, bright pickup box molding, bright wheel opening moldings, bright rocker panel moldings, bright roof drip moldings, full wheel trim covers, a bright windshield molding, a bright rear window molding, a padded instrument panel, steel-belted radial tires, self-adjusting front disc brakes with wear indicators, a High Energy Ignition system, a Freedom side-terminal battery, a dual-mode ventilation system, new interior styling with a delta-spoked soft vinyl steering wheel, a fully inflated compact spare tire, a bright left-hand outside rearview mirror, extensive corrosion-resisting treatments, visible ball-joint wear indicators, a front stabilizer bar, a Delcotron generator, a coolant recovery system, seat belts with push-button buckle releases for all passengers, two combination seat and inertia reel shoulder belts for driver and passenger (with reminder light and buzzer), an energy-absorbing steering column, passenger guard door locks, safety door latches with stamped steel hinges, a contoured windshield header, a thick laminate windshield, a safety steering wheel, side marker lights and reflectors, parking lights that illuminate with the headlamps, four-way hazard flashers, back-up lights, directional signals with a lane-change feature, a defroster, dual speed windshield wipers, windshield washers, a 10-in.-wide prismatic wide-view day/night inside rearview mirror with vinyl edging and a deflecting support, a left-hand outside rearview mirror, a dual master cylinder brake system with warning light, a starter safety switch, a dual-action safety hood latch, an ignition key reminder buzzer and a steering column lock. Standard interior trim included deluxe vinyl door and side trim panels, a cloth headliner with foam padding, full-depth padded armrests in both doors, color-keyed nylon cut-pile carpeting an a 4-in.-thick foam-cushioned 50/50 seat.

Model Number	Body/Style Number	Body Type & Seating	Factory Price	Shipping Weight	Production Total
EL CAMINO SERIES W (V-6)					
W	80	pickup	$5,187	—	Note 1
EL CAMINO SERIES W (BASE V-8)					
W	80	pickup	$5,377	3,242 lbs.	Note 1

EL CAMINO SS — SERIES W + Z15 V-8

In addition to the features of the base El Camino, the El Camino Super Sport (SS) came with a large front air dam, matching sport mirrors, a special black paint treatment around the grille openings, a choice of seven paint accent colors on the lower body, decal stripes to accent the paint-break lines, Rallye wheels painted to match the lower body color, black quarter window moldings and

EL CAMINO

large Supper Sport door graphics.

Model Number	Body/Style Number	Body Type & Seating	Factory Price	Shipping Weight	Production Total
W	80	pickup	$5,579	3,242 lbs.	Note 1

NOTE 1: Total El Camino production was 58,008.

MODEL OPTIONS

CONQUISTA PACKAGE: The 1979 El Camino Conquista package was highlighted by a striking molding and paint treatment. The basic body color appeared on the roof, the upper portion of the pickup box, the lower body sides and on the tailgate. The center section of the body side, the hood and the lower portion of the tailgate were set off by a special accent color. Also featured were bright paint-break moldings along the upper side of the pickup box and tailgate, bright moldings along the lower body sides and wheel house moldings. A Conquista decal was placed on the tailgate.

ROYAL KNIGHT PACKAGE: The Royal Knight package featured a distinctive exterior décor treatment for the El Camino Super Sport only. Most apparent was a large, bold hood decal depicting two dragons. Other ingredients of the option included color-keyed side striping, a large front air dam, matching Sport mirrors and Rallye wheels. The "Royal Knight" name appeared on the fenders as a decal.

ENGINES

EL CAMINO BASE 200-CID, 95-HP V-6 (FEDERAL): Overhead-valve. Cast-iron block and head. Displacement: 200 cid (3.3 liters). Bore & stroke: 3.50 x 3.48 in. Compression ratio: 8.2:1. Brake hp: 95 at 3800 rpm. Torque: 160 lbs.-ft. at 2000 rpm. Four main bearings. Hydraulic valve lifters. Carburetor: Rochester 2GC two-barrel. Sales Code: L26. VIN code: M.

EL CAMINO BASE 231-CID, 105 HP V-6 (CALIFORNIA): Overhead-valve V-6. Cast-iron block and head. Displacement: 231 cid (3.8 liters). Bore & stroke: 3.80 x 3.40 in. Compression ratio: 8.0:1. Brake hp: 105 at 3400 rpm Torque: 185 lbs.-ft. at 2000 rpm. Four main bearings. Hydraulic valve lifters. Carburetor: Rochester 2GE two-barrel. Sales Code: LD5. VIN code: A.

EL CAMINO BASE 267-CID, 125-HP V-8: Overhead-valve. Cast-iron block and head. Bore and stroke: 3.50 x 3.48 in. Displacement: 267 cid (4.4 liters). Compression ratio: 8.2:1. Net brake hp: 125 at 3800 rpm. Taxable hp: 39.20. Net torque: 215 lbs.-ft. at 2400 rpm. Five main bearings. Hydraulic valve lifters. Carburetor: Rochester M2MC two-barrel. VIN Code: J.

EL CAMINO OPTIONAL 305-CID, 155-HP V-8: Overhead-valve. Cast-iron block and head. Bore and stroke: 3.74 x 3.48 in. Displacement: 305 cid (5.0 liters). Compression ratio: 8.4:1. Net brake hp: 155 at 4000 rpm. Taxable hp: 44.66. Net torque: 235 lbs.-ft. at 2400 rpm. Five main bearings. Hydraulic valve lifters. Carburetor: Rochester M4MC four-barrel. VIN Code: H.

EL CAMINO OPTIONAL 350-CID, 165-HP V-8: Overhead-valve. Cast-iron block and head. Bore and stroke: 4.00 x 3.48 in. Displacement: 350 cid (5.7 liters). Compression ratio: 8.2:1. Net brake hp: 165-170 at 3800 rpm. Taxable hp: 51.20. Net torque: 260-270 lbs-ft. at 2400 rpm. Five main bearings. Hydraulic valve lifters. Carburetor: Rochester M4MC four-barrel. VIN Code: L.

CHASSIS

Wheelbase: 117.1 in. Overall length: 201.60 in. Height: 53.8 in. Front tread: 58.5 in. Rear tread: 57.8 in. Cargo box length from back of cab to top of tailgate: 79.5 in. Bed width between rear wheel housings: 45 in. Bed width above rear wheel housings: 59.5 in. Tires: G78-14B. Transmission: Three-speed synchromesh. Gears: 3F/1R. Column-mounted gearshift lever. Single-plate, dry-disc clutch (with V-6). Rear axle: semi-floating. Hydraulic four-wheel brakes. Kelsey-Hayes pressed steel wheels.

OPTIONS

A01 tinted body glass. A02 tinted windshield. A31 electric windows. A42 six-way power seat control. AG1 six-way power 60/40 seat adjuster. AK1 deluxe safety belts. AU3 power door locks. AV3 pickup box tie downs. B32 front floor mats. BS1 acoustical insulation. BW2 deluxe body molding exterior ornamentation. BX8 moldings and two-tone paint. BW3 advance price sheet. C60 all-weather air conditioning. C95 ASM dome and reading lamp. CD4 pulse type windshield wipers. D24 litter container. D33 remote-control driver's mirror. D34 visor-vanity mirror. D35 Classic remote-control left-hand outside rearview mirror. D55 front compartment floor console. D64 visor mirror. D68 dual Sport-style exterior rearview mirrors. D73 pickup box handrail. D84 custom two-tone paint. D85 lower body side accent stripe. D91 special two-tone paint. F40 heavy-duty front and rear suspension. F41 special heavy-duty suspension front and rear. G80 Positraction. G92 3.08:1 rear axle. J50 power brakes. K05 engine block heater. K30 speed and cruise control. K81 63-amp Delcotron. K97 80-amp. Delcotron. L26 200-cid V-6 engine. L39 267-cid V-8 engine. LC6 231-cid V-6. LD5 231-cid V-6. LG4 305-cid V-8. LM1 350-cid four-barrel V-8. MM3 three-speed manual transmission. MM4 four-speed manual transmission. MX1 automatic transmission. N23 22-gallon fuel tank. N33 tilt steering. N41 variable-ratio power steering. N95 simulated wire wheel covers. NA5 federal emission requirements. NA6 alternative emissions requirements. P01 wheel trim covers. P40 export tire equipment. PB2 ABS plastic wheel trim covers. QFK P205-70R14 steel-belted radial white sidewall tires. QVF P205-70R14 steel-belted radial white-letter tires. QFZ P195-75R steel-belted radial white stripe tires. QJY P205-75R steel-belted radial white-stripe tires. QKL P205-75R steel-belted radial white-letter tires. QKQ P185-75R steel-belted radial white stripe tires. QKR P195-75R steel-belted radial black sidewall tires. QKP P195-75R steel-belted radial white stripe tires. QKS P195-75R14 glass-belted white-stripe radial tires. T72 required dual left-hand headlights for export. T84 right-hand headlamp for export. T85 left-hand headlight for export. Export turn signal and marker lamps. TR9 lamp group. U05 dual horns. U14 gauge package. U18 export speedometer. U35 electric clock. U58 AM/FM stereo. U63 push-button radio. U69 AM/FM push-button radio. U75 power antenna. U76 windshield antenna. U80 auxiliary speaker. UA1 heavy-duty battery. UF7 gauges package. UM1 AM push-button radio and stereo tape player. UM2 AM-FM push-button radio and stereo tape player. UN3 AM/FM stereo cassette radio, less clock. UP5 AM/FM mono CB radio. UP6 AM/FM stereo CB radio. UX6 dual front dash speakers. UY8 AM/FM stereo radio with digital clock. V01 heavy-duty radiator. V30 front and rear bumper guards. V31 front bumper guards. V78 less certificate of compliance plate. VE5 bumper impact strip. YC8 demo option drive. YF5 California emission requirements. YG6 Royal Sierra, Bonanza package A. YG7 Royal Sierra, Bonanza package B. YG8 Royal Sierra, Bonanza package C. YJ7 demo drive. Z03 Landau equipment. Z15 SS package. Z16 Royal Knight. Z49 mandatory Canadian base equipment modifications. ZJ7 special hub caps and trim rings. ZN7 color-keyed rally spare wheel.

OPTION INSTALLATION RATES

267-cid V-8 engine (22.2 percent). 305-cid V-8 engine (58.2 percent). V-8 engine 350 cid (3.6 percent). V-6 (16 percent). Automatic transmission (93.4 percent). Four-speed transmission (3.1 percent). Power steering (99.3 percent). Steel-belted radial tires (100 percent). Styled wheels (84 percent). Standard wheel covers (16 percent). Regular bumpers (100 percent). Exterior trim package (44.9 percent). Bucket seats (10.4 percent). Tinted glass (93.9 percent). Air conditioning (83.0 percent). Cruise control (41.1 percent). Adjustable steering column (61.9 percent). Power windows (15.5 percent). Power door locks (13.2 percent). AM radio (42.1 percent). AM/FM radio (18.6 percent). Stereo (11.3 percent). Tape player (7.6 percent). CB radio (0.9 percent).

HISTORICAL

D.A. Bouchard was general sales manager for Chevrolet trucks. R.L. Higginbotham was merchandising manager for light- and medium-duty trucks. For the 1978 calendar year, Chevrolet built a record 1,215,995 commercial vehicles. El Camino model-year sales were 50,155 units compared to 50,189 the previous season. The new El Camino handily outsold the Ford Ranchero, which was in its next-to-last appearance in 1978.

The 1980 Conquista package consisted mainly of a bold molding and paint treatment.

"You won't believe you're in a pickup," said the 1980 El Camino sales brochure. Chevrolet's latest car-based pickup had a brighter, vertical-emphasis grille. Larger headlights, larger side marker lamps and a new 3.8-liter standard V-6 were the year's major revisions. The windshield washer system worked more precisely and Rallye wheels were a new option. The base V-6 and optional 5.0-liter V-8 could be had with a new automatic transmission with a "lock-up" torque converter.

I.D. NUMBERS

VIN embossed on the top left-hand side of the instrument panel and visible through the windshield. The first symbol 1 designates Chevrolet. The second symbol indicates series: W=El Camino. The third and fourth symbols indicate body style: 80=El Camino. The fifth symbol indicates engine (net hp): K=RPO LC3 229-cid/110-hp V-6, A=RPO LD5 231-cid/110-hp V-6 (California), J=RPO L39 267-cid/115-hp V-8, H=RPO LG4 305-cid/150-hp V-8 and L=RPO LM1 350-cid/170-hp El Camino only V-8. The sixth symbol designates the model year: A=1980. The seventh symbol designates the assembly plant location: B=Baltimore, Maryland, D=Doraville, Georgia, Z=Fremont, California, R=Arlington, Texas, K=Leeds, Missouri, and 1=Oshawa, Canada. The last six symbols are the sequential unit production number at the specific factory. The Fisher body tag riveted to the top of the cowl on the left side of the car below the hood provides additional vehicle identification information. The Fisher body STYLE NUMBER (ST) consists of a prefix identifying model and four or more symbols identifying the series and body style (example: 80-1AW for a 1980 El Camino). The BODY NUMBER consists of a prefix designating assembly plant and the sequential unit production number at the specific factory. The TRIM NUMBER (TR) identifies upholstery.

COLORS

(11) Antique White, (15) Silver Poly, (16) Gray Poly, (19) Black, (21) Light Blue Poly, (22) Medium Blue Poly, (24) Bright Blue Poly, (29) Dark Blue Poly, (40) Lime Green, (44) Dark Green Poly, (50) Yellow (51) Bright Yellow, (56) Yellow, (57) Gold Poly, (59) Beige, (63) Camel Poly, (67) Dark Brown Poly, (69) Medium Camel Poly, (72) Red, (75) Claret Ply, (76) Dark Claret Poly, (77) Cinnabar, (79) Red Orange, (80) Rust Poly, (84) Charcoal Poly and (85) Vapor Gray. Vinyl tops were available in: 11T=White, 19=Black, 21T=Light Blue Poly, 44T=Dark Green, 63T=Camel Poly, 76T=Dark Claret and 85T=Gray.

ENGINE CODES

Codes appear on the right side of the V-6 cylinder blocks behind the distributor and right-hand side of the V-8 engine blocks. Engine codes for 1980 were: (229-cid two-barrel V-6), DHB and DHA; (229-cid two-barrel V-6) CLA, CLB and CRC; (231-cid two-barrel V-6) OV, OW, OP and OR; (267-cid two-barrel V-8) CPA, CPB, CPM and CPR; (205-cid four-barrel V-8) CEA, CER, CEC, CMF, CMC, CMD and CMN; (350-cid four-barrel V-8) CHB.

EL CAMINO — SERIES W — V-6/V-8

Standard equipment features included a 3.8-liter V-6 (not available in California), frameless door glass and thin roof pillars, bright pickup box molding, bright wheel opening moldings, bright rocker panel moldings, bright roof drip moldings, full wheel trim covers, a bright windshield molding, a bright rear window molding, a padded instrument panel, steel-belted radial tires, self-adjusting front disc brakes with wear indicators, a High Energy Ignition system, a Freedom side-terminal battery, a dual-mode ventilation system, a delta-spoked soft vinyl steering wheel, a fully inflated compact spare tire, a bright left-hand outside rearview mirror, extensive corrosion-resisting treatments, visible ball-joint wear indicators, a front stabilizer bar, a Delcotron generator, a coolant recovery system, seat belts with push-button buckle releases for all passengers, two combination seat and inertia reel shoulder belts for driver and passenger (with reminder light and buzzer), an energy-absorbing steering column, passenger guard door locks, safety door latches with stamped steel hinges, a contoured windshield header, a thick laminate windshield, a safety steering wheel, side marker lights and reflectors, parking lights that illuminate with the headlamps, four-way hazard flashers, back-up lights, directional signals with a lane-change feature, a defroster, dual speed windshield wipers, windshield washers, a 10-in.-wide prismatic wide-view day/night inside rearview mirror with vinyl edging and a deflecting support, a left-hand outside rearview mirror, a dual master cylinder brake system with warning light, a starter safety switch, a dual-action safety hood latch, an ignition key reminder buzzer and a steering column lock. Standard interior trim included deluxe vinyl door and side trim panels, a cloth headliner with foam padding, full-depth padded armrests in both doors, color-keyed nylon cut-pile carpeting an a 4-in.-thick foam-cushioned 50/50 seat.

Model Number	Body/Style Number	Body Type & Seating	Factory Price	Shipping Weight	Production Total
EL CAMINO SERIES W (V-6)					
W	80	pickup	$5,731	—	Note 1
EL CAMINO SERIES W (BASE V-8)					
W	80	pickup	$5,911	3,238 lbs.	Note 1

EL CAMINO SS — SERIES W + Z15 V-8

In addition to the features of the base El Camino, the El Camino Super Sport (SS) came with a large front air dam, painted sport mirrors, a special black paint treatment around the grille openings, a choice of eight paint accent colors on the lower body, decal accent stripes, Rallye wheels, black quarter window moldings, large Super Sport door graphics and smaller Super Sport lettering on the right lower portion of the tailgate.

Model Number	Body/Style Number	Body Type & Seating	Factory Price	Shipping Weight	Production Total
W	80	Pickup	$6,128	3,238 lbs.	Note 1

NOTE 1: Total El Camino production was 40,932.

MODEL OPTIONS

CONQUISTA PACKAGE: The El Camino Conquista package was highlighted by a striking molding and paint treatment. The basic body color appeared on the roof, the upper portion of the pickup box, the lower body sides and on the tailgate. The center section of the body side, the hood and the lower portion of the tailgate were set off by a special accent color. Also featured were bright paint break moldings along the upper side of the pickup box and tailgate, bright moldings along the lower body sides and wheel-house moldings. A Conquista decal was placed on the tailgate. The Conquista package sold for $165 this year.

ROYAL KNIGHT PACKAGE: The Royal Knight package featured a distinctive exterior décor treatment for the El Camino Super Sport only. Most apparent was a large, bold hood decal depicting two dragons. Other ingredients of the option included color-keyed side striping, a large front air dam, matching sport mirrors and Rallye wheels. The "Royal Knight" name appeared on the fenders as a decal. Royal Knight trim was a $73 option for El Caminos with the Super Sport package only.

ENGINES

EL CAMINO BASE 229-CID, 115-HP V-6 (FEDERAL): Overhead-valve. Cast-iron block and head. Displacement: 229 cid (3.8 liters). Bore & stroke: 3.74 x 3.48 in. Compression ratio: 8.6:1. Brake hp: 115 at 4000 rpm. Torque: 175 lbs.-ft. at 2000 rpm. Four main bearings. Hydraulic valve lifters. Carburetor: Rochester two-barrel M2ME. Sales Code: LC3. VIN code: K.

EL CAMINO BASE 231-CID 11-HP V-6 (CALIFORNIA): Overhead-valve. Cast-iron block and head. Displacement: 231 cid (3.8 liters). Bore & stroke: 3.80 x 3.40 in. Compression ratio: 8.0:1. Brake hp: 110 at 3800 rpm Torque: 190 lbs.-ft. at 2000 rpm Four main bearings. Hydraulic valve lifters. Carburetor: Rochester M2ME two-barrel. Sales Code: LD5. VIN code: A.

EL CAMINO BASE 267-CID, 120-HP V-8: Overhead-valve. Cast-iron block and head. Bore and stroke:

The 1980 Super Sport was easy to spot with its large door graphics.

3.50 x 3.48 in. Displacement: 267 cid (4.4 liters). Compression ratio: 8.3:1. Net brake hp: 120 at 3600 rpm. Taxable hp: 39.20. Net torque: 215 lbs.-ft. at 2000 rpm. Five main bearings. Hydraulic valve lifters. Carburetor: Rochester M2ME two-barrel. VIN Code: J.

EL CAMINO OPTIONAL 305-CID, 155-HP V-8: Overhead-valve. Cast-iron block and head. Bore and stroke: 3.74 x 3.48 in. Displacement: 305 cid (5.0 liters). Compression ratio: 8.6:1. Net brake hp: 155 at 4000 rpm. Taxable hp: 44.66. Net torque: 240 lbs.-ft. at 1600 rpm. Five main bearings. Hydraulic valve lifters. Carburetor: Rochester M4ME four-barrel. VIN Code: H.

CHASSIS

Wheelbase: 117.1 in. Overall length: 201.60 in. Height: 53.8 in. Front tread: 58.5 in. Rear tread: 57.8 in. Cargo box length from back of cab to top of tailgate: 79.5 in. Bed width between rear wheel housings: 45 in. Bed width above rear wheel housings: 59.5 in. Tires: G78-14B. Transmission: Three-speed synchromesh. Gears: 3F/1R. Column-mounted gearshift lever. Single-plate, dry-disc clutch (with V-6). Rear axle: semi-floating. Hydraulic four-wheel brakes. Kelsey-Hayes pressed steel wheels.

OPTIONS

A01 tinted body glass ($75). A02 tinted windshield. A31 electric windows ($143). AG9 six-way power seat control ($175). AG1 six-way power 60/40 seat adjuster. AU3 power door locks ($93). AV3 pickup box tie downs ($20). B32 front floor mats. BS1 acoustical insulation. BW2 deluxe body molding exterior ornamentation ($57). BX8 moldings and two-tone paint. BW3 advance price sheet. C60 all-weather air conditioning ($601). C95 ASM dome and reading lamp. CD4 pulse type windshield wipers ($41). D24 litter container. D33 remote-control driver's mirror. D34 visor-vanity mirror. D35 remote-control left-hand outside rearview mirror. D55 front compartment floor console ($86). D64 visor mirror. D68 dual sport-style exterior rearview mirrors. D73 pickup box handrail ($79). D84 custom two-tone paint. D85 lower body side accent stripe. D91 special two-tone paint. F40 heavy-duty front and rear suspension. F41 special heavy-duty suspension front and rear. G80 Positraction. G92 3.08:1 rear axle. J50 power brakes. K05 engine block heater. K30 speed and cruise control ($112). K81 63-amp Delcotron. K97 80-amp. Delcotron. L26 200-cid V-6 engine. L39 267-cid V-8 engine ($80). LC6 231-cid V-6. LD5 231-cid V-6. LG4 305-cid V-8 ($195). MM3 three-speed manual transmission. MM4 four-speed manual transmission ($144). MX1 automatic transmission ($358). N23 22-gallon fuel tank ($23). N33 tilt steering. N41 variable-ratio power steering ($174). N95 simulated wire wheel covers ($125). NA5 federal emission requirements. NA6 alternative emissions requirements. P01 wheel trim covers. P40 export tire equipment. PB2 ABS plastic wheel trim covers ($56). QFK P205-70R14 steel-belted radial white sidewall tires. QVF P205-70R14 steel-belted radial white-letter tires. QFZ P195-75R steel-belted radial white stripe tires. QJY P205-75R steel-belted radial white stripe tires. QKL P205-75R steel-belted radial white letter tires. QKQ P185-75R steel-belted radial white stripe tires. QKR P195-75R steel-belted radial black sidewall tires. QKP P195-75R steel-belted radial white stripe tires. QKS P195-75R14 glass-belted white-stripe radial tires. T72 required dual left-hand headlights for export. T84 right-hand headlamp for export. T85 left-hand headlight for export. T90 Export turn signal and marker lamps. TR9 lamp group. U05 dual horns. U14 gauge package ($134). U18 export speedometer. U35 electric clock ($25). U58 AM/FM stereo. U63 push-button AM radio ($85). U69 AM/FM push-button radio ($158). U75 power antenna ($47). U76 windshield antenna ($27). U80 auxiliary speaker. UA1 heavy-duty battery. UF7 gauges package. UM1 AM push-button radio and stereo tape player ($248). UM2 AM-FM push-button radio and stereo tape player ($335). UN3 AM/FM stereo cassette radio, less clock ($341). UP5 AM/FM mono CB radio ($489). UP6 AM/FM stereo CB radio ($570). UX6 dual front dash speakers ($21). UY8 AM/FM stereo radio with digital clock ($395). V01 heavy-duty radiator ($36-$63). V30 front and rear bumper guards. V31 front bumper guards. V78 less certificate of compliance plate. VE5 bumper impact strip. YC8 demo option drive. YF5 California emission requirements. YG6 Royal Sierra, Bonanza package A. YG7 Royal Sierra, Bonanza package B. YG8 Royal Sierra, Bonanza package C. YJ7 demo drive. Z03 Landau equipment. Z15 SS package. Z16 Royal Knight ($73). Z49 mandatory Canadian base equipment modifications. ZJ7 special hubcaps and trim rings. ZN7 color-keyed Rallye wheels ($50). Conquista trim ($165). Cargo box tonneau cover ($116). Vinyl roof ($81). Cloth trim bucket seats ($91). Cloth trim 50/50 bench seat ($184). Vinyl bench seat ($28). Vinyl bucket seats ($91). Vinyl 50/50 bench seat ($212).

OPTION INSTALLATION RATES

267-cid V-8 engine (23.9 percent). 305-cid V-8 engine (26.1 percent). V-6 (50 percent). Automatic transmission (85.3 percent). Four-speed transmission (1.3 percent). Power front disc brakes (100 percent). Positraction (7.4 percent). Power steering (99.3 percent). Styled wheels (79.9 percent). Standard wheel covers (20.1 percent). Steel-belted radial tires (100 percent). Exterior trim package (34.7 percent). Bucket seats (9.6 percent). Tinted glass (89.5 percent). Air conditioning (75.70 percent). Cruise control (35.2 percent). Adjustable steering column (50.4 percent). Power windows (13.3 percent). Power door locks (11.4 percent). AM radio (44.9 percent). AM/FM radio (14.1 percent). Stereo (10.3 percent). Tape player (8.5 percent). CB radio (1 percent). Conventional rear bumper (100 percent).

HISTORICAL FOOTNOTES

Jim Perkins became sales manager for Chevrolet trucks. Jack L. Sherman became truck merchandising manager. For the 1980 calendar year, Chevrolet sold only 724,330 commercial vehicles, a 46 percent drop from 1979. El Camino model-year sales were 43,896 units compared to 50,284 the previous season. That drop came despite the fact that its main direct competitor, the Ford Ranchero, was not offered in the 1980 model year.

Striking paint, striping and decals made the 1981 Royal Knight hard to miss.

The El Caminos were relatively unchanged in 1981, other than a minor grille redesign dominated by eight prominent horizontal elements that "veed" outwards in the middle. The word "Chevrolet" in chrome block letters decorated the lower left-hand corner. A stand-up hood ornament with a red, six-sided badge with a gold Chevrolet bow tie sat atop the hood.

The major mechanical change was the adoption of General Motors' CCC (Computer Command Control) system for engine management, particularly of exhaust emission control, by electronic means. The base 3.8-liter V-6 with a two-barrel carburetor was available with a three-speed manual or automatic transmission. Only the automatic gearbox was offered with the optional 4.4-liter (267-cid) and 5.0-liter (305-cid) V-8s. The latter engine, with a four-barrel carburetor, was optional for El Caminos sold in California, which had a different (231-cid) base 3.8-liter V-6. Higher-pressure radial tires were standard for improved fuel economy. Conquista, Royal Knight and Super Sport packages were offered once again.

I.D. NUMBERS

VIN embossed on the top left-hand side of the instrument panel and visible through the windshield. The first designates the country of origin: 1=U.S. and 2=Canada. The second symbol indentifies the manufacturer: G=General Motors. The third symbol indicates the make: 1=Chevrolet. The fourth symbol indicates the type of restraint system: A=non-passive/manual seat belts; B=passive/automatic seat belts and C=passive/inflatable. The fifth symbol indicates series: W=El Camino. The sixth and seventh indicate body style: 80=El Camino. The eighth symbol indicates engine (net hp): K=RPO LC3 229-cid/110-hp V-6, A=RPO LD5 231-cid/110-hp V-6 (California), J=RPO L39 267-cid/115-hp V-8 and H=RPO LG4 305-cid/150-hp V-8. The ninth symbol is a check digit. The 10th symbol designates the model year: B=1981. The 11th symbol designates the assembly plant location: B=Baltimore, Maryland, D=Doraville, Georgia, Z=Fremont, California, R=Arlington, Texas, K=Leeds, Missouri, and 1=Oshawa, Canada. The last six symbols are the sequential unit production number at the specific factory. The Fisher body tag riveted to the top of the cowl on the left side of the car below the hood provides additional vehicle identification information. The Fisher body STYLE NUMBER (ST) consists of a prefix identifying model year and four or more symbols identifying the series and body style (example: 81-1AW for a 1981 El Camino). The BODY NUMBER consists of a prefix designating assembly plant and the sequential unit production number at the specific factory. The TRIM NUMBER (TR) identifies upholstery.

COLORS

(11) Antique White, (16) Silver Poly, (19) Black, (20) Bright Blue Poly; (21) Light Blue Poly, (22) Medium Blue Poly, (29) Dark Blue Poly, (35) Pastel Waxberry, (36) Light Waxberry Poly, (37) Medium Waxberry Poly, (45) Light Jadestone Poly, (47) Dark Jadestone Poly, (48) Dark Green Poly, (51) Bright Yellow, (54) Gold Poly, (56) Yellow, (57) Citrus Orange Poly, (58) Orange Poly, (63) Pastel Sandstone, (67) Dark Brown Poly, (68) Medium Sandstone Poly, (69) Dark Sandstone Poly, (72) Light Maple Poly, (75) Spectra Red, (77) Dark Maple Poly and (84) Charcoal Poly. Vinyl tops were available in: 11T=White, 19T=Black, 29T=Dark Blue Poly, 36T=Light waxberry Poly, 45T=Light Jadestone Poly, 63T=Pastel Sandstone Poly, 64T=Doeskin, 77T=Dark Maple and 85T=Medium Slate Poly.

ENGINE CODES

Codes appear on the right side of V-6 cylinder blocks behind the distributor and right-hand side of V-8 engine blocks. Engine codes for 1981 were: (229-cid two-barrel V-6) DAA, DAB, DAC, DAD, DAH, DAJ, DAK, D7A and D7B; (231-cid two-barrel V-6) NA, NB, NC, ND, NF, NL, LZ, RA, RB, NJ, RK, RL, RC, RD, NZ and NK; (267-cid two-barrel V-8) DFA, DFC, DFD, DFF, DFH, DBA, D8C, D8D, D8F, D8H and DFK; (305-cid four-barrel V-8) DHA, DHB, DHC, DHD, DKH, DHF, DHH, DHK, DHJ, DHZ, DKB, D6A, D6B, D6C, D6D, DHU and DKF; (350-cid four-barrel El Camino V-8) DMA, DMC, DMD, D5A, D5B, DMB, DMF and DMH.

EL CAMINO — SERIES W — V-6/V-8

Standard equipment features included a 3.8-liter (229-cid) V-6 (not available in California), a three-speed manual transmission, Computer Command Control, frameless door glass and thin roof pillars, bright roof drip moldings, new diamond-patterned full wheel trim covers, a bright windshield molding, a bright rear window molding, a padded instrument panel, steel-belted radial tires, self-adjusting front disc brakes with wear indicators, a High Energy Ignition system, a Freedom side-terminal battery, a dual-mode ventilation system, a fully inflated compact spare tire, a bright left-hand outside rearview mirror, extensive corrosion-resisting treatments, visible ball-joint wear indicators, a front stabilizer bar, a Delcotron generator, a coolant recovery system, seat belts with push-button buckle releases for all passengers, two combination seat and inertia reel shoulder belts for driver and passenger (with reminder light and buzzer), an energy-absorbing steering column, passenger guard door locks, safety door latches with stamped steel hinges, a contoured windshield header, a thick laminate windshield, a safety steering wheel, side marker lights and reflectors, parking lights that illuminate with the headlamps, four-way hazard flashers, back-up lights, directional signals with a lane-change feature, a defroster, dual speed windshield wipers, windshield washers, a 10-in.-wide prismatic wide-view day/night inside rearview mirror with vinyl edging and a deflecting support, a left-hand outside rearview mirror, a dual master cylinder brake system with warning light, a starter safety switch, a dual-action safety hood latch, an ignition key reminder buzzer and a steering column lock. For 1981, the El Camino's interior elegance was significantly improved. Convenient new door-pull straps graced the doors and even the standard split-back front seat was trimmed with luxurious fabrics. Power steering became standard equipment. The standard full-foam cushioned bench seat had the handy split back so El Camino owners could reach the concealed storage compartments behind it. The spare tire was stowed behind the passenger side seating position and now had an extractor for easy removal. Roomy contoured bucket seats were optional (with or without a floor console and floor shifter). A brand new option was a 55/45 seat option with a single folding armrest.

Model Number	Body/Style Number	Body Type & Seating	Factory Price	Shipping Weight	Production Total
EL CAMINO SERIES W (V-6)					
W	80	pickup	$6,938	—	Note 1
EL CAMINO SERIES W (BASE V-8)					
W	80	pickup	$6,988	3,181 lbs.	Note 1

EL CAMINO SS — SERIES W + Z15 V-8

The 1981 El Camino Super Sport was a blend of the El Camino's basic value, plus a lot of sporty character. The model option included a large front air dam, painted sport mirrors, a choice of eight accent colors on the lower body, decal striping, "Super Sport" decal identification on the lower doors and tailgate, color-keyed Rallye wheels and a new "Super Sport" dashboard nameplate. There was no SS identification on the radiator grille.

El Camino

Model Number	Body/Style Number	Body Type & Seating	Factory Price	Shipping Weight	Production Total
W	80	pickup	$7,217	3,238 lbs.	Note 1

NOTE 1 Total El Camino production was 37,533.

MODEL OPTIONS

CONQUISTA PACKAGE: The El Camino Conquista package was a dramatic paint treatment option featuring an accent color on the hood, body sides and lower portion of the tailgate to set off the basic body color. There were also bright paint break moldings along the pickup box and tailgate, bright lower body side moldings and bright wheel opening moldings. A Conquista decal on the tailgate and a dash nameplate completed the $161 package.

ROYAL KNIGHT PACKAGE: The Royal Knight package featured a color-keyed regal hood decal, tri-tone pin striping, color-keyed Royal Knight decals on the front fenders and tailgate, a large front air dam, Rallye wheels and painted Sport mirrors.

ENGINES

EL CAMINO BASE 229-CID, 110-HP V-6 (FEDERAL): Overhead-valve. Cast-iron block and head. Displacement: 229 cid (3.8 liters). Bore & stroke: 3.74 x 3.48 in. Compression ratio: 8.6:1. Brake hp: 110 at 4200 rpm. Torque: 170 lbs.-ft. at 2000 rpm. Four main bearings. Hydraulic valve lifters. Carburetor: Rochester two-barrel 2ME. Sales Code: LC3. VIN code: K.

EL CAMINO BASE 231-CID, 110-HP V-6 (CALIFORNIA): Overhead-valve. Cast-iron block and head. Displacement: 231 cid (3.8 liters). Bore & stroke: 3.80 x 3.40 in. Compression ratio: 8.0:1. Brake hp: 110 at 3800 rpm Torque: 190 lbs.-ft. at 1600 rpm. Four main bearings. Hydraulic valve lifters. Carburetor: Rochester E2ME two-barrel. Sales Code: LD5. VIN code: A.

EL CAMINO BASE 267-CID, 115-HP V-8: Overhead-valve. Cast-iron block and head. Bore and stroke: 3.50 x 3.48 in. Displacement: 267 cid (4.4 liters). Compression ratio: 8.3:1. Net brake hp: 115 at 4000 rpm. Taxable hp: 39.20. Net torque: 200 lbs.-ft. at 2400 rpm. Five main bearings. Hydraulic valve lifters. Carburetor: Rochester 2ME two-barrel. VIN Code: J.

EL CAMINO OPTIONAL 305-CID, 150-HP V-8: Overhead-valve. Cast-iron block and head. Bore and stroke: 3.74 x 3.48 in. Displacement: 305 cid (5.0 liters). Compression ratio: 8.6:1. Net brake hp: 150 at 3800 rpm. Taxable hp: 44.66. Net torque: 240 lbs.-ft. at 2400 rpm. Five main bearings. Hydraulic valve lifters. Carburetor: Rochester 4ME four-barrel. VIN Code: H.

CHASSIS

Wheelbase: 117.1 in. Overall length: 201.60 in. Height: 53.8 in. Front tread: 58.5 in. Rear tread: 57.8 in. Cargo box length from back of cab to top of tailgate: 79.5 in. Bed width between rear wheel housings: 45 in. Bed width above rear wheel housings: 59.5 in. Tires: G78-14B. Transmission: Three-speed synchromesh. Gears: 3F/1R. Column-mounted gearshift lever. Single-plate, dry-disc clutch (with V-6). Rear axle: semi-floating. Hydraulic four-wheel brakes. Kelsey-Hayes pressed steel wheels.

OPTIONS

A01 tinted body glass. A02 tinted windshield. A31 electric windows. A32 electric front door window. AG9 six-way power seat control. AU3 power door locks ($93). AU6 electric tailgate lock release. AV3 pickup box tie downs. B32 front floor mats. B90 side window moldings. B93 door edge guards. B96 wheel opening moldings. B3W preliminary price information. BS1 acoustical insulation. BW2 Deluxe body molding exterior ornamentation. BX8 moldings and two-tone paint. C60 manual air conditioning. CD4 pulse type windshield wipers. D28 right-hand outside rearview mirror. D33 remote-control driver's mirror. D35 remote-control left-hand outside rearview mirror. D36 10-in. tilting export inside rearview mirror. D55 front compartment floor console. D68 dual sport-style exterior rearview mirrors. D73 pickup box handrail. D84 custom two-tone paint. D85 lower body side accent stripe. D91 special two-tone paint. F40 heavy-duty front and rear suspension. F41 special

The 1981 Super Sport again featured a choice of eight different body accent colors and bold graphics on the doors.

heavy-duty suspension front and rear. G80 Positraction. K05 engine block heater. K35 speed and cruise control with resume. K73 70-amp generator. K81 63-amp generator. L39 267-cid V-8 engine. LC3 229-cid V-6. LD5 231-cid V-6. LG4 305-cid V-8. MM3 three-speed manual transmission. MM4 four-speed manual transmission. MX1 automatic transmission. N18 locking wire wheel covers. N23 22-gallon fuel tank. N33 tilt steering. N95 simulated wire wheel covers. NM5 non-closed-loop emission system (Canada). NM8 leaded gas conversion emissions modification. QXW P195-70R14 steel-belted radial white striped tires. QXX P205-70R14 steel-belted radial black sidewall tires. QXY P205-75R14 steel-belted radial white stripe tires. QXZ P205-75R14 steel-belted radial white letter tires. QYA P205-70R14 steel-belted radial black sidewall tires. QYB P205-70R14 steel-belted radial white stripe tires. QYC P205-70R steel-belted radial white letter tires. QYD P185-75R14 glass-belted radial black sidewall tires. QYE P185-75R14 glass-belted white-stripe radial tires. QYF P195-75R14 glass-belted black sidewall tires. QYG P195-75R14 glass-belted white-stripe tires. T72 required dual left-hand headlights for export. T84 right-hand headlamp for export. T85 left-hand headlight for export. T90 Export turn signal and marker lamps. TR9 lamp group. TT4 tungsten quartz halogen headlights. U05 dual horns. U14 gauge package. U18 export speedometer. U35 electric clock. U58 AM/FM stereo. U63 push-button AM radio. U69 AM/FM push-button radio. U75 power antenna. U76 windshield antenna. U80 auxiliary speaker. UA1 heavy-duty battery. UF7 gauges package. UM2 AM-FM push-button radio and stereo tape player. UN3 AM/FM stereo cassette radio, less clock. UP6 AM/FM stereo CB radio. V08 heavy-duty cooling. V30 front and rear bumper guards. V78 less certificate of compliance plate. V84 government export orders, U.S. vehicles. VB1 Japanese shipping label. VC3 U.S. Territory shipping label. VC4 Puerto Rico shipping label. VC5 price label, non-Japan. VE5 bumper impact strip. YC8 demo option drive. YF5 California emission requirements. YG6 Royal Sierra, Bonanza package A. YG7 Royal Sierra, Bonanza package B. YG8 Royal Sierra, Bonanza package C. YJ7 demo drive. Z15 SS package. Z16 Royal Knight. Z49 mandatory Canadian base equipment modifications. ZJ1 two-tone custom interior. ZJ2 custom exterior moldings. ZJ3 Chevy's '81 Value Bonus package. ZJ4 Chevy's '81 Value Bonus package. ZJ7 special hubcaps and trim rings. ZN7 color-keyed Rallye wheels. Conquista trim. Cargo box tonneau cover. Vinyl roof. ZL6 Chevy's '81 Value Bonus package phase II. ZL7 Chevy's '81 Value Bonus package phase II. ZL8 Chevy's '81 Value Bonus package phase II. ZL9 Chevy's '81 Value Bonus package phase II. Cloth 55/45 seating.

OPTION INSTALLATION RATES

267-cid V-8 engine (23.9 percent). 305-cid V-8 engine (26.1 percent). V-6 (50 percent). Automatic transmission (85.3 percent). Four-speed transmission (1.3 percent). Power front disc brakes (100 percent). Positraction (7.4 percent). Power steering (99.3 percent). Styled wheels (79.9 percent). Standard wheel covers (20.1 percent). Steel-belted radial tires (100 percent). Exterior trim package (34.7 percent). Bucket seats (9.6 percent). Tinted glass (89.5 percent). Air conditioning (75.7 percent). Cruise control (35.2 percent). Adjustable steering column (50.4 percent). Power windows (13.3 percent). Power door locks (11.4 percent). AM radio (44.9 percent). AM/FM radio (14.1 percent). Stereo (10.3 percent). Tape player (8.5 percent). CB radio (1 percent). Conventional rear bumper (100 percent).

HISTORICAL FOOTNOTES

Michael H. Erdman became sales manager for Chevrolet trucks. Jack L. Sherman became truck merchandising manager. For the 1981 calendar year, Chevrolet sold only 675,628 commercial vehicles, a 10.7 percent drop from 1980. El Camino model-year sales were 36,711 units compared to 43,896 the previous year.

The El Camino adopted the Malibu's new Caprice-style grille and side-by-side dual rectangular headlamps in 1982. The grille had three thin horizontal bars and 15 vertical ones. The Chevrolet name appeared at the lower left side and a stand-up hood ornament was seen again. Also revised was the seating and instrument panel and a new "Smart Switch" was added to the steering column.

The Malibu gained diesel power through the optional 5.7-liter (350-cid) V-8 or the new 4.3-liter (260-cid) V-6 engine. Chevrolet carried over the gas engine lineup from 1981, including the standard 3.8-liter (229-cid) V-6 and optional 4.4-liter (267-cid) V-8 and 5.0-liter (305-cid) V-8. In California the 231-cid 3.8-liter V-6 was standard and the LG4 5.0-liter V-8 was the only option.

I.D. NUMBERS

VIN embossed on the top left-hand side of the instrument panel and visible through the windshield. The first designates the country of origin: 1=U.S. and 2=Canada. The second symbol indentifies the manufacturer: G=General Motors. The third symbol indicates the make: 1=Chevrolet. The fourth symbol indicates the type of restraint system: A=non-passive/manual seat belts; B=passive/automatic seat belts and C=passive/inflatable. The fifth symbol indicates series: W=El Camino. The sixth and seventh indicate body style: 80=El Camino. The eighth symbol indicates engine (net hp): K=RPO LC3 229-cid/110-hp V-6, A=RPO LD5 231-cid/110-hp V-6 (California), J=RPO L39 267-cid/115-hp V-8, H=RPO LG4 305-cid/145-hp V-8, V=RPO

EL CAMINO

The 1982 Conquista package again gave El Camino buyers the option of a two-tone paint job.

LT6 260-cid/85-hp diesel V-6 and N=RPO LF9 350-cid-105-hp diesel V-8. The ninth symbol is a check digit. The 10th symbol designates the model year: C=1982. The 11th symbol designates the assembly plant location: R=Arlington, Texas. The last six symbols are the sequential unit production number at the specific factory. The Fisher body tag riveted to the top of the cowl on the left side of the car below the hood provides additional vehicle identification information. The Fisher body STYLE NUMBER (ST) consists of a prefix identifying model year and four or more symbols identifying the series and body style (example: 82-1GW for a 1982 El Camino). The BODY NUMBER consists of a prefix designating assembly plant and the sequential unit production number at the specific factory. The TRIM NUMBER (TR) identifies upholstery.

COLORS

(11) Antique White, (16) Silver Poly, (19) Black, (21) Light Blue Poly, (22) Bright Blue Poly, (29) Dark Blue Poly, (45) Light Jadestone Poly, (49) Dark Jadestone Poly, (55) Goldwing Poly, (57) Marigold, (63) Pastel Sandstone, (67) Dark Goldwing Poly, (68) Medium Sandstone Poly, (72) Light Redwood Poly, (74) Autumn Maple, (75) Spectra Red, (77) Dark Redwood Poly, (78) Dark Claret Poly, (80) Slate Gray, (84) Charcoal Poly, (85) Medium Slate Firemist and (88) Dark Brown Firemist. Vinyl tops were available in: 11T=White, 19T=Black, 29T=Dark Blue Poly, 36T=Light waxberry Poly, 45T=Light Jadestone Poly, 63T=Pastel Sandstone Poly, 64T=Doeskin, 77T=Dark Maple and 85T=Medium Slate Poly.

ENGINE CODES

Codes appear on the right side of V-6 cylinder blocks behind the distributor and right-hand side of V-8 engine blocks. Engine codes for 1982 were: (229-cid two-barrel V-6) CCA, CCH, CCM, CCR, CCC, CCK, CCN, CCS and CCF; (231-cid two-barrel V-6) ML and MG; (260-cid diesel V-6) UAA, UAD and UAJ; (267-cid two-barrel V-8) CDB, CDJ, C4S, C4U, CDC, C4N, C4T, C4W, CDD and C4R; (305-cid four-barrel V-8) CFA, CFH, CFZ, C2T, CFB, CFR, CRA, C2U, CFC, CFT, C2R, C2W, CFD, CFW, C2S, C2X, CFF and CFY; (350-cid diesel V-8) VAB, VAM, VAW, VBB, VAC, VAN, VAX, VBC, VAD, VAP, VAY, VBP, VAK, VAS, VAZ, VB4, VAL, VAU, VBA and VBW.

EL CAMINO — SERIES W — V-6/V-8

Standard equipment features included a 3.8-liter (229-cid) V-6 (not available in California), an automatic transmission, power steering, Computer Command Control, steering column "Smart Switch," frameless door glass and thin roof pillars, bright roof drip moldings, full wheel trim covers, a bright windshield molding, a bright rear window molding, a redesigned padded instrument panel, steel-belted radial tires, self-adjusting power front disc brakes with wear indicators and a new quick take-up master cylinder, a High Energy Ignition system, a Freedom side-terminal battery, a dual-mode ventilation system, a fully inflated compact spare tire, a bright left-hand outside rearview mirror, extensive corrosion-resisting treatments, visible ball-joint wear indicators, a front stabilizer bar, a generator, a coolant recovery system, seat belts with push-button buckle releases for all passengers, two combination seat and inertia reel shoulder belts for driver and passenger (with reminder light and buzzer), an energy-absorbing steering column, passenger guard door locks, safety door latches with stamped steel hinges, a contoured windshield header, a thick laminate windshield, a safety steering wheel, side marker lights and reflectors, parking lights that illuminate with the headlamps, four-way hazard flashers, back-up lights, directional signals with a lane-change feature, a defroster, dual speed windshield wipers, windshield washers, a 10-in.-wide prismatic wide-view day/night inside rearview mirror with vinyl edging and a deflecting support, a left-hand outside rearview mirror, a dual master cylinder brake system with warning light, a starter safety switch, a dual-action safety hood latch, an ignition key reminder buzzer and a steering column lock. For 1982, the El Camino's standard interior reflected a high level of comfort and businesslike practicality. It was outfitted with a padded headliner, armrests, door-to-door color-keyed carpeting and new notchback seats with a fold-down center armrest upholstered in knit cloth or vinyl. All El Camino interiors were made more attractive this year with the addition of a handsome new instrument panel featuring easy-to-read round gauges accented by simulated wood-grain trim. In addition, the new steering-column-mounted "Smart Switch" provided fingertip control for the headlights, bright lights, windshield wipers and washers and optional automatic speed control.

Model Number	Body/Style Number	Body Type & Seating	Factory Price	Shipping Weight	Production Total
EL CAMINO SERIES W (V-6)					
W	80	pickup	$7,925	—	Note 1
EL CAMINO SERIES W (BASE V-8)					
W	80	pickup	$7,995	3,294 lbs.	Note 1

EL CAMINO SS — SERIES W + Z15 V-8

The 1982 El Camino Super Sport was a blend of the El Camino's basic value, plus a lot of sporty character. The model option included a large front air dam, painted sport mirrors, a choice of seven accent colors on the lower body, decal striping, "Super Sport" decal identification on the lower doors and tailgate, color-keyed rally wheels and a new "Super Sport" dashboard nameplate. There was no SS identification on the radiator grille.

Model Number	Body/Style Number	Body Type & Seating	Factory Price	Shipping Weight	Production Total
W	80	pickup	$8,244	3,300 lbs.	Note 1

NOTE 1 Total El Camino production was 23,104.

MODEL OPTIONS

CONQUISTA PACKAGE: The El Camino Conquista package was a dramatic paint treatment option featuring an accent color on the hood, body sides and lower portion of the tailgate to set off the basic body color. There were also bright paint break moldings along the pickup box and tailgate, bright lower body side moldings and bright wheel opening moldings. A Conquista decal on the tailgate and a dash nameplate completed the $183 package.

ROYAL KNIGHT PACKAGE: The Royal Knight package featured a color-keyed regal hood decal, tri-tone pin striping, color-keyed Royal Knight decals on the front fenders and tailgate, a large front air dam, Rallye wheels and painted sport mirrors. We didn't change our description of this package and Chevrolet didn't change the photo of the El Camino Royal Knight used in the sales catalog, except to airbrush in the new Caprice-like grille with side-by-side rectangular headlights at each end.

The 1982 El Camino had a new grille and side-by-side dual rectangular headlights. This machine is heavily modified with a different hood, grille, badging, and aftermarket wheels.

ENGINES

EL CAMINO BASE 229-CID, 110-HP V-6: 90-degree, overhead-valve. Cast-iron block and head. Bore and stroke: 3.74 x 3.48 in. Displacement: 229 cid (3.8 liters). Compression ratio: 8.6:1. Brake hp: 110 at 4200 rpm. Torque: 170 lbs.-ft. at 2000 rpm. Four main bearings. Hydraulic valve lifters. Carburetor: Rochester two-barrel E2ME. VIN Code: K.

EL CAMINO BASE 231-CID, 110-HP V-6 (CALIFORNIA): Overhead-valve V-6. Cast-iron block and head. Displacement: 231 cid (3.8 liters). Bore & stroke: 3.80 x 3.40 in. Compression ratio: 8.0:1. Brake hp: 110 at 3800 rpm Torque: 190 lbs.-ft. at 1600 rpm Four main bearings. Hydraulic valve lifters. Carburetor: Rochester E2ME two-barrel. Sales Code: LD5. VIN code: A.

EL CAMINO OPTIONAL 267-CID, 115-HP V-8: Overhead-valve. Cast-iron block and head. Bore and stroke: 3.50 x 3.48 in. Displacement: 267 cid (4.4 liters). Compression ratio: 8.3:1. Net brake hp: 115 at 4000 rpm. Taxable hp: 39.20. Net brake hp: 120 at 3600 rpm. Net torque: 205 lbs.-ft. at 2400 rpm. Five main bearings. Hydraulic valve lifters. Carburetor: Rochester E2ME two-barrel. VIN Code: J.

EL CAMINO OPTIONAL 305-CID, 145-HP V-8: Overhead-valve. Cast-iron block and head. Bore and stroke: 3.74 x 3.48 in. Displacement: 305 cid (5.0 liters). Compression ratio: 8.6:1. Net brake hp: 145 at 4000 rpm. Taxable hp: 44.66. Net torque: 240 lbs.-ft. at 2000 rpm. Five main bearings. Hydraulic valve lifters. Carburetor: Rochester E4ME four-barrel. VIN Code: H.

CHASSIS

Wheelbase: 117.1 in. Overall length: 201.60 in. Width: 71.9 in. Height: 53.8 in. Front tread: 58.5 in. Rear tread: 57.8 in. Cargo box length from back of cab to top of tailgate: 79.5 in. Bed width between rear wheel housings: 45 in. Bed width above rear wheel housings: 59.5 in. Tires: G78-14B. Transmission: Automatic. Column-mounted gearshift lever. Rear axle: semi-floating. Hydraulic four-wheel brakes. Kelsey-Hayes pressed steel wheels.

OPTIONS

A01 tinted body glass. A02 tinted windshield. A31 electric windows. A32 electric front door window. AG9 six-way power seat control ($175). AU3 power door locks ($93). AU6 electric tailgate lock release. AV3 pickup box tie downs. B32 front floor mats. B90 side window moldings. B93 door edge guards. B96 wheel opening moldings. B3W preliminary price information. BS1 acoustical insulation. BW2 Deluxe body molding exterior ornamentation. BX8 moldings and two-tone paint. C60 manual air conditioning. CD4 pulse type windshield wipers. D28 right-hand outside rearview mirror. D33 remote-control driver's mirror. D35 remote-control left-hand outside rearview mirror. D36 10-in. tilting export inside rearview mirror. D55 front compartment floor console. D68 dual Sport-style exterior rearview mirrors. D73 pickup box handrail. D84 custom two-tone paint. D85 lower body side accent stripe. D91 special two-tone paint. F40 heavy-duty front and rear suspension. F41 special heavy-duty suspension front and rear. G80 Positraction. G84 high-altitude rear axle ratio. G92 performance ratio rear axle. GH2 2.29:1 rear axle ratio. GM7 2.39:1 rear axle ratio. GM8 2.56:1 rear axle ratio. GU1 2.41:1 rear axle ratio. GU2 2.73:1 rear axle ratio. GU3 2.93:1 rear axle ratio. GU4 3.08:1 rear axle ratio. GU5 3.23:1 rear axle ratio. GW9 2.93:1 rear axle ratio. JE1 European export brake system. K05 engine block heater. K35 Cruise and speed control with resume. K73 70-amp. Delcotron generator. LC3 229-cid V-6 engine (standard Federal engine). L39 267-cid V-8 engine. LD5 231-cid V-6 engine (standard California engine). LG4 305-cid V-8 engine in station wagon. LT6 4.3-liter diesel V-6. MX1 Turbo-Hydra-Matic automatic transmission. N18 simulated wire wheel covers. N23 22-gal. fuel tank. N33 Tilt steering wheel. N81 full-size spare radial tire. N95 simulated wire wheel covers with locks. NA6 alternate requirements emission system. NM5 Non-closed loop emission system on Canadian cars. NM8 leaded gas emissions modification. P41 export tire equipment. P42 self-sealing tire. QVJ P195-75R14 steel-belted white stripe radial tires. QVT P205-75R14B steel-belted radial tires with white stripe. QXW P195-75R14B steel-belted radial tires with white stripe. QXX P205-75R14B steel-belted radial black sidewall tires. QXY P205-75R14B steel-belted radial tires with white stripe. QXZ P205-75R14B steel-belted radial tires with raised white letters. QYD P185-75R14B radial black sidewall tires. QYE P185-75R14B radial tires with white stripes. QYF P195-75R14B radial black sidewall tires. QYG P195-75R14B radial tires with white stripes. T84 rectangular export-type right-hand headlight. T90 export-type signal light and marker lamp. TR9 lamp group. TT5 tungsten quartz halogen headlights. U14 special instrumentation gauge package. U18 export speedometer. U35 electric clock. U58 AM/FM push-button stereo. U63 AM push-button radio. U69 AM/FM push-button radio. U73 fixed antenna. U75 power antenna. U76 windshield antenna included with all radios. U81 dual rear radio speakers. UA1 heavy-duty battery. UF7 gauge package, except tachometer. UM2 AM/FM push-button radio and tape player. UN3 AM/FM stereo cassette radio less clock. V08 heavy-duty radiator. V10 cold climate package. V30 front and rear bumper guards. VC3 U.S. Territory shipping label. VC4 Puerto Rico shipping label. VE5 front and rear bumper impact strips. YC8 demo option drive. Z15 El Camino SS package. Z16 El Camino Black Knight Sport décor package. Z49 mandatory Canadian base equipment model. ZJ1 two-tone custom interior. ZJ2 custom exterior moldings. ZJ7 special wheel package with hubcap and trim rings. Dual horns.

OPTION INSTALLATION RATES

267-cid V-8 engine (18.5 percent). 305-cid V-8 engine (44.9 percent). V-6 (36.6 percent). Automatic transmission (100 percent). Power front disc brakes (100 percent). Positraction (8.7 percent). Power steering (100 percent). Styled wheels (81.9 percent). Steel-belted radial tires (100 percent). Base exterior/exterior trim package (42.8 percent). Level 2 exterior/exterior trim package (43.3 percent). Level 3 exterior/exterior trim package (10 percent). Level 4 exterior/exterior trim package (3.9 percent). Tinted glass (96.2 percent). Air conditioning (91.7 percent). Cruise control (62.8 percent). Adjustable steering column (74.7 percent). Power windows (28.1 percent). Power door locks (26.8 percent). AM radio (29.3 percent). AM/FM radio (11.4 percent). Stereo (28.7 percent). Cassette player (12.9 percent). 8-track tape player (2.7 percent).

HISTORICAL FOOTNOTES

Michael H. Erdman was sales manager for Chevrolet trucks. Jeffrey P. Hulbert became truck merchandising manager. For the 1982 calendar year, Chevrolet sold 758,387 trucks, an 8 percent gain over 1981. Calendar-year sales of El Caminos were 22,732 units. Production of El Camino's was actually quartered in GM's Arlington, Texas, plant where Buick Regals, Monte Carlos, Malibus, El Caminos and Caballeros were built this year.

The 1983 El Camino was luxurious. The base El Camino had dual, side-by-side, rectangular headlights on either side of a cross-hatch grille, with long, narrow parking lights directly below the headlights. The bumper was of a simple, straight-across design. This was the first year that the El Camino could be ordered with a 5.7-liter V-8.

I.D. NUMBERS

VIN embossed on the top left-hand side of the instrument panel and visible through the windshield. The first designates the country of origin: 1=U.S. and 2=Canada. The second symbol indentifies the manufacturer: G=General Motors. The third symbol indicates the make: 1=Chevrolet. The fourth symbol indicates the type of restraint system: A=non-passive/manual seat belts; B=passive/automatic seat belts and C=passive/inflatable. The fifth symbol indicates the car line/series: W=El Camino. The sixth and seventh symbols indicate body type: 80=El Camino. The eighth symbol indicates engine (net hp): 9=RPO LC3 229-cid/115-hp V-6, A=RPO LD5 231-cid/110-hp V-6 (California), H=RPO LG4 305-cid/150-hp V-8, V=RPO LT6 260-cid/85-hp diesel V-6 and N=RPO LF9 350-cid/125-hp diesel V-8. The ninth symbol is a check digit. The 10th symbol designates the model year: D=1983. The 11th symbol designates the assembly plant location: R=Arlington, Texas. The last six symbols are the sequential unit production number at the specific factory. The Fisher body tag riveted to the top of the cowl on the left side of the car below the hood provides additional vehicle identification information. The Fisher body STYLE NUMBER (ST) consists of a prefix identifying model year and four or more symbols identifying the series and body style (example: 83-1AW for a 1983 El Camino). The BODY NUMBER consists of a prefix designating assembly plant and the sequential unit production number at the specific factory. The TRIM NUMBER (TR) identifies upholstery.

COLORS

(11) White, (15) Silver Sand Poly, (19) Black, (22) Light Blue Poly, (27) Medium Dark Royal Blue Poly, (42) Light Grayfern Poly, (48) Dark Grayfern Poly, (60) Light Sand Gray, (62) Light Briar Brown Poly, (67) Dark Briar Brown Poly, (75) Spectra Red and (78) Dark Autumn

Standard equipment on the 1983 El Camino included a 3.8-liter V-6, redesigned instrument panel, self-adjusting front disc brakes, and Computer Command Control.

Maple Poly. Vinyl tops were available in: 11T=White, 19T=Black, 27T=Medium Dark Royal Blue, 42T=Light Grayfern, 60T Light Sand Gray, 67T Dark Briar Brown, 78T=Dark Autumn Maple and 91T=Light Flax Poly.

ENGINE CODES

Codes appear on the right side of V-6 cylinder blocks behind the distributor and right-hand side of V-8 engine blocks. Engine codes for 1982 were: (229-cid two-barrel V-6) DBA, DBB and DBC; (231-cid two-barrel V-6) NL, ND, NG, NH and NJ; (260-cid diesel V-6) UKA, UKB, UKC, UKJ and UKK; (305-cid four-barrel V-8) DDB, DDJ, DDK, DGN, D5F, DDD, D5B, D5H, DDF, DDN, D5C and DDH; (350-cid diesel V-8) VLB, VKZ and VLA.

EL CAMINO — SERIES W — V-6/V-8

Standard equipment features included a 3.8-liter (229-cid) V-6 (not available in California), an automatic transmission, power steering, Computer Command Control, a steering column "Smart Switch," frameless door glass and thin roof pillars, bright roof drip moldings, full wheel trim covers, a bright windshield molding, a bright rear window molding, a redesigned padded instrument panel, steel-belted radial tires, self-adjusting power front disc brakes with wear indicators and a quick take-up master cylinder, a High Energy Ignition system, a Freedom side-terminal battery, a dual-mode ventilation system, a fully inflated compact spare tire, a bright left-hand outside rearview mirror, extensive corrosion-resisting treatments, visible ball-joint wear indicators, a front stabilizer bar, a generator, a coolant recovery system, seat belts with push-button buckle releases for all passengers, two combination seat and inertia reel shoulder belts for driver and passenger (with reminder light and buzzer), an energy-absorbing steering column, passenger guard door locks, safety door latches with stamped steel hinges, a contoured windshield header, a thick laminate windshield, a safety steering wheel, side marker lights and reflectors, parking lights that illuminate with the headlamps, four-way hazard flashers, back-up lights, directional signals with a lane-change feature, a defroster, dual speed windshield wipers, windshield washers, a 10-in.-wide prismatic wide-view day/night inside rearview mirror with vinyl edging and a deflecting support, a left-hand outside rearview mirror, a dual master cylinder brake system with warning light, a starter safety switch, a dual-action safety hood latch, an ignition key reminder buzzer and a steering column lock. The standard El Camino interior featured a padded headliner, armrests, door-to-door color-keyed carpeting and notchback seats with a fold-down center armrest upholstered in knit cloth or vinyl.

Model Number	Body/Style Number	Body Type & Seating	Factory Price	Shipping Weight	Production Total
EL CAMINO SERIES W (V-6)					
W	80	pickup	$8,121	—	Note 1
EL CAMINO SERIES W (BASE V-8)					
W	80	pickup	$8,191	3,294 lbs.	Note 1

EL CAMINO SS — SERIES W + Z15 V-8

The El Camino Super Sport was a blend of the El Camino's basic value, plus a lot of sporty character. The model option included a large front air dam, painted sport mirrors, a choice of accent colors on the lower body, decal striping, "Super Sport" decal identification on the lower doors and tailgate, color-keyed rally wheels and a new "Super Sport" dashboard nameplate. There was no SS identification on the radiator grille.

Model Number	Body/Style Number	Body Type & Seating	Factory Price	Shipping Weight	Production Total
W	80	pickup	$8,445	3,337 lbs.	Note 1

NOTE 1: Total El Camino production was 22,429.

MODEL OPTIONS

CONQUISTA PACKAGE: The El Camino Conquista package was a dramatic paint treatment option featuring an accent color on the hood, body sides and lower portion of the tailgate to set off the basic body color. There were also bright paint break moldings along the pickup box and tailgate, bright lower body side moldings and bright wheel opening moldings. A Conquista decal on the tailgate and a dash nameplate completed the $189 package.

ROYAL KNIGHT PACKAGE: The Royal Knight package featured a color-keyed regal hood decal, tri-tone pin striping, color-keyed Royal Knight decals on the front fenders and tailgate, a large front air dam, Rallye wheels and painted sport mirrors. We didn't change our description of this package and Chevrolet didn't change the photo of the El Camino Royal Knight used in the sales catalog, except to airbrush in the new Caprice-like grille with side-by-side rectangular headlights at each end.

ENGINES

EL CAMINO BASE 229-CID, 115-HP V-6: 90-degree, overhead-valve. Cast-iron block and head. Bore and stroke: 3.74 x 3.48 in. Displacement: 229-cid (3.8 liters). Compression ratio: 8.6:1. Brake hp: 115 at 4200 rpm. Torque: 170 lbs.-ft. at 2000 rpm. Four main bearings. Hydraulic valve lifters. Carburetor: two-barrel Rochester E2ME. VIN Code: K or 9.
(**NOTE:** California models used a Buick 231-cid V-6.)

EL CAMINO OPTIONAL 305-CID, 150-HP V-8: 90-degree, overhead valve. Cast-iron block and head. Bore and stroke: 3.74 x 3.48 in. Displacement: 305-cid (5.0 liters). Compression ratio: 8.6:1. Brake hp: 150 at 4000 rpm. Torque: 240 lbs.-ft. at 2400 rpm. Five main bearings. Hydraulic valve lifters. Carburetor: four-barrel Rochester E4ME. VIN Code: H.

EL CAMINO OPTIONAL 350-CID, 105-HP DIESEL V-8: 90-degree, overhead-valve. Cast-iron block and head. Bore and stroke: 4.057 x 3.385 in. Displacement: 350-cid (5.7 liters). Compression ratio: 22.5:1. Brake hp: 105 at 3200 rpm. Torque: 200 lbs.-ft. at 1600 rpm. Five main bearings. Hydraulic valve lifters. Fuel injection. Olds-built. VIN Code: N.

CHASSIS

Wheelbase: 117.1 in. Overall length: 201.60 in. Width: 71.9 in. Height: 53.8 in. Front tread: 58.5 in. Rear tread: 57.8 in. Cargo box length from back of cab to top of tailgate: 79.5 in. Bed width between rear wheel housings: 45 in. Bed width above rear wheel housings: 59.5 in. Tires: G78-14B. Transmission: Automatic. Column-mounted gearshift lever. Rear axle: semi-floating.

Hydraulic four-wheel brakes. Kelsey-Hayes pressed steel wheels.

OPTIONS

A01 all tinted glass ($105). A02 tinted windshield. A26 United Kingdom and European Glazing Window. A31 power windows with electric control ($255). A32 electric front door window. AG9 six-way power seat adjuster. AU3 power door locks ($170). AU6 El Camino electric tailgate release ($40). AV3 El Camino pickup box tie downs. B37 color-keyed floor mats. B93 door edge guards ($15-$25). BS1 acoustical insulation. BW2 Deluxe body molding exterior decoration ($57). BX8 front fender and body moldings. B2L fleet early order option. B3W preliminary price information. B6W fleet A/C incentive program. C49 electric rear window defogger ($135). C60 manual air conditioning ($725). CD4 pulse-type windshield wipers and washers. D33 remote-control left-hand outside rearview mirror ($22). D35 custom outside rearview mirrors ($59). D73 pickup box hand rail. D84 custom two-tone paint ($138). D85 body side lower accent stripes. DG8 export breakaway mirror. F40 heavy-duty front and rear suspension ($26). G80 Positraction rear axle ($95). G84 high-altitude rear axle ratio. G92 performance ratio rear axle ($21). GH2 2.29:1 rear axle ratio. GM7 2.39:1 rear axle ratio. GM8 2.56:1 rear axle ratio. GM8 2.56:1 rear axle ratio. GT4 3.73:1 rear axle ratio. GU1 2.41:1 rear axle ratio. GU2 2.73:1 rear axle ratio. GU3 2.93:1 rear axle ratio. GU4 3.08:1 rear axle ratio. GU5 3.23:1 rear axle ratio. GU6 3.42:1 rear axle ratio. GW9 2.93:1 rear axle ratio. JE1 European export brake system. K05 engine block heater. K35 Cruise and speed control with resume. K64 78-amp. Delcotron generator. LC3 229-cid V-6 engine (standard Federal engine). LD5 231-cid V-6 engine (standard California engine). LF9 350-cid diesel V-8 ($700). LG4 305-cid V-8 engine ($225). LT6 4.3-liter diesel V-6 ($500). MX1 Turbo-Hydra-Matic automatic transmission (standard). N18 simulated wire wheel covers. N23 22-gal. fuel tank. N33 Tilt steering wheel ($105). N81 full-size spare radial tire. N95 simulated wire wheel covers with locks ($190). NA6 alternate requirements emission system. NM5 Non-closed loop emission system on Canadian cars. NM8 leaded gas emissions modification. P01 Deluxe wheel trim covers. P41 export tire equipment. PB2 ABS plastic wheel trim covers. QVJ P195-75R14 steel-belted white stripe radial tires. QVT P205-75R14B steel-belted radial tires with white stripe. QXX P205-75R14B steel-belted radial black sidewall tires. QYD P185-75R14B radial black sidewall tires. QYE P185-75R14B radial tires with white stripes. QYF P195-75R14B radial black sidewall tires. QYG P195-75R14B radial tires with white stripes. T90 export-type signal light and marker lamp. TR9 lamp group ($49-$56). TT5 tungsten quartz halogen headlights. U05 dual A note horn. U14 special instrumentation gauge package ($95). U18 export speedometer. U35 electric clock ($35). U58 AM/FM push-button stereo ($198). U63 AM push-button radio ($112). U69 AM/FM

Total production of the 1983 El Camino was 22,429.

push-button radio ($171). U73 fixed antenna ($41). U81 dual rear radio speakers. UA1 heavy-duty battery ($25). UN3 AM/FM stereo cassette radio less clock ($298). V08 heavy-duty radiator ($40-$70). V10 cold climate package ($99). V30 front and rear bumper guards ($50). V55 roof luggage carrier. V78 less certificate of compliance plate. VC3 U.S. Territory shipping label. VC4 Puerto Rico shipping label. VC5 export shipping label. VE5 front and rear bumper impact strips ($50). YF5 California emission requirements. Z15 El Camino SS package. Z16 El Camino Black Knight sport décor package. Z49 mandatory Canadian base equipment model. ZJ7 special wheel package with hubcaps and trim rings.

OPTION INSTALLATION RATES

Automatic transmission (100 percent). V-8 gas engine (71.0 percent). V-6 gas engine (26.5 percent). Diesel V-8 engine (2.5 percent). Automatic transmission (100 percent). Power front disc brakes (100 percent). Positraction (11.9 percent). Power steering (100 percent). Styled wheels (82.4 percent). Steel-belted radial tires (100 percent). Base exterior/exterior trim package (44.4 percent). Level 2 exterior/exterior trim package (42.6 percent). Level 3 exterior/exterior trim package (9.8 percent). Level 4 exterior/exterior trim package (3.2 percent). Tinted glass (96.8 percent). Air conditioning (92.3 percent). Cruise control (68.4 percent). Adjustable steering column (80 percent). Power windows (31.9 percent). Power door locks (30.3 percent). AM radio (19.8 percent). AM/FM radio (6.8 percent). Stereo (35.3 percent). Cassette player (21.9 percent).

HISTORICAL FOOTNOTES

Michael H. Erdman was again sales manager for Chevrolet trucks. Jeffrey P. Hulbert was truck merchandising manager. For the 1983 calendar year, Chevrolet sold 934,587 trucks. Calendar-year sales of El Caminos were 24,010 units. Production of El Camino's was again quartered in GM's Arlington, Texas plant where Oldsmobile Cutlass Supremes, Chevy Monte Carlos, El Caminos and Caballeros were manufactured. Model-year assemblies started August 23, 1982 and stopped on August 11, 1983.

Chevrolet dropped the mid-sized Malibu in 1983, but continued producing the El Camino. The 1984 El Camino was a very luxurious vehicle. It had dual, side-by-side, rectangular headlights on either side of a crosshatch grille, with long, narrow parking lights directly below the headlights. The bumper was of a simple, straight-across design. A 5.7-liter gas V-8 returned to the optional equipment list. A 5.7-liter diesel V-8 remained available.

I.D. NUMBERS

VIN embossed on the top left-hand side of the instrument panel and visible through the windshield. Beginning this year, GM used its Light Duty Truck, Multipurpose Passenger Vehicle and Incomplete Vehicle VIN coding system to code the El Camino, except that El Camino engine codes were those used for passenger cars. The first symbol designates the country of origin: 3=Mexico. The second symbol identifies the manufacturer: G=General Motors. The third symbol indicates the make and type: C=Chevrolet truck. The fourth symbol indicates the GVWR. The fifth symbol indicates the series: W=El Camino. The sixth and seventh symbols indicate body type 80=sedan-pickup. The eighth symbol indicates engine (net hp): 9=RPO LC3 229-cid/115-hp V-6, A=RPO LD5 231-cid/110-hp V-6 (California), H=RPO LG4 305-cid/150-hp V-8, 8=350-cid V-8 and N=RPO LF9 350-cid/125-hp diesel V-8. The ninth symbol is a check digit. The 10th symbol designates the model year: E=1984. The 11th symbol designates the assembly plant location: S=Ramos Arizpe, Mexico. The last six symbols are the sequential unit production number at the specific factory. The Fisher body tag riveted to the top of the cowl on the left side of the car below the hood provides additional vehicle identification information. The Fisher body STYLE NUMBER (ST) consists of a prefix identifying model year and four or more symbols identifying the series and body style (example: 84-1GW for a 1984 El Camino). The BODY NUMBER consists of a prefix designating assembly plant and the sequential unit production number at the specific factory. The TRIM NUMBER (TR) identifies upholstery.

COLORS

(11) White, (17) Silver Metallic, (19) Black, (22) Light Royal Blue, (27) Medium Dark Royal Blue, (42) Light Grayfern Metallic, (48) Dark Grayfern Metallic, (59) Cream Beige, (62) Light Briar Brown Metallic, (67) Dark Briar Brown Metallic, (73) Light Maple Metallic, (78) Dark Autumn Maple Poly, (22E) Light Royal Blue Metallic, (22W) Light Royal Blue Metallic, (27E) Medium Dark Royal Blue Metallic), (27W) Medium Dark Royal Blue Metallic, (62E) Light Briar Brown Metallic, (62W) Light Briar Brown Metallic, (67E) Dark Briar Brown Metallic) and (67W) Dark Briar Brown Metallic.

ENGINE CODES

Codes appear on the right side of V-6 cylinder blocks behind the distributor and right-hand side of V-8 engine blocks. Engine codes for 1984 were: (229-cid two-barrel V-6) SBA, SBC, SBF and SBJ; (231-cid two-barrel V-6) FUA, FSA, FXA, FYA, FZA, FRA and FWA; (305-cid four-barrel V-8) SDA, SDR, C4C, SDS, SDH, C4D, SDJ, SDN, C4B, C4W and SDU; (350-cid diesel V-8) RAA, RAB, RBL, RBM and RAF; (350-cid gas V-8) not available.

EL CAMINO — SERIES W — V-6/V-8

Standard equipment features included a 3.8-liter (229-cid) V-6 (not available in California), an automatic transmission, power steering, Computer Command Control, steering column "Smart Switch," frameless door glass and thin roof pillars, bright roof drip moldings, full wheel trim covers, a bright windshield molding, a bright rear window molding, a redesigned padded instrument panel, steel-belted radial tires, self-adjusting power front disc brakes with wear indicators and a quick take-up master cylinder, a High Energy Ignition system, a Freedom side-terminal battery, a dual-mode ventilation system, a fully inflated compact spare tire, a bright left-hand outside rearview mirror, extensive corrosion-resisting treatments, visible ball-joint wear indicators, a front stabilizer bar, a generator, a coolant recovery system, seat belts with push-button buckle releases for all passengers, two combination seat and inertia reel shoulder belts for driver and passenger (with reminder light and buzzer), an energy-absorbing steering column, passenger guard door locks, safety door latches with stamped steel hinges, a contoured windshield header, a thick laminate windshield, a safety steering wheel, side marker lights and reflectors, parking lights that illuminate with the headlamps, four-way hazard flashers, back-up lights, directional signals with a lane-change feature, a defroster, dual speed windshield wipers, windshield washers, a 10-in.-wide prismatic wide-view day/night inside rearview mirror with vinyl edging and a deflecting support, a left-hand outside rearview mirror, a dual master cylinder brake system with warning light, a starter safety switch, a dual-action safety hood latch, an ignition key reminder buzzer and a steering column lock.

Model Number	Body/Style Number	Body Type & Seating	Factory Price	Shipping Weight	Production Total
EL CAMINO SERIES W (V-6)					
W	80	pickup	$8,438	3,078 lbs.	Note 1
EL CAMINO SERIES W (BASE V-8)					
W	80	pickup	$8,522	3,298 lbs.	Note 1

EL CAMINO SS — SERIES W + Z15 V-8

The El Camino Super Sport was a blend of the El Camino's basic value, plus a lot of sporty character. The model option included a large front air dam, painted sport mirrors, a choice of accent colors on the lower body, decal striping, "Super Sport" decal identification on the lower doors and tailgate, color-keyed Rallye wheels and a new "Super Sport" dashboard nameplate. There was no SS identification on the radiator grille.

Model Number	Body/Style Number	Body Type & Seating	Factory Price	Shipping Weight	Production Total
W	80	pickup	$8,781	3,305 lbs.	Note 1

NOTE 1 Total El Camino production was 24,244.

MODEL OPTIONS

CONQUISTA PACKAGE: The El Camino Conquista package was a dramatic paint treatment option featuring an accent color on the hood, body sides and lower portion of the tailgate to set off the basic body color. There were also bright paint break moldings along the pickup box and tailgate, bright lower body side moldings and bright wheel opening moldings. A Conquista decal on the tailgate and a dash nameplate completed the package, which again sold for $189.

ENGINES

EL CAMINO BASE 229-CID, 115-HP V-6: 90-degree, overhead-valve. Cast-iron block and head. Bore and stroke: 3.74 x 3.48 in. Displacement: 229-cid (3.8 liters). Compression ratio: 8.6:1. Brake hp: 115 at 4200 rpm. Torque: 170 lbs.-ft. at 2000 rpm. Four main bearings. Hydraulic valve lifters. Carburetor: two-barrel Rochester E2ME. VIN Code: K or 9.
(NOTE: California models used a Buick 231-cid V-6.)

EL CAMINO OPTIONAL 305-CID, 150-HP V-8: 90-degree, overhead-valve. Cast-iron block and head. Bore and stroke: 3.74 x 3.48 in. Displacement: 305-cid (5.0 liters). Compression ratio: 8.6:1. Brake hp: 150 at 4000 rpm. Torque: 240 lbs.-ft. at 2400 rpm. Five main bearings. Hydraulic valve lifters. Carburetor: four-barrel Rochester E4ME. VIN Code: H.

EL CAMINO OPTIONAL 350-CID, 161-HP V-8: 90-degree, overhead-valve. Cast-iron block and head. Bore and stroke: 4.00 x 3.48 in. Displacement: 350-cid (5.7 liters). Compression ratio: 8.6:1. Brake hp: 161 at 3800 rpm. Torque: 275 lbs.-ft. at 1600 rpm. Five main bearings. Hydraulic valve lifters. Induction: CFI. VIN code: 8.

EL CAMINO OPTIONAL 350-CID, 105-HP DIESEL V-8: 90-degree, overhead-valve. Cast-iron block and head. Bore and stroke: 4.057 x 3.385 in. Displacement: 350-cid (5.7 liters). Compression ratio: 22.5:1. Brake hp: 105 at 3200 rpm. Torque: 200 lbs.-ft. at 1600 rpm. Five main bearings. Hydraulic valve lifters. Fuel injection. Olds-built. VIN Code: N.

CHASSIS

Wheelbase: 117.1 in. Overall length: 201.60 in. Width: 71.9 in. Height: 53.8 in. Front tread: 58.5 in. Rear tread: 57.8 in. Cargo box length from back of cab to top of tailgate: 79.5 in. Bed width between rear wheel housings: 45 in. Bed width above rear wheel housings: 59.5 in. Tires: G78-14B. Transmission: Automatic. Column-mounted gearshift lever. Rear axle: semi-floating. Hydraulic four-wheel brakes. Kelsey-Hayes pressed steel wheels.

OPTIONS

A01 all tinted glass. A02 tinted windshield. A31 power windows with electric control. AU3 power door locks. AV3 El Camino pickup box tie downs. BW2 Deluxe body molding exterior decoration. BX8 front fender and body moldings. B32 color-keyed floor mats. B93 door edge guards. B3W preliminary price information. C60 manual air conditioning. CD4 intermittent windshield wipers and washers. D35 Sport outside rearview mirrors. D55 center console. D73 pickup box hand rail. D91 Conquista package. F41 Sport suspension. G80 Positraction rear axle. G92 performance ratio rear axle. GH2 2.29:1 rear axle ratio. GU1 2.41:1 rear axle ratio. GU2 2.73:1 rear axle ratio. GU4 3.08:1 rear axle ratio. GU6 3.42:1 rear axle ratio. GT4 3.73:1 rear axle ratio. K05 engine block heater. K34 electric speed control. LC3 229-cid V-6 engine (standard Federal engine). LD5 231-cid V-6 engine (standard California engine). LF9 350-cid diesel V-8. LG4 305-cid V-8 engine. MXO automatic transmission with overdrive. MX1 Turbo-Hydra-Matic automatic transmission (standard). N18 simulated wire wheel covers. N23 22-gal. fuel tank. N33 tilt steering wheel. N95 wire wheel covers. NA6 alternate requirements emission system. QFT P205-75R14B steel-belted radial black sidewall tires. QJR P205-75R14B steel-belted radial white stripe tires. QSA P205-75R14B steel-belted radial white letter tires. TR9 lamp group. TT5 tungsten quartz halogen headlights. U14 special instrumentation gauge package. U35 electric clock. U58 AM/FM push-button stereo. U63 AM push-button radio. U73 fixed antenna. UA1 heavy-duty battery. UF7 instrument panel gauge with trip odometer. UN3 AM/FM stereo cassette radio less clock. V08 heavy-duty radiator. V10 cold climate package. VE5 front and rear bumper impact strips. YF5 California emission requirements. Z15 El Camino SS package. ZJ7 special wheel package with hubcap and trim rings.

OPTION INSTALLATION RATES

Automatic transmission (100 percent). V-8 gas engine (81.5 percent). V-6 gas engine (18.1 percent). Diesel V-8 engine (0.4 percent). Automatic transmission (100 percent). Power front disc brakes (100 percent). Positraction (13.6 percent). Power steering (100 percent). Styled wheels (86.3 percent). Steel-belted radial tires (100 percent). Base exterior/exterior trim package (44.6 percent). Level 2 exterior/exterior trim package (38.3 percent). Level 3 exterior/exterior trim package (17.1 percent). Tinted glass (97 percent). Air conditioning (93.6 percent). Cruise control (72 percent). Adjustable steering column (84.1 percent). Power windows (46.1 percent). Power door locks (45.1 percent). AM radio (10 percent). AM/FM radio (8.9 percent). Stereo (28.8 percent). Cassette player (38.7 percent).

HISTORICAL FOOTNOTES

Michael H. Erdman was again sales manager for Chevrolet trucks. Frank F. Raine, Jr., was truck merchandising manager. For the 1984 calendar year, Chevrolet sold 1,111,839 trucks. Calendar-year sales of El Caminos were 22,997 units. Model-year sales of El Caminos were 24,933. While sales of the El Camino were far from their high point of earlier years, deliveries of this model and the Suburban were very important to the Chevrolet Truck Division in this time period. Both were unique products with no competitors and this helped push Chevrolet's total truck sales ahead of those of archrival Ford. Under a unique arrangement, Chevrolet El Caminos and GMC Caballeros were assembled at a plant in Mexico from components supplied from the U.S. This freed up additional capacity at the GM assembly plant in Arlington, Texas, for the production of mid-size, rear-wheel-drive cars.

The El Camino was living on borrowed time, but was an important part of Chevrolet's truck arsenal. The Malibu that the El Camino was based on was dropped after 1983, but Chevrolet kept making the sedan-pickup because it was a unique product. The sales of the El Camino and the Suburban were helping to keep Chevrolet ahead of Ford in the all-important race for the title of America's leading truck maker. In addition to last year's standard equipment, the 1985 El Camino had a new 4.3-liter V-6.

I.D. NUMBERS

VIN embossed on the top left-hand side of the instrument panel and visible through the windshield. GM now used its light-duty truck, multipurpose passenger vehicle, and incomplete VIN coding system to code the El Camino, except that El Camino engine codes were those used for passenger cars. The first symbol designates the country of origin: 3=Mexico. The second symbol identifies the manufacturer: G=General Motors. The third symbol indicates the make and type: C=Chevrolet truck. The fourth symbol indicates the GVWR. The fifth symbol indicates the series: W=El Camino. The sixth and seventh symbols indicate body type 80=El Camino. The eighth symbol indicates engine (net hp): Z=RPO LB4 262-cid 130-hp V-6, H=RPO LG4 305-cid/165-hp V-8. The ninth symbol is a check digit. The 10th symbol designates the model year: F=1985. The 11th symbol designates the assembly plant location: S=Ramos Arizpe, Mexico. The last six symbols are the sequential unit production number at the specific factory. The Fisher body tag riveted to the top of the cowl on the left side of the car below the hood provides additional vehicle identification information. The Fisher body STYLE NUMBER (ST) consists of a prefix identifying model year and four or more symbols identifying the series and body style (example: 85-1GW for a 1985 El Camino). The BODY NUMBER consists of a prefix designating assembly plant and the sequential unit production number at the specific factory. The TRIM NUMBER (TR) identifies upholstery.

COLORS

(11) White, (12) Silver Metallic, (15) Medium Gray Metallic, (19) Black, (25) Light Blue Metallic, (31) Dark Blue Metallic, (43) Light Sage Green, (46) Medium Sage Metallic, (58) Light Chestnut Metallic, (59) cream Beige, (62) Dark Chestnut Metallic, (79) Dark Red Metallic, (12E) Silver Metallic, (12W) Silver Metallic, (15E) Medium Gray Metallic and (15W) Medium Gray Metallic.

ENGINE CODES

Codes appear on the right side of V-6 cylinder blocks behind the distributor and right-hand side of V-8 engine

There were only minor visable changes to the new 1985 El Caminos, but the sedan-pickup did get a new 4.3-liter V-6.

blocks. Engine codes for 1985 were: (262-cid TBI V-6) CCB, CLC, CLF, CLH, CLB and CLD; (305-cid four-barrel V-8) CDD, CDJ, C4R, C7A, CDF, C4P, CDL, C7B, CDH and CKA.

EL CAMINO — SERIES W — V-6/V-8

The El Camino grille was the same as last year and there were very few changes other than a larger V-6 engine. Standard equipment features included a 4.3-liter (262-cid) V-6, an automatic transmission, power steering, Computer Command Control, steering column "Smart Switch," frameless door glass and thin roof pillars, bright roof drip moldings, full wheel trim covers, a bright windshield molding, a bright rear window molding, steel-belted radial tires, self-adjusting power front disc brakes with wear indicators and a quick take-up master cylinder, a High Energy Ignition system, a Freedom side-terminal battery, a dual-mode ventilation system, a fully inflated compact spare tire, a bright left-hand outside rearview mirror, extensive corrosion-resisting treatments, visible ball-joint wear indicators, a front stabilizer bar, a generator, a coolant recovery system, seat belts with push-button buckle releases for all passengers, two combination seat and inertia reel shoulder belts for driver and passenger (with reminder light and buzzer), an energy-absorbing steering column, passenger guard door locks, safety door latches with stamped steel hinges, a contoured windshield header, a thick laminate windshield, a safety steering wheel, side marker lights and reflectors, parking lights that illuminate with the headlamps, four-way hazard flashers, back-up lights, directional signals with a lane-change feature, a defroster, dual speed windshield wipers, windshield washers, a 10-in.-wide prismatic wide-view day/night inside rearview mirror with vinyl edging and a deflecting support, a left-hand outside rearview mirror, a dual master cylinder brake system with warning light, a starter safety switch, a dual-action safety hood latch, an ignition key reminder buzzer and a steering column lock.

Model Number	Body/Style Number	Body Type & Seating	Factory Price	Shipping Weight	Production Total
EL CAMINO SERIES W (V-6)					
W	80	pickup	$8,849	—	Note 1
EL CAMINO SERIES W (BASE V-8)					
W	80	pickup	$8,933	3,252 lbs.	Note 1

EL CAMINO SS — SERIES W + Z15 V-8

The El Camino SS shared its aerodynamic-style plastic nose cap with the high-performance Monte Carlo SS coupe. The SS package also included dual, SS decal striping, "Super Sport" decal identification on the doors above the lower body feature line and Rallye wheels. A non-functional blister hood, dummy side pipes and pickup bed rails were optional. The SS came only in five distinctive exterior two-tone paint combinations.

Model Number	Body/Style Number	Body Type & Seating	Factory Price	Shipping Weight	Production Total
W	80	pickup	$9,198	3,263 lbs.	Note 1

MODEL OPTIONS

CONQUISTA PACKAGE: The El Camino Conquista package was a dramatic paint treatment option featuring an accent color on the hood, body sides and lower portion of the tailgate to set off the basic body color. There were also bright paint break moldings along the pickup box and tailgate, bright lower body side moldings and bright wheel opening moldings. A Conquista decal on the tailgate and a dash nameplate completed the package, which came only in five distinctive exterior two-tone paint combinations.

NOTE 1: Total El Camino production was 24,582.

ENGINES

EL CAMINO BASE 262-CID, 130-HP V-6: 90-degree, overhead-valve V-6. Cast-iron block and head. Bore and stroke: 4.00 x 3.43 in. Displacement: 262-cid (4.3 liters). Compression ratio: 9.3:1. Brake hp: 130 at 3600 rpm. Torque: 235 lbs.-ft. at 2400 rpm. Four main bearings. Hydraulic valve lifters. Induction: Throttle Body Injection (TBI). VIN Code: Z.

EL CAMINO OPTIONAL 305-CID, 165-HP V-8: 90-degree, overhead-valve V-8. Cast-iron block and head. Bore and stroke: 3.74 x 3.48 in. Displacement: 305-cid (5.0 liters). Compression ratio: 8.6:1. Brake hp: 165 at 4000 rpm. Torque: 255 lbs.-ft. at 2400 rpm. Five main bearings. Hydraulic valve lifters. Carburetor: four-barrel Rochester E4ME. VIN Code: H.

CHASSIS

Wheelbase: 117.1 in. Overall length: 201.60 in. Width: 71.9 in. Height: 53.8 in. Front tread: 58.5 in. Rear tread: 57.8 in. Cargo box length from back of cab to top of tailgate: 79.5 in. Bed width between rear wheel housings: 45 in. Bed width above rear wheel housings: 59.5 in. Tires: P205-75R14. Transmission: Automatic. Rear axle: semi-floating. Hydraulic four-wheel brakes. Kelsey-Hayes pressed steel wheels.

OPTIONS

A01 all tinted glass. A02 tinted windshield. A31 power windows with electric control. AU3 power door locks. AV3 El Camino pickup box tie downs. B32 color-keyed floor mats. B93 door edge guards. B3W preliminary price information. BW2 deluxe body molding exterior decoration. BX8 front fender and body moldings. C60 manual air conditioning. CD4 intermittent windshield wipers and washers. D35 sport outside rearview mirrors. D55 center console. D73 pickup box hand rail. D91 Conquista package. F41 Sport suspension. G80 Positraction rear axle. G92 performance ratio rear axle. GH2 2.29:1 rear axle ratio. GU1 2.41:1 rear axle ratio. GM8 2.56:1 rear axle ratio. GU2 2.73:1 rear axle ratio. GU4 3.08:1 rear axle ratio. GU6 3.42:1 rear axle ratio. GT4 3.73:1 rear axle ratio. K05 engine block heater. K34 electric speed control. LB4 4.3-liter V-6. LG4 305-cid V-8 engine. MXO automatic transmission with overdrive. MX1 Turbo-Hydra-Matic automatic transmission (standard). N18 simulated wire wheel covers. N23 22-gal. fuel tank. N33 Tilt steering wheel. N95 wire wheel covers. NA6 alternate requirements emission system. QFT P205-75R14B steel-belted radial black sidewall tires. QJR P205-75R14B steel-belted radial white stripe tires. QSA P205-75R14B steel-belted radial white letter tires. TR9 lamp group. TT4 tungsten quartz halogen headlights. U14 special instrumentation gauge package. U35 electric clock. U58 AM/FM push-button stereo. U63 AM push-button radio. U73 fixed antenna. UA1 heavy-duty battery. UF7 instrument panel gauge with trip odometer. UN3 AM/FM stereo cassette radio less clock. UX1 AM-FM stereo cassette radio with clock. V08 heavy-duty radiator. V30 bumper guards. VE5 front and rear bumper impact strips. YF5 California emission requirements. Z15 El Camino SS Sport décor package. ZJ7 special wheel package with hubcap and trim rings.

OPTION INSTALLATION RATES

V-8 gas engine (77.3 percent). V-6 gas engine (22.7 percent). Automatic transmission (100 percent). Styled wheels (87.1 percent). Base exterior/exterior trim package (46.1 percent). Level 2 exterior/exterior trim package (34.8 percent). Level 3 exterior/exterior trim package (19.1 percent). Power front disc brakes (100 percent). Power steering (100 percent). Positraction (16.3 percent). Steel-belted radial tires (100 percent). Air conditioning (94.8 percent). Bucket seats (13 percent). Tinted glass (97.6 percent). Cruise control (71 percent). Adjustable steering column (84.6 percent). Power windows (50.3 percent). Power door locks (49.2 percent). AM radio (5.1 percent). AM/FM radio (2.3 percent). Stereo (28.3 percent). Cassette player (51.8 percent).

HISTORICAL FOOTNOTES

For the 1985 calendar year, Chevrolet sold 1,300,130 trucks, a gain of 2.2 percent, though not quite enough to break the record of 1,340,259 set back in 1978. Calendar-year sales of El Caminos were 21,816 units. Model-year sales of El Caminos were 20,233. Chevrolet truck production in Mexico increased from 28,379 units in 1984 to 37,038 units in 1985. Most of these were El Caminos, but the Caballero was also included.

The El Camino featured a new instrument panel and revised gauge cluster graphics to modernize it. It continued to offer 35.5 cubic feet or cargo capacity and a 1,250-lb. payload.

I.D. NUMBERS

VIN embossed on the top left-hand side of the instrument panel and visible through the windshield. GM again used its light-duty truck, multipurpose passenger vehicle and incomplete vehicle VIN coding system to code the El Camino, except that El Camino engine codes were those used for passenger cars. The first symbol designates the country of origin: 3=Mexico. The second symbol identifies the manufacturer: G=General Motors. The third symbol indicates the make and type: C=Chevrolet truck. The fourth symbol indicates the gross vehicle weight ratio. The fifth symbol indicates the series: W=El Camino. The sixth and seventh symbols indicate body type 80=El Camino. The eighth symbol indicates engine (net horsepower): Z=RPO LB4 262-cid/140-hp V-6, H=RPO LG4 305-cid/165-hp V-8. The ninth symbol is a check digit. The 10th symbol designates the model year: G=1986. The 11th symbol designates the assembly plant location: S=Ramos Arizpe, Mexico. The last six symbols are the sequential unit production number at the specific factory. A new service parts identification label located on the glove box door or behind the seat bore the VIN, option codes, paint type, paint code and trim code.

COLORS

(11) White, (12) Silver Metallic, (13S) Silver Metallic, (15) Medium Gray Metallic, (19) Black, (25) Light Blue Metallic, (31) Dark Blue Metallic, (43) Light Sage Metallic, (54) Yellow Beige, (58) Light Chestnut Metallic, (62) Dark Chestnut Metallic, (71) Medium Red Metallic and (79) Dark Red Metallic. Engine codes appear on the right side of V-6 cylinder blocks behind the distributor and right-hand side of V-8 engine blocks. Engine codes for 1986 were: (262-cid EFI V-6) DPC, DPA, DPD and DPF; (305-cid four-barrel V-8) D4A, DDK, DDJ, DDU, B4T, DDL, DFM, D4B, T9U and T9W.

EL CAMINO — SERIES W — V-6/V-8

The El Camino's standard "ice-cube-tray" grille had 16 vertical cars crossed by three wide horizontal bars. Dual, side-by-side rectangular headlights sat above the long, slim parking lamps. Standard equipment features included a 4.3-liter (262-cid) V-6, an automatic trans-

The El Camino was largely unchanged for 1986. Only 16,229 units were produced, leading to its removal from the assembly lines one year later. This modified truck has aftermarket whitewalls and fender skrts, along with a different air dam.

mission, power steering, Computer Command Control, steering column "Smart Switch," frameless door glass and thin roof pillars, bright roof drip moldings, full wheel trim covers, a bright windshield molding, a bright rear window molding, a padded instrument panel, steel-belted radial tires, self-adjusting power front disc brakes with wear indicators, a quick take-up master cylinder, a High Energy Ignition system, a Freedom side-terminal battery, a dual-mode ventilation system, a fully inflated compact spare tire, a bright left-hand outside rearview mirror, extensive corrosion-resisting treatments, visible ball-joint wear indicators, a front stabilizer bar, a generator, a coolant recovery system, seat belts with push-button buckle releases for all passengers, two combination seat and inertia reel shoulder belts for driver and passenger (with reminder light and buzzer), an energy-absorbing steering column, passenger guard door locks, safety door latches with stamped steel hinges, a contoured windshield header, a thick laminate windshield, a safety steering wheel, side marker lights and reflectors, parking lights that illuminate with the headlamps, four-way hazard flashers, back-up lights, directional signals with a lane-change feature, a defroster, dual speed windshield wipers, windshield washers, a 10-in.-wide prismatic wide-view day/night inside rearview mirror with vinyl edging and a deflecting support, a left-hand outside rearview mirror, a dual master cylinder brake system with warning light, a starter safety switch, a dual-action safety hood latch, an ignition key reminder buzzer and a steering column lock.

Model Number	Body/Style Number	Body Type & Seating	Factory Price	Shipping Weight	Production Total
EL CAMINO SERIES W (V-6)					
W	80	pickup	$9,488	3,234 lbs.	Note 1
EL CAMINO SERIES W (BASE V-8)					
W	80	pickup	$9,572	3,234 lbs.	Note 1

EL CAMINO SS — SERIES W + Z15 V-8

The El Camino SS shared its aerodynamic-style plastic nose cap with the high-performance Monte Carlo SS coupe. The SS package also included dual sport mirrors, SS decal striping, "Super Sport" decal identification on the front air dam and doors above the lower body feature line and rally wheels. A non-functional blister hood, dummy side pipes and pickup bed rails were optional. The SS came only in five distinctive two-tone exterior color combinations: Black and Silver Metallic, Dark Blue Metallic and Light Blue Metallic, Light Brown Metallic and Medium Brown Metallic, Dark Maroon Metallic and Silver Metallic and Silver Metallic and Medium Gray Metallic. Interior recommendations were color coordinated.

Model Number	Body/Style Number	Body Type & Seating	Factory Price	Shipping Weight	Production Total
W	80	pickup	$9,885	3,239 lbs.	Note 1

NOTE 1 Total El Camino production was 16,229.

MODEL OPTIONS

CONQUISTA PACKAGE: The El Camino Conquista package was a dramatic paint treatment option featuring an accent color on the hood, body sides and lower portion of the tailgate to set off the basic body color. There were also bright paint break moldings along the pickup box and tailgate, bright lower body side moldings and bright wheel opening moldings. A Conquista decal on the tailgate and a dash nameplate completed the package, which came only in five distinctive exterior two-tone paint combinations. The Conquista package was also offered in only five two-tone color combinations: Light Blue Metallic and Dark Blue Metallic, Medium Brown Metallic and Light Brown Metallic, Medium Gray Metallic and Silver Metallic, Silver Metallic and Dark Maroon Metallic and Silver Metallic and Black. The package was priced at $225 this year.

ENGINES

EL CAMINO BASE 262-CID, 140-HP V-6: 90-degree, overhead-valve. Cast-iron block and head. Bore and stroke: 4.00 x 3.43 in. Displacement: 262-cid (4.3 liters). Compression ratio: 9.3:1. Brake hp: 140 at 4000 rpm. Torque: 225 lbs.-ft. at 2000 rpm. Four main bearings. Hydraulic valve lifters. Induction: Throttle Body Injection (TBI). VIN Code: Z.

EL CAMINO OPTIONAL 305-CID, 150-HP V-8: 90-degree, overhead-valve. Cast-iron block and head. Bore and stroke: 3.74 x 3.48 in. Displacement: 305-cid (5.0 liters). Compression ratio: 8.6:1. Brake hp: 150 at 4000 rpm. Torque: 240 lbs.-ft. at 2000 rpm. Five main bearings. Hydraulic valve lifters. Carburetor: four-barrel Rochester E4ME. VIN Code: H.

CHASSIS

Wheelbase: 117.1 in. Overall length: 201.60 in. Width: 71.9 in. Height: 53.8 in. Front tread: 58.5 in. Rear tread: 57.8 in. Cargo box length from back of cab to top of tailgate: 79.5 in. Bed width between rear wheel housings: 45 in. Bed width above rear wheel housings: 59.5 in. Tires: P205-75R14. Transmission: Automatic. Rear axle: semi-floating. Hydraulic four-wheel brakes. Kelsey-Hayes pressed steel wheels.

OPTIONS

A01 all tinted glass. A02 tinted windshield. A31 power windows with electric control. A65 bench seat. AM6 55/45 cloth seat. AR9 bucket seats. AU3 power door locks. AV3 El Camino pickup box tie downs. B32 color-keyed floor mats. B93 door edge guards. B3W preliminary price information. BW2 deluxe body molding exterior decoration. BX8 front fender and body moldings. C60 manual air conditioning. CD4 intermittent windshield wipers and washers. D35 Sport outside rearview mirrors. D55 center console. D73 pickup box hand rail. D91 Conquista package. F41 Sport suspension. G80 Positraction rear axle. G92 performance ratio rear axle. GH2 2.29:1 rear axle ratio. GU1 2.41:1 rear axle ratio. GM8 2.56:1 rear axle ratio. GU2 2.73:1 rear axle ratio. GU4 3.08:1 rear axle ratio. GU6 3.42:1 rear axle ratio. GT4 3.73:1 rear axle ratio. K05 engine block heater. K34 electric speed control. LB4 4.3-liter V-6. LG4 305-cid V-8 engine. MXO automatic transmission with overdrive. MX1 Turbo-Hydra-Matic automatic transmission (standard). N18 simulated wire wheel covers. N23 22-gal. fuel tank. N33 tilt steering wheel. N91 wire wheel covers. QFT P205-75R14B steel-belted radial black sidewall tires. QJR P205-75R14B steel-belted radial white stripe

The 1986 El Camino SS featured an aerodynamic front end, and non-functioning blister hood and side pipes. This car was modified by Choo-Choo Customs.

tires. QSA P205-75R14B steel-belted radial white letter tires. TR9 lamp group. TT4 tungsten quartz halogen headlights. U16 tachometer. U39 gauge package with odometer. U63 AM push-button radio. U73 fixed antenna. UA1 heavy-duty battery. UK4 AM-FM seek-and-scan stereo. UM6 AM/FM seek-and-scan stereo with cassette and clock, UM7 AM/FM seek-and-scan stereo with cassette. UX1 AM-FM seek-and-scan stereo cassette radio with clock. V08 heavy-duty cooling. V30 bumper guards. VE5 front and rear bumper impact strips. YF5 California emission requirements. Z15 El Camino SS Sport décor package. ZJ7 Rallye wheel package.

OPTION INSTALLATION RATES

V-8 gas engine (76 percent). V-6 gas engine (24 percent). Automatic transmission (100 percent). Base exterior/exterior trim package (59 percent). Level 2 exterior/exterior trim package (41 percent). Power front disc brakes (100 percent). Power steering (100 percent). Positraction (19 percent). Steel-belted radial tires (100 percent). Air conditioning (96 percent). Tinted glass (98 percent). Cruise control (83 percent). Adjustable steering column (91 percent). Power windows (71 percent). Power door locks (70 percent). AM radio (3 percent). Stereo (22 percent). Cassette player (71 percent).

HISTORICAL FOOTNOTES

John M. Kelly was sales manager for Chevrolet trucks. Tom P. Cutler was truck merchandising manager. For the 1986 calendar year, Chevrolet sold 1,247,594 trucks. Calendar-year sales of El Caminos were 21,508 units. Model-year sales of El Caminos were 23,767. Chevrolet truck production in Mexico in calendar 1986 was 21,547 units. Most of these were El Caminos, but the Caballero was also included.

The El Camino combined the utility of a pickup truck with the beauty of a sport coupe passenger car. Apparently, this was a combination that was no longer in great demand, as this was the last full year for El Camino production. A few hundred were built in the first four months of 1988, before the model was dropped. Chevrolet's separate sales catalog for the 1987 El Camino said, "The end product makes a uniquely bold, personal statement." The El Camino's trim lines and sleek good looks were available in three ways.

I.D. NUMBERS

VIN embossed on the top left-hand side of the instrument panel and visible through the windshield. GM again used its light-duty truck, multipurpose passenger vehicle and incomplete vehicle VIN coding system to code the El Camino, except that El Camino engine codes were those used for passenger cars. The first symbol designates the country of origin: 3=Mexico. The second symbol identifies the manufacturer: G=General Motors. The third symbol indicates the make and type: C=Chevrolet truck. The fourth symbol indicates the gross vehicle weight ratio. The fifth symbol indicates the series: W=El Camino. The sixth and seventh symbols indicate body type 80=El Camino. The eighth symbol indicates engine (net hp): Z=RPO LB4 262-cid/140-hp V-6, H=RPO LG4 305-cid/165-hp V-8. The ninth symbol is a check digit. The 10th symbol designates the model year: H=1987. The 11th symbol designates the assembly plant location: S=Ramos Arizpe, Mexico. The last six symbols are the

El Camino

This 1987 El Camino was a product of Choo Choo Customs of Chattanooga, Tennessee. Such "factory" customs are now valuable collector cars.

Jerry Heasley photo

sequential unit production number at the specific factory. The service parts identification label located on the glove box door or behind the seat bore the VIN, option codes, paint type, paint code and trim code.

COLORS

11=White, 12, 13S= Silver Metallic, 15=Medium Gray metallic, 19=Black, 25=Light Blue Metallic; 31=Dark Blue Metallic, 43=Light Sage Metallic, 54=Yellow Beige, 58=Light Chestnut Metallic, 62=Dark Chestnut Metallic, 71=Medium Red Metallic, Dark Red Metallic.

ENGINE CODES

Codes appear on the right side of V-6 cylinder blocks behind the distributor and right-hand side of V-8 engine blocks. Engine codes for 1986 were: (262-cid EFI V-6) SBB, SBC, SBD, DPK and SBA; (305-cid four-barrel V-8) C7J, C7K, C7X, CKH, SDA, SDC, SFC, SFD and SFF.

EL CAMINO — SERIES W — V-6/V-8

Standard equipment included left- and right-hand air vents and padded arm rests, a lighted instrument panel ash tray, color-keyed carpeting, an outside air heater and defroster, gauges (for speedometer, odometer and fuel level), switches (for lights, directional signals and ignition), warning lights (for generator, oil pressure, temperature, seat belts, parking brake, directional lights, hazard lamps and headlight high-beams), sound deadening insulation (on firewall and under floor), lights for instrument panel and dome and glove box, a 10-in. prismatic rear view mirror, safety belts, a behind-passenger-seat spare tire, a color-keyed plastic steering wheel with energy-absorbing column, a glove box with light and key, left- and right-hand sun shades, air-adjustable rear shocks, chromed front and rear bumpers, a plastic grille with bright trim, a dual-note electric horn, back-up lights, tail and stop lights, front and rear parking lights, side marker lights, dual rectangular headlights, a black left-hand rearview mirror with styled head, a mechanical jack and wheel wrench, painted wheels with bright full wheel covers and two-speed electric windshield wipers and washers. The standard El Camino was elegantly understated with solid color paint, a bright grille and bright appearance items throughout. Standard interior features included a full-width cloth bench seat with pull-down center arm rest, cut-pile carpeting, a cleanly designed instrument panel and gauges, a storage space hidden behind the driver's seat, door-pull straps, a color-keyed cloth-over-foam headliner, a lighted ash tray, a lighted glove box and vinyl door trim panels. Options included bucket seats or a 55/45 split bench seat in cloth or custom cloth fabric, a front console, air conditioning, power windows, tinted glass, and a full complement of audio equipment. Standard interiors were offered in blue, gray, light green, maroon and saddle. Options included cloth bench, cloth bucket, cloth 55/45 bench, vinyl bench and custom cloth 55/45 bench seats. The standard engine was the 4.3-liter V-6. A 5.0-liter V-8 was optional.

Model Number	Body/Style Number	Body Type & Seating	Factory Price	Shipping Weight	Production Total

EL CAMINO SERIES W (V-6)					
W	80	pickup	$10,369	3,234 lbs.	Note 1
EL CAMINO SERIES W (BASE V-8)					
W	80	pickup	$10,453	3,239 lbs.	Note 1

EL CAMINO SS — SERIES W + Z15 V-8

The no-holds-barred SS Sport Decor model incorporated a front air dam, dual aerodynamic mirrors, a lower body accent color emphasized by a pin striping decal, Rallye wheel rims, and blacked-out trim. The SS Sport Decor models offered a limited number of two-tone exterior color choices. Shown on the back of the 1987 El Camino sales catalog was the optional El Camino SS in white with a decorative hood treatment, aero style front fascia, non-functional side pipes, and box side rails that were provided by an independent supplier that marketed this package through authorized Chevrolet dealers. (Choo-Choo Customs of Tennessee supplied such packages.)

Model Number	Body/Style Number	Body Type & Seating	Factory Price	Shipping Weight	Production Total
W	80	pickup	$10,784	3,244 lbs.	Note 1

NOTE 1 Total El Camino production was 15,589.

MODEL OPTIONS

CONQUISTA PACKAGE: The optional El Camino Conquista model featured two-tone paint marked by bright moldings. The Conquista Sport Decor models offered a limited number of two-tone exterior color choices. The package was priced at $238 this year.

ENGINES

EL CAMINO BASE 262-CID, 140-HP V-6: 90-degree, overhead-valve V-6. Cast-iron block and head. Bore and stroke: 4.00 x 3.43 in. Displacement: 262-cid (4.3 liters). Compression ratio: 9.3:1. Brake hp: 140 at 4000 rpm. Torque: 225 lbs.-ft. at 2000 rpm. Four main bearings. Hydraulic valve lifters. Induction: Throttle Body Injection (TBI). VIN Code: Z.

EL CAMINO OPTIONAL 305-CID, 150-HP V-8: 90-degree, overhead-valve V-8. Cast-iron block and head. Bore and stroke: 3.74 x 3.48 in. Displacement: 305-cid (5.0 liters). Compression ratio: 8.6:1. Brake hp: 150 at 4000 rpm. Torque: 240 lbs.-ft. at 2000 rpm. Five main bearings. Hydraulic valve lifters. Carburetor: four-barrel Rochester E4ME. VIN Code: H.

CHASSIS

Wheelbase: 117.1 in. Overall length: 201.60 in. Width: 71.9 in. Height: 53.8 in. Front tread: 58.5 in. Rear tread: 57.8 in. Cargo box length from back of cab to top of tailgate: 79.5 in. Bed width between rear wheel housings: 45 in. Bed width above rear wheel housings: 59.5 in. Tires: P205-75R14. Transmission: Automatic. Rear axle: semi-floating. Hydraulic four-wheel brakes. Kelsey-Hayes pressed steel wheels.

OPTIONS

A01 all tinted glass. A02 tinted windshield. A31 power windows with electric control. A65 bench seat. AM6 55/45 cloth seat. AR9 bucket seats. AU3 power door locks. AV3 El Camino pickup box tie downs. B32 color-keyed floor mats. B93 door edge guards. B3W preliminary price information. BW2 deluxe body molding exterior decoration. BX8 front fender and body moldings. C60 manual air conditioning. CD4 intermittent windshield wipers and washers. D35 sport outside rearview mirrors. D55 center console. D73 pickup box hand rail. D91 Conquista package. F41 Sport suspension. G80 Positraction rear axle. G92 performance ratio rear axle. G72 2.14:1 rear axle ratio. GH2 2.29:1 rear axle ratio. GU1 2.41:1 rear axle ratio. GM8 2.56:1 rear axle ratio. GU2 2.73:1 rear axle ratio. GU4 3.08:1 rear axle ratio. GU5 3.23:1 rear axle ratio. GU6 3.42:1 rear axle ratio. GT4 3.73:1 rear axle ratio. K05 engine block heater. K34 electric speed control. LB4 4.3-liter V-6. LG4 305-cid V-8 engine. MXO automatic transmission with overdrive. MX1 Turbo-Hydra-Matic automatic transmission (standard). N23 22-gal. fuel tank. N33 tilt steering wheel. N91 wire wheel covers. QFT P205-75R14B steel-belted radial black sidewall tires. QJR P205-75R14B steel-belted radial white stripe tires. QSA P205-75R14B steel-belted radial white-letter tires. TR9 lamp group. TT4 tungsten quartz halogen headlights. U16 tachometer. U39 gauge package with odometer. U63 AM push-button radio. U73 fixed antenna. UA1 heavy-duty battery. UK4 AM-FM seek-and-scan stereo. UM6 AM/FM seek-and-scan stereo with cassette and clock. UM7 AM/FM seek-and-scan stereo with cassette. UX1 AM-FM seek-and-scan stereo cassette radio with clock. V08 heavy-duty cooling. V30 bumper guards. VE5 front and rear bumper impact strips. YF5 California emission requirements. Z15 El Camino SS sport décor package. ZJ7 Rallye wheel package.

OPTION INSTALLATION RATES

V-8 gas engine (84 percent). V-6 gas engine (16 percent). Automatic transmission (100 percent). Power steering (100 percent). Power front disc brakes (100 percent). Positraction (25.8 percent). Steel-belted radial tires (100 percent). Manual air conditioning (97.4 percent). Tinted glass (98 percent). Power windows (78.5 percent). Power door locks (78 percent). Base exterior/exterior trim package (40.4 percent). Level 2 exterior/exterior trim package (34.2 percent). Level 3 exterior/exterior trim package (25.4 percent). AM radio (2.5 percent). Stereo (25.2 percent). Cassette player (54.6 percent). Premium sound package (13.7 percent). Tilt steering (92.7 percent). Cruise control (78.5 percent). Intermittent wipers (65.4 percent). Analog clock (0.9 percent). Digital clock (39.5 percent).

HISTORICAL FOOTNOTES

Robert D. Burger was Chevrolet Division General Manager. John M. Kelly was marketing manager for Chevrolet trucks. Tom P. Cutler was truck advertising manager. For the 1987 calendar year, Chevrolet sold 1,191,848 trucks. Model-year sales of El Caminos were 15,626 units. Calendar-year sales of El Caminos were 13,743 units. Chevrolet truck production in Mexico in calendar 1987 was 11,266 units. Most of these were El Caminos, but the Caballero was also included. Richard C. Nerod was managing director of General Motors de Mexico S.A. de C.V.

Sprint
1971-1977

1971

The big news for 1971 at GMC was the introduction of the Sprint. Based on the Chevrolet El Camino, this was a sedan-pickup that combined passenger car sheet metal with a pickup box.

The first Sprint had a two-tier grille with double-horizontal-slot front parking lights as visual characteristics. The idea behind this example of GM badge engineering was to achieve more sales of the El Camino-type model by making it available at GM dealerships. The more stores you have, the more units you sell.

I.D. NUMBERS

The VIN is stamped on a plate on the top left side of the instrument panel and visible through the windshield. The first symbol 5 designates GMC. The second and third symbols designate the series: (six-cylinder) 33=Sprint, 34=Custom Sprint; (V-8) 36=Custom Sprint. The fourth and fifth symbols designate body type: 80=two-door sedan pickup. The sixth symbol designates the model year: 1=1971. The seventh symbol indicated assembly plant: B=Baltimore, Maryland; F=Flint, Michigan; K=Kansas City/Leeds, Missouri; L=Los Angles/Van Nuys, California; R=Arlington, Texas and 1-Oshawa, Canada. The last six symbols are the sequential unit production number at the specific factory.

SPRINT — SERIES 33/34 — SIX/V-8

Standard models had bright windshield frames, back-up lights on the tailgate, and a base six-cylinder engine. A plain cloth and vinyl interior was standard. The pickup box, used through 1972, had an outside width of 75 1/2 in. The inside width behind the cab was 59 in. and the inside width near the tailgate was 64 1/2 in. The width between the wheel housings was 44 in. The bottom bed length measured 79 1/4 in. Tailgate measurements were 54 1/2 x 22 1/2 in.

Model Number	Body/Style Number	Body Type & Seating	Factory Price	Shipping Weight	Production Total
SPRINT SERIES 33 (6-CYL)					
533	80	pickup	$2,640	3,302 lbs.	Note 1
SPRINT SERIES 34 (V-8)					
534	80	pickup	$2,730	3,418 lbs.	Note 1

SPRINT CUSTOM — SERIES 36 — V-8

Customs added a V-8 as base engine, body side moldings, wheelhouse moldings, pickup box rim moldings, rear body corner moldings, two moldings on the tailgate, and silver anodized lower body perimeter. The Custom interior had vinyl seats, vinyl door panels, vinyl sidewall panels, color-keyed carpeting and wood-grained vinyl dash accents.

Model Number	Body/Style Number	Body Type & Seating	Factory Price	Shipping Weight	Production Total
536	80	custom pickup	$2,809	3,442 lbs.	Note 1

NOTE 1 Total GMC Sprint production for the model year is 5,536.

MODEL OPTIONS

SPRINT SP: An SP package was available. The basic SP package was $365 extra and the engine selections were separate options. The performance and appearance package included a black-accented grille with SP emblems, SP badges behind the front wheel cutouts, a sport suspension, power front disc brakes, a domed hood with lock pins and 15 x 7 Sport wheels with F60-15 raised white-letter tires. The 400-cid and 454-cid V-8s were optional.

ENGINES

SPRINT BASE 250-CID, 145-HP SIX-CYL: Inline. Overhead-valve. Cast-iron block. Displacement: 250 cid. Bore and stroke: 3.875 x 3.53 in. Compression ratio: 8.5:1. Brake hp: 145 at 4200 rpm. Net brake hp: 110 at

The SP series was the top-of-the-line Sprint. The SP had a starting price of $2,809, but a 454 like this one was more than that.

The first GMC Sprint arrived in 1971. This SP 454 model showed off how the grille and front end differed from the El Camino, on which the Sprint was based.

3800 rpm. Taxable hp: 36. Torque: 230 lbs.-ft. at 1600 rpm. Seven main bearings. Hydraulic valve lifters. Crankcase capacity: 4 qt. (add 1 qt. for new filter). Cooling system capacity: 12 qt (add 6 qt. for heater). Carburetor: Rochester one-barrel Model 7028017. Sales code L22. Available standard with three-speed fully synchronized manual transmission and Powerglide automatic transmission.

SPRINT BASE 307-CID, 200-HP V-8: Overhead-valve. Cast-iron block and head. Bore and stroke: 3.88 x 3.25 in. Displacement: 307 cid. Compression ratio: 8.50:1. Gross brake hp: 200 at 4600 rpm. Net brake hp: 140 at 4400 rpm. Taxable hp: 48. Gross torque: 300 lbs.-ft. at 2400. Net torque: 235 lbs.-ft. at 2400 rpm. Five main bearings. Hydraulic valve lifters. Crankcase capacity: 4 qt. (add 1 qt. for new filter). Cooling system capacity: 15 qt. (add 1 qt. for heater). Carburetor: Two-barrel.

SPRINT OPTIONAL 350-CID, 165-HP V-8: Overhead-valve. Cast-iron block and head. Bore and stroke: 4.00 x 3.48 in. Displacement: 350 cid. Compression ratio: 8.50:1. Gross brake hp: 245 at 4800 rpm. Net brake hp: 165 at 4000 rpm. Taxable hp: 51.20. Gross torque: 350 lbs.-ft. at 2800. Net torque: 280 lbs.-ft. at 2400 rpm. Five main bearings. Hydraulic valve lifters. Crankcase capacity: 4 qt. (add 1 qt. for new filter). Cooling system capacity: 15 qt. (add 1 qt. for heater). Carburetor: Two-barrel. Sales code L65.

SPRINT OPTIONAL 350-CID, 270-HP V-8: Overhead-valve. Cast-iron block and head. Bore and stroke: 4.00 x 3.48 in. Displacement: 350 cid. Compression ratio: 8.50:1. Gross brake hp: 270 at 4800 rpm. Net brake hp: 210 at 4400 rpm. Taxable hp: 51.20. Gross torque: 360 lbs.-ft. at 3200. Net torque: 300 lbs.-ft. at 2800 rpm. Five main bearings. Hydraulic valve lifters. Crankcase capacity: 4 qt. (add 1 qt. for new filter). Cooling system capacity: (full-size) 14 qt.; (others) 15 qt. (add 1 qt. for heater). Carburetor: Four-barrel. Sales code L48.

SPRINT OPTIONAL 402-CID, 300-HP V-8: Overhead-valve. Cast-iron block and head. Bore and stroke: 4.13 x 3.76 in. Displacement: 402 cid (400 cid). Compression ratio: 8.50:1. Gross brake hp: 300 at 4800 rpm. Net brake hp: 260 at 4400 rpm. Taxable hp: 54.50. Gross torque: 400 lbs.-ft. at 3200. Net torque: 345 lbs.-ft. at 3200 rpm. Five main bearings. Hydraulic valve lifters. Crankcase capacity: 4 qt. (add 1 qt. for new filter). Cooling system capacity: 22 qt. (add 1 qt. for heater). Carburetor: Four-barrel. Sales code LS3.

SPRINT OPTIONAL 454-CID, 365-HP V-8: Over-

The GMC and 454 badges were visible on the grille.

head-valve. Cast-iron block and head. Bore and stroke: 4.25 x 4.00 in. Displacement: 454 cid. Compression ratio: 8.50:1. Gross brake hp: 365 at 4800 rpm. Net brake hp: 285 at 4000 rpm. Taxable hp: 57.80. Gross torque: 465 lbs.-ft. at 3200. Net torque: 390 lbs.-ft. at 3200 rpm. Five main bearings. Hydraulic valve lifters. Crankcase capacity: 4 qt. (add 1 qt. for new filter). Cooling system capacity: 21 qt. (add 1 qt. for heater). Dual exhaust. Carburetor: Four-barrel. Sales code LS5.

SPRINT OPTIONAL 454-CID, 325-HP V-8: Overhead-valve. Cast-iron block and head. Bore and stroke: 4.25 x 4.00 in. Displacement: 454 cid. Compression ratio: 9.00:1. Gross brake hp: 425 at 5600 rpm. Net brake hp: 325 at 5600 rpm. Taxable hp: 57.80. Gross torque: 475 lbs.-ft. at 4000. Net torque: 390 lbs.-ft. at 3600 rpm. Five main bearings. Hydraulic valve lifters. Crankcase capacity: 4 qt. (add 1 qt. for new filter). Cooling system capacity: 21 qt. (add 1 qt. for heater). Dual exhaust. Carburetor: Four-barrel. Sales code LS6.

CHASSIS

Wheelbase: 116 in. Overall length: 206.8 in. Height: 54.4 in. Front tread: 60.2. Rear tread: 59.2 in. Tires: E78-14B. GVW: 4,100 lb. Saginaw manual, fully synchronized, transmission. Speeds: 3F/1R. Column-mounted gearshift lever. Single-plate dry-disc clutch (six-cylinder) or coil spring single-dry-plate (V-8). Rear axle: semi-floating. Hydraulic, four-wheel brakes. Kelsey-Hayes pressed steel wheels.

OPTIONS

A01 tinted body glass. A02 tinted windshield. A31 electric windows. A39 front and rear seat belts with retractors. A41 four-way power seat. A42 six-way electric front seat control. A46 power driver's bucket seat. A51 Astro bucket seats. A85 front shoulder belts. AK1 deluxe safety belts. AU3 power door locks. B37 floor mats. B85 belt reveal molding. B90 door edge and window frame moldings. B93 door edge guards. C08 vinyl top. C60 all-weather air conditioning. C75 automatic temperature control. D33 remote-control driver's mirror. D34 visor-vanity mirror. D55 front compartment floor console. F40 heavy-duty suspension. F41 special performance suspension. G67 level-control rear shock absorbers. G80 Positraction. J50 power brakes. J52 front disc brakes. JL2 front disc brakes. K85 63-amp Delcotron. L48 350-cid four-barrel V-8. L65 350-cid two-barrel V-8. L78 396-cid special high-performance V-8. LS3 402-cid four-barrel V-8. LS5 454-cid four-barrel V-8. M11 floor shifter. M20 four-speed manual transmission. M22 heavy-duty four-speed manual transmission. M35

The Sport wheels were standard on the Sprint SPs.

The box of the '71 Sprint measured 79 1/4 in. in length and 64 1/2 in. in width at the tailgate.

SPRINT

Powerglide automatic transmission. M38 three-speed automatic transmission. M40 three-speed automatic transmission. MC1 heavy-duty three-speed manual transmission. N33 tilt steering. N40 power steering. NK2 deluxe vinyl steering wheel. NK4 Sport steering wheel. P01 wheel trim covers. P02 simulated wire wheel covers. P90 G70-15 B white stripe tires. PA3 special wheel covers. PK2 G78-14 B glass-belted white stripe tires. PL3 E78-14 B glass-belted white stripe tires. PM6 G78-14 B glass-belted white stripe tires. PM7 F60-15 B glass-belted white letter tires. PU8 G78-15 B glass-belted white stripe tires. PX6 F78-14 B glass-belted white stripe tires. T60 heavy-duty battery. U14 instrument panel gauges. U35 electric clock. U63 push-button radio. U69 AM/FM push-button radio. U76 windshield antenna. U79 stereo radio. U80 auxiliary speaker. UM1 AM push-button radio and tape player. UM2 AM-FM push-button radio and tape player. V01 heavy-duty radiator. V30 bumper guards. YD1 trailering rear axle ratio. ZJ7 special hubcaps and trim rings. ZJ9 auxiliary lighting group. ZL2 special ducted hood air system. ZQ9 performance ratio rear axle.

HISTORICAL FOOTNOTES

Production start-up date 1971 models was Aug. 21, 1970. They hit the showrooms about five weeks later. The GMC Sprint used the same seven engines offered in El Caminos, which were modified to operate on unleaded gasoline. Front disc brakes were standard. Model-year sales were 3,963.

As they were with El Caminos, bucket seats were optional in the Sprint interior.

The Sprint badge was centered on the tailgate.

The 454 engine option helped the Sprint appeal to muscle car fans.

The deluxe vinyl steering wheel.

The 1972 GMC Sprint had a new three-tier grille with two thin, horizontal moldings running the full-width across the center of each tier. The tiers were separated by thicker, full-width horizontal moldings. There was GMC lettering in the middle of the center of the grille and engine call-out badges in the lower left-hand (driver's side) corner. The front parking lights were larger, one-piece lenses. They were more or less square, but were angled to wrap around the front body corners to do double duty as side marker lights. Chrome GMC block letters appeared on the body sides, just behind the front wheel openings.

I.D. NUMBERS

The VIN is stamped on a plate on the top left side of the instrument panel and visible through the windshield. The first symbol 5 designates GMC. The second and third symbols designate the series: (six-cylinder) 33=Sprint, 34=Custom Sprint. (V-8) 36=Custom Sprint. The fourth and fifth symbols designate body type: 80=two-door sedan pickup. The sixth symbol designates the model year: 2=1972. The seventh symbol indicated assembly plant: B=Baltimore, Maryland; F=Flint, Michigan; K=Kansas City/Leeds, Missouri; L=Los Angles/Van Nuys, California; R=Arlington, Texas and 1-Oshawa, Canada. The last six symbols are the sequential unit production number at the specific factory.

SPRINT — SERIES 33/34 — SIX/V-8

Standard models had bright windshield frames, back-up lights on the tailgate, and a base six-cylinder engine. A plain cloth and vinyl interior was standard. The pickup box had an outside width of 75 1/2 in. The inside width behind the cab was 59 in. and the inside width near the tailgate was 64 1/2 in. The width between the wheel housings was 44 in. The bottom bed length measured 79 1/4 in. Tailgate measurements were 54 1/2 x 22 1/2 in.

Model Number	Body/Style Number	Body Type & Seating	Factory Price	Shipping Weight	Production Total
SPRINT SERIES 33 (6-CYL)					
533	80	pickup	$2,790	3,302 lbs.	Note 1
SPRINT SERIES 34 (V-8)					
534	80	pickup	$2,880	3,418 lbs.	Note 1

SPRINT CUSTOM — SERIES 36 — V-8

Customs added a V-8 as base engine, body side moldings, wheel house moldings, pickup box rim moldings, rear body corner moldings, two moldings on the tailgate, and silver anodized lower body perimeter. The Custom interior had vinyl seats, vinyl door panels, vinyl sidewall panels, color-keyed carpeting and wood-grained vinyl dash accents.

Model Number	Body/Style Number	Body Type & Seating	Factory Price	Shipping Weight	Production Total
536	80	Custom pickup	$2,960	3,442 lbs.	Note 1

NOTE 1: Total GMC Sprint production for the model year is 6,473.

MODEL OPTIONS

SPRINT SP: An SP package was available. The basic SP package was $365 extra and the engine selections were separate options. The performance and appearance package included a black-accented grille with SP emblems, SP badges behind the front wheel cutouts, a Sport suspension, power front disc brakes, a domed hood with lock pins and 15 x 7 Sport wheels with F60-15 raised white letter tires. The 400-cid and 454-cid V-8s were optional.

ENGINES

SPRINT BASE 250-CID, 110-HP SIX-CYL: Inline. Overhead-valve. Cast-iron block. Displacement: 250 cid. Bore and stroke: 3.875 x 3.53 in. Compression ratio: 8.5:1. Brake hp: 145 at 4200 rpm. Net brake hp: 110 at 3800 rpm. Taxable hp: 36. Torque: 230 lbs.-ft. at 1600 rpm. Seven main bearings. Hydraulic valve lifters. Crankcase capacity: 4 qt. (add 1 qt. for new filter). Cooling system capacity: 12 qt (add 6 qt. for heater). Carburetor: Rochester one-barrel Model 7028017. Sales code L22. Available standard with three-speed fully synchronized manual transmission and Powerglide automatic transmission.

SPRINT BASE 307-CID, 130-HP V-8: Overhead-valve. Cast-iron block and head. Bore and stroke: 3.88 x 3.25 in. Displacement: 307 cid. Compression ratio: 8.50:1. Net brake hp: 130 at 4000 rpm. Taxable hp: 48. Net torque. 230 lbs.-ft. at 2400 rpm. Five main bearings. Hydraulic valve lifters. Crankcase capacity: 4 qt. (add 1 qt. for new filter). Cooling system capacity: 14 qt.; (add 1 qt. for heater). Carburetor: Two-barrel.

SPRINT OPTIONAL 350-CID, 165-HP V-8: Overhead-valve. Cast-iron block and head. Bore and stroke: 4.00 x 3.48 in. Displacement: 350 cid. Compression ratio: 8.50:1. Net brake hp: 165 at 4000 rpm. Taxable hp: 51.20. Net torque: 280 lbs.-ft. at 2400 rpm. Five main bearings. Hydraulic valve lifters. Crankcase capacity: 4 qt. (add 1 qt. for new filter). Cooling system capacity: 15 qt. (add 1 qt. for heater). Sales code L65. Carburetor: Two-barrel.

SPRINT OPTIONAL 350-CID, 175-HP V-8: Overhead-valve. Cast-iron block and head. Bore and stroke: 4.00 x 3.48 in. Displacement: 350 cid. Compression ratio: 8.50:1. Net brake hp: 175 at 4000 rpm. Taxable hp: 51.20. Net torque: 280 lbs.-ft. at 2400 rpm. Five main bearings. Hydraulic valve lifters. Crankcase capacity: 4 qt. (add 1 qt. for new filter). Cooling system capacity: 15 qt. (add 1 qt. for heater). Sales code: L48. Carburetor: Four-barrel.

SPRINT OPTIONAL 402-CID, 350-HP V-8: Overhead-valve. Cast-iron block and head. Bore and stroke: 4.126 x 3.76 in. Displacement: 402 cid (a.k.a. 396 cid). Compression ratio: 8.50:1. Net brake hp: 240 at 4400 rpm. Taxable hp: 54.50. Net torque: 345 lbs.-ft. at 3200 rpm. Five main bearings. Hydraulic valve lifters. Crankcase capacity: 4 qt. (add 1 qt. for new filter). Cooling system capacity: 22 qt. (add 1 qt. for heater). Sales code LS3. Carburetor: Four-barrel.

SPRINT SP ONLY OPTIONAL 454-CID, 270-HP V-8: Overhead-valve. Cast-iron block and head. Bore and stroke: 4.251 x 4.00 in. Displacement: 454 cid. Compression ratio: 8.50:1. Net brake hp: 270 at 4000 rpm. Taxable hp: 57.80. Net torque. 390 lbs.-ft. at 3200 rpm. Five main bearings. Hydraulic valve lifters. Crankcase capacity: 4 qt. (add 1 qt. for new filter). Cooling system capacity: 22 qt. (add 1 qt. for heater). Dual exhaust. Sales code: LS5. Carburetor: Four-barrel.

CHASSIS

Wheelbase: 116 in. Overall length: 206.8 in. Height: 54.4 in. Front tread: 60.2. Rear tread: 59.2 in. Tires: E78-14B. Gross vehicle weight: 4,100 lbs. Saginaw manual, fully synchronized, transmission. Speeds: 3F/1R. Column-mounted gearshift lever. Single-plate dry-disc clutch (six-cylinder) or coil spring single-dry-plate (V-8). Rear axle: semi-floating. Hydraulic, four-wheel brakes. Kelsey-Hayes pressed steel wheels.

OPTIONS

A01 tinted body glass. A02 tinted windshield. A31 electric windows. A39 front and rear seat belts with retractors. A41 four-way power seat. A42 six-way electric front seat control. A46 power driver's bucket seat. A51 Astro bucket seats. A85 front shoulder belts. AK1 deluxe safety belts. AU3 power door locks. B37 floor mats. B85 belt reveal molding. B90 door edge and window frame moldings. B93 door edge guards. C08 vinyl top. C60 all-weather air conditioning. C75 automatic temperature control. D33 remote-control driver's mirror. D34 visor-vanity mirror. D55 front compartment floor console. F40 heavy-duty suspension. F41 special performance suspension. G67 level-control rear shock absorbers. G80 Positraction. J50 power brakes. J52 front disc brakes. JL2 front disc brakes. K85 63-amp. Delcotron. L48 350-cid four-barrel V-8. L65 350-cid two-barrel V-8. L78 396-cid special high-performance V-8. LS3 402-cid four-barrel V-8. LS5 454-cid four-barrel V-8. M11 floor shifter. M20 four-speed manual transmission. M22 heavy-duty four-speed manual transmission. M35 Powerglide automatic transmission. M38 three-speed automatic transmission. M40 three-speed automatic transmission. MC1 heavy-duty three-speed manual transmission. N33 tilt steering. N40 power steering. NK2 deluxe vinyl steering wheel. NK4 Sport steering wheel. P01 wheel trim covers. P02 simulated wire wheel covers. P90 G70-15 B white stripe tires. PA3 special wheel covers. PK2 G78-14 B glass-belted white stripe tires. PL3 E78-14 B glass-belted white stripe tires. PM6 G78-14 B glass-belted white stripe tires. PM7 F60-15 B glass-belted white letter tires. PU8 G78-15 B glass-belted white stripe tires. PX6 F78-14 B glass-belted white stripe tires. T60 heavy-duty battery. U14 instrument panel gauges. U35 electric clock. U63 push-button radio. U69 AM/FM push-button radio. U76 windshield antenna. U79 stereo radio. U80 auxiliary speaker. UM1 AM push-button radio and tape player. UM2 AM-FM push-button radio and tape player. V01 heavy-duty radiator. V30 bumper guards. YD1 trailering rear axle ratio. ZJ7 special hubcaps and trim rings. ZJ9 auxiliary lighting group. ZL2 special ducted hood air system. ZQ9 performance ratio rear axle.

HISTORICAL FOOTNOTES

Alex Mair took over as the general manager of GMC. Model-year sales of Sprints was 6,492, representing 10.2 percent of combined sales of El Camino and Sprint models.

The Sprint SP model option featured a domed hood and lock pins.

The all-new 1973 Sprint shared the first new El Camino body since 1968. New looks, a bit more length and cleaner exhaust were featured. The SP package was carried over and a new High Sierra trim option was available for Custom models. The sedan-pickup was a bit taller than the previous models and about 5 inches longer overall. All models had impact-resistant front bumpers and were said to be substantially improved in roadability, comfort and styling.

Engine availability included a de-tuned version of the 250-cid in-line six, a base 307-cid V-8, two versions of the 350-cid V-8, and a 454-cid V-8. The base series was called the Sprint. The one-step-up line was called the Sprint Custom. A new full-width grille was topped off with a heavier molding that dropped down the sides of the grille insert and extended horizontally under the headlights. The insert had a fine mesh of thin vertical and horizontal moldings. There was a small GMC badge in the center and Sprint lettering at the lower left-hand side. Square headlights were sunk into rectangular housings ahead of squarish bulges that flared into the hood and fender lines for a classic look. There were rectangular parking lights in the full-width bumper. The new High sierra trim option had wood-grained body side and tailgate panels.

I.D. NUMBERS

The VIN is stamped on a plate on the top left side of the instrument panel and visible through the windshield. The first symbol 5 designates GMC. The second and third symbols designate the series: C=Sprint, D=Custom Sprint. The third and fourth symbols designate body type: 80=two-door sedan pickup. The fifth symbol indicates the engine: D=250-cid six, F=307-cid V-8, H=350-cid V-8 (two-barrel), K=350-cid V-8 (four-barrel) and Y=454-cid V-8. The sixth symbol designates the model year: 3=1973. The seventh symbol indicates assembly plant: B=Baltimore, Maryland.; F=Flint, Michigan; K=Kansas City/Leeds, Missouri; L=Los Angles/Van Nuys, California; R=Arlington, Texas and 1-Oshawa, Canada. The last six symbols are the sequential unit production number at the specific factory.

SPRINT — SERIES C — SIX/V-8

Standard equipment on all 1973 Sprints included a bright Sprint nameplate on the left-hand grille panel, a bright GMC grille center emblem, bright back window reveal moldings, a bright Sprint nameplate on the lower right-hand side of the tailgate, chrome front and rear bumpers, bright door lock handles, bright door lock cylinder covers, bright Sprint nameplates on the front fender sides, a bright grille outer edge molding, a bright headlight bezel bead, a bright hood molding, bright hubcaps, a bright left-hand outside rearview mirror, bright body side, tailgate, drip rail and wheel opening moldings, bright windshield reveal moldings, side doors with a lift-bar latch release and key lock cylinders, a rear tailgate with a single-handle double latch mechanism, safety glass (in windshield, back glass and side windows), an Argent Silver plastic grid grille insert, instrument panel knobs marked with function symbols, back-up lights, two single-lens front park/turn lights, two Class A rear lamps with tail/stop/signal and side marker functions, two Power-Beam headlights, a single rear license plate light, win front and rear side marker lights, a single D note horn, steel side door guard beams, a mechanical jack and wheel lug nut wrench, partial under body and full-wheel well undercoating, body-color steel wheels, two-speed electric windshield wipers with hideaway wipers and arms, left- and right-hand cowl air vents with individual controls, dual armrests, bright seat back latch and adjuster knobs, bright window regulator knobs, a cigarette lighter, color-coordinated upholstery with black trim, a door-actuated dome lamp, push-button door locks, closed-cell rubber door seals, color-keyed vinyl covered rubber floor mats, a speedometer, an odometer, a fuel gauge, directional signals with a lane-change feature, a hazard warning, a heater and defroster, warning lights (for generator, oil pressure, temperature, brake-on, directionals and headlight high beams), a fiberglass-filled plastic instrument panel, sound deadening insulation, a 12-in. inside rearview mirror, full-width seats with textured all-vinyl trim, seat and shoulder safety belts, a black grained plastic steering wheel with soft rim and brushed chrome insert with the GMC name, dual sun shades, side door opening scuff plates and floor mat retainers, a spare tire carrier behind the driver seating position, a lockable steering column, vinyl door trim panels with bright trim, vinyl-coated cowl side panels, a vinyl-coated headliner, an ignition key warning buzzer, bright metal window regulators, padded windshield pillars, a 250-cid in-line six-cylinder engine, three-speed manual transmission and G78-14B black sidewall tires.

Model Number	Body/Style Number	Body Type & Seating	Factory Price	Shipping Weight	Production Total
SPRINT SERIES C (6-CYL)					
C	80	pickup	—	—	Note 1
SPRINT SERIES C (V-8)					
C	80	pickup	$2,976	3,625 lbs.	Note 1

SPRINT CUSTOM — SERIES D — V-8

In addition to standard Sprint equipment, the Sprint Custom included a 307-cid V-8 engine, lower body sill moldings, color-keyed carpeting, a choice of black or light neutral color interior trim, a deluxe vinyl-coated headliner, an instrument with a panel crown pad and dull paint finish, an inside rearview mirror with black finish on the back and mirror support and a full-width seat with custom vinyl trim.

Model Number	Body/Style Number	Body Type & Seating	Factory Price	Shipping Weight	Production Total
D	80	Custom pickup	$3,038	3,635 lbs.	Note 1

NOTE 1 Total GMC Sprint production for the model year was 8,552 units.

MODEL OPTIONS

SPRINT SP: GMC continued to list an SP Sport equipment package for the 1973 Sprint. In addition to or in place of the standard equipment listed above, the SP equipment package included a black-finished grille with an SP emblem, a remote-control left-hand outside Sport-style rearview mirror, a manual right-hand Sport-style outside rearview mirror, SP fender emblems, SP door trim, an SP steering wheel, an SP emblem above the rear bumper, bright roof drip moldings, lower body side and wheel opening stripes keyed to the body color, black-accented taillight frames, a special instrument cluster, special front and rear stabilizer bars, 14 x 7-in. Rallye wheels with special center caps and trim rings and G70-14 white letter tires. The SP equipment package cost $250.

SPRINT HIGH SIERRA: Accentuating the appearance of the Sprint Custom was a new High Sierra trim package. It consisted of full-body side and tailgate accents with a wood-grain vinyl trim. Chrome scripts calling out the "High Sierra" name were located on the front fenders below the Sprint nameplates. Also included were special vinyl-covered pattern door trim panels. The High Sierra package cost $131.

ENGINES

SPRINT BASE 250-CID, 100-HP SIX-CYL: Inline. Overhead-valve. Cast-iron block. Displacement: 250 cid. Bore and stroke: 3.875 x 3.53 in. Compression ratio: 8.25:1. Net brake hp: 100 at 3800 rpm. Taxable hp: 36. Torque: 175 lbs.-ft. at 1600 rpm. Seven main bearings. Hydraulic valve lifters. Crankcase capacity: 4 qt. (add 1 qt. for new filter). Cooling system capacity: 12 qt (add 6 qt. for heater). Carburetor: Rochester one-barrel Model 7028017. Sales code L22.

SPRINT BASE 307-CID, 115-HP V-8: Overhead-valve. Cast-iron block and head. Bore and stroke: 3.88 x 3.25 in. Displacement: 307 cid. Compression ratio: 8.50:1. Net brake hp: 115 at 4000 rpm. Taxable hp: 48. Net torque. 205 lbs.-ft. at 2000 rpm. Five main bearings. Hydraulic valve lifters. Crankcase capacity: 4 qt. (add 1 qt. for new filter). Cooling system capacity: 15 qt.; (add 1 qt. for heater). Carburetor: Two-barrel.

SPRINT OPTIONAL 350-CID, 145-HP V-8: Overhead-valve. Cast-iron block and head. Bore and stroke: 4.00 x 3.48 in. Displacement: 350 cid. Compression ratio: 8.50:1. Net brake hp: 145 at 4000 rpm. Taxable hp: 51.20. Net torque: 255 lbs.-ft. at 2400 rpm. Five main bearings. Hydraulic valve lifters. Crankcase capacity: 4 qt. (add 1 qt. for new filter). Cooling system capacity: 15 qt. (add 1 qt. for heater). Carburetor: Two-barrel. Sales code L65.

SPRINT OPTIONAL 350-CID, 175-HP V-8: Overhead-valve. Cast-iron block and head. Bore and stroke: 4.00 x 3.48 in. Displacement: 350 cid. Compression ratio: 8.50:1. Net brake hp: 175 at 4000 rpm. Taxable hp: 51.20. Net torque: 270 lbs.-ft. at 2400 rpm. Five main bearings. Hydraulic valve lifters. Crankcase capacity: 4 qt. (add 1 qt. for new filter). Cooling system capacity: (Nova) 17 qt.; (Chevrolet) 16 qt. (others) 15 qt. (add 1 qt. for heater). Carburetor: Four-barrel. Sales code L48.

SPRINT OPTIONAL 454-CID, 245-HP V-8: Overhead-valve. Cast-iron block and head. Bore and stroke: 4.25 x 4.00 in. Displacement: 454 cid. Compression ratio: 8.50:1. Net brake hp: 245 at 4000 rpm. Taxable hp: 57.80. Net torque: 375 lbs.-ft. at 2800 rpm. Five main bearings. Hydraulic valve lifters. Crankcase capacity: 4 qt. (add 1 qt. for new filter). Cooling system capacity: (Chevelle, Monte Carlo) 22 qt.; (Chevrolet) 23 qt. (add 1 qt. for heater). Dual exhaust. Carburetor: Four-barrel. Sales code LS5.

CHASSIS

Wheelbase: 116 in. Overall length: 206.8 in. Height: 54.4 in. Front tread: 60.2. Rear tread: 59.2 in. Tires: E78-14B. Gross vehicle weight: 4,100 lbs. Saginaw manual, fully synchronized, transmission. Speeds: 3F/1R. Column-mounted gearshift lever. Single-plate dry-disc clutch (six-cylinder) or coil spring single-dry-plate (V-8). Rear axle: semi-floating. Hydraulic, four-wheel brakes. Kelsey-Hayes pressed steel wheels.

OPTIONS

A01 tinted body glass. A02 tinted windshield. A31 electric windows. A39 front and rear seat belts with retractors. A41 four-way power seat. A42 six-way electric front seat control. A46 power driver's bucket seat. A51 Astro bucket seats. A85 front shoulder belts. AK1 deluxe safety belts. AU3 power door locks. B37 floor mats. B85 belt reveal molding. B90 door edge and window frame moldings. B93 door edge guards. C08 vinyl top. C60 all-weather air conditioning. C75 automatic temperature control. D33 remote-control driver's mirror. D34 visor-vanity mirror. D55 front compartment floor console. F40 heavy-duty suspension. F41 special performance suspension. G67 level-control rear shock absorbers. G80 Positraction. J50 power brakes. J52 front disc brakes. JL2 front disc brakes. K85 63-amp. Delcotron. L48 350-cid four-barrel V-8. L65 350-cid two-barrel V-8. L78 396-cid special high-performance V-8. LS3 402-cid four-barrel V-8. LS5 454-cid four-barrel V-8. M11 floor shifter. M20 four-speed manual transmission. M22 heavy-duty four-speed manual transmission. M35 Powerglide automatic transmission. M38 three-speed automatic transmission. M40 three-speed automatic transmission. MC1 heavy-duty three-speed manual transmission. N33 tilt steering. N40 power steering. NK2 deluxe vinyl steering wheel. NK4 Sport steering wheel. P01 wheel trim covers. P02 simulated wire wheel covers. P90 G70-15 B white stripe tires. PA3 special wheel covers. PK2 G78-14 B glass-belted white stripe tires. PL3 E78-14 B glass-belted white stripe tires. PM6 G78-14 B glass-belted white-stripe tires. PM7 F60-15 B glass-belted white-letter tires. PU8 G78-15 B glass-belted white stripe tires. PX6 F78-14 B glass-belted white stripe tires. T60 heavy-duty battery. U14 instrument panel gauges. U35 electric clock. U63 push-button radio. U69 AM/FM push-button radio. U76 windshield antenna. U79 stereo radio. U80 auxiliary speaker. UM1 AM push-button radio and tape player. UM2 AM-FM push-button radio and tape player. V01 heavy-duty radiator. V30 bumper guards. YD1 trailering rear axle ratio. ZJ7 special hubcaps and trim rings. ZJ9 auxiliary lighting group. ZL2 special ducted hood air system. ZQ9 performance ratio rear axle.

OPTION INSTALLATION RATES

Automatic transmission (87.5). Power brakes (100 percent). Disc brakes (100 percent). Power steering (97.1 percent). AM radio (76.5 percent). AM/FM stereo radio (18.2 percent). V-8 engine 350-cid or less (90.1 percent). V-8 engine over 350-cid (9.9 percent). Air conditioning (71.9 percent). Positraction (13.7 percent). Tinted glass (83.8 percent).

HISTORICAL FOOTNOTES

Alex Mair took over as the general manager of GMC. Model-year sales of Sprints was 6,766, representing 9.4 percent of combined sales of El Camino and Sprint models.

The 1974 Sprint had a new grille with GMC lettering in the center of three large, rectangular segments. Optional engine call-outs were seen in the lower portion of the left-hand rectangle. The square headlights were still sunk into rectangular housings ahead of squarish bulges that flared into the hood and fender lines for a classic look. There were rectangular parking lights below the main bar. A body-colored panel showed through the center of the front bumper. All 1974 Sprints had a V-8 engine.

I.D. NUMBERS

The VIN is stamped on a plate on the top left side of the instrument panel and visible through the windshield. The first symbol 5 designates GMC. The second and third symbols designate the series: C=Sprint, D=Custom Sprint. The third and fourth symbols designate body type: 80=two-door sedan pickup. The fifth symbol indicates the engine: H=350-cid V-8 (two-barrel), L=350-cid V-8 (four-barrel), R=400-cid V-8 (two-barrel), U=400-cid V-8 (four-barrel) and Y=454-cid V-8. The sixth symbol designates the model year: 4=1974. The seventh symbol indicates assembly plant: B=Baltimore, Maryland; F=Flint, Michigan; K-=Kansas City/Leeds, Missouri; L=Los Angles/Van Nuys, California; R=Arlington, Texas and 1-Oshawa, Canada. The last six symbols are the sequential unit production number at the specific factory.

SPRINT — SERIES C — V-8

Standard equipment on all 1974 Sprints included a bright GMC grille emblem, bright back window reveal moldings, chrome front and rear bumpers, bright door lock handles, bright door lock cylinder covers, a bright grille outer edge molding, a bright headlight bezel bead, a bright hood molding, bright hubcaps, a bright left-hand outside rearview mirror, bright body side, tailgate, drip rail and wheel opening moldings, bright windshield reveal moldings, side doors with a lift-bar latch release and key lock cylinders, a rear tailgate with a single-handle double latch mechanism, safety glass (in windshield, back glass and side windows), instrument panel knobs marked with function symbols, back-up lights, two single-lens front park/turn lights, two Class A rear lamps with tail/stop/signal and side marker functions, two Power-Beam headlights, a single rear license plate light, win front and rear side marker lights, a single D note horn, steel side door guard beams, a mechanical jack and wheel lug nut wrench, partial under body and full wheel well undercoating, body-color steel wheels, two-speed electric windshield wipers with hideaway wipers and arms, left- and right-hand cowl air vents with individual controls, dual armrests, bright seat back latch and adjuster knobs, bright window regulator knobs, a cigarette lighter, color-coordinated upholstery with black trim, a door-actuated dome lamp, push-button door locks, closed-cell rubber door seals, color-keyed vinyl covered rubber floor mats, a speedometer, an odometer, a fuel gauge, directional signals with a lane-change feature, a hazard warning, a heater and defroster, warning lights (for generator, oil pressure, temperature, brake-on, directionals and headlight high beams), a fiberglass-filled plastic instrument panel, sound deadening insulation, a 12-in.-inside rearview mirror, full-width seats with textured all-vinyl trim, seat and shoulder safety belts, dual sun shades, side door opening scuff plates and floor mat retainers, a spare tire carrier behind the driver seating position, a lockable steering column, vinyl door trim panels with bright trim, vinyl-coated cowl side panels, a vinyl-coated headliner, an ignition key warning buzzer, bright metal window regulators, padded windshield pillars, a V-8 engine, a three-speed manual transmission and G78-14B black-sidewall tires.

Model Number	Body/Style Number	Body Type & Seating	Factory Price	Shipping Weight	Production Total
C	80	pickup	$3,119	3,817 lbs.	Note 1

SPRINT CUSTOM — SERIES D — V-8

In addition to standard Sprint equipment, the Sprint Custom included a 350-cid V-8 engine, lower body sill moldings, color-keyed carpeting, a choice of black or light neutral color interior trim, a deluxe vinyl-coated headliner, an instrument with a panel crown pad and dull paint finish, an inside rearview mirror with black finish on the back and mirror support and a full-width seat with custom vinyl trim.

Model Number	Body/Style Number	Body Type & Seating	Factory Price	Shipping Weight	Production Total
D	80	Custom pickup	$3,277	3,832 lbs.	Note 1

NOTE 1 Total GMC Sprint production for the model year was 4,502 units.

MODEL OPTIONS

SPRINT SP GMC continued to list an SP Sport equipment package for the 1974 Sprint. In addition to or in place of the standard equipment listed above, the SP equipment package included a black-finished grille with an SP emblem, a remote-control left-hand outside Sport-style rearview mirror, a manual right-hand Sport-style outside rearview mirror, SP fender emblems, SP door trim, an SP steering wheel, an SP emblem above the rear bumper, bright roof drip moldings, lower body side and wheel opening stripes keyed to the body color, black-accented taillight frames, a special instrument cluster, special front and rear stabilizer bars, 14 x 7-in. Rallye wheels with special center caps and trim rings and G70-14 white-letter tires. The SP equipment package cost $250.

SPRINT HIGH SIERRA: Accentuating the appearance of the Sprint Custom was a new High Sierra trim package. It consisted of full body side and tailgate accents with a wood-grain vinyl trim. Chrome scripts calling out the "High Sierra" name were located on the front fenders below the Sprint nameplates. Also included were special vinyl-covered pattern door trim panels. The price of the High Sierra package was $131.

ENGINES

SPRINT BASE 350-CID, 145-HP V-8: Overhead-valve. Cast-iron block and head. Bore and stroke: 4.00 x 3.48 in. Displacement: 350 cid. Compression ratio: 8.50:1. Net brake hp: 145 at 3600 rpm. Taxable hp: 51.20. Net torque: 250 lbs.-ft. at 2200 rpm. Five main bearings. Hydraulic valve lifters. Crankcase capacity: 4 qt. (add 1 qt. for new filter). Cooling system capacity with heater: 18 qt. Carburetor: Two-barrel. Sales code L65.

SPRINT OPTIONAL 400-CID, 150-HP V-8: Overhead-valve. Cast-iron block and head. Bore and stroke: 4.13 x 3.75 in. Displacement: 400 cid. Compression ratio: 8.50:1. Net brake hp: 150 at 3200 rpm. Taxable hp: 54.40. Net torque. 295 lbs.-ft. at 2000 rpm. Five main bearings. Hydraulic valve lifters. Crankcase capacity: 4 qt. (add 1 qt. for new filter). Cooling system capacity with heater: 18 qt. Carburetor: Two-barrel. Sales code LF6.

SPRINT OPTIONAL 350-CID, 160-HP V-8: Overhead-valve. Cast-iron block and head. Bore and stroke: 4.00 x 3.48 in. Displacement: 350 cid. Compression ratio: 8.50:1. Net brake hp: 160 at 3800 rpm. Taxable hp: 51.20. Net torque: 250 lbs.-ft. at 2400 rpm. Five main bearings. Hydraulic valve lifters. Crankcase capacity: 4 qt. (add 1 qt. for new filter). Cooling system capacity with heater: 18 qt. Carburetor: Four-barrel. Sales code LM1.

SPRINT OPTIONAL 400-CID, 180-HP V-8: Overhead-valve. Cast-iron block and head. Bore and stroke: 4.13 x 3.75 in. Displacement: 400 cid. Compression ratio: 8.50:1. Net brake hp: 180 at 3800 rpm. Taxable hp: 54.40. Net torque: 290 lbs.-ft. at 2400 rpm. Five main bearings. Hydraulic valve lifters. Crankcase capacity: 4 qt. (add 1 qt. for new filter). Cooling system capacity with heater: 16.5 qt. Carburetor: Four-barrel. Sales code LT4.

SPRINT OPTIONAL 454-CID, 235-HP V-8: Overhead-valve. Cast-iron block and head. Bore and stroke: 4.25 x 4.00 in. Displacement: 454 cid. Compression ratio: 8.50:1. Net brake hp: 235 at 4000 rpm. Taxable hp: 57.80. Net torque. 360 lbs.-ft. at 2800 rpm. Five main bearings. Hydraulic valve lifters. Crankcase capacity: 5 qt. (add 1 qt. for new filter). Cooling system capacity with heater: 23 qt. Dual exhaust. Carburetor: Four-barrel. Sales code LS4.

CHASSIS

Wheelbase: 116 in. Overall length: 206.8 in. Height: 54.4 in. Front tread: 60.2. Rear tread: 59.2 in. Tires: E78-14B. GVW: 4,100 lb. Saginaw manual, fully synchronized, transmission. Speeds: 3F/1R. Column-mounted gearshift lever. Single-plate dry-disc clutch (six-cylinder) or coil spring single-dry-plate (V-8). Rear axle: semi-floating. Hydraulic, four-wheel brakes. Kelsey-Hayes pressed steel wheels.

OPTIONS

A01 tinted body glass. A02 tinted windshield. A31 electric windows. A39 front and rear seat belts with retractors. A41 four-way power seat. A42 six-way electric front seat control. A46 power driver's bucket seat. A51 Astro bucket seats. A85 front shoulder belts. AK1 deluxe safety belts. AU3 power door locks. B37 floor mats. B85 belt reveal molding. B90 door edge and window frame moldings. B93 door edge guards. C08 vinyl top. C60 all-weather air conditioning. C75 automatic temperature control. D33 remote-control driver's mirror. D34 visor-vanity mirror. D55 front compartment floor console. F40 heavy-duty suspension. F41 special performance suspension. G67 level-control rear shock absorbers. G80 Positraction. J50 power brakes. J52 front disc brakes. JL2 front disc brakes. K85 63-amp. Delcotron generator. L48 350-cid four-barrel V-8. L65 350-cid two-barrel V-8. L78 396-cid special high-performance V-8. LS3 402-cid four-barrel V-8. LS5 454-cid four-barrel V-8. M11 floor shifter. M20 four-speed manual transmission. M22 heavy-duty four-speed manual transmission. M35 Powerglide automatic transmission. M38 three-speed automatic transmission. M40 three-speed automatic transmission. MC1 heavy-duty three-speed manual transmission. N33 tilt steering. N40 power steering. NK2 deluxe vinyl steering wheel. NK4 Sport steering wheel. P01 wheel trim covers. P02 simulated wire wheel covers. P90 G70-15 B white stripe tires. PA3 special wheel covers. PK2 G78-14 B glass-belted white stripe tires. PL3 E78-14 B glass-belted white stripe tires. PM6 G78-14 B glass-belted white stripe tires. PM7 F60-15 B glass-belted white-letter tires. PU8 G78-15 B glass-belted white-stripe tires. PX6 F78-14 B glass-belted white stripe tires. T60 heavy-duty battery. U14 instrument panel gauges. U35 electric clock. U63 push-button radio. U69 AM/FM push-button radio. U76 windshield antenna. U79 stereo radio. U80 auxiliary speaker. UM1 AM push-button radio and tape player. UM2 AM-FM push-button radio and tape player. V01 heavy-duty radiator. V30 bumper guards. YD1 trailering rear axle ratio. ZJ7 special hubcaps and trim rings. ZJ9 auxiliary lighting group. ZL2 special ducted hood air system. ZQ9 performance ratio rear axle.

OPTION INSTALLATION RATES

Automatic transmission (97.3 percent). Manual disc

brakes (4 percent). Power disc brakes (4 percent). Power steering (97.9 percent). AM radio (70 percent). AM/FM stereo radio (29.5 percent). V-8 engine (100 percent). Air conditioning (76.6 percent). Positraction (14.1 percent). Tinted glass (85.5 percent). Streel-belted radial tires (13.8 percent). Wheel covers (56.6 percent).

HISTORICAL FOOTNOTES

Alex Mair continued as the general manager of GMC. Model-year sales of Sprints was 4,873, representing 8.7 percent of combined sales of El Camino and Sprint models. The GMC Truck & Coach Division recorded its second best sales year in history.

The 1975 Sprint had a new grille pattern with bright vertical division bars creating 10 segments with a crosshatch insert behind them. A small, squarish badge was in the next to last left-hand segment. The square headlights were still sunk into rectangular housings ahead of squarish bulges that flared into the hood and fender lines for a classic look. There were rectangular parking lights below the main bar. A body-colored panel showed through the center of the front bumper. The Custom model was now called the Classic.

I.D. NUMBERS

The VIN is stamped on a plate on the top left side of the instrument panel and visible through the windshield. The first symbol 5 designates GMC. The second and third symbols designate the series: C=Sprint, D=Classic Sprint. The third and fourth symbols designate body type: 80=two-door sedan pickup. The fifth symbol indicates the engine: D=250-cid six, H=350-cid V-8 (two-barrel), L=350-cid V-8 (four-barrel), U=400-cid V-8 (four-barrel) and Y=454-cid V-8. The sixth symbol designates the model year: 5=1975. The seventh symbol indicates assembly plant: B=Baltimore, Maryland; F=Flint, Michigan; K=Kansas City/Leeds, Missouri; L=Los Angles/Van Nuys, California; R=Arlington, Texas and 1-Oshawa, Canada. The last six symbols are the sequential unit production number at the specific factory.

SPRINT — SERIES C — SIX/V-8

Standard equipment on all 1975 Sprints included a bright GMC grille emblem, bright back window reveal moldings, chrome front and rear bumpers, bright door lock handles, bright door lock cylinder covers, a bright grille outer edge molding, a bright headlight bezel bead, a bright hood molding, bright hubcaps, a bright left-hand outside rearview mirror, bright body side, tailgate, drip rail and wheel opening moldings, bright windshield reveal moldings, side doors with a lift-bar latch release and key lock cylinders, a rear tailgate with a single-handle double latch mechanism, safety glass (in windshield, back glass and side windows), instrument panel knobs marked with function symbols, back-up lights, two single-lens front park/turn lights, two Class A rear lamps with tail/stop/signal and side marker functions, two Power-Beam headlights, a single rear license plate light, win front and rear side marker lights, a single D note horn, steel side door guard beams, a mechanical jack and wheel lug nut wrench, partial under body and full wheel well undercoating, body-color steel wheels, two-speed electric windshield wipers with hideaway wipers and arms, left- and right-hand cowl air vents with individual controls, dual armrests, bright seat back latch and adjuster knobs, bright window regulator knobs, a cigarette lighter, color-coordinated upholstery with black trim, a door-actuated dome lamp, push-button door locks, closed-cell rubber door seals, color-keyed vinyl covered rubber floor mats, a speedometer, an odometer, a fuel gauge, directional signals with a lane-change feature, a hazard warning, a heater and defroster, warning lights (for generator, oil pressure, temperature, brake-on, directionals and headlight high beams), a fiberglass-filled plastic instrument panel, sound deadening insulation, a 12-in. inside rearview mirror, full-width seats with textured all-vinyl trim, seat and shoulder safety belts, dual sun shades, side door opening scuff plates and floor mat retainers, a spare tire carrier behind the driver seating position, a lockable steering column, vinyl door trim panels with bright trim, vinyl-coated cowl side panels, a vinyl-coated headliner, an ignition key warning buzzer, bright metal window regulators, padded windshield pillars, a 250-cid inline six-cylinder engine, three-speed manual transmission and G78-14B black-sidewall tires.

Model Number	Body/Style Number	Body Type & Seating	Factory Price	Shipping Weight	Production Total
SPRINT SERIES C (6-CYL)					
C	80	pickup	—	—	Note 1
SPRINT SERIES C (V-8)					
C	80	pickup	$3,828	3,706 lbs.	Note 1

SPRINT CLASSIC — SERIES D — V-8

In addition to standard Sprint equipment, the Sprint Classic included lower body sill moldings, color-keyed carpeting, a choice of black or light neutral color interior trim, a deluxe vinyl-coated headliner, an instrument with a panel crown pad and dull paint finish, an inside rearview mirror with black finish on the back and mirror support and a full-width seat with custom vinyl trim.

Model Number	Body/Style Number	Body Type & Seating	Factory Price	Shipping Weight	Production Total
D	80	Classic pickup	$3,966	3,748 lbs.	Note 1

NOTE 1: Total GMC Sprint production for the model year was 3,988 units.

MODEL OPTIONS

SPRINT SP: GMC continued to list an SP Sport equipment package for the 1975 Sprint. In addition to or in place of the standard equipment listed above, the SP equipment package included a black-finished grille with an SP emblem, a remote-control left-hand outside Sport-style rearview mirror, a manual right-hand Sport-style outside rearview mirror, SP fender emblems, SP door trim, an SP steering wheel, an SP emblem above the rear bumper, bright roof drip moldings, lower body side and wheel opening stripes keyed to the body color, black-accented taillight frames, a special instrument cluster, special front and rear stabilizer bars, 14 x 7-in. Rallye wheels with special center caps and trim rings and G70-14 white-letter tires. The cost of the SP equipment package was $215.

SPRINT HIGH SIERRA: Accentuating the appearance of the Sprint Classic was a new High Sierra trim package. It consisted of full-body side and tailgate accents with a wood-grain vinyl trim. Chrome scripts calling out the "High Sierra" name were located on the front fenders below the Sprint nameplates. Also included were special vinyl-covered pattern door trim panels. The price of the High Sierra package was $157.

ENGINES

SPRINT BASE 250-CID, 100-HP SIX-CYL: Inline. Overhead-valve. Cast-iron block. Displacement: 250 cid. Bore and stroke: 3.875 x 3.53 in. Compression ratio: 8.25:1. Net brake hp: 100 at 3800 rpm. Taxable hp: 36. Torque: 175 lbs.-ft. at 1600 rpm. Seven main bearings. Hydraulic valve lifters. Crankcase capacity: 4 qt. (add 1 qt. for new filter). Cooling system capacity: 12 qt (add 6 qt. for heater). Carburetor: Rochester one-barrel Model 7028017. Sales code L22.

SPRINT BASE 350-CID, 145-HP V-8: Overhead-valve. Cast-iron block and head. Bore and stroke: 4.00 x 3.48 in. Displacement: 350 cid. Compression ratio: 8.50:1. Net brake hp: 145 at 3600 rpm. Taxable hp: 51.20. Net torque: 250 lbs.-ft. at 2200 rpm. Five main bearings. Hydraulic valve lifters. Crankcase capacity: 4 qt. (add 1 qt. for new filter). Cooling system capacity with heater: 18 qt. Carburetor: Two-barrel. Sales code L65.

SPRINT OPTIONAL 400-CID, 150-HP V-8: Overhead-valve. Cast-iron block and head. Bore and stroke: 4.13 x 3.75 in. Displacement: 400 cid. Compression ratio: 8.50:1. Net brake hp: 150 at 3200 rpm. Taxable hp: 54.40. Net torque: 295 lbs.-ft. at 2000 rpm. Five main bearings. Hydraulic valve lifters. Crankcase capacity: 4 qt. (add 1 qt. for new filter). Cooling system capacity with heater: 18 qt. Carburetor: Two-barrel. Sales code LF6.

SPRINT OPTIONAL 350-CID, 160-HP V-8: Overhead-valve. Cast-iron block and head. Bore and stroke: 4.00 x 3.48 in. Displacement: 350 cid. Compression ratio: 8.50:1. Net brake hp: 160 at 3800 rpm. Taxable hp: 51.20. Net torque: 250 lbs.-ft. at 2400 rpm. Five main bearings. Hydraulic valve lifters. Crankcase capacity: 4 qt. (add 1 qt. for new filter). Cooling system capacity with heater: 18 qt. Carburetor: Four-barrel. Sales code LM1.

SPRINT OPTIONAL 400-CID, 180-HP V-8: Overhead-valve. Cast-iron block and head. Bore and stroke: 4.13 x 3.75 in. Displacement: 400 cid. Compression ratio: 8.50:1. Net brake hp: 180 at 3800 rpm. Taxable hp: 54.40. Net torque: 290 lbs.-ft. at 2400 rpm. Five main bearings. Hydraulic valve lifters. Crankcase capacity: 4 qt. (add 1 qt. for new filter). Cooling system capacity with heater: 16.5 qt. Carburetor: Four-barrel. Sales code LT4.

SPRINT OPTIONAL 454-CID, 235-HP V-8: Overhead-valve. Cast-iron block and head. Bore and stroke: 4.25 x 4.00 in. Displacement: 454 cid. Compression ratio: 8.50:1. Net brake hp: 235 at 4000 rpm. Taxable hp: 57.80. Net torque. 360 lbs.-ft. at 2800 rpm. Five main bearings. Hydraulic valve lifters. Crankcase capacity: 5 qt. (add 1 qt. for new filter). Cooling system capacity with heater: 23 qt. Dual exhaust. Carburetor: Four-barrel. Sales code LS4.

CHASSIS

Wheelbase: 116 in. Overall length: 206.8 in. Height: 54.4 in. Front tread: 60.2. Rear tread: 59.2 in. Tires: E78-14B. GVW: 4,100 lbs. Saginaw manual, fully synchronized, transmission. Speeds: 3F/1R. Column-mounted gearshift lever. Single-plate dry-disc clutch (6-cylinder) or coil spring single-dry-plate (V-8). Rear axle: semi-floating. Hydraulic, four-wheel brakes. Kelsey-Hayes pressed steel wheels.

OPTIONS

A01 tinted body glass. A02 tinted windshield. A31 electric windows. A39 front and rear seat belts with retractors. A41 four-way power seat. A42 six-way electric front seat control. A46 power driver's bucket seat. A51 Astro bucket seats. A85 front shoulder belts. AK1 deluxe safety belts. AU3 power door locks. B37 floor mats. B85 belt reveal molding. B90 door edge and window frame moldings. B93 door edge guards. C08 vinyl top. C60 all-weather air conditioning. C75 automatic temperature control. D33 remote-control driver's mirror. D34 visor-vanity mirror. D55 front compartment floor console. F40 heavy-duty suspension. F41 special performance suspension. G67 level-control rear shock absorbers. G80 Positraction. J50 power brakes. J52 front disc brakes. JL2 front disc brakes. K85 63-amp Delcotron generator. L48 350-cid four-barrel V-8. L65 350-cid two-barrel V-8. L78 396-cid special high-performance V-8. LS3 402-cid four-barrel V-8. LS5 454-cid four-barrel V-8. M11 floor shifter. M20 four-speed manual transmission. M22 heavy-duty four-speed manual transmission. M35 Powerglide automatic transmission. M38 three-speed automatic transmission. M40 three-speed automatic transmission. MC1 heavy-duty three-speed manual transmission. N33 tilt steering. N40 power steering. NK2 Deluxe vinyl steering wheel. NK4 Sport steering wheel. P01 wheel trim covers. P02 simulated wire wheel covers. P90 G70-15 B white stripe tires. PA3 special wheel covers. PK2 G78-14 B glass-belted white stripe tires. PL3 E78-14 B glass-belted white stripe tires. PM6 G78-14 B glass-belted white stripe tires. PM7 F60-15 B glass-belted white-letter tires. PU8 G78-15 B glass-belted white-stripe tires. PX6 F78-14 B glass-belted white stripe tires. T60 heavy-duty battery. U14 instrument panel gauges. U35 electric clock. U63 push-button radio. U69 AM/FM push-button radio. U76 windshield antenna. U79 stereo radio. U80 auxiliary speaker. UM1 AM push-button radio and tape player. UM2 AM-FM push-button radio and tape player. V01 heavy-duty radiator. V30 bumper guards. YD1 trailering rear axle ratio. ZJ7 special hubcaps and trim rings. ZJ9 auxiliary lighting group. ZL2 special ducted hood air system. ZQ9 performance ratio rear axle.

OPTION INSTALLATION RATES

Automatic transmission (94 percent). Power disc brakes (100 percent). Power steering (92.4 percent). V-8 engine 350-cid or less (79 percent). V-8 engine over 350-cid (19.7 percent). Six-cylinder engine (2.2 percent). Positraction (11.8 percent). Steel-belted radial tires (100 percent). Wheel covers (60.9 percent). Interior trim package (27.7 percent). Exterior trim package (45.2 percent). Tilt steering (57.6 percent). Cruise control (12.8 percent). AM radio (70.3 percent). AM/FM stereo radio (0.1 percent). Air conditioning (76.2 percent). Tinted glass (87.2 percent).

HISTORICAL FOOTNOTES

R.W. Truxell became general manager of GMC. Model-year sales of Sprints was 3,051, representing 8.3 percent of combined sales of El Camino and Sprint models. The GMC Truck & Coach Division recorded its second-best sales year in history.

The 1976 Sprint had a wide "Mercedes-like" grille with a fine mesh-patterned insert and a small GMC nameplate at the center. The headlamps were changed to two squares stacked on top of each other. The bulges sculptured into the hood and fender lines looked great with the new grille. The Sprint was offered in base and Classic models with SP, and Sierra Madre Del Sur trim options available.

I.D. NUMBERS

The VIN is stamped on a plate on the top left side of the instrument panel and visible through the windshield. The first symbol 5 designates GMC. The second and third symbols designate the series: C=Sprint, D=Classic Sprint. The third and fourth symbols designate body type: 80=two-door sedan pickup. The fifth symbol indicates the engine: D=250-cid six-cylinder, L=350-cid V-8 (four-barrel), Q=305-cid V-8, U=400-cid V-8 (four-barrel) and V=350-cid V-8 (two-barrel). The sixth symbol designates the model year: 6=1976. The seventh symbol indicates assembly plant: D=Doraville, Georgia, R=Arlington, Texas and 1=Oshawa, Canada. The last six symbols are the sequential unit production number at the specific factory.

SPRINT — SERIES C — SIX/V-8

The base Sprint featured a wide "Mercedes-Benz" style grille There were seven wide-spaced vertical members and 11 horizontal members with tighter spacing. Standard equipment on base Sprints included a bright GMC grille emblem, bright back window reveal moldings, chrome front and rear bumpers with a hydraulic/pneumatic impact cushioning system, bright door lock handles, bright door lock cylinder covers, a bright grille outer edge molding, a bright headlight bezel bead, a bright hood molding, bright hubcaps, a bright left-hand outside rearview mirror, bright body side, tailgate, drip rail and wheel opening moldings, bright windshield reveal moldings, side doors with a lift-bar latch release and key lock cylinders, a rear tailgate with a single-handle double latch mechanism, safety glass (in windshield, back glass and side windows), instrument panel knobs marked with function symbols, back-up lights, two single-lens front park/turn lights, two Class A rear lamps with tail/stop/signal and side marker functions, two Power-Beam headlights, a single rear license plate light, front and rear side marker lights, a single D note horn, steel side door guard beams, a mechanical jack and wheel lug nut wrench, partial under-body and full wheel well undercoating, body-color steel wheels, two-speed electric windshield wipers with hideaway wipers and arms, left- and right-hand cowl air vents with individual controls, dual armrests, bright seat back latch and adjuster knobs, bright window regulator knobs, a cigarette lighter, color-coordinated upholstery with black trim, a door-actuated dome lamp, push-button door locks, closed-cell rubber door seals, color-keyed vinyl covered rubber floor mats, a speedometer, an odometer, a fuel gauge, directional signals with a lane-change feature, a hazard warning, a heater and defroster, warning lights (for generator, oil pressure, temperature, brake-on, directionals and headlight high beams), a fiberglass-filled plastic instrument panel, sound deadening insulation, a 12-in. inside rearview mirror, seat and shoulder safety belts, dual sun shades, side door opening scuff plates and floor mat retainers, a spare tire carrier behind the passenger seating position, a lockable steering column, vinyl door trim panels with bright trim, vinyl-coated cowl side panels, a vinyl-coated headliner, an ignition key warning buzzer, bright metal window regulators, padded windshield pillars, a 250-cid inline six-cylinder engine, three-speed manual transmission, G78-14B black sidewall tires, front disc/rear drum brakes with disc brake lining sensors, a concealed storage compartment for tools and small items behind the driver's seat, front suspension ball joint wear indicators, tough double-walled body panel construction, a full-coil spring suspension, air-adjustable shock absorbers, an integrated voltage regulator, a catalytic converter, a durable new aluminized muffler and a Delco sealed side terminal battery.

Model Number	Body/Style Number	Body Type & Seating	Factory Price	Shipping Weight	Production Total
SPRINT SERIES C (6-CYL)					
C	80	pickup	—	—	Note 1
SPRINT SERIES C (V-8)					
C	80	pickup	$4,333	3,791 lbs.	Note 1

SPRINT CLASSIC — SERIES D — V-8

In addition to standard Sprint equipment, the Sprint Classic included lower body sill moldings, color-keyed carpeting, a choice of interior trim colors, a deluxe vinyl-coated headliner, an instrument panel with a crown pad and dull paint finish, an inside rearview mirror with black finish on the back and mirror support and a full-width seat with custom vinyl trim.

Model Number	Body/Style Number	Body Type & Seating	Factory Price	Shipping Weight	Production Total
D	80	Classic pickup	$4,468	3,821 lbs.	Note 1

NOTE 1 Total GMC Sprint production for the model year was 5,884 units.

MODEL OPTIONS

SPRINT SP: GMC continued to list an SP Sport equipment package for the 1976 Sprint. In addition to or in place of the standard equipment listed above, the SP equipment package included a black-finished grille with an SP emblem, a remote-control left-hand outside Sport-style rearview mirror, a manual right-hand Sport-style outside rearview mirror, SP fender emblems, SP door trim, an SP steering wheel, an SP emblem above the rear bumper, bright roof drip moldings, lower body side and wheel opening stripes keyed to the body color, black-accented taillight frames, a special instrument cluster, special front and rear stabilizer bars, 14 x 7-in. Rallye wheels with special center caps and trim rings and G70-14 white letter tires. The SP equipment package cost $226.

SPRINT SIERRA MADRE DEL SUR: Accentuating the appearance of the Sprint Classic was a new Sierra Madre del Sur trim package. This was very much like the El Camino Conquista package. The Sierra Madre del Sur package cost $128.

ENGINES

SPRINT BASE 250-CID, 105-HP SIX-CYL: Inline. Overhead-valve. Cast-iron block. Displacement: 250 cid. Bore and stroke: 3.875 x 3.53 in. Compression ratio: 8.25:1. Net brake hp: 105 at 3800 rpm. Taxable hp: 36. Torque: 185 lbs.-ft. at 1200 rpm. Seven main bearings. Hydraulic valve lifters. Crankcase capacity: 4 qt. (add 1 qt. for new filter). Cooling system capacity: 12 qt (add 6 qt. for heater). Carburetor: Rochester one-barrel. Sales code L22.

SPRINT BASE 305-CID, 140-HP V-8: Overhead-valve. Cast-iron block and head. Bore and stroke: 4.00 x 3.48 in. Displacement: 305 cid. Compression ratio: 8.50:1. Net brake hp: 140 at 3800 rpm. Taxable hp: 44.66. Net torque: 245 lbs.-ft. at 2000 rpm. Five main bearings. Hydraulic valve lifters. Crankcase capacity: 4 qt. (add 1 qt. for new filter). Cooling system capacity with heater: 16 qt. Carburetor: Two-barrel. Sales code LG3.

SPRINT OPTIONAL 350-CID, 145-HP V-8: Overhead-valve. Cast-iron block and head. Bore and stroke: 4.00 x 3.48 in. Displacement: 350 cid. Compression ratio: 8.50:1. Net brake hp: 145 at 3800 rpm. Taxable hp: 51.20. Net torque: 250 lbs.-ft. at 2200 rpm. Five main bearings. Hydraulic valve lifters. Crankcase capacity: 4 qt. (add 1 qt. for new filter). Cooling system capacity with heater: 16 qt. Carburetor: Two-barrel. Sales code L65.

SPRINT OPTIONAL 350-CID, 165-HP V-8: Overhead-valve. Cast-iron block and head. Bore and stroke: 4.00 x 3.48 in. Displacement: 350 cid. Compression ratio: 8.50:1. Net brake hp: 165 at 3800 rpm. Taxable hp: 51.20. Net torque: 260 lbs.-ft. at 2400 rpm. Five main bearings. Hydraulic valve lifters. Crankcase capacity: 4 qt. (add 1 qt. for new filter). Cooling system capacity with heater: 16 qt. Carburetor: Four-barrel. Sales code: LM1.

SPRINT OPTIONAL 400-CID, 175-HP V-8: Overhead-valve. Cast-iron block and head. Bore and stroke: 4.13 x 3.75 in. Displacement: 400 cid. Compression ratio: 8.50:1. Net brake hp: 175 at 3600 rpm. Taxable hp: 54.40. Net torque: 305 lbs.-ft. at 2000 rpm. Five main bearings. Hydraulic valve lifters. Crankcase capacity: 4 qt. (add 1 qt. for new filter). Cooling system capacity with heater 16 qt. Carburetor: Four-barrel. Sales code LT4.

CHASSIS

Wheelbase: 116 in. Overall length: 206.8 in. Height: 54.4 in. Front tread: 60.2. Rear tread: 59.2 in. Tires: E78-14B. Gross vehicle weight: 4,100 lbs. Saginaw manual, fully synchronized, transmission. Speeds: 3F/1R. Column-mounted gearshift lever. Single-plate dry-disc clutch (six-cylinder) or coil spring single-dry-plate (V-8). Rear axle: semi-floating. Hydraulic, four-wheel brakes. Kelsey-Hayes pressed steel wheels.

OPTIONS

A01 tinted body glass. A02 tinted windshield. A31 electric windows. A39 front and rear seat belts with retractors. A41 four-way power seat. A42 six-way electric front seat control. A46 power driver's bucket seat. A51 Astro bucket seats. A85 front shoulder belts. AK1 deluxe safety belts. AU3 power door locks. B37 floor mats. B85 belt reveal molding. B90 door edge and window frame moldings. B93 door edge guards. C08 vinyl top. C60 all-weather air conditioning. C75 automatic temperature control. D33 remote-control driver's mirror. D34 visor-vanity mirror. D55 front compartment floor console. F40 heavy-duty suspension. F41 special performance suspension. G67 level-control rear shock absorbers. G80 Positraction. J50 power brakes. J52 front disc brakes. JL2 front disc brakes. K85 63-amp. Delcotron. L48 350-cid four-barrel V-8. L65 350-cid two-barrel V-8. L78 396-cid special high-performance V-8. LS3 402-cid four-barrel V-8. LS5 454-cid four-barrel V-8. M11 floor shifter. M20 four-speed manual transmission. M22 heavy-duty four-speed manual transmission. M35 Powerglide automatic transmission. M38 three-speed automatic transmission. M40 three-speed automatic transmission. MC1 heavy-duty three-speed manual transmission. N33 tilt steering. N40 power steering. NK2 deluxe vinyl steering wheel. NK4 Sport steering wheel. P01 wheel trim covers. P02 simulated wire wheel covers. P90 G70-15 B white stripe tires. PA3 special wheel covers. PK2 G78-14 B glass-belted white stripe tires. PL3 E78-14 B glass-belted white stripe tires. PM6 G78-14 B glass-belted white stripe tires. PM7 F60-15 B glass-belted white letter tires. PU8 G78-15 B glass-belted white stripe tires. PX6 F78-14 B glass-belted white stripe tires. T60 heavy-duty battery. U14 instrument panel gauges. U35 electric clock. U63 push-button radio. U69 AM/FM push-button radio. U76 windshield antenna. U79 stereo radio. U80 auxiliary speaker. UM1 AM push-button radio and tape player. UM2 AM-FM push-button radio and tape player. V01 heavy-duty radiator. V30 bumper guards.

YD1 trailering rear axle ratio. ZJ7 special hubcaps and trim rings. ZJ9 auxiliary lighting group. ZL2 special ducted hood air system. ZQ9 performance ratio rear axle.

OPTION INSTALLATION RATES

V-8 engine 350-cid or less (62.5 percent). V-8 engine over 350-cid (34 percent). Six-cylinder engine (3.5 percent). Automatic transmission (98 percent). Power disc brakes (100 percent). Power steering (98.4 percent). Positraction (11.1 percent). Streel-belted radial tires (99.5 percent). Bumper guards (54.8 percent). Rear bumper (100 percent). Wheel covers (61.4 percent). Styled wheels (38.6 percent). Interior/exterior trim packages (88.2 percent). Bucket seats (11 percent). Tinted glass (89.8 percent). Air conditioning (78.1 percent). Tilt steering (62.4 percent). Cruise control (30 percent). AM radio (48.8 percent). AM/FM stereo radio (24.2 percent). Stereo (17.2 percent).

HISTORICAL FOOTNOTES

R.W. Truxell became GM of GMC. Model-year sales of Sprints were 5,436, representing 10.8 percent of combined sales of El Camino and Sprint models.

The 1977 Sprint was the last of its generation and therefore had few changes. Only three engines were offered this year, the 250-cid inline six-cylinder, the 305-cid V-8 (which was not available in California) and the 350-cid four-barrel V-8. Exterior color offerings were revised and the interval for changing the automatic transmission fluid and filter was extended to every 60,000 miles. In addition to the base and Classic models, there was an SP model-option for the Classic and a Siera adre del Sur trim package. This was the last GMC sedan-pickup to be called a Sprint.

I.D. NUMBERS

The VIN is stamped on a plate on the top left side of the instrument panel and visible through the windshield. The first symbol 5 designates GMC. The second and third symbols designate the series: C=Sprint, D=Sprint Classic. The third and fourth symbols designate body type: 80=two-door sedan pickup. The fifth symbol indicates the engine: D=250-cid six-cylinder, U=305-cid V-8 (four-barrel) and L=350-cid V-8 (four-barrel). The sixth symbol designates the model year: 7=1977. The seventh symbol indicates assembly plant: D=Doraville, Georgia, and R=Arlington, Texas. The last six symbols are the sequential unit production number at the specific factory.

SPRINT — SERIES C — SIX/V-8

Standard equipment included a bright GMC grille center emblem, bright back window reveal moldings, a Sprint decal on the upper left-hand side of the tailgate, chrome front and rear bumpers with a hydraulic/pneumatic impact cushioning system, bright door lock handles, bright door lock cylinder covers, bright Sprint nameplates on sale panels, a bright grille outer edge molding, a bright headlight bezel bead, a bright hood molding, bright hubcaps, a bright left-hand outside rearview mirror, bright body side, tailgate, drip rail and wheel opening moldings, bright windshield reveal moldings, side doors with a lift-bar latch release and key lock cylinders, a rear tailgate with a single-handle double latch mechanism, safety glass (in windshield, back glass and side windows), instrument panel knobs marked with function symbols, back-up lights, two single-lens front park/turn lights, two Class A rear lamps with tail/stop/signal and side marker functions, two Power-Beam headlights, a single rear license plate light, front and rear side marker lights, a single D note horn, steel side door guard beams, a mechanical jack and wheel lug nut wrench, partial under-body and full wheel well undercoating, body-color steel wheels, two-speed electric windshield wipers with hideaway wipers and arms, left- and right-hand cowl air vents with individual controls, dual armrests, bright seat back latch and adjuster knobs, bright window regulator knobs, a cigarette lighter, color-coordinated upholstery with black trim, a door-actuated dome lamp, push-button door locks, closed-cell rubber door seals, color-keyed vinyl covered rubber floor mats, a speedometer, an odometer, a fuel gauge, directional signals with a lane-change feature, a hazard warning, a heater and defroster, warning lights (for generator, oil pressure, temperature, brake-on, directionals and headlight high beams), a fiberglass-filled plastic instrument panel, sound deadening insulation, a 12-in. inside rearview mirror, seat and shoulder safety belts, dual sun shades, side door opening scuff plates and floor mat retainers, a spare tire carrier behind the passenger seating position, a lockable steering column, vinyl door trim panels with bright trim, vinyl-coated cowl side panels, a vinyl-coated headliner, an ignition key warning buzzer, bright metal window regulators, padded windshield pillars, a 250-cid inline six-cylinder engine, three-speed manual transmission, G78-14B black sidewall tires, front disc/rear drum brakes with disc brake lining sensors, a concealed storage compartment for tools and small items behind the driver's seat, front suspension ball joint wear indicators, tough double-walled body panel construction, a full-coil spring suspension, air-adjustable shock absorbers, an integrated voltage regulator, a catalytic converter, a new durable aluminized muffler and a Delco sealed side terminal battery.

Model Number	Body/Style Number	Body Type & Seating	Factory Price	Shipping Weight	Production Total
SPRINT SERIES C (6-CYL)					
C	80	pickup	—	—	Note 1
SPRINT SERIES C (V-8)					
C	80	pickup	$4,268	3,791 lbs.	Note 1

SPRINT

SPRINT CLASSIC — SERIES D — V-8

In addition to standard Sprint equipment, the Sprint Classic included lower-body sill moldings, color-keyed carpeting, a choice of interior trim colors, a deluxe vinyl-coated headliner, an instrument with a panel crown pad and dull paint finish, an inside rearview mirror with black finish on the back and mirror support and a full-width seat with custom vinyl trim.

Model Number	Body/Style Number	Body Type & Seating	Factory Price	Shipping Weight	Production Total
D	80	Classic pickup	$4,403	3,821 lbs.	Note 1

NOTE 1 Total GMC Sprint production for the model year was 7,118 units.

MODEL OPTIONS

SPRINT SP: In addition to or in place of the standard equipment listed above, the SP equipment package included a black-finished grille with an SP emblem, a remote-control left-hand outside Sport-style rearview mirror, a manual right-hand Sport-style outside rearview mirror, SP fender emblems, SP door trim, an SP steering wheel, an SP emblem above the rear bumper, bright roof drip moldings, lower body side and wheel opening stripes keyed to the body color, black-accented taillight frames, a special instrument cluster, special front and rear stabilizer bars, 14 x 7-in. Rallye wheels with special center caps and trim rings and G70-14 white letter tires.

SPRINT SIERRA MADRE DEL SUR: Accentuating the appearance of the Sprint Classic was a new Sierra Madre del Sur trim package. This was very much like the El Camino Conquista package.

ENGINES

SPRINT BASE 250-CID, 110-HP SIX-CYL: Inline. Overhead-valve. Cast-iron block. Displacement: 250 cid. Bore and stroke: 3.875 x 3.53 in. Compression ratio: 8.25:1. Net brake hp: 110 at 3800 rpm. Taxable hp: 36. Torque: 185 lbs.-ft. at 1200 rpm. Seven main bearings. Hydraulic valve lifters. Crankcase capacity: 4 qt. (add 1 qt. for new filter). Cooling system capacity: 12 qt (add 6 qt. for heater). Carburetor: Rochester one-barrel. VIN code: D. Sales code L22.

SPRINT BASE 305-CID, 145-HP V-8: Overhead-valve. Cast-iron block and head. Bore and stroke: 3.74 x 3.48 in. Displacement: 305 cid (5.0 liters). Compression ratio: 8.5:1. Net brake hp: 145 at 3800 rpm. Taxable hp: 44.66. Net torque: 245 lbs.-ft. at 2400 rpm. Five main bearings. Hydraulic valve lifters. Carburetor: Rochester 2GC two-barrel. VIN Code: U. Sales code: LG3.

SPRINT OPTIONAL 350-CID, 170-HP V-8: Overhead-valve. Cast-iron block and head. Bore and stroke: 4.00 x 3.48 in. Displacement: 350 cid (5.7 liters). Compression ratio: 8.5:1. Net brake hp: 170 at 3800 rpm. Taxable hp: 51.20. Net torque: 270 lbs.-ft. at 2400 rpm. Five main bearings. Hydraulic valve lifters. Carburetor: Rochester M4MC four-barrel. VIN Code: L. Sales code: LM1.

CHASSIS

Wheelbase: 116 in. Overall length: 206.8 in. Height: 54.4 in. Front tread: 60.2. Rear tread: 59.2 in. Tires: E78-14B. GVW: 4,100 lbs. Automatic transmission. Rear axle: semi-floating. Hydraulic, four-wheel brakes. Kelsey-Hayes pressed steel wheels.

OPTIONS

A01 tinted body glass. A02 tinted windshield. A31 electric windows. A39 front and rear seat belts with retractors. A41 four-way power seat. A42 six-way electric front seat control. A46 power driver's bucket seat. A51 Astro bucket seats. A85 front shoulder belts. AK1 deluxe safety belts. AU3 power door locks. B37 floor mats. B85 belt reveal molding. B90 door edge and window frame moldings. B93 door edge guards. C08 vinyl top. C60 all-weather air conditioning. C75 automatic temperature control. D33 remote-control driver's mirror. D34 visor-vanity mirror. D55 front compartment floor console. F40 heavy-duty suspension. F41 special performance suspension. G67 level-control rear shock absorbers. G80 Positraction. J50 power brakes. J52 front disc brakes. JL2 front disc brakes. K85 63-amp. Delcotron. L48 350-cid four-barrel V-8. L65 350-cid two-barrel V-8. L78 396-cid special high-performance V-8. LS3 402-cid four-barrel V-8. LS5 454-cid four-barrel V-8. M11 floor shifter. M20 four-speed manual transmission. M22 heavy-duty four-speed manual transmission. M35 Powerglide automatic transmission. M38 three-speed automatic transmission. M40 three-speed automatic transmission. MC1 heavy-duty three-speed manual transmission. N33 tilt steering. N40 power steering. NK2 deluxe vinyl steering wheel. NK4 Sport steering wheel. P01 wheel trim covers. P02 simulated wire wheel covers. P90 G70-15 B white stripe tires. PA3 special wheel covers. PK2 G78-14 B glass-belted white stripe tires. PL3 E78-14 B glass-belted white stripe tires. PM6 G78-14 B glass-belted white stripe tires. PM7 F60-15 B glass-belted white letter tires. PU8 G78-15 B glass-belted white stripe tires. PX6 F78-14 B glass-belted white stripe tires. T60 heavy-duty battery. U14 instrument panel gauges. U35 electric clock. U63 push-button radio. U69 AM/FM push-button radio. U76 windshield antenna. U79 stereo radio. U80 auxiliary speaker. UM1 AM push-button radio and tape player. UM2 AM-FM push-button radio and tape player. V01 heavy-duty radiator. V30 bumper guards. YD1 trailering rear axle ratio. ZJ7 special hubcaps and trim rings. ZJ9 auxiliary lighting group. ZL2 special ducted hood air system. ZQ9 performance ratio rear axle.

OPTION INSTALLATION RATES

V-8 engine 350-cid or less (97.8 percent). Six-cylinder engine (2.2 percent). Automatic transmission (99.6 percent). Power disc brakes (100 percent). Power steering (99.5 percent). Steel-belted radial tires (99.5 percent). Front bumper guards (54.0 percent). Rear bumper (100 percent). Bucket seats (10.6 percent). Tinted glass (92.5 percent). Air conditioning (83.2 percent). Tilt steering (74.3 percent). Cruise control (52.5 percent). AM radio (36.7 percent). AM/FM stereo radio (24.1 percent). Stereo (21.9 percent).

HISTORICAL FOOTNOTES

Model-year sales of Sprints were 5,955, representing 9.9 percent of combined sales of El Caminos and Sprints.

Caballero
1978-1985

CABALLERO

1978

This 1978 Caballero with the Diablo package is a rare find. The package included a large front air dam, Sport mirrors and special decals.

Downsizing was in at GM in the late 1970s and the GMC sedan-pickup got a partial treatment in 1978. The new version was called the Caballero, instead of Sprint. The engineers who designed the Caballero felt that a complete downsizing would have compromised the sedan-pickup's already limited cargo capacity.

The result was a new-sized vehicle with a wheelbase that was about an inch longer than the 1977 Sprint's wheelbase. However, the Caballero body was several inches shorter than the old Sprint body and the weight was reduced by hundreds of pounds. Interior head and legroom were actually increased as well.

In addition to the base Caballero, there were two model-options called the Caballero Laredo and the Caballero Diablo. The standard engine was a thrifty V-6. Full-frame construction was retained. Other selling features included a standard front stabilizer bar, extensive corrosion-resisting treatments, 14 noise-insulating body mounts (for a quieter ride) and double-panel doors, hood and deck lid construction.

I.D. NUMBERS

VIN embossed on the top left-hand side of the instrument panel and visible through the windshield. The first symbol 5 designates GMC. The second symbol indicates series: W=Caballero. The third and fourth symbols indicate body style: 80=sedan-pickup. The fifth symbol indicates engine (net hp): M=RPO L26 200-cid 94-hp V-6, A=RPO LD5 231-cid 105-hp V-6 (California), U=RPO LG3 305-cid 145-hp V-8 and L=RPO LM1 350-cid 170-hp V-8. The sixth symbol designates the model year: 8=1978. The seventh symbol designates the assembly plant location: B=Baltimore, Maryland, D=Doraville, Georgia, Z=Fremont, California, R=Arlington, Texas, L=Leeds, Missouri. and 1=Oshawa, Canada. The last six symbols are the sequential unit production number at the specific factory.

CABALLERO — SERIES W — V-6/V-8

Sitting on a 117.1-in. wheelbase, the new Caballero's overall length was reduced to 201.6 in., or 11.7 in. less than in 1977. Key styling features included a sweeping roofline with small side quarter windows, a wraparound rear window and single rectangular headlights. Despite the reduction in curb weight, load capacity remained at 800 lbs. The standard 3.3-liter V-6 was a derivative of the small-block Chevy V-8. It weighed almost 80 lbs. less than the inline six it replaced. A second V-6, with a 3.8-liter displacement, was mandatory for trucks sold in California. The new Caballero pickup box was 79.5 in. long, 45 in. wide between the wheel housings and 59.1 in. wide above the wheel housings. The radiator grille was a chrome rectangle with an "egg-crate" style insert and a six-sided badge at the center of the upper surround. The headlamps were large, rectangular units set in an even larger bright housing that canted backwards at each corner, on the bottom. The parking lamps were positioned vertically between the grille and the headlamps, with amber-colored side marker lamps and directionals at the outboard ends. The front body sides had a curvature to them and angled forward at the front and at the rear. The rear end featured a drop-down tailgate with a chrome-rimmed license plate recess in its center and a bright Chevrolet bow tie logo above the recess. The rectangular taillights were placed in the rear bumper. Separate rectangular side markers were placed on the body sides, just ahead of the wraparound bumper corners. The front bumper was of a simple, straight-across design. Black rubber impact strips and bumper guards were optional. A new vertical-style instrument panel, mounted well forward, helped to enhance the spaciousness of the interior. A separate module held the radio controls, heater controls and instruments. Plug-in components and a swing-down glove compartment made behind-the-dash servicing easier. The headlight dimmer switch was moved to the turn-signal lever. A new ventilation system delivered outside air under all driving conditions, whether power assisted or ram vented. The chassis featured coil springs all around, a single-piece propeller shaft, lower rear axle ratios, relay-type steering and front disc, rear drum brakes. The new fuel tank held 17.5 gallons. The Caballero rode on radial-ply tires on 14-in. wheels. Standard equipment included self-adjusting front disc brakes with wear indicators, a High Energy Ignition system, a Freedom side-terminal battery, a dual-mode ventilation system, full carpeting, radial tires, new interior styling with a delta-spoked soft vinyl steering wheel, a fully inflated compact spare tire, rectangular headlights with chrome-plated bezels, bright windshield and rear window reveal moldings, bright belt side and roof drip moldings, a bright left-hand outside rearview mirror, extensive corrosion-resisting treatments, full wheel covers, wheel opening moldings, visible ball-joint wear indicators, a front stabilizer bar, a Delcotron generator, a coolant recovery system, seat belts with push-button buckle releases for all passengers, two combination seat and inertia reel shoulder belts for driver and passenger (with reminder light and buzzer), an energy-absorbing steering column, passenger guard door locks, safety door latches with stamped steel hinges, an energy-absorbing padded instrument panel, a contoured windshield header, a thick laminate windshield, safety armrests, a safety steering wheel, side marker lights and reflectors, parking lights that illuminate with the headlamps, four-way hazard flashers, back-up lights, directional signals with a lane-change feature, a defroster, dual speed windshield wipers, windshield washers, a wide-view day/night inside rearview mirror with vinyl edging and a deflecting support, a left-hand outside rearview mirror, a dual master cylinder brake system with warning light, a starter safety switch, a dual-action safety hood latch, an ignition key reminder buzzer and a steering column lock. Standard interior trim included a four-inch thick, foam-cushioned 50/50 seat with a handy split back. All controls were easily accessible in the trim rectangular instrument cluster. For added convenience, GMC offered an optional split-back bench seat with fold-down center armrest. Options included a six-way power driver's seat or Strato bucket seats (with or without a center console and optional integral shift lever.

Model Number	Body/Style Number	Body Type & Seating	Factory Price	Shipping Weight	Production Total
CABALLERO SERIES W (V-6)					
W	80	pickup	—	—	Note 1
CABALLERO SERIES W (305-CID V-8)					
W	80	pickup	$4,774	3,184 lbs.	Note 1

CABALLERO DIABLO — SERIES W + YE7 V-8

In addition to the features of the base Caballero, the Diablo came with a large front air dam, matching sport mirrors, a special large color-coordinated hood decal, a choice of accent colors on the lower body with Diablo graphics, decal stripes to accent the paint-break lines, Rallye wheels painted to match the lower body color, black quarter window moldings and Diablo identification on the lower right-hand side of the tailgate.

Model Number	Body/Style Number	Body Type & Seating	Factory Price	Shipping Weight	Production Total
W	80	pickup	$4,953	3,184 lbs.	Note 1

NOTE 1: Total Caballero production was 7,661.

MODEL OPTIONS

LAREDO PACKAGE: The Caballero Laredo package was highlighted by a striking molding and paint treatment. The basic body color appeared on the roof, the upper portion of the pickup box, the lower body sides and on the tailgate. The center section of the body side, the hood and the lower portion of the tailgate were set off by a special accent color. Also featured were bright paint break moldings along the upper side of the pickup box and tailgate, bright moldings along the lower body sides and wheel house moldings. A Laredo decal was placed on the tailgate.

ENGINES

CABALLERO BASE 200-CID, 95-HP V-6 (FEDERAL): Overhead-valve. Cast-iron block and head. Displacement: 200 cid (3.3 liters). Bore & stroke: 3.50 x 3.48 in. Compression ratio: 8.2:1. Brake hp: 95 at 3800 rpm. Torque: 160 lbs.-ft. at 2000 rpm. Four main bearings. Hydraulic valve lifters. Carburetor: Rochester 2GC two-barrel. Sales Code: L26. VIN code: M.

CABALLERO BASE 231-CID, 105-HP V-6 (CALIFORNIA): Overhead-valve. Cast-iron block and head. Displacement: 231 cid (3.8 liters). Bore & stroke: 3.80 x 3.40 in. Compression ratio: 8.0:1. Brake hp: 105 at 3400

CABALLERO

rpm Torque: 185 lbs.-ft. at 2000 rpm. Four main bearings. Hydraulic valve lifters. Carburetor: Rochester 2GE two-barrel. Sales Code: LD5. VIN code: A.

CABALLERO BASE 305-CID, 145-HP V-8: Overhead-valve. Cast-iron block and head. Bore and stroke: 3.74 x 3.48 in. Displacement: 305 cid (5.0 liters). Compression ratio: 8.4:1. Net brake hp: 145 at 3800 rpm. Taxable hp: 44.66. Net torque: 245 lbs.-ft. at 2400 rpm. Five main bearings. Hydraulic valve lifters. Carburetor: Rochester 2GC two-barrel. Sales Code: LG3. VIN code: U.

CABALLERO OPTIONAL 350-CID, 170-HP V-8: Overhead-valve. Cast-iron block and head. Bore and stroke: 4.00 x 3.48 in. Displacement: 350 cid (5.7 liters). Compression ratio: 8.2:1. Net brake hp: 170 at 3800 rpm. Taxable hp: 51.20. Net torque: 270 lbs.-ft. at 2400 rpm. Five main bearings. Hydraulic valve lifters. Carburetor: Rochester M4MC four-barrel. Sales Code: LM1. VIN code: L.

CHASSIS

Wheelbase: 117.1 in. Overall length: 201.60 in. Height: 53.8 in. Front tread: 58.5 in. Rear tread: 57.8 in. Cargo box length from back of cab to top of tailgate: 79.5 in. Bed width between rear wheel housings: 45 in. Bed width above rear wheel housings: 59.5 in. Tires: G78-14B. Transmission: Automatic transmission standard. Three-speed manual transmission available with 3.3-liter V-6. Four-speed manual transmission available with 5.0- and 5.7-liter V-8s. Rear axle: semi-floating. Hydraulic four-wheel brakes. Kelsey-Hayes pressed steel wheels.

OPTIONS

A01 tinted body glass. A02 tinted windshield. A31 electric windows. AG7 six-way electric 50/50 front seat control. AK1 Deluxe safety belts. AU3 power door locks. AV3 pickup box tie downs. B32 front floor mats. B90 side window moldings. B93 door edge guards. B96 wheel

The Diablo was the only Caballero with this unique hood decal.

The Diablos were easy to spot from behind.

opening moldings. BS1 acoustical insulation. BW2 deluxe body molding exterior ornamentation. BX8 moldings and two-tone paint. BW3 advance price sheet. C60 all-weather air conditioning. C95 ASM dome and reading lamp. CD4 pulse type windshield wipers. D24 litter container. D33 remote-control driver's mirror. D34 visor-vanity mirror. D35 Classic remote-control left-hand outside rearview mirror. D55 front compartment floor console. D64 visor mirror. D68 dual Sport-style exterior rearview mirrors. D73 pickup box handrail. D84 custom two-tone paint. D85 lower body side accent stripe. D91 special two-tone paint. F40 heavy-duty front and rear suspension. F41 special heavy-duty suspension front and rear. G80 Positraction. G92 3.08:1 rear axle. J50 power brakes. K05 engine block heater. K30 speed and cruise control. K76 61-amp Delcotron generator. K97 80-amp. Delcotron generator. L26 200-cid V-6 engine. LD5 231-cid V-6 engine. LG3 305-cid two-barrel V-8. LM1 350-cid four-barrel V-8. MM3 three-speed manual transmission. MM4 four-speed manual transmission. MX1 automatic transmission. N23 22-gallon fuel tank. N33 tilt steering. N41 variable-ratio power steering. N95 simulated wire wheel covers. NA6 alternative emissions requirements. P01 wheel trim covers. PB2 ABS plastic wheel trim covers. QFZ P195-75R steel-belted radial white-sidewall tires. QKH P205-75R steel-belted radial black sidewall tires. QKJ P205-75R steel-belted radial white-sidewall tires. QKK P205-75R steel-belted radial white-letter tires. QKP P185-75R steel-belted radial black-sidewall tires. QKQ P185-75R steel-belted radial white-stripe tires. QKR P195-75R steel-belted radial black-sidewall tires. QKP P195-75R steel-belted radial white-stripe tires. T59 conventional battery. U05 dual horns. U14 gauge package. U35 electric clock. U58 AM/FM stereo. U63 push-button radio. U69 AM/FM push-button radio. U75 power antenna. U76 windshield antenna. U80 auxil-

CABALLERO

iary speaker. UA1 heavy-duty battery. UF7 gauges package. UM1 AM push-button radio and stereo tape player. UM2 AM-FM push-button radio and stereo tape player. V01 heavy-duty radiator. V30 bumper guards. VE5 bumper impact strip. Y57 demo drive. YC8 demo option drive. YE7 Diablo model-option. YJ6 economy décor package. Z49 mandatory Canadian base equipment modifications. ZJ7 special hubcaps and trim rings. ZJ9 auxiliary lighting group.

OPTION INSTALLATION RATES

V-8 engine under 350 cid (34 percent). V-8 engine 350 cid or more (54 percent). V-6 (12 percent). Automatic transmission (93 percent). Four-speed transmission (4 percent). Power front disc brakes (99.9 percent). Manual front disc brakes (0.1 percent). Power steering (99 percent). Steel-belted radial tires (100 percent). Positraction (13 percent). Regular bumpers (100 percent). Two-tone paint (66.3 percent). Exterior striping (66.3 percent). Bucket seats (9 percent). Tinted glass (88 percent). Air conditioning (80 percent). Cruise control (53 percent). Adjustable steering column (71 percent). Power windows (28 percent). Power door locks (23 percent). AM radio (25 percent). AM/FM radio (18 percent). Stereo (20 percent).

HISTORICAL FOOTNOTES

Robert W. Truxell was general sales manager for GMC trucks. Caballero model-year sales were 6,700 units compared to 5,955 the previous season. That represented a record of almost 11 percent of combined El Camino and Sprint/Caballero sales

The 1979 Caballero received a new grille with a prominent horizontal emphasis. A new engine option was a 267-cid V-8, but this engine wasn't available in California.

I.D. NUMBERS

VIN embossed on the top left-hand side of the instrument panel and visible through the windshield. The first symbol 5 designates GMC. The second symbol indicates series: W=Caballero. The third and fourth symbols indicate body style: 80=sedan-pickup. The fifth symbol indicates engine (net hp): M=RPO L26 200-cid 94-hp V-6, A=RPO LD5 231-cid 105-hp V-6 (California), J=RPO L39 267-cid 125-hp V-8, H=RPO LG4 305-cid 155-hp V-8 and L=RPO LM1 350-cid 170-hp V-8. The sixth symbol designates the model year: 9=1979. The seventh symbol designates the assembly plant location: B=Baltimore, Maryland, D=Doraville, Georgia, Z=Fremont, California, R=Arlington, Texas, K=Leeds, Missouri, and 1=Oshawa, Canada. The last six symbols are the sequential unit production number at the specific factory.

CABALLERO — SERIES W — V-6/V-8

The base model came with an impressive array of standard equipment features, including a 3.3-liter V-6 (not available in California), frameless door glass and thin roof pillars, bright pickup box molding, bright wheel opening moldings, bright rocker panel moldings, bright roof drip moldings, full wheel trim covers, a bright windshield molding, a bright rear window molding, a padded instrument panel, steel-belted radial tires, self-adjusting front disc brakes with wear indicators, a High Energy Ignition system, a Freedom side-terminal battery, a dual-mode ventilation system, new interior styling with a delta-spoked soft vinyl steering wheel, a fully inflated compact spare tire, a bright left-hand outside rearview mirror, extensive corrosion-resisting treatments, visible ball-joint wear indicators, a front stabilizer bar, a Delcotron generator, a coolant recovery system, seat belts with push-button buckle releases for all passengers, two combination seat and inertia reel shoulder belts for driver and passenger (with reminder light and buzzer), an energy-absorbing steering column, passenger guard door locks, safety door latches with stamped steel hinges, a contoured windshield header, a thick laminate windshield, a safety steering wheel, side marker lights and reflectors, parking lights that illuminate with the headlamps, four-way hazard flashers, back-up lights, directional signals with a lane-change feature, a defroster, dual speed windshield wipers, windshield washers, a 10-in.-wide prismatic wide-view day/night inside rearview mirror with vinyl edging and a deflecting support, a left-hand outside rearview mirror, a dual master cylinder brake system with warning light, a starter safety switch, a dual-action safety hood latch, an ignition key reminder buzzer and a steering column lock. Standard interior trim included Deluxe vinyl door and side trim panels, a cloth headliner with foam padding, full-depth padded armrests in both doors, color-keyed nylon cut-pile carpeting an a 4-in.-thick foam-cushioned 50/50 seat.

Model Number	Body/Style Number	Body Type & Seating	Factory Price	Shipping Weight	Production Total
CABALLERO SERIES W (V-6)					
W	80	pickup	—	—	Note 1
CABALLERO SERIES W (305-CID V-8)					
W	80	pickup	$5,378	3,188 lbs.	Note 1

CABALLERO DIABLO — SERIES W + YE7 — V-8

The Diablo was similar to an El Camino SS with the Royal Knight package. In addition to the features of the base Caballero, the Diablo came with a large front air dam, matching sport mirrors, a special large color-coordinated hood decal, a choice of accent colors on the lower body with Diablo graphics, decal stripes to accent the paint-break lines, Rallye wheels painted to match the lower body color, black quarter window moldings and Diablo identification on the lower right-hand side of the tailgate.

Model Number	Body/Style Number	Body Type & Seating	Factory Price	Shipping Weight	Production Total
CABALLERO DIABLO — SERIES W + YE7 — V-8					
W	80	Pickup	$5,580	3,328 lbs.	Note 1

NOTE 1: Total Caballero production was 7,642.

MODEL OPTIONS

LAREDO PACKAGE The Caballero Laredo package was similar to the base El Camino with Conquista trim. The Laredo highlighted by a striking molding and paint treatment. The basic body color appeared on the roof, the upper portion of the pickup box, the lower body sides and on the tailgate. The center section of the body side, the hood and the lower portion of the tailgate were set off by a special accent color. Also featured were bright paint break moldings along the upper side of the pickup box and tailgate, bright moldings along the lower body sides and wheel house moldings. A Laredo decal was placed on the tailgate. The package cost $155 this year.

ENGINES

CABALLERO BASE 200-CID, 95-HP V-6 (FEDERAL): Overhead-valve V-6. Cast-iron block and head. Displacement: 200 cid (3.3 liters). Bore & stroke: 3.50 x 3.48 in. Compression ratio: 8.2:1. Brake hp: 95 at 3800 rpm. Torque: 160 lbs.-ft. at 2000 rpm. Four main bearings. Hydraulic valve lifters. Carburetor: Rochester 2GC two-barrel. Sales Code: L26. VIN code: M.

CABALLERO BASE 231-CID, 105-HP V-6 (CALIFORNIA): Overhead-valve V-6. Cast-iron block and head. Displacement: 231 cid (3.8 liters). Bore & stroke: 3.80 x 3.40 in. Compression ratio: 8.0:1. Brake hp: 105 at 3400 rpm. Torque: 185 lbs.-ft. at 2000 rpm Four main bearings. Hydraulic valve lifters. Carburetor: Rochester 2GE two-barrel. Sales Code: LD5. VIN code: A.

CABALLERO BASE 267-CID, 125-HP V-8: Overhead-valve. Cast-iron block and head. Bore and stroke: 3.50 x 3.48 in. Displacement: 267 cid (4.4 liters). Compression ratio: 8.2:1. Net brake hp: 125 at 3800 rpm. Taxable hp: 39.20. Net torque: 215 lbs.-ft. at 2400 rpm. Five main bearings. Hydraulic valve lifters. Carburetor: Rochester M2MC two-barrel. VIN Code: J.

CABALLERO OPTIONAL 305-CID, 155-HP V-8: Overhead-valve. Cast-iron block and head. Bore and stroke: 3.74 x 3.48 in. Displacement: 305 cid (5.0 liters). Compression ratio: 8.4:1. Net brake hp: 155 at 4000 rpm. Taxable hp: 44.66. Net torque: 235 lbs.-ft. at 2400 rpm. Five main bearings. Hydraulic valve lifters. Carburetor: Rochester M4MC four-barrel. VIN Code: H.

CABALLERO OPTIONAL 350-CID, 170-HP V-8: Overhead-valve. Cast-iron block and head. Bore and stroke: 4.00 x 3.48 in. Displacement: 350 cid (5.7 liters). Compression ratio: 8.2:1. Net brake hp: 165-170 at 3800 rpm. Taxable hp: 51.20. Net torque: 260-270 lbs.-ft. at 2400 rpm. Five main bearings. Hydraulic valve lifters. Carburetor: Rochester M4MC four-barrel. VIN Code: L.

CHASSIS

Wheelbase: 117.1 in. Overall length: 201.60 in. Height: 53.8 in. Front tread: 58.5 in. Rear tread: 57.8 in. Cargo box length from back of cab to top of tailgate: 79.5 in. Bed width between rear wheel housings: 45 in. Bed width above rear wheel housings: 59.5 in. Tires: G78-14B. Transmission: Automatic transmission standard. Three-speed manual transmission available with 3.3-liter V-6. Four-speed manual transmission available with 5.0- and 5.7-liter V-8s. Rear axle: semi-floating. Hydraulic four-wheel brakes. Kelsey-Hayes pressed steel wheels.

OPTIONS

A01 tinted body glass. A02 tinted windshield. A31 electric windows. AG7 six-way electric 50/50 front seat control. AK1 Deluxe safety belts. AU3 power door locks. AV3 pickup box tie downs. B32 front floor mats. B90 side window moldings. B93 door edge guards. B96 wheel opening moldings. BS1 acoustical insulation. BW2 deluxe body molding exterior ornamentation. BX8 moldings and two-tone paint. BW3 advance price sheet. C60 all-weather air conditioning. C95 ASM dome and reading lamp. CD4 pulse type windshield wipers. D24 litter container. D33 remote-control driver's mirror. D34 visor-vanity mirror. D35 Classic remote-control left-hand outside rearview mirror. D55 front compartment floor console. D64 visor mirror. D68 dual sport-style exterior rearview mirrors. D73 pickup box handrail. D84 custom two-tone paint. D85 lower body side accent stripe. D91 special two-tone paint. F40 heavy-duty front and rear suspension. F41 special heavy-duty suspension front and rear. G80 Positraction. G92 3.08:1 rear axle. J50 power brakes. K05 engine block heater. K30 speed and cruise control. K76 61-amp Delcotron generator. K97 80-amp Delcotron generator. L26 200-cid V-6 engine. LD5 231-cid V-6 engine. LG3 305-cid two-barrel V-8. LM1 350-cid four-barrel V-8. MM3 three-speed manual transmission. MM4 four-speed manual transmission. MX1 automatic transmission. N23 22-gallon fuel tank. N33 tilt steering. N41 variable-ratio power steering. N95 simulated wire wheel covers. NA6 alternative emissions requirements. P01 wheel trim covers. PB2 ABS plastic wheel trim covers. QFZ P195-75R steel-belted radial white sidewall tires. QKH P205-75R steel-belted radial black sidewall tires. QKJ P205-75R steel-belted radial white sidewall tires. QKK P205-75R steel-belted radial white letter tires. QKP P185-75R steel-belted radial black sidewall tires. QKQ P185-75R steel-belted radial white-stripe tires. QKR P195-75R steel-belted radial black sidewall tires. QKP P195-75R steel-belted radial white stripe tires. T59 conventional battery. U05 dual horns. U14 gauge package. U35 electric clock. U58 AM/FM stereo. U63 push-button radio. U69 AM/FM push-button radio. U75 power antenna. U76 windshield antenna. U80 auxiliary speaker. UA1 heavy-duty battery. UF7 gauges package. UM1 AM push-button radio and stereo tape player. UM2 AM-FM push-button radio and stereo tape player. V01 heavy-duty radiator. V30 bumper guards. VE5 bumper impact strip. Y57 demo drive. YC8 demo option drive. YE7 Diablo model-option. YJ6 economy décor package. Z49 mandatory Canadian base equipment modifications. ZJ7 special hubcaps and trim rings. ZJ9 auxiliary lighting group.

CABALLERO

OPTION INSTALLATION RATES

V-8 under 300 cid (22.2 percent). V-8 301-349 cid (58.2 percent). V-8 engine 350 cid or more (3.6 percent). V-6 under 250-cid (12.1 percent). V-6 250-cid up (3.9 percent). Automatic transmission (93.4 percent). Four-speed transmission (3.1 percent). Power front disc brakes (100 percent). Power steering (99.3 percent). Styled steel wheels (84 percent). Wheel covers (16 percent). Steel-belted radial tires (100 percent). Exterior trim group (44.9 percent). Bucket seats (10.4 percent). Tinted glass (83 percent). Air conditioning (83 percent). Cruise control (41.1 percent). Adjustable steering column (61.9 percent). Power windows (15.5 percent). Power door locks (13.2 percent). AM radio (42 percent). AM/FM radio (18.6 percent). Stereo (11.3 percent). Radio with tape player (7.6 percent). Radio with CB (0.9 percent). Regular bumpers (100 percent).

HISTORICAL FOOTNOTES

Robert W. Truxell was general sales manager for GMC trucks. Caballero model-year sales were 6,952 units compared to 6,700 the previous season. That represented 10.7 percent of combined El Camino and Sprint/Caballero sales

GMC's latest car-based pickup had a revised grille design with three rows of short, thin, vertical blades. Slightly heavier horizontal moldings separated the rows and there was a vertical center molding. A stand-up hood ornament was used. Trim variations included base, Diablo and Laredo packages. Larger headlights, larger side marker lamps and a new 3.8-liter standard V-6 were the year's major revisions. The windshield washer system worked more precisely and Rallye wheels were a new option. The base V-6 and optional 5.0-liter V-8 could be had with a new automatic transmission with a "lock-up" torque converter.

I.D. NUMBERS

VIN embossed on the top left-hand side of the instrument panel and visible through the windshield. The first symbol 5 designates GMC. The second symbol indicates series: W=Caballero. The third and fourth symbols indicate body style: 80=sedan-pickup. The fifth symbol indicates engine (net hp): K=RPO LC3 229-cid/110-hp V-6, A=RPO LD5 231-cid/110-hp V-6 (California), J=RPO L39 267-cid/115-hp V-8, H=RPO LG4 305-cid/150-hp V-8 and L=RPO LM1 350-cid/170-hp El Camino only V-8. The sixth symbol designates the model year: A=1980. The seventh symbol designates the assembly plant location: B=Baltimore, Maryland; D=Doraville, Georgia; Z=Fremont, California; R=Arlington, Texas; K=Leeds, Missouri; and 1=Oshawa, Canada. The last six symbols are the sequential unit production number at the specific factory.

CABALLERO — SERIES W — V-6/V-8

Standard equipment features included a 3.8-liter V-6 (not available in California), frameless door glass and thin roof pillars, bright pickup box molding, bright wheel opening moldings, bright rocker panel moldings, bright roof drip moldings, full wheel trim covers, a bright windshield molding, a bright rear window molding, a padded instrument panel, steel-belted radial tires, self-adjusting front disc brakes with wear indicators, a High Energy Ignition system, a Freedom side-terminal battery, a dual-mode ventilation system, a delta-spoked soft vinyl steering wheel, a fully inflated compact spare tire, a bright left-hand outside rearview mirror, extensive corrosion-resisting treatments, visible ball-joint wear indicators, a front stabilizer bar, a Delcotron generator, a coolant recovery system, seat belts with push-button buckle releases for all passengers, two combination seat and inertia reel shoulder belts for driver and passenger (with reminder light and buzzer), an energy-absorbing steering column, passenger guard door locks, safety door latches with stamped steel hinges, a contoured windshield header, a thick laminate windshield, a safety steering wheel, side marker lights and reflectors, parking lights that illuminate with the headlamps, four-way hazard flashers, back-up lights, directional signals with a lane-change feature, a defroster, dual speed windshield wipers, windshield washers, a 10-in.-wide prismatic wide-view day/night inside rearview mirror with vinyl edging and a deflecting support, a left-hand outside rearview mirror, a dual master cylinder brake system with warning light, a starter safety switch, a dual-action safety hood latch, an ignition key reminder buzzer and a steering column lock. Standard interior trim included deluxe vinyl door and side trim panels, a cloth headliner with foam padding, full-depth padded armrests in both doors, color-keyed nylon cut-pile carpeting an a 4-in.-thick foam-cushioned 50/50 seat.

Model Number	Body/Style Number	Body Type & Seating	Factory Price	Shipping Weight	Production Total
CABALLERO SERIES W (V-6)					
W	80	pickup	—	—	Note 1
CABALLERO SERIES W (305-CID V-8)					
W	80	pickup	$5,911	3,098 lbs.	Note 1

NOTE 1 Total Caballero production was 4,703.

CABALLERO DIABLO — SERIES W + YE7 V-8

The Diablo was similar to an El Camino SS with the Royal Knight package. In addition to the features of the base Caballero, the Diablo came with a large front air dam, matching Sport mirrors, a special large color-coordinated hood decal, a choice of accent colors on the lower body with Diablo graphics, decal stripes to accent the paint-break lines, Rallye wheels painted to match the lower body color, black quarter window moldings and Diablo identification on the lower right-hand side of the tailgate.

Model Number	Body/Style Number	Body Type & Seating	Factory Price	Shipping Weight	Production Total
W	80	pickup	$6,129	3,328 lbs.	Note 1

MODEL OPTIONS

LAREDO PACKAGE: The Caballero Laredo package was similar to the base El Camino with Conquista trim. The Laredo highlighted by a striking molding and paint treatment. The basic body color appeared on the roof, the upper portion of the pickup box, the lower body sides and on the tailgate. The center section of the body side, the hood and the lower portion of the tailgate were set off by a special accent color. Also featured were bright paint break moldings along the upper side of the pickup box and tailgate, bright moldings along the lower body sides and wheel house moldings. A Laredo decal was placed on the tailgate. The package cost $165 this year.

ENGINES

CABALLERO BASE V-6 229-CID, 115-HP (FEDERAL): Overhead-valve V-6. Cast-iron block and head. Displacement: 229 cid (3.8 liters). Bore & stroke: 3.74 x 3.48 in. Compression ratio: 8.6:1. Brake hp: 115 at 4000 rpm. Torque: 175 lbs.-ft. at 2000 rpm. Four main bearings. Hydraulic valve lifters. Carburetor: Rochester two-barrel M2ME. Sales Code: LC3. VIN code: K.

CABALLERO BASE 231-CID, 110-HP V-6 (CALIFORNIA): Overhead-valve V-6. Cast-iron block and head. Displacement: 231 cid (3.8 liters). Bore & stroke: 3.80 x 3.40 in. Compression ratio: 8.0:1. Brake hp: 110 at 3800 rpm Torque: 190 lbs.-ft. at 2000 rpm Four main bearings. Hydraulic valve lifters. Carburetor: Rochester M2ME two-barrel. Sales Code: LD5. VIN code: A.

CABALLERO BASE 267-CID, 120-HP V-8: Overhead-valve. Cast-iron block and head. Bore and stroke: 3.50 x 3.48 in. Displacement: 267 cid (4.4 liters). Compression ratio: 8.3:1. Net brake hp: 120 at 3600 rpm. Taxable hp: 39.20. Net torque: 215 lbs.-ft. at 2000 rpm. Five main bearings. Hydraulic valve lifters. Carburetor: Rochester M2ME two-barrel. VIN Code: J.

CABALLERO OPTIONAL 305-CID, 155-HP V-8: Overhead-valve. Cast-iron block and head. Bore and stroke: 3.74 x 3.48 in. Displacement: 305 cid (5.0 liters). Compression ratio: 8.6:1. Net brake hp: 155 at 4000 rpm. Taxable hp: 44.66. Net torque: 240 lbs.-ft. at 1600 rpm. Five main bearings. Hydraulic valve lifters. Carburetor: Rochester M4ME four-barrel. VIN Code: H.

CHASSIS

Wheelbase: 117.1 in. Overall length: 201.60 in. Height: 53.8 in. Width: 71.9 in. Front tread: 58.5 in. Rear tread: 57.8 in. Cargo box length from back of cab to top of tailgate: 79.5 inches. Bed width between rear wheel housings: 45 in. Bed width above rear wheel housings: 59.5 in. Tires: G78-14B. Transmission: Automatic transmission standard. Three-speed manual transmission available with 3.3-liter V-6. Four-speed manual transmission available with 5.0- and 5.7-liter V-8s. Rear axle: semi-floating. Hydraulic four-wheel brakes. Kelsey Hayes pressed steel wheels.

OPTIONS

A01 tinted body glass ($75). A02 tinted windshield. A31 electric windows ($143). AG9 six-way power seat control ($175). AG1 six-way power 60/40 seat adjuster. AU3 power door locks ($93). AV3 pickup box tie downs ($20). B32 front floor mats. BS1 acoustical insulation. BW2 deluxe body molding exterior ornamentation ($57). BX8 moldings and two-tone paint. BW3 advance price sheet. C60 all-weather air conditioning ($601). C95 ASM dome and reading lamp. CD4 pulse type windshield wipers ($41). D24 litter container. D33 remote-control driver's mirror. D34 visor-vanity mirror. D35 remote-control left-hand outside rearview mirror. D55 front compartment floor console ($86). D64 visor mirror. D68 dual Sport-style exterior rearview mirrors. D73 pickup box handrail ($79). D84 custom two-tone paint. D85 lower body side accent stripe. D91 special two-tone paint. F40 heavy-duty front and rear suspension. F41 special heavy-duty suspension front and rear. G80 Positraction. G92 3.08:1 rear axle. J50 power brakes. K05 engine block heater. K30 speed and cruise control ($112). K81 63-amp Delcotron generator. K97 80-amp Delcotron generator. L26 200-cid V-6 engine. L39 267-cid V-8 engine ($80). LC6 231-cid V-6. LD5 231-cid V-6. LG4 305-cid V-8 ($195). MM3 three-speed manual transmission. MM4 four-speed manual transmission ($144). MX1 automatic transmission ($358). N23 22-gallon fuel tank ($23). N33 tilt steering. N41 variable-ratio power steering ($174). N95 simulated wire wheel covers ($125). NA5 federal emission requirements. NA6 alternative emissions requirements. P01 wheel trim covers. P40 export tire equipment. PB2 ABS plastic wheel trim covers ($56). QFK P205-70R14 steel-belted radial white sidewall tires. QVF P205-70R14 steel-belted radial white letter tires. QFZ P195-75R steel-belted radial white stripe tires. QJY P205-75R steel-belted radial white stripe tires. QKL P205-75R steel-belted radial white letter tires. QKQ P185-75R steel-belted radial white stripe tires. QKR P195-75R steel-belted radial black sidewall tires. QKP P195-75R steel-belted radial white stripe tires. QKS P195-75R14 glass-belted white stripe radial tires. T72 required dual left-hand headlights for export. T84 right-hand headlamp for export. T85 left-hand headlight for export. T90 Export turn signal and marker lamps. TR9 lamp group. U05 dual horns. U14 gauge package ($134). U18 export speedometer. U35 electric clock ($25). U58 AM/FM stereo. U63 push-button AM radio ($85). U69 AM/FM push-button radio ($158). U75 power antenna ($47). U76 windshield antenna ($27). U80 auxiliary speaker. UA1 heavy-duty battery. UF7 gauges package. UM1 AM push-button radio and stereo tape player ($248). UM2 AM-FM push-button radio and stereo tape player ($335). UN3 AM/FM stereo cassette radio, less clock ($341). UP5 AM/FM mono CB radio ($489). UP6 AM/FM stereo CB radio ($570). UX6 dual front dash speakers ($21). UY8 AM/FM stereo radio with digital clock ($395). V01 heavy-duty radiator ($36-$63). V30 front and rear bumper guards. V31 front bumper guards. V78 less certificate of compliance plate. VE5 bumper impact strip. YC8 demo option drive. YF5 California emission requirements. YE7 Diablo package. YJ7 demo drive. Z03 Landau equipment. Z49 mandatory Canadian base equipment modifications. ZJ7 special hubcaps and trim rings. ZN7 color-keyed Rallye wheels ($50). Cargo box tonneau cover ($116). Vinyl roof ($81). Cloth trim bucket seats ($91). Cloth trim 50/50 bench seat ($184). Vinyl bench seat ($28). Vinyl bucket seats ($91). Vinyl 50/50 bench seat ($212).

OPTION INSTALLATION RATES

V-8 under 300 cid (23.9 percent). V-8 301-349 cid (26.1 percent). V-6 under 250-cid (50 percent). Automatic transmission (85.3 percent). Four-speed transmission (1.3 percent). Power front disc brakes (100 percent). Positraction (7.4 percent). Power steering (99.3 percent). Styled steel wheels (79.9 percent). Wheel covers (20.1 percent). Steel-belted radial tires (100 percent). Exterior trim group (34.7 percent). Bucket seats (9.6 percent). Tinted glass (89.5 percent). Air conditioning (75.7 percent). Cruise control (35.2 percent). Adjustable steering column (50.4 percent). Power windows (13.3 percent). Power door locks (11.4 percent). AM radio (44.9 percent). AM/FM radio (14.1 percent). Stereo (10.3 percent). Radio with tape player (8.5 percent). Radio with CB (1 percent). Regular bumpers (100 percent).

HISTORICAL

Robert W. Truxell was general sales manager for GMC trucks. Caballero model-year sales were 4,742 units compared to 6,952 the previous season. That represented 10.4 percent of combined El Camino and Sprint/Caballero sales.

A new grille in the Caballero had eight thin, full-width horizontal bars and bright upper and lower moldings. The Caballero name was on the lower left-hand (driver's side) corner. New wheel covers were seen. Inside was a restyled instrument panel with a new pad and a glossy appliqué, new seat trim and international symbols for controls.

New options included a 55/45 split bench seat, trip odometer and resume-speed cruise control system. The Diablo models came with contrasting lower-body perimeter finish and the Diablo name on the lower door sections. There was a new Caballero Amarillo package with the roof and lower body perimeter finished in a matching color that contrasted with the main body color. Also new were high-pressure tires that decreased rolling resistance and upped fuel economy. Power trains were carried over from 1980, but with GM's Computer Command Control engine management system.

I.D. NUMBERS

VIN embossed on the top left-hand side of the instrument panel and visible through the windshield. The first designates the country of origin: 1=U.S. and 2=Canada. The second symbol indentifies the manufacturer: G=General Motors. The third symbol indicates the make: 1=GMC. The fourth symbol indicates the type of restraint system: A=non-passive/manual seat belts; B=passive/automatic seat belts and C=passive/inflatable. The fifth symbol indicates series: W=Caballero. The sixth and seventh indicate body style: 80=sedan-pickup. The eighth symbol indicates engine (net hp): K=RPO LC3 229-cid/110-hp V-6, A=RPO LD5 231-cid/110-hp V-6 (California), J=RPO L39 267-cid/115-hp V-8 and H=RPO LG4 305-cid/150-hp V-8. The ninth symbol is a check digit. The 10th symbol designates the model year: B=1981. The 11th symbol designates the assembly plant location: B=Baltimore, Maryland, D=Doraville, Georgia, Z=Fremont, California, R=Arlington, Texas, K=Leeds, Missouri. and 1=Oshawa, Canada. The last six symbols are the sequential unit production number at the specific factory.

CABALLERO — SERIES W — V-6/V-8

Standard equipment features included a 3.8-liter (229-cid) V-6 (not available in California), a three-speed manual transmission, Computer Command Control, frameless door glass and thin roof pillars, bright roof drip moldings, new diamond-patterned full-wheel trim covers, a bright windshield molding, a bright rear window molding, a padded instrument panel, steel-belted radial tires, self-adjusting front disc brakes with wear indicators, a High Energy Ignition system, a Freedom side-terminal battery, a dual-mode ventilation system, a fully inflated compact spare tire, a bright left-hand outside rearview mirror, extensive corrosion-resisting treatments, visible ball-joint wear indicators, a front stabilizer bar, a Delcotron generator, a coolant recovery system, seat belts with push-button buckle releases for all passengers, two combination seat and inertia reel shoulder belts for driver and passenger (with reminder light and buzzer), an energy-absorbing steering column, passenger guard door locks, safety door latches with stamped steel hinges, a contoured windshield header, a thick laminate windshield, a safety steering wheel, side marker lights and reflectors, parking lights that illuminate with the headlamps, four-way hazard flashers, back-up lights, directional signals with a lane-change feature, a defroster, dual speed windshield wipers, windshield washers, a 10-in.-wide prismatic wide-view day/night inside rearview mirror with vinyl edging and a deflecting support, a left-hand outside rearview mirror, a dual master cylinder brake system with warning light, a starter safety switch, a dual-action safety hood latch, an ignition key reminder buzzer and a steering column lock. For 1981, the interior elegance was upgraded with convenient new door-pull straps. Power steering became standard equipment. The spare tire was stowed behind the passenger side seating position and now had an extractor for easy removal.

Model Number	Body/Style Number	Body Type & Seating	Factory Price	Shipping Weight	Production Total
CABALLERO SERIES W (V-6)					
W	80	pickup	—	—	Note 1
CABALLERO SERIES W (305-CID V-8)					
W	80	pickup	$6,988	3,181 lbs.	Note 1

CABALLERO DIABLO — SERIES W + YE7 V-8

The Diablo was similar to an El Camino SS with the Royal Knight package. In addition to the features of the base Caballero, the Diablo came with a large front air dam, matching Sport mirrors, a special large color-coordinated hood decal, a choice of accent colors on the lower body with Diablo graphics, decal stripes to accent the paint-break lines, Rallye wheels painted to match the lower body color, black quarter window moldings and Diablo identification on the lower right-hand side of the tailgate.

Model Number	Body/Style Number	Body Type & Seating	Factory Price	Shipping Weight	Production Total
W	80	pickup	$7,217	3,328 lbs.	Note 1

NOTE 1 Total Caballero production was 4,493.

MODEL OPTIONS

AMARILLO PACKAGE: The new Amarillo package was similar to the El Camino Conquista with a two-tone paint treatment. The basic body color appeared on the roof, the upper portion of the pickup box, the lower body sides and on the tailgate. The center section of the body side, the hood and the lower portion of the tailgate were set off by a special accent color. Also featured were bright paint break moldings along the upper side of the pickup box and tailgate, bright moldings along the lower body sides and wheel house moldings. A Laredo decal was placed on the tailgate. The package cost $161 this year.

ENGINES

CABALLERO BASE 229-CID, 110-HP V-6 (FEDERAL) Overhead-valve. Cast-iron block and head. Displacement: 229 cid (3.8 liters). Bore & stroke: 3.74 x 3.48 in. Compression ratio: 8.6:1. Brake hp: 110 at 4200 rpm. Torque: 170 lbs.-ft. at 2000 rpm. Four main bearings. Hydraulic valve lifters. Carburetor: Rochester two-barrel 2ME. Sales Code: LC3. VIN code: K.

CABALLERO BASE 231-CID, 110-HP V-6 (CALIFORNIA): Overhead-valve V-6. Cast-iron block and head. Displacement: 231 cid (3.8 liters). Bore & stroke: 3.80 x 3.40 in. Compression ratio: 8.0:1. Brake hp: 110 at 3800 rpm. Torque: 190 lbs.-ft. at 1600 rpm. Four main bearings. Hydraulic valve lifters. Carburetor: Rochester E2ME two-barrel. Sales Code: LD5. VIN code: A.

CABALLERO BASE V-8: Overhead-valve. Cast-iron block and head. Bore and stroke: 3.50 x 3.48 in. Displacement: 267 cid (4.4 liters). Compression ratio: 8.3:1. Net brake hp: 115 at 4000 rpm. Taxable hp: 39.20. Net torque: 200 lbs.-ft. at 2400 rpm. Five main bearings. Hydraulic valve lifters. Carburetor: Rochester 2ME two-barrel. VIN Code: J.

CABALLERO OPTIONAL V-8: Overhead-valve. Cast-iron block and head. Bore and stroke: 3.74 x 3.48 in. Displacement: 305 cid (5.0 liters). Compression ratio: 8.6:1. Net brake hp: 150 lbs.-ft. at 3800 rpm. Taxable hp: 44.66. Net torque: 240 lbs.-ft. at 2400 rpm. Five main bearings. Hydraulic valve lifters. Carburetor: Rochester 4ME four-barrel. VIN Code: H.

CHASSIS

Wheelbase: 117.1 in. Overall length: 201.60 in. Height: 53.8 in. Width: 71.9 in. Front tread: 58.5 in. Rear tread: 57.8 in. Cargo box length from back of cab to top of tailgate: 79.5 in. Bed width between rear wheel housings: 45 in. Bed width above rear wheel housings: 59.5 in. Tires: G78-14B. Transmission: Automatic transmission standard. Hydraulic four-wheel brakes (front disc/rear drums). Pressed steel wheels.

OPTIONS

A01 tinted body glass. A02 tinted windshield. A31 electric windows. A32 electric front door window. AG9 six-way power seat control. AU3 power door locks ($93). AU6 electric tailgate lock release. AV3 pickup box tie downs. B32 front floor mats. B90 side window moldings. B93 door edge guards. B96 wheel opening moldings. B3W preliminary price information. BS1 acoustical insulation. BW2 Deluxe body molding exterior ornamentation. BX8 moldings and two-tone paint. C60 manual air conditioning. CD4 pulse type windshield wipers. D28 right-hand outside rearview mirror. D33 remote-control driver's mirror. D35 remote-control left-hand outside rearview mirror. D36 10-in. tilting export inside rearview mirror. D55 front compartment floor console. D68 dual Sport-style exterior rearview mirrors. D73 pickup box handrail. D84 custom two-tone paint. D85 lower body side accent stripe. D91 special two-tone paint. F40 heavy-duty front and rear suspension. F41 special heavy-duty suspension front and rear. G80 Positraction. K05 engine block heater. K35 speed and cruise control with resume. K73 70-amp generator. K81 63-amp generator. L39 267-cid V-8 engine. LC3 229-cid V-6. LD5 231-cid V-6. LG4 305-cid V-8. MM3 three-speed manual transmission. MM4 four-speed manual transmission. MX1 automatic transmission. N18 locking wire wheel covers. N23 22-gallon fuel tank. N33 tilt steering. N95 simulated wire wheel covers. NM5 non-closed-loop emission system (Canada). NM8 leaded gas conversion emissions modification. QXW P195-70R14 steel-belted radial white striped tires. QXX P205-70R14 steel-belted radial black sidewall tires. QXY P205-75R14 steel-belted radial white stripe tires. QXZ P205-75R14 steel-belted radial white-letter tires. QYA P205-70R14 steel-belted radial black sidewall tires. QYB P205-70R14 steel-belted radial white stripe tires. QYC P205-70R steel-belted radial white-letter tires. QYD P185-75R14 glass-belted radial black-sidewall tires. QYE P185-75R14 glass-belted white-stripe radial tires. QYF P195-75R14 glass-belted black-sidewall tires. QYG P195-75R14 glass-belted white-stripe tires. T72 required dual left-hand headlights for export. T84 right-hand headlamp for export. T85 left-hand headlight for export. T90 Export turn signal and marker lamps. TR9 lamp group. TT4 tungsten quartz halogen headlights. U05 dual horns. U14 gauge package.

U18 export speedometer. U35 electric clock. U58 AM/FM stereo. U63 push-button AM radio. U69 AM/FM push-button radio. U75 power antenna. U76 windshield antenna. U80 auxiliary speaker. UA1 heavy-duty battery. UF7 gauges package. UM2 AM-FM push-button radio and stereo tape player. UN3 AM/FM stereo cassette radio, less clock. UP6 AM/FM stereo CB radio. V08 heavy-duty cooling. V30 front and rear bumper guards. V78 less certificate of compliance plate. V84 government export orders, U.S. vehicles. VB1 Japanese shipping label. VC3 U.S. Territory shipping label. VC4 Puerto Rico shipping label. VC5 price label, non-Japan. VE5 bumper impact strip. YC8 demo option drive. YF5 California emission requirements. YJ7 demo drive. Z49 mandatory Canadian base equipment modifications. ZJ1 two-tone custom interior. ZJ2 custom exterior moldings. ZJ7 special hubcaps and trim rings. ZN7 color-keyed Rallye wheels. YE7 Diablo trim. Cargo box tonneau cover. Vinyl roof. Cloth 55/45 seating.

OPTION INSTALLATION RATES

V-8 under 300 cid (18.1 percent). V-8 301-349 cid (24.8 percent). V-6 under 250-cid (57.1 percent). Automatic transmission (90.3 percent). Four-speed transmission (1.7 percent). Power front disc brakes (100 percent). Positraction (6.2 percent). Power steering (100 percent). Styled steel wheels (81.5 percent). Wheel covers (20.1 percent). Fiberglass-belted radial tires (100 percent). Base exterior/interior trim level (54.2 percent). Second level exterior/interior trim (35.8 percent). Third level exterior/interior trim (6.3 percent). Fourth level exterior/interior trim (3.7 percent). Bucket seats (8.5 percent). Tinted glass (93.6 percent). Air conditioning (83.2 percent). Cruise control (44.5 percent). Adjustable steering column (59.6 percent). Power windows (17 percent). Power door locks (15.2 percent). AM radio (39.9 percent). AM/FM radio (12 percent). Stereo (16.5 percent). Radio with tape player (10.6 percent). Radio with CB (0.6 percent). Regular bumpers (100 percent).

HISTORICAL FOOTNOTES

Robert W. Truxell was general sales manager for GMC trucks. Caballero model-year sales were 4,380 units compared to 4,742 the previous season. That represented 10.7 percent of combined El Camino and Sprint/Caballero sales

"A bright new face for '82" was how the Caballero sales catalog described the sedan-pickup's restyled ice-cube-tray grille and side-by-side dual rectangular headlamps. The grille had three thin horizontal bars and 15 vertical ones. The Caballero name appeared at the lower left side and a stand-up hood ornament holding a GMC badge was seen again. Exterior color choices included five new colors and new two-tone combinations. Dual cowl-mounted "fluidic" windshield washers provided a fan spray for effective cleaning. A fender-mounted fixed-mast antenna replaced the in-the-windshield type and enhanced fringe-area radio reception. It could be unscrewed and taken in for protection while in a car wash.

Caballero models for 1982 came equipped with a three-speed automatic transmission coupled with either the standard 3.8-liter V-6, available 4.4-liter V-8 (except in California) or available 5.0-liter V-8. Front disc brakes with new low-drag calipers helped reduce friction and increased fuel economy. New deep-foam notchback style bench seats came in a choice of cloth or vinyl upholstery. A new color-styled instrument panel featured a simulated wood-grain appliqué.

I.D. NUMBERS

VIN embossed on the top left-hand side of the instrument panel and visible through the windshield. The first designates the country of origin: 1=U.S. and 2=Canada. The second symbol indentifies the manufacturer: G=General Motors. The third symbol indicates the make: 1=GMC. The fourth symbol indicates the type of restraint system: A=non-passive/manual seat belts; B=passive/automatic seat belts and C=passive/inflatable. The fifth symbol indicates series: W=Caballero. The sixth and seventh indicate body style: 80=sedan-pickup. The eighth symbol indicates engine (net hp): K=RPO LC3 229-cid/110-hp V-6, A=RPO LD5 231-cid/110-hp V-6 (California), J=RPO L39 267-cid/115-hp V-8, H=RPO LG4 305-cid/145-hp V-8, V=RPO LT6 260-cid/85-hp diesel V-6 and N=RPO LF9 350-cid/105-hp diesel V-8. The ninth symbol is a check digit. The 10th symbol designates the model year: C=1982. The 11th symbol designates the assembly plant location: R=Arlington, Texas. The last six symbols are the sequential unit production number at the specific factory.

CABALLERO — SERIES W — V-6/V-8

Characterized by GMC as "the elegant pickup that looks good and thrives on hard work, the Caballero for 1982 featured new interiors, new front end styling, new comfort, new color, new features and new value." The new front-end design gave the sedan-pickup a broader road stance and sleeker appearance. Standard features included the new grille, dual rectangular headlamps, bright grille moldings, chromed front and rear bumpers, a chromed left-hand outside rearview mirror, a dual-note horn, new fluidic windshield washers, two-speed electric windshield wipers, a new deep-foam notchback-style front bench seat in cloth or vinyl, full-floor carpeting, a new color-styled instrument panel with simulated wood-grain appliqué, a lighted ash tray, a cigarette lighter, dual padded sunshades, an energy-absorbing steering column

1982

The Diablo option package returned for the 1982 Caballero.

with new "smart switch," a heater and defroster system, an anti-theft ignition key warning buzzer and steering column lock, an inside hood release, door-actuated courtesy lights, padded armrests, a lighted glove compartment, a foam-backed cloth headliner, concealed storage for the spare tire and luggage, a color-keyed steering wheel, self-adjusting low-drag power front disc brakes with wear indicators, power rear drum brakes, a Freedom II battery, a High Energy ignition system, a Delcotron generator, a computer-selected full-coil suspension system with air-adjustable shocks, power steering, a three-speed automatic transmission, an engine coolant recovery system, a 3.8-liter Chevrolet-built V-6 and the GM Computer Command Control engine management system. A 4.4-liter V-8 and a 5.0-liter V-8 were optional. The standard new notchback bench seat with cloth or up-level textured-all-vinyl interior trims featured a fold-down center armrest and adjustable headrests. Standard seat colors were new silver gray, blue, camel or maroon. An optional 55/45 split bench seat with a fold-down armrest could be ordered in the same fabrics and colors as the standard seat trim. Also optional was a new custom interior featuring the new notchback bench seat in custom knit velour cloth in dark blue, jade, camel or maroon.

Model Number	Body/Style Number	Body Type & Seating	Factory Price	Shipping Weight	Production Total
CABALLERO SERIES W (V-6)					
W	80	pickup	—	—	Note 1
CABALLERO SERIES W (305-CID V-8)					
W	80	pickup	$7,995	3,294 lbs.	Note 1

CABALLERO DIABLO — SERIES W + YE7 V-8

The real eye-catcher on the Caballero Diablo was a hood decal sporting a striking large scroll motif of the devil (or "Diablo" in Spanish). Large Diablo lettering also appeared on the exterior lower door panels. Diablo identification also appeared on the tailgate and above the glove box door. Available two-tone exteriors for this model came in seven color combinations and color-keyed pin striping covered the paint break line. Interiors came in camel, maroon, dark blue or silver gray. Sport mirrors were painted the upper body color. New Rallye wheels with a GMC center emblem were standard.

Model Number	Body/Style Number	Body Type & Seating	Factory Price	Shipping Weight	Production Total
W	80	pickup	$8,244	3,300 lbs.	Note 1

NOTE 1 Total Caballero production was 2,738.

MODEL OPTIONS

AMARILLO PACKAGE The 1982 Amarillo package was similar to the El Camino Conquista and was offered in eight two-tone paint combinations for 1982. The basic body color appeared on the roof, the upper portion of the pickup box, the lower body sides and on the tailgate. The center section of the body side, the hood and the lower portion of the tailgate were set off by a special accent color. Also featured were bright paint break moldings along the upper side of the pickup box and tailgate, bright moldings along the lower body sides and wheel house moldings. An Amarillo decal was placed on the upper right tailgate and above the glove box door. Interior color offerings were dark blue, camel, silver gray or maroon. The package cost $183 this year.

ENGINES

CABALLERO BASE 229-CID, 110-HP V-6: 90-degree, overhead-valve. Cast-iron block and head. Bore and stroke: 3.74 x 3.48 in. Displacement: 229 cid (3.8 liters). Compression ratio: 8.6:1. Brake hp: 110 at 4200 rpm. Torque: 170 lbs.-ft. at 2000 rpm. Four main bearings. Hydraulic valve lifters. Carburetor: Rochester two-barrel E2ME. VIN Code: K.

CABALLERO BASE 231-CID, 110-HP V-6: (CALIFORNIA) Overhead-valve. Cast-iron block and head. Displacement: 231 cid (3.8 liters). Bore & stroke: 3.80 x 3.40 in. Compression ratio: 8.0:1. Brake hp: 110 at 3800 rpm Torque: 190 lbs.-ft. at 1600 rpm Four main bearings. Hydraulic valve lifters. Carburetor: Rochester E2ME two-barrel. Sales Code: LD5. VIN code: A.

CABALLERO OPTIONAL 267-CID, 115-HP V-8: Overhead-valve. Cast-iron block and head. Bore and stroke: 3.50 x 3.48 in. Displacement: 267 cid (4.4 liters). Compression ratio: 8.3:1. Net brake hp: 115 at 4000 rpm. Taxable hp: 39.20. Net brake hp: 120 at 3600 rpm. Net torque: 205 lbs.-ft. at 2400 rpm. Five main bearings. Hydraulic valve lifters. Carburetor: Rochester E2ME two-barrel. VIN Code: J.

CABALLERO OPTIONAL 305-CID, 145-HP V-8: Overhead-valve. Cast-iron block and head. Bore and stroke: 3.74 x 3.48 in. Displacement: 305 cid (5.0 liters). Compression ratio: 8.6:1. Net brake hp: 145 at 4000 rpm. Taxable hp: 44.66. Net torque: 240 lbs.-ft. at 2000 rpm. Five main bearings. Hydraulic valve lifters. Carburetor: Rochester E4ME four-barrel. VIN Code: H.

CHASSIS

Wheelbase: 117.1 in. Overall length: 201.60 in. Width: 71.9 in. Height: 53.8 in. Front tread: 58.5 in. Rear tread: 57.8 in. Cargo box length from back of cab to top of tailgate: 79.5 in Bed width between rear wheel housings: 45 in. Bed width above rear wheel housings: 59.5 in. Tires: G78-14B. Transmission: Automatic. Column-mounted gearshift lever. Rear axle: semi-floating. Hydraulic four-wheel brakes. Kelsey-Hayes pressed steel wheels.

OPTIONS

A01 tinted body glass. A02 tinted windshield. A31 electric windows. A32 electric front door window. AG9 six-way power seat control ($175). AU3 power door locks ($93). AU6 electric tailgate lock release. AV3 pickup box tie downs. B32 front floor mats. B90 side window moldings. B93 door edge guards. B96 wheel opening moldings. B3W preliminary price information. BS1 acoustical insulation. BW2 deluxe body molding exterior ornamentation. BX8 moldings and two-tone paint. C60 manual air conditioning. CD4 pulse type windshield wipers. D28 right-hand outside rearview mirror. D33 remote-control driver's mirror. D35 remote-control left-hand outside rearview mirror. D36 10-in. tilting export inside rearview mirror. D55 front compartment floor console. D68 dual sport-style exterior rearview mirrors. D73 pickup box handrail. D84 custom two-tone paint. D85 lower body side accent stripe. D91 special two-tone paint. F40 heavy-duty front and rear suspension. F41 special heavy-duty suspension front and rear. G80 Positraction. G84 high-altitude rear axle ratio. G92 performance ratio rear axle. GH2 2.29:1 rear axle ratio. GM7 2.39:1 rear axle ratio. GM8 2.56:1 rear axle ratio. GU1 2.41:1 rear axle ratio. GU2 2.73:1 rear axle ratio. GU3 2.93:1 rear axle ratio. GU4 3.08:1 rear axle ratio. GU5 3.23:1 rear axle ratio. GW9 2.93:1 rear axle ratio. JE1 European export brake system. K05 engine block heater. K35 Cruise and speed control with resume. K73 70-amp Delcotron generator. LC3 229-cid V-6 engine (standard Federal engine). L39 267-cid V-8 engine. LD5 231-cid V-6 engine (standard California engine). LG4 305-cid V-8 engine in station wagon. LT6 4.3-liter diesel V-6. MX1 Turbo-Hydra-Matic automatic transmission. N18 simulated wire wheel covers. N23 22-gal. fuel tank. N33 Tilt steering wheel. N81 full-size spare radial tire. N95 simulated wire wheel covers with locks. NA6 alternate requirements emission system. NM5 Non-closed loop emission system on Canadian cars. NM8 leaded gas emissions modification. P41 export tire equipment. P42 self-sealing tire. QVJ P195-75R14 steel-belted white-

1982

NEW STYLING FOR '82...
GMC CABALLERO

QUALITY BUILT FOR VALUE

The 1982 Caballero received new colors, new interior styling, and a new front end.

stripe radial tires. QVT P205-75R14B steel-belted radial tires with white stripe. QXW P195-75R14B steel-belted radial tires with white stripe. QXX P205-75R14B steel-belted radial black-sidewall tires. QXY P205-75R14B steel-belted radial tires with white stripe. QXZ P205-75R14B steel-belted radial tires with raised white letters. QYD P185-75R14B radial black-sidewall tires. QYE P185-75R14B radial tires with white stripes. QYF P195-75R14B radial black-sidewall tires. QYG P195-75R14B radial tires with white stripes. T84 rectangular export-type right-hand headlight. T90 export-type signal light and marker lamp. TR9 lamp group. TT5 tungsten quartz halogen headlights. U14 special instrumentation gauge package. U18 export speedometer. U35 electric clock. U58 AM/FM push-button stereo. U63 AM push-button radio. U69 AM/FM push-button radio. U73 fixed antenna. U75 power antenna. U76 windshield antenna included with all radios. U81 dual rear radio speakers. UA1 heavy-duty battery. UF7 gauge package, except tachometer. UM2 AM/FM push-button radio and tape player. UN3 AM/FM stereo cassette radio less clock. V08 heavy-duty radiator. V10 cold climate package. V30 front and rear bumper guards. VC3 U.S. Territory shipping label. VC4 Puerto Rico shipping label. VE5 front and rear bumper impact strips. YC8 demo option drive. YE7 Diablo package. Z49 mandatory Canadian base equipment model. ZJ1 two-tone custom interior. ZJ2 custom exterior moldings. ZJ7 special wheel package with hubcap and trim rings. Dual horns.

OPTION INSTALLATION RATES

4.4-liter V-8 engine (18.5 percent). 305-cid V-8 engine (44.9 percent). V-6 (36.6 percent). Automatic transmission (100 percent). Power front disc brakes (100 percent). Positraction (8.7 percent). Power steering (100 percent). Air conditioning (92 percent). Steel styled wheels (82 percent). Steel-belted radial tires (100 percent). Base exterior/exterior trim package (43 percent). Level 2 exterior/exterior trim package (43 percent). Level 3 exterior/exterior trim package (10 percent). Level 4 exterior/exterior trim package (4 percent). Tinted glass (96 percent). Cruise control (63 percent). Adjustable steering column (75 percent). Power windows (28 percent). Power door locks (27 percent). AM radio (29 percent). AM/FM radio (11 percent). Stereo (29 percent). Cassette player (13 percent). Eight-track tape player (3 percent).

HISTORICAL FOOTNOTES

Robert W. Truxell was general sales manager for GMC trucks in 1982, but Donald J. Atwood took over as head of the division by 1983. Atwood held the new title of group executive of the Truck & Buss Group. He was also a General Motors vice president. Caballero calendar-year sales were 2,573 units. Model-year sales were 2,654 units compared to 4,380 in 1981 and 4,742 in 1980.

The 1983 Caballero looked so much like the 1982 model that the picture of the base model used in the sales catalogs from the two years was exactly the same, except for size. The picture of the Caballero Amarillo in front of an antiques shop was also identical, except that the two-tone color combination was changed by the catalog artists.

The main news this year was the offering of a 5.7-liter diesel V-8. There was also new simulated leather-grain trim on the instrument panel and steering wheel shroud, replacing the previous wood-grain trim, and five new interior trim colors.

I.D. NUMBERS

VIN embossed on the top left-hand side of the instrument panel and visible through the windshield. The first designates the country of origin: 1=U.S. and 2=Canada. The second symbol indentifies the manufacturer: G=General Motors. The third symbol indicates the make: 5=GMC. The fourth symbol indicates the type of restraint system: A=non-passive/manual seat belts; B=passive/automatic seat belts and C=passive/inflatable. The fifth symbol indicates the car line/series: W=Caballero. The sixth and seventh symbols indicate body type: 80=sedan-pickup. The eighth symbol indicates engine (net hp): 9=RPO LC3 229-cid/115-hp V-6, A=RPO LD5 231-cid/110-hp V-6 (California), H=RPO LG4 305-cid/150-hp V-8, V=RPO LT6 260-cid/85-hp diesel V-6 and N=RPO LF9 350-cid/125-hp diesel V-8. The ninth symbol is a check digit. The 10th symbol designates the model year: D=1983. The 11th symbol designates the assembly plant location: R=Arlington, Texas. The last six symbols are the sequential unit production number at the specific factory.

CABALLERO — SERIES W — V-6/V-8

Standard features for 1983 included an ice-cube-tray grille, dual rectangular headlamps, bright grille moldings, a bright windshield molding, a bright rear window molding, a bright belt line bead molding, pickup box side rail moldings, bright rocker panel moldings, bright wheel opening moldings, bright drip rail moldings, chromed front and rear bumpers, a chromed left-hand outside rearview mirror, a selection of 10 solid paint colors (nine of them new), a dual-note horn, fluidic windshield washers, two-speed electric windshield wipers with concealed blades and arms, a deep-foam notchback-style front bench seat in cloth or vinyl, full-floor carpeting, a color-styled instrument panel with new simulated leather-grain appliqué, a simulated leather-grain steering wheel shroud, a lighted ash tray, a cigarette lighter, dual padded sunshades, an energy-absorbing steering column with "smart switch," a heater and defroster system, an anti-theft ignition key warning buzzer and steering column lock, an inside hood release, door-actuated dome and courtesy lights, padded armrests, a lighted glove compartment with lock, a foam-backed cloth headliner, concealed storage for the spare tire and luggage, a color-keyed steering wheel, bright wheel covers, self-adjusting low-drag power front disc brakes with wear indicators, steel-belted radial tires, power rear drum brakes, a 355 cold-cranking amps Freedom II battery, a High Energy

The 1983 Caballero was almost identical to the 1982 model. The biggest change was the arrival of a V-8 diesel engine option.

ignition system, a 37-amp Delcotron generator, a computer-selected full-coil suspension system with air-adjustable shocks, power steering, a three-speed automatic transmission, an engine coolant recovery system, a 3.8-liter Chevrolet-built V-6 and the GM Computer Command Control engine management system. A 5.0-liter V-8 and a 5.7-liter diesel V-8 were optional. The standard new notchback bench seat with cloth or up-level textured-all-vinyl interior trims featured a fold-down center armrest and adjustable headrests. Standard seat colors were new dark blue, dark brown, fern, maroon or sand gray. These colors, except fern, were also used for the optional vinyl-trimmed seats.

Model Number	Body/Style Number	Body Type & Seating	Factory Price	Shipping Weight	Production Total
CABALLERO SERIES W (V-6)					
W	80	pickup	—	—	Note 1
CABALLERO SERIES W (305-CID V-8)					
W	80	pickup	$8,191	3,332 lbs.	Note 1

CABALLERO DIABLO — SERIES W + YE7 V-8

The Caballero Diablo again had a "devil" hood decal ("Diablo" meant "devil" in Spanish), large Diablo lettering on the exterior lower door panels, Diablo identification on the tailgate and above the glove box door, two-tone exterior finish and color-keyed pin striping on the paint break line. The Sport mirrors were painted the upper-body color. Rallye wheels with a GMC center emblem and trim rings were standard.

Model Number	Body/Style Number	Body Type & Seating	Factory Price	Shipping Weight	Production Total
W	80	pickup	$8,445	3,337 lbs.	Note 1

NOTE 1: Total Caballero production was 2,738.

MODEL OPTIONS

AMARILLO PACKAGE: The 1984 Amarillo package was similar to the El Camino Conquista and was offered in striking two-tone paint combinations. The basic body color appeared on the roof, the upper portion of the pickup box, the lower body sides and on the tailgate. The center section of the body side, the hood and the lower portion of the tailgate were set off by a special accent color. Also featured were bright paint break moldings along the upper side of the pickup box and tailgate, bright moldings along the lower body sides and wheel house moldings. An Amarillo decal was placed on the upper right tailgate and above the glove box door. The

CABALLERO

package cost $189 this year.

ENGINES

CABALLERO BASE 229-CID, 115-HP V-6: 90-degree, overhead-valve V-6. Cast-iron block and head. Bore and stroke: 3.74 x 3.48 in. Displacement: 229-cid (3.8 liters). Compression ratio: 8.6:1. Brake hp: 115 at 4200 rpm. Torque: 170 lbs.-ft. at 2000 rpm. Four main bearings. Hydraulic valve lifters. Carburetor: two-barrel Rochester E2ME. VIN Code: K or 9.

(**NOTE** California models used a Buick 231-cid V-6.)

CABALLERO OPTIONAL 305-CID, 150-HP V-6: 90-degree, overhead-valve. Cast-iron block and head. Bore and stroke: 3.74 x 3.48 in. Displacement: 305-cid (5.0 liters). Compression ratio: 8.6:1. Brake hp: 150 at 4000 rpm. Torque: 240 lbs.-ft. at 2400 rpm. Five main bearings. Hydraulic valve lifters. Carburetor: four-barrel Rochester E4ME. VIN Code: H.

CABALLERO OPTIONAL 350-CID, 105-HP DIESEL V-8: 90-degree, overhead-valve. Cast-iron block and head. Bore and stroke: 4.057 x 3.385 in. Displacement: 350-cid (5.7 liters). Compression ratio: 22.5:1. Brake hp: 105 at 3200 rpm. Torque: 200 lbs.-ft. at 1600 rpm. Five main bearings. Hydraulic valve lifters. Fuel injection. Olds-built. VIN Code: N.

CHASSIS

Wheelbase: 117.1 in. Overall length: 201.60 in. Width: 71.9 in. Height: 53.8 in. Front tread: 58.5 in. Rear tread: 57.8 in. Cargo box length from back of cab to top of tailgate: 79.5 in. Bed width between rear wheel housings: 45 in. Bed width above rear wheel housings: 59.5 in. Tires: G78-14B. Transmission: Automatic. Column-mounted gearshift lever. Rear axle: semi-floating. Hydraulic four-wheel brakes. Kelsey-Hayes pressed steel wheels.

OPTIONS

A01 all tinted glass ($105). A02 tinted windshield. A26 United Kingdom and European Glazing Window. A31 power windows with electric control ($255). A32 electric front door window. AG9 six-way power seat adjuster. AU3 power door locks ($170). AU6 electric tailgate release ($40). AV3 pickup box tie downs. B37 color-keyed floor mats. B93 door edge guards ($15-$25). BS1 acoustical insulation. BW2 deluxe body molding exterior decoration ($57). BX8 front fender and body moldings. B2L fleet early order option. B3W preliminary price

The "devil's head" motif was still included in the flashy Diablo package.

The 1983 Caballeros had a new leather-grain accent trim on the instrument panel. The standard interior included a fold-down split bench seat and fold-down armrest.

information. B6W fleet A/C incentive program. C49 electric rear window defogger ($135). C60 manual air conditioning ($725). CD4 pulse-type windshield wipers and washers. D33 remote-control left-hand outside rearview mirror ($22). D35 custom outside rearview mirrors ($59). D73 pickup box hand rail. D84 custom two-tone paint ($138). D85 body side lower accent stripes. DG8 export breakaway mirror. F40 heavy-duty front and rear suspension ($26). G80 Positraction rear axle ($95). G84 high-altitude rear axle ratio. G92 performance ratio rear axle ($21). GH2 2.29:1 rear axle ratio. GM7 2.39:1 rear axle ratio. GM8 2.56:1 rear axle ratio. GM8 2.56:1 rear axle ratio. GT4 3.73:1 rear axle ratio. GU1 2.41:1 rear axle ratio. GU2 2.73:1 rear axle ratio. GU3 2.93:1 rear axle ratio. GU4 3.08:1 rear axle ratio. GU5 3.23:1 rear axle ratio. GU6 3.42:1 rear axle ratio. GW9 2.93:1 rear axle ratio. JE1 European export brake system. K05 engine block heater. K35 Cruise and speed control with resume. K64 78-amp Delcotron generator. LC3 229-cid V-6 engine (standard Federal engine). LD5 231-cid V-6 engine (standard California engine). LF9 350-cid diesel V-8 ($700). LG4 305-cid V-8 engine ($225). LT6 4.3-liter diesel V-6 ($500). MX1 Turbo-Hydra-Matic automatic transmission (standard). N18 simulated wire wheel covers. N23 22-gal. fuel tank. N33 Tilt steering wheel ($105).

N81 full-size spare radial tire. N95 simulated wire wheel covers with locks ($190). NA6 alternate requirements emission system. NM5 Non-closed loop emission system on Canadian cars. NM8 leaded gas emissions modification. P01 deluxe wheel trim covers. P41 export tire equipment. PB2 ABS plastic wheel trim covers. QVJ P195-75R14 steel-belted white-stripe radial tires. QVT P205-75R14B steel-belted radial tires with white stripe. QXX P205-75R14B steel-belted radial black sidewall tires. QYD P185-75R14B radial black-sidewall tires. QYE P185-75R14B radial tires with white stripes. QYF P195-75R14B radial black-sidewall tires. QYG P195-75R14B radial tires with white stripes. T90 export-type signal light and marker lamp. TR9 lamp group ($49-$56). TT5 tungsten quartz halogen headlights. U05 dual A note horn. U14 special instrumentation gauge package ($95). U18 export speedometer. U35 electric clock ($35). U58 AM/FM push-button stereo ($198). U63 AM push-button radio ($112). U69 AM/FM push-button radio ($171). U73 fixed antenna ($41). U81 dual rear radio speakers. UA1 heavy-duty battery ($25). UN3 AM/FM stereo cassette radio less clock ($298). V08 heavy-duty radiator ($40-$70). V10 cold climate package ($99). V30 front and rear bumper guards ($50). V55 roof luggage carrier. V78 less certificate of compliance plate. VC3 U.S. Territory shipping label. VC4 Puerto Rico shipping label. VC5 export shipping label. VE5 front and rear bumper impact strips (850). YF5 California emission requirements. YE7 Diablo package. Z49 mandatory Canadian base equipment model. ZJ7 special wheel package with hubcap and trim rings.

OPTION INSTALLATION RATES

5.0-liter V-8 engine (63.8 percent). 350-cid diesel V-8 engine (6.9 percent). V-6 (29.3 percent). Automatic transmission (100 percent). Power front disc brakes (100 percent). Positraction (16.2 percent). Power steering (100 percent). Steel-belted radial tires (100 percent). Air conditioning (92.9 percent). Steel styled wheels (79 percent). Base exterior/exterior trim package (42.6 percent). Level 2 exterior/exterior trim package (7.7 percent). Level 3 exterior/exterior trim package (49.7 percent). Tinted glass (95.8 percent). Cruise control (75.5 percent). Adjustable steering column (81.8 percent). Power windows (46.3 percent). Power door locks (41.2 percent). AM radio (13.7 percent). AM/FM radio (6.4 percent). Stereo (38.5 percent). Cassette player (33.2 percent).

HISTORICAL FOOTNOTES

Donald J. Atwood continued as executive of the Truck & Bus Group. He was also a General Motors vice president. Caballero calendar-year sales were 2,160 units. Model-year sales were 2,126 compared to 2,654 in 1982, 4,380 in 1981 and 4,742 in 1980.

General Motors dropped the mid-sized Chevrolet Malibu in 1983, but continued producing the Chevy El Camino and GMC Caballero sedan-pickups derived from the passenger car. The 1984 Caballero was a very luxurious vehicle. It had dual, side-by-side, rectangular headlights on either side of a cross-hatch grille, with long, narrow parking lights directly below the headlights. The bumper was of a simple, straight-across design. A 5.7-liter gas V-8 returned to the optional equipment list. A 5.7-liter diesel V-8 remained available.

I.D. NUMBERS

VIN embossed on the top left-hand side of the instrument panel and visible through the windshield. Beginning this year, GM used its light-duty truck, multipurpose passenger vehicle and Incomplete Vehicle VIN coding system to code the Caballero, except that Caballero engine codes were those used for passenger cars. The first symbol designates the country of origin: 3=Mexico. The second symbol identifies the manufacturer: G=General Motors. The third symbol indicates the make and type: T=GMC truck. The fourth symbol indicates the GVWR. The fifth symbol indicates the series: W=Caballero. The sixth and seventh symbols indicate body type 80=sedan-pickup. The eighth symbol indicates engine (net hp): 9=RPO LC3 229-cid/115-hp V-6, A=RPO LD5 231-cid/110-hp V-6 (California), H=RPO LG4 305-cid/150-hp V-8, 8=350-cid V-8 and N=RPO LF9 350-cid/125-hp diesel V-8. The ninth symbol is a check digit. The 10th symbol designates the model year: E=1984. The 11th symbol designates the assembly plant location: S=Ramos Arizpe, Mexico. The last six symbols are the sequential unit production number at the specific factory.

CABALLERO — SERIES W — V-6/V-8

Standard features for included an ice-cube-tray grille, dual rectangular headlamps, bright grille moldings, a bright windshield molding, a bright rear window molding, a bright belt line bead molding, pickup box side rail moldings, bright rocker panel moldings, bright wheel opening moldings, bright drip rail moldings, chromed front and rear bumpers, a chromed left-hand outside rearview mirror, a selection of 10 solid paint colors (nine of them new), a dual-note horn, fluidic windshield washers, two-speed electric windshield wipers with concealed blades and arms, a deep-foam notchback-style front bench seat in cloth or vinyl, full-floor carpeting, a color-styled instrument panel with new simulated leather-grain appliqué, a simulated leather-grain steering wheel shroud, a lighted ash tray, a cigarette lighter, dual padded sunshades, an energy-absorbing steering column with "smart switch," a heater and defroster system, an anti-theft ignition key warning buzzer and steering column lock, an inside hood release, door-actuated dome and courtesy lights, padded armrests, a lighted glove compartment with lock, a foam-backed cloth headliner, concealed storage for the spare tire and luggage, a color-keyed steering wheel, bright wheel covers, self-adjusting low-drag power front disc brakes with wear indicators, steel-belted radial tires, power rear drum brakes, a 355 cold cranking amps Freedom II battery, a High Energy ignition system, a 37-amp. Delcotron generator, a computer-selected full-coil suspension system with air-adjustable shocks, power steering, a three-speed automatic transmission, an engine coolant recovery system, a 3.8-liter Chevrolet-built V-6 and the GM Computer Command Control engine management system. A 5.0-liter V-8 and a 5.7-liter diesel V-8 were optional. The standard notchback bench seat with cloth or up-level textured-all-vinyl interior trims featured a fold-down center armrest and adjustable headrests.

Model Number	Body/Style Number	Body Type & Seating	Factory Price	Shipping Weight	Production Total
CABALLERO SERIES W (V-6)					
W	80	pickup	—	—	Note 1
CABALLERO SERIES W (305-CID V-8)					
W	80	pickup	$8,522	3,298 lbs.	Note 1

CABALLERO DIABLO SS — SERIES W + YE7 — V-8

The Caballero Diablo again had large Diablo lettering on the exterior lower door panels, Diablo identification on the tailgate and above the glove box door, two-tone exterior finish and color-keyed pin striping on the paint break line. The Sport mirrors were painted the upper body color. Rallye wheels with a GMC center emblem and trim rings were standard.

Model Number	Body/Style Number	Body Type & Seating	Factory Price	Shipping Weight	Production Total
W	80	pickup	$8,781	3,305 lbs.	Note 1

NOTE 1 Total Caballero production was 2,797.

MODEL OPTIONS

AMARILLO PACKAGE: The 1984 Amarillo package was offered in striking two-tone paint combinations. The basic body color appeared on the roof, the upper portion of the pickup box, the lower body sides and on the tailgate. The center section of the body side, the hood and the lower portion of the tailgate were set off by a special accent color. Also featured were bright paint break moldings along the upper side of the pickup box and tailgate, bright moldings along the lower body sides and wheel house moldings. An Amarillo decal was placed on the upper right tailgate and above the glove box door.

ENGINES

CABALLERO BASE 229-CID, 115-HP V-6: 90-degree, overhead-valve. Cast-iron block and head. Bore and stroke: 3.74 x 3.48 in. Displacement: 229-cid (3.8 liters). Compression ratio: 8.6:1. Brake hp: 115 at 4200 rpm. Torque: 170 lbs.-ft. at 2000 rpm. Four main bearings. Hydraulic valve lifters. Carburetor: two-barrel Rochester E2ME. VIN Code: K or 9.

(**NOTE** California models used a Buick 231-cid V-6.)

CABALLERO OPTIONAL 305-CID, 150-HP V-8: 90-degree, overhead-valve. Cast-iron block and head. Bore and stroke: 3.74 x 3.48 in. Displacement: 305-cid (5.0 liters). Compression ratio: 8.6:1. Brake hp: 150 at 4000 rpm. Torque: 240 lbs.-ft. at 2400 rpm. Five main bearings. Hydraulic valve lifters. Carburetor: four-barrel Rochester E4ME. VIN Code: H.

CABALLERO OPTIONAL 350-CID, 161-HP V-8: 90-degree, overhead-valve. Cast-iron block and head. Bore and stroke: 4.00 x 3.48 in. Displacement: 350-cid (5.7 liters). Compression ratio: 8.6:1. Brake hp: 161 at 3800 rpm. Torque: 275 lbs.-ft. at 1600 rpm. Five main bearings. Hydraulic valve lifters. Induction: CFI. VIN code: 8.

CABALLERO OPTIONAL 350-CID, 105-HP DIESEL V-8: 90-degree, overhead-valve. Cast-iron block and head. Bore and stroke: 4.057 x 3.385 in. Displacement: 350-cid (5.7 liters). Compression ratio: 22.5:1. Brake hp: 105 at 3200 rpm. Torque: 200 lbs.-ft. at 1600 rpm. Five main bearings. Hydraulic valve lifters. Fuel injection. Olds-built. VIN Code: N.

CHASSIS

Wheelbase: 117.1 in. Overall length: 201.60 in. Width: 71.9 in. Height: 53.8 in. Front tread: 58.5 in. Rear tread: 57.8 in. Cargo box length from back of cab to top of tailgate: 79.5 in. Bed width between rear wheel housings: 45 in. Bed width above rear wheel housings: 59.5 in. Tires: G78-14B. Transmission: Automatic. Column-mounted gearshift lever. Rear axle: semi-floating. Hydraulic four-wheel brakes. Kelsey-Hayes pressed steel wheels.

OPTIONS

A01 all tinted glass. A02 tinted windshield. A31 power windows with electric control. AU3 power door locks. AV3 El Camino pickup box tie downs. BW2 deluxe body molding exterior decoration. BX8 front fender and body moldings. B32 color-keyed floor mats. B93 door edge guards. B3W preliminary price information. C60 manual air conditioning. CD4 intermittent windshield wipers and washers. D35 sport outside rearview mirrors. D55 center console. D73 pickup box hand rail. D91 Conquista package. F41 Sport suspension. G80 Positraction rear axle. G92 performance ratio rear axle. GH2 2.29:1 rear axle ratio. GU1 2.41:1 rear axle ratio. GU2 2.73:1 rear axle ratio. GU4 3.08:1 rear axle ratio. GU6 3.42:1 rear axle ratio. GT4 3.73:1 rear axle ratio. K05 engine block heater. K34 electric speed control. LC3 229-cid V-6 engine (standard Federal engine). LD5 231-cid V-6 engine (standard California engine). LF9 350-cid diesel V-8. LG4 305-cid V-8 engine. MXO automatic transmission with overdrive. MX1 Turbo-Hydra-Matic automatic transmission (standard). N18 simulated wire wheel covers. N23 22-gal. fuel tank. N33 tilt steering wheel. N95 wire wheel covers. NA6 alternate requirements emission system. QFT P205-75R14B steel-belted radial black-sidewall tires. QJR P205-75R14B steel-belted radial white-stripe tires. QSA P205-75R14B steel-belted radial white-letter tires. TR9 lamp group. TT5 tungsten quartz halogen headlights. U14 special instrumentation gauge package. U35 electric clock. U58 AM/FM push-button stereo. U63 AM push-button radio. U73 fixed antenna. UA1 heavy-duty battery. UF7 instrument panel gauge with trip odometer. UN3 AM/FM stereo cassette radio less clock. V08 heavy-duty radiator. V10 cold climate package. VE5 front and rear bumper impact strips. YF5 California emission requirements. YE7 Diablo package. ZJ7 special wheel package with hubcap and trim rings.

OPTION INSTALLATION RATES

Automatic transmission (100 percent). V-8 gas engine (79.2 percent). V-6 gas engine (19.9 percent). Diesel V-8 engine (0.9 percent). Automatic transmission (100 percent). Base exterior/exterior trim package (99 percent). Level 2 exterior/exterior trim package (1 percent). Power front disc brakes (100 percent). Positraction (16.8 percent). Steel-belted radial tires (100 percent). Power steering (100 percent). Bucket seats (8 percent). Tinted glass (43.4 percent). Air conditioning (92.3 percent). Cruise control (82.1 percent). Adjustable steering column (89.2 percent). Power windows (60.8 percent). Power door locks (60.5 percent). AM radio (6.4 percent). AM/FM radio (7.4 percent). Stereo (27.8 percent). Cassette player (54.1 percent).

HISTORICAL FOOTNOTES

Donald J. Atwood continued as executive of the Truck & Bus Group. He was also a General Motors vice president. Caballero calendar-year sales were 2,702 units. Model-year sales were 2,751.

CABALLERO

The Caballero Diablo SS had a two-tone paint scheme without the body side moldings.

The 1985 Caballero was promoted as "a truck you can live with." There were no drastic styling changes this year, but nine new solid paint colors were offered along with three carryover shades. New stainless steel wheel covers had a brush-finished center with GMC lettering. All-new interior colors were Blue, Light Green, Saddle, Maroon and Gray. There was also a new standard velour cloth upholstery trim. Under the hood, Caballero buyers could now get a 4.3-liter Vortec V-6 as standard equipment. The 5.0-liter V-8 had improvements such as a 9.5:1 compression ratio and electronic spark control to help prevent spark knock. A new higher-capacity generator was automatically included on air-conditioned trucks.

I.D. NUMBERS

VIN embossed on the top left-hand side of the instrument panel and visible through the windshield. Beginning this year, GM used its light-duty truck, multipurpose passenger vehicle and incomplete vehicle VIN coding system to code the Caballero, except that Caballero engine codes were those used for passenger cars. The first symbol designates the country of origin: 3=Mexico. The second symbol identifies the manufacturer: G=General Motors. The third symbol indicates the make and type: T=GMC truck. The fourth symbol indicates the GVWR. The fifth symbol indicates the series: W=Caballero. The sixth and seventh symbols indicate body type 80=sedan-pickup. The eighth symbol indicates engine (net hp): Z=RPO LB4 262-cid/130-hp V-6, H=RPO LG4 305-cid/165hp V-8. The ninth symbol is a check digit. The 10th symbol designates the model year: F=1985. The 11th symbol designates the assembly plant location: S=Ramos Arizpe, Mexico. The last six symbols are the sequential unit production number at the specific factory.

COLORS

(11) White, (12) Silver Metallic, (15) Medium Gray Metallic, (19) Black, (25) Light Blue Metallic, (31) Dark Blue Metallic, (43) Light Green Metallic, (46) Medium Green Metallic, (58) Light Brown Metallic, (59) Cream

Beige, (62) Medium Brown Metallic and (79) Dark Maroon Metallic.

CABALLERO — SERIES W — V-6/V-8

features for included an ice-cube-tray grille, dual rectangular headlamps, bright grille moldings, a bright windshield molding, a bright rear window molding, a bright belt line bead molding, pickup box side rail moldings, bright rocker panel moldings, bright wheel opening moldings, bright drip rail moldings, chromed front and rear bumpers, a chromed left-hand outside rearview mirror, a new "4.3 Fuel Injection" nameplate on the left side, a selection of 12 solid paint colors (nine of them new), a dual-note horn, fluidic windshield washers, two-speed electric windshield wipers with concealed blades and arms, a deep-foam notchback-style front bench seat in cloth or vinyl, full-floor carpeting, a color-styled instrument panel with new simulated leather-grain appliqué, a simulated leather-grain steering wheel shroud, a lighted ash tray, a cigarette lighter, dual padded sunshades, an energy-absorbing steering column with "smart switch," an outside air heater and defogger system, an anti-theft ignition key warning buzzer and steering column lock, an inside hood release, door-actuated dome and courtesy lights, padded armrests, a lighted glove compartment with lock, a foam-backed cloth headliner, concealed storage for the spare tire and luggage, a color-keyed steering wheel, bright wheel covers, self-adjusting low-drag power front disc brakes with wear indicators, steel-belted radial tires, power rear drum brakes, a 355 cold-cranking amps Freedom II battery, a High Energy ignition system, a 37-amp Delcotron generator, a computer-selected full-coil suspension system with air-adjustable shocks, power steering, a three-speed automatic transmission, an engine coolant recovery system, a 4.3-liter V-6 and the GM Computer Command Control engine management system. A 5.0-liter V-8 was optional. New interior color offerings were blue, light green, saddle, maroon and gray and the standard trim changed to velour cloth.

Model Number	Body/Style Number	Body Type & Seating	Factory Price	Shipping Weight	Production Total
CABALLERO SERIES W (V-6)					
W	80	pickup	—	—	Note 1
CABALLERO SERIES W (305-CID V-8)					
W	80	pickup	$8,933	3,252 lbs.	Note 1

CABALLERO DIABLO SS — SERIES W + YE7 — V-8

The Caballero Diablo SS featured a large front air dam, a Diablo nameplate on the instrument panel, black quarter window moldings, rally wheels with bright trim rings, dual Sport-style mirrors and a two-tone paint scheme with an accent color along the lower body sides highlighted by color-keyed pin striping on the paint break.

Model Number	Body/Style Number	Body Type & Seating	Factory Price	Shipping Weight	Production Total
W	80	pickup	$9,198	3,263 lbs.	Note 1

NOTE 1: Total Caballero production was 3,320.

MODEL OPTIONS

AMARILLO PACKAGE: The 1984 Amarillo package was offered in striking two-tone paint combinations. The basic body color appeared on the roof, the upper portion of the pickup box, the lower body sides and on the tailgate. The center section of the body side, the hood and the lower portion of the tailgate were set off by a special accent color. Also featured were bright paint break moldings along the upper side of the pickup box and tailgate, bright moldings along the lower body sides and wheel house moldings. An Amarillo decal was placed on the upper right tailgate and above the glove box door.

ENGINES

CABALLERO BASE V-6: 90-degree, overhead-valve V-6. Cast-iron block and head. Bore and stroke: 4.00 x 3.43 in. Displacement: 262-cid (4.3 liters). Compression ratio: 9.3:1. Brake hp: 130 at 3600 rpm. Torque: 235 lbs.-ft. at 2400 rpm. Four main bearings. Hydraulic valve lifters. Induction: Throttle Body Injection (TBI). VIN

The Amarillo package was again a model option for 1984. The package included decals, two-tone paint schemes and paint-break moldings.

Code: Z.

CABALLERO OPTIONAL V-8: 90-degree, overhead-valve V-8. Cast-iron block and head. Bore and stroke: 3.74 x 3.48 in. Displacement: 305-cid (5.0 liters). Compression ratio: 8.6:1. Brake hp: 165 at 4000 rpm. Torque: 255 lbs.-ft. at 2400 rpm. Five main bearings. Hydraulic valve lifters. Carburetor: four-barrel Rochester E4ME. VIN Code: H.

CHASSIS

Wheelbase: 117.1 in. Overall length: 201.60 in. Width: 71.9 in. Height: 53.8 in. Front tread: 58.5 in. Rear tread: 57.8 in. Cargo box length from back of cab to top of tailgate: 79.5 in. Bed width between rear wheel housings: 45 in. Bed width above rear wheel housings: 59.5 in. Tires: P205-75R14. Transmission: Automatic. Rear axle: semi-floating. Hydraulic four-wheel brakes. Kelsey-Hayes pressed steel wheels.

OPTIONS

A01 all tinted glass. A02 tinted windshield. A31 power windows with electric control. AU3 power door locks. AV3 El Camino pickup box tie downs. B32 color-keyed floor mats. B93 door edge guards. B3W preliminary price information. BW2 deluxe body molding exterior decoration. BX8 front fender and body moldings. C60 manual air conditioning. CD4 intermittent windshield wipers and washers. D35 Sport outside rearview mirrors. D55 center console. D73 pickup box hand rail. D91 Conquista package. F41 Sport suspension. G80 Positraction rear axle. G92 performance ratio rear axle. GH2 2.29:1 rear axle ratio. GU1 2.41:1 rear axle ratio. GM8 2.56:1 rear axle ratio. GU2 2.73:1 rear axle ratio. GU4 3.08:1 rear axle ratio. GU6 3.42:1 rear axle ratio. GT4 3.73:1 rear axle ratio. K05 engine block heater. K34 electric speed control. LB4 4.3-liter V-6. LG4 305-cid V-8 engine. MXO automatic transmission with overdrive. MX1 Turbo-Hydra-Matic automatic transmission (standard). N18 simulated wire wheel covers. N23 22-gal. fuel tank. N33 tilt steering wheel. N95 wire wheel covers. NA6 alternate requirements emission system. QFT P205-75R14B steel-belted radial black sidewall tires. QJR P205-75R14B steel-belted radial white stripe tires. QSA P205-75R14B steel-belted radial white letter tires. TR9 lamp group. TT4 tungsten quartz halogen headlights. U14 special instrumentation gauge package. U35 electric clock. U58 AM/FM push-button stereo. U63 AM push-button radio. U73 fixed antenna. UA1 heavy-duty battery. UF7 instrument panel gauge with trip odometer. UN3 AM/FM stereo cassette radio less clock. UX1 AM-FM stereo cassette radio with clock. V08 heavy-duty radiator. V30 bumper guards. VE5 front and rear bumper impact strips. YF5 California emission requirements. YE7 Diablo SS package. ZJ7 special wheel package with hub cap and trim rings.

OPTION INSTALLATION RATES

V-8 gas engine (77.3 percent). V-6 gas engine (22.7 percent). Automatic transmission (100 percent). Styled wheels (87.1 percent). Base exterior/exterior trim package (46.1 percent). Level 2 exterior/exterior trim package (34.8 percent). Level 3 exterior/exterior trim package (19.1 percent). Power front disc brakes (100 percent). Power steering (100 Percent). Positraction (16.3 percent). Steel-belted radial tires (100 Percent). Air conditioning (94.8 percent). Bucket seats (13 percent). Tinted glass (97.6 Percent). Cruise control (71 percent). Adjustable steering column (84.6 percent). Power windows (50.3 percent). Power door locks (49.2 percent). AM radio (5.1 percent). AM/FM radio (2.3 percent). Stereo (28.3 percent). Cassette player (51.8 percent).

HISTORICAL FOOTNOTES

Donald J. Atwood continued as executive of the Truck & Bus Group. He was also a General Motors vice president. Caballero calendar-year sales were 2,605 units. Model-year sales were 2,504. The Caballero was built in Mexico.

The 1986 Caballero featured a new instrument panel and revised gauge cluster graphics to modernize it. New Electronically Tuned Receiver (ETR) radios offered Caballero buyers a new experience in automotive audio systems with channelized tuning that electronically locked onto a frequency for clear, crisp sound.

The Caballero continued to offer 35.5 cubic feet or cargo capacity and a 1,250-lb. payload. Also new were a black-finished left-hand outside rearview mirror, two new solid paint colors, a new color-keyed steering wheel and CL (custom level) interior trims with pillow-back seats. A new "service engine soon" light warned Caballero owners whenever their engine needed attention.

I.D. NUMBERS

VIN embossed on the top left-hand side of the instrument panel and visible through the windshield. Beginning this year, GM used its light-duty truck, multipurpose passenger vehicle and incomplete vehicle VIN coding system to code the Caballero, except that Caballero engine codes were those used for passenger cars. The first symbol designates the country of origin: 3=Mexico. The second symbol identifies the manufacturer: G=General Motors. The third symbol indicates the make and type: T=GMC truck. The fourth symbol indicates the GVWR. The fifth symbol indicates the series: W=-Caballero. The sixth and seventh symbols indicate body type 80=sedan-pickup. The eighth symbol indicates

1986

The Amarillo package sold for $225 in 1986. The base Caballero with a V-8 was priced at $9,623.

engine (net hp): Z=RPO LB4 262-cid/130-hp V-6, H=RPO LG4 305-cid/165-hp V-8. The ninth symbol is a check digit. The 10th symbol designates the model year: G=1986. The 11th symbol designates the assembly plant location: S=Ramos Arizpe, Mexico. The last six symbols are the sequential unit production number at the specific factory.

COLORS

White, Silver Metallic, Medium Gray Metallic, Light Blue Metallic, Dark Blue Metallic, Light Green Metallic, Maroon Metallic, Light Brown Metallic, Yellow Beige, Medium Brown Metallic, dark Maroon Metallic and Black.

CABALLERO — SERIES W — V-6/V-8

Standard features for included an ice-cube-tray grille, dual rectangular headlamps, bright grille moldings, a bright windshield molding, a bright rear window molding, a bright belt line bead molding, pickup box side rail moldings, bright rocker panel moldings, bright wheel opening moldings, bright drip rail moldings, chromed front and rear bumpers, a new black left-hand outside rearview mirror, a selection of 12 solid paint colors (two of them new), a dual-note horn, fluidic windshield washers, two-speed electric windshield wipers with concealed blades and arms, bright wheel covers, a deep-foam notchback-style front bench seat with fold-down center armrest, color-keyed full-floor carpeting, a lighted ash tray, a cigarette lighter, dual padded sunshades, an energy-absorbing steering column with "smart switch," an outside air heater and defogger system, an anti-theft ignition key warning buzzer and steering column lock, an inside hood release, door-actuated dome and courtesy lights, padded armrests, a lighted glove compartment with lock, a foam-backed cloth headliner, concealed storage for the spare tire and luggage, a color-keyed steering wheel, Quiet Sound interior insulation, self-adjusting low-drag power front disc brakes with wear indicators, steel-belted radial tires, power rear drum brakes, a 355 cold-cranking amps Freedom II battery, a High Energy ignition system, a 37-amp Delcotron generator, a computer-selected full-coil suspension system with air-adjustable shocks, power steering, a three-speed automatic transmission, an engine coolant recovery system, a 4.3-liter V-6 and the GM Computer Command Control engine management system. A 5.0-liter V-8 was optional. A new standard knit velour cloth interior was offered in five colors and the optional vinyl trim came in four colors.

Model Number	Body/Style Number	Body Type & Seating	Factory Price	Shipping Weight	Production Total
CABALLERO SERIES W (V-6)					
W	80	pickup	—	—	Note 1
CABALLERO SERIES W (305-CID V-8)					
W	80	pickup	$9,623	3,234 lbs.	Note 1

CABALLERO

CABALLERO DIABLO SS SERIES W + YE7 — V-8

The Caballero Diablo SS featured a large front air dam, a Diablo nameplate on the instrument panel, black quarter window moldings, rally wheels with bright trim rings, dual Sport-style mirrors and a two-tone paint scheme with an accent color along the lower body sides highlighted by color-keyed pin striping on the paint break.

Model Number	Body/Style Number	Body Type & Seating	Factory Price	Shipping Weight	Production Total
W	80	pickup	$9,936	3,239 lbs.	Note 1

NOTE 1: Total Caballero production was 2,192.

MODEL OPTIONS

AMARILLO PACKAGE: The 1984 Amarillo package was offered in striking two-tone paint combinations. The basic body color appeared on the roof, the upper portion of the pickup box, the lower body sides and on the tailgate. The center section of the body side, the hood and the lower portion of the tailgate were set off by a special accent color. Also featured were bright paint break moldings along the upper side of the pickup box and tailgate, bright moldings along the lower body sides and wheel house moldings. An Amarillo decal was placed on the upper right tailgate and above the glove box door. This package sold for $225 in 1986.

ENGINES

CABALLERO BASE 262-CID, 140-HP V-6: 90-degree, overhead-valve. Cast-iron block and head. Bore and stroke: 4.00 x 3.43 in. Displacement: 262-cid (4.3 liters). Compression ratio: 9.3:1. Brake hp: 140 at 4000 rpm. Torque: 225 lbs.-ft. at 2000 rpm. Four main bearings. Hydraulic valve lifters. Induction: Throttle Body Injection (TBI). VIN Code: Z.

CABALLERO OPTIONAL 305-CID, 150-HP V-8: 90-degree, overhead-valve. Cast-iron block and head. Bore and stroke: 3.74 x 3.48 in. Displacement: 305-cid (5.0 liters). Compression ratio: 8.6:1. Brake hp: 150 at 4000 rpm. Torque: 240 lbs.-ft. at 2000 rpm. Five main bearings. Hydraulic valve lifters. Carburetor: four-barrel Rochester E4ME. VIN Code: H.

CHASSIS

Wheelbase: 117.1 in. Overall length: 201.60 in. Width: 71.9 in. Height: 53.8 in. Front tread: 58.5 in. Rear tread: 57.8 in. Cargo box length from back of cab to top of tailgate: 79.5 in. Bed width between rear wheel housings: 45 in. Bed width above rear wheel housings: 59.5 in. Tires: P205-75R14. Transmission: Automatic. Rear axle: semi-floating. Hydraulic four-wheel brakes. Kelsey-Hayes pressed steel wheels.

OPTIONS

A01 all tinted glass. A02 tinted windshield. A31 power windows with electric control. A65 bench seat. AM6 55/45 cloth seat. AR9 bucket seats. AU3 power door locks. AV3 El Camino pickup box tie downs. B32 color-keyed floor mats. B93 door edge guards. B3W preliminary price information. BW2 Deluxe body molding exterior decoration. BX8 front fender and body moldings. C60 manual air conditioning. CD4 intermittent wind-

The Diablo was billed as the "dashing" model in the Caballero line.

shield wipers and washers. D35 sport outside rearview mirrors. D55 center console. D73 pickup box hand rail. D91 Conquista package. F41 Sport suspension. G80 Positraction rear axle. G92 performance ratio rear axle. GH2 2.29:1 rear axle ratio. GU1 2.41:1 rear axle ratio. GM8 2.56:1 rear axle ratio. GU2 2.73:1 rear axle ratio. GU4 3.08:1 rear axle ratio. GU6 3.42:1 rear axle ratio. GT4 3.73:1 rear axle ratio. K05 engine block heater. K34 electric speed control. LB4 4.3-liter V-6. LG4 305-cid V-8 engine. MXO automatic transmission with overdrive. MX1 Turbo-Hydra-Matic automatic transmission (standard). N18 simulated wire wheel covers. N23 22-gal. fuel tank. N33 Tilt steering wheel. N91 wire wheel covers. QFT P205-75R14B steel-belted radial black-sidewall tires. QJR P205-75R14B steel-belted radial white-stripe tires. QSA P205-75R14B steel-belted radial white-letter tires. TR9 lamp group. TT4 tungsten quartz halogen headlights. U16 tachometer. U39 gauge package with odometer. U63 AM push-button radio. U73 fixed antenna. UA1 heavy-duty battery. UK4 AM-FM seek-and-scan stereo. UM6 AM/FM seek-and-scan stereo with cassette and clock, UM7 AM/FM seek-and-scan stereo with cassette. UX1 AM-FM seek-and-scan stereo cassette radio with clock. V08 heavy-duty cooling. V30 bumper guards. VE5 front and rear bumper impact strips. YF5 California emission requirements. YE7 Diablo SS package. ZJ7 Rallye-wheel package.

OPTION INSTALLATION RATES

V-8 gas engine (76.7 percent). V-6 gas engine (23.3 percent). Automatic transmission (100 percent). Base exterior/exterior trim package (59.9 percent). Level 2 exterior/exterior trim package (40.1 percent). Power front disc brakes (100 percent). Power steering (100 percent). Positraction (19.1 percent). Steel-belted radial tires (100 percent). Air conditioning (97.5 percent). Tinted glass (98.5 percent). Cruise control (84.2 percent). Adjustable steering column (93.9 percent). Power windows (71.9 percent). Power door locks (70.5 percent). AM radio (3.1 percent). ETR radio (0.3 percent). ETR stereo (21.9 percent). ETR stereo with cassette (71.5 percent).

HISTORICAL FOOTNOTES

John D. Rock became manager of Truck & Coach Operations. Caballero calendar-year sales were 2,542 units. Model-year sales were 2,795. The Caballero was built in Mexico.

The 1987 Caballero underwent minimal change in its last year on the market. The G-car-based sedan-pickup was eliminated by the start of model-year 1988 and left only a minor gap in the GMC product lineup.

I.D. NUMBERS

VIN embossed on the top left-hand side of the instrument panel and visible through the windshield. Beginning this year, GM used its light-duty truck, multipurpose passenger vehicle and incomplete vehicle VIN coding system to code the Caballero, except that Caballero engine codes were those used for passenger cars. The first symbol designates the country of origin: 3=Mexico. The second symbol identifies the manufacturer: G=General Motors. The third symbol indicates the make and type: T=GMC truck. The fourth symbol indicates the GVWR. The fifth symbol indicates the series: W=Caballero. The sixth and seventh symbols indicate body type 80=sedan-pickup. The eighth symbol indicates engine (net hp): Z=RPO LB4 262-cid/130-hp V-6, H=RPO LG4 305-cid/165hp V-8. The ninth symbol is a check digit. The 10th symbol designates the model year: G=1987. The 11th symbol designates the assembly plant location: S=Ramos Arizpe, Mexico. The last six symbols are the sequential unit production number at the specific factory.

COLORS

Black, Medium Gray Metallic, Light Blue Metallic, Dark Blue Metallic, Light Brown Metallic, Medium Brown Metallic, Light Green Metallic, Maroon Metallic, Dark Maroon Metallic, Silver Metallic, White, and Yellow Beige.

CABALLERO — SERIES W — V-6/V-8

Standard features for included an ice-cube-tray grille, dual rectangular headlamps, bright grille moldings, a bright windshield molding, a bright rear window molding, a bright beltline bead molding, pickup box side rail moldings, bright rocker panel moldings, bright wheel opening moldings, bright drip rail moldings, chromed front and rear bumpers, a black left-hand outside rearview mirror, a selection of 12 solid paint colors, a dual-note horn, fluidic windshield washers, two-speed electric windshield wipers with concealed blades and arms, bright wheel covers, a deep-foam notchback-style front bench seat with fold-down center armrest, color-keyed full-floor carpeting, a lighted ash tray, a cigarette lighter, dual padded sunshades, an energy-absorbing steering column with "smart switch," an outside air heater and defogger system, an anti-theft ignition key warning buzzer and steering column lock, an inside hood release, door-actuated dome and courtesy lights, padded armrests, a lighted glove compartment with lock, a foam-backed cloth headliner, concealed storage for the spare tire and luggage, a color-keyed steering wheel, Quiet Sound interior insulation, self-adjusting low-drag power front disc brakes with wear indicators, steel-belted radial tires, power rear drum brakes, a 355 cold-cranking amps Freedom II battery, a High Energy ignition system, a 37-amp Delcotron generator, a computer-selected full-coil suspension system with air-adjustable shocks, power steering, a three-speed automatic transmission, an engine coolant recovery system, a 4.3-liter V-6 and the GM Computer Command Control engine management system. A 5.0-liter V-8 was optional. The standard interior featured knit velour cloth. Vinyl trim was optional.

Model Number	Body/Style Number	Body Type & Seating	Factory Price	Shipping Weight	Production Total
CABALLERO SERIES W (V-6)					
W	80	pickup	—	—	Note 1
CABALLERO SERIES W (305-CID V-8)					
W	80	pickup	$10,504	3,239 lbs.	Note 1

CABALLERO DIABLO SS SERIES W + YE7 — V-8

The Caballero Diablo SS featured a large front air dam, a Diablo nameplate on the instrument panel, black quarter window moldings, Rally wheels with bright trim rings, dual Sport-style mirrors and a two-tone paint scheme with an accent color along the lower body sides highlighted by color-keyed pin striping on the paint break.

Model Number	Body/Style Number	Body Type & Seating	Factory Price	Shipping Weight	Production Total
W	80	pickup	$10,835	3,244 lbs.	Note 1

NOTE 1 Total Caballero production was 1,907.

MODEL OPTIONS

AMARILLO PACKAGE: The Amarillo package was offered in striking two-tone paint combinations. The basic body color appeared on the roof, the upper portion of the pickup box, the lower body sides and on the tailgate. The center section of the body side, the hood and the lower portion of the tailgate were set off by a special accent color. Also featured were bright paint break moldings along the upper side of the pickup box and tailgate, bright moldings along the lower body sides and wheel house moldings. An Amarillo decal was placed on the upper right tailgate and above the glove box door. This package sold for $238 in 1987.

ENGINES

CABALLERO BASE V-6: 90-degree, overhead-valve. Cast-iron block and head. Bore and stroke: 4.00 x 3.43 in. Displacement: 262-cid (4.3 liters). Compression ratio: 9.3:1. Brake hp: 140 at 4000 rpm. Torque: 225 lbs.-ft. at 2000 rpm. Four main bearings. Hydraulic valve lifters. Induction: Throttle Body Injection (TBI). VIN Code: Z.

CABALLERO OPTIONAL V-8: 90-degree, overhead-valve. Cast-iron block and head. Bore and stroke: 3.74 x 3.48 in. Displacement: 305-cid (5.0 liters). Compression ratio: 8.6:1. Brake hp: 150 at 4000 rpm. Torque: 240 lbs.-ft. at 2000 rpm. Five main bearings. Hydraulic valve lifters. Carburetor: four-barrel Rochester E4ME. VIN Code: H.

CHASSIS

Wheelbase: 117.1 in. Overall length: 201.60 in. Width: 71.9 in. Height: 53.8 in. Front tread: 58.5 in. Rear tread: 57.8 in. Cargo box length from back of cab to top of tailgate: 79.5 inches. Bed width between rear wheel housings: 45 in. Bed width above rear wheel housings: 59.5 in. Tires: P205-75R14. Transmission: Automatic. Rear axle: semi-floating. Hydraulic four-wheel brakes. Kelsey-Hayes pressed steel wheels.

OPTIONS

A01 all tinted glass. A02 tinted windshield. A31 power windows with electric control. A65 bench seat. AM6 55/45 cloth seat. AR9 bucket seats. AU3 power door locks. AV3 pickup box tie downs. B32 color-keyed floor mats. B93 door edge guards. B3W preliminary price information. BW2 Deluxe body molding exterior decoration. BX8 front fender and body moldings. C60 manual air conditioning. CD4 intermittent windshield wipers and washers. D35 sport outside rearview mirrors. D55 center console. D73 pickup box hand rail. F41 sport suspension. G80 Positraction rear axle. G92 performance ratio rear axle. G72 2.14:1 rear axle ratio. GH2 2.29:1 rear axle ratio. GU1 2.41:1 rear axle ratio. GM8 2.56:1 rear axle ratio. GU2 2.73:1 rear axle ratio. GU4 3.08:1 rear axle ratio. GU5 3.23:1 rear axle ratio. GU6 3.42:1 rear axle ratio. GT4 3.73:1 rear axle ratio. K05 engine block heater. K34 electric speed control. LB4 4.3-liter V-6. LG4 305-cid V-8 engine. MXO automatic transmission with overdrive. MX1 Turbo-Hydra-Matic automatic transmission (standard). N23 22-gal. fuel tank. N33 tilt steering wheel. N91 wire wheel covers. QFT P205-75R14B steel-belted radial black-sidewall tires. QJR P205-75R14B steel-belted radial white stripe tires. QSA P205-75R14B steel-belted radial white letter tires. TR9 lamp group. TT4 tungsten quartz halogen headlights. U16 tachometer. U39 gauge package with odometer. U63 AM push-button radio. U73 fixed antenna. UA1 heavy-duty battery. UK4 AM-FM seek-and-scan stereo. UM6 AM/FM seek-and-scan stereo with cassette and clock. UM7 AM/FM seek-and-scan stereo with cassette. UX1 AM-FM seek-and-scan stereo cassette radio with clock. V08 heavy-duty cooling. V30 bumper guards. VE5 front and rear bumper impact strips. YF5 California emission requirements. YE7 Diablo SS package. ZJ7 Rallye wheel package.

OPTION INSTALLATION RATES

V-8 gas engine (80 percent). V-6 gas engine (20 percent). Automatic transmission (100 percent). Power steering (100 percent). Power front disc brakes (100 percent). Positraction (22.6 percent). Steel-belted radial tires (100 percent). Air conditioning (98.5 percent). Tinted glass (100 percent). Power windows (87.3 percent). Power door locks (86.9 percent). Base exterior/exterior trim package (33 percent). Level 2 exterior/exterior trim package (28.3 percent). Level 3 exterior/exterior trim package (38.7 percent). ETR AM radio (1.3 percent). ETR AM/FM stereo (20.6 percent). Cassette radio (61.1 percent). Premium sound system (15 percent). Cruise control (86.9 percent). Adjustable steering column (92.9 percent). Delay wipers (87.2 percent). Digital clock (65.9 percent). Left-hand remote-control mirror (97.6 percent). Right-hand remote-control mirror (38.6 percent).

HISTORICAL FOOTNOTES

Calendar-year sales of the Mexican-built Caballero were 1,705 units. Model-year sales were 1,882.

Price Guide

Vehicle Condition Scale

1: **Excellent:** Restored to current maximum professional standards of quality in every area, or perfect original with components operating and apearing as new. A 95-plus point show car that is not driven.

2: **Fine:** Well-restored or a combination of superior restoration and excellent original parts. Also, extremely well-maintained original vehicle showing minimal wear.

3: **Very Good:** Complete operable original or older restoration. Also, a very good amateur restoration, all presentable and serviceable inside and out. Plus, a combination of well-done restoration and good operable components or a partially restored car with all parts necessary to compete and/or valuable NOS parts.

4: **Good:** A driveable vehicle needing no or only minor work to be functional. Also, a deteriorated restoration or a very poor amateur restoration. All components may need restoration to be "excellent," but the car is mostly useable "as is."

5. **Restorable:** Needs complete restoration of body, chassis and interior. May or may not be running, but isn't weathered, wrecked or stripped to the point of being useful only for parts.

6. **Parts car:** May or may not be running, but is weathered, wrecked and/or stripped to the point of being useful primarily for parts.

Chevelle and Malibu

1964 Chevelle

	6	5	4	3	2	1
2d Sed	450	1,400	2,300	4,650	8,100	11,600
4d Sed	450	1,400	2,300	4,600	8,050	11,500
2d Sta Wag	600	1,850	3,100	6,150	10,800	15,400
4d Sta Wag	600	1,800	3,050	6,100	10,600	15,200

1964 Malibu Series, V-8

	6	5	4	3	2	1
4d Sed	450	1,400	2,300	4,650	8,100	11,600
2d HT*	900	2,650	4,400	8,800	15,400	22,000
2d Conv*	1,300	3,950	6,600	13,200	23,100	33,000
4d Sta Wag	600	1,800	3,000	6,000	10,500	15,000

NOTE: Add 15 percent for Super Sport option. Deduct 10 percent for 6-cyl.

1965 Chevelle

	6	5	4	3	2	1
2d Sed	450	1,400	2,300	4,600	8,050	11,500
4d Sed	450	1,350	2,300	4,550	8,000	11,400
2d Sta Wag	600	1,850	3,100	6,200	10,900	15,500
4d Sta Wag	600	1,850	3,100	6,200	10,900	15,500

1965 Malibu, V-8

	6	5	4	3	2	1
4d Sed	450	1,400	2,350	4,700	8,250	11,800
2d HT	900	2,750	4,600	9,200	16,100	23,000
2d Conv	1,350	4,100	6,800	13,600	23,800	34,000
4d Sta Wag	600	1,800	3,000	6,050	10,600	15,100

1969 Malibu four-door sedan

Price Guide

1965 Malibu Super Sport, V-8

	6	5	4	3	2	1
2d HT	1,100	3,250	5,400	10,800	18,900	27,000
2d Conv	1,450	4,300	7,200	14,400	25,200	36,000

NOTE: Add 100 percent for RPO Z16 SS 396 option on hardtop only. Add 35 percent for 396 cid, 325 hp.

1966 Chevelle

	6	5	4	3	2	1
2d Sed	450	1,400	2,300	4,600	8,050	11,500
4d Sed	450	1,350	2,300	4,550	8,000	11,400
4d Sta Wag	450	1,400	2,350	4,700	8,200	11,700

1971 Chevelle

245

1968 Malibu sport coupe

1966 Malibu, V-8

	6	5	4	3	2	1
4d Sed	450	1,400	2,350	4,700	8,250	11,800
4d HT	500	1,450	2,400	4,800	8,400	12,000
2d HT	900	2,750	4,600	9,200	16,100	23,000
2d Conv	1,200	3,600	6,000	12,000	21,000	30,000
4d Sta Wag	500	1,450	2,400	4,800	8,400	12,000

1967 Chevelle 300, V-8

	6	5	4	3	2	1
2d Sed	450	1,400	2,300	4,600	8,050	11,500
4d Sed	450	1,350	2,300	4,550	8,000	11,400

1967 Chevelle 300 DeLuxe, V-8

	6	5	4	3	2	1
2d Sed	450	1,400	2,350	4,700	8,250	11,800
4d Sed	450	1,400	2,350	4,700	8,200	11,700
4d Sta Wag	600	1,800	3,000	6,000	10,500	15,000

1967 Chevelle Malibu, V-8

	6	5	4	3	2	1
4d Sed	500	1,450	2,400	4,800	8,400	12,000
4d HT	600	1,800	3,000	6,000	10,500	15,000
2d HT	850	2,500	4,200	8,400	14,700	21,000
2d Conv	1,150	3,500	5,800	11,600	20,300	29,000
4d Sta Wag	500	1,500	2,500	5,000	8,750	12,500

NOTE: Add 50 percent for 327 cid, 325 hp.

1967 Chevelle Concours, V-8

	6	5	4	3	2	1
4d Sta Wag	600	1,850	3,100	6,200	10,900	15,500

1967 Chevelle Super Sport 396

	6	5	4	3	2	1
2d HT	1,300	3,850	6,400	12,800	22,400	32,000
2d Conv	1,450	4,300	7,200	14,400	25,200	36,000

NOTE: Add 10 percent for 396 cid, 350 hp. Add 30 percent for 396 cid, 375 hp.

1968 Chevelle 300

	6	5	4	3	2	1
2d Sed	350	1,000	1,700	3,350	5,900	8,400
4d Sta Wag	350	1,000	1,700	3,400	5,950	8,500

1968 Chevelle 300 DeLuxe

	6	5	4	3	2	1
4d Sed	350	1,000	1,700	3,350	5,900	8,400
4d HT	350	1,050	1,800	3,550	6,250	8,900
2d Cpe	350	1,000	1,700	3,400	5,950	8,500
4d Sta Wag	450	1,300	2,200	4,400	7,700	11,000

1968 Chevelle Malibu

	6	5	4	3	2	1
4d Sed	350	1,000	1,700	3,400	5,950	8,500
4d HT	450	1,400	2,300	4,600	8,050	11,500
2d HT	750	2,300	3,800	7,600	13,300	19,000
2d Conv	1,150	3,500	5,800	11,600	20,300	29,000
4d Sta Wag	450	1,400	2,300	4,600	8,050	11,500

NOTE: Add 10 percent for 396 cid, 350 hp. Add 30 percent for 396 cid, 375 hp. Add 5 percent for Concourse Package.

1968 Chevelle Concourse Estate

	6	5	4	3	2	1
4d Sta Wag	500	1,450	2,400	4,800	8,400	12,000

1968 Chevelle SS 396

	6	5	4	3	2	1
2d HT	1,100	3,350	5,600	11,200	19,600	28,000
2d Conv	1,400	4,200	7,000	14,000	24,500	35,000

1968 Chevelle 300

	6	5	4	3	2	1

NOTE: Only 1,270 Nova 4s were built in 1968.

1969 Chevelle 300 DeLuxe

	6	5	4	3	2	1
4d Sed	300	850	1,400	2,800	4,900	7,000
2d HT	450	1,400	2,300	4,600	8,050	11,500
2d Cpe	300	900	1,500	3,000	5,250	7,500
4d Nomad	300	900	1,550	3,100	5,400	7,700
4d Dual Nom	300	950	1,600	3,200	5,600	8,000
4d GB Wag	300	900	1,500	3,000	5,250	7,500
4d 6P GB						
Dual Wag	300	900	1,500	3,000	5,250	7,500
4d 9P GB						
Dual Wag	300	900	1,500	3,050	5,300	7,600

1966 Chevelle convertible

1969 Chevelle Malibu, Concourse, V-8

	6	5	4	3	2	1
4d Sed	300	900	1,500	3,000	5,250	7,500
4d HT	300	950	1,600	3,200	5,600	8,000
2d HT	700	2,150	3,600	7,200	12,600	18,000
2d Conv	1,000	3,000	5,000	10,000	17,500	25,000
4d HT	450	1,400	2,300	4,600	8,050	11,500
4d 9P Estate	300	900	1,500	3,050	5,300	7,600
4d 6P Estate	300	900	1,500	3,000	5,250	7,500

NOTE: Add 10 percent for 396 cid, 350 hp. Add 30 percent for 396 cid, 375 hp.

1969 Chevelle Malibu SS 396

	6	5	4	3	2	1
2d HT	1,000	3,000	5,000	10,000	17,500	25,000
2d Conv	1,250	3,700	6,200	12,400	21,700	31,000

NOTE: Add 60 percent for Yenko hardtop.

1970 Chevelle

	6	5	4	3	2	1
2d Cpe	350	1,050	1,750	3,500	6,150	8,800
4d Sed	300	900	1,500	3,000	5,250	7,500
4d Nomad	300	950	1,600	3,200	5,600	8,000

1970 Malibu, V-8

	6	5	4	3	2	1
4d Sed	300	900	1,500	3,050	5,300	7,600
4d HT	300	950	1,600	3,200	5,600	8,000
2d HT	700	2,050	3,400	6,800	11,900	17,000
2d Conv	950	2,900	4,800	9,600	16,800	24,000
4d Concourse Est Wag	350	1,050	1,700	3,450	6,000	8,600

1970 Chevelle Malibu SS 396

	6	5	4	3	2	1
2d HT	1,100	3,250	5,400	10,800	18,900	27,000
2d Conv	1,300	3,850	6,400	12,800	22,400	32,000

1970 Chevelle Malibu SS 454

	6	5	4	3	2	1
2d HT	1,250	3,700	6,200	12,400	21,700	31,000
2d Conv	1,450	4,300	7,200	14,400	25,200	36,000

NOTE: Add 30 percent for 396 cid, 375 hp. Add 50 percent for LS6 engine option.

1971 Chevelle

	6	5	4	3	2	1
2d HT	700	2,050	3,400	6,800	11,900	17,000
2d Malibu HT	900	2,650	4,400	8,800	15,400	22,000
2d Mal Conv	1,100	3,250	5,400	10,800	18,900	27,000
4d HT	500	1,450	2,400	4,800	8,400	12,000
4d Sed	300	900	1,500	3,000	5,250	7,500
4d Concours						
Est Wag	450	1,300	2,200	4,400	7,700	11,000

1971 Chevelle Malibu SS

	6	5	4	3	2	1
2d HT	900	2,750	4,600	9,200	16,100	23,000
2d Conv	1,150	3,500	5,800	11,600	20,300	29,000

1964 Chevelle Malibu

Price Guide

1980 El Camino with Olympic Cargo Box Cap

1971 Chevelle Malibu SS 454

	6	5	4	3	2	1
2d HT	1,050	3,100	5,200	10,400	18,200	26,000
2d Conv	1,300	3,850	6,400	12,800	22,400	32,000

1972 Chevelle

	6	5	4	3	2	1
2d Malibu HT	800	2,400	4,000	8,000	14,000	20,000
2d Mal Conv	1,100	3,250	5,400	10,800	18,900	27,000
4d HT	500	1,450	2,400	4,800	8,400	12,000
4d Sed	300	900	1,500	3,000	5,250	7,500
4d Concours Est Wag	450	1,300	2,200	4,400	7,700	11,000

1972 Chevelle Malibu SS

	6	5	4	3	2	1
2d HT	900	2,750	4,600	9,200	16,100	23,000
2d Conv	1,150	3,500	5,800	11,600	20,300	29,000

1972 Chevelle Malibu SS 454

	6	5	4	3	2	1
2d HT	1,000	3,000	5,000	10,000	17,500	25,000
2d Conv	1,250	3,700	6,200	12,400	21,700	31,000

1973 Chevelle Malibu V8

	6	5	4	3	2	1
2d Cpe	300	900	1,500	3,050	5,300	7,600
4d Sed	300	900	1,500	3,000	5,250	7,500

NOTE: Add 15 percent for SS option.

1974 Malibu

	6	5	4	3	2	1
2d Col Cpe	300	950	1,600	3,200	5,600	8,000
4d Col Sed	300	900	1,500	3,050	5,300	7,600
4d Sta Wag	300	850	1,450	2,900	5,050	7,200

1974 Malibu Classic

	6	5	4	3	2	1
2d Col Cpe	300	900	1,550	3,100	5,400	7,700
2d Lan Cpe	300	900	1,500	2,950	5,200	7,400
4d Col Sed	300	850	1,400	2,850	4,950	7,100
4d Sta Wag	300	850	1,400	2,800	4,900	7,000

1974 Malibu Classic Estate

	6	5	4	3	2	1
4d Sta Wag	300	850	1,400	2,850	4,950	7,100

1975 Malibu

	6	5	4	3	2	1
2d Col Cpe	300	900	1,500	3,000	5,250	7,500
2d Col Sed	300	850	1,400	2,800	4,900	7,000
4d Sta Wag	300	850	1,400	2,850	4,950	7,100

1975 Malibu Classic

	6	5	4	3	2	1
2d Col Cpe	300	950	1,600	3,200	5,600	8,000
2d Lan	350	1,000	1,650	3,300	5,750	8,200
4d Col Sed	300	850	1,450	2,900	5,050	7,200
4d Sta Wag	300	850	1,400	2,850	4,950	7,100
4d Est Wag	300	850	1,450	2,900	5,050	7,200

1976 Malibu, V-8

	6	5	4	3	2	1
2d Sed	300	850	1,400	2,850	4,950	7,100
4d Sed	300	850	1,400	2,800	4,900	7,000
4d 2s Sta Wag ES	300	850	1,400	2,800	4,900	7,000
4d 3s Sta Wag ES	300	850	1,400	2,800	4,900	7,000

1972 Malibu (left)

PRICE GUIDE

A pre-production 1965 Chevelle SS coupe

1976 Malibu Classic, V-8

	6	5	4	3	2	1
2d Sed	300	900	1,500	3,000	5,250	7,500
2d Lan Cpe	300	900	1,550	3,100	5,400	7,700
4d Sed	300	850	1,400	2,800	4,900	7,000

1977 Malibu, V-8

	6	5	4	3	2	1
2d Cpe	250	750	1,300	2,550	4,500	6,400
4d Sed	250	800	1,300	2,600	4,550	6,500
4d 2s Sta Wag	250	750	1,200	2,450	4,250	6,100
3s Sta Wag	250	750	1,250	2,500	4,350	6,200

1968 Malibu sport coupe

251

1977 Malibu Classic, V-8

	6	5	4	3	2	1
2d Cpe	250	800	1,300	2,600	4,550	6,500
2d Lan Cpe	300	850	1,400	2,800	4,900	7,000
4d Sed	250	800	1,300	2,650	4,600	6,600
4d 2s Sta Wag	250	750	1,250	2,500	4,400	6,300
4d 3s Sta Wag	250	750	1,300	2,550	4,500	6,400

1978 Malibu

	6	5	4	3	2	1
2d Spt Cpe	184	552	920	1,840	3,220	4,600
4d Sed	180	540	900	1,800	3,150	4,500
4d Sta Wag	180	540	900	1,800	3,150	4,500

1978 Malibu Classic

	6	5	4	3	2	1
2d Spt Cpe	188	564	940	1,880	3,290	4,700
4d Sed	184	552	920	1,840	3,220	4,600
4d Sta Wag	184	552	920	1,840	3,220	4,600

1979 Malibu, V-8

	6	5	4	3	2	1
4d Sed	184	552	920	1,840	3,220	4,600
2d Spt Cpe	192	576	960	1,920	3,360	4,800
4d Sta Wag	188	564	940	1,880	3,290	4,700

1979 Malibu Classic, V-8

	6	5	4	3	2	1
4d Sed	188	564	940	1,880	3,290	4,700
2d Spt Cpe	196	588	980	1,960	3,430	4,900
2d Lan Cpe	200	600	1,000	2,000	3,500	5,000
4d Sta Wag	192	576	960	1,920	3,360	4,800

NOTE: Deduct 5 percent for 6-cyl.

1980 Malibu, V-8

	6	5	4	3	2	1
4d Sed	144	432	720	1,440	2,520	3,600
2d Cpe Spt	152	456	760	1,520	2,660	3,800
4d Sta Wag	148	444	740	1,480	2,590	3,700

NOTE: Deduct 10 percent for V-6.

1980 Malibu Classic, V-8

	6	5	4	3	2	1
4d Sed	148	444	740	1,480	2,590	3,700
2d Cpe Spt	156	468	780	1,560	2,730	3,900
2d Cpe Lan	160	480	800	1,600	2,800	4,000
4d Sta Wag	152	456	760	1,520	2,660	3,800

NOTE: Deduct 10 percent for 6-cyl.

1974 El Camino SS

Price Guige

1965 Chevelle 300 Deluxe two-door sedan

1981 Malibu, V-8

	6	5	4	3	2	1
4d Sed Spt	148	444	740	1,480	2,590	3,700
2d Cpe Spt	152	456	760	1,520	2,660	3,800
4d Sta Wag	152	456	760	1,520	2,660	3,800

NOTE: Deduct 10 percent for 6-cyl.

1981 Malibu Classic, V-8

	6	5	4	3	2	1
4d Sed Spt	152	456	760	1,520	2,660	3,800
2d Cpe Spt	156	468	780	1,560	2,730	3,900
2d Cpe Lan	160	480	800	1,600	2,800	4,000
4d Sta Wag	156	468	780	1,560	2,730	3,900

1986 El Camino

1966 El Camino

1982 Malibu, V-8

	6	5	4	3	2	1
4d Sed	164	492	820	1,640	2,870	4,100
4d Sta Wag	168	504	840	1,680	2,940	4,200

NOTE: Deduct 10 percent for 6-cyl.

1983 Malibu, V-8

	6	5	4	3	2	1
4d Sed	168	504	840	1,680	2,940	4,200
4d Sta Wag	172	516	860	1,720	3,010	4,300

NOTE: Deduct 10 percent for 6-cyl.

El Camino

1964-1966 1/2-ton, V-8

	6	5	4	3	2	1
El Camino	800	2,400	4,000	8,000	14,000	20,000

1967-1968 El Camino Series, V-8

	6	5	4	3	2	1
Spt PU	800	2,400	4,000	8,000	14,000	20,000
Cus Spt PU	840	2,520	4,200	8,400	14,700	21,000

1965 El Camino Custom

1969-1970 El Camino Series, V-8

	6	5	4	3	2	1
Spt PU	760	2,280	3,800	7,600	13,300	19,000
Cus Spt PU	800	2,400	4,000	8,000	14,000	20,000

NOTE: Add 15 percent for SS 396 option.

1971-1972 El Camino, V-8

	6	5	4	3	2	1
Spt PU	760	2,280	3,800	7,600	13,300	19,000
Cus Spt PU	800	2,400	4,000	8,000	14,000	20,000
SS PU	880	2,640	4,400	8,800	15,400	22,000

NOTE: Add 30 percent for 350, 40 percent for 402, 45 percent for 454 engine options. Deduct 20 percent for 6-cyl.

1973-1977 El Camino, V-8

	6	5	4	3	2	1
PU	550	1,600	2,700	5,400	9,450	13,500
Cus PU	550	1,700	2,800	5,600	9,800	14,000

1978-1982 El Camino, V-8

	6	5	4	3	2	1
PU	450	1,400	2,300	4,600	8,050	11,500
Cus PU	500	1,450	2,400	4,800	8,400	12,000

NOTE: Deduct 20 percent for V-6.

1983-1987 El Camino, V-8

	6	5	4	3	2	1
PU	400	1,250	2,100	4,200	7,350	10,500
Cus PU	450	1,300	2,200	4,400	7,700	11,000

NOTE: Deduct 20 percent for V-6. Add 30 percent for Choo Choo model where available.

GMC Sprint

1971-1972 Sprint, 1/2-ton, V-8

	6	5	4	3	2	1
PU	750	2,300	3,800	7,600	13,300	19,000

NOTE: Add 30 percent for 350, 40 percent for 402, 45 percent for 454 engine options.

1973-1977 Sprint 1/2-ton, V-8

	6	5	4	3	2	1
Sprint Cus	550	1,600	2,700	5,400	9,450	13,500

GMC Caballero

1978-1981 Caballero, V-8

	6	5	4	3	2	1
PU	450	1,400	2,300	4,600	8,050	11,500
Cus PU	500	1,450	2,400	4,800	8,400	12,000

NOTE: Deduct 20 percent for V-6.

1967 El Camino

255

1987 Caballero, V-8

	6	5	4	3	2	1
	400	1,250	2,100	4,200	7,350	10,500
	450	1,300	2,200	4,400	7,700	11,000

20 percent for V-6. Add 30 percent for Choo Choo model where available.

1983-1987 Caballero, 1/2-ton

	6	5	4	3	2	1
Caballero PU	300	900	1,500	3,000	5,250	7,500
Diablo PU	360	1,080	1,800	3,600	6,300	9,000

1981-1982 Caballero, 1/2-ton

	6	5	4	3	2	1
Caballero PU	220	660	1,100	2,200	3,850	5,500
Diablo PU	240	720	1,200	2,400	4,200	6,000

1973 El Camino Estate